Biolog

for CAPE® Examinations

Myda Ramesar, Mary Jones and Geoff Jones

CAMBRIDGE
UNIVERSITY PRESS

CAMBRIDGE UNIVERSITY PRESS
Cambridge, New York, Melbourne, Madrid, Cape Town,
Singapore, São Paulo, Delhi, Tokyo, Mexico City

Cambridge University Press
The Edinburgh Building, Cambridge CB2 8RU, UK

www.cambridge.org
Information on this title: www.cambridge.org/9780521176910

First published 2011

Printed in India by Replika Press Pvt Ltd

A catalogue record for this publication is available from the British Library

ISBN 978-0-521-17691-0 Paperback

Additional resources for this publication at
www.cambridge.org/capebiology/resources

Contents

Introduction

The new *Biology for CAPE® Examinations* course provides complete coverage of the CAPE® Biology syllabus. There are two books, one covering Unit 1 and one covering Unit 2. Some of the material is based on the *Cambridge OCR Advanced Sciences Biology 1 for OCR* and *Biology 2 for OCR*, but much is new. It has been brought up to date with new findings in numerous topics. Examples have generally been drawn from Caribbean contexts – for example, ecosystems are dealt with in the context of coral reefs, and the chapters covering health and disease address Caribbean issues.

The books address each of the learning outcomes in the CAPE® Biology syllabus. The material is organised in the same sequence as in the syllabus. It is written to ensure it will be accessible to students who have studied the Caribbean Secondary Education Certificate (CSEC®) Biology course, or other Biology courses at a similar level.

The depth and breadth of treatment of each topic is pitched at the appropriate level for CAPE® Biology students. Most chapters also include boxes containing material that goes a little beyond the requirements of the syllabus, to interest and stretch more able students.

The illustrations include numerous micrographs, some of which have accompanying interpretive diagrams. The diagrams have all been drawn by a biologist, and students should find them very helpful in developing their understanding of structures and processes.

Each chapter also includes self assessment questions (SAQs). These provide opportunities to check understanding and sometimes to make links back to earlier work. They often address misunderstandings that commonly appear in examination answers, and will help students to avoid such errors. Answers to the SAQs can be found at the back of the book.

Each chapter ends with numerous questions in the style of those that students will meet in the CAPE® examination papers, written by an experienced CAPE® examiner. These include three styles of question – multiple choice, structured and essay questions. The answers to these questions are on the free Cambridge Learning website: www.cambridge.org/capebiology/resources

There is a glossary at the end of the book, where brief definitions of important biological terms are given.

Chapter 1
Photosynthesis and ATP synthesis

By the end of this chapter you should be able to:

a describe the structure of a dicotyledonous leaf, a palisade cell and a chloroplast, relating these structures to their roles in the process of photosynthesis;

b make drawings from prepared slides of a transverse section of a dicotyledonous leaf and a palisade cell;

c explain the process of photophosphorylation;

d outline the essential stages of the Calvin cycle involving the light-independent fixation of carbon dioxide;

e discuss the concept of limiting factors in photosynthesis;

f discuss the extent to which knowledge of limiting factors can be used to improve plant productivity.

Humans, like all animals and fungi, are **heterotrophs**. This means that we need to eat food containing organic molecules, especially carbohydrates, fats and proteins. These organic molecules are our only source of energy.

Plants, however, do not need to take in any organic molecules at all. They obtain their energy from sunlight. They can use this energy to build their own organic molecules for themselves, using simple inorganic substances. They first produce carbohydrates from carbon dioxide and water, by **photosynthesis**. They can then use these carbohydrates, plus inorganic ions such as nitrate, phosphate and magnesium, to manufacture all the organic molecules that they need. Organisms that feed in this way – self-sufficient, not needing any organic molecules that another organism has made – are **autotrophs**.

So heterotrophs depend on autotrophs for the supply of organic molecules on which they feed. Some heterotrophs feed directly on plants, while others feed further along a food chain. But eventually all of an animal's or fungus's food can be traced back to plants, and the energy of sunlight.

In this chapter, we will look in detail at how plants transfer energy from sunlight to chemical energy in organic molecules. In Chapter 2, we will see how all living organisms can then release the trapped energy from these molecules and convert it into a form that their cells can use. This process is called **respiration**, and it involves oxidation of the energy-containing organic substances, forming another energy-containing substance called **ATP**. Every cell has to make its own ATP. You can find out more about ATP in Chapter 2.

An overview of photosynthesis

Photosynthesis happens in several different kinds of organisms, not only plants. There are many kinds of bacteria that can photosynthesise. Photosynthesis also takes place in **phytoplankton**, tiny organisms that float in the upper layers of the sea and lakes. Here, though, we will concentrate on photosynthesis in green plants, which takes place in the chloroplasts of several plant tissues, especially the palisade mesophyll and spongy mesophyll tissues of leaves (Figure 1.1). This photosynthesis is the ultimate source of almost all of our food.

The overall equation for photosynthesis is:

$$6CO_2 + 6H_2O \longrightarrow C_6H_{12}O_6 + 6O_2$$

The xylem tissues of roots, stems and leaf vascular bundles bring water to the photosynthesising cells of the leaf. The carbon dioxide diffuses into the leaf through stomata, the tiny holes usually found in the lower epidermis of the leaf. It then

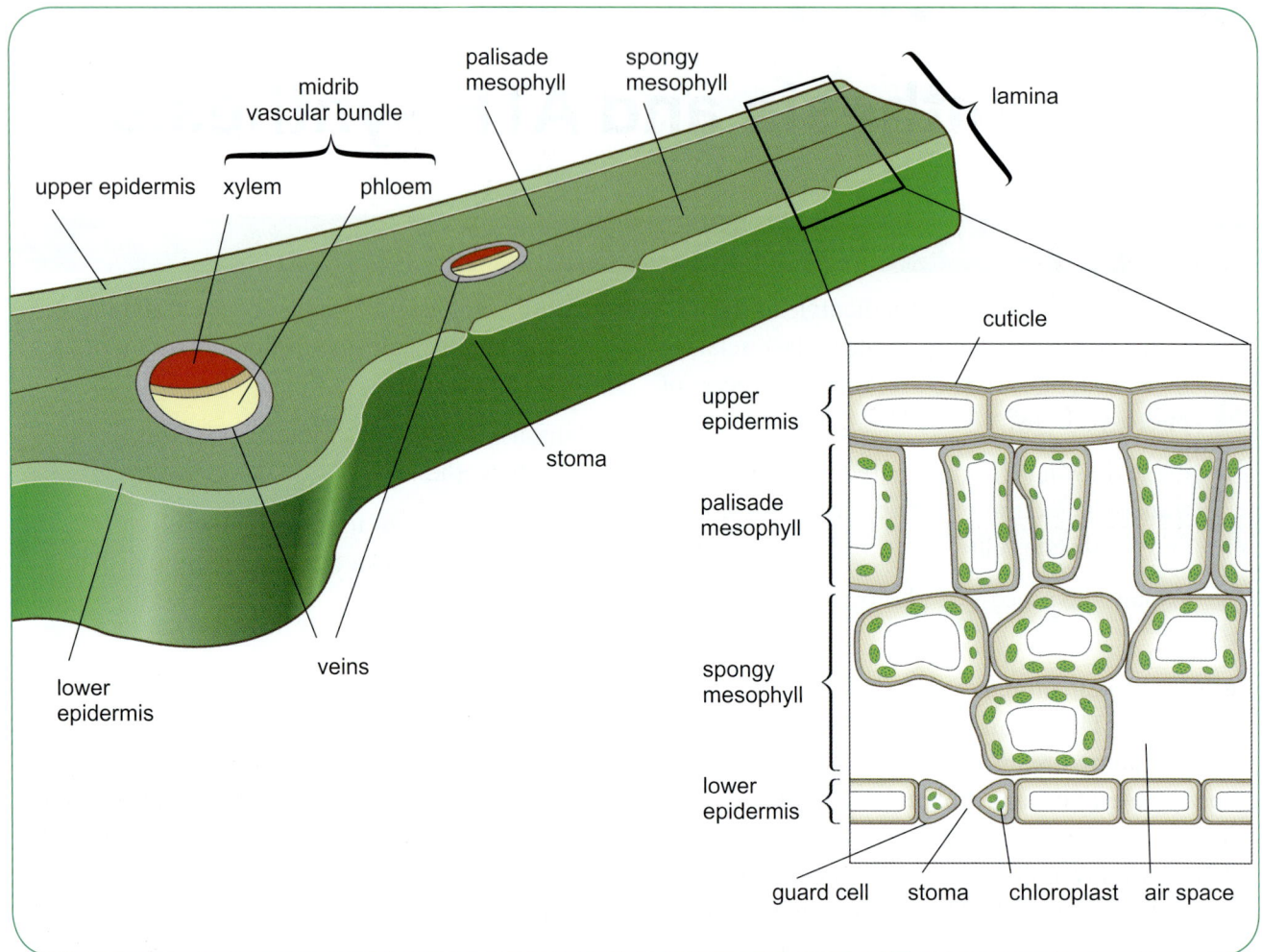

Figure 1.1   The structure of a leaf.

diffuses through air spaces and into mesophyll cells and finally into chloroplasts, where photosynthesis takes place.

Leaf structure and function

The leaf has a broad, thin lamina, a midrib and a network of veins.

It may also have a leaf stalk (petiole). Figure 1.2 is a photomicrograph of a section of a typical leaf from a mesophyte – that is, a plant adapted for normal terrestrial conditions (it is adapted neither for living in water nor for withstanding excessive drought).

To perform its function the leaf must:
● contain chlorophyll and other photosynthetic pigments arranged in such a way that they can absorb light;
● be able to absorb carbon dioxide and dispose of the waste product, oxygen;
● have a water supply and be able to export manufactured carbohydrate to the rest of the plant.

The large surface area and thinness of the lamina allows it to absorb a lot of light. Its thinness minimises the length of the diffusion pathway for gaseous exchange. The arrangement of leaves on the plant (the leaf mosaic) helps the plant to absorb as much light as possible.

The upper epidermis is made of thin, flat, transparent cells which allow light through to the cells of the mesophyll below, where photosynthesis takes place. A waxy transparent cuticle, which is secreted by the epidermal cells, provides a watertight layer preventing water loss other than through the stomata, which can be closed in dry

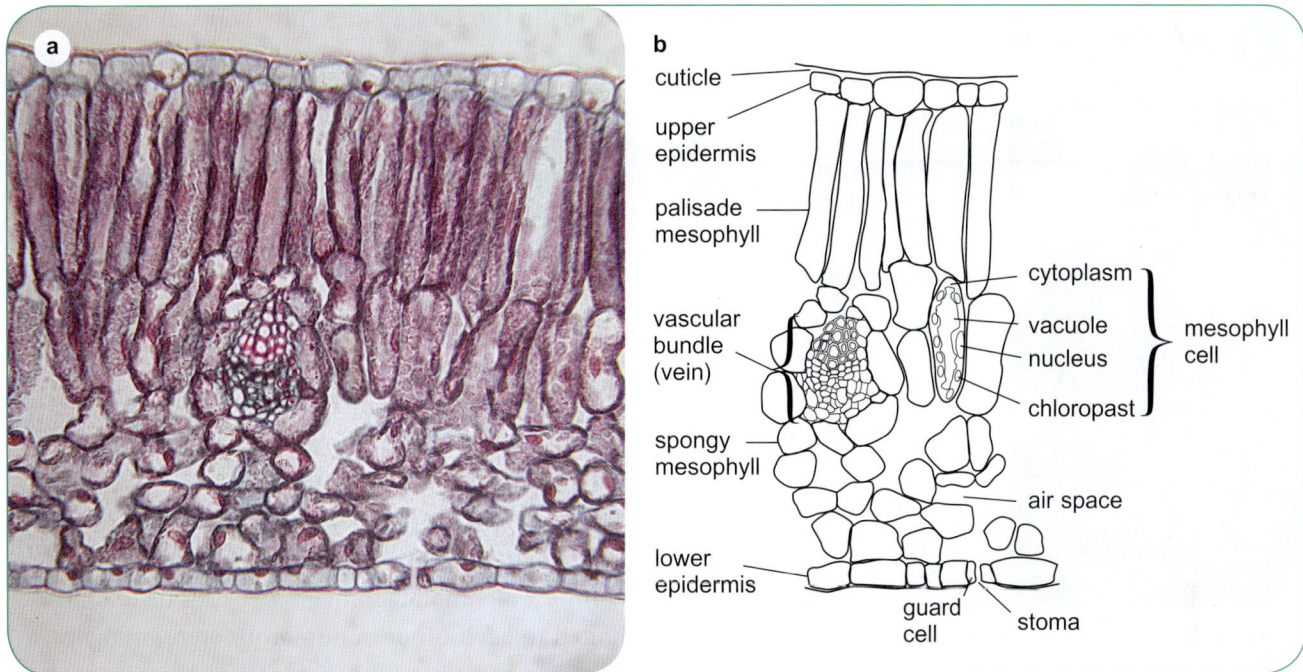

Figure 1.2 **a** Photomicrograph of a TS of a leaf (×300), **b** drawing of part of **a**.

conditions. The cuticle and epidermis together form a protective layer against microorganisms and some insects.

The structure of the lower epidermis is similar to that of the upper, except that most mesophytes have many stomata in the lower epidermis. (Some have a few stomata in the upper epidermis also.) Stomata are the pores in the epidermis through which diffusion of gases occurs, including carbon dioxide. Each stoma is bounded by two sausage-shaped guard cells (Figure 1.3). Changes in the turgidity of these guard cells cause them to change shape so that they open and close the pore. When the guard cells gain water, the pore opens; as they lose water it closes. Guard cells have unevenly thickened cell walls. The wall adjacent to the pore is very thick, whilst the wall furthest from the pore is thin. Bundles of cellulose microfibrils are arranged as hoops around each guard cell and, as the cell becomes turgid, these hoops ensure that the cell mostly increases in length and not diameter. Since the ends of the two guard cells are joined and the thin outer wall bends more readily than the thick inner one, the guard cells become curved. This makes the pore between the cells open.

Guard cells gain and lose water by osmosis. A decrease in water potential is needed before water can enter the cells by osmosis. This is achieved by the active removal of hydrogen ions, using energy from ATP, and then intake of potassium ions (indirect active transport).

An electron micrograph and a drawing of a palisade cell is shown in Unit 1 on page 41. Figure 1.4 shows a photomicrograph of palisade cells. The palisade mesophyll is the main site of photosynthesis, as there are more chloroplasts per cell than in the spongy mesophyll.

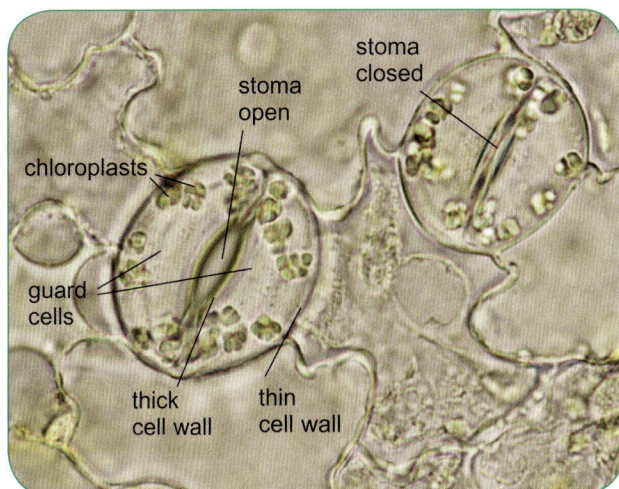

Figure 1.3 Photomicrograph of stomata and guard cells in *Tradescantia* leaf epidermis (×2000).

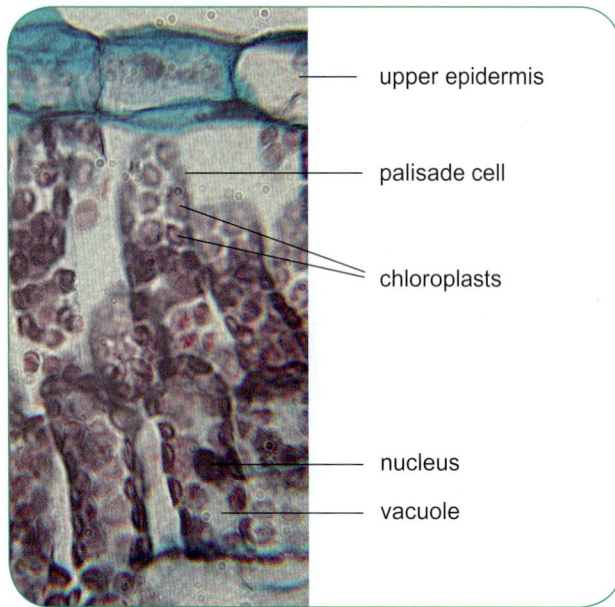

Figure 1.4 Photomicrograph of palisade cells (×600).

Palisade cells show several adaptations for light absorption.

- They are long cylinders arranged at right-angles to the upper epidermis. This reduces the number of light-absorbing cross walls in the upper part of the leaf so that as much light as possible can reach the chloroplasts.
- The cells have a large vacuole with a thin peripheral layer of cytoplasm. This restricts the chloroplasts to a layer near the outside of the cell where light can reach them most easily.
- The chloroplasts can be moved (by proteins in the cytoplasm, as they cannot move themselves) within the cells, to absorb the most light or to protect the chloroplasts from excessive light intensities.

The palisade cells also show adaptations for gaseous exchange.

- The cylindrical cells pack together with long, narrow air spaces between them. This gives a large surface area of contact between cell and air.
- The cell walls are thin, so that gases can diffuse through them more easily.

Spongy mesophyll is mainly adapted as a surface for the exchange of carbon dioxide and oxygen. The cells contain chloroplasts, but in smaller numbers than in palisade cells. Photosynthesis

occurs in the spongy mesophyll only at high light intensities. The irregular packing of the cells and the large air spaces thus produced provide a large surface area of moist cell wall for gaseous exchange.

The veins in the leaf help to support the large surface area of the leaf. They contain xylem, which brings in the water necessary for photosynthesis and for cell turgor, and phloem, which takes the products of photosynthesis to other parts of the plant.

Chloroplast structure and function

The equation on page 1 is a simplification of photosynthesis. In reality photosynthesis is a complex **metabolic pathway** – a series of reactions linked to each other in numerous steps, many of which are catalysed by enzymes. These reactions take place in two stages. The first is the **light-dependent stage**, and this is followed by the **light-independent stage**. Both of these stages take place inside chloroplasts within cells of the leaves and often stems of plants (Figure 1.5).

Figure 1.6 shows the structure of a typical chloroplast. Each cell in a photosynthesising tissue may have ten or even 100 chloroplasts inside it.

A chloroplast is surrounded by two membranes, forming an **envelope**. There are more membranes inside the chloroplast, which are arranged so that they enclose fluid-filled sacs between them. The membranes are called **lamellae** and the fluid-

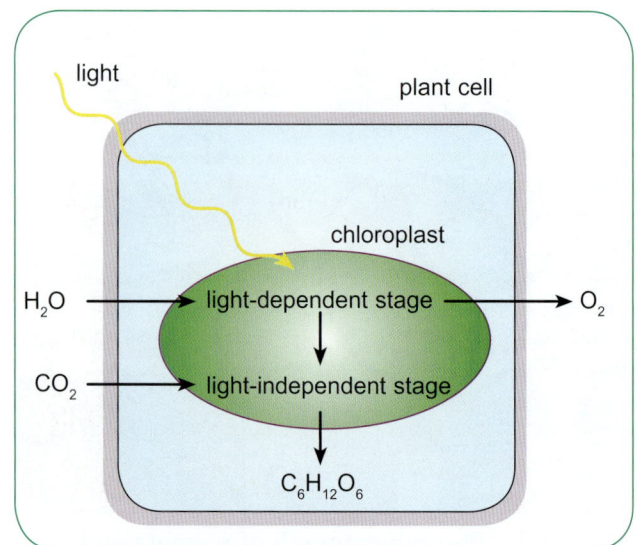

Figure 1.5 The stages of photosynthesis.

Electron micrograph of a chloroplast

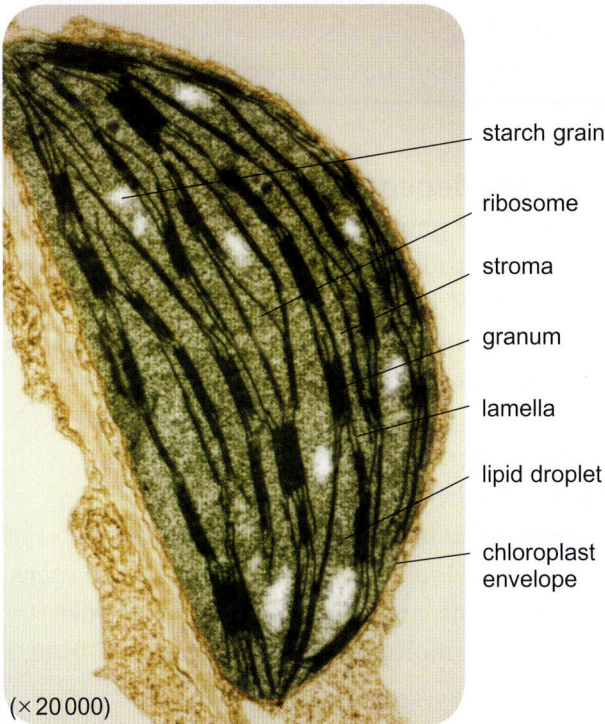

starch grain

ribosome

stroma

granum

lamella

lipid droplet

chloroplast envelope

(×20 000)

Diagram of a chloroplast

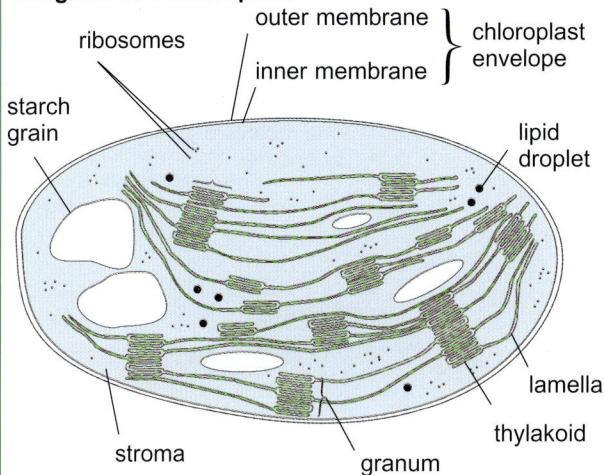

ribosomes

outer membrane

inner membrane

} chloroplast envelope

starch grain

lipid droplet

stroma

granum

lamella

thylakoid

Electron micrograph of part of a chloroplast

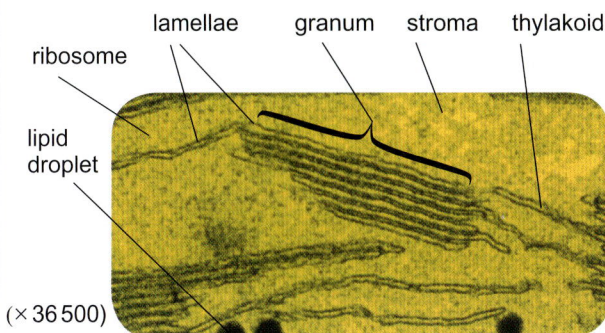

lamellae   granum   stroma   thylakoid

ribosome

lipid droplet

(×36 500)

Figure 1.6   The structure of a chloroplast.

filled sacs are **thylakoids**. In some parts of the chloroplasts, the thylakoids are stacked up like a pile of pancakes, and these stacks are called **grana**. The 'background material' inside the chloroplast is called the **stroma**.

Embedded tightly in the membranes inside the chloroplast are several different kinds of **photosynthetic pigments**. These are coloured substances that absorb energy from certain wavelengths (colours) of light. The most abundant pigment is **chlorophyll**, which comes in two forms, **chlorophyll *a*** and **chlorophyll *b***.

The stacked membranes have a large surface area and so their photosynthetic pigments can capture light very efficiently. The transformation of light energy into chemical energy is carried out by other chemicals in the membranes closely associated with the photosynthetic pigments. The membranes not only hold chemicals allowing them to function correctly, but also create the thylakoid spaces. The space inside each thylakoid, the thylakoid lumen, is needed for the accumulation of hydrogen ions, H^+, used in the production of ATP (see page 7 and Chapter 2).

Chloroplasts often contain **starch grains**, because starch is the form in which plants store the carbohydrate that they make by photosynthesis. They also contain **ribosomes** and their own small circular strand of **DNA**. (You may remember that chloroplasts are thought to have evolved from bacteria that first invaded eukaryotic cells over a thousand million years ago.)

SAQ

1 List the features of a chloroplast that aid photosynthesis.

Photosynthetic pigments

A pigment is a substance whose molecules absorb some wavelengths (colours) of light, but not others. The wavelengths it does not absorb are either reflected or transmitted through the substance. These unabsorbed wavelengths reach our eyes, so we see the pigment in these colours.

The majority of the pigments in a chloroplast are chlorophyll *a* and chlorophyll *b* (Figure 1.7).

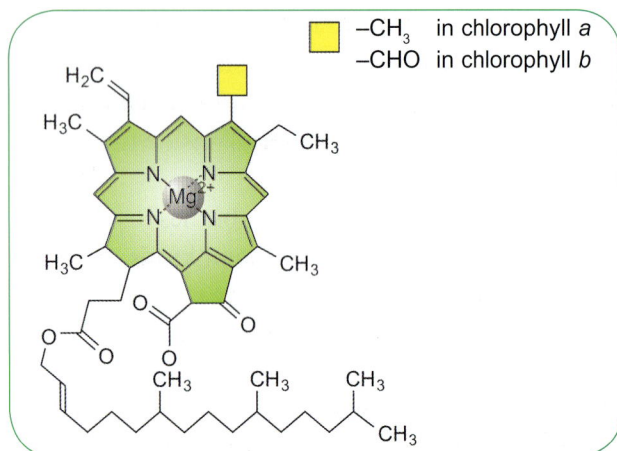

Figure 1.7   A chlorophyll molecule.

These are the primary pigments.. Both types of chlorophyll absorb similar wavelengths of light, but chlorophyll *a* absorbs slightly longer wavelengths than chlorophyll *b*. This can be shown in a graph called an **absorption spectrum** (Figure 1.8).

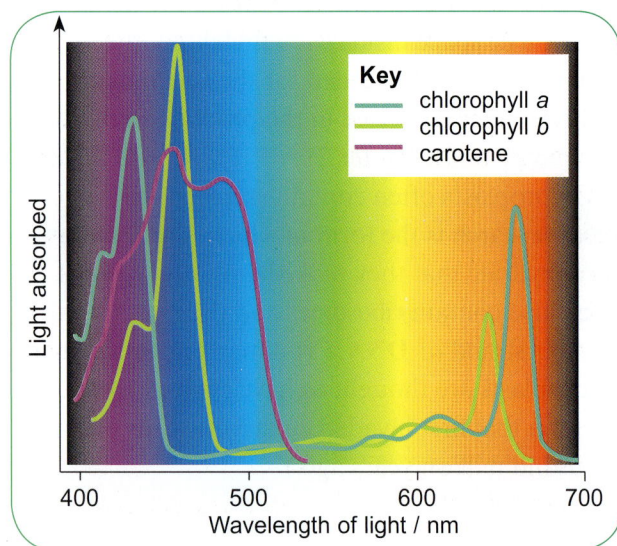

Figure 1.8   Absorption spectra for chlorophyll and carotene.

Other pigments found in chloroplasts include **carotenoids**, such as carotene and xanthophylls. These absorb a wide range of short wavelength light, including more blue-green light than the chlorophylls. They are **accessory pigments**. They help by absorbing wavelengths of light that would otherwise not be used by the plant. They pass on some of this energy to chlorophyll. They probably also help to protect chlorophyll from damage by very intense light.

2 **a** Use Figure 1.8 to explain why chlorophyll looks green.

b What colour are carotenoids?

The light-dependent stage

This stage of photosynthesis takes place on the thylakoids inside the chloroplast. It involves the absorption of light energy by chlorophyll, and the use of that energy and the products from splitting water to make ATP and reduced NADP.

Photosystems

The chlorophyll molecules are arranged in clusters called **photosystems** in the thylakoid membranes (Figure 1.9). Each photosystem spans the membrane, and contains protein molecules and pigment molecules. Energy is captured from

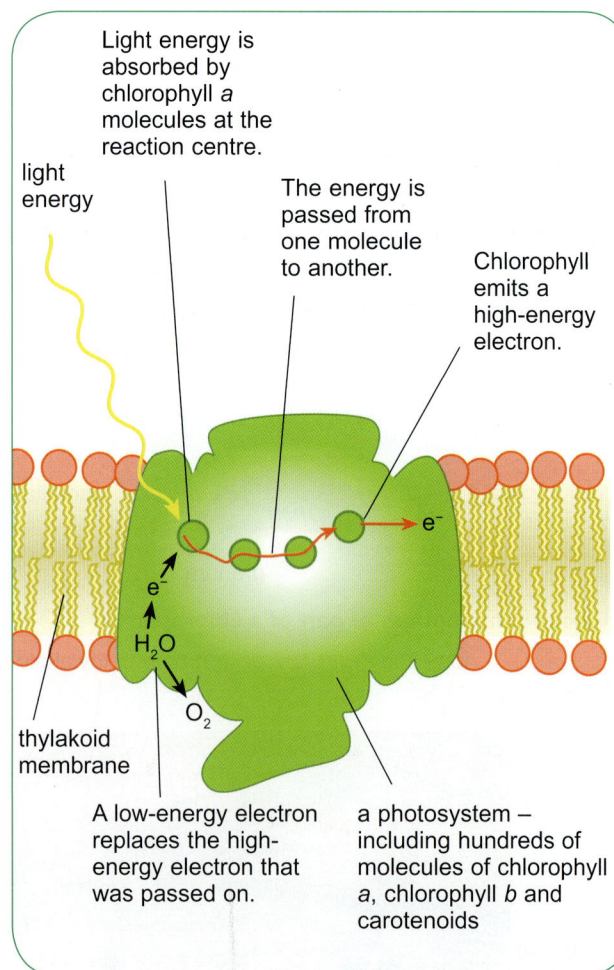

Figure 1.9   A photosystem in a thylakoid membrane showing photoactivation of chlorophyll.

photons of light that hit the photosystem, and is funnelled down to a pair of molecules at the **reaction centre** of the photosystem complex.

There are two different sorts of photosystem, **PSI** and **PSII**, both with a small number of molecules of chlorophyll *a* at the reaction centre.

Photophosphorylation

Photophosphorylation means 'phosphorylation using light'. It refers to the production of ATP, by combining a phosphate group with ADP, using energy that originally came from light:

ADP + phosphate $\longrightarrow$ ATP

Photophosphorylation happens when an electron is passed along a series of **electron carriers**, forming an **electron transport chain** in the thylakoid membranes. The electron starts off with a lot of energy, and it gradually loses some of it as it moves from one carrier to the next. The energy is used to cause a phosphate group to react with ADP.

Cyclic photophosphorylation

This process involves only PSI, not PSII. It results in the formation of ATP, but not reduced NADP (Figure 1.10).

Light is absorbed by PSI and the energy passed on to electrons in the chlorophyll *a* molecules at the reaction centre. In each chlorophyll *a* molecule, one of the electrons becomes so energetic that it

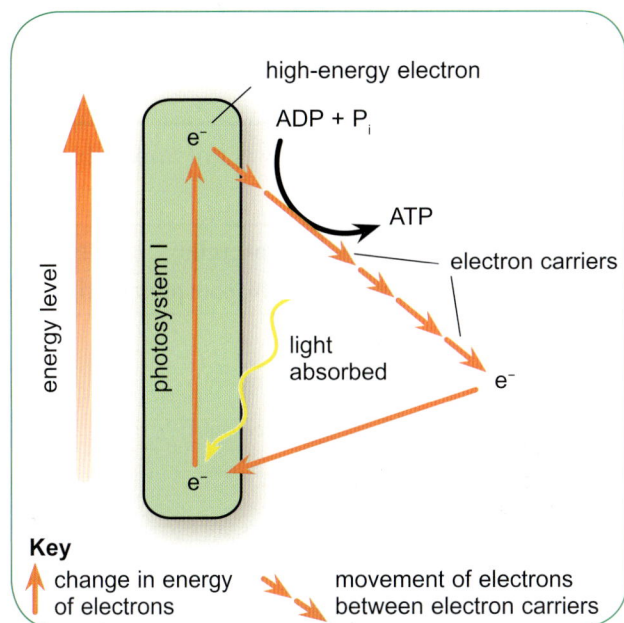

Key

↑ change in energy of electrons

⬂ movement of electrons between electron carriers

Figure 1.10   Cyclic photophosphorylation.

leaves the chlorophyll molecules completely. The electron is then passed along the chain of electron carriers. The energy from the electron is used to make ATP. The electron, now having lost its extra energy, eventually returns to chlorophyll *a* in PSI.

Non-cyclic photophosphorylation

This process involves both kinds of photosystem. It results not only in the production of ATP, but also of reduced NADP.

Light hitting either PSI or PSII causes electrons to be emitted. The electrons from PSII pass down the electron carrier chain, generating ATP by photophosphorylation. However, instead of going back to PSII, the electrons instead replace the electrons lost from PSI.

The phosphorylation of ADP to ATP involves the movement of H^+ across the thylakoid membrane. This process also occurs in respiration and is described in detail in Chapter 2.

The electrons emitted from PSI are not used to make ATP. Instead, they help to reduce NADP.

For this to happen, hydrogen ions are required. These come from another event that happens when light hits PSII. PSII contains an enzyme that splits water when it is activated by light. The reaction is called **photolysis**:

$2H_2O \longrightarrow 4H^+ + 4e^- + O_2$

The hydrogen ions are taken up by NADP, forming reduced NADP. The electrons replace the ones that were emitted from PSII when light hit it. The oxygen diffuses out of the chloroplast and eventually out of the leaf, as an excretory product.

The Z-scheme

The **Z-scheme** is simply a way of summarising what happens to electrons during the light-dependent reactions. It is a kind of graph, with the *y*-axis indicating the 'energy level' of the electron (Figure 1.11).

Start at the bottom left, where light hits photosystem II. The red vertical line going up shows the increase in the energy level of electrons as they are emitted from this photosystem. You can also see where these electrons came from – the splitting of water molecules. (In fact, it probably isn't the same electrons – but the electrons from the

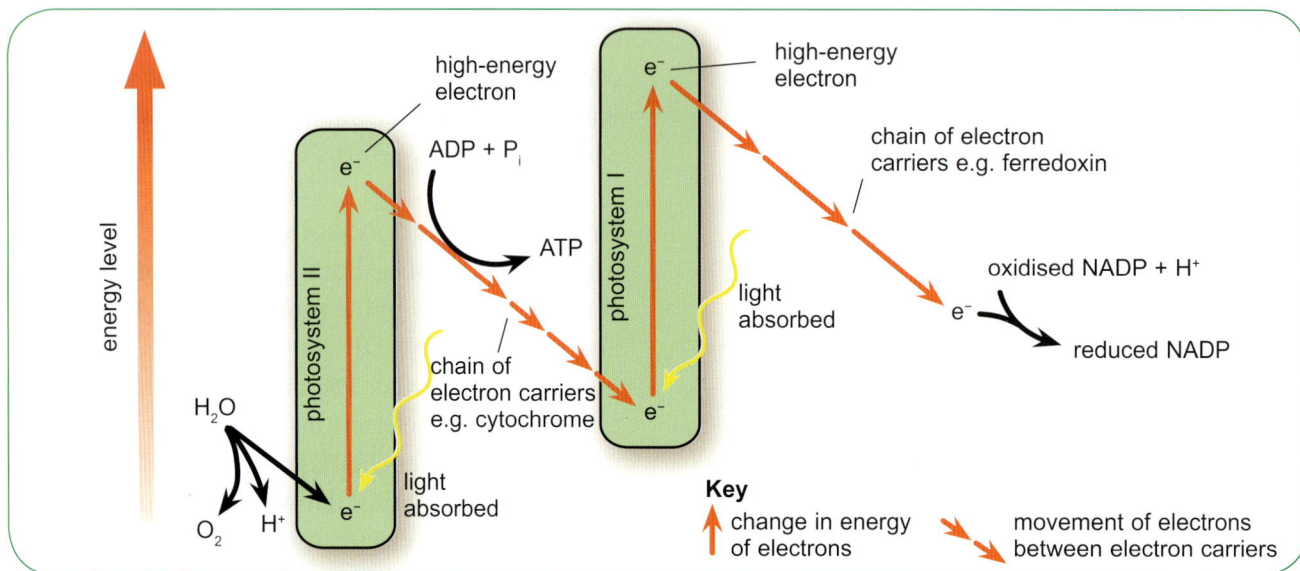

Figure 1.11 The Z-scheme, summarising non-cyclic photophosphorylation.

water replace the ones that are emitted from the photosystem.)

If you keep following the vertical line showing the increasing energy in the electrons, you arrive at a point where it starts a steep dive downwards. This shows the electrons losing their energy as they pass along the electron carrier chain. Eventually they arrive at photosystem I.

You can then track the movement of the electrons to a higher energy level when PSI is hit by light, before they fall back downwards as they lose energy and become part of a reduced NADP molecule.

The light-independent stage

Now the ATP and reduced NADP that have been formed in the light-dependent stage are used to help to produce carbohydrates from carbon dioxide. These events take place in the stroma of the chloroplast. The cyclic series of reactions is known as the Calvin cycle (Figure 1.12).

The chloroplast stroma contains an enzyme called **rubisco** (its full name is ribulose bisphosphate carboxylase). This is thought to be the most abundant enzyme in the world. Its function is to catalyse the reaction in which carbon dioxide combines with a substance called **RuBP**

SAQ

3 Copy and complete the table to compare cyclic and non-cyclic photophosphorylation.

(If a box in a particular row is not applicable, write n/a.)

	Cyclic photophosphorylation	Non-cyclic photophosphorylation
Is PSI involved?		
Is PSII involved?		
Where does PSI obtain replacement electrons from?		
Where does PSII obtain replacement electrons from?		
Is ATP made?		
Is reduced NADP made?		

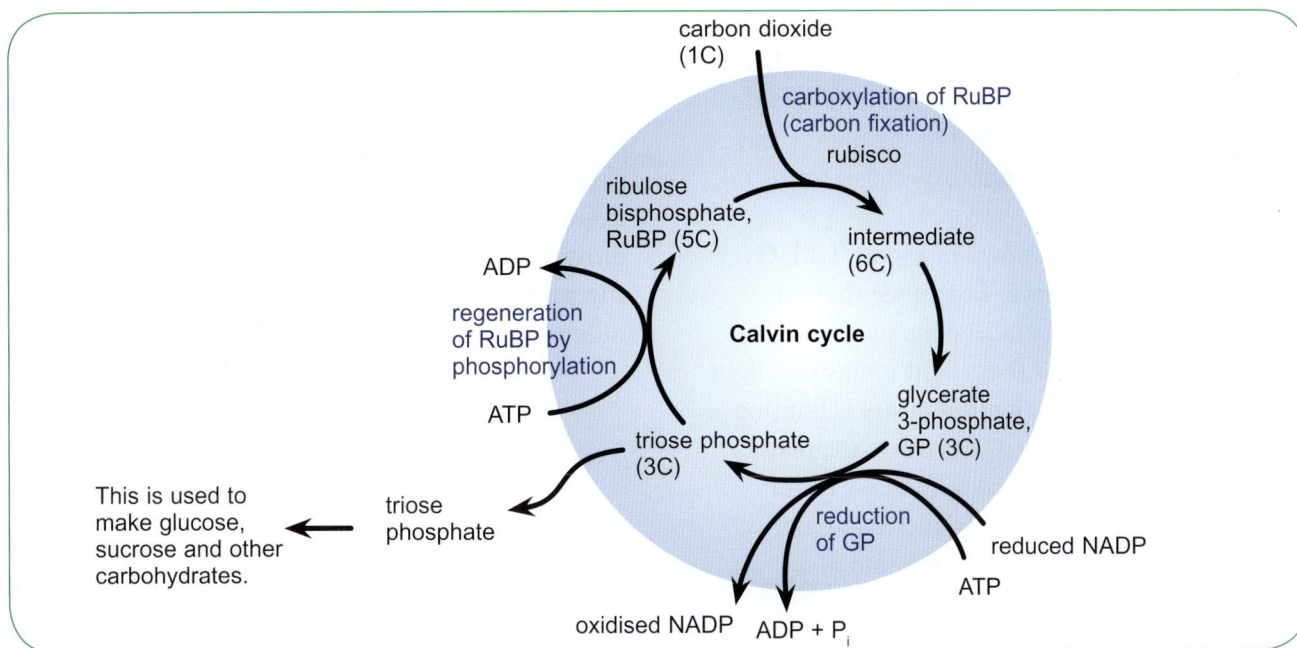

Figure 1.12 The Calvin cycle.

(ribulose bisphosphate).

RuBP molecules each contain five atoms of carbon. The reaction with carbon dioxide therefore produces a six-carbon molecule, but this immediately splits to form two three-carbon molecules. This three-carbon substance is **glycerate 3-phosphate**, usually known as **GP**. An alternative name is phosphoglyceric acid (PGA).

Now the two products of the light-dependent stages come into play. The reduced NADP and the ATP are used to provide energy and phosphate groups, which change the GP into a three-carbon sugar called **triose phosphate** (**TP** or **GALP**). This is the first carbohydrate that is made in photosynthesis.

There are many possible fates of the triose phosphate. Five-sixths of it are used to regenerate RuBP. The remainder can be converted into other carbohydrates. For example, two triose phosphates can combine to produce a hexose phosphate molecule. From these, glucose, fructose, sucrose, starch and cellulose can be formed.

The triose phosphate can also be used to make lipids and amino acids. For amino acid production, nitrogen needs to be added, which plants obtain from the soil in the form of nitrate ions or ammonium ions.

SAQ

4 Suggest what happens to the ADP, inorganic phosphate and NADP that are formed during the Calvin cycle.

Factors affecting the rate of photosynthesis

Photosynthesis requires several inputs. It needs raw materials in the form of carbon dioxide and water, and energy in the form of sunlight. The light-independent stage also requires a reasonably high temperature, because the rates of reactions are affected by the kinetic energy of the molecules involved.

If any of these requirements is in short supply, it can limit the rate at which the reactions of photosynthesis are able to take place.

Light intensity

Light provides the energy that drives the light-dependent reactions, so it is obvious that when there is no light, there is no photosynthesis. If we provide a plant with more light, then it will photosynthesise faster.

However, this can only happen up to a point. We would eventually reach a light intensity where, if we give the plant more light, its rate of photosynthesis does not change. We can say that 'light saturation' has occurred. Some other factor, such as the availability of carbon dioxide or the quantity of chlorophyll in the plant's leaves, is preventing the rate of photosynthesis from continuing to increase.

This relationship is shown in Figure 1.13. Over the first part of the curve, we can see that rate of photosynthesis does indeed increase as light intensity increases. For these light intensities, light is a **limiting factor**. The light intensity is limiting the rate of photosynthesis. If we give the plant more light, then it will photosynthesise faster.

But, from point **X** onwards, increasing the light intensity has no effect on the rate of photosynthesis. Along this part of the curve, light is no longer a limiting factor. Something else is. It is most likely to be the carbon dioxide concentration.

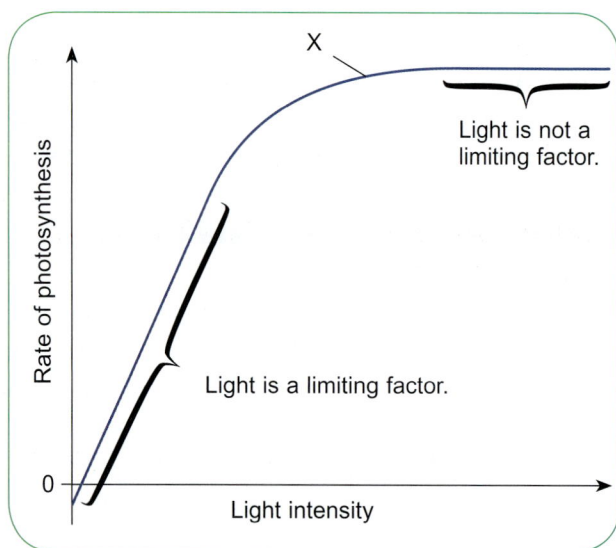

Figure 1.13 The effect of light intensity on the rate of photosynthesis.

Carbon dioxide concentration

The concentration of carbon dioxide in the air is very low, only about 0.04%. Yet this substance is needed for the formation of every organic molecule inside every living thing on Earth.

Plants absorb carbon dioxide into their leaves by diffusion through the stomata. During daylight, carbon dioxide is used in the Calvin cycle in the chloroplasts, so the concentration of carbon dioxide inside the leaf is even lower than in the air

outside, providing the diffusion gradient that keeps it moving into the leaf.

Carbon dioxide concentration is often a limiting factor for photosynthesis. If we give plants extra carbon dioxide, they can photosynthesise faster. Figure 1.14 shows the relationship between carbon dioxide concentration and rate of photosynthesis. Figure 1.15 shows the effect of carbon dioxide at different light intensities.

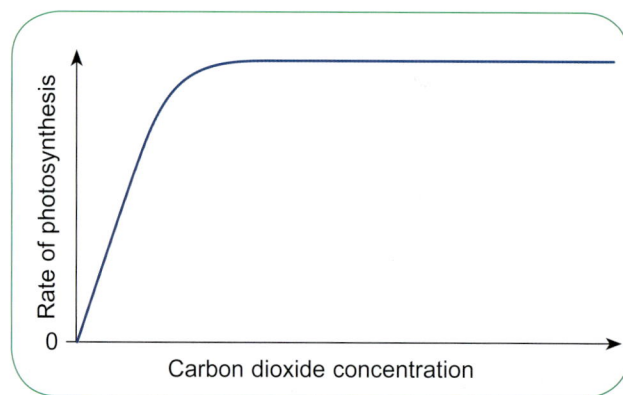

Figure 1.14 The effect of carbon dioxide on rate of photosynthesis.

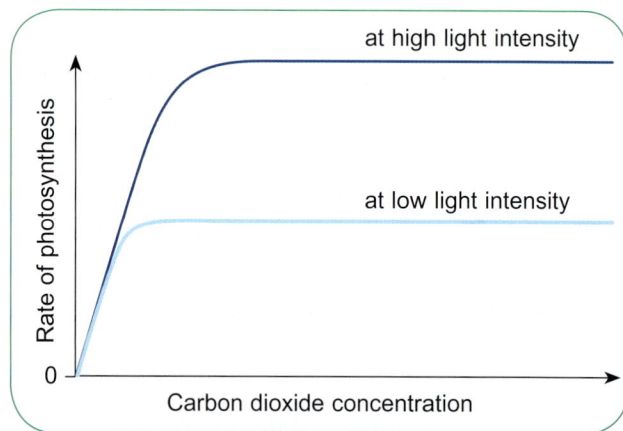

Figure 1.15 The effect of carbon dioxide concentration on the rate of photosynthesis at different light intensities.

SAQ

5 a Over which part of the curve in Figure 1.14 is carbon dioxide a limiting factor for photosynthesis?

   b Suggest why the curve flattens out at high levels of CO_2.

Temperature

Temperature affects the kinetic energy of molecules. The higher the temperature, the faster molecules move, and the more frequently they collide with one another. They also collide with more energy. The greater frequency and energy of collisions means that the reaction rate increases.

In photosynthesis, though, this effect is only seen in the light-independent reactions. The rate of the light-dependent reactions is not directly affected by temperature, because the energy that drives them comes from light, not the kinetic energy of molecules.

In living organisms, most reactions are catalysed by enzymes, so we also need to consider the effect of temperature on them. Just like any molecules, their kinetic energy increases as temperature increases. However, as you will remember, beyond a certain temperature (different for different enzymes) they begin to lose their shape, and therefore their catalytic properties. Plant enzymes often have lower optimum temperatures than enzymes found in mammals, because they have evolved to work in the environmental temperatures in which the plant normally lives.

Things are complicated, however, by a peculiar property of the enzyme rubisco. Rubisco has an unfortunate tendency to stop doing what it is supposed to do – catalyse the combination of carbon dioxide with RuBP – and start doing something else when temperature rises. It switches to catalysing a reaction in which *oxygen* is combined with RuBP. This is very wasteful, as it wastes RuBP. It is called **photorespiration**, and it can seriously reduce the rate of photosynthesis in many plant species, when temperature and light intensity are high. (Photorespiration is a misleading name, as it is not really respiration at all.)

The effect of light on the Calvin cycle

The Calvin cycle is the light-independent stage of photosynthesis. It is given that name because it does not require energy input from light. It *does*, however, need energy input from the light-dependent stage, in the form of ATP and reduced NADP.

Imagine that light is shining on a chloroplast. The light-dependent stage is generating ATP and reduced NADP, and the reactions of the Calvin cycle are working continuously.

Now the light is switched off. The light-dependent stage stops, so the supply of ATP and NADP to the Calvin cycle also stops. These substances are needed to fuel the conversion of GP to TP. So now GP can no longer be converted into TP, and the GP just builds up. The rest of the cycle keeps running, until most of the TP is used up. Then it grinds to a halt.

Figure 1.16 shows what happens to the relative amounts of GP and TP when the light is switched off. As we would expect, the levels of TP plummet, while the levels of GP rise. If the light is switched on again, they go back to their 'normal' relative levels.

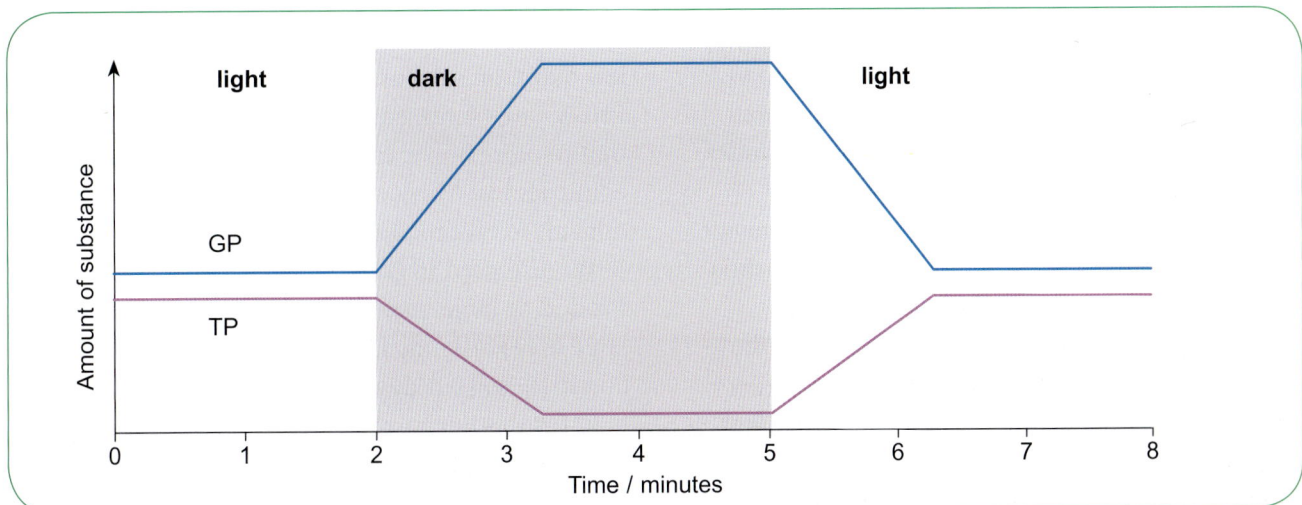

Figure 1.16 The effect of light and dark on the relative levels of TP and GP in a chloroplast.

SAQ

6 a Explain why the Calvin cycle stops running when there is no light and the TP is used up.

b Make a copy of Figure 1.16. Add another line to show what you would expect to happen to the levels of RuBP during this eight-minute period.

7 What effect would you expect a rise or a fall in temperature to have on the relative levels of GP, TP and RuBP? (Assume that the temperature does not go high enough to denature enzymes.) Explain your reasoning.

Limiting factors and crop production

If one factor is rate limiting, increasing the supply of any other factor has no effect on the rate of photosynthesis and therefore no effect on crop production. On the other hand, increasing the supply of the limiting factor will have a dramatic impact on crop production.

For photosynthesis, light or carbon dioxide could be rate limiting at temperatures within the range tolerated by the crop. However, a farmer has limited capacity to affect light or carbon dioxide levels in order to increase the rate of photosynthesis, unless a crop is being grown in a specialised glasshouse.

But photosynthesis is not the only process which may have limiting factors that affect crop production. Water and each mineral nutrient required by a plant can also limit the rate of growth. If the supply of, for example, potassium is limited in the soil, potassium may be rate limiting for crop growth. So, increasing the light intensity will have no or little effect on crop production in these circumstances.

Analysis of the climate, soil and atmospheric environment of a crop can reveal which factor is going to be rate limiting in a range of circumstances and therefore which factor could be increased to make maximum impact on crop production at any one time.

Biofuels

The ability of plants to transfer light energy into chemical energy means that they can be used to provide fuels for us to use – for example, for generating electricity or in vehicle engines. As stocks of fossil fuels run down, and as carbon dioxide levels in the atmosphere continue to increase, there has been a sharp increase in the use of crop plants to produce fuels rather than food. For example, rape seed is being used to produce biodiesel, rather than food for animals or humans.

At first sight, this would appear to be very good for the environment. Using plants to provide fuels is theoretically 'carbon-neutral'. The carbon dioxide that is given out when the fuels are burnt is matched by the carbon dioxide that the plants take in as they photosynthesise and grow. However, if we take into account the energy that is used in harvesting the plants, converting the biomass to a useful form of fuel and transporting that fuel to points of sale, then there is still a net emission of carbon dioxide to the atmosphere.

But the greatest problem is the effect that the increasing quantity of crops to produce biofuels is having on the availability and price of food. For example, as huge areas of land in the USA are taken over to grow corn (maize) for fuel, there is less maize on sale for cattle feed or human food. Prices have increased, in some cases so much so that poorer people, especially in neighbouring countries like Mexico, are finding it much more difficult to buy enough food for their needs.

We also need to consider effects on ecosystems. Producing large quantities of biofuels will take up large areas of land. There is a danger that some countries will cut down forests to provide extra land for this purpose, damaging habitats and endangering species that live there.

Summary

- Photosynthesis uses light energy to cause carbon dioxide and water to react to produce carbohydrates and oxygen. The light energy is transformed to chemical energy in the carbohydrates.

- Most photosynthesis takes place inside chloroplasts in palisade cells in leaves.

- Leaf structure helps to ensure good supplies of raw materials for photosynthesis. Most leaves have a thin, broad lamina to maximise the amount of light that can be absorbed. Their thinness also minimises the diffusion pathway for carbon dioxide. Stomata and air spaces allow carbon dioxide to diffuse easily to photosynthesising cells. Xylem vessels bring water.

- Palisade cells contain large numbers of chloroplasts. They are tall and thin, so light does not have to pass through too many cell walls before reaching a chloroplast. The chloroplasts are arranged in the cytoplasm around the outer edge of the cell, and can be moved to maximise light absorption.

- Chloroplasts are surrounded by an envelope enclosing the stroma. Inside the chloroplast, membranes form fluid-filled sacs called thylakoids, which in turn form stacks called grana. Chlorophyll molecules are embedded in the membranes. The chlorophyll molecules are found within photosystems I and II.

- The light-dependent stage of photosynthesis takes place in the thylakoids. Light energy raises the energy level of an electron in a chlorophyll molecule. The electron is passed down a series of carriers, generating ATP by photophosphorylation. If only PSI is involved, the electron is returned to PSI and this is called cyclic photophosphorylation. If the electron is passed to PSII, then reduced NADP is also produced, using hydrogen ions from the splitting of water. This is called non-cyclic photophosphorylation.

- The light-independent stage of photosynthesis is also known as the Calvin cycle, and takes place in the stroma. The enzyme rubisco catalyses the reaction of carbon dioxide with ribulose bisphosphate (RuBP) to form two molecules of glycerate 3-phosphate (GP). This reacts with reduced NADP and ATP to produce triose phosphate (TP). Most TP is reconverted to RuBP, but one sixth is used to make carbohydrates such as glucose, sucrose or starch.

- Light intensity, carbon dioxide concentration and temperature all affect the rate at which photosynthesis can take place. The factor that is in the shortest supply at any one time is known as the limiting factor. If crops are grown in glasshouses, these factors can be adjusted to increase the rate of photosynthesis and therefore the productivity of the crop.

Questions

Multiple choice questions

1   The micrograph represents a cross-section of a dicotyledonous leaf. Which region is the main site of light absorption?

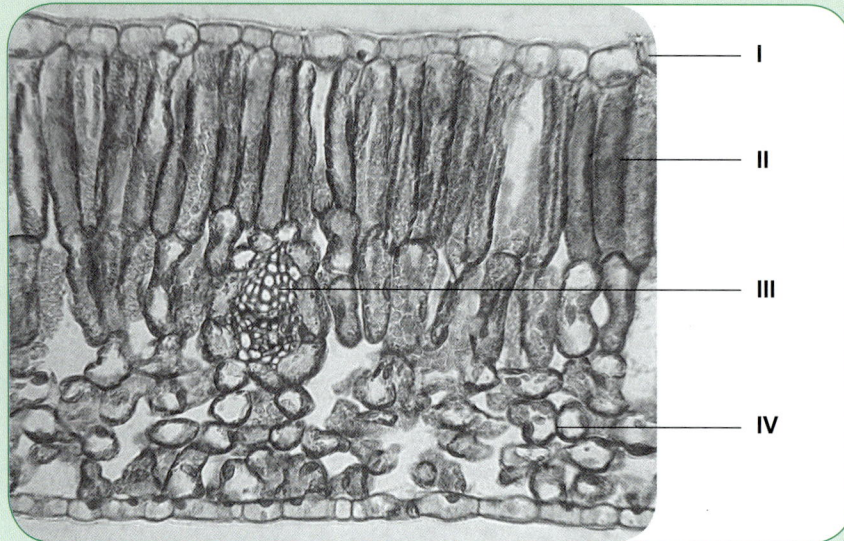

    A I
    B II
    C III
    D IV

2   Where do the light-independent reactions of photosynthesis occur in the chloroplast?
    A thylakoid membranes
    B stroma
    C grana
    D matrix

3   The main photosynthetic pigments found in the reaction centre of photosystem II is or are:
    A carotenoids.
    B xanthophylls.
    C chlorophyll *a*.
    D chlorophyll *b*.

4   In which part of a chloroplast is light energy transferred to chemical energy?
    A envelope
    B granum
    C stroma
    D starch grain

continued …

5 What are the steps numbered 1–4 in the diagram of the Calvin cycle shown below?

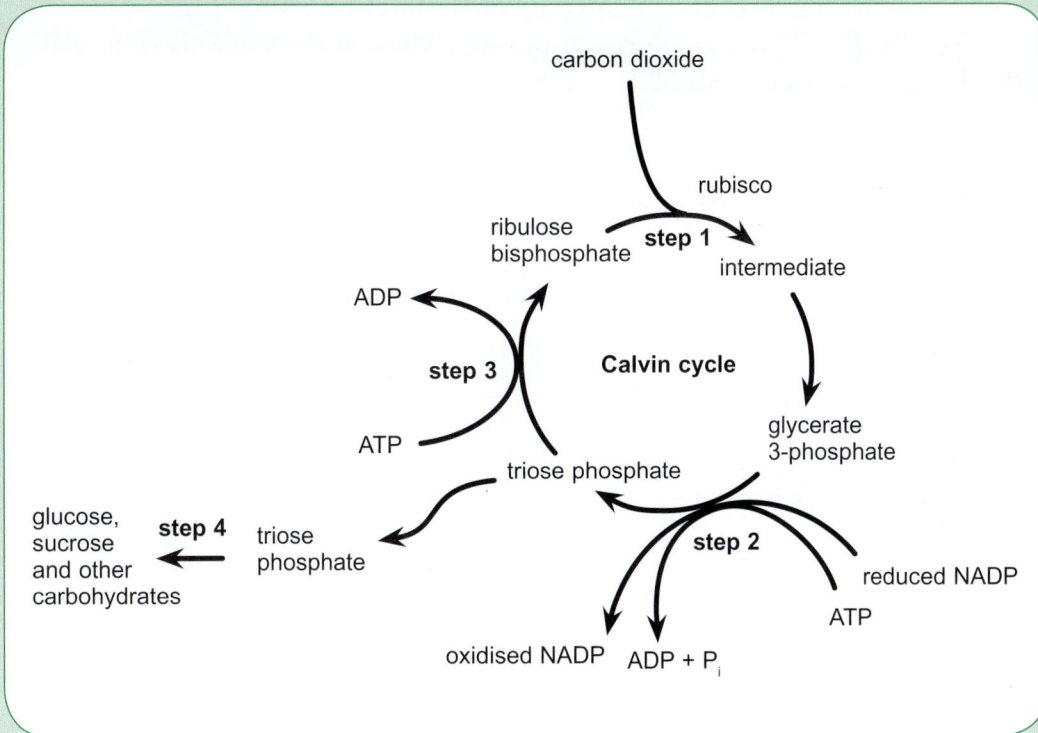

	Step 1	Step 2	Step 3	Step 4
A	oxidation	carboxylation	product synthesis	regeneration of RuBP
B	regeneration of RuBP	product synthesis	carboxylation	oxidation
C	product synthesis	regeneration of RuBP	oxidation	carboxylation
D	carboxylation	reduction	regeneration of RuBP	product synthesis

6 The electrons lost from chlorophyll *a* in the reaction centre in photosystem II are replaced by electrons from:
   A reduced NADP.
   B photosystem I.
   C hydroxyl ions from water.
   D hydrogen ions from water.

7 The products of non-cyclic photophosphorylation during the light-dependent reactions of photosynthesis are:
   A glucose, reduced NADP and ATP.
   B ATP, oxygen and reduced NADP.
   C ADP, carbon dioxide and RuBP.
   D hydrogen ions, oxygen and ATP.

continued ...

8 The graph below illustrates the effect of light intensity on the rate of photosynthesis of a suspension of *Chlorella* at 150 °C and 0.4% carbon dioxide. Which of the following is the **most** likely explanation for the plateau labelled Y?

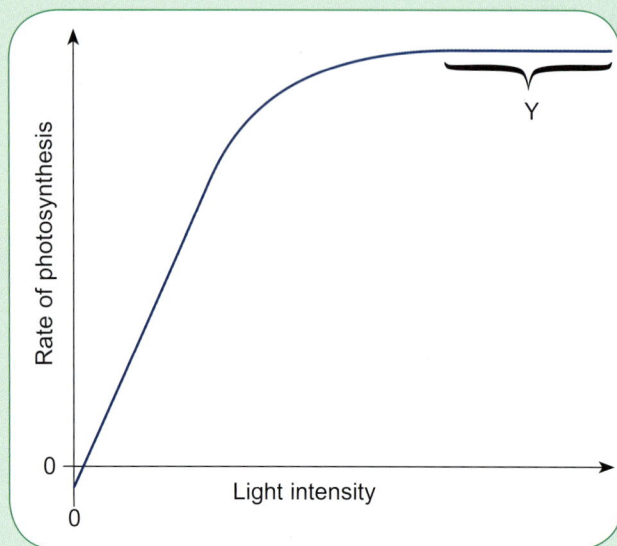

A Light saturation has occurred.
B Light saturation has occurred and carbon dioxide concentration is now the limiting factor.
C Light saturation has occurred and temperature is now the limiting factor.
D Light intensity is the limiting factor.

9 ATP is used in the Calvin cycle in the:
A reduction of GP to TP (GALP) and regeneration of RuBP.
B reduction of GP to TP (GALP).
C carboxylation and regeneration of RuBP.
D reduction of GP to TP (GALP) and carboxylation.

10 The chloroplasts of some guard cells possess photosystem I only. Which of the following can be produced by these chloroplasts?
A ATP only
B sugars only
C sugars, ATP and NADP
D ATP, O_2 and reduced NADP

continued …

Structured questions

11 a The rate of photosynthesis is limited by certain environmental factors known as limiting factors.

   i What do you understand by the term 'limiting factor'? [2 marks]

   ii Identify **three** environmental limiting factors of photosynthesis. [2 marks]

b The apparatus (Audus microburette), shown below, is used to measure the rate of photosynthesis.

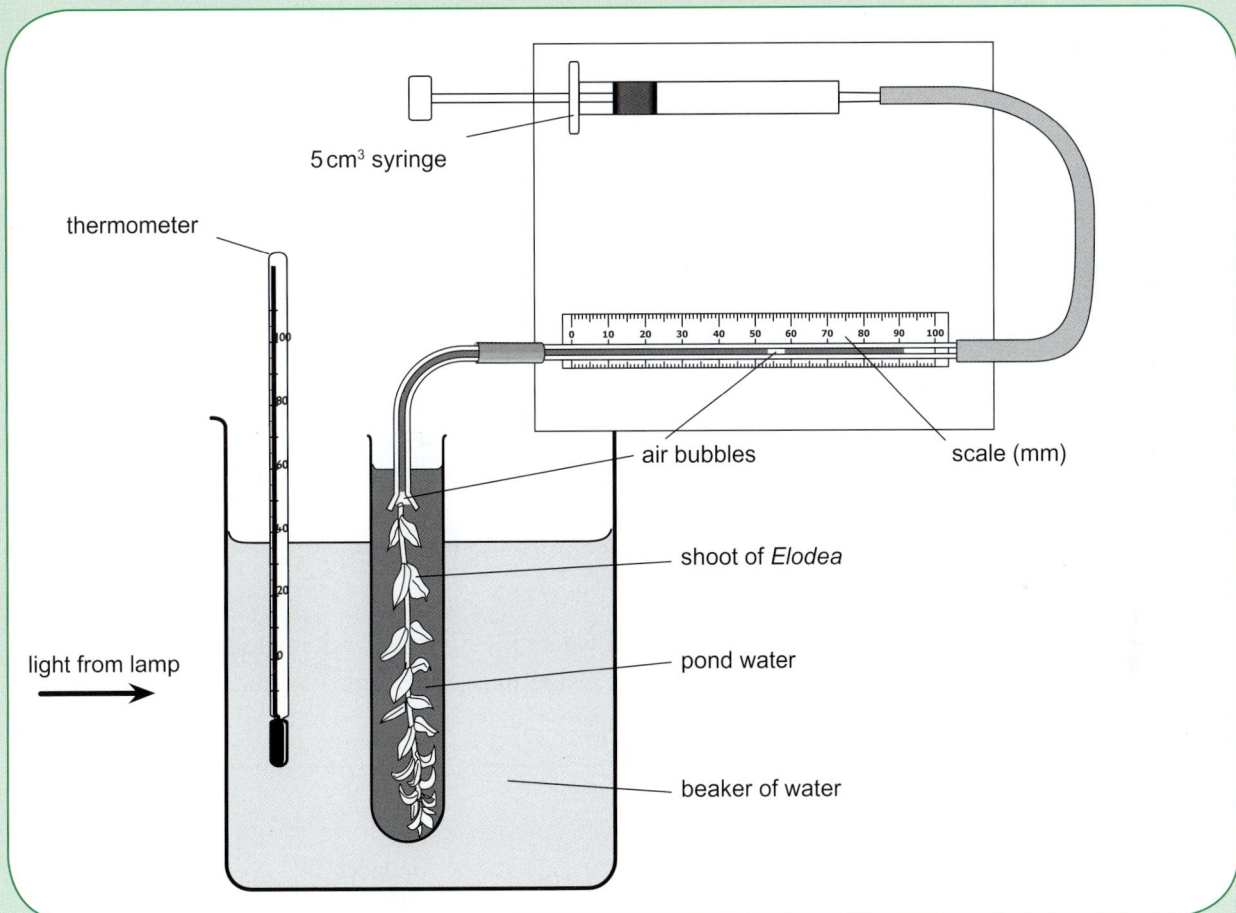

   i Describe how the apparatus shown in this diagram can be used to investigate the effect of different concentrations of carbon dioxide on the rate of photosynthesis. [4 marks]

   ii Describe **two** precautions which should be taken in setting up and conducting the experiment to ensure that the results obtained are valid measures of the rate of photosynthesis under the given conditions. [2 marks]

continued …

c   The graph below shows how the rate of photosynthesis varies with light intensity at different concentrations of carbon dioxide.

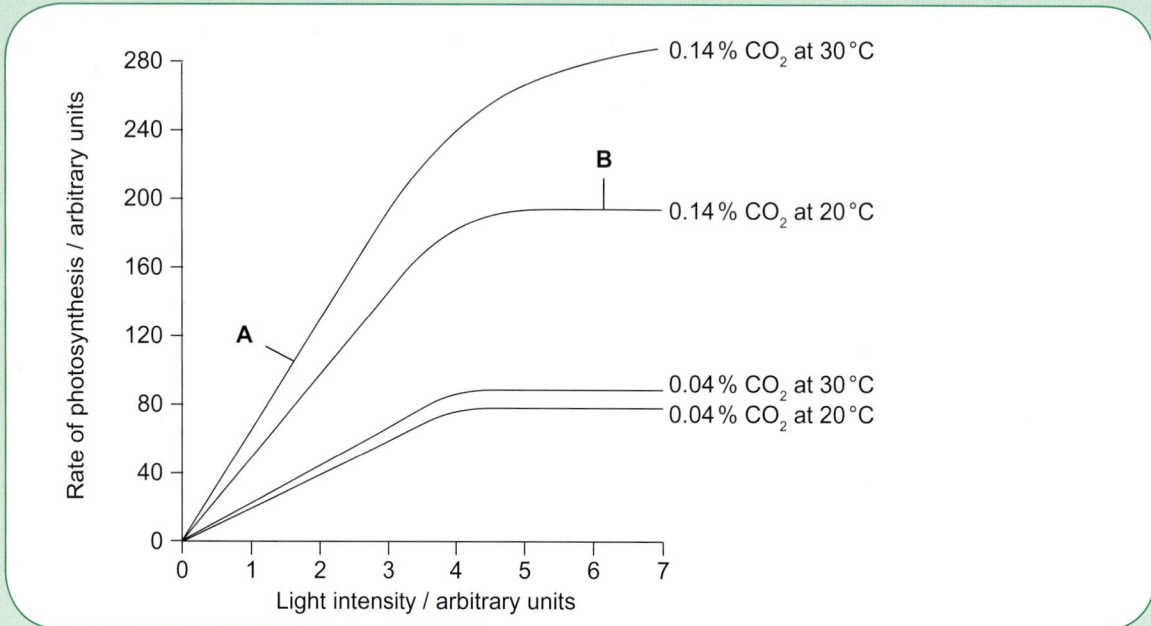

i   Identify any factors limiting the rate of photosynthesis in regions **A** and **B**. Give reasons for your answer.   [3 marks]

ii Suggest how knowledge of limiting factors can be used to increase plant productivity.   [2 marks]

12 The thylakoid membranes of the chloroplast are where the light-dependent stage of photosynthesis takes place. The diagram below summarises the light-dependent stage of photosynthesis.

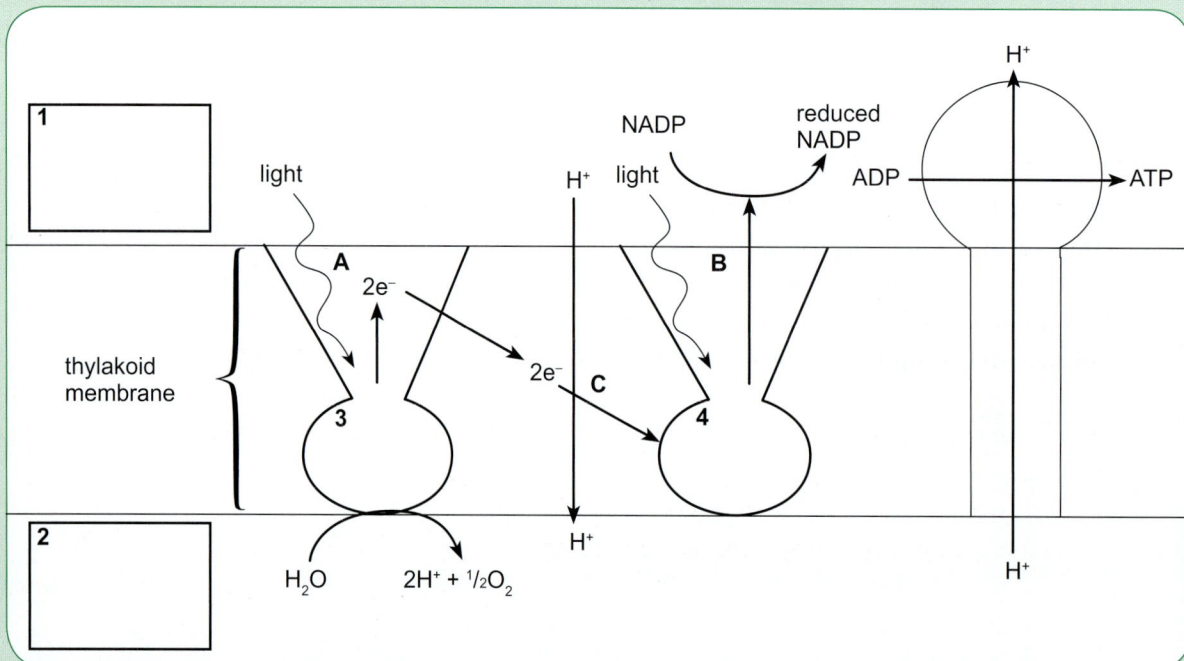

continued ...

a Copy the diagram. Write the labels 'stroma' and 'thylakoid lumen' in the appropriate boxes labelled **1** and **2** in the diagram. In each case, give a reason for your answer. [4 marks]

b **A** and **B** represent photosystems.
  i What do you understand by the term 'photosystem'?
  ii Write PSI and PSII in the appropriate boxes labelled **3** and **4**.
  iii Make a labelled drawing to show the generalised structure of a photosystem. [5 marks]

c Describe the photoactivation of chlorophyll. [3 marks]

d What type of molecule is represented by label **C**? [1 mark]

e Explain the function of the proton (hydrogen ion) gradient which is produced across the thylakoid membrane. [3 marks]

f Identify the type of photophosphorylation shown on the diagram. Give a reason for your answer. [2 marks]

13 Fixation of carbon dioxide occurs during the light-independent reactions of the Calvin cycle. The diagram below is a summary of the Calvin cycle.

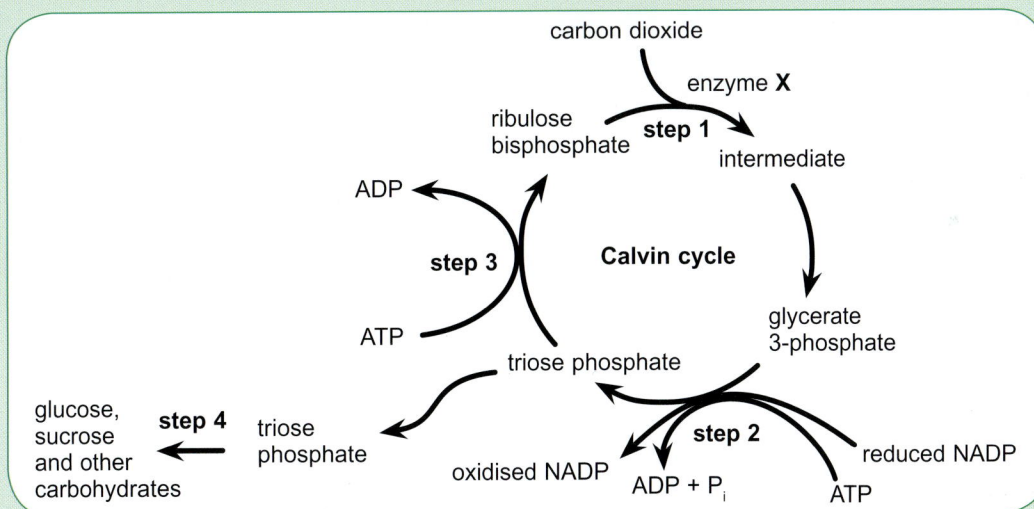

a i State where in the chloroplast the Calvin cycle takes place. [1 mark]
  ii The light-independent reactions of the Calvin cycle occur in steps. Copy the diagram above and identify steps **1** to **4**. [4 marks]
  iii Name the enzyme **X** which catalyses the reaction of carbon dioxide with the carbon dioxide acceptor, RuBP. [1 mark]
  iv Name **two** products of the light-dependent reactions of photosynthesis that are needed in the Calvin cycle. [2 marks]
  v Identify on the diagram the stages where the chemicals identified in **iv** are used in the Calvin cycle. [3 marks]

b Gramoxone™ is a widely used weed killer in the Caribbean. It prevents the light-dependent stage of photosynthesis from occurring. Explain how it causes the weeds to die. [4 marks]

continued …

Essay questions

14 a By means of annotated diagrams only, describe the structure and functions in photosynthesis of:

    i the external structure of the dicotyledonous leaf. [3 marks]

    i a palisade cell. [3 marks]

    iii a chloroplast. [5 marks]

  b Explain what is meant by the term 'photosynthetic pigment' and explain the difference between a 'primary pigment' and an 'accessory pigment'. [4 marks]

15 a Describe how light energy is converted into chemical energy in the light-dependent stage of photosynthesis. [7 marks]

  b Explain the main stages of the Calvin cycle. [8 marks]

16 a **i** Define the term 'photosynthesis'. [2 marks]

    ii Photosynthesis is represented by the following equation:

$$6CO_2 + 6H_2O \rightarrow C_6H_{12}O_6 + 6O_2$$

    Give **four** reasons why this equation does not fully represent photosynthesis. [4 marks]

  b Discuss the roles of the following in photosynthesis:

    i light

    ii water

    iii photosystems [9 marks]

Chapter 2
Cellular respiration and ATP synthesis

By the end of this chapter you should be able to:

a   outline the stepwise breakdown of glucose in cellular respiration;

b   explain the sequence of steps in glycolysis;

c   describe the structure of a mitochondrion, relating its structure to its function;

d   state the fate of pyruvate in the cytosol when oxygen is available;

e   outline the Krebs cycle;

f   explain the significance of the Krebs cycle in ATP formation;

g   explain the process of oxidative phosphorylation with reference to the electron transport chain;

h   investigate the rate of oxygen uptake during respiration using a simple respirometer;

i   compare the fate of pyruvate in the absence of oxygen in animals and yeast.

All living cells, and therefore all living organisms, need energy in order to survive. Energy is required for many different purposes. Every living cell, for example, must be able to move substances across its membranes against their concentration gradients, by **active transport**. Cells need to use energy to drive many of their **metabolic reactions**, such as building protein molecules from amino acids, or making copies of DNA molecules. Energy is used to move chromosomes around during mitosis and meiosis. Most animals also have specialised **muscle cells**, which use energy to make themselves contract and so produce movement.

Cells obtain energy by metabolic pathways known as **respiration**. Respiration releases chemical potential energy from glucose and other energy-containing organic molecules.

ATP

ATP stands for **adenosine triphosphate**. Every living cell uses ATP as its immediate source of energy. When energy is released from glucose or other molecules during respiration, it is used to make ATP.

Figure 2.1 shows the structure of an ATP molecule. ATP is a phosphorylated nucleotide. It is similar in structure to the nucleotides that make up RNA and DNA.

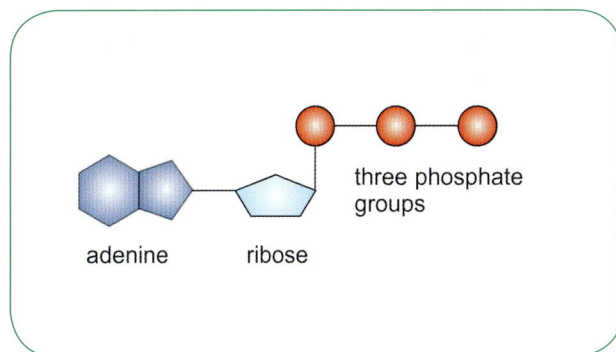

Figure 2.1   The structure of ATP.

ATP molecules contain energy. When one phosphate group is removed from each molecule in one mole of ATP, 30.5 kJ of energy is released (Figure 2.2). This is a hydrolysis reaction, and it is catalysed by enzymes called **ATPases**. Most cells contain many different types of ATPases. The products of the reaction are ADP (adenosine diphosphate) and a phosphate group (P_i).

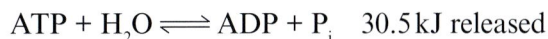

$$ATP + H_2O \rightleftharpoons ADP + P_i \quad 30.5\,kJ \text{ released}$$

More energy can be obtained if a second phosphate group is removed. AMP stands for adenosine monophosphate.

$$ADP + H_2O \rightleftharpoons AMP + P_i \quad 30.5\,kJ \text{ released}$$

The each-way arrows in these equations mean that the reaction can go either way. ATPases may catalyse the synthesis of ATP, or its breakdown.

ATP is used for almost every energy-demanding activity in the body. The amount of energy contained in one ATP molecule is often a suitable quantity to use for a particular purpose. One glucose molecule would contain too much, so a lot would be wasted if all the energy in a glucose molecule was released to make a particular event happen. ATP can provide energy in small packages. Also, the energy in ATP can be released very quickly and easily, at exactly the right time and in exactly the right place in a cell, just when and where it is needed. ATP is often known as the 'energy currency' of a cell. Each cell has to make its own ATP – it cannot be transported from one cell to another. However, within a cell ATP can be likened to money – a kind of energy currency – that can be used to provide energy for a wide range of processes.

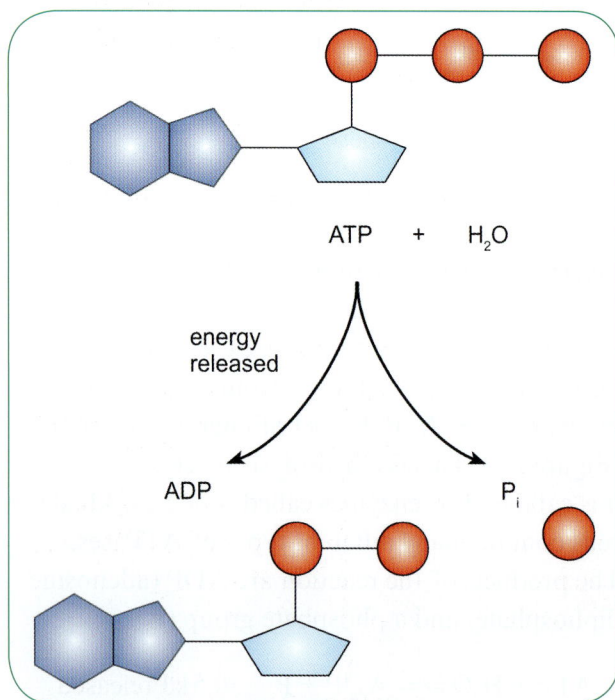

Figure 2.2 Energy is released when ATP is hydrolysed.

SAQ

1 Outline why energy is needed for each of these processes. (You may need to look them up.)
   a the transport of sucrose in a plant
   b the transmission of an action potential along a nerve axon
   c the selective reabsorption of glucose from a kidney nephron.
2 a What are the similarities between an ATP molecule and a nucleotide in DNA?
   b What are the differences between them?

Glycolysis

Glycolysis is the first group of reactions that takes place in respiration. It means 'breaking glucose apart'. Glycolysis is a metabolic pathway that takes place in the cytoplasm of the cell. Glucose is broken down in a series of steps, each catalysed by an enzyme. In the process, a small proportion of the energy in each glucose molecule is released, and used to make a small amount of ATP. Figure 2.3 shows the main steps in glycolysis.

The first step in glycolysis involves adding a phosphate group to a glucose molecule. This produces glucose-6-phosphate. The process is called **phosphorylation**. It raises the energy level of the compound, making it able to participate in the steps that follow. The phosphate group comes from an ATP molecule, which is converted to ADP in the process.

Next, the atoms in the glucose-6-phosphate are reorganised to produce fructose-6-phosphate. No atoms are added or removed. Glucose-6-phosphate and fructose-6-phosphate are therefore **isomers**, and the process of changing one to the other is called **isomerisation**. Once again, this is necessary to make the next step in the pathway possible.

The next step is another phosphorylation, this time adding a phosphate group to the fructose-6-phosphate to form fructose bisphosphate. This undergoes a **catabolic** reaction by being split (**lysis**) into two molecules of three-carbon sugars, **triose phosphate**. The two are actually slightly different from each other – they are the isomers dihydroxyacetone phosphate and glyceraldehyde-3-phosphate.

The triose phosphates are then oxidised to **pyruvate**, by having hydrogen removed from them. This **oxidation** is catalysed by a **dehydrogenase** enzyme. The enzyme can only work if there is another molecule present that can take up the hydrogen that it removes. This molecule is called **NAD**, which stands for nicotinamide adenine dinucleotide. NAD is a **coenzyme** – a substance that is needed to help an enzyme to catalyse its reactions. The addition of hydrogen to a substance is called **reduction**, so NAD becomes **reduced NAD** (Figure 2.4). This is sometimes written as NADH.

If you look at Figure 2.3, you will see that something else happens when triose phosphate is oxidised to pyruvate. Two ADP molecules are converted to ATP for each triose phosphate. This uses some of the energy that was in the original glucose molecule. Glycolysis transfers some of the energy from within the glucose molecule to energy in ATP molecules. This is an example of **substrate-level phosphorylation**, which distinguishes it from the way ATP is synthesised in oxidative phosphorylation (see page 26).

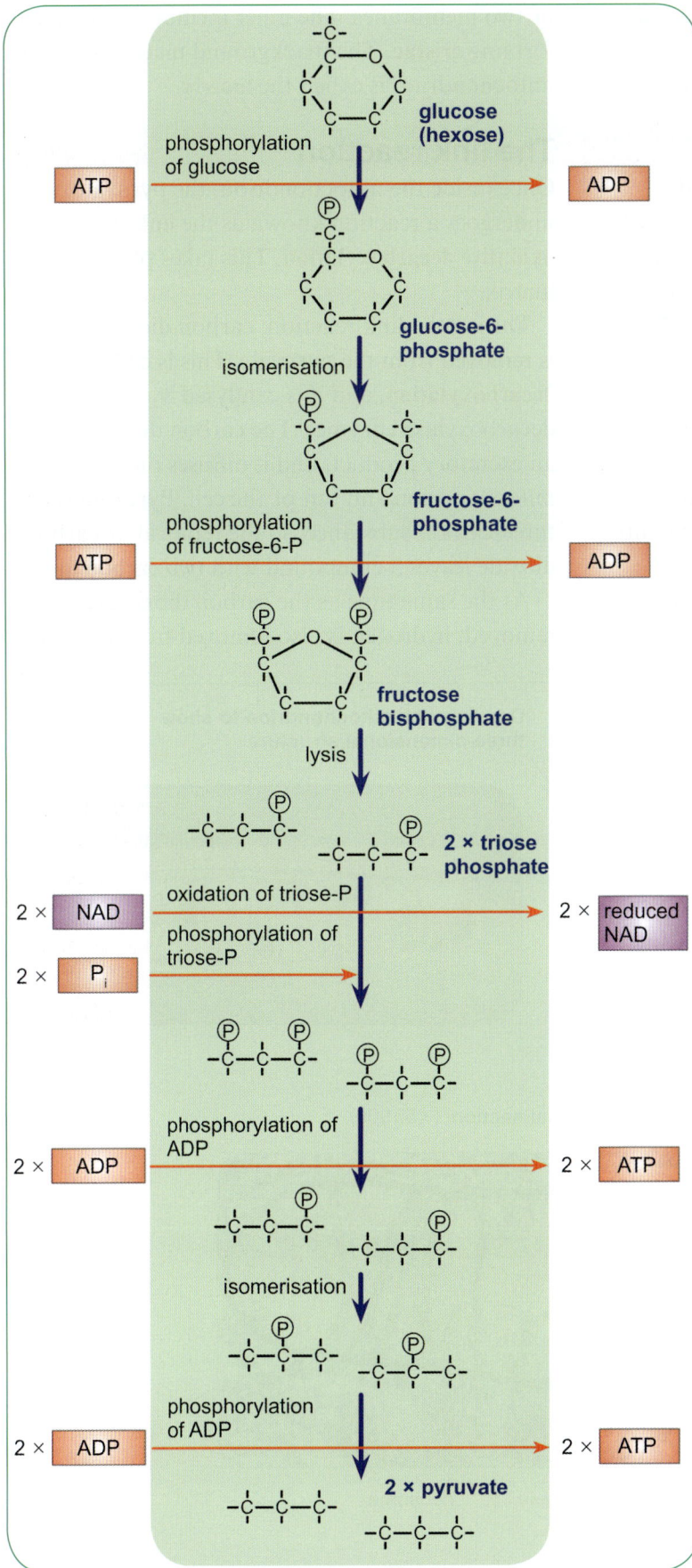

Figure 2.3 The main steps of glycolysis.

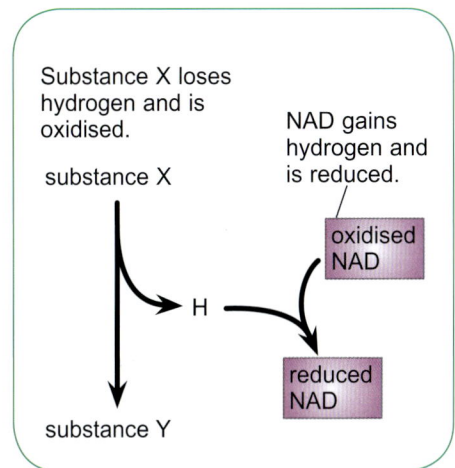

Figure 2.4 Oxidation and reduction.

SAQ _____

3 Look at Figure 2.3 to answer these questions.

   a Explain why ATP is actually used up during the first step in glycolysis.

   b How many ATP molecules are used?

   c How many ATP molecules are produced during glycolysis, from one glucose molecule?

   d What is the net gain in ATP molecules when one glucose molecule undergoes glycolysis?

Into a mitochondrion

What happens to the pyruvate depends on the availability of oxygen in the cell. If there is plenty, then **aerobic respiration** can take place. The pyruvate is moved into a mitochondrion. This is done by active transport (so again, we are using up ATP before we can make it).

Figure 2.5 shows the structure of a mitochondrion. Like a chloroplast, it is surrounded by an **envelope**

of two membranes. The inner membrane is folded, forming **cristae**. The 'background material' inside a mitochondrion is called the **matrix**.

The link reaction

Once inside the mitochondrion, the pyruvate undergoes a reaction known as the **link reaction** or **oxidative decarboxylation**. This takes place in the matrix.

During the link reaction, carbon dioxide is removed from the pyruvate. This is called **decarboxylation**, and it is catalysed by decarboxylase enzymes. The carbon dioxide is an excretory product, and it diffuses out of the mitochondrion and out of the cell. Pyruvate is a three-carbon substance, so the removal of carbon dioxide leaves a compound with two carbon atoms.

At the same time as the carbon dioxide is removed, hydrogen is also removed from pyruvate.

Diagram of a mitochondrion in longitudinal section

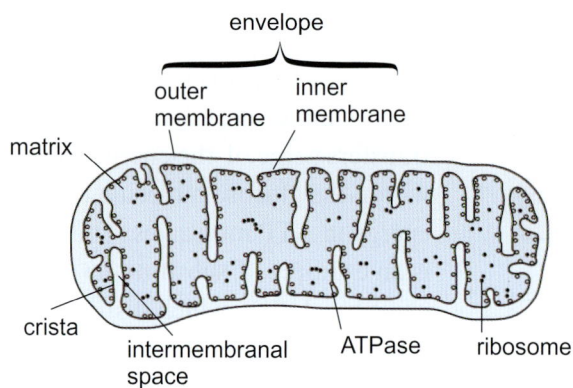

Drawing of a mitochondrion to show three-dimensional structure

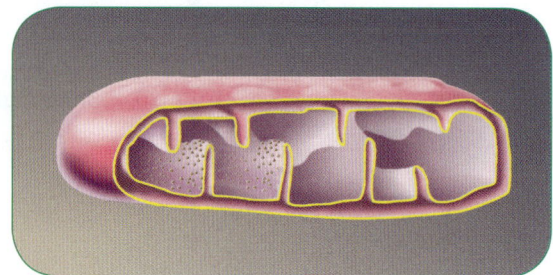

Electron micrograph of a mitochondrion in longitudinal section (×55 900)

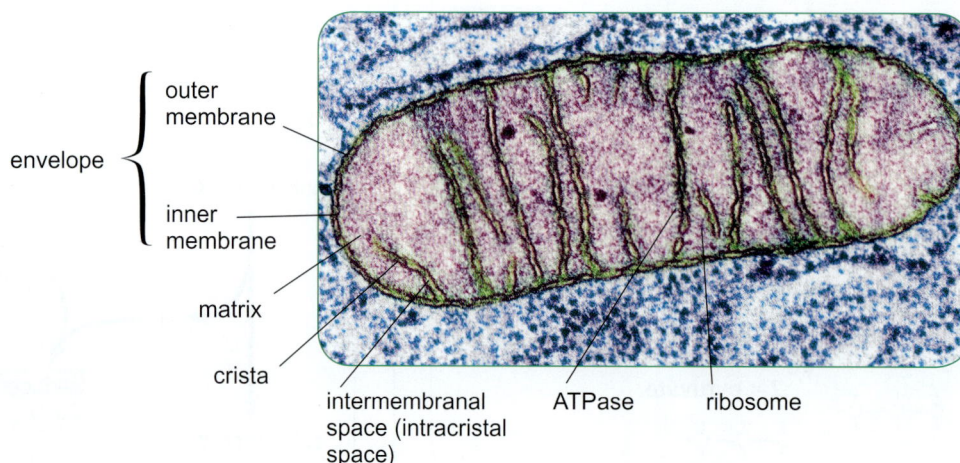

Figure 2.5   The structure of a mitochondrion.

This is again picked up by NAD, producing reduced NAD.

The remainder of the pyruvate combines with **coenzyme A** (often known as CoA) to produce **acetyl CoA** (Figure 2.6).

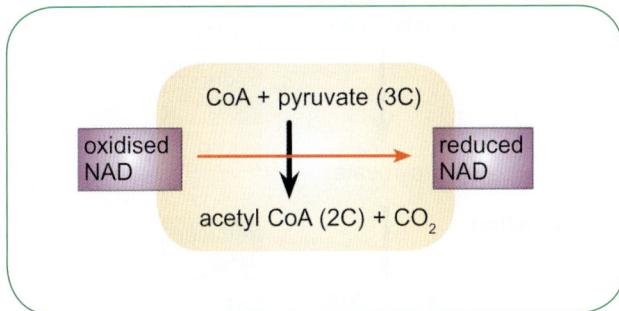

Figure 2.6 The link reaction.

The Krebs cycle

The link reaction is given that name because it provides the link between the two main series of reactions in aerobic respiration – glycolysis and the **Krebs cycle**.

The Krebs cycle takes place in the matrix of the mitochondrion. It is a series of reactions in which a six-carbon compound is gradually changed to a four-carbon compound.

First, the acetyl CoA made in the link reaction combines with a four-carbon compound called **oxaloacetate**. You can see in Figure 2.7 that coenzyme A is released at this point, ready to combine with more pyruvate. It is has served its function of passing the two-carbon acetyl group from pyruvate to oxaloacetate.

This converts oxaloacetate into a six-carbon compound called **citrate**. In a series of small steps, the citrate is converted back to oxaloacetate. As this happens, more carbon dioxide is released and more NAD is reduced as it accepts hydrogen. In one stage, a different coenzyme, called **FAD**, accepts hydrogen. And at one point in the cycle a molecule of ATP is made.

Each of the steps in the Krebs cycle is catalysed by a specific enzyme. These enzymes are all present in the matrix of the mitochondrion. Those that

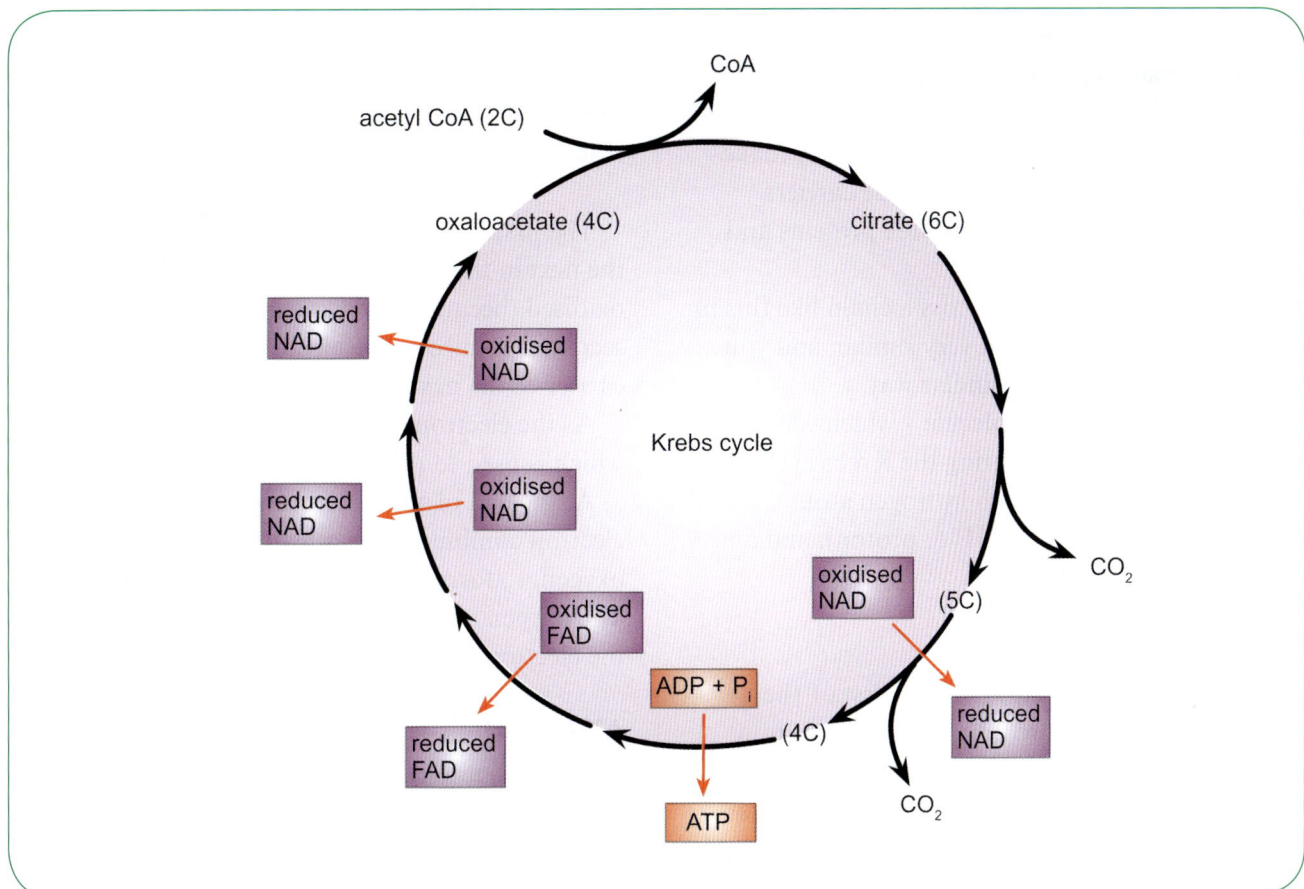

Figure 2.7 The Krebs cycle.

cause oxidation are called oxidoreductases or dehydrogenases. Those that remove carbon dioxide are decarboxylases.

Remember that the whole purpose of respiration is to produce ATP for the cell to use as an energy source. At first sight, it looks as though the contribution of the Krebs cycle to this is not very large, because only one ATP molecule is produced during one 'turn' of the cycle. This direct production of ATP is called **substrate-level phosphorylation**. However, as you will see, all those reduced NADs and reduced FADs are used to generate a very significant amount of ATP – much more than can be done from glycolysis.

Figure 2.8 shows how glycolysis, the link reaction and the Krebs cycle link together.

Oxidative phosphorylation

The last stages of aerobic respiration involve **oxidative phosphorylation**: the use of oxygen to produce ATP from ADP and P_i. (You'll remember from page 7 that photophosphorylation is the production of ATP using light.)

The electron transport chain

Held in the inner membrane of the mitochondrion are molecules called **electron carriers**. They make up the **electron transport chain**. These carriers are complex molecules, and include proteins and cytochromes.

You have already come across a chain like this in photosynthesis. It is indeed very similar, and you will see that it works in a similar way.

Each reduced NAD molecule – which was produced in the matrix during the Krebs cycle – releases its hydrogens. Each hydrogen atom splits into a hydrogen ion, H^+ (a proton), and an electron, e^-.

$$H \longrightarrow H^+ + e^-$$

The electrons are picked up by the first of the electron carriers (Figure 2.9). The carrier is now reduced, because it has gained an electron. The reduced NAD has been oxidised, because it has lost hydrogen. The NAD can now go back to the Krebs cycle cand be re-used as a coenzyme to pick up hydrogen again.

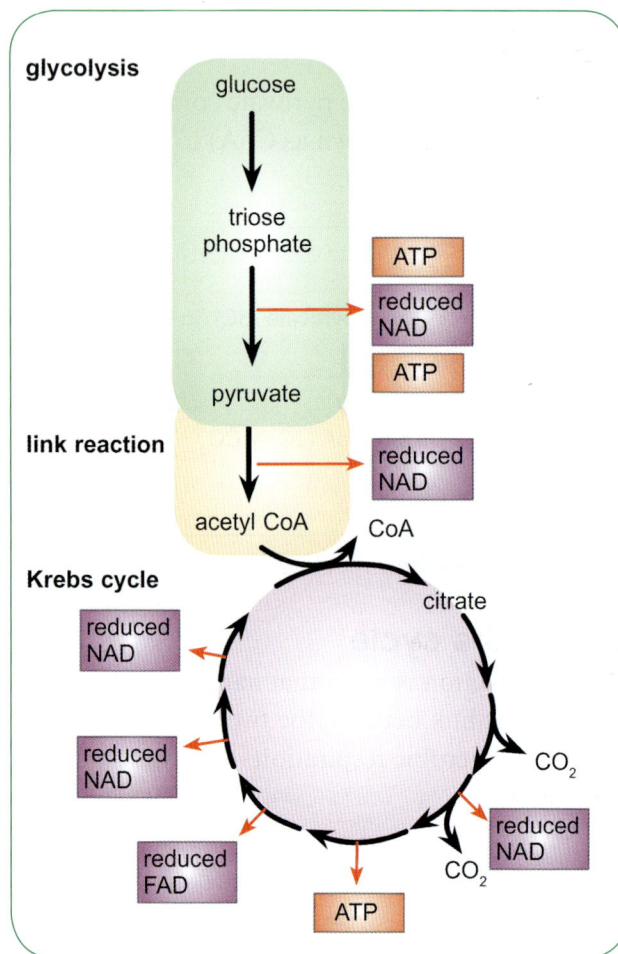

Figure 2.8 Summary of glycolysis, the link reaction and the Krebs cycle.

The first electron carrier passes its electron to the next in the chain. The first carrier is therefore oxidised (because it has lost an electron) and the second is reduced. The electron is passed from one carrier to the next all the way along the chain.

As the electron is moved along, it releases energy which is used to make ATP.

At the end of the electron transport chain, the electron combines with a hydrogen ion and with oxygen, to form water. This is why we need oxygen. The oxygen acts as the final electron acceptor for the electron transport chain.

ATP synthesis

We have seen that when hydrogens were donated to the electron transport chain by reduced NAD, they split into hydrogen ions and electrons. These both have an important role to play.

The electrons release energy as they pass along

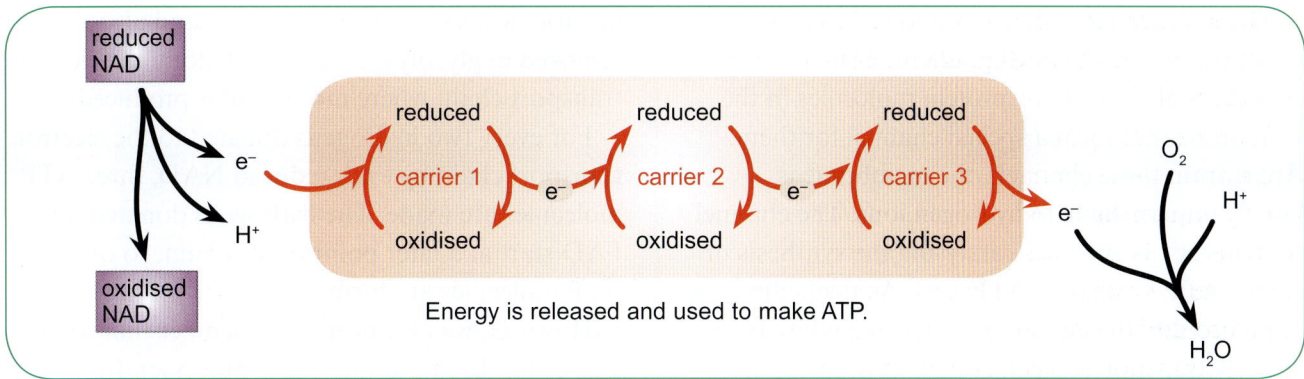

Figure 2.9 The electron transport chain.

the electron transport chain. Some of this energy is used to pump hydrogen ions across the inner membrane of the mitochondrion and into the space between the inner and outer membranes (Figure 2.10) – the intermembranal space. This builds up a concentration gradient for the hydrogen ions, because there are more of them on one side of the inner membrane than the other. It is also an electrical gradient, because the hydrogen ions, H^+, have a positive charge. So there is now a greater positive charge on one side of the membrane than the other. There is an **electrochemical gradient**.

One of the carriers is cytochrome c. A very large protein that spans the membrane, called **cytochrome oxidase**, allows the electron carried by cytochrome c to be used to make water and allow the energy from the electron to be used to pump H^+ across the membrane.

1 The electron transport chain provides energy to pump hydrogen ions from the matrix into the space between the two mitochondrial membranes.

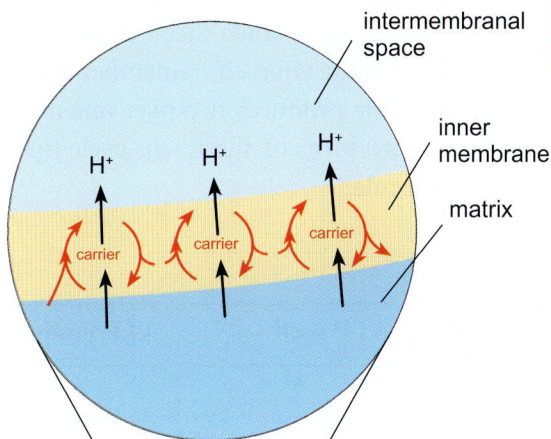

2 When the hydrogen ions are allowed to diffuse back through ATPase, the transferred energy is used to make ATP from ADP and P_i.

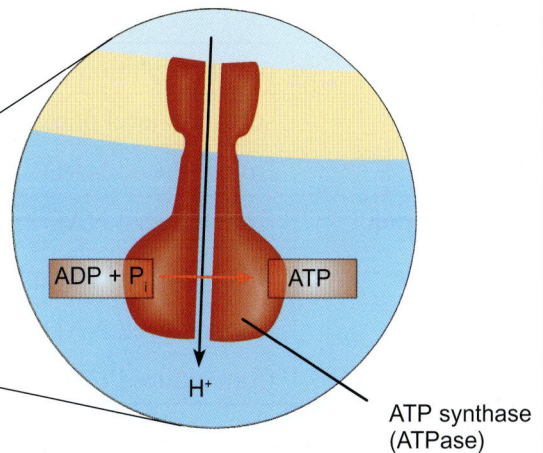

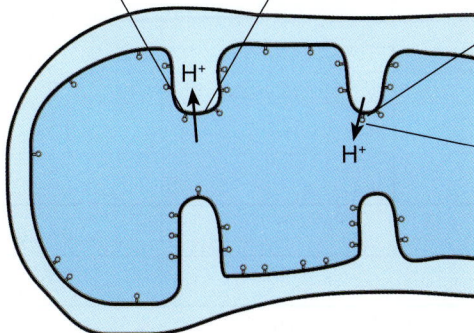

Figure 2.10 Oxidative phosphorylation.

The hydrogen ions are now allowed to diffuse down the electrochemical gradient. They have to pass through a group of protein molecules in the membrane that form a special channel for them. Apart from these channels, the membrane is largely impermeable to hydrogen ions. The channel proteins act as enzymes catalysing the synthesis of ATP – **ATP synthases** (ATPases). As the hydrogens pass through, the energy that they gained by being actively transported against their concentration gradient is used to make ATP from ADP and P_i.

This process is sometimes called **chemiosmosis**, which is rather confusing as it has nothing to do with water or water potentials.

SAQ

4 a Across which membranes in a mitochondrion would you expect there to be a pH gradient?
  b Which side would have the lower pH?
  c Across which membranes in a chloroplast would you expect there to be a pH gradient?
  d Which side would have the lower pH?

How much ATP?

We have seen that, in aerobic respiration, glucose is first oxidised to pyruvate in glycolysis. Then the pyruvate is oxidised in the Krebs cycle, which produces some ATP directly. Hydrogens removed at various steps in the Krebs cycle, and also those removed in glycolysis, are passed along the electron transport chain where more ATP is produced.

For every two hydrogens donated to the electron transport chain by each reduced NAD, three ATP molecules are made. The hydrogens donated by FAD start at a later point in the chain, so only two ATP molecules are formed.

However, we also need to remember that some energy has been put into these processes. In particular, energy is needed to transport ADP from the cytoplasm and into the mitochondrion. (You can't make ATP unless you have ADP and P_i to make it from.) Energy is also needed to transport ATP from the mitochondrion, where it is made, into the cytoplasm, where it will be used. Taking this into account, we can say that overall the hydrogens from each reduced NAD produce about two and a half ATPs (not three) while those from reduced FAD produce about one a half ATPs (not two).

Now we can count up how much ATP is made from the oxidation of one glucose molecule. Table 2.1 shows the balance sheet. If you want to work this out for yourself, remember that one glucose molecule produces two pyruvate molecules, so there are two turns of the Krebs cycle for each glucose molecule.

Process		ATP used	ATP produced
Glycolysis	phosphorylation of glucose	2	
	substrate-level phosphorylation of ADP		4
	from reduced NAD		5
Link reaction	from reduced NAD		5
Krebs cycle	substrate-level phosphorylation of ADP		2
	from reduced NAD		15
	from reduced FAD		3
Totals		2	34
Net yield			32

Table 2.1 ATP molecules that can theoretically be produced from one glucose molecule. Note: these are maximum values, and the actual yield will vary from tissue to tissue.

Structure and function in mitochondria

The number of mitochondria in a cell depends on its activity. Mammalian liver cells, which are very active, contain between 1000 and 2000 mitochondria. Their shape and size are variable but they remain quite narrow, rarely more than 1 μm in diameter. This keeps the distances down for the diffusion of the materials that pass into and out of the mitochondrion (Figure 2.11).

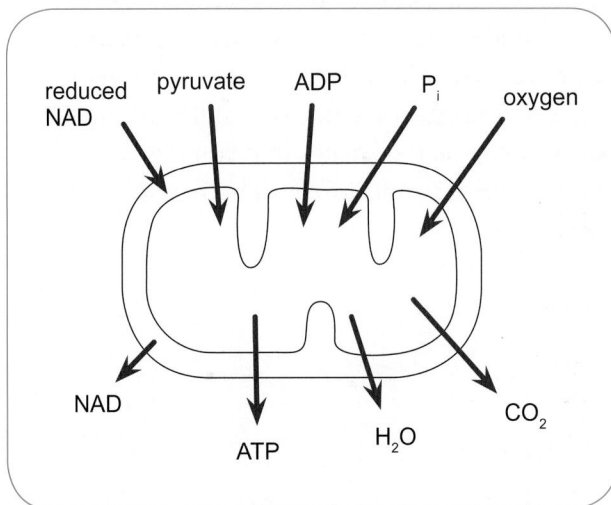

Figure 2.11 Exchange of substances between the mitochondrion and the cytoplasm.

The inner mitochondrial membrane is folded inwards to form cristae. This membrane is the site of the electron transport chain and oxidative phosphorylation and contains the proteins necessary for this, including the ATPase molecules attached to the surface of the inner membrane. The space between the two mitochondrial membranes usually has a lower pH than the matrix of the mitochondrion as a result of the H^+ that are transported into the intermembranal space by the activity of the electron transport chain. They are contained there until they are allowed out during ATP synthesis.

These cristae give the inner membrane a large total surface area, so it can hold many molecules of the electron transport chain and ATPase. The more membrane there is, the more ATP can be produced. Cristae in mitochondria from different types of cells show considerable variation in appearance, but, in general, mitochondria from active cells have longer, more densely packed cristae than those from less active cells (Figure 2.12).

The outer and inner mitochondrial membranes have different compositions and properties, particularly in terms of the movement of substances across them. For example, reduced NAD generated in the cytoplasm has to be moved into the intermembranal spaces to provide electrons for the electron transport chain. Electrons have to be transported back and forth between the faces of the inner membrane along the elctron transport chain to move H^+ into the intermembranal spaces. ATPase molecules attached to the inner membrane allow the movement of H^+ through them from the intermembranal space to the matrix. All of these are necessary for ATP synthesis.

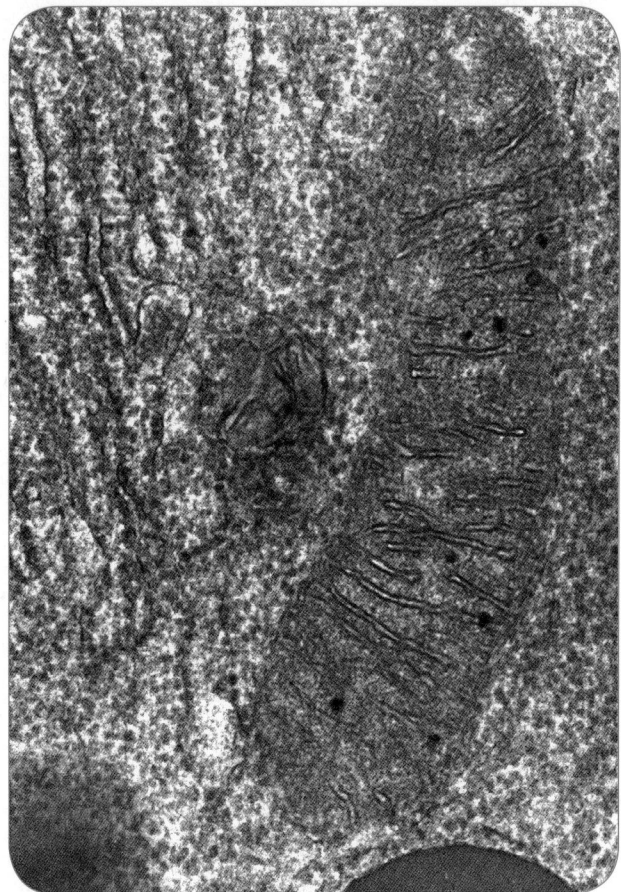

Figure 2.12 TEM of a mitochondrion inside a pancreatic cell, where much ATP is required for the synthesis of enzymes.

Using energy to keep warm

Going through the ATPases is not the only way that hydrogen ions (protons) can move down the electrochemical gradient from the space between the mitochondrial membranes into its matrix. Some of the protons are able to leak through other parts of the inner membrane. This is called proton leak.

Proton leak is important in generating heat. In babies, in a special tissue known as brown fat, the inner mitochondrial membrane contains a transport protein called uncoupling protein (UCP), which allows protons to leak through the membrane. The energy involved is not used to make ATP – in other words, the movement of the protons has been uncoupled from ATP production. Instead, the energy is transferred to heat energy. Brown fat in babies can produce a lot of heat.

Some people's mitochondrial membranes are leakier than others, and it is likely that this difference can at least partly account for people's different metabolic rates.

During the First World War in Britain, women helped to make artillery shells. One of the chemicals used was 2,4-dinitrophenol. Some of the women became very thin after exposure to this chemical. For a short time in the 1930s, it was actually used as a diet pill. Now we know that dinitrophenol increases the leakiness of the inner mitochondrial membrane. It is banned from use as a diet pill because it increases the likelihood of developing cataracts and it can damage the nervous system. However, several pharmaceutical companies are still working on the development of drugs that could be used to help obese people lose weight, based on this same idea.

Anaerobic respiration

The processes described so far – glycolysis followed by the link reaction, the Krebs cycle and the electron transport chain – make up the metabolic reactions that we call **aerobic respiration**. They can all only take place when oxygen is present. This is because oxygen is needed as the final electron acceptor from the electron transport chain. If there is no oxygen, then the electron carriers cannot pass on their electrons, so they cannot accept any more from reduced NAD. So the reduced NAD cannot be reconverted to NAD, meaning that there is nothing available to accept hydrogens from the reactions in the link reaction or Krebs cycle. The link reaction, Krebs cycle and the electron transport chain all grind to a halt. It is like a traffic jam building up on a blocked road. The whole process of respiration backs up all the way from the formation of pyruvate.

However, glycolysis can still take place – so long as something can be done with the pyruvate. And, indeed, pyruvate does have an alternative, unblocked route that it can go down. In many organisms it can be changed into **lactate**.

$$\text{pyruvate} + \text{reduced NAD} \longrightarrow \text{lactate} + \text{NAD}$$

This reaction requires the addition of hydrogen, which is taken from reduced NAD. The pyruvate is acting as an alternative hydrogen acceptor.

These NAD molecules can now accept hydrogen as glycolysis takes place, just as they normally do. So at least some ATP can be made, because glycolysis can carry on as usual.

The oxidation of glucose by means of glycolysis and the lactate pathway is known as **anaerobic respiration** or **lactic fermentation** (Figure 2.13).

You can probably see that anaerobic respiration only generates a tiny amount of ATP compared with aerobic respiration. None of the ATP that could have been generated in the Krebs cycle or electron transport chain is made. Instead of the theoretical maximum of 32 molecules of ATP from each molecule of glucose, anaerobic respiration produces only 2. (Remember that the reduced NAD produced in glycolysis is not able to pass on its hydrogens to the electron transport chain – it gives them to pyruvate instead.)

Dealing with the lactate

The lactate pathway is most likely to occur in skeletal muscle cells. When they are exercising vigorously, they may need more oxygen than can be supplied to them by the blood. They carry on using whatever oxygen they can in aerobic respiration, but may also 'top up' their ATP production by using the lactate pathway. This means that lactate can build up in the muscle cells.

The lactate diffuses into the blood, where it dissolves in the plasma and is carried around the body. A high concentration of lactate can make a person feel disorientated and nauseous, as it affects the cells in the brain. If it builds up too much, it can stop the muscles from contracting. A 400 m race is notorious for producing high concentrations of lactate in the blood, and some athletes actually vomit after running this race.

When the lactate reaches the liver, the hepatocytes (liver cells) absorb it and use it. They first convert it back to pyruvate. Later, when the exercise has stopped and oxygen is plentiful again, they will oxidise the pyruvate using the link reaction and the Krebs cycle. They also convert some of it to glycogen, which they store as an energy reserve.

This removal of the lactate by the hepatocytes requires oxygen. This is why you go on breathing heavily after strenuous exercise. You are providing extra oxygen to your liver cells, to enable them to metabolise the lactate. The extra oxygen required is often known as the **oxygen debt**.

Anaerobic respiration in yeast

All mammals use the lactate pathway in anaerobic respiration. Fungi and plants, however, have a different pathway, in which **ethanol** is produced (Figure 2.14). This is also called fermentation.

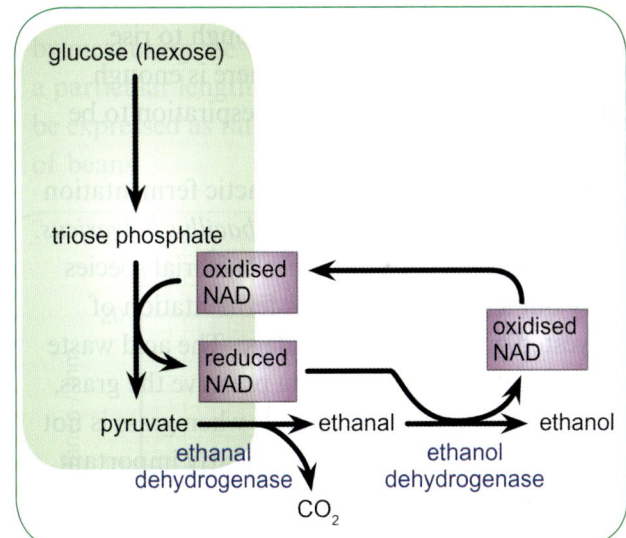

Figure 2.14   Fermentation (anaerobic respiration) in yeast.

SAQ

5 a Outline the differences between the metabolism of pyruvate in humans and in yeast, in anaerobic respiration.

   b How are these two processes similar?

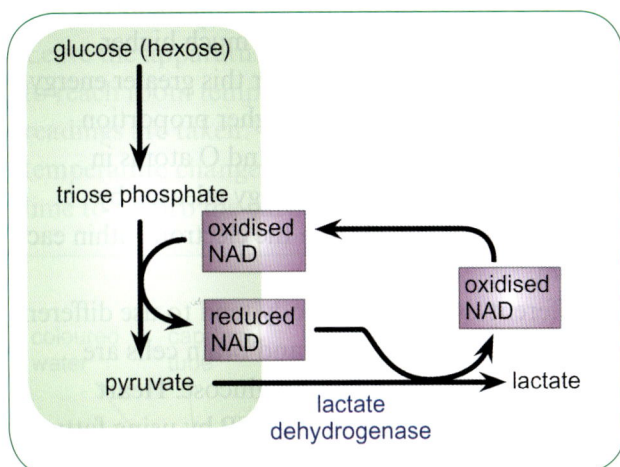

Figure 2.13   Lactic fermentation (anaerobic respiration); the production of lactate from pyruvate generates oxidised NAD and allows glycolysis to continue.

Errors involved in measuring gas volume

Gas volumes are extremely sensitive to temperature and pressure. If the air temperature rises during an experiment, the drop in the volume of air inside the apparatus will be less than that you would expect from the uptake of oxygen. Water baths are commonly used to maintain stable temperatures, but this respirometer cannot be used in a water bath.

Error is also introduced if there is a change in the atmospheric pressure of the laboratory air outside the apparatus during the experiment.

Both of these errors can be corrected by using a second simple respirometer, without respiring organisms, at the same time as the experimental respirometer. The apparatus without organisms acts as a control and readings have to be taken at the same time with both pieces of apparatus. The control apparatus measures volume changes due to changes in atmospheric pressure and air temperature. The readings can be subtracted from the experimental results, to find the changes due to respiration alone.

A more complicated apparatus that can be used with a water bath to stabilise temperature, and which can reduce error due to changes in laboratory air pressure, is shown in Figure 2.18. This apparatus uses a U-tube manometer to measure pressure difference between the air in the two tubes. Any gas volume change due to temperature or laboratory air pressure fluctuations will affect both the control tube, without respiring organisms, and the tube containing the organisms. As the two tubes are connected by the manometer these pressure changes are cancelled out. Pressure changes affecting one tube but not the other will cause the manometer fluid to show a difference in height on the two sides of the U-tube.

The apparatus is assembled with both three-way taps open to the air, to prevent the manometer fluid being pushed into the tubes. However, during an experiment both three-way taps are closed to prevent air movement between the air in the apparatus and air in the laboratory, as shown in Figure 2.18. The difference between the levels of manometer fluid on the two sides of the U-tube represents the pressure difference between the air in the two tubes. This can be recorded over time.

However, there is both a pressure and volume change in the experimental tube. If the syringe is used to equalise the levels of the manometer fluid on both sides, while the taps remain in the position shown in the diagram, the syringe will record just the volume.

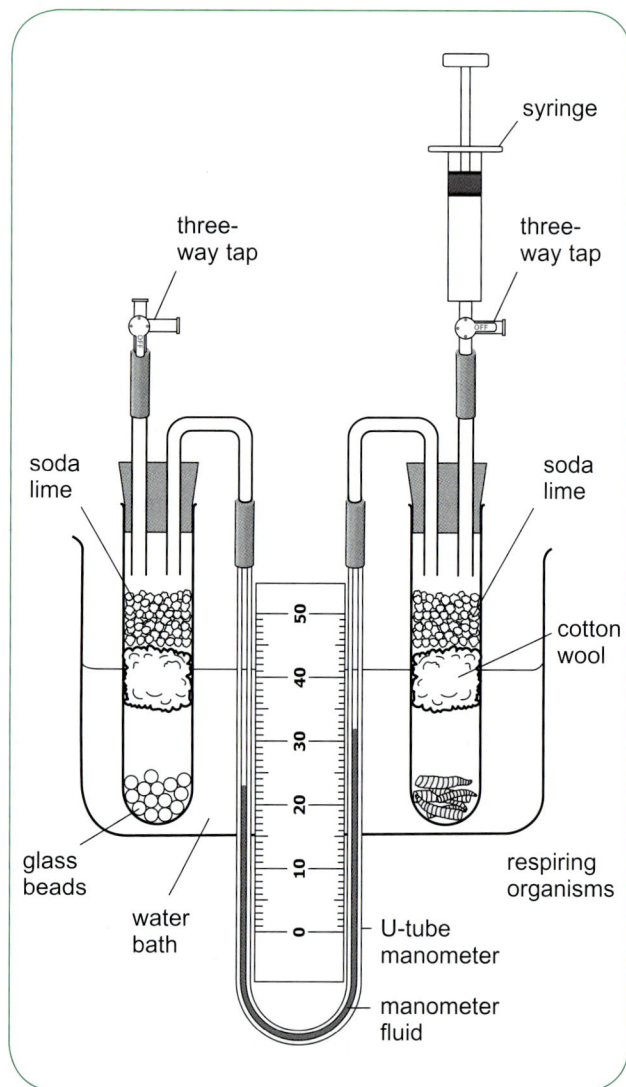

Figure 2.18 A differential respirometer.

SAQ

8 Design an investigation to determine the effect of temperature on the rate of respiration of germinating mung beans using the differential respirometer. Include step by step instructions. Describe the main sources of error and the steps taken to minimise or eliminate them.

Summary

- ATP is the energy currency of every living cell. ATP is made by a metabolic pathway known as respiration. This involves the stepwise breakdown of glucose or other substrates.

- The first series of steps in respiration is known as glycolysis and takes place in the cytoplasm. Each glucose molecule is converted to two pyruvate molecules. In this process, two ATP molecules are used and four produced. Reduced NAD is also formed.

- When oxygen is available, aerobic respiration can take place, and the pyruvate is moved into the matrix of a mitochondrion where it is converted to acetyl CoA in the link reaction. The 2C acetyl CoA combines with the 4C compound oxaloacetate and enters the Krebs cycle.

- The Krebs cycle also takes place in the mitochondrial matrix. It converts the 6C compound citrate to oxaloacetate in a series of steps. Dehydrogenation reactions remove hydrogen, which is taken up by NAD to produce reduced NAD, or by FAD to produce reduced FAD. Decarboxylation reactions remove carbon dioxide, which diffuses out of the cell and is excreted. Substrate-level phosphorylation occurs, in which ATP is made directly.

- The reduced NAD and reduced FAD pass their electrons to the electron transport chain in the inner membrane of the cristae. As the electrons pass along the chain, they lose energy which is transferred to hydrogen ions, moving these ions across the membrane from the matrix to the intermembranal space. At the end of the chain, the electrons combine with hydrogen ions and oxygen atoms to form water molecules.

- The hydrogen ions that have accumulated in the intermembranal space diffuse back through the membrane into the matrix. They pass through ATPase molecules, which use their energy to convert ADP and P_i to ATP. This is oxidative phosphorylation.

- If oxygen is not available, anaerobic respiration occurs. Glycolysis proceeds as normal, but the pyruvate does not enter a mitochondrion. Instead, it is converted to lactate (in animals) or ethanol (in yeast). These reactions convert reduced NAD back to NAD, allowing glycolysis to continue.

- A respirometer can be used to measure the rate of oxygen uptake by aerobically respiring organisms. A carbon dioxide absorbant such as soda lime or potassium hydroxide solution removes carbon dioxide from the air, so that the drop in volume of the air inside the apparatus results directly from the use of oxygen by the organisms.

Questions

Multiple choice questions

1 Which of the following cellular processes in living organisms does **not** require ATP ?
   A division of a cell by mitosis
   B uptake of carbon dioxide by leaves
   C protein synthesis
   D movement of a sperm cell

2 ATP made during glycolysis is generated by:
   A substrate-level phosphorylation.
   B oxidative phosphorylation.
   C reduction of NAD.
   D oxidation of reduced NAD.

continued ...

3 The diagram below shows a mitochondrion in a cell. Which of the following correctly identifies where the Krebs cycle and oxidative phosphorylation occur?

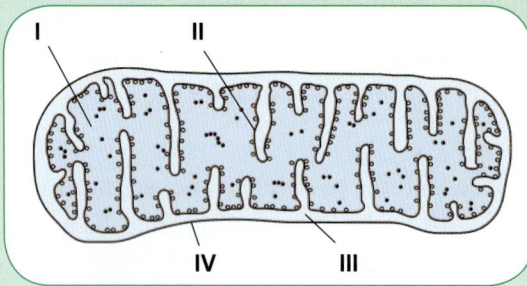

	Krebs cycle	Oxidative phosphorylation
A	I	II
B	I	III
C	II	IV
D	IV	II

4 The diagram below shows some of the stages of respiration. Which of the following identifies molecules **X** and **Y** respectively?

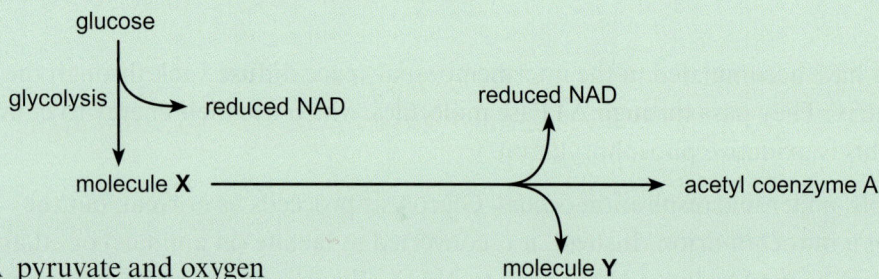

A pyruvate and oxygen
B pyruvate and carbon dioxide
C lactate and hydrogen
D fructose bisphosphate and carbon dioxide

5 The diagram below shows a simple respirometer.

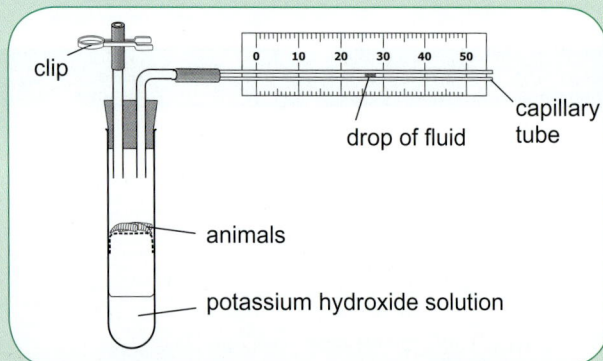

What can the apparatus be used to measure?
A oxygen uptake
B oxygen uptake minus carbon dioxide production
C carbon dioxide uptake
D carbon dioxide production minus oxygen production

continued …

6 Which of the following enters and leaves the mitochondrion during aerobic respiration?

	Enters	Leaves
A	reduced NAD	phosphate
B	ATP	NAD
C	pyruvate	ADP
D	oxygen	water

7 During strenuous exercise, muscles in humans respire anaerobically. What product(s) is (are) formed during this process?

A carbon dioxide and alcohol
B alcohol only
C lactate only
D lactate and carbon dioxide

8 Which of the following statements about respiration is true?

A In the absence of NAD, glycolysis can function.
B Carbon dioxide is released in the conversion of glucose to pyruvate.
C Glucose is oxidised and oxygen is reduced.
D The end products of glycolysis are reduced NAD and pyruvate.

9 The diagram below shows the Krebs cycle. Which correctly identifies the 4-carbon and 6-carbon compounds?

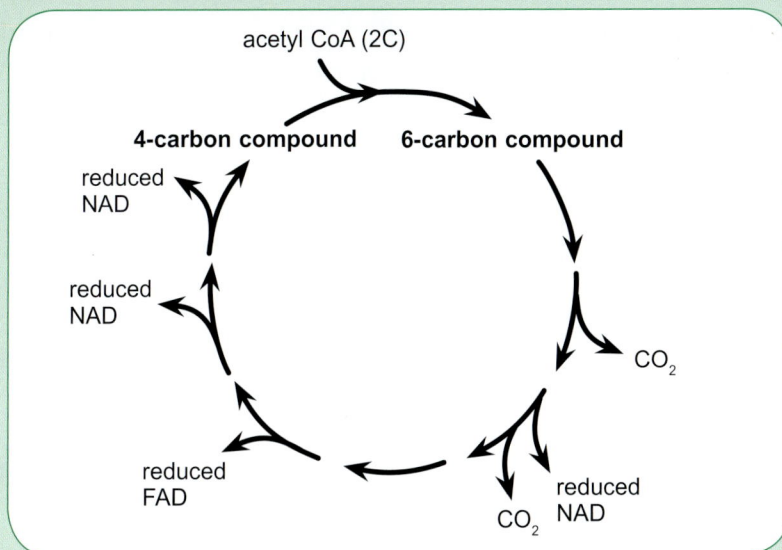

	4-carbon compound	6-carbon compound
A	citrate	oxaloacetate
B	pyruvate	citrate
C	acetyl CoA	oxaloacetate
D	oxaloacetate	citrate

continued ...

10 If oxygen is available during the process of aerobic respiration, the maximum net number of ATP molecules that can theoretically be produced from a molecule of glucose is:

A 2.

B 4.

C 32.

D 38.

Structured questions

11 The apparatus below is a simple respirometer. Some students in a CAPE® Biology class used it to determine the rate of oxygen uptake by germinating mung beans.

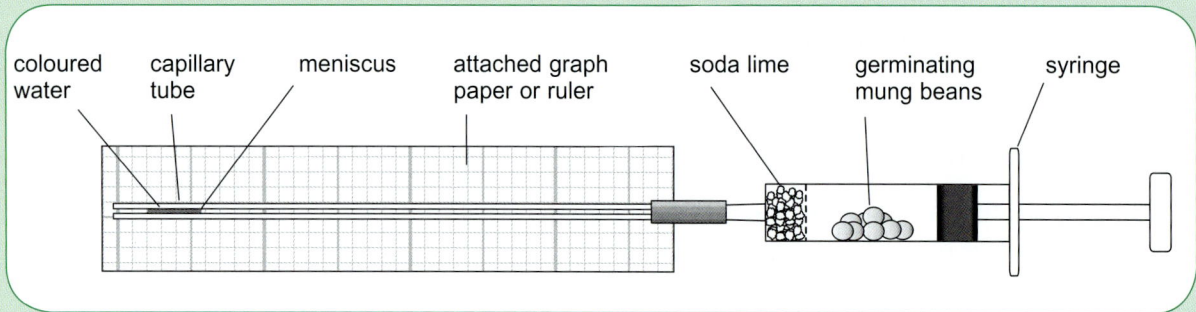

a Explain how the apparatus shown in the diagram can be used to measure the rate of oxygen uptake in $mm^3 min^{-1} g^{-1}$. [3 marks]

b Apart from lack of a control, describe **two** other limitations of the procedure described in **a**. [2 marks]

c Describe a control which should be set up to obtain valid results. [3 marks]

d The results in the table below were obtained by the students when measuring the uptake of oxygen by the mung beans.
Plot a graph of the results.

Time / s	0	30	60	90	120	150	180
Distance moved by meniscus / mm	0.0	10.0	20.5	32.0	43.5	52.0	67.0

[4 marks]

e Using the data in **d**, calculate the average volume of oxygen taken up in $mm^3 min^{-1} g^{-1}$. Assume that the diameter of the capillary tube is 0.2 mm and 0.5 g of mung beans was used. The formula to calculate the volume of a cylinder is $\pi r^2 d$. [2 marks]

f Explain how the apparatus could be used to measure the volume of carbon dioxide produced per minute. [2 marks]

continued ...

g The diagram below shows a differential respirometer. It eliminates some limitations of a simple respirometer.

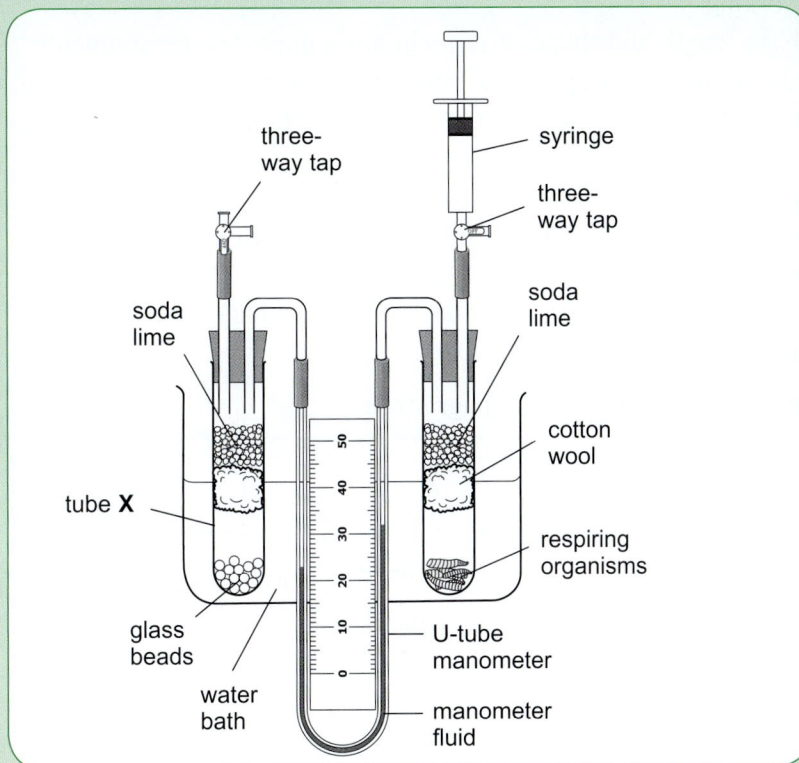

Explain the functions of the following:

i tube **X**

ii the three-way taps

iii the syringe

iv the water bath

[4 marks]

12 The electron micrograph below shows a cross-section of a mitochondrion.

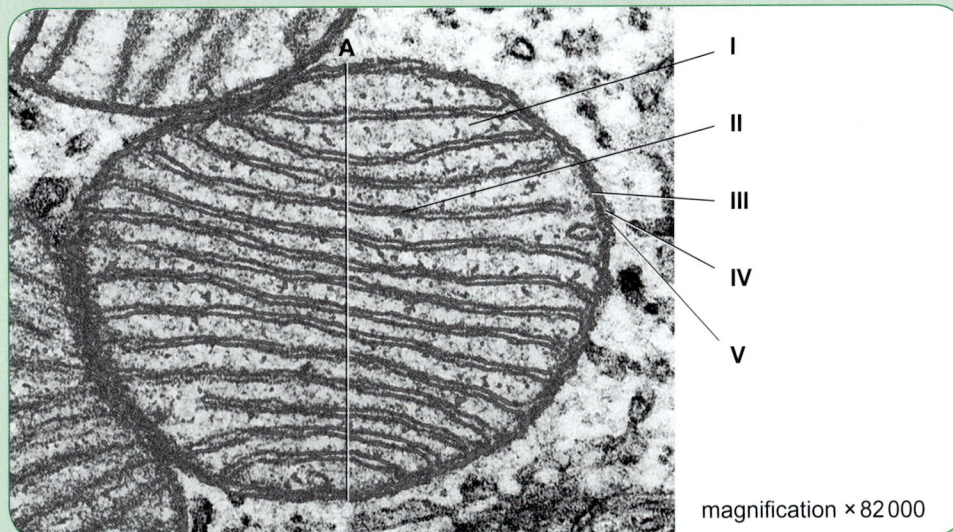

magnification × 82 000

continued …

a   Identify the structures labelled **I** to **V**. [5 marks]

b   i   Calculate the diameter of the mitochondrion at **A** in micrometres (microns) (µm). Show your working. [2 marks]

   ii   Even though the length and shape of mitochondria may vary, the diameter remains small, rarely exceeding 1.0 µm. Suggest a reason for this observation. [1 mark]

c   Use the numbered labels on the micrograph to indicate where:

   i   the Krebs cycle occurs.

   ii   oxidative phosphorylation occurs. [2 marks]

d   Describe **four** ways in which the structure of the mitochondrion is adapted for aerobic respiration. [4 marks]

e   Identify **one** compound which enters and one compound which leaves the mitochondrion. [1 mark]

13 Some stages of glycolysis are shown in the diagram below.

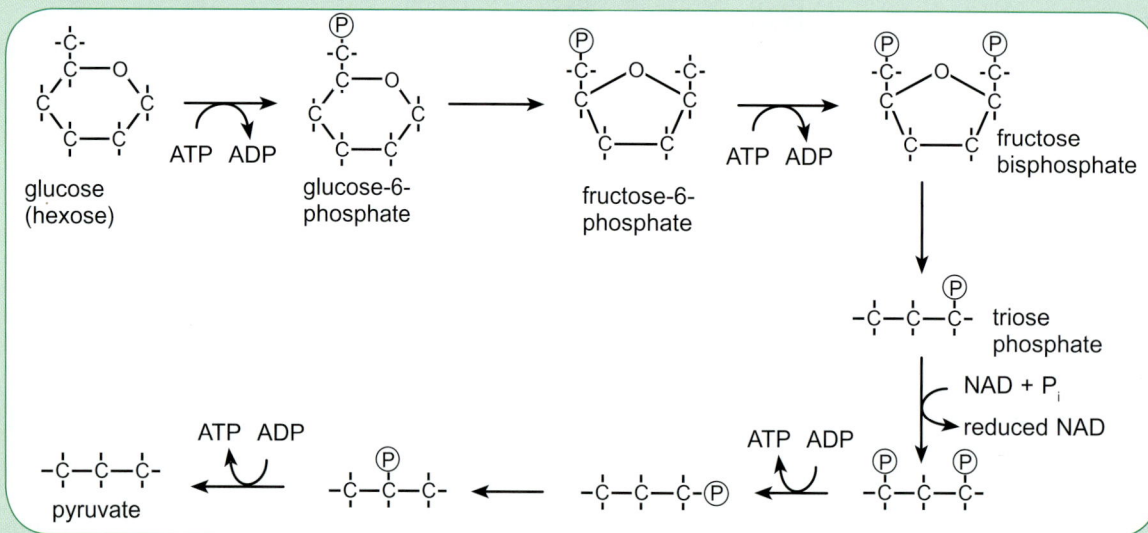

a   What is meant by the term 'glycolysis' and where does it occur? [2 marks]

b   Explain why glucose is broken down in a series of steps. [2 marks]

c   i   Copy the diagram of glycolysis above. Write the label 'phosphorylation' to show where phosphorylation involving the breakdown of ATP to ADP occurs. [2 marks]

   ii   Give **two** reasons for the phosphorylation of glucose. [2 marks]

d   Suggest a reason for the rearrangement of glucose-6-phosphate to fructose-6-phosphate. [1 mark]

e   i   Write the label 'lysis' on your diagram to show where the lysis of the hexose sugar into triose sugars occurs. [1 mark]

   ii   Give **two** reasons for the lysis of the hexose sugar. [2 marks]

f   Show on the diagram where oxidation occurs. [1 mark]

g   Explain why inorganic phosphate is added to glyceraldehyde-3-phosphate. [1 mark]

h   i   State the net gain of ATP molecules when one molecule of glucose is broken down to pyruvic acid (pyruvate).

   ii   Name the process by which ATP is produced in glycolysis. [2 marks]

i   What are the products of glycolysis? [2 marks]

j   State **two** possible fates of the pyruvate in a muscle cell. [2 marks]

continued ...

Essay questions

14 a Describe the role of NAD in aerobic respiration. [2 marks]

    b Explain the terms 'decarboxylation' and 'dehydrogenation'. [2 marks]

    c Describe the reactions which link glycolysis to the Krebs cycle. [4 marks]

    d Discuss the main features of the Krebs cycle. [7 marks]

15 a i ATP is often described as the 'universal currency of cells'. What do you understand by the term? [2 marks]

    ii Identify **two** cellular processes in living organisms that require ATP. [2 marks]

Most of the ATP produced in cellular respiration is made by a process known as oxidative phosphorylation.

    b By means of a diagram, describe the main features of oxidative phosphorylation. [8 marks]

    c Oxygen acts as the final electron acceptor in the electron transport chain. The poison cyanide binds to the electron carrier, cytochrome oxidase. Explain how cyanide stops ATP production by the mitochondria. [3 marks]

16 a i Describe the fate of pyruvate and reduced NAD molecules formed under anaerobic conditions in both yeast and mammalian muscle cells. [5 marks]

    ii Describe how anaerobic respiration in yeast and mammalian muscle cells differs. [2 marks]

    b Discuss the commercial uses of anaerobic respiration in yeast cells. [3 marks]

    c i What do you understand by the term 'oxygen debt'? [2 marks]

    ii Describe the fate of the product formed in respiring muscle cells during vigorous exercise. [3 marks]

Chapter 3
Energy flow and nutrient cycling

By the end of this chapter you should be able to:

a distinguish among the terms ecosystem, habitat, ecological niche;

b discuss the way in which energy flows in an ecosystem;

c discuss the efficiency of energy transfer between trophic levels;

d discuss the concept of biological pyramids;

e describe how nitrogen is cycled within an ecosystem;

f distinguish between energy flow and nutrient cycling within an ecosystem;

g explain how energy flow and nutrient cycling are important for ecosystems to remain self-sustaining units.

Some terms used in ecology

A **habitat** is a place where organisms live – for example, a coral reef crest. One **species** of organism you will probably find in this habitat in the Caribbean is the elkhorn coral, *Acropora palmata* (Figure 3.1). We can actually describe the habitat for elkhorn coral a little more precisely. It lives in and around exposed reef crests and in the forereef, in depths of generally less than 6 m (Figure 3.2).

Figure 3.1 Elkhorn coral (*Acropora palmata*) Belize, Caribbean Sea.

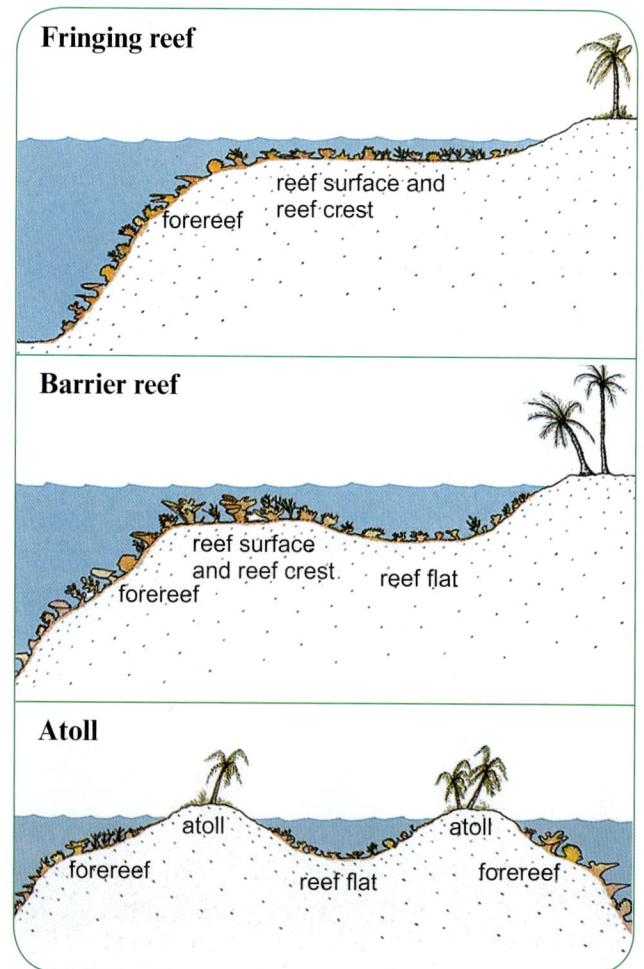

Figure 3.2 Some types of coral reef. Within each, there will be many habitats suitable for individual species.

Within this habitat there may be a **population** of, for example, the queen parrotfish (*Scarus vetula*) (Figure 3.3). A population is a group of organisms of the same species, living in the same place at the same time, and able to interbreed with each other. There will be populations of many other species here too. All the populations of all the species living in this habitat at one time make up a **community**.

In ecology you can study individual species, but it is the study of the interaction of one species with others and with the non-living environment that reveals most about the world we live in. To help us with this study, a name has been given to the concept of the system that is made up of all the interactions within an area – the **ecosystem**. An ecosystem can be considered as a relatively self-contained system including all the living organisms and their environment, interacting with each other. An ecosystem is a system rather than a place, but there is often a relatively identifiable place in which any particular ecosytem exists. We can think, for example, of a coral reef as being an ecosystem, but the term really means the ways in which all the organisms in the reef interact with each other and also with the non-living components of their habitat, such as seawater, the reef substrate, the sediment in hollows, the air dissolved in the water and the light that falls onto the reef.

The way in which an organism interacts with others and with the physical environment has impacts on other organisms and their lives. The precise way of life of an organism is therefore important and the term **ecological niche** is used to describe this. A niche can be defined as the role of an organism in an ecosystem: the effects that it has on other components of the ecosystem, and the effects that they have on it. As we will see in Chapter 4, the niches of some organisms can be very significant. For example, the niche of the queen parrotfish, which includes grazing on seaweeds, is important in the recovery of reefs following damage.

As reef-building corals cannot live at depths where the light is weak, coral reefs only occur to maximum depths up to about 70 m and most are in tropical areas. The coral reef ecosystem is quite uncommon globally and the Caribbean contains a significant proportion of the world's coral reefs. The large numbers of different species found in coral reefs make them one of the most diverse ecosystems there are. Reefs are generally under threat around the world, which makes their study a matter of international importance (Figure 3.4).

Figure 3.3 Queen parrotfish (*Scarus vetula*) and stove-pipe sponge (*Aplysina archeri*), Bonaire, Caribbean.

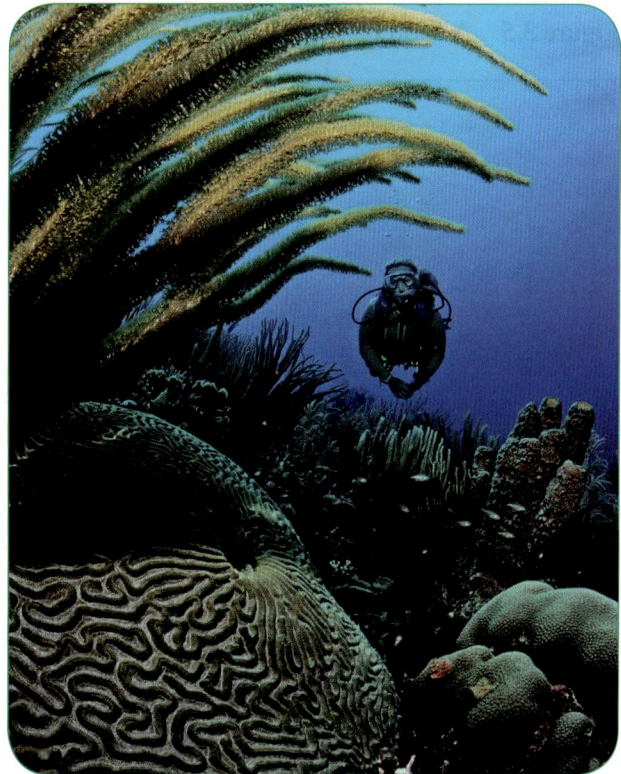

Figure 3.4 Reef at Bonaire, Caribbean.

products), while the larger animals are called **detritivores**, meaning 'detritus feeders'.

Part of the decomposer food web that belongs to the St Martin ecosystem contains the following food chain (Figure 3.8):

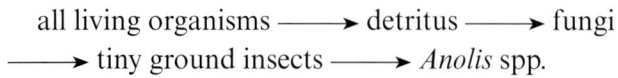

all living organisms ⟶ detritus ⟶ fungi ⟶ tiny ground insects ⟶ *Anolis* spp.

Decomposers are a largely unseen but vitally important group within every ecosystem. You will find out more about their roles in the nitrogen cycle on pages 51–56.

The significance of food webs

The complex feeding relationships in an ecosystem are linked to effective cycling of important nutrients, such as nitrogen compounds, carbon compounds and many mineral elements.

Complex food webs are also linked to the stability of ecosystems. This is discussed in Chapter 4, on page 70. Knowledge of food webs may help us reduce the damage done by humans to vulnerable ecosystems.

Pyramids of number and biomass

The numbers of organisms feeding at each trophic level in an ecosystem can be represented as a **pyramid of numbers**. Figure 3.9 shows a common shape of such a pyramid.

Table 3.1 gives data for the numbers of organisms in a coral reef ecosystem in Bermuda. You will see from the table that the organisms are listed as herbivore and carnivore, not primary, secondary and tertiary consumer. This highlights a difficulty with the use of pyramids. It is very difficult and time-consuming to collect data and sort it into trophic levels. As a consequence, this has not been carried out in detail for many ecosystems. Part of the problem is that many species can feed at different trophic levels, and the proportion of feeding at the different levels can vary through the year and from one year to another.

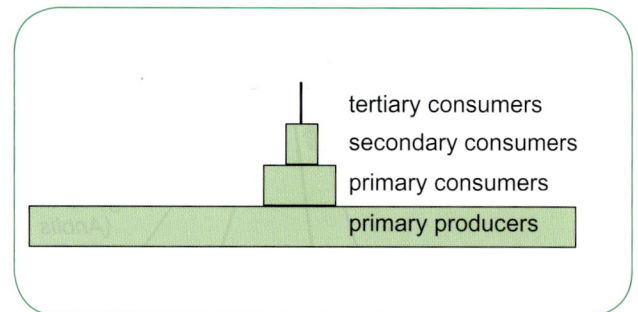

Figure 3.9 Pyramid of numbers for summer grassland in the USA.

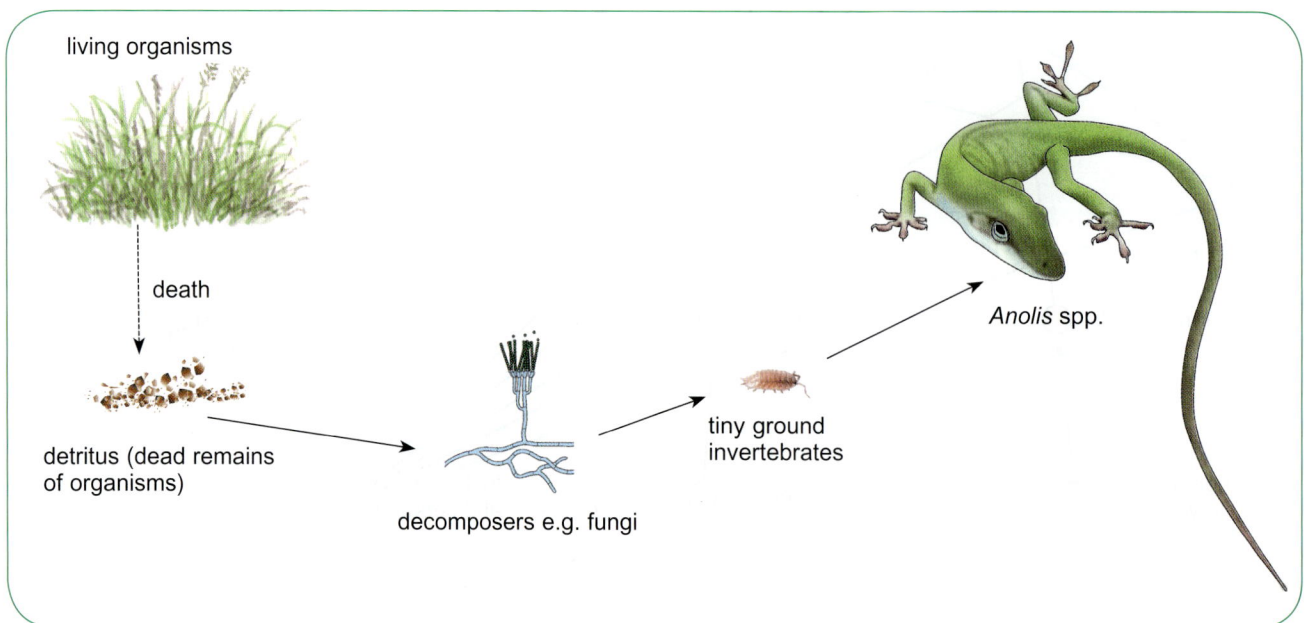

Figure 3.8 A food chain which includes decomposers.

Name of organism	Feeding	Number
algal turf	producer	700
jointed seaweed	producer	500
phytoplankton	producer	10 000
zooplankton	herbivore	1000
finger coral	carnivore	7500
common sea fan	herbivore	7000
brain coral	herbivore	6000
sponges	carnivore	1000
spotlight parrot fish	herbivore	5
squid	carnivore	2
purple sea urchin	herbivore	6
Nassau grouper	carnivore	24
four-eyed butterfly fish	herbivore	2
silver porgy	carnivore	3
surgeon fish	herbivore	4
blue tang	herbivore	2
barracuda	carnivore	1

Table 3.1   Numbers of organisms in a Bermudan coral reef.

SAQ

1 Using the data in Table 3.1, construct a three-step pyramid of numbers for this reef.

Sometimes the pyramid of numbers for an ecosystem can have a different shape, such as the one below for temperate forest (Figure 3.10).

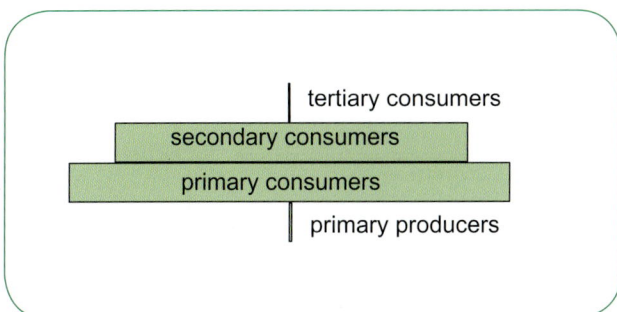

Figure 3.10   Pyramid of numbers for temperate forest.

The small number of primary producers is simply a result of the small number of large trees that are the most significant producers in this ecosystem.

Biomass is the total mass of living organisms of a species (or defined group of species) living in an area (or volume) of environment at one time. In Figure 3.11, tropical forest biomass is described using units of $g\,m^{-2}$. In this example, it tells us that there are 4 g of primary consumers for every square metre of rainforest in Panama. Biomass can be measured using dried organisms or organisms as they are in life, containing water.

A pyramid of biomass is useful because it prevents size of individual organisms from affecting the shape of the pyramid.

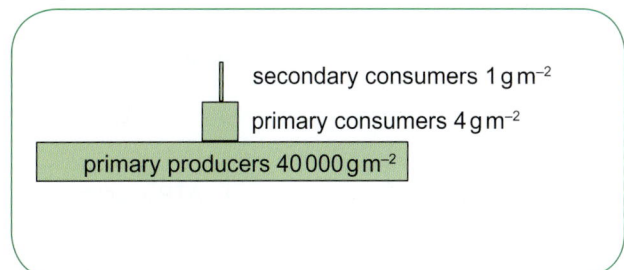

Figure 3.11   Pyramid of biomass for tropical rainforest in Panama.

Energy flow through an ecosystem

The reason for pyramids of biomass (and often pyramids of number) getting significantly smaller as you move to higher trophic levels – having a pyramidal shape – is related to the flow of energy within an ecosystem (Figure 3.12).

Within most living cells, the immediate source of energy is ATP. Most metabolic reactions within cells require input of energy from ATP, used to fuel active transport, the synthesis of proteins and many other processes.

The initial entry of energy into most ecosystems takes place during photosynthesis. Some of the energy in the sunlight hitting a plant's leaves is used to make carbohydrates, proteins and fats whose molecules contain a proportion of this energy. Plants are **primary producers** (or just producers). The carbohydrates and other organic substances that they synthesise serve as supplies of chemical energy to all of the other organisms in the ecosystem. These other organisms, which include all the animals and fungi, and many of the microorganisms, consume the organic substances made by plants. They are **consumers**.

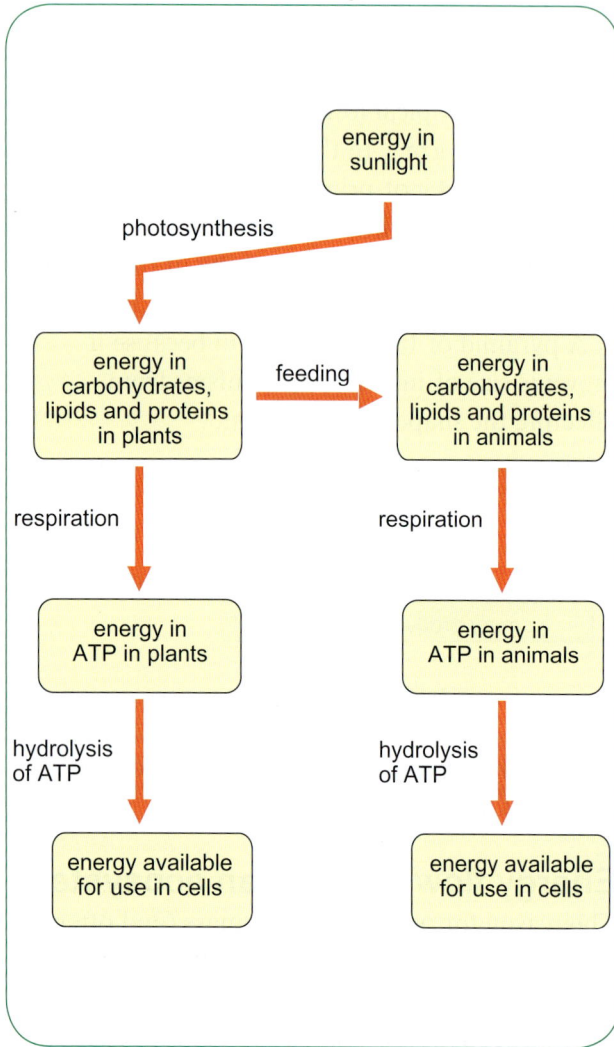

Figure 3.12 Energy flow through ecosystems.

Energy losses along food chains

Whenever energy is transferred from one form, or one system, to another, some is always lost as heat. As energy passes along a food chain, large losses from the food chain occur at each transfer, both within and between the organisms. Figure 3.13 shows these losses for a simple terrestrial food chain.

Of all the sunlight energy falling onto a terrestrial ecosystem, only a very small percentage is converted by the green plants into chemical energy (Figure 3.14). In most ecosystems, the plants convert less than 3% of this sunlight to chemical energy. The reasons for this inefficiency include:

- some sunlight missing leaves entirely, and falling onto the ground or other non-photosynthesising surfaces
- some sunlight being reflected from the surfaces of leaves
- some sunlight passing through leaves, without encountering chlorophyll molecules
- only certain wavelengths of light being absorbed by chlorophyll
- energy losses as energy absorbed by chlorophyll is transferred to carbohydrates during the reactions of photosynthesis.

The chemical potential energy, now in the plant's tissues, is contained in various organic molecules, especially carbohydrates, lipids and proteins. It is from these molecules that the primary consumers in the ecosystem obtain all of their energy. However, in most plants, almost half of the

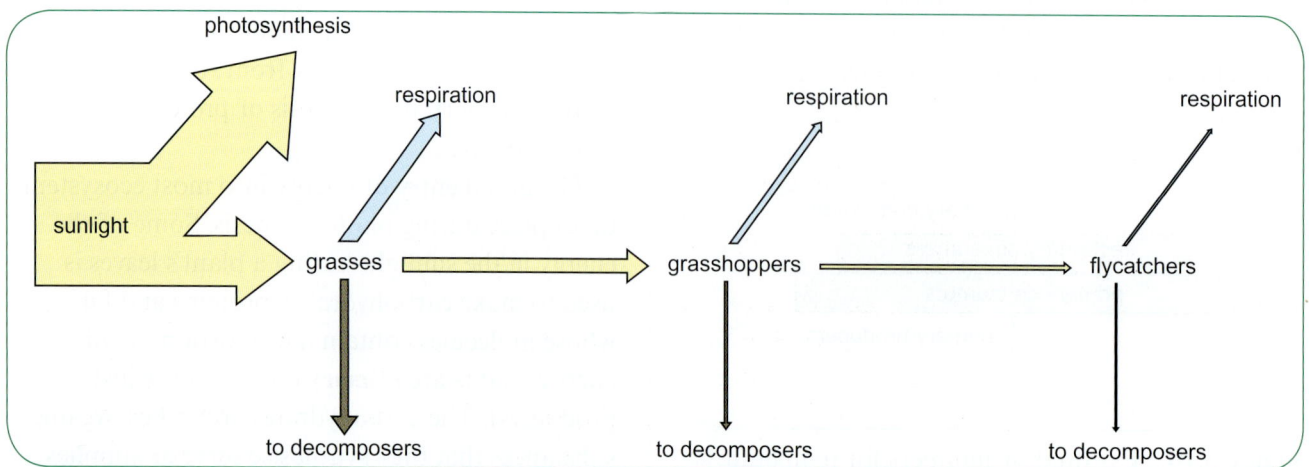

Figure 3.13 Energy losses along a food chain. Arrow width is representing the amount of energy transfer.

chemical potential energy that they store is used by the plants themselves. They break down the organic molecules by respiration, releasing some of the energy from them and using it to make ATP. During this process, and also when the energy in the ATP is used for activities in the plant cells, much energy is lost to the environment as heat.

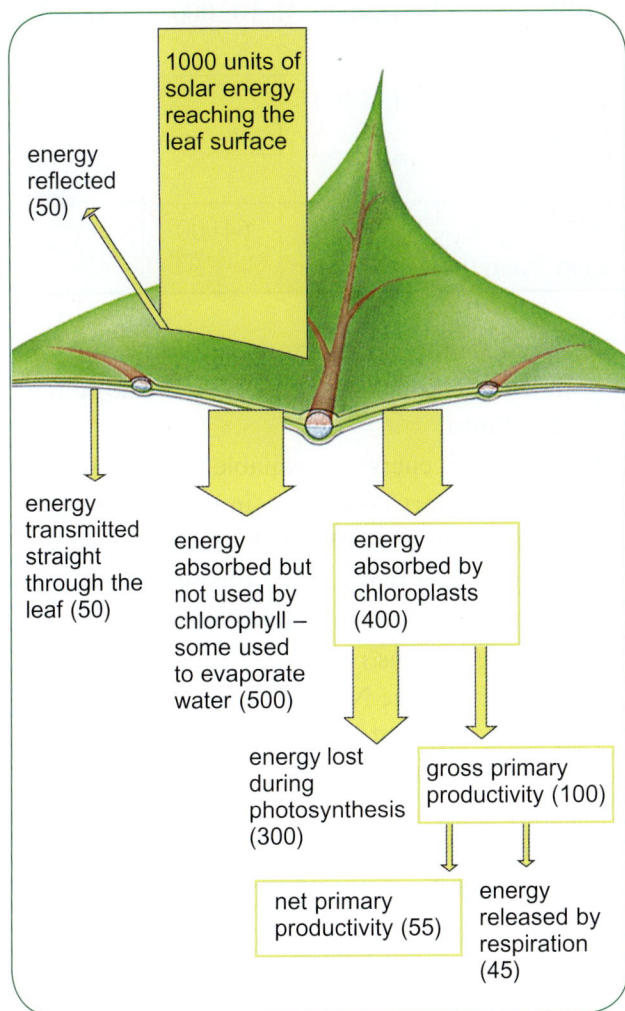

Figure 3.14 Photosynthetic efficiency.

What is left is then available for other organisms, which feed on the plants. Once again, losses occur between the plants and the primary consumers. The reasons for these losses include:

- not all parts of all the plants being eaten – for example, woody tissues or roots may be left
- not all the plant material that is eaten being fully digested, so that not all of the molecules are absorbed by the consumer (the rest is lost as faeces, and therefore becomes available to decomposers)

- energy being lost as heat within the consumer's digestive system as the food molecules are hydrolysed.

As a result of the loss of energy during respiration in plants, and the three reasons above, the overall **efficiency** of transfer of energy from producers to primary consumers is rarely greater than 10%.

Similar losses occur at each trophic level. So, as energy is passed along a food chain, less and less is available at each successive trophic level. Food chains rarely have more than four or five links in them, because there simply would not be enough energy left to support animals so far removed from the original energy input to the producers. If you *can* pick out a five-organism food chain from a food web, you will probably find that the 'top' carnivore also feeds at a lower level in a different food chain – or that it is extremely scarce.

SAQ

2 Energy losses from mammals and birds tend to be significantly greater than from other organisms. Suggest why this is.

Pyramids of energy

You can show data for energy transfer from one trophic level to another as a pyramid of energy. Figure 3.15 shows an example for a temperate lake ecosytem in the USA. Such diagrams clearly show that there are limitations for organisms which feed solely at the tertiary consumer level or higher, because there is insufficient energy available to them to sustain a viable population.

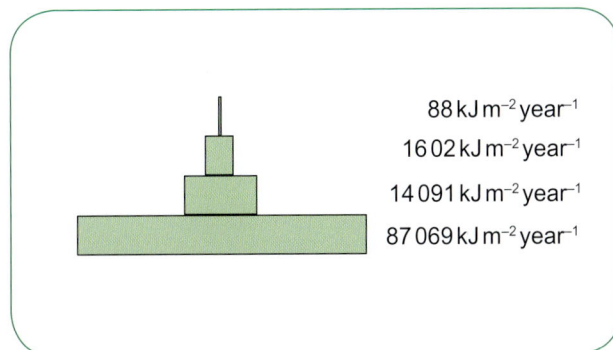

Figure 3.15 Pyramid of energy showing the energy transfer between trophic levels in a lake.

Productivity

The *rate* at which plants convert light energy into chemical potential energy is called **productivity**, or **primary productivity**. It is usually measured in kilojoules of energy transferred per square metre per year ($kJ\,m^{-2}\,year^{-1}$).

Ecologists often differentiate between **gross primary productivity (GPP)** and **net primary productivity (NPP)**. GPP is the total quantity of energy transferred by plants from sunlight into plant tissues. NPP is the energy that is left as chemical energy after the plants have supplied their own needs by respiration. Figure 3.16 shows some ecosystems and their primary productivity.

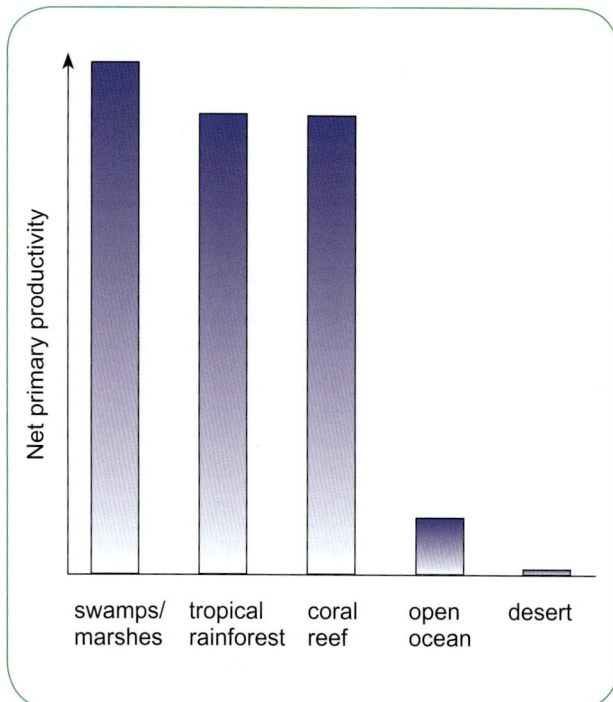

Figure 3.16 Different ecosystems have very different net primary productivity.

SAQ

3 The table shows some information about energy transfers in three ecosystems.

	Rainforest in Puerto Rico	Alfalfa field in the USA	Pine forest in England
GPP/ $kJ\,m^{-2}\,year^{-1}$	188 000	102 000	51 000
Respiration by plants/ $kJ\,m^{-2}\,year^{-1}$	134 000		20 000
NPP/ $kJ\,m^{-2}\,year^{-1}$	54 000	64 000	

a Calculate the figures for respiration by plants in the alfalfa field, and the NPP of the young pine forest.

b How much energy is available to be passed on to the primary consumers in the rainforest?

c Suggest why the GPP of the rainforest is so much greater than that of the pine forest. (You should be able to think of several possible reasons.)

d Suggest why the NPP of the alfalfa field is greater than that of the rainforest. (Again, you may be able to think of several reasons.)

4 The table shows some typical values for NPP in a range of different ecosystems.

Type of ecosystem	NPP / $kJ\,m^{-2}\,year^{-1}$
desert	280
subsistence farming	3 000
temperate grassland	15 000
temperate forest	26 000
intensive agriculture	30 000
tropical rainforest	40 000

a Explain why the NPP in desert is so low.

b Suggest why the NPP of temperate forest is greater than that of temperate grassland.

Productivity at different trophic levels

The productivity of photosynthesising organisms is often call *primary* productivity because these organisms are in the *first* trophic level in most ecosystems. But the concepts of gross productivity and net productivity can be applied to all trophic levels. One way to represent this for an ecosystem is shown in Figure 3.17, where the energy that is potentially available to organisms in the next trophic level, the net production, is shown between each trophic level.

Cycling matter in ecosystems

In addition to energy, organisms pass matter between themselves – atoms of various elements that they use to build their bodies. Carbon, oxygen and hydrogen are needed to make carbohydrates and fats and also proteins, which in addition require nitrogen. Other elements, such as potassium, calcium, magnesium and iodine, are needed in smaller quantities to make particular molecules, to act as enzyme cofactors or to produce potential differences across membranes.

By definition, an ecosystem is to a large extent a self-contained entity. But there is a difference between the ways in which energy and matter are moved within the ecosystem. Matter, unlike energy, tends to be cycled *within* the ecosystem rather than passing through it. In other words, it tends to be recycled. When an organism dies or sheds a part of itself, excretes or egests, the molecules from its body are used as nutrients by decomposers. The decomposers break down the organic molecules and liberate atoms and ions that can be used by other organisms. Decomposers have a vital part to play in returning 'used' materials to the ecosystem so that they become available to other organisms.

We will look at just one example of how an element is cycled within an ecosystem – the nitrogen cycle.

The nitrogen cycle

Nitrogen is an essential element for all living organisms and is cycled in ecosystems (Figure 3.18). It is essential because of its presence in proteins and nucleic acids. There is a large quantity of nitrogen in the air, which is around 78% nitrogen gas. However, most organisms cannot use this nitrogen. This is because nitrogen gas exists as molecular nitrogen, in which two nitrogen atoms are linked with a triple covalent bond (N_2). In this form, nitrogen is very unreactive. With each breath

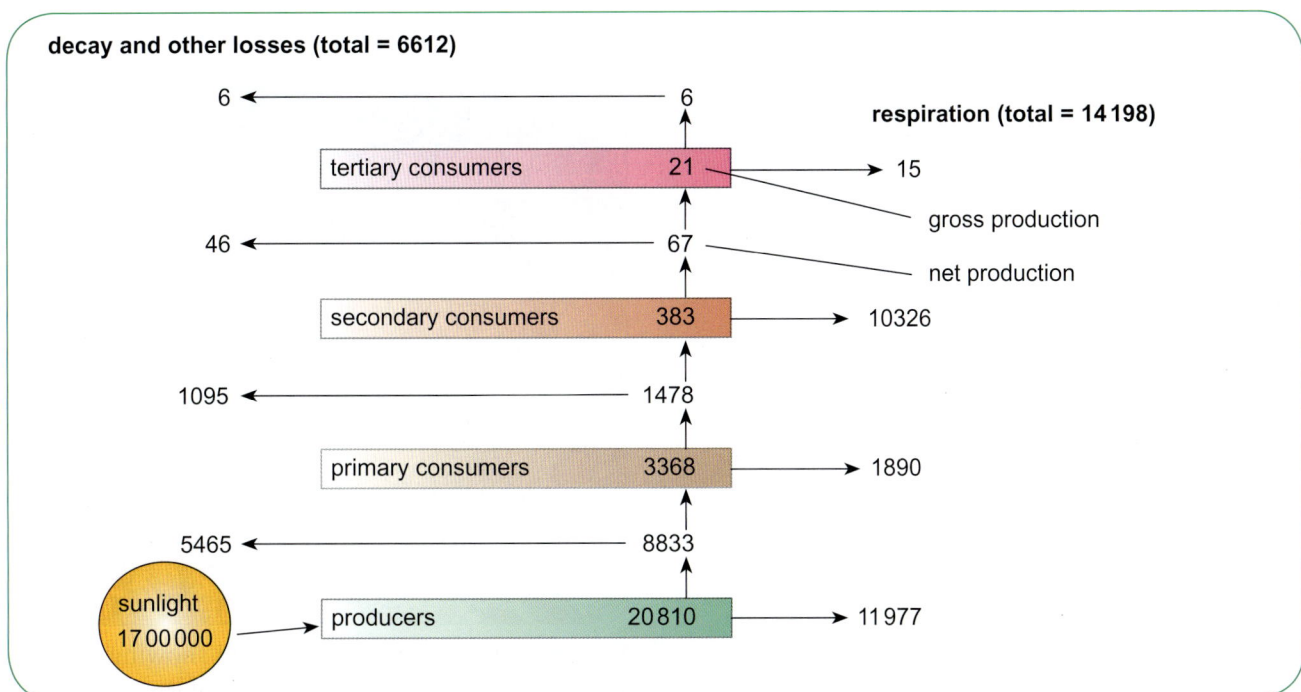

Figure 3.17   Energy flow in a river ecosystem in Silver Springs, Florida, USA. The units of energy flow are kilojoules per square metre per year ($kJ\,m^{-2}\,year^{-1}$).

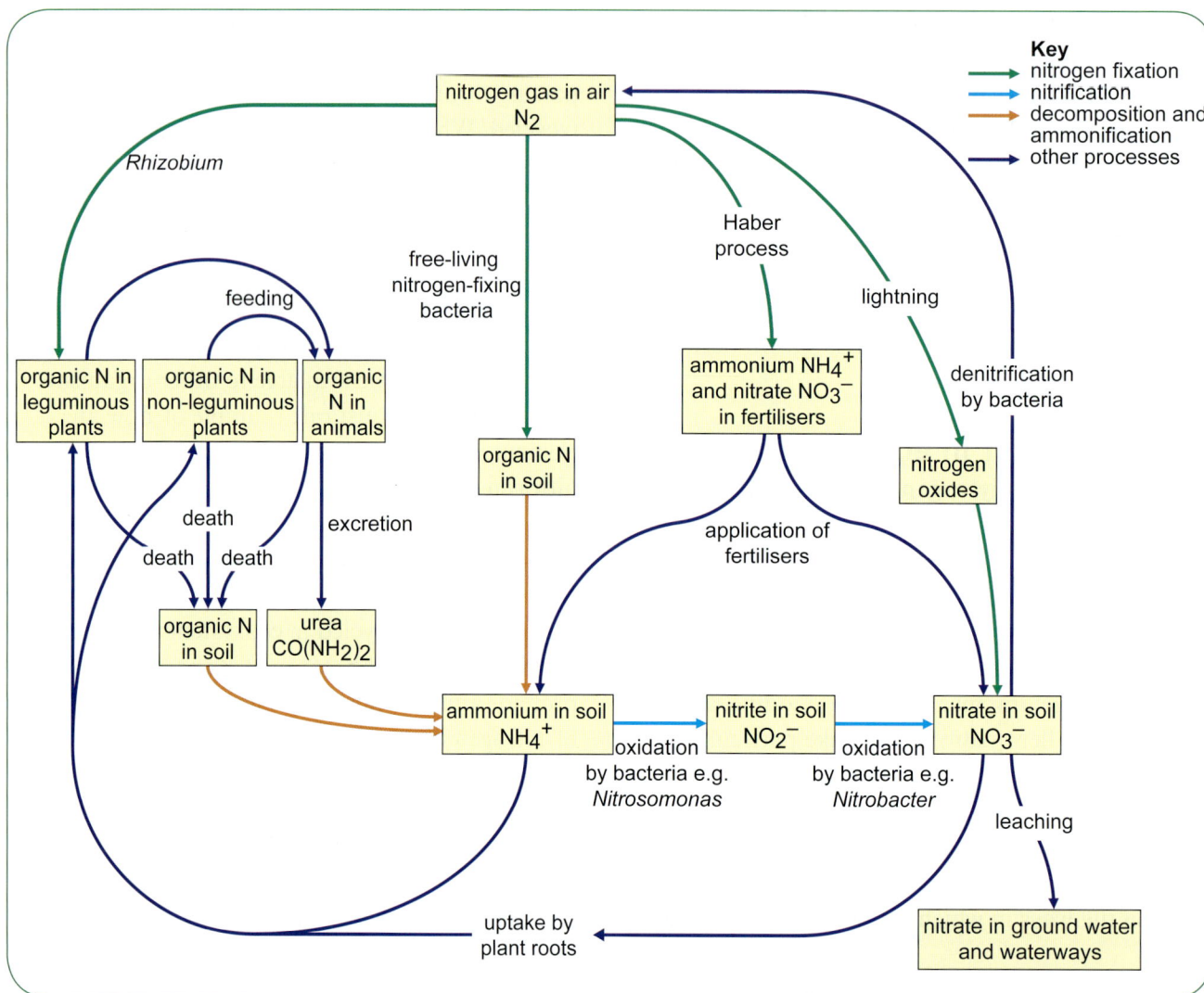

Figure 3.18 The nitrogen cycle.

you take in around 350 cm³ of nitrogen gas, but this is completely useless to you. It simply passes in and out of your body unchanged. Similarly, N_2 passes freely in and out of a plant's stomata, with the plant unable to make any use of it.

Before nitrogen can be used by living organisms it must be converted from N_2 into some more reactive form, such as ammonia (NH_3) or nitrate (NO_3^-). This conversion is called **nitrogen fixation**.

Nitrogen fixation by living organisms

Only prokaryotes and archeans are capable of fixing nitrogen. One of the best-known nitrogen-fixing bacteria is *Rhizobium* (Figure 3.19). This bacterium lives freely in the soil, and also in the roots of many species of plants, especially leguminous plants (belonging to the pea family)

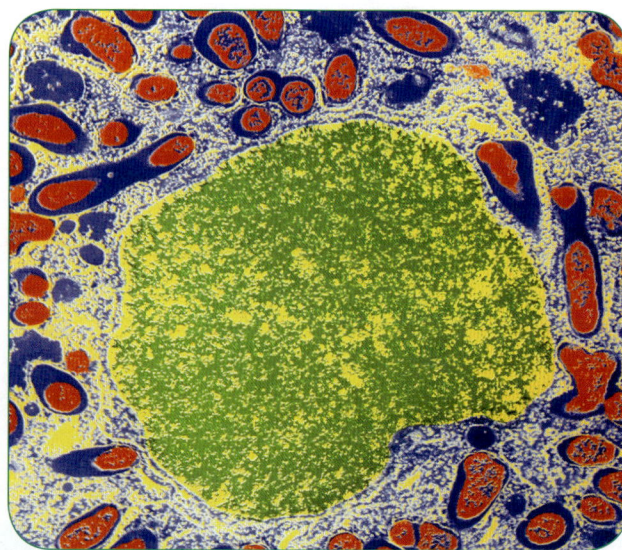

Figure 3.19 Electron micrograph showing *Rhizobium* bacteria inside the cytoplasm of a root nodule cell. The large green area is the cell nucleus. The bacteria are red ($\times 4480$).

such as peas, beans and clover. They live in nodules on the roots (Figure 3.20). When living freely in the soil, *Rhizobium* can only fix nitrogen to a very limited extent. Most nitrogen fixation by *Rhizobium* occurs when it is living in plant roots. The plant and the bacterium coexist in a rather remarkable way, each benefiting from the presence of the other.

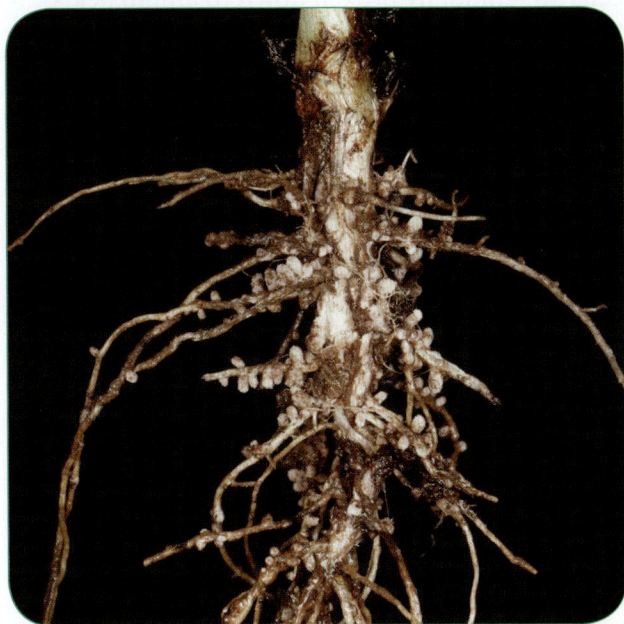

Figure 3.20   Root nodules on the roots of a broad bean plant.

Rhizobium is found in most soils. When a leguminous plant germinates, its roots produce proteins called lectins, which bind to polysaccharides on the cell surface of the bacteria. The bacteria invade the roots, spreading along the root hairs. They stimulate some of the cells in the root to divide and develop into small lumps called nodules, inside which the bacteria form colonies.

The bacteria fix nitrogen with the help of an enzyme called **nitrogenase**. This enzyme catalyses the conversion of nitrogen gas, N_2, to ammonium ions, NH_4^+. To do this, it needs:

- a supply of hydrogen
- a supply of ATP
- anaerobic conditions – that is, the absence of oxygen.

The hydrogen comes from reduced NADP, which is produced by the plant. The ATP comes from the metabolism of sucrose, produced by photosynthesis in the plant's leaves and transported down into the root nodules. Here the sucrose is processed and used in respiration to generate ATP. Anaerobic conditions are maintained through the production, by the plant, of a protein called leghaemoglobin. This molecule has a high affinity for oxygen, and effectively 'mops up' oxygen that diffuses into the nodules.

The relationship between the plant and the bacteria is therefore a very close one. The plant supplies living space, and the conditions required by the bacteria to fix nitrogen. The bacteria supply the plant with fixed nitrogen. This is an example of **mutualism**, in which two organisms of different species live very closely together, each meeting some of the other's needs.

Nitrogen fixation in the atmosphere

When lightning passes through the atmosphere, the huge quantities of energy involved can cause nitrogen molecules to react with oxygen, forming nitrogen oxides. These dissolve in rain, and are carried to the ground. In countries where there are frequent thunderstorms – for example, many tropical countries – this is a very significant source of fixed nitrogen.

Fixation by the Haber process

The production of fertilisers containing fixed nitrogen is a major industry. In the Haber process, nitrogen and hydrogen gases are reacted together to produce ammonia. This requires considerable energy input, so the resulting fertilisers are not cheap. The ammonia is often converted to ammonium nitrate, which is the most widely used inorganic fertiliser in the world.

Use of fixed nitrogen by plants

In legumes, the fixed nitrogen produced by *Rhizobium* in their root nodules is used to make amino acids. These are transported out of the nodules into the xylem, distributed to all parts of the plant and used within cells to synthesise proteins (Figure 3.21).

Other plants rely on supplies of fixed nitrogen in the soil. Their root hairs take up nitrate ions by active transport. In many plants, the nitrate is converted in the roots, first to nitrite (NO_2^-), then to ammonia and then to amino acids which are transported to other parts of the plant through the xylem. In other plant species, the nitrate ions are transported, in xylem, to the leaves before undergoing these processes. Again, most of the nitrogen ends up as part of protein molecules in the plant, especially in seeds and storage tissues.

Assimilation of nitrogen by animals

Animals, including humans, can only use nitrogen when it is part of an organic molecule. Most of our nitrogen supply comes from proteins in the diet, with a small amount from nucleic acids. During digestion, proteins are broken down to amino acids, before being absorbed into the blood and distributed to all cells in the body. Here they are built up again into proteins. Excess amino acids are deaminated in the liver, where the nitrogen becomes part of urea molecules. These are excreted in urine.

Return of nitrate to the soil from living organisms

When an animal or plant dies, the proteins in its cells are gradually broken down to amino acids. This is done by decomposers, especially bacteria and fungi, which produce protease enzymes. The decomposers use some of the amino acids for their own growth, while some are broken down and the nitrogen released as ammonia. Ammonia is also produced from the urea in animal urine. The production of ammonia is called **ammonification**.

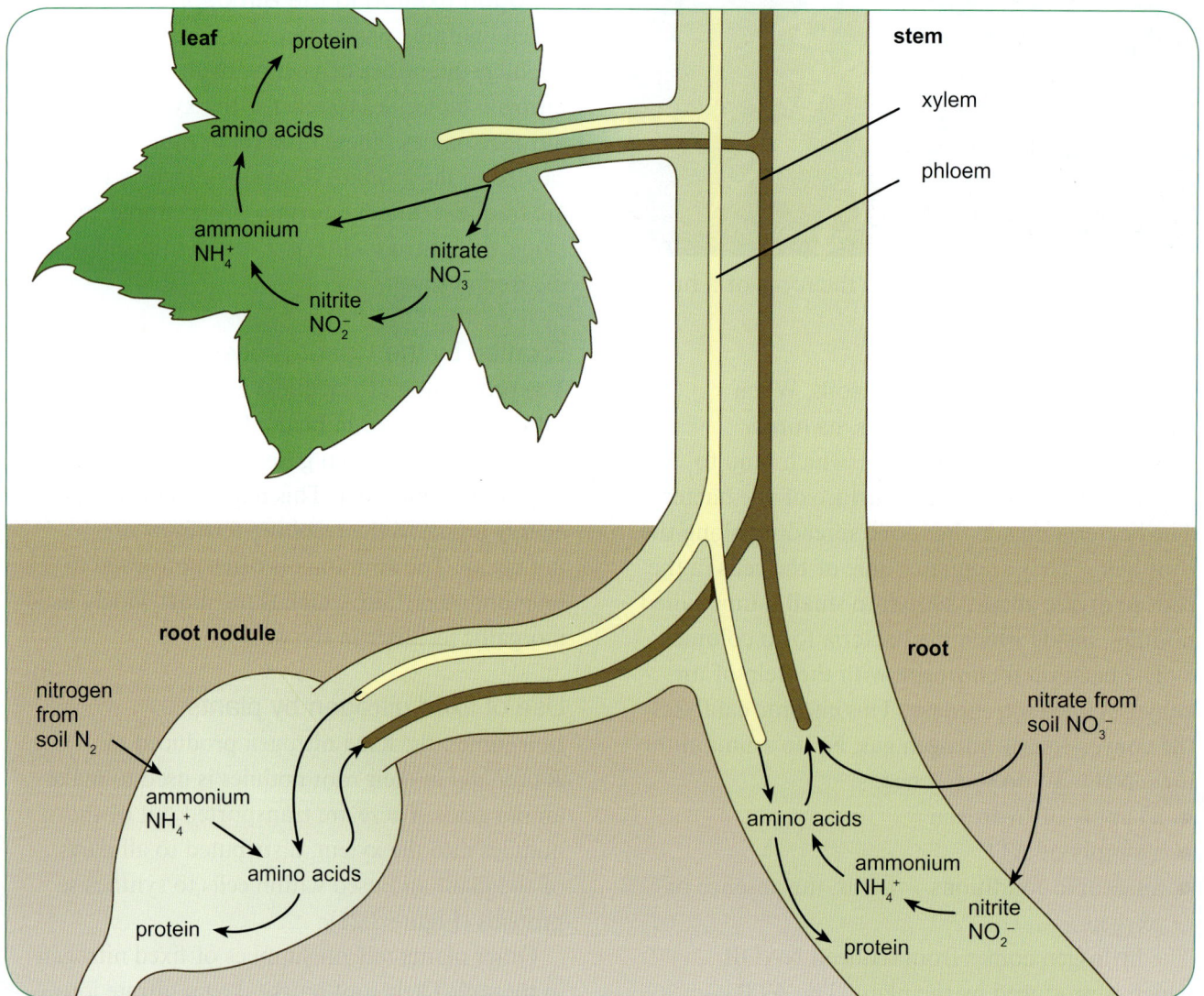

Figure 3.21 A summary of nitrogen metabolism and transport in plants.

Ammonia in the soil is rapidly converted to nitrite ions (NO_2^-) and nitrate ions (NO_3^-) by a group of bacteria called **nitrifying bacteria**. They include *Nitrosomonas* and *Nitrobacter*. These bacteria derive their energy from **nitrification**. In contrast to nitrogen fixation, this only occurs freely provided the soil is well aerated. Boggy soils are therefore often short of nitrates. Some plants have become adapted to growing in such soils by supplementing their nitrogen intake using animal protein. These carnivorous plants trap insects, whose proteins are digested and absorbed by the plant (Figure 3.22).

Denitrification

Denitrifying bacteria provide themselves with energy by reversing nitrogen fixation and converting nitrate to nitrogen gas, which is returned to the air (**denitrification**). They are common in places such as sewage treatment plants, compost heaps and wet soils. This brings the nitrogen cycle full circle.

Figure 3.22   Nitrate and ammonium ions are in very short supply in waterlogged soils, but carnivorous plants, such as this venus fly trap (*Dionaea muscipula*), survive by obtaining nitrogen from insects.

Summary

- An ecosystem is the interactions between all the living organisms, and between the organisms and their environment, in a relatively self-contained area.

- All the living organisms of one species living in an area at the same time, and able to interbreed with one another, is called a population. All the populations of all the different species living in the same area at the same time is called a community.

- The place where an organism lives is called its habitat. Each species of organism plays a particular role in a community or ecosystem, known as its niche.

- A food chain shows how energy flows from one organism to another, in the form of chemical energy in food. A food web is a diagram showing many interconnecting food chains.

- The level at which an organism feeds in a food chain is called a trophic level. There are rarely more than five trophic levels, because energy is lost at each transfer in the food chain, so there is little energy left to support higher trophic levels. This is the reason for the shape of pyramids of number, biomass and energy.

- Energy flows through ecosystems, and is eventually lost from the ecosystem as heat. Matter tends to cycle within an ecosystem.

- Nitrogen gas is inert and cannot be used by most living organisms. It must first be fixed – that is, converted into a more reactive compound. Nitrogen-fixing bacteria convert nitrogen gas into ammonium ions, which are used by plants to make amino acids and proteins. Lightning causes nitrogen to react with oxygen in the air, forming nitrogen oxides which fall to the ground in rain. The Haber process converts nitrogen and hydrogen to ammonia, much of which is used to make ammonium nitrate fertiliser.

- When organisms excrete, egest or die, their waste products are acted on by decomposers which convert many of their nitrogen-containing compounds to ammonium ions. These are oxidised to nitrite and nitrate by nitrifying bacteria. Denitrifying bacteria convert nitrate to nitrogen gas.

Questions

Multiple choice questions

1   What is the ecological definition of the term 'niche'?
   A all the food webs in an ecosystem
   B the role that a species plays in the community in which it lives
   C the living organisms and their non-living environment
   D the place where the organism lives

2   Which of the following best describes an ecosystem?
   A environment where the organism lives, eats and reproduces
   B specific set of environmental conditions
   C relatively self-contained community of organisms and their physical environment
   D individuals of one species living in a particular habitat

continued ...

3 Which statement correctly describes some organisms in the forest food web shown below?

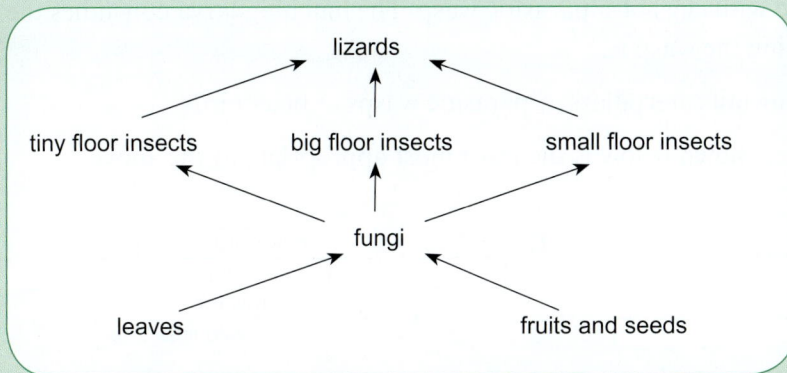

A Fungi are decomposers.
B Tiny floor insects and small floor insects are omnivores.
C Lizards are secondary consumers only.
D Big floor insects are primary consumers.

4 What limits the number of trophic levels in a food chain?
A efficiency of energy conversion between trophic levels
B gross productivity of the ecosystem
C net productivity of the ecosystem
D the respiration rate of the producers

5 The diagram below shows part of the nitrogen cycle.

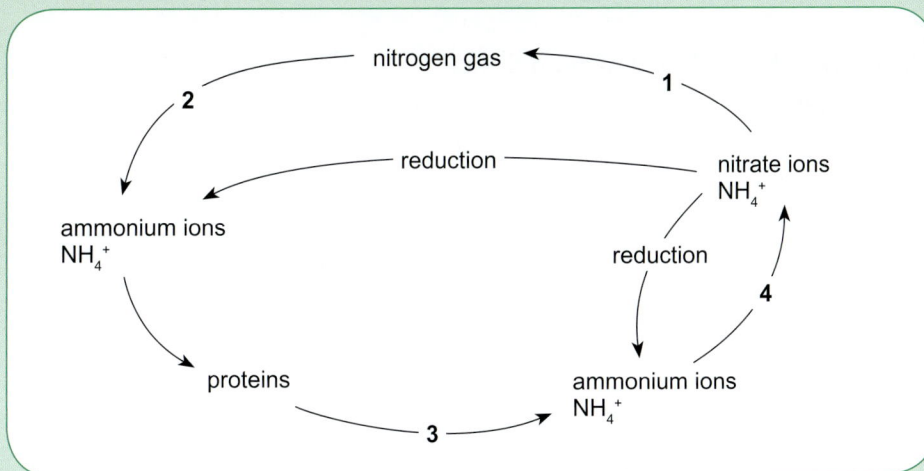

Which sequence of numbers correctly shows the roles of different types of microorganism in the nitrogen cycle?

	Decomposing (putrefying) bacteria	Denitrifying bacteria	Nitrifying bacteria
A	2	4	3
B	3	1	2
C	3	1	4
D	4	2	1

continued ...

6 The Bahamian swallowtail butterfly lays its eggs on the leaves of the wild lime tree. The caterpillar may eat leaves of the tree infested with eggs of a parasitic wasp. The hatching larva consumes the caterpillar. A food chain containing the wasp is:

wild lime tree → Bahamian swallowtail caterpillars → parasitic wasps → blackbirds

Which of the pyramids of number shown below is the most most appropriate to the above food chain?

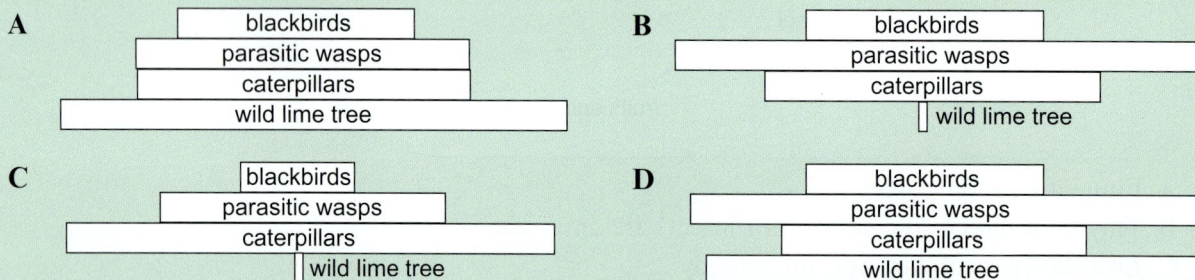

A
| blackbirds |
| parasitic wasps |
| caterpillars |
| wild lime tree |

B
| blackbirds |
| parasitic wasps |
| caterpillars |
| wild lime tree |

C
| blackbirds |
| parasitic wasps |
| caterpillars |
| wild lime tree |

D
| blackbirds |
| parasitic wasps |
| caterpillars |
| wild lime tree |

7 The light energy absorbed by producers in an ecosystem is 80 000 kJ. The energy trapped by producers and converted into biomass is 10 000 kJ. The amount of energy lost as heat by the producers is 45 600 kJ and 20 800 kJ is lost as detritus. What is the net primary productivity of the producers in kJ ?
   A 80 000 kJ   B 45 600 kJ   C 20 800 kJ   D 13 600 kJ

8 The energy striking producers that is converted into chemical energy is less than 3%. Which of the following explains what happens to the energy striking the producers that is **not** converted into chemical energy?
   A Most of the light is absorbed by the leaves of producers.
   B Only red and blue wavelengths of light are absorbed by chlorophyll.
   C Most of the energy is lost by producers through respiration.
   D Producers are made up of indigestible parts.

9 The diagram below shows part of the nitrogen cycle.

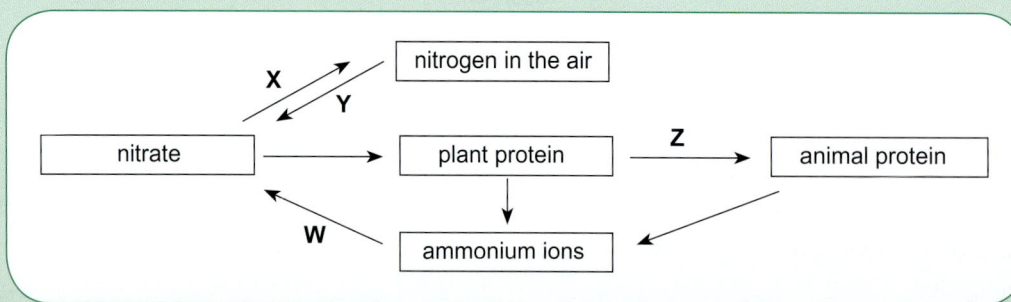

Which of the following correctly identifies processes **W**, **X**, **Y** and **Z**?

	W	X	Y	Z
A	feeding	nitrogen fixation	nitrification	denitrification
B	nitrification	denitrification	nitrogen fixation	feeding
C	nitrogen fixation	nitrification	feeding	denitrification
D	nitrification	feeding	denitrification	nitrogen fixation

continued ...

10 What is the function of nitrifying bacteria in the soil?

    A reduction of nitrates to nitrogen gas

    B oxidation of nitrates to nitrogen gas

    C oxidation of ammonium compounds to nitrates

    D reduction of ammonium compounds to nitrates

Structured questions

11 The diagram below shows part of a food web found in a coral ecosystem.

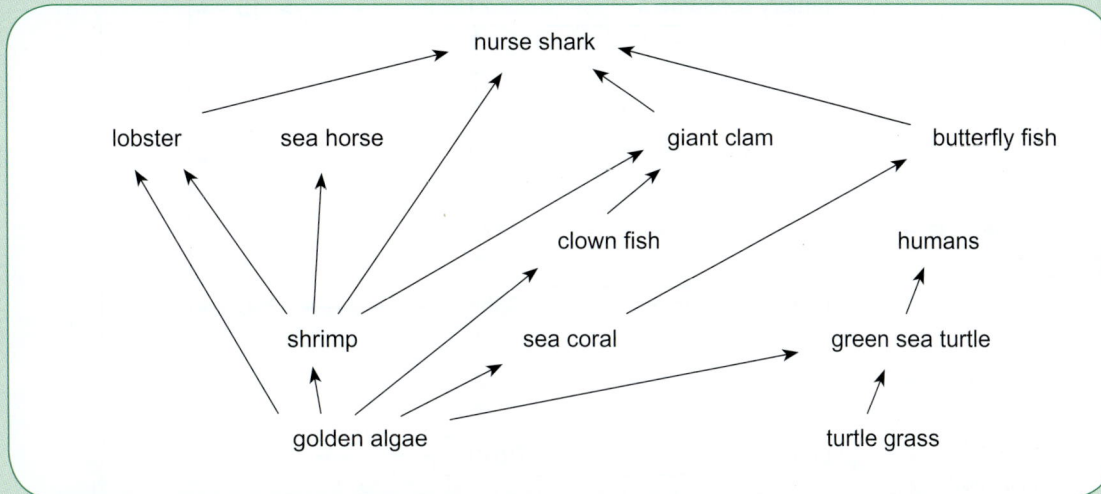

  a Using the information from the food web above write **two** food chains that are made up of three and four trophic levels respectively. [2 marks]

  b What do food webs, such as the one above, tell us about the flow of food and energy in an ecosystem? [3 marks]

  c **i** Identify the trophic levels at which the nurse shark feeds. [2 marks]

     ii What are the advantages to a species of feeding at different trophic levels? [3 marks]

  d Draw a diagram to show the expected pyramid of biomass for the organisms in the following food chain.

    golden algae → lobster → nurse shark [2 marks]

  e Explain why food chains are generally limited to four or five links. [3 marks]

continued …

12 The diagram below shows the flow of energy through a river ecosystem in Silver Springs, Florida. The figures are given in kilojoules per square metre per year ($kJ\,m^{-2}\,year^{-1}$).

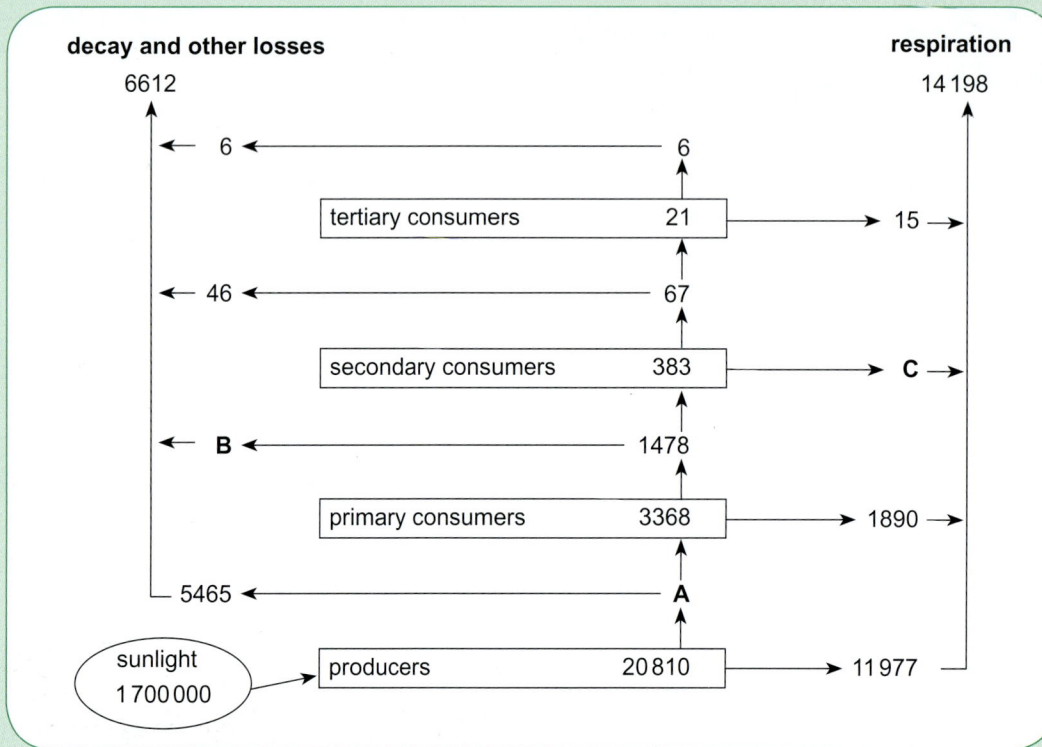

```
decay and other losses                                          respiration
      6612                                                        14 198
       ↑                                                             ↑
   ← 6 ←──────────────────────────────── 6                          │
                                          ↑                          │
              ┌──────────────────────────────────┐                  │
              │ tertiary consumers          21    │──→ 15 →          │
              └──────────────────────────────────┘                  │
                                          ↑                          │
   ← 46 ←─────────────────────── 67                                 │
              ┌──────────────────────────────────┐                  │
              │ secondary consumers        383    │──→ C →           │
              └──────────────────────────────────┘                  │
                                          ↑                          │
   ← B ←──────────────────────── 1478                               │
              ┌──────────────────────────────────┐                  │
              │ primary consumers         3368    │──→ 1890 →        │
              └──────────────────────────────────┘                  │
                                          ↑                          │
   └ 5465 ←──────────────────────── A                               │
   ⌒⌒⌒⌒⌒    ┌──────────────────────────────────┐                  │
  ( sunlight )→│ producers               20 810  │──→ 11 977 ┘
  ( 1 700 000 )└──────────────────────────────────┘
   ⌣⌣⌣⌣⌣
```

a Calculate the percentage of sunlight striking the producers that is converted to chemical energy by the producers. [2 marks]

b Suggest **two** reasons why not all the energy striking the producers is converted into chemical energy. [2 marks]

c Calculate the amount of energy in each of **A**, **B** and **C** in the diagram above. [3 marks]

d i Explain the difference between gross primary productivity (GPP) and net primary productivity (NPP). [2 marks]

  ii What is the GPP and NPP of the producers in the ecosystem? [2 marks]

e What is the percentage energy transfer between the secondary and tertiary consumers? [1 mark]

f Explain what happens to the rest of the energy that is **not** passed from secondary to tertiary consumers. [2 marks]

g It is often stated that '10% of energy passes from one trophic level to the next'. With reference to the diagram above, discuss whether this statement is true. [3 marks]

h Draw a pyramid of energy of the ecosystem illustrated in the diagram above. [3 marks]

continued …

13 The diagram below shows a nitrogen cycle.

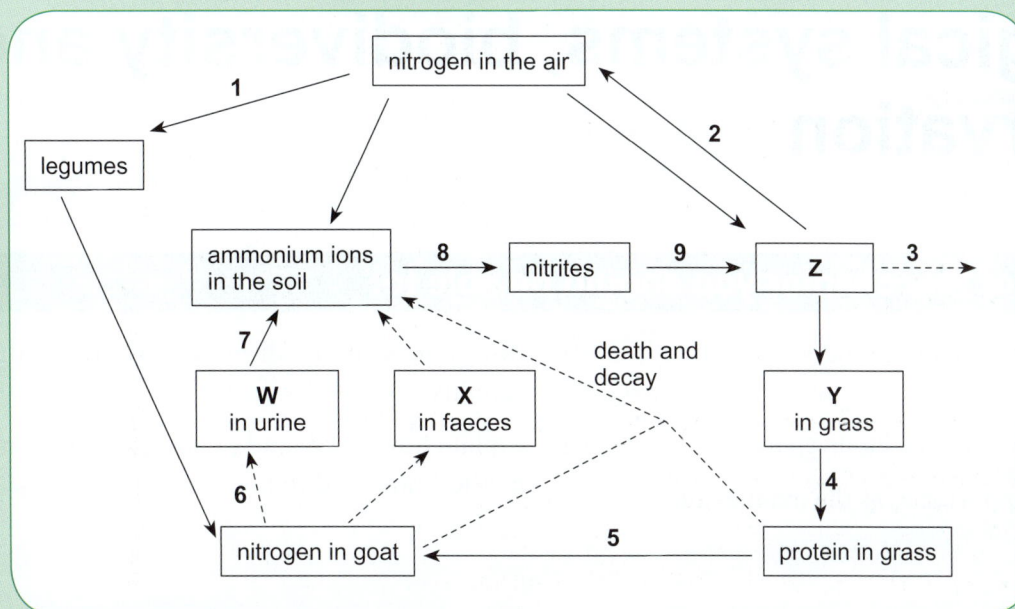

a Name the processes labelled **1** to **9**. [9 marks]
b Name the substances labelled **W**, **X**, **Y** and **Z**. [4 marks]
c Name the types of bacteria which carry out the processes at **1**, **2**, **8** and **9**. [4 marks]
d State the process that converts nitrogen in the air to **Z** directly. [1 mark]
e By what process does the grass take up **Z**? [1 mark]
f Pea seeds are often planted together with corn seeds by farmers in the Caribbean. Explain how this combination of plants helps with soil fertility. [3 marks]

Essay questions

14 a What do you understand by the terms 'food chain' and 'food web'? [2 marks]
b Discuss the composition of an ecosystem and how the parts of the ecosystem interact with each other. [8 marks]
c Energy flows through food chains and food webs in an ecosystem. Discuss the efficiency of energy transfer in an ecosystem. [5 marks]

15 a What do you understand by the term 'ecological pyramid'? [2 marks]
b Using examples, discuss the following types of pyramid:
i pyramid of numbers
ii pyramid of biomass
iii pyramid of energy. [13 marks]

16 a Using a simple diagram of the nitrogen cycle, explain how nitrogen is cycled in an ecosystem. Include in your answer the role of microorganisms. [7 marks]
b i Distinguish between energy flow and nutrient cycling in an ecosystem. [4 marks]
ii Explain how energy flow and nutrient cycling are important to maintain self-sustaining ecosystems. [4 marks]

Chapter 4

Ecological systems, biodiversity and conservation

By the end of this chapter you should be able to:

a discuss how ecosystems function as dynamic systems;

b explain the concept of biodiversity;

c discuss the importance of the maintenance of biodiversity;

d discuss how species diversity is related to the stability of an ecosystem;

e explain how *in situ* and *ex situ* conservation methods are used to maintain biodiversity.

An ecosystem is a relatively self-contained system including all the living organisms and the environment, interacting with each other. The word 'interacting' is very important. An ecosystem is dynamic – changes are happening in it all the time, as interactions take place. As we learned in Chapter 3, energy constantly flows through it, from one organism to another and between organisms and the non-living environment. Materials, too, pass between the environment and the organisms, and between the different organisms in the ecosystem. In this chapter we will look at further examples of interactions within ecosytems, which explain why ecosystems are so dynamic.

Biotic and abiotic factors

The components of an ecosystem that affect the organisms within it can be divided into **biotic factors** and **abiotic factors**.

Biotic factors

Biotic factors are ones that involve other living organisms. They include:

- the **feeding** of herbivores on plants or algae (Figure 4.1)
- **predation**, in which one organism (the predator) kills and eats another (the prey)
- **parasitism**, in which one organism (the parasite) lives in close association with an organism of a different species (the host) and does it harm

Figure 4.1   A queen parrotfish, *Scarus vetula*, feeding on algae on the reef surface, Antilles.

- **mutualism**, in which two organisms of different species live in close association, both benefiting from the relationship
- **competition**, in which two organisms both require something that is in short supply.

Abiotic factors

Abiotic factors are ones that involve non-living components of the environment. They include:

- **temperature**, which affects the rate of metabolic reactions in both endothermic and ectothermic organisms
- **light intensity**, which affects the rate of photosynthesis in plants and also the behaviour of animals
- **oxygen concentration**, which affects any organism that respires aerobically
- **carbon dioxide concentration**, which affects photosynthesising plants and algae
- **water supply**, affecting all terrestrial organisms
- **pH** of water or soil, which affects all organisms living in them
- **availability of inorganic ions** such as nitrate or potassium, which affects the growth of plants
- **factors relating to the soil**, known as **edaphic** factors, such as aeration, size of soil particles, drainage and mineral content
- **atmospheric humidity**, which affects the rate of water loss by evaporation from an organism's body
- **wind speed**, which affects transpiration rate of plants and can also greatly increase cooling effects if the environmental temperature is low
- **wave action**, which can damage organisms but also helps to move nutrients and gases around.

SAQ

1 Classify each of these factors as biotic or abiotic.
  a The speed of water flow in a river.
  b The density of seaweed growing in a rock pool.
  c Hurricane damage to a reef.
  d The population density of guppies in a pool.

Some examples of biotic and abiotic factors and their interactions

The coral reef ecosystem was introduced in Chapter 3 and here we give some examples of interactions and their relevance to this ecosystem.

Wave action

Reefs can be damaged by wave action due to the high winds in a hurricane. This is destructive but does not necessarily mean that the reef is permanently damaged as we will see below.

Wave action is not all destructive. Normal wave action is important in constantly causing water movement, bringing oxygen to respiring organisms and plankton to stationary organisms that feed on it, such as anemones.

Feeding

In Chapter 3 we discussed the ecological niche of the queen parrotfish (*Scarus vetula*). A significant proportion of its diet includes seaweeds that are present on a coral reef.

Parrotfish are now thought to be vital to the survival of coral reef that has been seriously damaged. This might be due to severe wave action in a hurricane or it might be due to the death of large areas of coral in a reef after attack by a large population of sea urchins (e.g. *Diadema antillarum*), which eat coral. Following the death of the coral there is a massive growth of seaweed, totally covering the area. The parrotfish feed actively on the seaweed. Without the fish reducing seaweed growth, from 100% to 40% for example, coral is not able to re-establish in this area. If the populations of the different species of parrotfish are low due to overfishing, only about 5% of reef is grazed down sufficiently to allow coral to grow again and it does not recover.

Predation

There is a formidable **predator** of larger fish on a coral reef. Barracuda (*Sphyraena* spp.) patrol outer reef areas in large schools (Figure 4.2). Like many aquatic predators, they have evolved into fast swimmers with a very rapid acceleration. They kill their prey using conical, razor-sharp teeth. The selection pressure of this on their prey has resulted

Light intensity

Light intensity also has an impact on oxygen supply through the photosynthesis of the zooxanthellae in the corals on a bright day. If the water is not cloudy due to sediment, the coral releases oxygen into the water at a rate greater than it can dissolve and bubbles of oxygen can be seen on the coral. At low light intensities and at night the respiration of all organisms of the reef, including the coral and the zooxanthellae, will reduce the oxygen concentration of the water. This may affect the most active of the fish which have a high demand for oxygen when swimming rapidly.

Carbon dioxide

In seawater, **carbon dioxide concentration** is rarely limiting, though it is a raw material for photosynthesis. Seawater contains much dissolved hydrogencarbonate (HCO_3^-) and carbonic acid (H_2CO_3). If dissolved carbon dioxide is used up, some hydrogencarbonate breaks down to release carbon dioxide. Then some carbonic acid breaks down to release hydrogencarbonate.

For a coral reef, the problem with carbon dioxide is that there is generally too much. The rising atmospheric levels of carbon dioxide cause a rise in hydrogencarbonate and carbonic acid in seawater. This lowers the **pH** of the water and is referred to as **acidification**. Many experiments have shown that the rise in carbon dioxide levels over the past 300 years has caused a 40% reduction in the synthesis of the main mineral used by reef-building corals. If it continues this way, many reefs will stop growing, and will then turn from coral-dominated reefs to algal-dominated reefs.

A food web affected by pollution

In Chapter 3 (page 44) we saw an example of a partial food web for a seagrass bed in the Dominican Republic. The **availability of inorganic ions** is an important factor in all food webs and this is no exception. Studies of seagrass beds that have been enriched by mineral ions running off agricultural land and sewage from urban areas show that the food web is dramatically changed (Figure 4.5). The helmet snail, yellow stingray and queen conch disappear. But there is a great increase in the biomass of phytoplankton and epiphytes growing on the leaves of seagrass. There is also a large increase in the biomass of variegated sea urchins that feed on the phytoplankton and epiphytes and detritus arising from the dead phytoplankton.

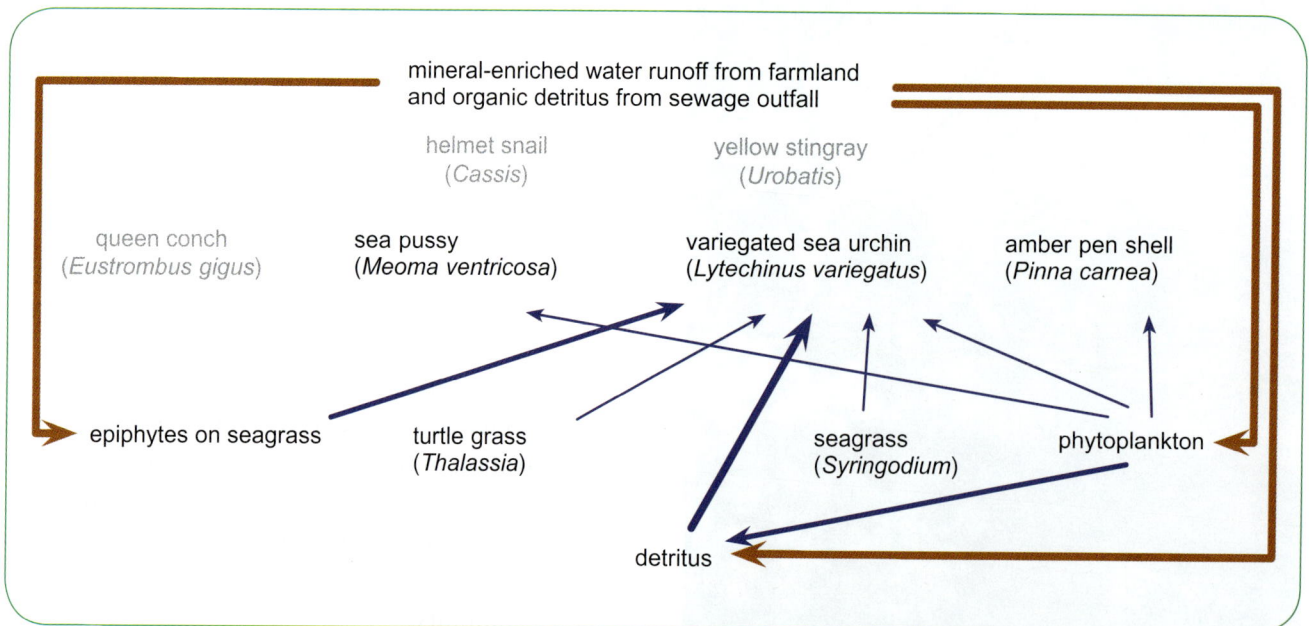

Figure 4.5 Seagrass partial food web in the Dominican Republic badly affected by human activity. The thickness of the arrows gives some indication of the amount of nutrient transfer. The grey text indicates organisms expected in unpolluted seagrass beds but missing when they are badly polluted.

Feedback controls in an ecosystem

A food web is only one way to indicate the complex interactions in an ecosystem. Figure 4.6 shows some control systems in a coral reef. If you study an ecosystem in this way and identify the processes that are most affected by such things as global warming and its associated acidification of seawater, it becomes more possible to predict the impact of these in the future. Figure 4.6 suggests that warming and acidification will have a major impact on reef ecosystems. This may be so severe that it has been suggested that most reef ecosystems may be lost in the not too distant future. If so, there will be serious consequences for reef-associated fisheries, tourism, coastal protection and the human communities dependent on these.

The impact of humans on ecosystems contrasts with the observation that ecosystems with less human interference appear to be quite stable. It has been suggested that this is a consequence of the high complexity of the ecosystem. Small disturbances affect organisms within the ecosystem, but recovery to former conditions is possible. If an ecosystem is seriously disturbed by the complete removal of one or more significant species from that ecosystem, it can

often be followed by extreme instability with large fluctuations in the population sizes of species that remain. Understanding what stabilises ecosystems will help us prevent excessive damage to the environment and the impact of that on human societies.

Biodiversity

No-one knows how many different species of living organisms there are on Earth. More than 1.5 million species of animals have been described and named to date. There were thought to be around a million flowering plant species. However, in a recent study to eliminate multiple entries in the list of species and correction of errors, the probable number of flowering plant species has been reduced to around 400 000. But there are thousands of other plants (such as ferns and mosses). When you consider species in all groups of organisms, you can see that there is a huge number of species on Earth.

And these are only the ones that we know about. Some biologists think that there may be as many as 100 million species on Earth. Alternatively, if the recent work on flowering plant numbers also applies to the other groups, it might be as low as 6 million. One tree in a tropical rainforest can

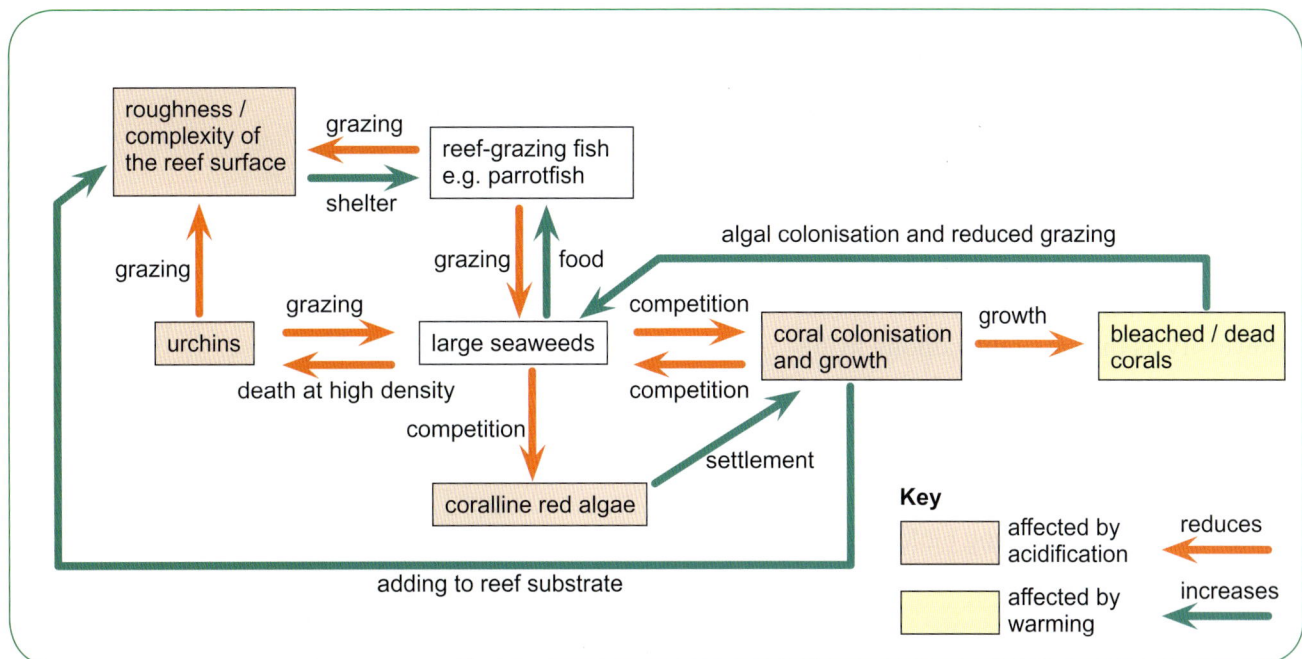

Figure 4.6 Control processes in a Caribbean reef ecosystem and impacts of global warming and seawater acidification.

contain as many as 1200 species of beetles, and almost every time a biologist does a thorough count of beetles in a small area of rainforest they find many previously unknown species.

There is much interest in **biodiversity**. It is fundamental to sustainable life on Earth and we have at last recognised how much human activities affect it – generally in a negative way, because our increasing population and the demands that we put on the environment damage habitats and cause species extinction. But our influence is not always negative. For example, sunken ships can become new habitats for marine organisms, and worked-out quarries can form new lakes and wetlands that are valuable for wildlife.

An understanding of biodiversity can help us to understand, and hopefully limit, the damage that we do, and even to reverse it.

What is biodiversity?

The number of species in a quadrat, a habitat, an ecosytem or geographical region defines the **species diversity** or **species richness** of that area. Dividing this by the area in which they were counted gives a figure describing **species density**.

A single species has variability within it. If this variation is inherited this is **genetic diversity** and is just as relevant to biodiversity as the number of different species.

Finally, the number of ecosystems there are in an area is also a significant aspect of biodiversity and is called **ecosytem diversity**.

All of these aspects of diversity can be combined into one concept – that of **biological diversity**. The United Nations' Article 2 of the Convention on Biological Diversity defines biodiversity as the variability among living organisms from all sources, including terrestrial, marine and other aquatic ecosystems, the ecological complexes and diversity within species, between species and of ecosystems. Such a wide definition makes quantifying biological diversity rather difficult.

Species diversity

If we count the number of species of all animals, plants and fungi in a community, the total number of species can be large. For example, the number of animal species (this includes insects, of course) in a tropical rainforest community can be in the high hundreds. This will also be the case for plants and fungi.

In habitats further away from the tropics, in general, there is less species diversity, but in all regions of the world there are 'hotspots' for diversity.

With hundreds of species in any one community, it is perhaps not surprising that much work on species diversity concentrates on a particular category of species within a community, as in the examples shown Figure 4.7 and Figure 4.8.

Both these figures show the general decline in species richness as you go further away from the equator. However, there are clearly other factors at work as well as latitude.

It appears that tree species richness is linked to temperature, solar radiation and the rate of water loss from leaves. Highest tree species richness occurs in areas with high humidity, high solar radiation and low rates of water loss from leaves. It is not so easy to find a reason for the variation in mammalian species richness, but this also partly

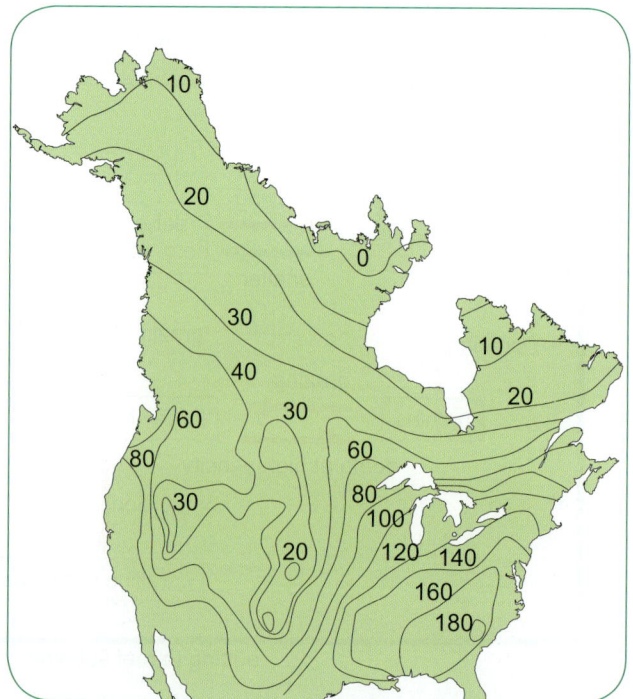

Figure 4.7 Tree species diversity across USA and Canada. The numbers are total tree species in quadrats 280 by 280 km.

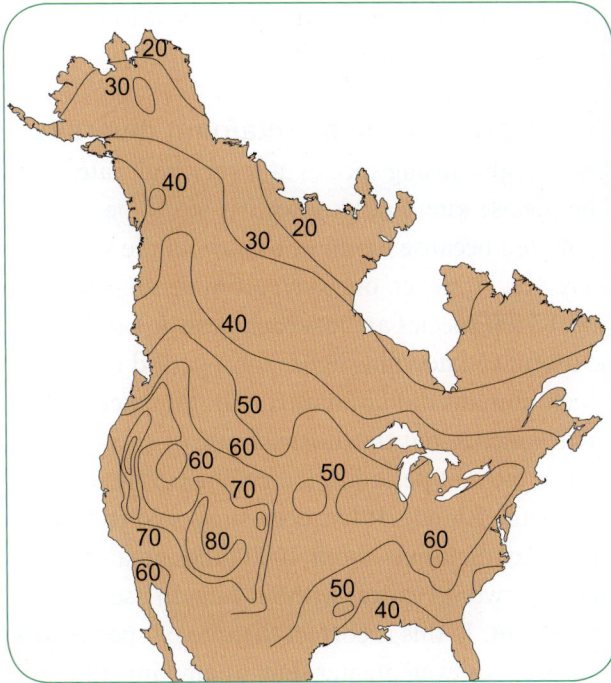

Figure 4.8 Mammal species diversity across USA and Canada. The numbers are total mammal species in quadrats 280 by 280 km.

links to low rates of water loss from leaves and may be a product of plant species diversity.

Ecosystem diversity

You would expect the number of different ecosytems in an area to have an effect on species diversity, with more ecosystems giving rise to greater species richness. To determine the relationship between the two, bird species richness and ecosystem richness were studied across the whole of the South American continent. Here bird diversity is great, including about one third of the world's bird species.

The continent was divided into large quadrats of up to about 1 million square kilometres in size. Within these quadrats, species richness ranged from 200 to 782 species and ecosystem diversity ranged from 12 to 24 per quadrat. As expected, greater ecosystem diversity was correlated with greater species diversity. However, it was calculated that ecosystem diversity could account for only about 30 to 50% of the species diversity. This shows that these two measurements give different information about the biodiversity of an area.

Genetic diversity

A species with low genetic diversity is less likely to survive in a changing environment than one with high genetic diversity. Loss of genetic diversity is almost inevitable when the species falls to a very low population size, if the species cannot cross-fertilise with other populations in other areas.

Proving that genetic diversity does increase chances of survival is not easy. However, in one study of the seagrass, *Zostera marina*, plots of $1 m^2$ in a natural habitat were planted with populations of *Zostera* of increasing genetic diversity. The plots contained 1, 2, 4 or 8 genotypes and were surrounded by natural *Zostera* populations.

The plots were left and were subjected to normal grazing by geese. After two weeks there was a clear relationship between the number of remaining *Zostera* shoots and number of genotypes planted. With one genotype only 55% of shoots remained but with eight genotypes 75% of shoots remained. This indicates that high genetic diversity in the seagrass increases its resistance to grazing geese.

SAQ

2 **a** Suggest why the seagrass beds with greater genetic diversity were less affected by grazing.
  b How would you test your suggestion experimentally?

Advantages and disadvantages of different measurements of diversity

Species diversity is a simple concept and that is one of its advantages. However, it has limitations. Collecting the data is time consuming, depending on the sampling methods chosen. Another limitation is that the presence or absence of a particular species tells you nothing about the ecological 'health' of that species. It gives no measure of the abundance of the species, if it is present. Neither does it describe the genetic diversity of any one species. Both the abundance and genetic diversity of a species can be important in determining survival of a species in a community.

When the abundance of a species falls very low in an area, there is a risk that it may become extinct in that area by chance – because of an extreme weather event, for example. This risk is also affected by genetic diversity, which is generally low in very small populations or in populations that have been reduced to a very low level in the past ('genetic bottleneck'). Though genetic diversity is important, it is quite difficult to determine.

Species diversity takes no account of species abundance. Take, for example, two communities made up of the same four species. In one, the four species are roughly equal in abundance, but in the other, one species is very abundant and the others are quite uncommon. We would consider the diversity of the first community to be greater than that of the second.

Ecosystem stability

In Chapter 3 it was mentioned that ecosystems with complex food webs tended to be more stable. A complex food web is an inevitable consequence of high biodiversity in an ecosystem.

There is a simple argument predicting a link between high biodiversity and increased stability. If an environmental change adversely affects one species within an ecosystem of low diversity, you would expect a proportionally bigger impact than for an ecosystem with very many species.

This argument has been challenged and there is still debate about it. However, there are a few experimental studies giving some support to the idea that higher diversity promotes stability in ecosystems.

In field grassland experimental plots in Minnesota, USA, data on plant species richness, community biomass and population biomass were collected over ten years. Using 200 experimental plots, with different plant species diversities, resistance to drought was measured. When the species diversity was low, drought reduced the growth in the plot more severely and increased the time taken to recover by several years, when compared to high diversity plots.

There are only a few investigations testing stability at the level of food webs, but there is one that looked at a grazing ecosystem in the Serengeti,

Tanzania. High biodiversity did appear to be linked to ecosystem stability.

The importance of maintaining diversity

The world is losing species at a very high rate. The precise rate is not known – it has to be estimated because we do not know all the species there are. However, one such estimate suggests that 17 500 species are lost each year. It would be useful to know this figure for a period in which humans did not have a major impact on environments, but the 'normal' rate of species loss for our current period in the geological time scale is also an estimate. It has been suggested that the rate of extinction is about 1000 times greater now than you would expect without human use of the environent. If this is correct the rate of species loss is as great or even greater than at any time in the past history of the Earth.

An **endemic species** is one that is found in one country only. Major habitat loss in that country can easily lead to the extinction of that species. Excessive hunting, however, can also result in extinction, which was the fate of the Caribbean monk seal (Figure 4.9). The highest rates of land vertebrate extinctions since 1500 have occurred in Madagascar and the Caribbean, with over 40 extinctions in each. Deforestation has contributed to many of these. In 2009, however, the country in which there was the highest number of threatened species was the Philippines, mainly due to the loss of tropical rainforest.

Figure 4.9   The extinct Caribbean monk seal. The last confirmed sighting was in 1952 at Seranilla Bank, between Jamaica and the Yucatan Peninsula.

One reason why we should try to maintain high biodiversity is to maintain the stability of ecosystems around the world. It is feared that low diversity would result in widescale ecosystem instability, with possible adverse consequences for human communities and climate change.

A second reason is that we may be losing species that contain chemicals that could make effective medical drugs, or have genes that could be beneficial if bred into crop plants. We are losing useful products and genes before we even know they exist. For example, around 7000 drugs that are prescribed by doctors are derived from plants. Almost 70% of these plants grow in tropical rainforests, which are being lost at an alarming rate.

One example of this is the discovery of the drug vincristine in the rosy periwinkle plant (Figure 4.10). This drug is very effective in the treatment of leukaemia. The plant is endemic to Madagascar, where there is a high rate of extinction of endemic plants.

Figure 4.10   The rosy periwinkle growing wild in Madagascar.

One of the greatest growth areas in the tourism industry is 'ecotourism', in which a main objective of tourists is to observe the biodiversity of the country they are visiting. Maintaining biodiversity is essential for this.

It is argued that waiting to see if the predictions of severe consequences of low biodiversity are correct would leave us in a situation in which it is too late to reverse the damage. If so, taking precautions now would be the sensible thing to do – by conserving species and halting biodiversity loss.

For many people, however, there is no need to justify conserving species for economic, ecological or climatic reasons. For them, it is simply our responsibility to look after our planet.

Conservation

Conservation is the protection of species, habitats and ecosystems in order to maintain biodiversity.

Conservation measures can be applied at the site in which a threatened organism lives – *in situ* **conservation**. Alternatively the conservation involves a site remote from the one in which the threatened species normally lives – *ex situ* **conservation**.

Examples of such *ex situ* conservation sites are specially created parks, wildlife reserves and nature reserves, in which there is natural habitat or nearly natural habitat that suits the moved organisms. *Ex situ* conservation sites also include zoos for captive breeding programmes, botanic gardens to grow endangered plants, and seed banks or embryo banks to preserve genetic material for future use.

In situ conservation measures are extremely diverse. They include protection of habitats from erosion, desertification, deforestation, sea acidification, introduced (alien) species, poaching, human collection of food and medicinal plants and animals, pollution and farming. They also include the use of specific management regimes intended to favour threatened species, such as the removal of introduced species, selective culling, cutting vegetation or mowing meadows. In all of these, humans are, to a varying degree, to blame for the need for conservation in the first place but they are also key to achieving successful conservation now and into the future.

The International Union for the Conservation of Nature and Natural Resources (IUCN) publishes a list of threatened species – the Red List. It is updated annually. The highest risk category is 'critically endangered'. The Red List draws the attention of governments and non-governmental organisations to the most vulnerable species on Earth.

Protection of habitat

Habitat loss may be the biggest threat to biodiversity at this moment. This is particularly so in areas which are unusually rich in biodiversity – **biodiversity hotspots** – such as the coral reefs of the Caribbean. If a particular habitat is lost in an area, so too are the communities of organisms that live in it. To protect habitat, you need to understand how and why it is being lost.

Natural habitats are lost by direct human activity and by climate change, which is, at least in part, an indirect result of human activities.

Loss of rainforest

Humans are significantly reducing biodiversity by reducing the area of tropical rainforest. It is estimated that 4.6 million hectares (17 760 square miles) are deforested each year. Some of this deforestation is to create plantations of rubber or oil palm, some for charcoal production (Figure 4.11), some for the timber only and some for subsistence farming. After deforestation there can be serious soil erosion, which leaves the land permanently degraded (Figure 4.12).

However, the relationship between the reduction in habitat area and its effect on biodiversity is not fully understood. When a rainforest is cut into sections, each forest 'island' may appear to retain the diversity of the original large forest. But if the islands are small, diversity within each island is reduced and some species may be lost from all the islands in an area. Habitat connectivity providing corridors for organisms to pass from island to island, may help to maintain diversity.

It might be thought that the loss of a habitat in one area, when the same habitat exists in other places, would not affect biodiversity. However, the assumption that two habitats are precisely the same may be not always be correct. In England a rare terrestrial snail of marshlands, Desmoulin's

Figure 4.11   Selling charcoal on the street in Gonaives, Haiti, from wood obtained by deforestation.

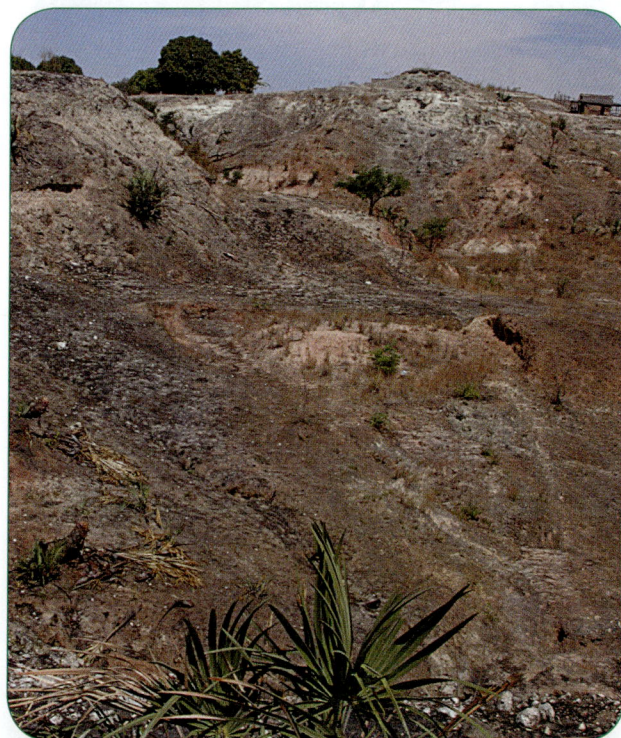

Figure 4.12   Deforestation in the central highlands of Madagascar has produced large areas that are now prone to drought and badly eroded.

whorl snail, is under threat, most probably by habitat loss. It was discovered at a marshland site through which a road was going to be built. It was moved to an apparently identical habitat nearby, but within six years it had died out at the new site.

Conserving tropical rainforest

How do we stop or reverse habitat loss? There is rarely a simple solution, and this is true with tropical rainforest. Understanding the diversity of pressures promoting deforestation has to be the first step.

In poor areas of the world, slash-and-burn agriculture is the only option for some people, where an area of forest is cleared and the wood burned to release nutrients for a few years of agricultural cropping before it is abandoned and another area cleared. At low levels, this may not be damaging to an area of forest, but, if it becomes more extensive, permanent damage will be done. A political solution to this is probably required, with feasible alternatives to this method of living provided or encouraged by national and local governments. The need of local people to live, feed and obtain fuel wood has to coexist with the need to conserve. Local people have to be included in the solution – their support is vital.

The clear-felling of an area of forest may provide a greater income for the owner if the cleared land is used to graze cattle, or turned into plantation. The pressure to plant oil palm trees has been high in recent years in south east Asia. In the Caribbean, the pressure to clear-fell forest has been high, but is now less than it was. The financial gain from creating banana plantations, for example, are not as great as they used to be (Figure 4.13). Nevertheless, some islands have shown considerable decline in forests since 1980. The loss of forest in some Caribbean islands is shown in Figure 4.14.

Rainforest retains water in the soil. When the land is clear-felled and used for agriculture rainwater quickly runs off, into streams and rivers and then into the sea. Rainforest is therefore a valuable source of drinking water for adjacent populations and this is an important issue in the Caribbean.

Figure 4.13 Banana plantation in St Lucia.

Old-growth rainforest contains a proportion of large hardwood trees of high value as timber. The felling of an area of this forest may therefore provide high profit. That area may never return to the state it was in before being logged. There are pressures on people and officials encouraging

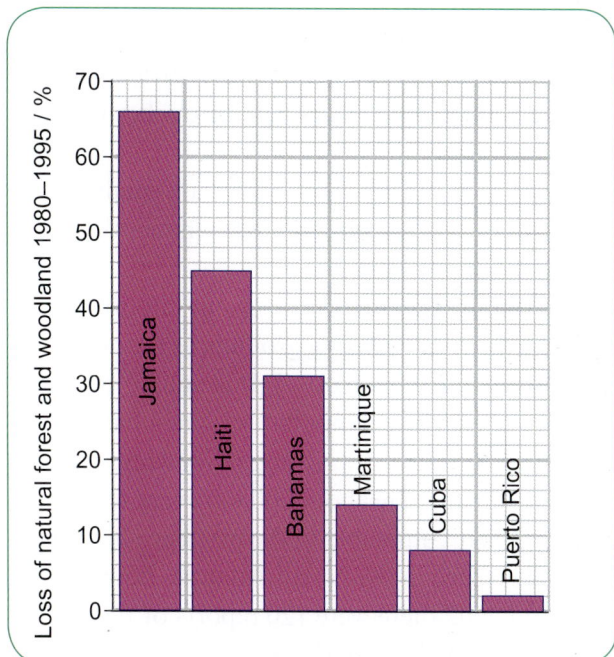

Figure 4.14 Deforestation on some Caribbean islands between 1980 and 1995.

short-term financial gain and insufficient pressures encouraging future prosperity which could well depend on keeping the rainforest intact.

Solutions to this pressure will need a combination of actions. National legislation could protect rainforest, as long as there is no political corruption and there is effective policing of the law. End-users of the products produced can be targeted to encourage them not to use the tropical hardwoods.

SAQ

3 Summarise the reasons for deforestation as a series of short bullet points.

In situ reserves

If a habitat is threatened, the designation of areas of that habitat to become a protected reserve of some sort may be able to protect the habitat and the biodiversity within it. If hunting is threatening a species, the extra protection provided by a reserve may be highly significant.

The leatherback turtle is threatened by fishing, habitat loss, nest disturbance and climate change and is critically endangered (Figure 4.15). The Pacuare Nature Reserve includes 1000 hectares of tropical rainforest on the Caribbean coast of Costa Rica and has the most important beach in Costa Rica for the nesting of these turtles, which is protected from poachers here throughout the breeding season.

However, if the areas of reserve are small, the problems of species vulnerability remain, through accidental catastrophe.

The leatherback turtle ranges out into the Atlantic from its breeding grounds as far north as England and even Iceland. It is limited by the summer sea surface temperature, which has to be at least 15 °C. Global warming is allowing it to increase its range by about 200 km every ten years. This makes it vulnerable to the extensive fishing that takes place in the North Atlantic. Between 1985 and 2002 there were 120 reports of dead leatherback turtles in UK waters, for example.

Figure 4.15   On the island of Grenada this leatherback turtle nest has been fenced off to prevent it from being disturbed.

Protection from introduced species

If a species is a new coloniser of a habitat, it sometimes spreads and becomes so dominant in that habitat that other members of the community are eliminated. Colonisations can be natural or due to human introductions and some are particularly damaging to biodiversity. The cause of the dramatic spread is usually the absence of natural predators (if the introduced organism is an animal) or herbivores (if a plant).

One particularly dramatic example is the accidental introduction of the brown treesnake (*Boiga irregularis*) to the Western Pacific island of Guam around 1950. The native birds (Figure 4.16), bats and reptiles were predated and by 1990 most forested areas of Guam retained only three native vertebrates, all small lizards.

Although islands are particularly vulnerable in this way, they are also places where it is sometimes feasible for humans to totally eradicate the invading organism. Feral goats, which were causing damage to the native vegetation on Round

Island in Mauritius, were successfully eliminated by a single marksman.

Though this method has been successful in this case, it has not been successfully carried out in very large areas for animals or plants.

It would appear that the best protection is not to introduce a potentially damaging organism intentionally and to minimise the introduction of them accidentally.

Some countries, such as Australia, expend much effort on biosecurity measures at all points of entry for people and cargo, in order to protect themselves from the introduction of new species. They have, after all, suffered one of the most serious events of this kind through the introduction of the rabbit in 1859.

Captive breeding and *ex situ* reserves

The scimitar-horned oryx, *Oryx damma*, lives in semi-desert habitats in northern Africa (Figure 4.17). By the 1970s there were few left due to hunting. Some were captured and a number of zoos around the world attempted to breed the oryx. Care was taken to avoid inbreeding and this required transport of animals from one zoo to another or the use of *in vitro* fertilisation techniques. A population was built up and in 1985 the oryx were introduced into a new reserve in

Figure 4.16   The flightless Guam rail is critically endangered and has not been present on the island since the 1980s. It has been bred in captivity. Some birds were introduced to the island of Rota in the Commonwealth of the Northern Mariana Islands but with little success.

Figure 4.17   Scimitar-horned oryx are now commonly bred in zoos around the world, like this one in England.

northern Africa that contained no native oryx. It is now thriving there.

This programme is a great success, but such programmes are expensive and generally only get the political support they require for particularly appealing or 'significant' animals. The approach is unlikely to be successful for most of the thousands of species that may become extinct in the near future.

However, most zoos are very active in breeding endangered animals, even when there is no plan for reintroduction. The hope is that a plan for reintroduction of a threatened species to a natural habitat could be started at some time, just so long as zoos keep a viable population alive.

There are other problems with captive breeding. For example, animals bred in captivity are unlikely to acquire immunity to diseases contacted in the wild and may be more susceptible to disease when released.

Dominica has two endemic parrot species – the sisserou parrot (*Amazona imperialis*), also known as the imperial parrot or imperial amazon, and the jaco parrot (*Amazona arausiaca*) or red-necked parrot.

The sisserou is classified as an endangered species; the jaco, which is more abundant, is vulnerable. The continued success of the Dominican parrot conservation programme depends on maintaining the quantity and quality of the parrots' preferred highland forest habitat.

Both parrots have been the subject of intensive conservation efforts in Dominica since the late 1970s. As a result, their numbers and range have increased. In 2000 the Morne Diablotin National Park was established, primarily to protect the parrots' habitats.

Botanic gardens can carry out a similar role for plants. Many are protecting very threatened species and are involved in programmes of reintroduction into natural habitats or distribution to gardens, parks and reserves.

SAQ

4 a Suggest why some animals cannot be bred in captivity.

b Explain why it is important to avoid inbreeding in a captive breeding programme.

Seed banks

The Royal Botanic Gardens at Kew, England, maintain the Millennium Seed Bank. In 2010 they had collected seeds from 10% of the world's plants. The aim is to collect seeds from 25% of the world's plants by 2020 and this is the most ambitious plant conservation project in the world. It is hoped that the seeds will prevent the extinction of these plants (Figure 4.18).

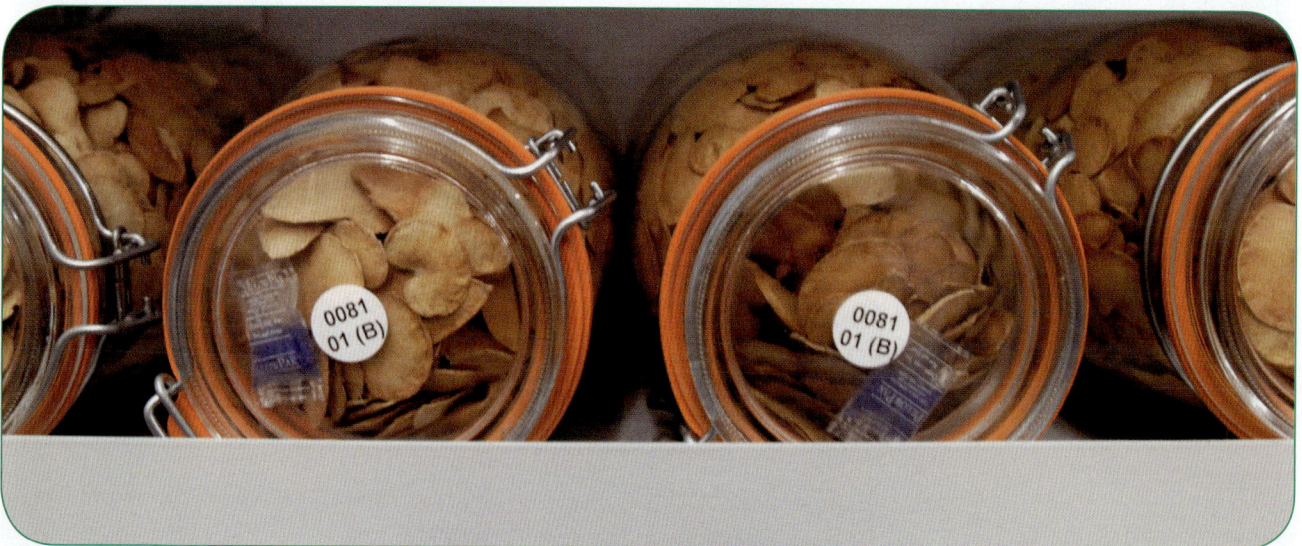

Figure 4.18 Seeds in storage at −20 °C in Kew's Millennium Seed Bank.

Not all seeds can be preserved in the same manner. Kew works in partnership with other seed banks and they are researching to find the conditions that allow different types of seed to remain viable for as long as possible. They have found that seeds from the majority of species can be treated in the same way (orthodox seeds). The seeds are dried at 15 °C until they reach a moisture content in equilibrium with air around them at 15% relative humidity. They are then cooled to −20 °C and stored at that temperature. Seeds from some species may remain viable for hundreds of years in these conditions, but others may only survive a few years. Periodically, seed are removed from storage and germinated to determine their viability.

Kew often works closely with local communities to protect species for threatened habitats. For example, the Centre Hills of Monserrat is a biodiversity hotspot but is under threat, and the volcanic eruption of 1995 to 1997 destroyed about 60% of Monserrat's forest ecosystems. Seeds from the most threatened species have been collected. The aim is for some of the seeds to be used to grow into plants with the hope of reintroducing the plants back to their natural habitat in the future.

SAQ

5 It has been suggested that seed banks put selection pressures on seeds that are different from the selection pressures the plants would experience in the wild.
   a How might these selection pressures differ?
   b How might this affect the chances of success when returning the plant to the wild?

Sperm and embryo banks

Attempts are being made to achieve similar results for animals as seed banks are now doing for plants. There are, in principle, several options for animals – sperm banks, gene banks or embryo banks. All of these are more difficult to store than plant seeds.

As a final resort, the possibility of regenerating an extinct organism from stored DNA from tissue of that organism is theoretically possible, but not very feasible at this moment.

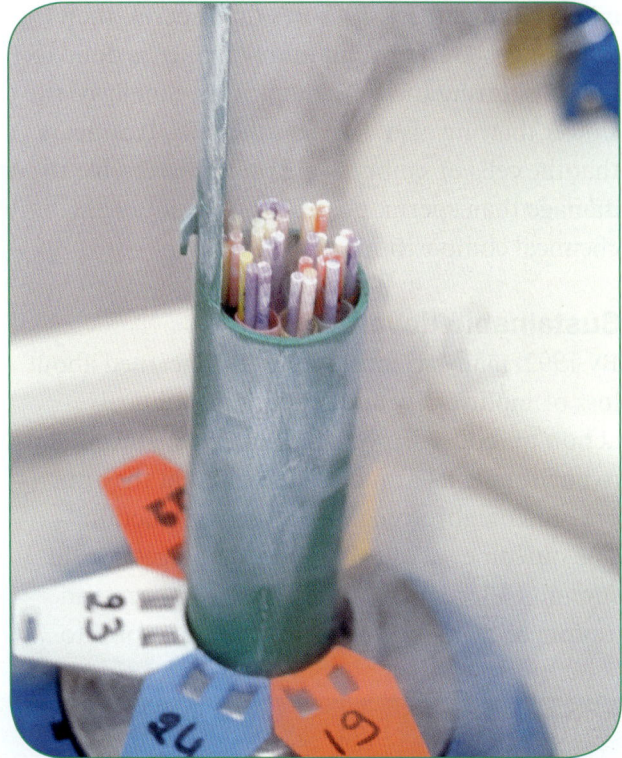

Figure 4.19 Straws of semen being removed from a container which is surrounded by liquid nitrogen at −196 °C.

The storage of sperm in sperm banks clearly cannot preserve a species unless there is also corresponding egg storage and the possibility of *in vitro* fertilisation.

To prepare the sperm for storage, they are washed to remove the liquid component of the semen and then immersed in a fluid that increases their viability storage. There are several variants of this fluid, but they often contain egg yolk and buffers, such as citrate, which keep the pH constant. A small narrow tube (a straw) is filled with sperm and preserving fluid. Usually less than 1 cm^3 is stored in each straw. It is cooled, then stored surrounded by liquid nitrogen at −196 °C (Figure 4.19).

It appears that the viability of the sperm falls over time, but there is evidence of viability after 20 years of storage. However, viability is unknown much beyond this and it is also not known if the pattern of viability is the same for all species.

In animal egg and embryo banking, it is difficult to maintain viability of the egg or embryo. There are a number of reasons for this. As eggs and embryos are larger structures than sperm, they take longer to freeze and more damage is done to the cells during the freezing process. Similarly, the slower thawing also damages the cells. It appears that the cells of embryos are more susceptible to damage than sperm, possibly as a result of their chemical composition.

Sustainable development

By 1992, many scientists were so concerned about loss of biodiversity and the lack of political action to reduce irreversible damage being done to environments around the world that they put pressure on governments to take some action. The outcome was, at that time, the largest world summit of leaders that there had ever been and a promise by most governments in the world to introduce sustainable development, in contrast to development causing permanently damaging changes to environments. The idea was to make sustainability a consideration in all decisions made by governments, public organisations and private organisations within a country. A key component of this Earth Summit in Rio de Janeiro was a pledge by governments to reduce the loss of biodiversity.

A repeat summit took place in Johannesburg in 2002. It remains to be seen if the impact of sustainable policies may have had a significant impact, but at least biodiversity in now a subject in the political arena, which is encouraging.

Summary

- An ecosystem is a dynamic system in which living organisms and their non-living environment constantly interact with one another.

- Biotic factors are those involving the effect of other living things on an organism. They include feeding, predation, parasitism, mutualism and competition.

- Abiotic factors are those involving the effect of non-living components of the environment on an organism. They include temperature, light intensity, availability of water, oxygen and carbon dioxide, pH, wind speed and wave action.

- Biotic and abiotic factors interact with one another in an ecosystem.

- Biodiversity is a measure of the variability among living organisms. It includes species diversity, genetic diversity and ecosystem diversity.

- There is some evidence that ecosystems with complex food webs and high biodiversity are more stable than those with lower biodiversity.

- Conservation aims to maintain high biodiversity. *In situ* conservation of a species involves working in the species' natural habitat, such as by maintaining a protected area or reserve. *Ex situ* conservation involves building up the species' population in another environment, such as a zoo, botanic garden, sperm bank, embryo bank or seed bank.

Questions

Multiple choice questions

1 Ecosystems are dynamic systems. Which of the following factors interact within an ecosystem?
   A biotic
   B abiotic
   C abiotic and biotic
   D abiotic and physical

2 Wild cilantro (shado beni, *Eryngium foetidum*) is a herb that requires moist fertile soil and is grown in backyard gardens. Which of the following are abiotic factors that might affect its distribution?
   A parasites and nutrient availability
   B nutrient availability and water
   C wind speed and temperature of the atmosphere
   D pH and caterpillars

3 The table below shows the number of species in four different ecosystems.

Organism	Number of individuals in ecosystem 1	Number of individuals in ecosystem 2	Number of individuals in ecosystem 3	Number of individuals in ecosystem 4
butterflies	5	42	0	12
earthworms	1	15	0	0
snails	0	8	12	0
blackbirds	2	8	0	3

Which ecosystem would be expected to show the greatest stability?
   A 1
   B 2
   C 3
   D 4

4 Biodiversity includes:
   A species, genetic and ecosystem diversity.
   B species and ecosystem diversity.
   C species diversity only.
   D ecosystem diversity only.

5 Which of the following is **not** a biotic factor?
   A competition between two species of barnacles on a rocky shore
   B oxygen concentration in the seawater around a coral reef
   C grazing of seagrass by manatees
   D the mutualistic relationship between sharks and remora fish

continued …

6 Which of the following is **not** a reason to maintain biodiversity?
A Many plant species are a possible source of medicines.
B Biodiversity provides inspiration to writers and poets.
C High biodiversity helps to keep biochemical cycles in balance.
D Increasing human populations require more land for agriculture.

7 Most seeds stored in seed banks are stored at:
A 35 °C and dehydrated to a moisture content of 5% relative humidity.
B −20 °C and dehydrated to a moisture content of 15% relative humidity.
C −20 °C and dehydrated to a moisture content of 5% relative humidity.
D −5 °C and dehydrated to a moisture content of 25% relative humidity.

8 Sperm is stored in a sperm bank in:
A straws kept at −160 °C.
B test-tubes kept at 350 °C.
C straws, buffered and kept at −196 °C.
D straws, buffered with citrate and kept at 196 °C.

9 Which row correctly describes *in situ* and *ex situ* conservation?

	Type of *in situ* conservation	Example of *in situ* conservation	Type of *ex situ* conservation	Example of *ex situ* conservation
A	preservation of species in their natural habitat	sperm bank	preservation of species outside their natural habitat	forest reserve
B	preservation of species in their natural habitat	wildlife sanctuary	preservation of species outside their natural habitat	seed bank
C	preservation of species outside their natural habitat	embryo bank	preservation of species in their natural habitat	wildlife sanctuary
D	preservation of species outside their natural habitat	forest reserve	preservation of species in their natural habitat	botanic garden

10 One advantage of captive breeding is that:
A it is a form of conservation of a species.
B the animals being conserved do not need their natural habitats.
C the conditions experienced by a conserved animal in captivity may be stressful to it.
D the conserved animals may be susceptible to diseases when released into the wild.

continued ...

Structured questions

11 Healthy coral reefs provide a complex habitat that promotes species diversity and abundance. The coral reefs of Jamaica demonstrated the dynamic nature of an ecosystem when they shifted from a healthy to a damaged state. The diagram below shows a food web for some of the organisms in the healthy coral reef.

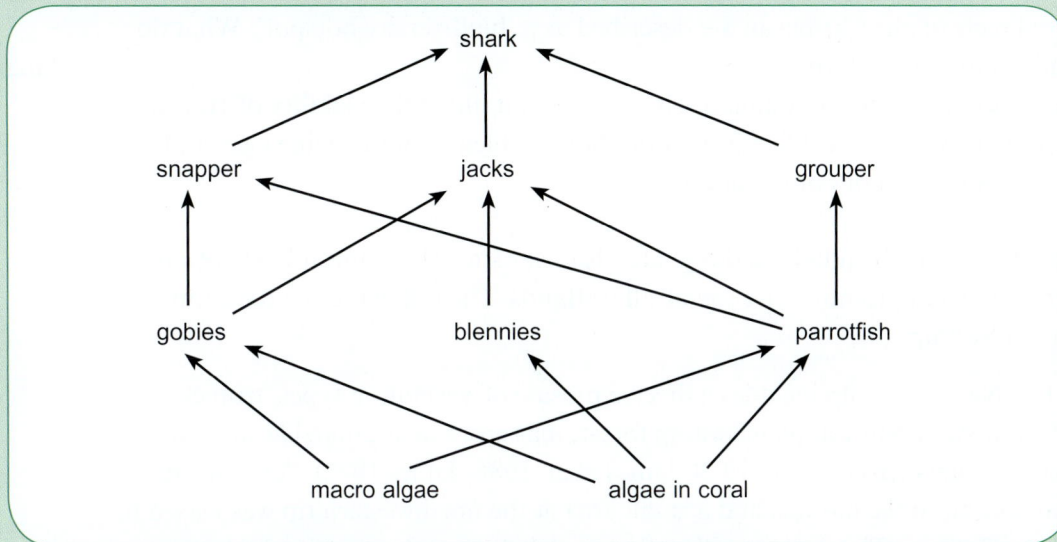

a i Sharks can be described as 'apex predators'. In relation to the food web above, what does this mean? [1 mark]

   ii Suggest **two** functions of an apex predator such as a shark in the ecosystem. [2 marks]

b Sharks are generally overfished in coral reef ecosystems. What might be a consequence of severe overfishing of sharks on the secondary consumers in the food web? [1 mark]

c What effect on the primary consumers would you expect from the consequence you describe in **b**? [1 mark]

d Symbiotic corals compete with macro algae for physical space to grow and settle. What would be the effect on both organisms if the apex predator was removed? [2 marks]

e i What type of algae would the habitat consist of if the sharks were removed? [1 mark]

   ii Explain what effect this would have on species diversity and abundance. [1 mark]

f Sharks, groupers, jacks and snappers have been almost completely absent due to human activities. Small herbivorous fish are now more numerous than they were. What effect would you expect the abundance of small herbivorous fish to have on corals with symbiotic algae? [1 mark]

g Hard coral abundance in the Caribbean has declined from 50% cover to less than 10% cover in the last 30 years. Suggest a reason for this. [1 mark]

h Explain how apex predators like the shark help to increase species diversity and abundance. [2 marks]

i Name an abiotic factor which would affect coral reef ecosystems. [1 mark]

j A conservation effort known as the Caribbean Challenge has the aim of protecting 20% of the region's marine and coastal habitat by 2020. Suggest one action which may be taken to achieve the aim. [1 mark]

continued ...

12 a Distinguish between:
   i *in situ* and *ex situ* conservation
   ii zoological gardens and botanic gardens
   iii habitat and ecosystem
   iv species richness and species abundance. [8 marks]
   b The coral reefs of the Caribbean are described as a 'biodiversity hotspot'. What do you understand by the term? [3 marks]
   c Sperm banks are relatively common. However, maintaining the viability of frozen eggs and embryos is more difficult. Identify **four** problems with freezing eggs and embryos as a method of conservation. [4 marks]

13 The Nariva Swamp in Trinidad is a designated Ramsar site. The Ramsar convention seeks to conserve and promote wise use of all wetlands. The following is a description of the Nariva Swamp.

> The Nariva Swamp includes a diverse mosaic of vegetation types: tropical forest, swamp forest, palm swamp forest, mangrove areas, marshland, and open waters (Bacon et al. 1979, James et al. 1986, James 1992). Agricultural areas add to the mosaic, and a small area at the northwestern tip was leased to local farmers. This area was illegally expanded through squatting by large rice farmers, and the negative impacts of this incursion will be explained below.

> There are three small communities surrounding Nariva Swamp. Most of the inhabitants of these communities depend on the natural resources of the area for food, mainly the cascadura fish (*Hoplosternum littorale*), blue crab (*Cardisoma guanhumi*), and black conch (*Pomacea urceus*). These are highly valued by the local communities not only for subsistence but also for commercial purposes. Many people in the local communities also have gardens with annual crops such as peppers, cucumbers, watermelon and rice.

> The area is exceedingly rich in biological resources. There are over 175 species of birds recorded for Nariva Swamp (Bacon et al. 1979) out of the 433 total bird species for Trinidad and Tobago (French 1980). The star is undoubtedly the blue and gold macaw (*Ara ararauna*), the object of a venture with the Cincinnati Zoo for reintroduction to the area. Despite the diversity existing in Nariva swamp, no comprehensive bird studies or regular bird surveys have been conducted. It is hoped that with the implementation of the restoration work in the area, the development of a monitoring program based on the avifauna may become possible.

> From: *Nariva Swamp Ramsar Site, Trinidad and Tobago (West Indies) Wetland Habitat Restoration Initiative* by Montserrat Carbonell and Nadra Nathai-Gyan

continued ...

a **i** What do you understand by the term 'biodiversity'? [2 marks]

    ii Using the information in the passage above, do you think the Nariva swamp has high biodiversity? Give reasons for your answer. [6 marks]

b The swamp is described as "exceedingly rich in biological resources". Do you think that the Nariva Swamp would be a stable ecosytem? Give reasons for your answer. [2 marks]

c Identify two reasons why the nearby communities would want to maintain the biodiversity of the Nariva Swamp. [2 marks]

d The Bush Bush Wildlife Sanctuary in the Nariva Swamp has many rare and threatened species like the blue and gold macaw.

    i What method of conservation has been employed by declaring it a wildlife sanctuary? [1 mark]

    ii Identify **two** steps that should be undertaken for this method of conservation to be successful. [2 marks]

Essay questions

14 a Outline the case for preventing the extinction of a species of living organism. [6 marks]

b Conservation methods include *in situ* and *ex situ* methods.

    i Distinguish clearly between the two types of conservation methods.

    ii Suggest some actions that may be needed to conserve an endangered species using *in situ* methods. [5 marks]

c The local community is sometimes opposed to establishment of conservation areas. Suggest **two** reasons for this opposition. [4 marks]

15 a The United Nations Convention on Biological Diversity defines biological diversity as the variability among living organisms from all sources, including terrestrial, marine and other aquatic ecosystems, the ecological complexes and diversity within species, between species and of ecosystems.
Geneticists, biologists and ecologists can use this definition of biological diversity. Discuss how the term 'biological diversity' would be important to each group of scientists. [6 marks]

b Briefly discuss the following methods of *ex situ* conservation.

    i sperm banks

    ii seed banks

    iii zoos

    iv embryo banks [8 marks]

16 a Using a named example, discuss why ecosystems are considered to be dynamic systems. [10 marks]

b Describe how the stability of an ecosystem might be related to the number of species it contains. [5 marks]

Chapter 5
Transport in plants

By the end of this chapter you should be able to:

a   explain the uptake of ions by active transport in roots, and the role of the endodermis;

b   describe the entry of water into plant roots in terms of water potential;

c   relate the structure of xylem vessels to their functions in transport and support;

d   make drawings from prepared slides of xylem vessels;

e   outline the ascent of water in plants, including the roles of root pressure, capillarity, cohesion, adhesion and transpiration pull, and the role of stomata in transpiration;

f   investigate the impact of environmental factors, including light and air movements, on the rate of transpiration;

g   relate the structure of sieve tubes and companion cells to their function;

h   make drawings of sieve tubes and companion cells from prepared microscope slides;

i   label pertinent features in an electron micrograph of a sieve tube and companion cell;

j   explain how phloem loading in the leaves occurs against a concentration gradient;

k   discuss mass (pressure) flow as a possible method of translocation, including experimental evidence for and against this hypothesis.

Plant transport systems

Plant cells, like animal cells, need a regular supply of oxygen and nutrients. All plants are multicellular, and some of them are very large. Most plants, however, have a much more branching shape than animals, and this provides a much larger surface area : volume ratio for exchange with their environment than in an animal of the same body mass.

The requirements of plants differ from those of animals in several ways, both in the nature of the nutrients and gases required and the rate at which these need to be supplied.

- **Carbon dioxide**: Photosynthesising plant cells need a supply of carbon dioxide during daylight. They obtain this from the air. Aquatic plants get carbon dioxide from the water that surrounds them.

- **Oxygen**: All living plant cells need oxygen for respiration. Cells that are actively photosynthesising produce more than enough oxygen for their needs. Cells that are not photosynthesising have to take in oxygen from their environment, but they do not respire at such a high rate as mammals and so they do not need such a rapid oxygen supply.

- **Organic nutrients**: Some plant cells make many of their own organic food materials, such as glucose, by photosynthesis. However, many plant cells do not photosynthesise and need to be supplied with organic nutrients from photosynthetic or storage cells.

- **Inorganic ions and water**: All plant cells require a range of inorganic ions and also water. These are taken up from the soil, by roots, and are transported to all areas of the plant.

The energy requirements of plant cells are, on average, far lower than those of cells in a mammal. This means that their rate of respiration and, therefore, their requirement for oxygen and glucose are considerably less than those of mammals. Plants can therefore manage with a much slower transport system.

One of the main requirements of the photosynthetic regions of a plant is sunlight. Plants have evolved thin, flat leaves which present a large surface area to the Sun. This also makes it easy for oxygen and carbon dioxide to diffuse into and out of the leaves, reaching and leaving every cell quickly enough so that there is no need for a transport system to carry gases.

As a result of these differences between the structures and requirements of a plant and a mammal, it is not surprising that they have evolved different transport systems. In fact, plants have two transport systems, one for carrying mainly water and inorganic ions from the roots to the parts above ground, and one for carrying substances made by photosynthesis from the leaves to other areas. In neither of these systems do fluids move as rapidly as blood does in a mammal, nor is there an obvious pump. Neither plant transport system carries oxygen or carbon dioxide, which travel to and from cells and the environment by diffusion alone.

SAQ
1 Explain why plants do not need a transport system to distribute oxygen or carbon dioxide.

Uptake of ions
Plants take up inorganic ions from the solution that is present between soil particles. Ions are absorbed into the **root hairs** (Figure 5.1), transported across the root, and then into the xylem. They then travel, in solution in water, to all parts of the plant. The structure and function of xylem tissue, and the way in which water moves in it, is described on pages 88–90.

The mechanism by which ions are taken up by root hairs depends on their concentration in the soil solution. If a particular type of ion is in a higher concentration in the soil than inside the root hair cell, then it will be absorbed by **facilitated diffusion**. This does not require any energy input by the plant. If, however, the concentration of the ion in the soil is lower than that inside the root hair cell, then it must be absorbed by **active transport** (Unit 1, Chapter 3, page 70). Specific transporter proteins use energy, derived from the hydrolysis of ATP, to move ions through the cell membrane, into the cytoplasm.

Water transport
Figure 5.2 outlines the pathway taken by water as it is transported through a plant. Water from the soil enters a plant through its root hairs and then moves across the root into the xylem tissue in the centre. It then moves upwards in the xylem vessels through the root into the stem and finally into the leaves.

From soil into root hair
The roots of plants have very thin, single-celled extensions of some of the cells that make up the outer layer (epidermis) of the root. These root hairs are a specialised exchange surface for the uptake of water and mineral ions.

Figure 5.1 A root of a young radish showing the root hairs.

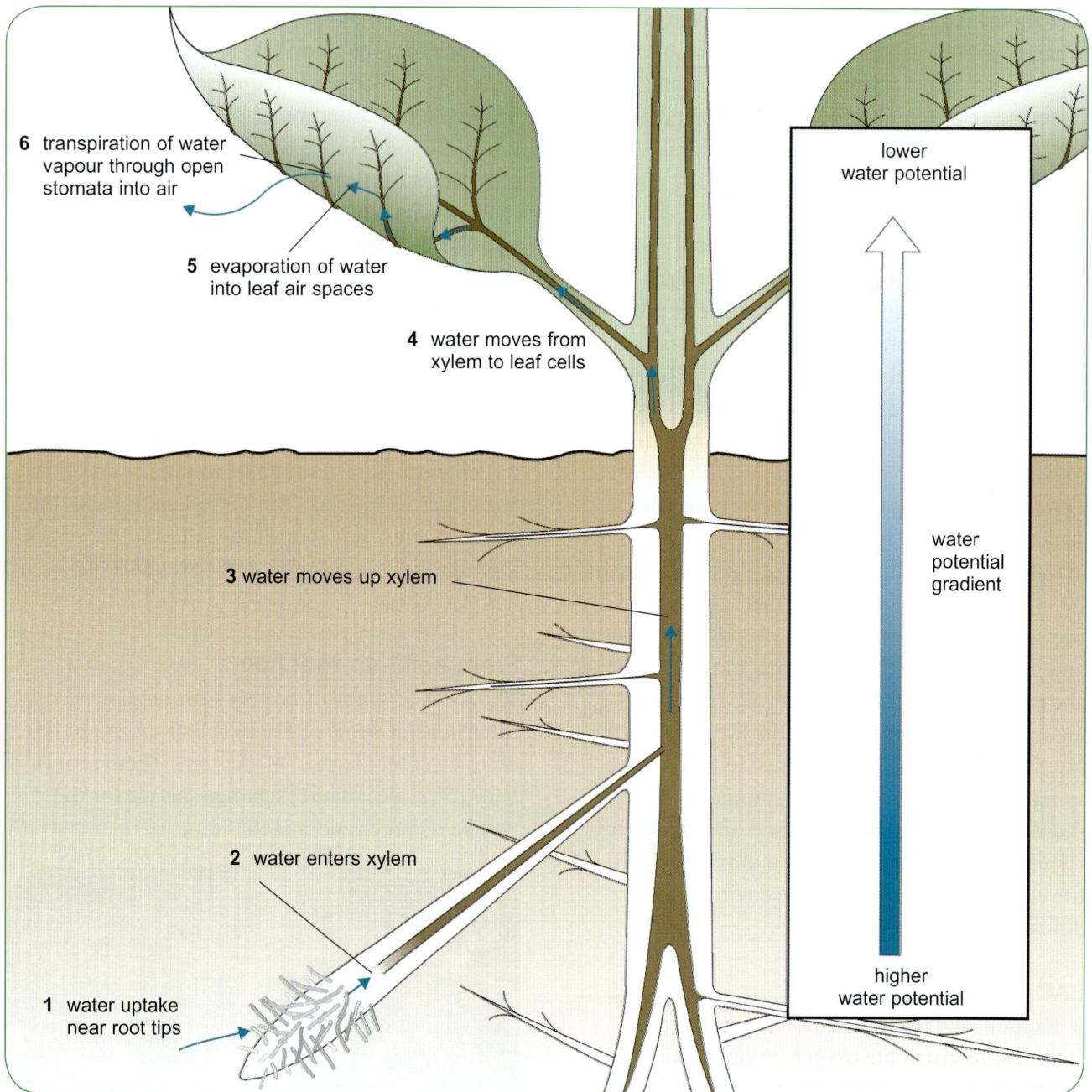

6 transpiration of water vapour through open stomata into air

5 evaporation of water into leaf air spaces

4 water moves from xylem to leaf cells

3 water moves up xylem

2 water enters xylem

1 water uptake near root tips

lower water potential

water potential gradient

higher water potential

Figure 5.2 An overview of the movement of water through a plant; water moves down a water potential gradient from the soil to the air.

Each root hair is only about 200–250 µm across, but this is large enough for them to be visible with the naked eye. There may be thousands of them on each tiny branch of a root, so together they provide an enormous surface area that is in contact with the soil surrounding the root.

Soil is made up of particles of minerals and humus. Between the soil particles there are air spaces. Unless the soil is very dry, there is a thin layer of water covering each soil particle. The root hairs make contact with this water, and absorb it by osmosis. The water moves into the root hair because there is a lower concentration of solutes in the soil than there is inside the root hair cell. The water potential outside the root hair is therefore higher than the water potential inside, so water moves passively down the water potential gradient into the cells (Figure 5.3).

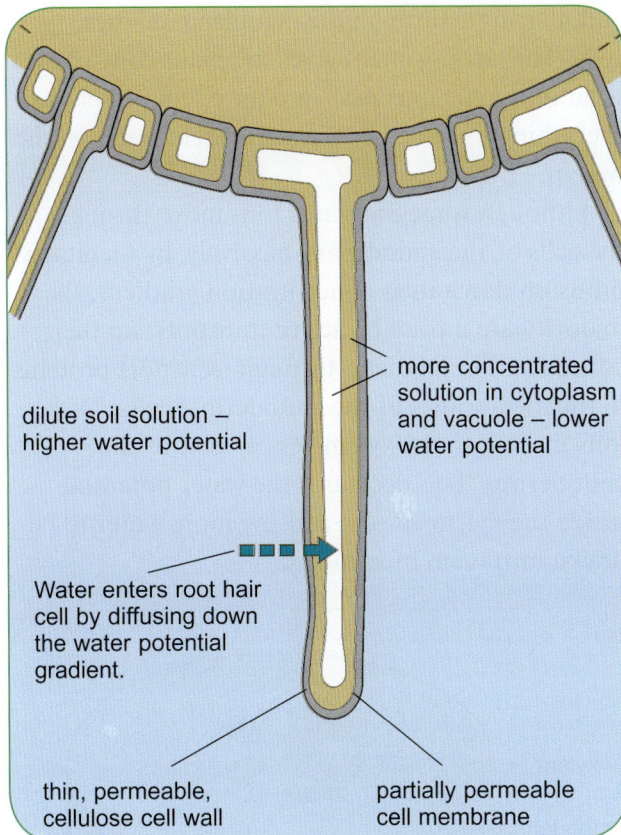

Figure 5.3 Water uptake by a root hair cell.

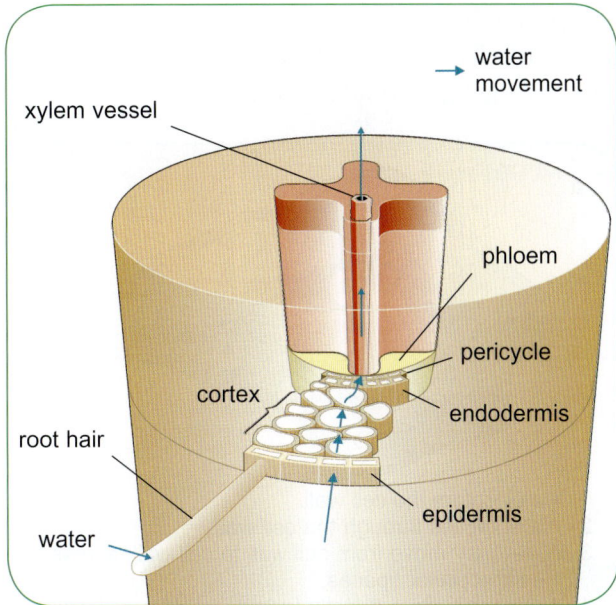

Figure 5.4 The pathway of water movement from root hair to xylem.

Water can also enter the root without going into a cell at all. It can seep into the cell walls of the root hair cells, and then move through these and other cell walls all the way into the centre of the root.

SAQ

2 Summarise the ways in which a root hair cell is adapted for its functions.

From root hair to xylem

Figures 5.4 and 5.5 show the internal structure of a young root. Water that has been taken up by the root hairs travels across the **cortex** and into the centre of the root. It does this because the water potential inside the xylem vessels is lower than the water potential in the root hairs and the cells in between. Water moves passively down its water potential gradient, from the edge of the root to the xylem in the centre.

The water takes two different routes through the cortex. The cells of the cortex, like all plant cells,

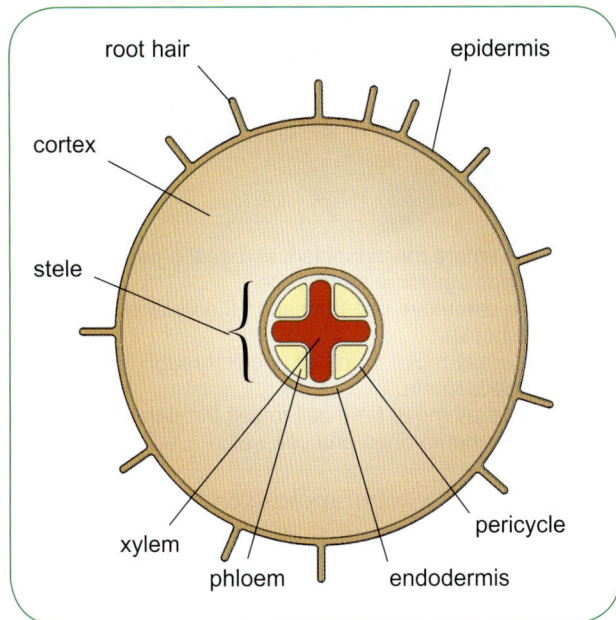

Figure 5.5 Transverse section of a young root to show the distribution of tissues.

are surrounded by cell walls made of many layers of cellulose fibres criss-crossing each other. Water soaks into these walls rather as it would soak into filter paper, and then seeps across the root from cell wall to cell wall, and through the spaces between the cells, without ever entering a cell. This route is called the **apoplast pathway** (Figure 5.6a). Some water, however, enters the cells and moves from cell to cell by osmosis, or through strands of cytoplasm that make direct connections between adjacent cells, called **plasmodesmata** (Figure 5.6b). This is called the **symplast pathway**.

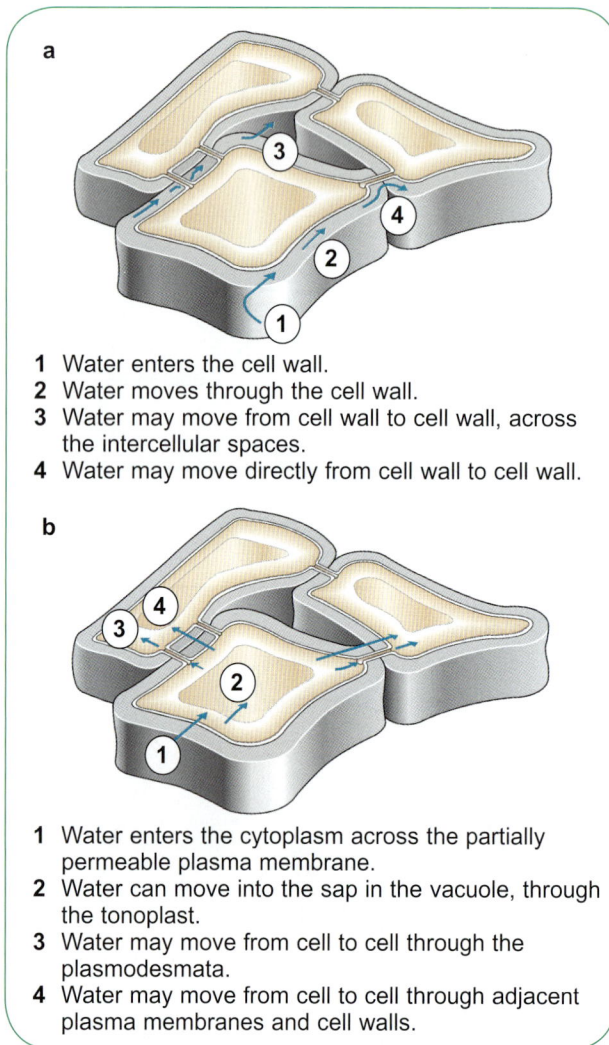

1 Water enters the cell wall.
2 Water moves through the cell wall.
3 Water may move from cell wall to cell wall, across the intercellular spaces.
4 Water may move directly from cell wall to cell wall.

1 Water enters the cytoplasm across the partially permeable plasma membrane.
2 Water can move into the sap in the vacuole, through the tonoplast.
3 Water may move from cell to cell through the plasmodesmata.
4 Water may move from cell to cell through adjacent plasma membranes and cell walls.

Figure 5.6 How water moves across a root: **a** the apoplast pathway, **b** the symplast pathway.

The relative importance of these two pathways depends on the species of plant and the environmental conditions. In most plants, for most of the time, the majority of water movement across the root is by the apoplast pathway.

When the water reaches the **stele** (Figure 5.5), the apoplast pathway is barred. The cells in the outer layer of the stele, called the **endodermis**, have a thick, waterproof, waxy substance called **suberin** in their walls (Figure 5.7). This band of suberin, called the **Casparian strip**, forms an impenetrable barrier to water in the walls of the endodermis cells. The only way for the water to cross the

endodermis is through the cytoplasm of these cells. This arrangement gives the plant control over what inorganic ions pass into its xylem vessels, as everything has to cross a plasma membrane on the way in.

Although some inorganic ions move through the cells of the endodermis passively, by facilitated diffusion down their concentration gradient, the majority are moved by active transport, up their concentration gradient, through transport proteins in the membranes of the endodermal cells. These ions move into the xylem vessels next to the endodermis. This decreases the water potential inside the xylem vessels, causing more water to be drawn into them by osmosis.

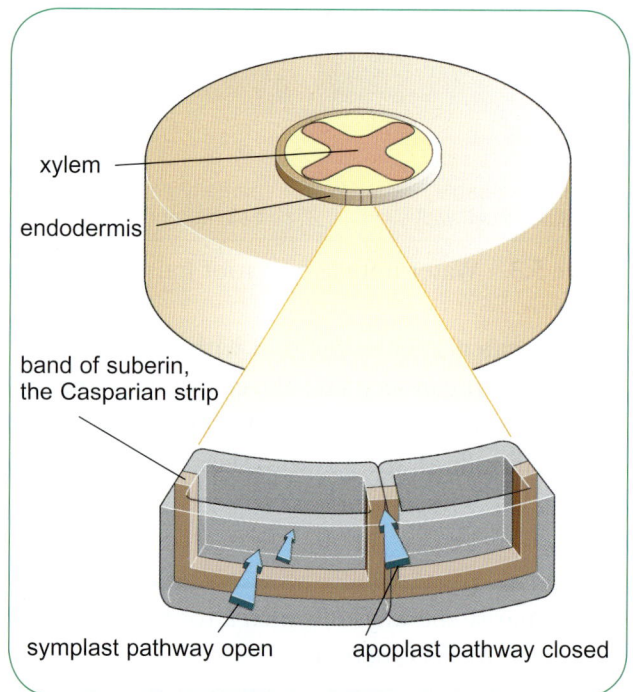

Figure 5.7 The Casparian strip.

Up through the xylem vessels

Water is carried from the roots all the way up to the top of the plant inside xylem vessels. In a large tree, the distance from the roots to the topmost leaf could be tens of metres. Yet there is no pump making the water move. What forces cause water to travel up a plant?

To answer this question, we need to understand what is happening to the water in the leaves, because this is what drives the process. It is also important to know something about the structure of the xylem vessels, as this too helps to keep the water moving.

We have already looked at the structure of xylem vessels (Unit 1, Chapter 2, page 51). Xylem vessels are made up of many long, narrow cells called **xylem elements** stacked end to end. Xylem elements began as living cells, with cytoplasm, nucleus and cellulose cell walls. However, they then differentiated into extremely specialised structures – and died. Xylem elements contain no living material, and are just the empty shells of the cells from which they developed.

Figures 5.8, 5.9, 5.10 and 5.11 show the structure of xylem vessels. Each xylem element has a wall made of cellulose and a substance called **lignin**. Lignin is a very strong, waterproof material.

It is important not only in keeping water inside the xylem vessels, but also in helping to support the plant. The wood of tree trunks and branches is made of xylem vessels.

The end walls of the xylem elements usually disappear completely, so that the stack of elements makes up a continuous tube, like a drainpipe, reaching all the way from the roots, through the stem and up to the very top of the plant. Figure 5.12 shows the position of xylem tissue in a stem. There are usually several xylem vessels side by side. Water can move sideways between them, and out of the xylem vessel into the surrounding cells, through **pits** in their walls. These are small gaps where no lignin has been deposited, leaving just the cellulose cell wall, through which water can easily move.

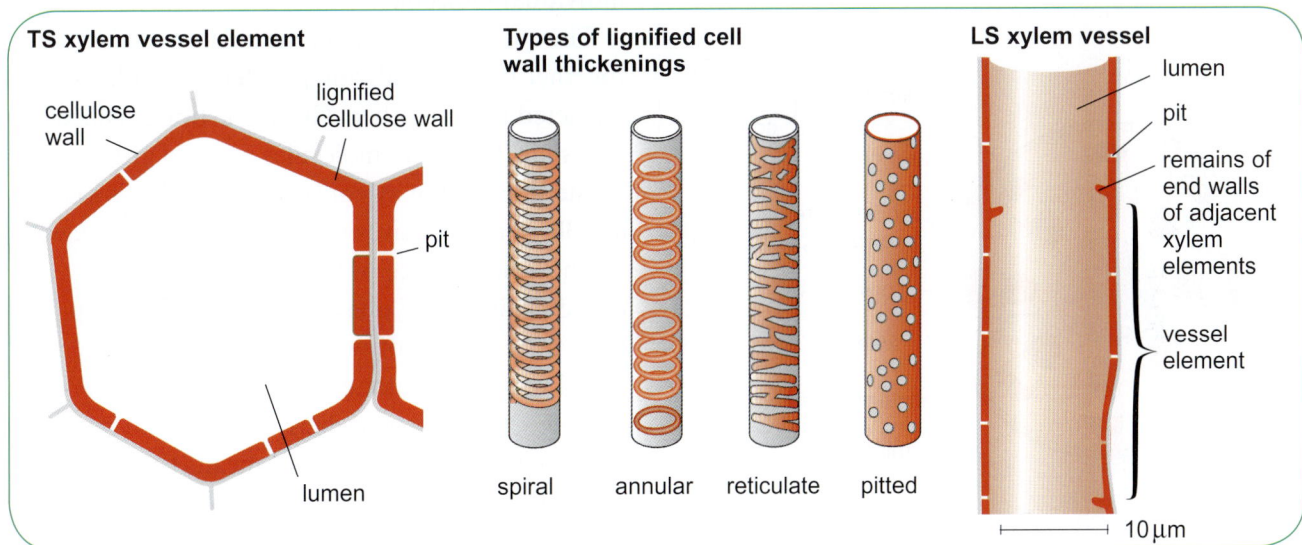

Figure 5.8 The structure of xylem vessels.

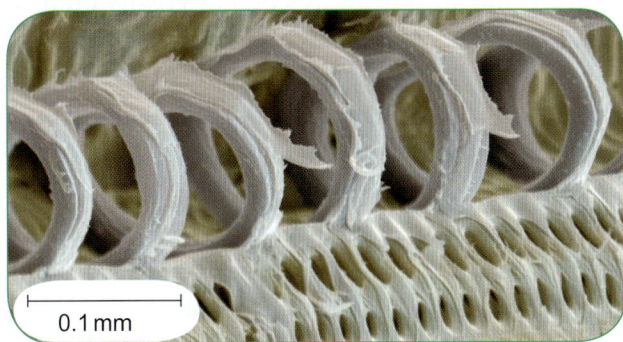

Figure 5.9 SEM of a longitudinal section through part of a bamboo stem, showing xylem vessels. The vessel at the top has a spiral band of lignin around it. The one below is older and has more extensive covering of lignin with many pits.

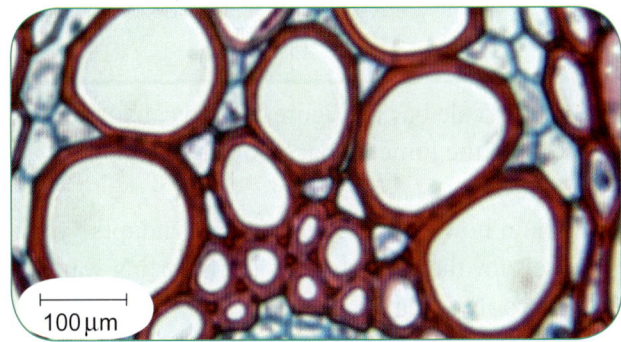

Figure 5.10 Photomicrograph of a transverse section of xylem vessels. They have been stained so that the lignin appears red. The xylem vessels are the large empty cells. You can also see smaller parenchyma cells between them.

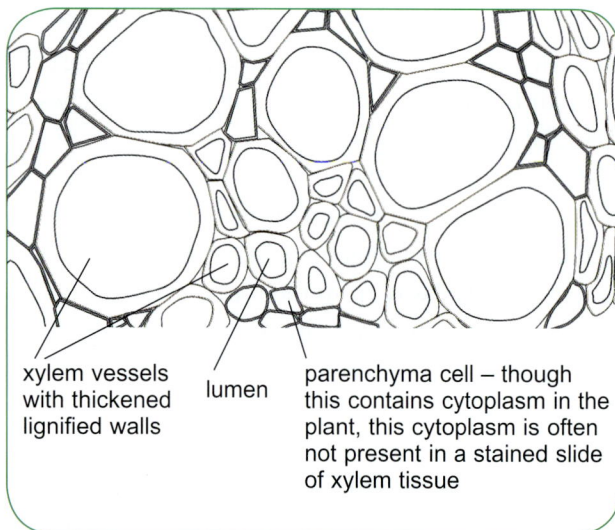

Figure 5.11 Drawing of xylem tissue in transverse section.

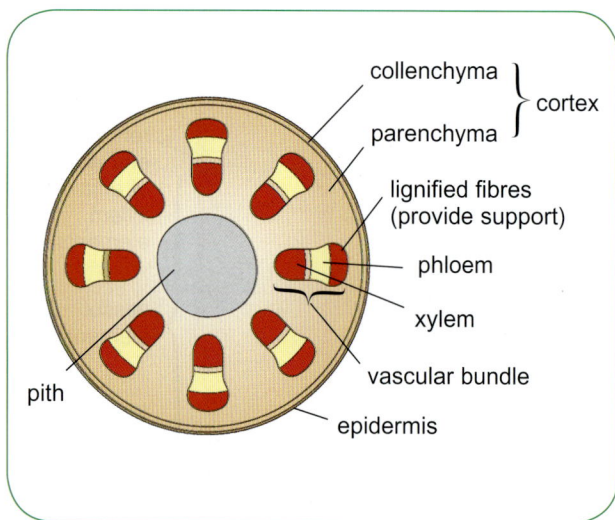

Figure 5.12 Transverse section through a young stem to show the distribution of tissues.

SAQ

3 Use the scale bar in Figure 5.10 to calculate the width of the lumen (space) inside one of the xylem vessels.

4 Explain how each of these features adapts xylem vessels for their function of transporting water from roots to leaves.

   a total lack of cell contents
   b no end walls in individual xylem elements
   c a diameter of between 0.01 mm and 0.2 mm
   d lignified walls
   e pits

You can think of xylem vessels as being like a group of drinking straws. To pull water up a straw, you put your mouth over the top and suck. 'Sucking' means reducing the pressure. Because you have reduced the hydrostatic pressure at the top of the straw, there is a pressure gradient from the bottom of the straw to the top. The liquid flows down this pressure gradient, from the relatively high pressure at the bottom to the relatively low pressure at the top.

The liquid moves up the straw, and up through xylem vessels, by **mass flow**. Mass flow is the way that water moves in a river, or up a drinking straw, or out of a tap. A whole body of water flows along together. This is very different from diffusion or osmosis, which rely on the random movements of individual molecules.

The column of water in the xylem vessels holds together because individual water molecules are attracted to each other. This attraction is called **cohesion**. The water molecules are also attracted to the sides of the xylem vessels, and this is known as **adhesion**. This gives them a tendency to 'crawl' up the inner surface of the vessel, a process called **capillarity**. Cohesion and adhesion help the whole column of water to flow up the xylem vessel without breaking. Xylem vessels are very narrow – usually somewhere between 0.01 mm and 0.2 mm in diameter – and this means that more of the water is in contact with the sides of the vessel than would be the case if the vessels were wider. Adhesive forces are therefore relatively high, able to overcome the downwards pull of gravity on the water column, and helping capillarity to work.

From leaf to atmosphere – transpiration

Figure 5.13 shows the structure of a leaf.

The cells in the spongy mesophyll layers are not tightly packed, and there are many spaces around them filled with air. The water in the cells seeps into the walls, so these cell walls are always wet. Some of this water evaporates into the air spaces, so that the air inside a leaf is usually saturated with water vapour.

These air spaces are in direct contact with the air outside the leaf, through small pores called **stomata**. If the air outside the leaf contains less

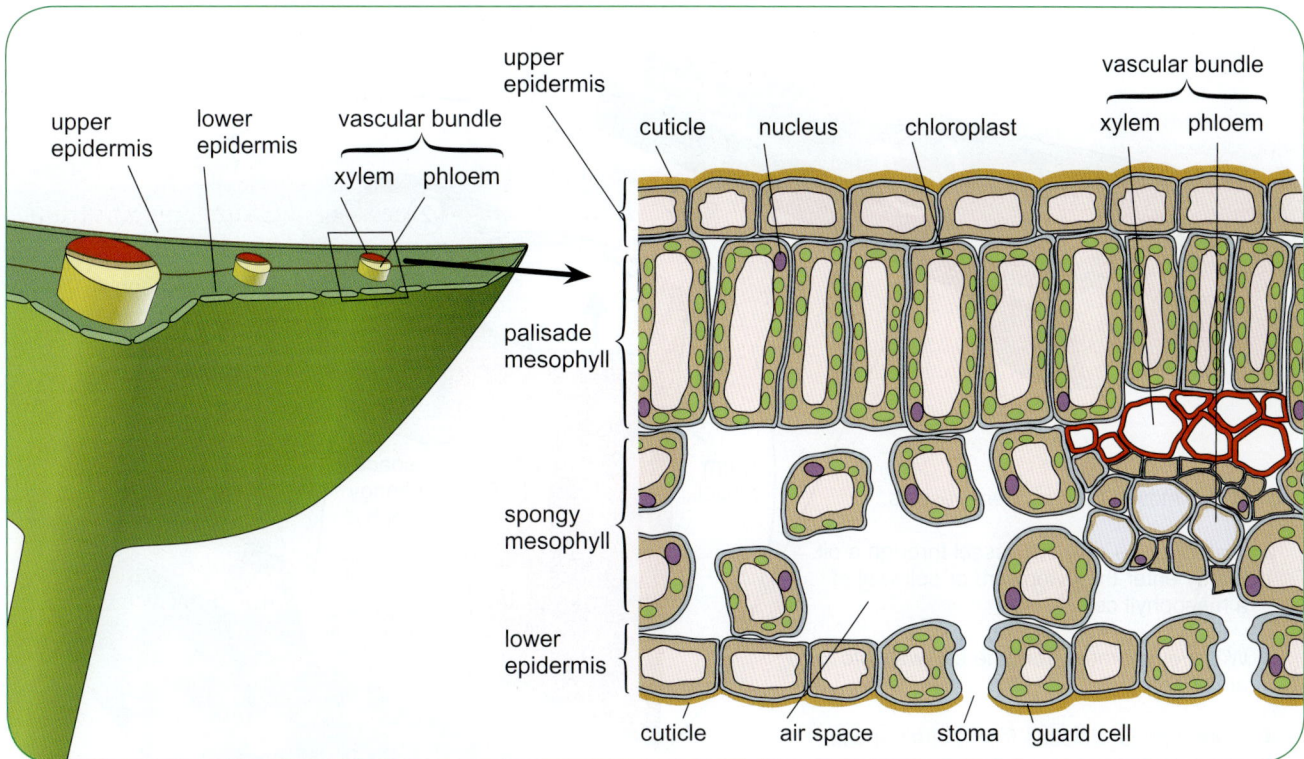

Figure 5.13 The structure of a leaf.

water vapour than inside it, then there is a water potential gradient from the air spaces inside the leaf to the outside. Water vapour therefore diffuses out through the stomata. This is called **transpiration** (Figure 5.14).

As water evaporates from the cell walls of the mesophyll cells, water moves into them to replace it. This water comes from the xylem vessels in the leaf. This removal of water from the top of the xylem vessels reduces its pressure. The water pressure at the top of the xylem vessel is therefore less than the water pressure at the bottom, so water flows up the vessel – just like water up a drinking straw (transpirational pull). Cohesion between the water molecules keeps them moving together without the column breaking, all the way up to the top of even the tallest trees.

The continuous movement of water from the roots, up through the xylem, into the leaves and then out into the atmosphere is known as the **transpiration stream**. Apart from the small contribution made by root pressure, the plant does not have to provide any energy at all to make it happen. The main driving force is supplied by the difference in water potential between the air and

the soil. The water moves down a water potential gradient.

In some plants and in some circumstances another force can contribute to the movement of water in the xylem. This force is **root pressure**. The process of active transport of ions through the endodermis draws water into the xylem vessels in the roots. This increases the hydrostatic pressure inside the xylem vessels, pushing the water upwards to regions where the hydrostatic pressure is lower. If air humidity is very high and rate of transpiration very low, root pressure can be sufficient to move water in the xylem.

However, root pressure is nowhere near enough to explain how water is forced to move all the way up a tall tree, or even a large plant.

Though the primary role for transpiration is to transport water and mineral ions from roots to all other parts of a plant, there is one other benefit. In hot conditions, the evaporation of water from the plant's leaves can have a very useful cooling effect, in a similar manner to the evaporation of sweat from your skin.

1 Water moves up the xylem vessels.

2 Water leaves a xylem vessel through a pit. It may enter the cytoplasm or cell wall of a mesophyll cell.

3 Water evaporates from the cell wall into an air space.

4 Water vapour diffuses from the air space through an open stoma.

5 Water vapour is carried away from the leaf surface by air movements.

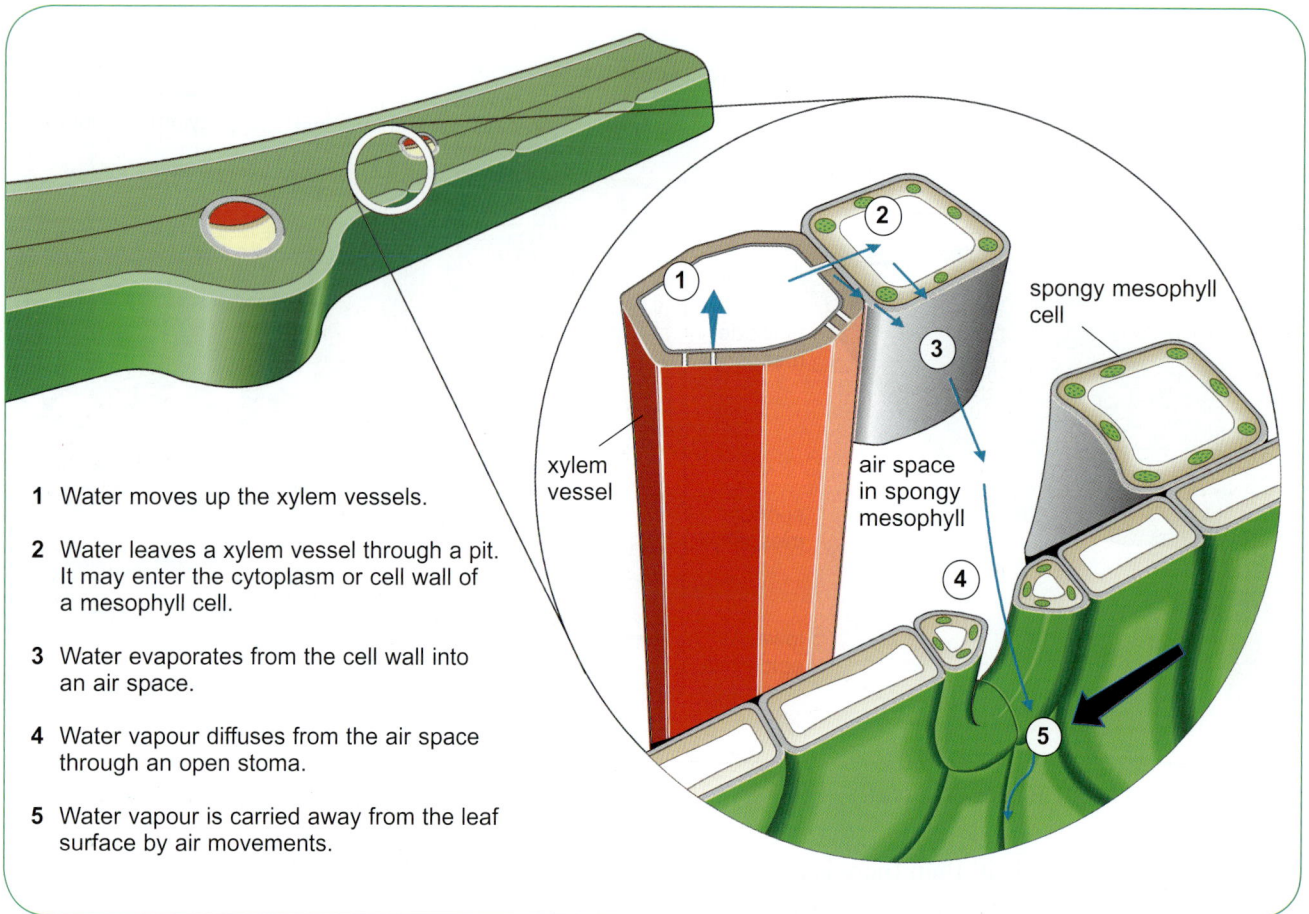

Figure 5.14 Water movement through a leaf.

Stomatal opening and closure

A stoma is a hole in the epidermis of a leaf, usually on the underside, that is surrounded by two sausage-shaped guard cells. When the guard cells are turgid, they swell and open the stoma. When they are flaccid, the stoma closes.

The diagram explains how this happens.

Stoma closed

Stoma open

1 ATP-powered proton pump actively transports H⁺ out of the guard cell.

2 The low H⁺ concentration and negative charge inside the cell cause K⁺ channels to open. K⁺ diffuses into the cell down an electrochemical gradient.

3 The high concentration of K⁺ inside the guard cell lowers the water potential (ψ).

4 Water moves in by osmosis, down a water potential gradient.

5 The entry of water increases the volume of the guard cells, so they expand. The thin outer wall expands most, so the cells curve apart.

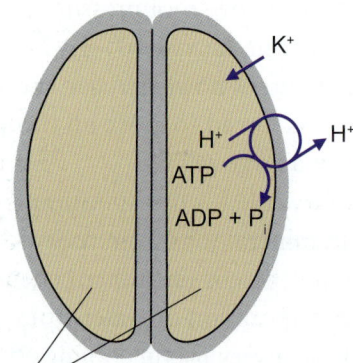

flaccid guard cells

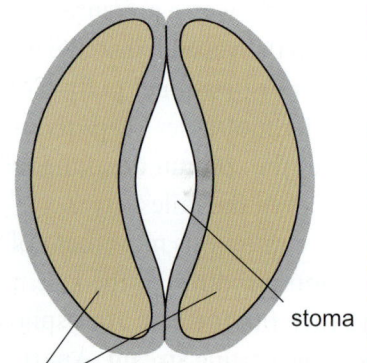

turgid guard cells

stoma

Factors affecting transpiration

Anything that increases the water potential gradient between the air spaces in the leaf and the air outside, or that speeds up the movement of the water molecules, will increase the rate of transpiration. Generally, transpirational pull is the most important mechanism for water movement in xylem.

- **Humidity**: Humidity is a measure of how much water vapour is held in the air. In conditions of low humidity – that is, when the air is dry – there is a steep water potential gradient between the leaf and the air. Transpiration rates are therefore greater in low humidity than in high humidity.
- **Temperature**: An increase in temperature causes an increase in the kinetic energy of water molecules. This increases the rate of evaporation of water from the cell walls into the air spaces, and also the rate of diffusion of the water vapour out of the leaf. An increase in temperature therefore increases the rate of transpiration.
- **Light intensity**: Light does not normally have any direct effect on the rate of transpiration during the daytime. However, many plants close their stomata at night, when it is dark and they are unable to photosynthesise and so do not need to use carbon dioxide from the air.
- **Air movements**: The more the air around the plant's leaves is moving, the faster the humid air surrounding them is carried away. This helps to prevent the leaf becoming surrounded by air that is saturated with water vapour, and maintains a water potential gradient from the air spaces inside the leaf to the air outside. Transpiration therefore happens faster on a windy day than on a still day (Figure 5.15).
- **Stomatal aperture**: In many plants, stomata close at night (Figure 5.16). In especially dry conditions, the plant may close its stomata even when light levels are ideal for photosynthesis, to avoid losing too much water from its leaves. There is often a compromise to be reached between allowing in enough carbon dioxide for photosynthesis, and not letting out too much water vapour.

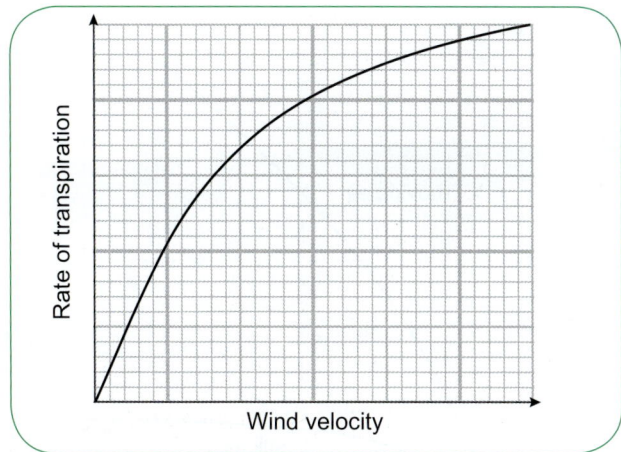

Figure 5.15   How wind affects transpiration.

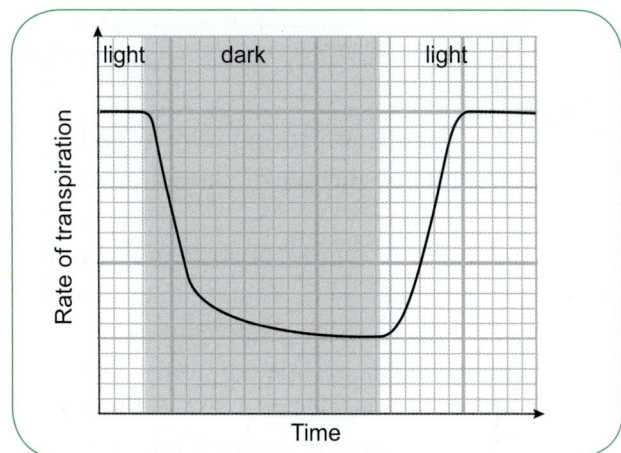

Figure 5.16   How stomatal closure affects transpiration. Stomatal closure has occurred at night in this plant.

The rate of transpiration is higher the greater the aperture (Figure 5.17). However, if you look at this graph, you will see that in still air, the increase in the rate of transpiration is very little at larger apertures, whereas in windy conditions, the rate continues to increase even with larger apertures.

- **Plant structure**: Transpiration occurs from the surface of leaves and green stems. For plants that need to conserve water, reducing the area of these surfaces will limit the rate of transpiration. This can be done by dropping leaves in dry seasons, having small leaves or having no leaves (relying on green stems for photosynthesis).

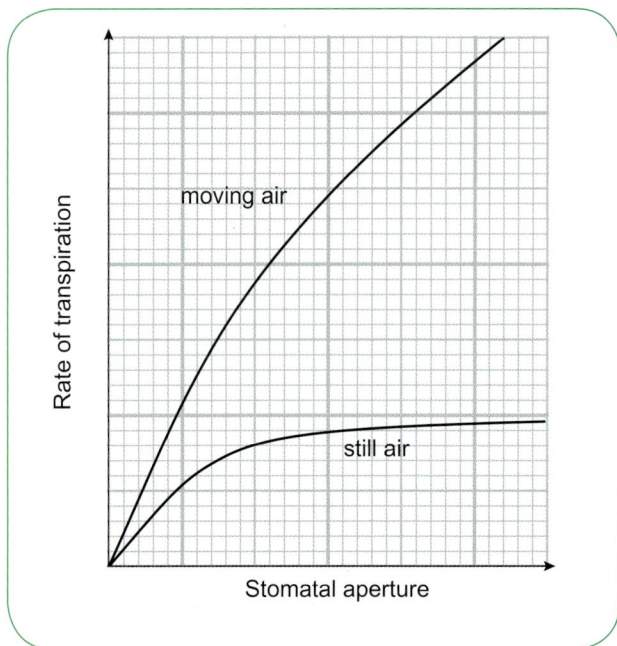

Figure 5.17 The effects of wind velocity and stomatal aperture on the rate of transpiration.

- **Leaf anatomy:** A number of structural features can reduce the rate of transpiration, even when stomata are open. All of these features act by trapping still air outside the stoma. This increases the distance water has to diffuse before it can be carried away in the mass flow of air in the wind. The further the distance water has to diffuse, the slower the rate of transpiration (Figure 5.18). This is achieved by one or more of the following; having stomata set in pits

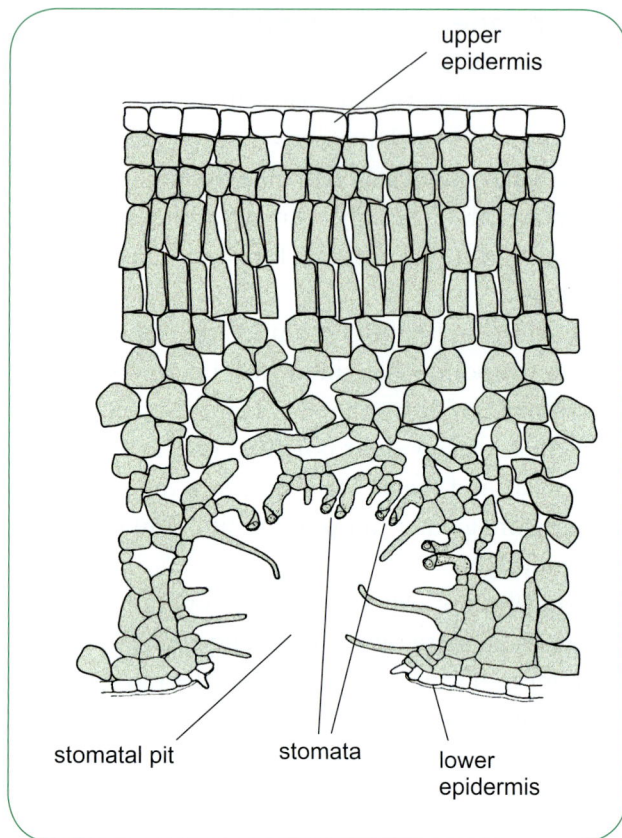

Figure 5.19 A cross-section of an *Oleander* leaf showing a pit on the underside where the stomata are found. This reduces the rate of transpiration.

(Figure 5.19), having stomata on a leaf surface that is on the inside of a rolled leaf, having dense hairs on the leaf surface or having a thick layer of wax on the leaf.

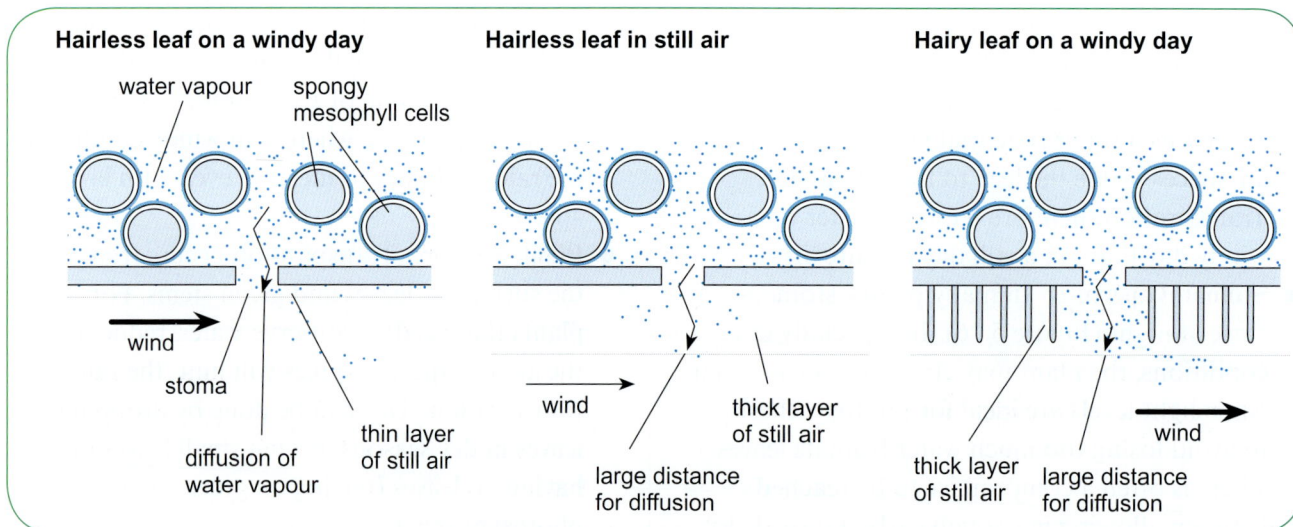

Figure 5.18 The effects of wind velocity and leaf hairiness on the rate of transpiration.

Comparing rates of transpiration

It is not easy to measure the rate at which water vapour is leaving a plant's leaves. This makes it very difficult to investigate directly how different factors, such as light or air movement, affect the rate of transpiration. However, it is relatively easy to measure the rate at which a plant stem takes up water. A very high proportion of the water taken up by a stem is lost in transpiration. As the rate at which transpiration is happening directly affects the rate of water uptake, this measurement can give a very good approximation of the rate of transpiration.

The apparatus used for this is called a **potometer** (Figure 5.20). It is essential that everything in the potometer is completely watertight and airtight, so that no leakage of water occurs and so that no air bubbles break the continuous water column. To achieve this, it helps if you can insert the plant stem into the apparatus with everything submerged in water, so that air bubbles cannot enter the xylem when you cut the stem. It also helps to cut the end of the stem with a slanting cut, as air bubbles are less likely to get trapped against it.

Potometers can be simpler than the one in Figure 5.20. You can manage without the reservoir (though this does mean it takes more time and

effort to refill the potometer) and the tubing can be straight rather than bent. In other words, you can manage with just a straight piece of glass tubing.

As water evaporates from the leaves, more water is drawn into the xylem vessels that are exposed at the cut end of the stem. Water is drawn along the capillary tubing. If you record the position of the meniscus at set time intervals, you can plot a graph of distance moved against time. If you expose the plant to different conditions, you can compare the rate of water uptake.

Transport in phloem

The transport of soluble organic substances within a plant is called **translocation**. These are substances that the plant itself has made – such as sugars, which are made by photosynthesis in the leaves. These substances are sometimes called **assimilates**. The main substance transported in phloem is **sucrose**.

Assimilates are transported in **sieve elements**. Sieve elements are found in **phloem** tissue, together with several other types of cells including **companion cells**. Sieve elements and companion cells work closely together to achieve translocation.

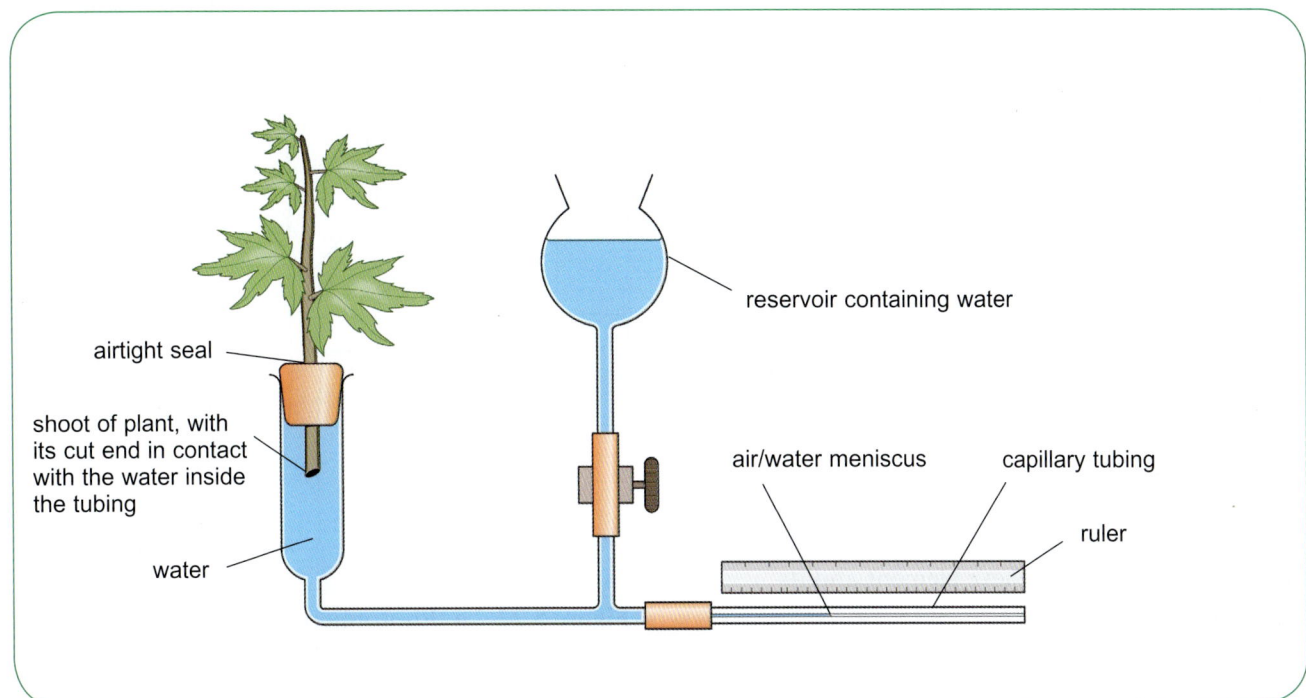

Figure 5.20   A potometer.

Sieve elements

Figure 5.21 shows the structure of a sieve element and its accompanying companion cell. A **sieve tube** is made up of many elongated sieve elements, joined end to end vertically to form a continuous column. Each sieve element is a living cell. They are very narrow, often between 10 and 15 µm in diameter. Like a normal plant cell, a sieve element has a cellulose cell wall, a plasma membrane and cytoplasm containing endoplasmic reticulum and mitochondria. However, the amount of cytoplasm is very small and only forms a thin layer lining the inside of the wall of the cell. There is no nucleus, nor are there any ribosomes. Figure 5.22 shows the appearance of phloem tissue through a light microscope, and Figure 5.23 shows its appearance using a scanning electron microscope.

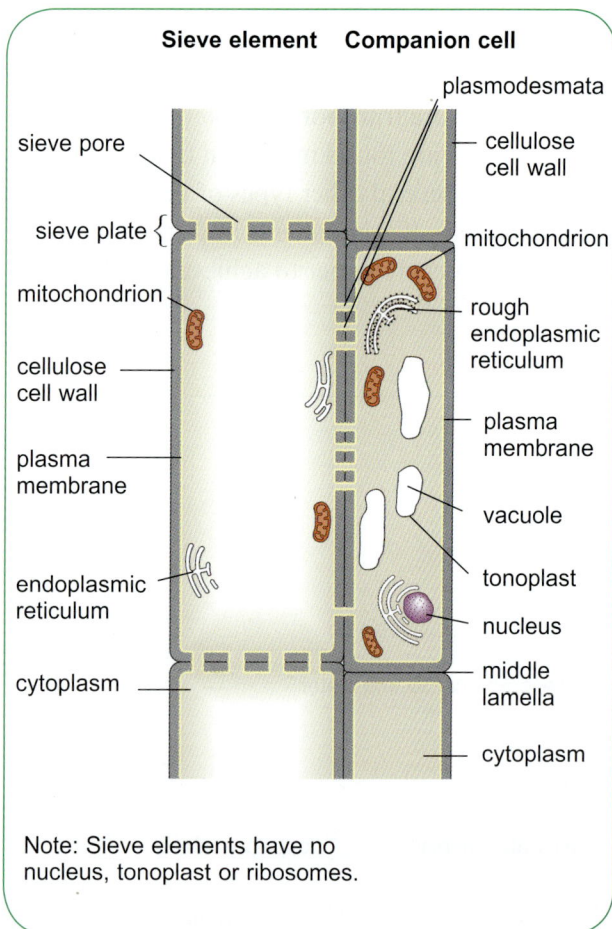

Note: Sieve elements have no nucleus, tonoplast or ribosomes.

Figure 5.21 A phloem sieve element and its companion cell.

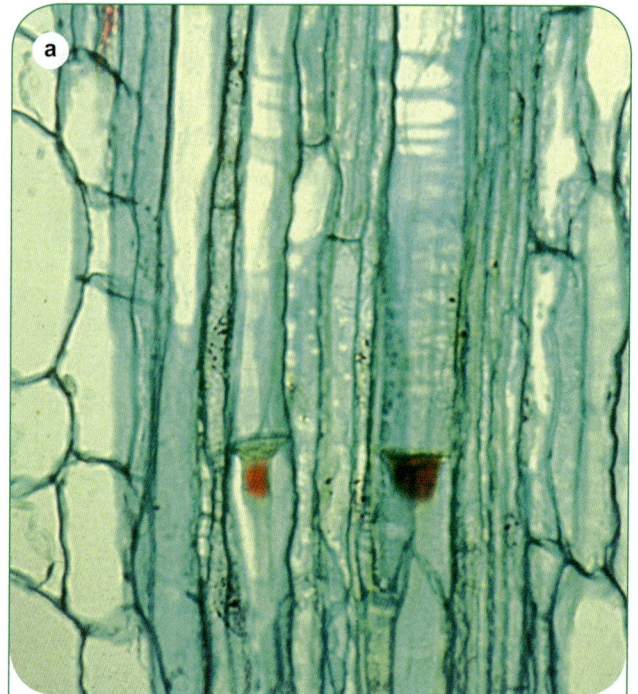

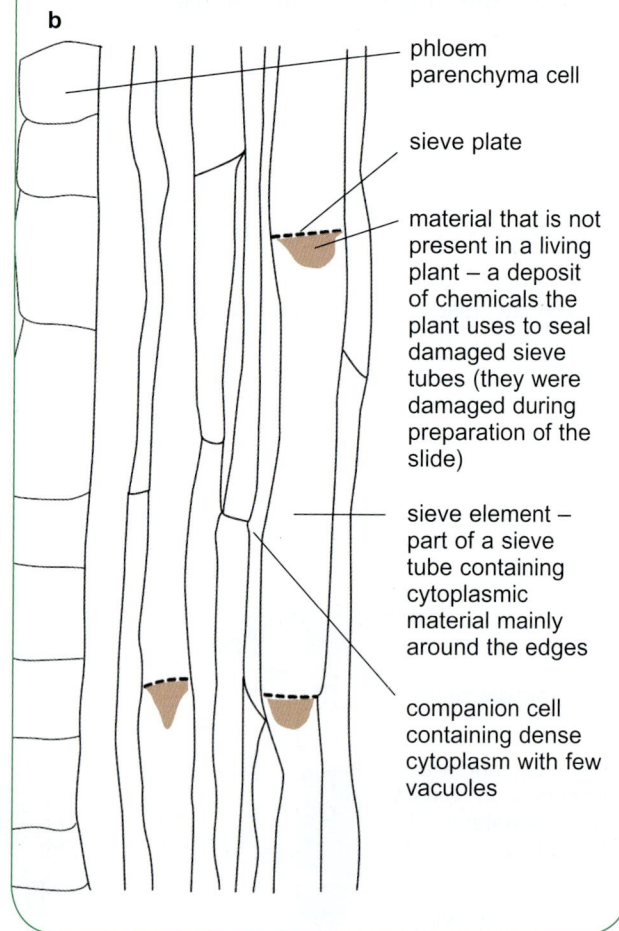

Figure 5.22 **a** Photomicrograph showing phloem sieve elements (×600), **b** drawing of phloem tissue.

Companion cells

Each sieve element has at least one **companion cell** lying close beside it. Companion cells have the structure of a 'normal' plant cell, with a cellulose cell wall, a plasma membrane, cytoplasm, a vacuole and a nucleus. However, the number of mitochondria and ribosomes is rather larger than usual, and the cells are metabolically very active. Also, the vacuole remains small and does not form a large central vacuole.

Companion cells are very closely associated with the neighbouring sieve elements. Many **plasmodesmata** (strands of cytoplasm) pass through their cell walls, providing a direct pathway between the cytoplasm of the companion cell and the cytoplasm of the sieve element.

Plasmodesmata

A plasmodesma (plural: plasmodesmata) is a strand of cytoplasm that runs directly from one plant cell to the next. In a tissue containing closely packed plant cells, each cell may have as many as 10 000 plasmodesmata.

The electron microscope shows that the gap in the cell wall is about 25 nm wide at its narrowest point. The plasma membranes of the cells run right through this gap and are continuous with each other. The membranes enclose cytoplasm and endoplasmic reticulum. This arrangement makes it easy for many different types of molecules to pass directly from one cell to the next, without having to cross a membrane.

The presence of these plasmodesmata means that all the cells of a plant are connected, which is a very different situation from that found in animal bodies, where most cells have no large pores in their plasma membranes connecting adjacent cells. Most pores in animal cells just connect with the extracellular solution.

Small molecules can diffuse freely, but it appears that the pores can, at times, allow larger molecules through, including small proteins. Indeed, it has long been known that many plant viruses can pass from cell to cell this way.

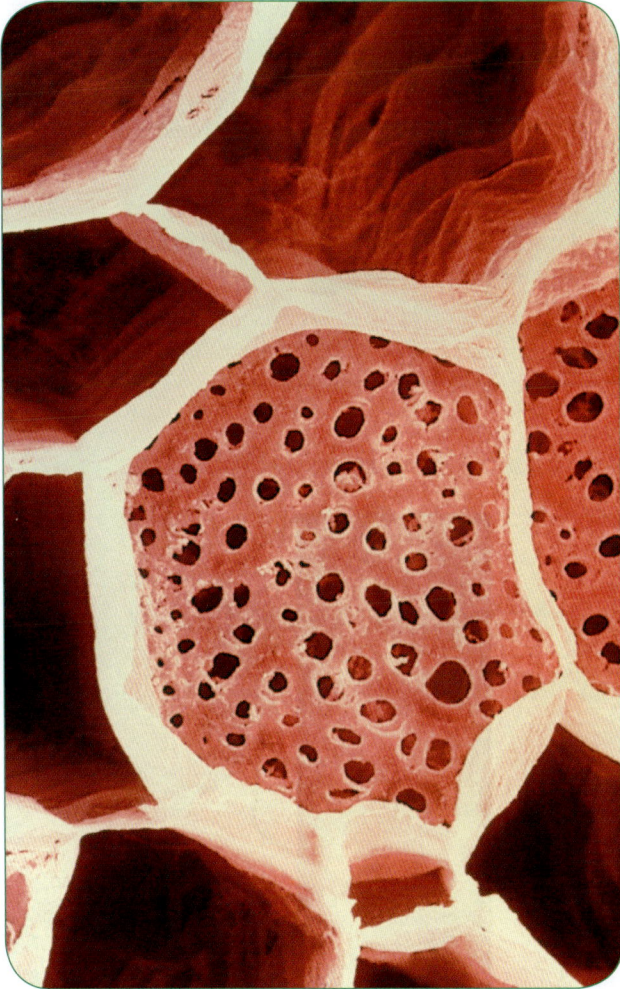

Figure 5.23 SEM of a sieve tube with a sieve plate and a companion cell below it (×4600).

Perhaps the most striking feature of sieve elements is their end walls. Where the end walls of two sieve elements meet, a **sieve plate** is formed. This is made up of the walls of both elements, perforated by large pores. These pores are easily visible with a good light microscope. When sieve plates are viewed using a transmission electron microscope in longitudinal section, strands of fibrous protein can sometimes be seen passing through these pores from one sieve element to another. However, these strands are produced by the sieve element in response to the damage caused when the tissue is cut during preparation of the specimen for viewing. In living phloem, the protein strands are not present, and so the pores are open and present little barrier to the free flow of liquid through them.

The contents of sieve tubes

The liquid inside phloem sieve tubes is called phloem sap, or just sap. Table 5.1 shows the composition of the sap of the castor oil plant, *Ricinus communis*.

Solute	Concentration / $mol\,dm^{-3}$
sucrose	250
potassium ions, K^+	80
amino acids	40
chloride ions, Cl^-	15
phosphate ions, PO_4^{3-}	10
magnesium ions, Mg^{2+}	5
sodium ions, Na^+	2
nitrate ions, NO_3^-	0
plant growth substances (e.g. auxin)	small traces

Table 5.1 Composition of sap in *Ricinus communis*.

SAQ

5 Which of the substances in Table 5.1 are synthesised by the plant?

It is not easy to collect enough phloem sap to analyse its contents. When phloem tissue is cut, the sieve elements respond by rapidly blocking the sieve pores. The pores are blocked first by plugs of phloem protein, and then, within hours, by a carbohydrate called **callose**. However, castor oil plants are unusual in that their phloem sap does continue to flow for a while, making it relatively easy to collect.

Aphids are a good way of collecting sap. Aphids, such as greenfly, feed by inserting their tubular mouthparts, called stylets, into the phloem of plant stems and leaves (Figure 5.24). Phloem sap flows through the stylet into the aphid. If the stylet is cut near the aphid's head, the sap continues to flow. It seems that the small diameter of the stylet does not allow sap to flow out rapidly enough to switch on the plant's phloem 'clotting' mechanism.

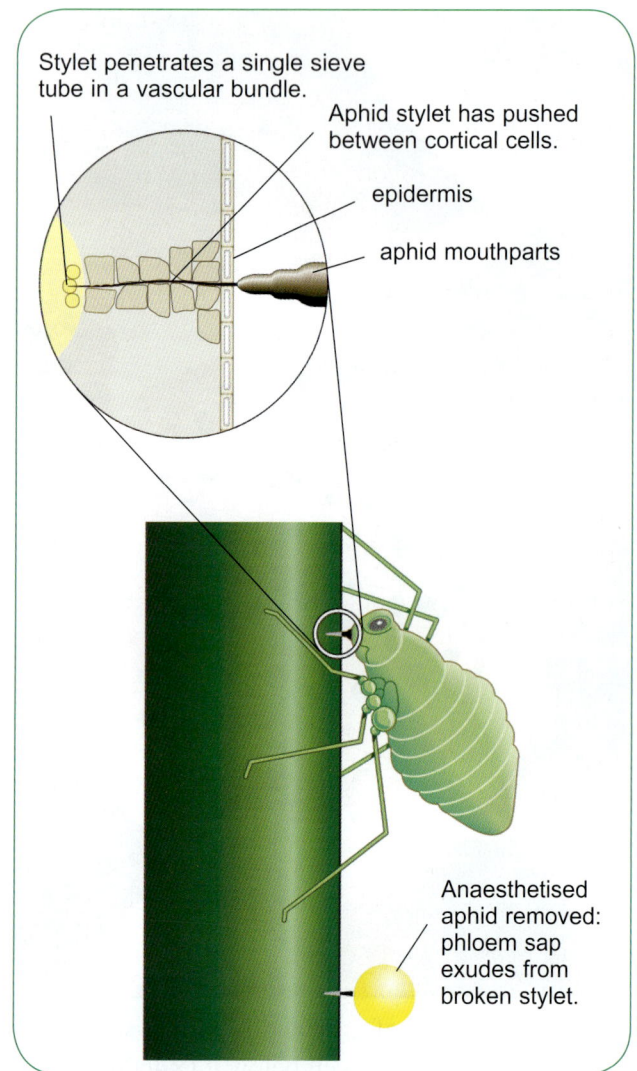

Stylet penetrates a single sieve tube in a vascular bundle.

Aphid stylet has pushed between cortical cells.

epidermis

aphid mouthparts

Anaesthetised aphid removed: phloem sap exudes from broken stylet.

Figure 5.24 Using an aphid to collect phloem sap.

How translocation occurs

Phloem sap, like the contents of xylem vessels, moves by mass flow. However, whereas in xylem vessels differences in pressure are produced by a water potential gradient between soil and air, requiring no energy input from the plant, this is not so in phloem transport. To create the pressure differences needed for mass flow in phloem, the plant has to use its own energy. Phloem transport is therefore an active process, in contrast to the passive transport in xylem.

The pressure difference is produced by active loading of sucrose into the sieve elements at the place from which sucrose is to be transported. This is typically in a photosynthesising leaf. As sucrose is loaded into the sieve element, this decreases the water potential in the sap inside it.

Therefore, water follows the sucrose into the sieve element, moving down a water potential gradient by osmosis.

At another point along the sieve tube, sucrose may be removed by other cells. Root cells, for example, may use sucrose delivered by phloem. Sucrose will often be at a relatively low concentration in these cells, because they are using it up. So sucrose simply diffuses out of the phloem and into the root cell, and water follows by osmosis.

So, in the leaf, water moves into the sieve tube. In the root, it moves out of it. This creates a pressure difference, with the pressure at the 'leaf' end of the phloem sieve tube being greater than that at the 'root' end. The pressure difference causes the liquid inside the tube to flow from the high pressure area to the lower one, by mass flow.

Any area of a plant from which sucrose is loaded into the phloem is called a **source**. An area that takes sucrose out of the phloem is called a **sink** (Figure 5.25).

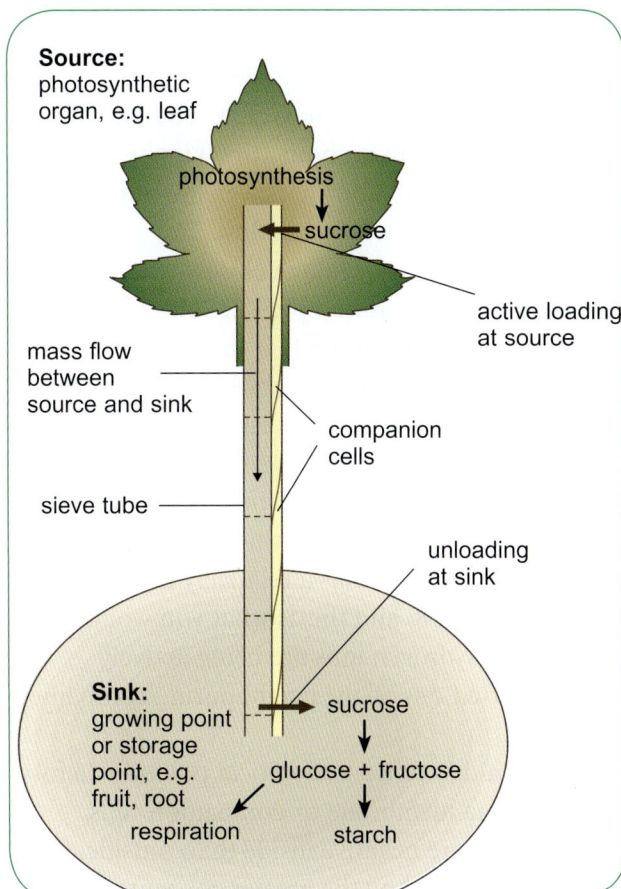

Figure 5.25   Sources, sinks and mass flow in phloem.

Sinks can be anywhere in the plant, both above and below the photosynthesising leaves. So sap flows both upwards and downwards. This contrasts with the situation in xylem, where flow is always upwards. Within any one phloem sieve tube, however, the flow is all in one direction.

SAQ
6 Which of the following are sources, and which are sinks?
   a a nectary in a flower
   b a developing fruit
   c the storage tissue of a potato tuber when the potato is just starting to sprout
   d a growing potato tuber

Loading sucrose into phloem

In leaf mesophyll cells, photosynthesis produces sugars. Some of these are converted into sucrose, which can be transported in the phloem to other parts of the plant.

Sucrose is soluble, so it dissolves in the water in the cell. It can move out of a mesophyll cell and across the leaf, by either the apoplast or symplast pathway.

Sucrose is loaded into companion cells by active transport (Figure 5.26). This is done in a rather roundabout way. First, hydrogen ions are pumped out of the cell by active transport, using ATP as the energy source. This creates a large excess of hydrogen ions outside the cell. They can move back into the cell down their concentration gradient, through a protein that acts as a carrier for both hydrogen ions and sucrose at the same time. The sucrose molecules are carried through this co-transporter into the companion cell, against the concentration gradient for sucrose. The sucrose molecules can then move from the companion cell into the sieve tube, through the plasmodesmata that connect them.

Unloading sucrose from phloem

Unloading occurs in any tissue that requires sucrose. It is likely that the sucrose moves out of the phloem and into the tissue by facilitated diffusion. Once in the tissue, the sucrose is

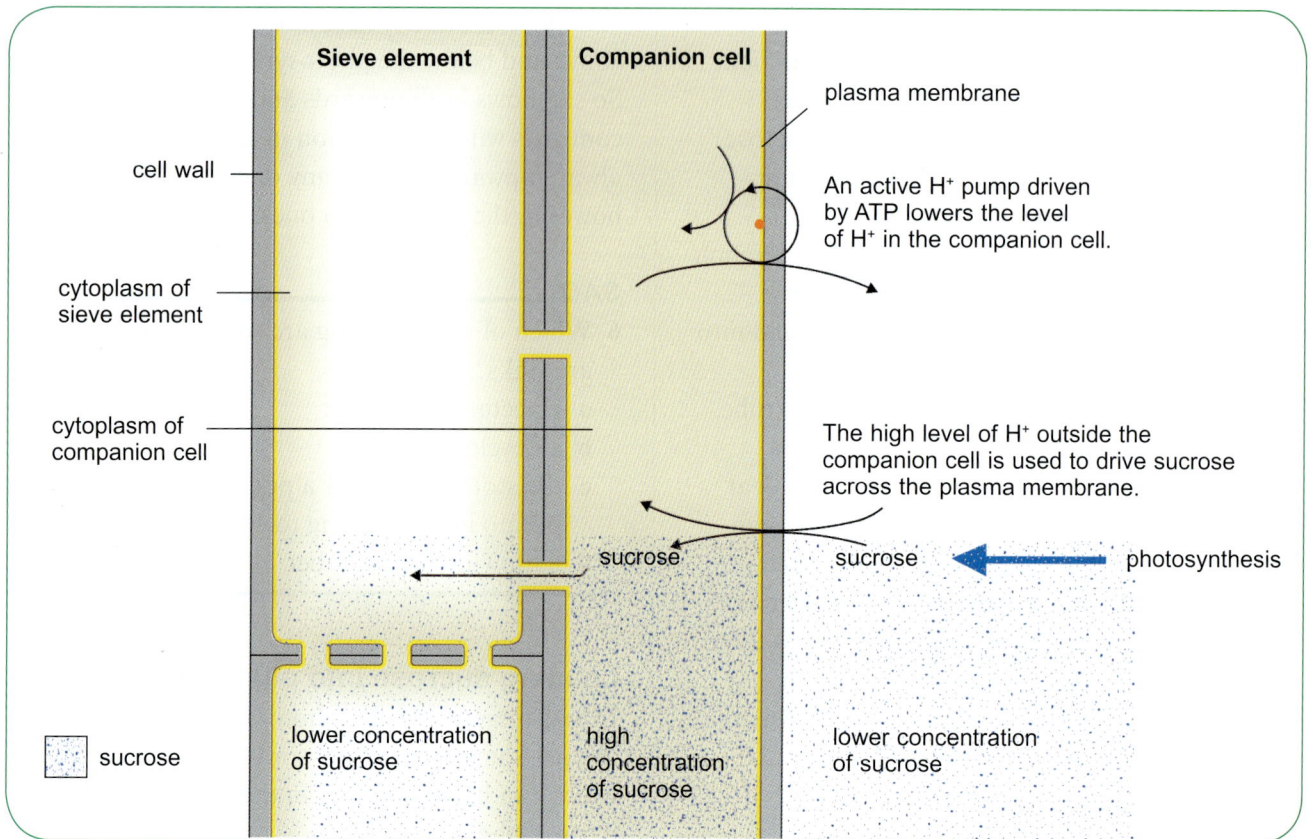

Figure 5.26 The method by which sucrose is loaded into phloem.

converted into something else by enzymes. This decreases its concentration and therefore maintains a concentration gradient from the phloem into the tissue. One such enzyme is invertase, which converts sucrose to glucose and fructose.

Evidence for the mechanism of phloem transport

Until the late 1970s and 1980s, there was considerable argument about whether or not phloem sap did or did not move by mass flow, in the way we have described. The stumbling block was the presence of the sieve pores and phloem protein, as it was felt that these must have some important role. Several hypotheses were put forward, which tried to provide a role for the phloem protein. It is now known that the phloem protein is not present in living, active phloem tissue, and so there is no need to provide it with a role when explaining the mechanism of phloem transport.

There is now a lot of evidence that phloem

transport does occur by mass flow. The rate of transport in phloem is about 10 000 times faster than it would be if substances were moving by diffusion rather than by mass flow. The actual rates of transport measured match closely with those calculated from measured pressure differences at source and sink, assuming that the pores in the sieve plates are open and unobstructed.

Experimental work has investigated the sucrose–hydrogen co-transporter in plant cells, and it is understood how this works. There is also plenty of circumstantial evidence that this takes place:

- phloem sap always has a relatively high pH, often around 8, and this is what you would expect if hydrogen ions are being actively transported out of the neighbouring companion cell;
- there is a difference in electrical potential across the plasma membrane of companion cells, which is more negative inside than outside; this could be caused by the greater concentration of positively charged hydrogen ions outside the cell than inside.

SAQ

7 Draw a table and use it to compare the structure of xylem vessels and phloem sieve tubes. You could include cell structure (walls, diameter, cell contents and so on), substances transported and methods of transport.

Transpiration and climate

Most of us are aware that cutting down rainforests reduces photosynthesis, increasing the amount of carbon dioxide in the air and contributing to global warming. But fewer people realise how transpiration can affect climate.

Aerial photographs, historical records and data and computer models from NASA have been used to look at the effects of changes in land cover on climate in the USA. In the midwest, the natural vegetation was grassland, but as this has been replaced by agricultural land, the average temperature in those regions has dropped by almost 1 °C. This is because grass does not transpire as much as crops. The extra transpiration from the crop plants increases the humidity of the air and has a cooling effect.

In contrast, when forest is removed to grow crops, as has happened on the east coast of the USA, the reverse effect is seen. Forest trees transpire much more than most crop plants, and so the air above the farmland often contains less water vapour than the air above a forest. As forest has been replaced by farmland, the climate in these regions has become warmer.

There have also been effects on local rainfall – slightly more rainfall where there are forests, compared to areas where forest has been replaced by crops. But these are much less marked than the temperature changes.

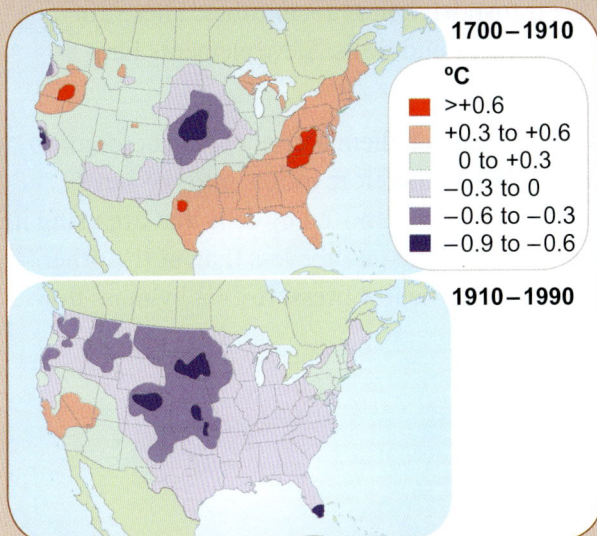

Change in average surface air temperature in July between 1700 and 1910, and between 1910 and 1990.

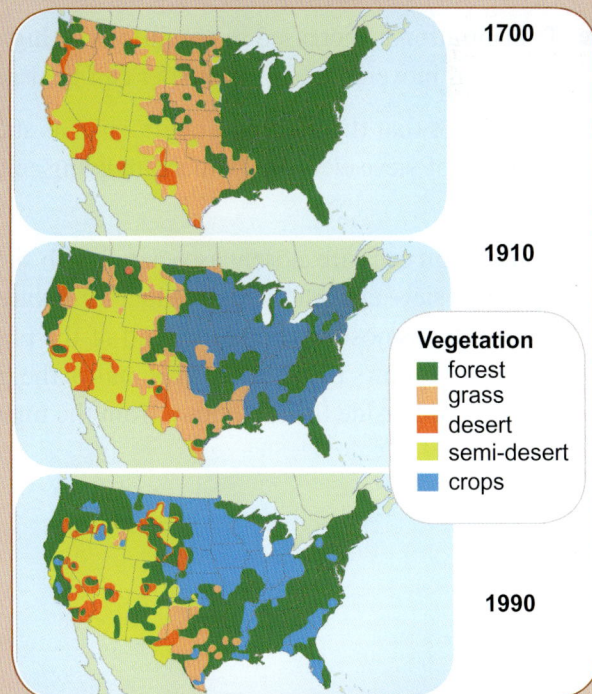

Vegetation in 1700, 1910 and 1990.

101

Summary

- Inorganic ions are absorbed into a plant through its root hairs, by facilitated diffusion or active transport.

- Water, containing inorganic ions in solution, is transported in xylem vessels. The water moves passively, down a water potential gradient from the soil to the air.

- Water moves into the root hairs by osmosis, and crosses the root cortex by the apoplast pathway (between the cells) and the symplast pathway (through the cells).

- The Casparian strip blocks the apoplast pathway, so water must pass through the cells of the endodermis. The membranes of these cells move inorganic ions by active transport. Water follows by osmosis, moving into xylem vessels and helping to increase the hydrostatic pressure at their bases (root pressure).

- Xylem vessels are stacks of dead, empty xylem elements. These have no end walls, and their side walls are impregnated with lignin. Adhesion of water molecules to their walls and cohesion of water molecules to each other help the water column inside xylem vessels to move upwards by mass flow without breaking.

- Transpiration in the leaves provides the major driving force for water movement through the plant. Water evaporates from the wet cell walls of cells inside the leaf, and then diffuses out through stomata into the air. Water moves from xylem vessels into the leaf cells by osmosis. This lowers the pressure at the top of the water column in the xylem so that water moves up xylem by mass flow, down a pressure gradient.

- Transpiration is increased in conditions of high light intensity, high temperature, low humidity and strong air movements. A potometer can be used to compare rates of transpiration.

- Substances that the plant has made, such as sucrose, are transported in phloem tubes. These are made up of sieve elements, which are living cells with perforated end walls. Sieve elements have no nucleus.

- Companion cells are closely associated with sieve elements. Some of them actively load sucrose into a phloem sieve element, which reduces the water potential. Water therefore moves into the sieve element by osmosis. At the other end of the phloem tube, sucrose is removed by cells that are using it, and water follows by osmosis. This makes the pressure at one end of the tube less than at the other, so the liquid inside the tube flows from the high pressure area to the low pressure area by mass flow.

Questions

Multiple choice questions

1 The uptake of mineral ions from the soil into the root hair cells lowers the water potential of the cell. Water then enters the cell. Which of the following correctly identifies the processes by which the ions and water are taken up?

	Ions	Water
A	active transport	active transport
B	active transport	osmosis
C	osmosis	osmosis
D	osmosis	active transport

2 Water moves across the root down a water potential gradient. Which of the following is responsible for producing the water potential gradient?

A root pressure

B capillarity

C transpiration pull

D adhesion

3 The diagram below shows a cross-section of a root.

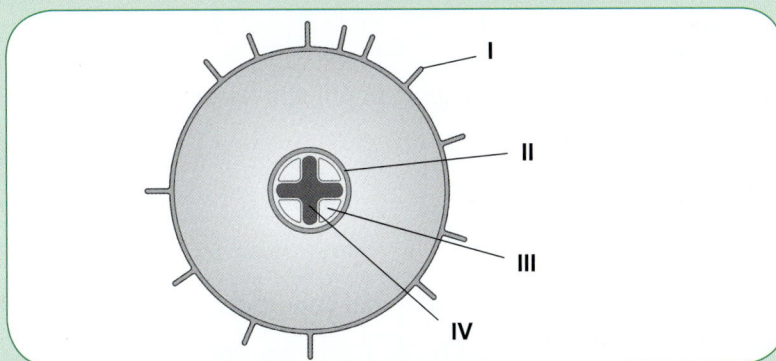

Which of the following correctly identifies the structure that controls the amounts of mineral ions taken into the xylem of the root?

A I B II C III D IV

4 Which feature of the xylem vessels allows them to transport water with little resistance?

A narrow lumen

B lignified walls

C pits

D lack of cell contents

continued ...

5 The photomicrograph below shows a longitudinal section through transport tissue in a plant stem.

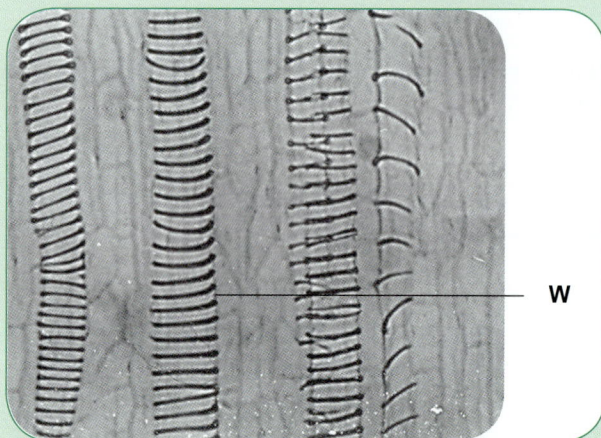

Which of the following correctly identifies the structure labelled **W** and the tissue in which it is found?

	Structure W	Tissue
A	xylem vessel	xylem
B	xylem vessel	phloem
C	sieve tube	xylem
D	sieve tube	phloem

6 Which of the following correctly describes a feature of transport in phloem tissue?
A Movement of metabolites is only unidirectional.
B No salts are translocated in the phloem.
C Uptake of sucrose into the phloem is passive.
D Uptake of sucrose into the phloem requires ATP.

7 The movement of water through xylem vessels is affected by external conditions. A decrease in which external factor would cause an increase in transpiration?
A temperature
B humidity
C light intensity
D wind speed

continued ...

8 The photomicrograph shows a longitudinal section of transport tissue in a plant stem.

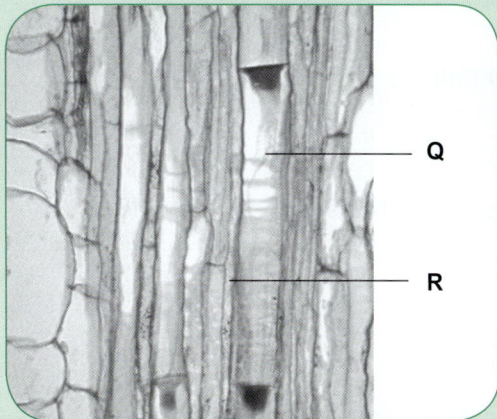

What are the names of the structures labelled **Q** and **R** and the tissue in which they are found?

	Structure Q	Structure R	Tissue
A	companion cell	sieve tube	phloem
B	xylem vessel	companion cell	xylem
C	sieve tube	companion cell	phloem
D	sieve tube	xylem vessel	xylem

9 The diagram shows a model which can be used to demonstrate mass flow.

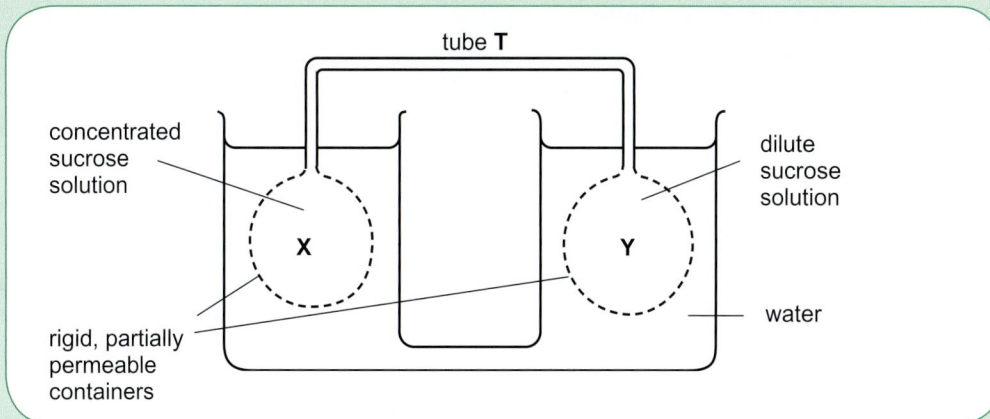

X and **Y** are filled with sucrose solutions of different concentration, causing water to move in or out of **X** and **Y** by osmosis or as a result of hydrostatic pressure. Sucrose solution then moves through the tube **T** joining **X** and **Y**.

Which description of this is correct?

	Water potential in X compared with Y	Direction of movement of sucrose solution in tube T
A	higher (less negative)	from **X** to **Y**
B	higher (less negative)	from **Y** to **X**
C	lower (more negative)	from **X** to **Y**
D	lower (more negative)	from **Y** to **X**

continued …

10 Which of the following cause the ascent of water in the stem of a plant?
   A osmosis, root pressure and capillarity
   B active transport, capillarity and transpiration pull
   C root pressure, capillarity, cohesion and transpiration pull
   D osmosis, active transport and root pressure

Structured questions

11 The apparatus shown below can be used to measure the rate of transpiration from a leafy shoot.

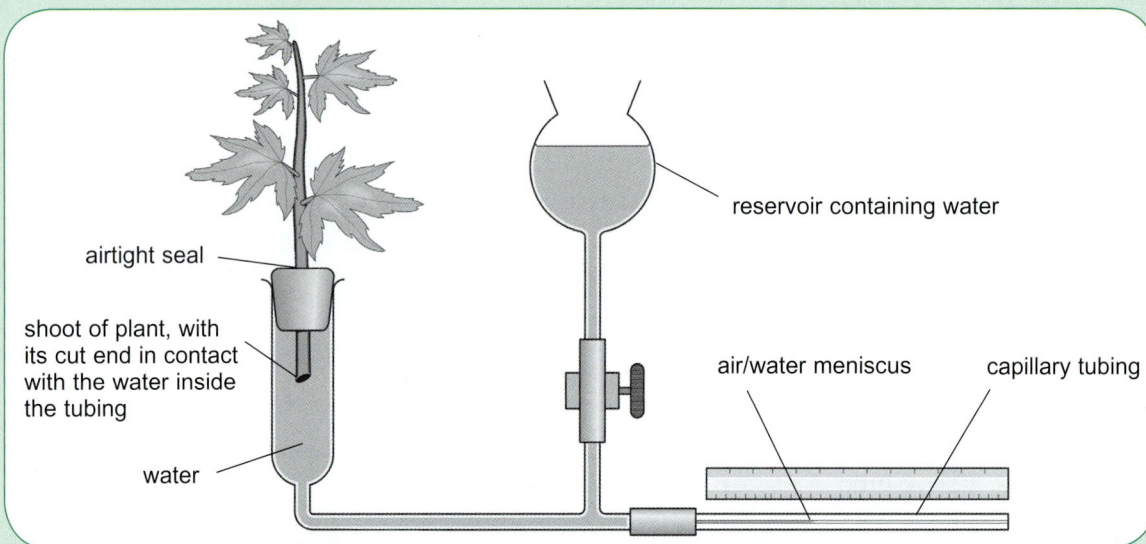

a What is the name for this kind of apparatus? [1 mark]
b Define the term 'transpiration'. [2 marks]
c **i** Identify **four** precautions that should be taken in setting up the apparatus to ensure valid measurements can be obtained under the given conditions. [4 marks]
   ii Describe how the apparatus can be used to measure the rate of water uptake in $cm^3 min^{-1}$. [3 marks]
d Explain why the apparatus shown above does **not** accurately measure the rate of transpiration in a plant. [2 marks]
e A student investigated the effect of varying wind speed. Wind speed was varied using a fan.
   The results are recorded in the table below.

Distance of fan from shoot / cm	Time taken for meniscus to move 30 mm / s	Time taken for meniscus to move 1 mm / s	Rate of movement of meniscus / mm s⁻¹
100	240.0	8.0	0.125
75	180.0	6.0	0.167
50	115.0	3.8	0.263
25	42.0		

continued ...

     i Calculate the rate of movement of the meniscus when the fan was at a distance of 25 cm. Show your working. [2 marks]

     ii Plot a graph of the results to illustrate the effect of distance of fan on the rate of movement of the meniscus. [4 marks]

f The results the student obtained for different light intensities are shown in the table below.

Condition	Distance moved in five minutes / mm
room (daylight)	25.0
bright light	42.0
dark cupboard	1.0

    Using the data in **both** tables, describe and explain the effect of wind speed and light intensity on the rate of water uptake. [5 marks]

g Describe a control that should have been set up to compare the results obtained in the student's investigations. [2 marks]

12 The diagrams below show sections of two organs from a dicotyledonous plant.

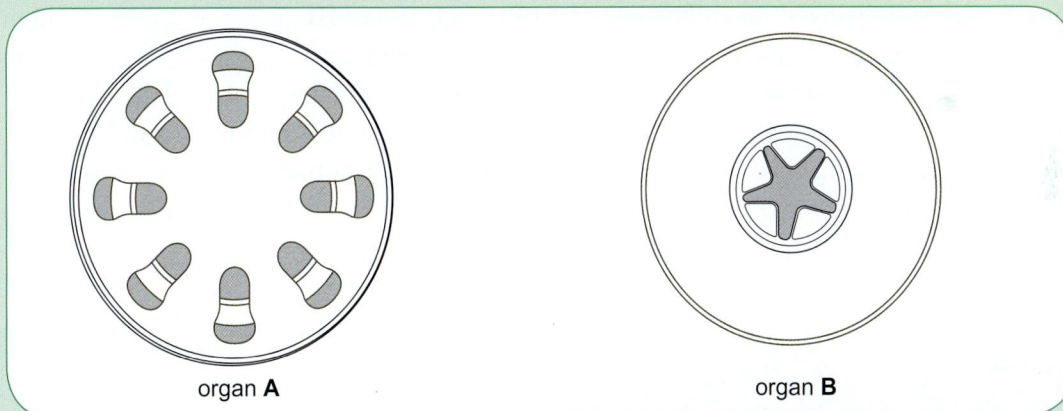

organ **A**   organ **B**

a Identify organs **A** and **B**, giving a reason for each of your answers. [2 marks]

b **i** Copy each diagram and shade in an area in both organs to show where translocation of assimilates occurs. [2 marks]

     ii Name the tissue which is specialised for translocation. [1 mark]

continued ...

c   The micrographs below are a transverse section and a longitudinal section of the same plant structure found in a vascular bundle.

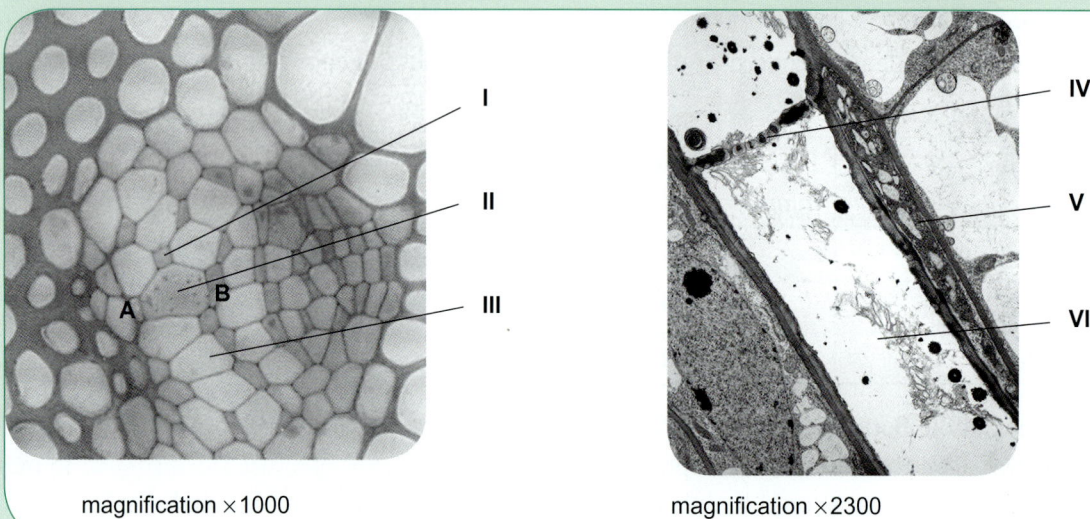

magnification ×1000

magnification ×2300

   i   Identify structures labelled **I** to **VI**.   [3 marks]
   ii   State how each of the structures **IV**, **V** and **VI** is adapted for its function.   [3 marks]
   iii Make a large drawing at magnification ×1.5 of cells **I**, **II** and **III**.   [3 marks]
   iv   Calculate the actual diameter of cell **II** between **A** and **B** in μm.   [2 marks]

d   Clothes lines can be made by tying wire to branches of trees. Bulging is observed above the wire but the branches do not die. If the bark of the tree is removed from the lower trunk, bulging occurs above the girdle and the tree eventually dies. Suggest an explanation for these observations.   [4 marks]

13 The photomicrograph below shows part of a mature root of buttercup, *Ranunculus*, viewed under high power.

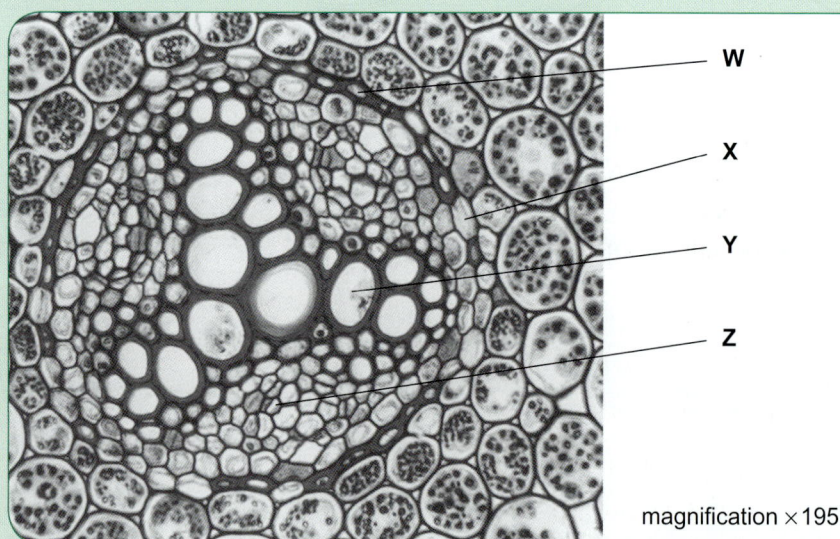

magnification ×195

continued …

a Identify the structures labelled **W, X ,Y** and **Z**. [4 marks]

b Describe the role of **W** in the root. [3 marks]

c Describe **two** features of xylem vessels that facilitate water transport. [2 marks]

Water travels up xylem vessels from the root to the leaves. Most of this water is lost by transpiration.

d List **two** functions of transpiration in the plant. [2 marks]

Transpiration is affected by many external environmental factors as well as structural features of the leaf.

e Identify **one** environmental and **one** structural factor that affect transpiration rates. [2 marks]

f The graph below shows the effect of stomatal aperture on the rate of transpiration. Describe and explain the relationship shown in the graph below.

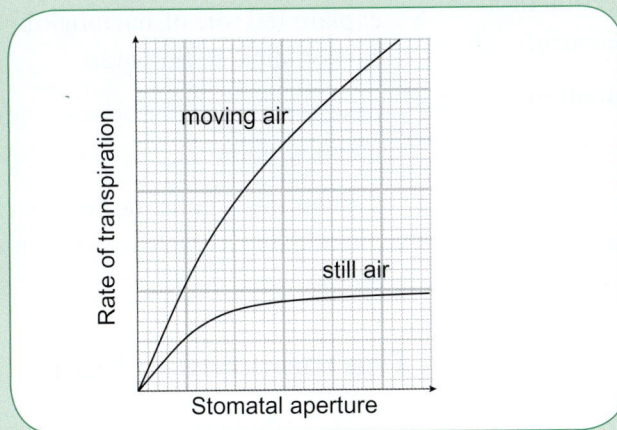

[4 marks]

g Some plants have leaves that contain sunken stomata and hairs. Explain how these adaptations help the plant to conserve water. [3 marks]

Essay questions

14 a Describe how water passes from the soil to the xylem vessels of the root. Illustrate your answer with a diagram. [7 marks]

b Explain how water travels up the stem and into the leaf of a mango tree. [5 marks]

c Explain how water moves from the vascular tissue in the leaf to the atmosphere. [3 marks]

15 a Plants transport organic solutes from the source to the sink. Giving examples, explain what is meant by the terms 'source' and 'sink'. [2 marks]

b i Describe how sugars produced during photosynthesis in the leaves are transported to the roots by mass (pressure) flow. [6 marks]

ii The mass (pressure) flow mechanism of transport of solutes is one hypothesis to explain the movement of organic assimilates. Critically assess the pressure flow hypothesis. [5 marks]

c Explain how the root of a plant can act as both a source and a sink at different times. [2 marks]

16 a The xylem transports water from the root to the leaves of plants. Describe and explain how the cells of the xylem are adapted for this function. [7 marks]

b i What do you understand by the term 'translocation'? [2 marks]

ii The phloem transports organic assimilates throughout the plant. Describe and explain how the phloem is adapted to perform this function. [6 marks]

Chapter 6
The circulatory system of mammals

By the end of this chapter you should be able to:

a   describe, and make annotated diagrams of, the structure of the heart and its associated major blood vessels;

b   make drawings of a longitudinal section of a heart from a fresh or preserved specimen;

c   explain the cardiac cycle and its initiation;

d   discuss the internal factors that control heart action;

e   define the terms blood pressure and pulse;

f   discuss factors affecting blood pressure;

g   make drawings of leucocytes and erythrocytes from prepared slides;

h   explain the role of haemoglobin in oxygen and carbon dioxide transport;

i   describe oxygen dissociation curves for adult haemoglobin;

j   explain the significance of the effect of carbon dioxide on oxygen dissociation curves (Bohr effect).

Transport in mammals

The mammalian transport system is made up of the heart and blood vessels. Unlike plants, mammals require a transport system that moves oxygen and carbon dioxide around their bodies. This is partly because mammals are much more active than plants, which means that their cells require more energy and therefore respire more rapidly. Cells therefore need constant deliveries of oxygen and must have the carbon dioxide produced in respiration taken away. Moreover, mammals do not have branching bodies like those of plants, so their surface area : volume ratio is usually much smaller. Many cells in a mammal are a long way from the gas exchange surface, so diffusion would not be sufficient to supply them with their needs.

In this chapter, we will look first at the heart, and then consider the different types of blood vessels and the blood that flows within them.

The mammalian heart

Structure of a human heart

The heart of an adult human has a mass of around 300 g and is about the size of your fist (Figure 6.1).

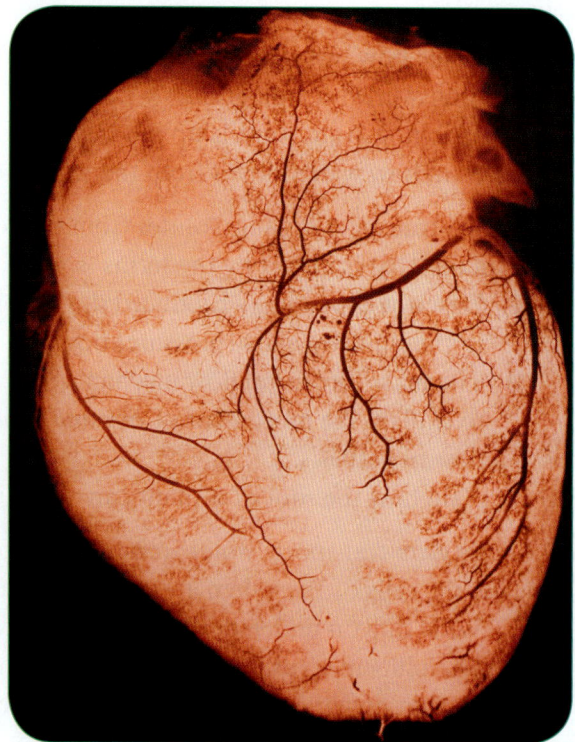

Figure 6.1   A human heart.

It is a bag of muscle, filled with blood. Figure 6.2 shows a drawing of a human heart, looking at it from the front of the body.

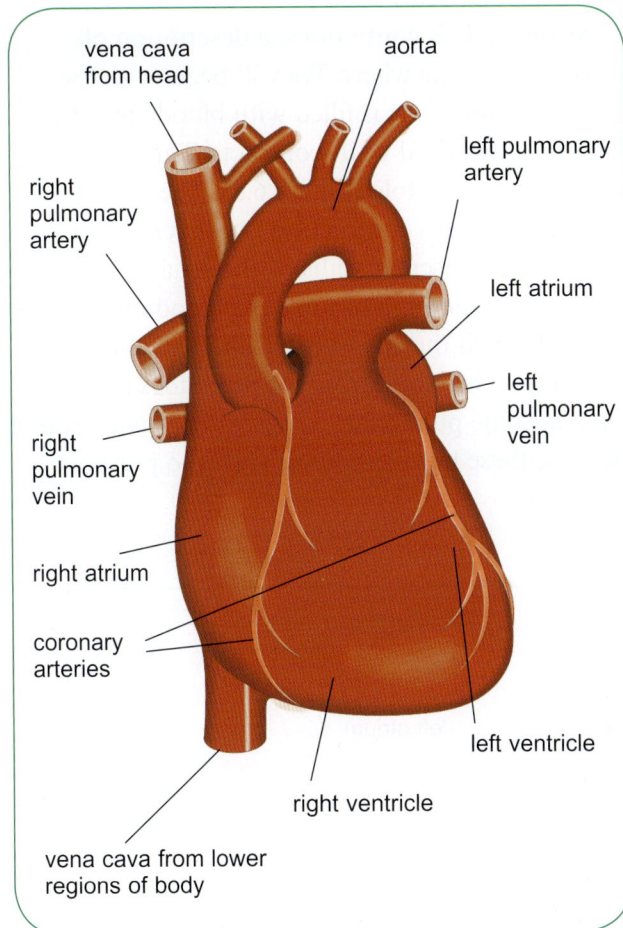

Figure 6.2 Diagram of the external structure of a human heart, seen from the front.

The muscle of which the heart is made is called **cardiac muscle**. This muscle is able to contract and relax rhythmically, 24 hours a day, throughout your life.

In Figure 6.2, you can see the blood vessels that carry blood into and out of the heart. The large, arching blood vessel is the largest artery, the **aorta**, with branches leading upwards towards the head and the main flow turning back downwards to the rest of the body. The other blood vessel leaving the heart is the **pulmonary artery**. This, too, branches very quickly after leaving the heart, into two arteries, one taking blood to the left lung and one to the right. Running vertically on the right-hand side of the heart are the two large veins, the **venae cavae** (singular: vena cava), one bringing blood

downwards from the head and the other bringing it upwards from the rest of the body. The **pulmonary veins** bring blood back to the heart from the left and right lungs.

On the surface of the heart, the **coronary arteries** can be seen (Figures 6.1 and 6.2). These branch from the aorta and deliver oxygenated blood to the muscle of the walls of the heart.

If the heart is cut open vertically (Figure 6.3 and Figure 6.4), it can be seen to contain four chambers. The two chambers on the left of the heart are completely separated from those on the right by a wall of muscle called the **septum**. Blood cannot pass through this septum; the only way for

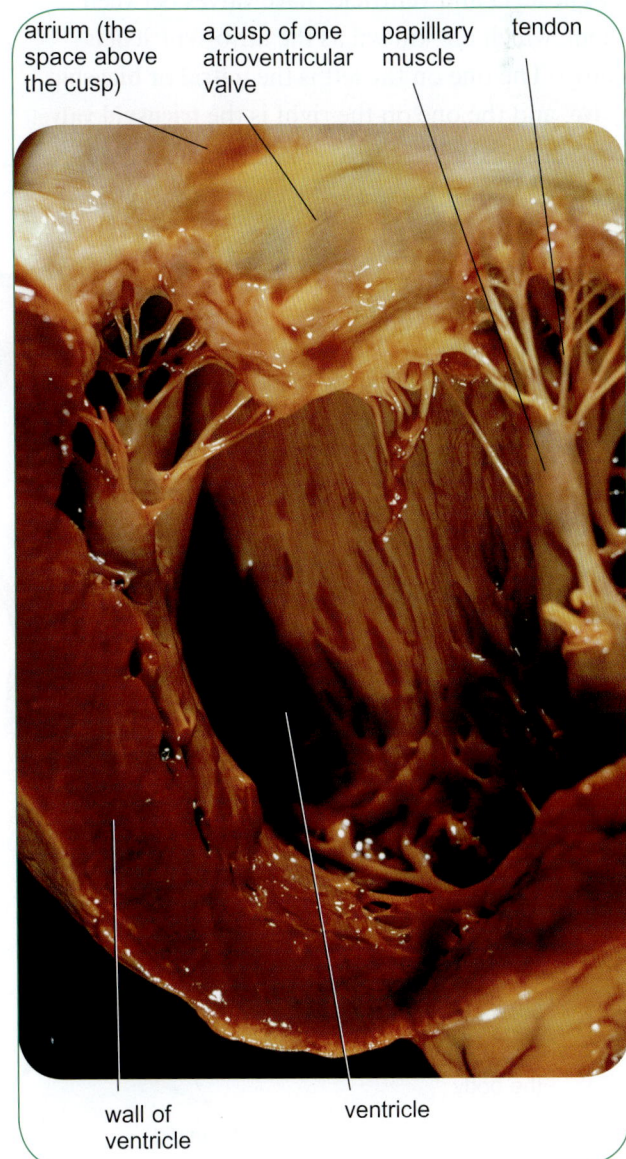

Figure 6.3 Section through part of one side of the heart.

blood to get from one side of the heart to the other is to leave the heart, circulate around either the lungs or the rest of the body, and then return to the heart.

The upper chamber on each side is called an **atrium**. The two atria receive blood from the veins. You can see from Figure 6.4 that blood from the venae cavae flows into the right atrium, while blood from the pulmonary veins flows into the left atrium.

The lower chambers are **ventricles**. Blood flows into the ventricles from the atria, and is then squeezed out into the arteries. Blood from the left ventricle flows into the aorta, while blood from the right ventricle flows into the pulmonary arteries.

The atria and ventricles have valves between them, which are known as the **atrio-ventricular valves**. The one on the left is the **mitral** or **bicuspid valve**, and the one on the right is the **tricuspid valve**.

The cardiac cycle

Your heart beats around 70 times a minute at rest. The **cardiac cycle** is the sequence of events that makes up one heart beat.

As the cycle is continuous, a description of it could begin anywhere. We will begin with the time when the heart is filled with blood, and the muscle in the atrial walls contracts. This stage is called **atrial systole** (Figure 6.5). The pressure developed by this contraction is not very great, because the muscular walls of the atria are only thin, but it is enough to force the blood in the atria down through the atrio-ventricular valves into the ventricles. The blood from the atria does not go back into the pulmonary veins or the venae cavae, because these have semilunar valves to prevent backflow.

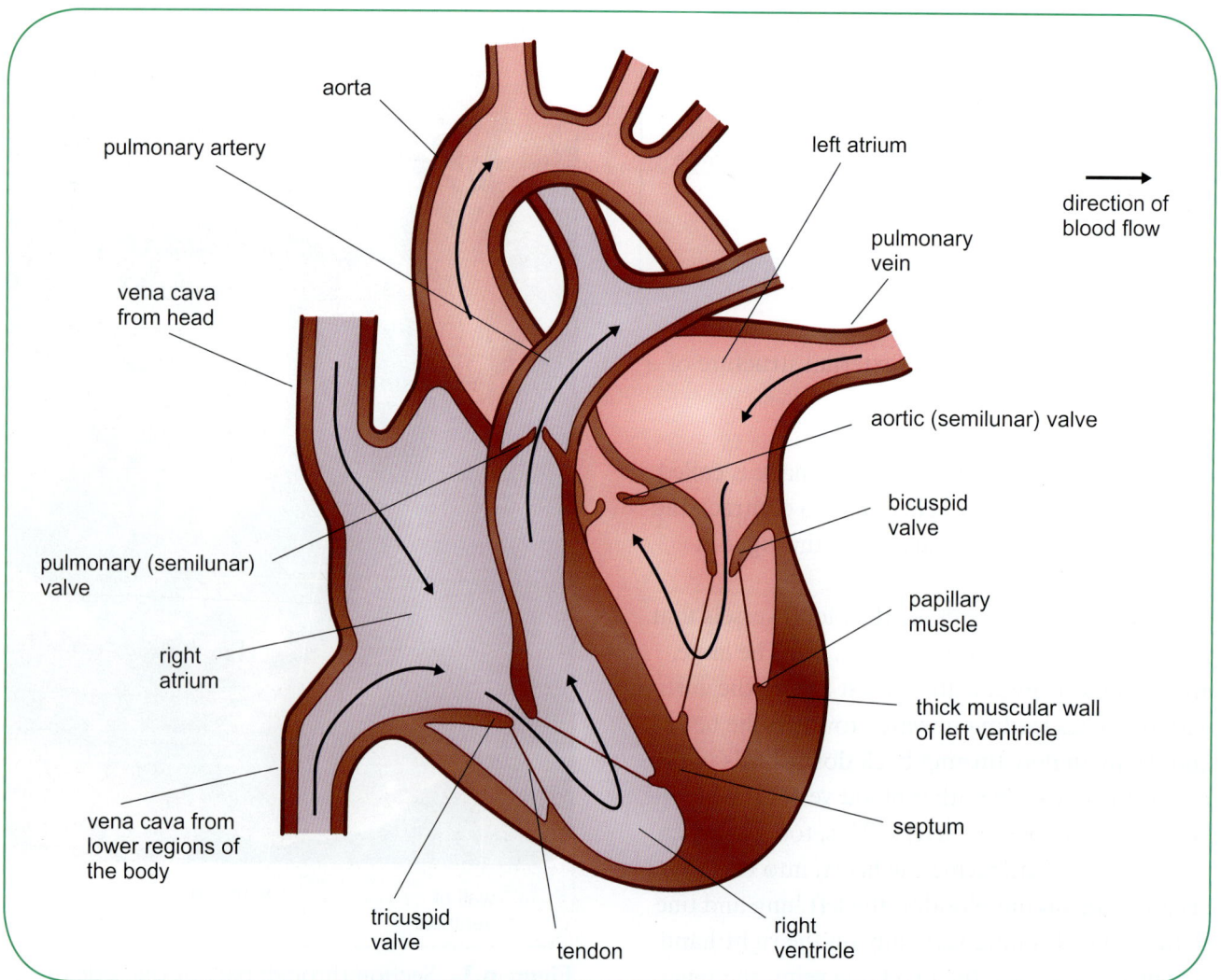

Figure 6.4   Diagramatic section through a heart.

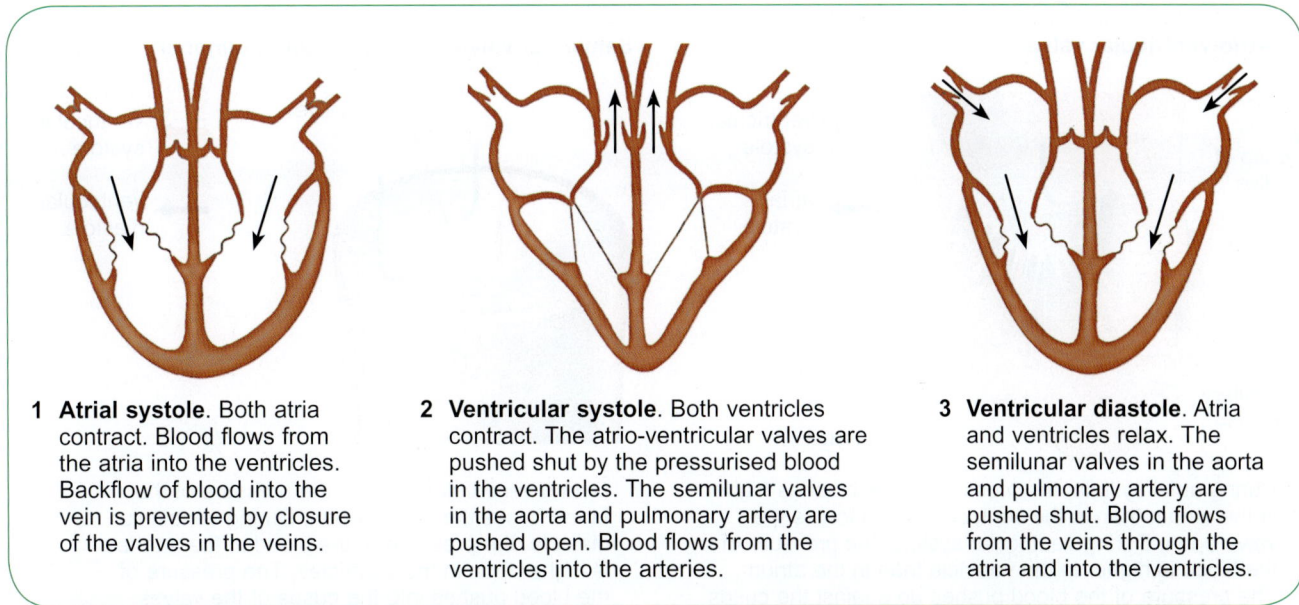

1 **Atrial systole**. Both atria contract. Blood flows from the atria into the ventricles. Backflow of blood into the vein is prevented by closure of the valves in the veins.

2 **Ventricular systole**. Both ventricles contract. The atrio-ventricular valves are pushed shut by the pressurised blood in the ventricles. The semilunar valves in the aorta and pulmonary artery are pushed open. Blood flows from the ventricles into the arteries.

3 **Ventricular diastole**. Atria and ventricles relax. The semilunar valves in the aorta and pulmonary artery are pushed shut. Blood flows from the veins through the atria and into the ventricles.

Figure 6.5 The cardiac cycle. Only three stages in this continuous process are shown.

About 0.1 s after the atria contract, the ventricles contract. This is called **ventricular systole**. The thick, muscular walls of the ventricles squeeze inwards on the blood, increasing its pressure and pushing it out of the heart. As soon as the pressure in the ventricles becomes greater than that in the atria, this pressure difference forces the atrio-ventricular valves shut, preventing blood from going back into the atria. Instead, the blood rushes upwards into the aorta and pulmonary artery, pushing open the semilunar valves in these vessels as it does so.

Ventricular systole lasts for about 0.3 s. The muscle then relaxes, and the stage called **ventricular diastole** begins. The pressure in the ventricles drops. The high-pressure blood which has just been pushed into the arteries would flow back into the ventricles, but for the presence of the semilunar valves, which snap shut as the blood fills their cusps.

During diastole, as the whole of the heart muscle relaxes, blood from the veins flows into the two atria. The blood is at a very low pressure, but the thin walls of the atria are easily distended, providing very little resistance to the blood flow. Some of the blood flows down into the ventricles. The atrial muscle then begins to contract, pushing blood forcefully down into the ventricles, and the whole cycle begins again.

Figure 6.6 shows how the atrio-ventricular and semilunar valves work. Figure 6.7 shows the pressure and volume changes in the heart, which are associated with the opening and closing of these valves.

The walls of the ventricles are much thicker than the walls of the atria, because the ventricles need to develop much more force when they contract, to push the blood out of the heart and around the body. For the right ventricle, the force required is relatively small, as the blood goes only to the lungs, which are very close to the heart. The left ventricle has to develop sufficient force to push blood all around the rest of the body. So the muscular wall of the left ventricle needs to be thicker than that of the right ventricle.

Interpreting the graphs in Figure 6.7 requires you to remember that the opening and closing of valves is caused by changes in pressure that alter which side of a valve has the highest pressure. Points on the graph where the highest pressure switches from one side of a valve to the other are where pressure lines cross. The second thing to remember is that contraction of muscle in the wall of a chamber causes pressure to rise in that chamber. SAQ 1 asks you to analyse these graphs.

Atrio-ventricular valve

cusp of valve

ventricular systole

atrial systole

cusp of valve

papillary muscle

tendon

During atrial systole, the pressure of the blood is higher in the atrium than in the ventricle and so forces the valve open. During ventricular systole, the pressure of the blood is higher in the ventricle than in the atrium. The pressure of the blood pushes up against the cusps of the valve, pushing it shut. Contraction of the papillary muscles, attached to the valve by tendons, prevents the valve from being forced inside-out.

Semilunar valve in the aorta and pulmonary artery

cusp of valve

ventricular systole

ventricular diastole

During ventricular systole, the pressure of the blood forces the valves open. During ventricular diastole, the pressure of the blood in the arteries is higher than in the ventricles. The pressure of the blood pushes into the cusps of the valves, squeezing them shut.

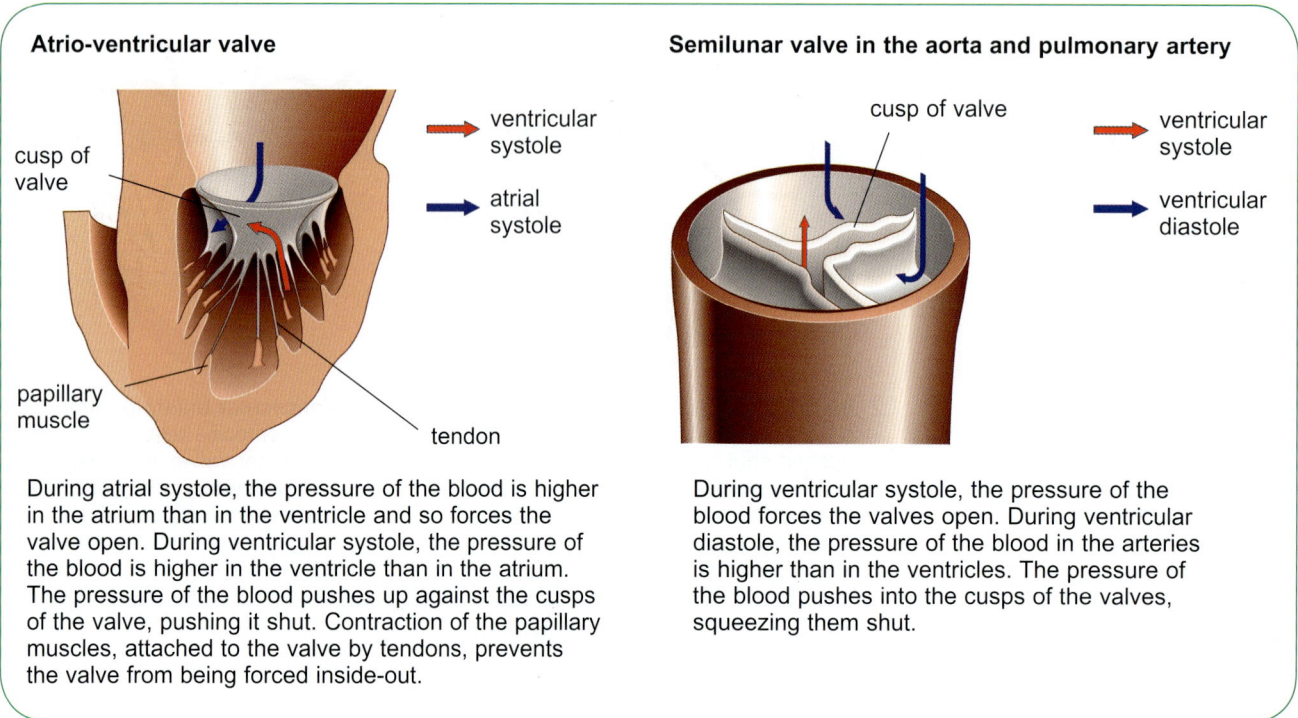

Fig 6.6   How the heart valves function.

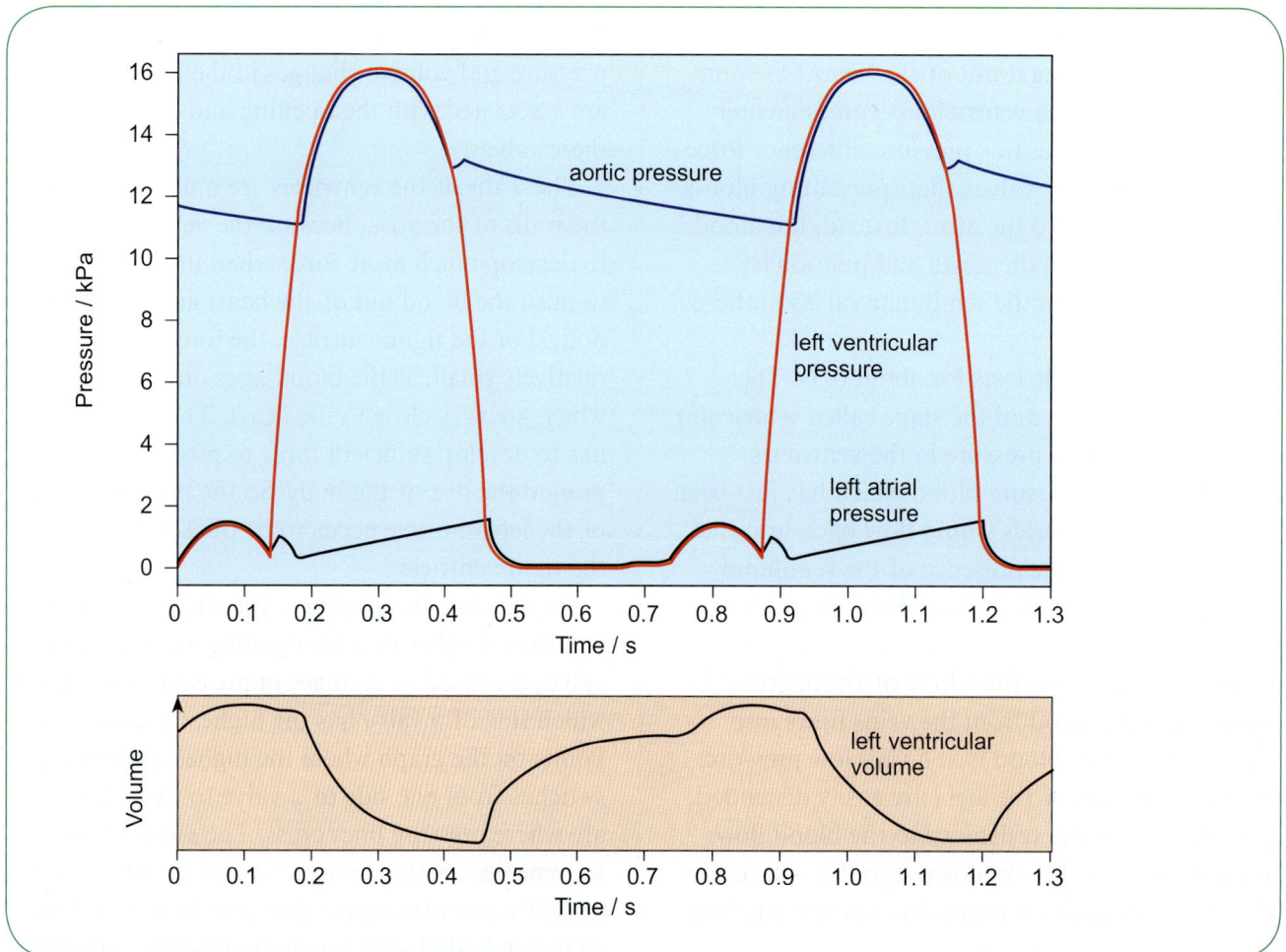

aortic pressure

left ventricular pressure

left atrial pressure

left ventricular volume

Figure 6.7   Pressure and volume changes in the heart during the cardiac cycle.

SAQ

1 Figure 6.7 shows the pressure changes in the left atrium, left ventricle and aorta throughout two cardiac cycles. Make a copy of this diagram.

    a i   How long does one heart beat (one cardiac cycle) last?

       ii What is the heart rate represented on this graph, in beats per minute?

    b The contraction of the muscles in the ventricle wall causes the pressure inside the ventricle to rise. When the muscles relax, the pressure drops again. On your copy of the diagram, mark the following periods:

       i   the time when the ventricle is contracting (ventricular systole)

       ii the time when the ventricle is relaxing (ventricular diastole).

    c The contraction of muscles in the wall of the atrium raises the pressure inside the atrium. This pressure is also raised when blood flows into the atrium from the veins, while the atrial walls are relaxed. On your copy of the diagram, mark the following periods:

       i   the time when the atrium is contracting (atrial systole)

       ii the time when the atrium is relaxing (atrial diastole).

    d The atrio-ventricular valves open when the pressure of the blood in the atria is greater than that in the ventricles. They snap shut when the pressure of the blood in the ventricles is greater than that in the atria. On your diagram, mark the points at which these valves open and close.

    e The opening and closing of the semilunar valves in the aorta depends, in a similar way, on the relative pressures in the aorta and ventricles. On your diagram, mark the points at which these valves open and close.

    f The right ventricle has much less muscle in its walls than the left ventricle, and only develops about one-quarter of the pressure developed on the left side of the heart. On your diagram, draw a line to represent the probable pressure inside the right ventricle during the 1.3 s shown.

    g Left ventricular volume is falling between 0.2 s and 0.45 s. Explain what is happening.

    h Over what stages of the cardiac cycle is the left ventricle filling with blood?

    i The heart sounds – 'lub' followed by 'dup' – are produced by heart valves snapping shut. The two atrio-ventricular valves (bicuspid and tricuspid valves) shut at the same time and produce the 'lub' sound. The two semilunar valves (aortic and pulmonary valves) shut at the same time producing the 'dup' sound. Mark on your graph 'lub' and 'dup' at the appropriate times.

Control of the heart beat

Cardiac muscle differs from the muscle in all other areas of the body in that it is **myogenic**. This means that it automatically contracts and relaxes; it does not need to receive impulses from a nerve to make it contract. If cardiac muscle cells are cultured in a warm, oxygenated solution containing nutrients, they contract and relax rhythmically, all by themselves. Cardiac muscle cells joined together contract together, in unison.

However, the individual muscle cells in a heart cannot be allowed to contract at their own natural rhythms. If they did, parts of the heart would contract out of sequence with other parts; the cardiac cycle would become disordered and the heart would stop working as a pump. The heart has its own built-in controlling and coordinating system which prevents this happening.

The cardiac cycle is initiated in a small patch of muscle in the wall of the right atrium, called the **sino-atrial node** or **SAN** (Figure 6.8). It is often called the pacemaker. The muscle cells in the SAN set the pace and rhythm for all the other cardiac muscle cells. Their natural rhythm of contraction is slightly faster than the rest of the heart muscle. Each time they contract, they set up a wave of electrical activity, which spreads out rapidly over the whole of the atrial walls. The cardiac muscle in the atrial walls responds to this excitation wave by contracting, in the same rhythm as the SAN.

1 Each cardiac cycle begins in the right atrium. There is a small patch of muscle tissue in the right atrium wall, called the sino-atrial node (SAN), which automatically contracts and relaxes all the time. It doesn't need a nerve impulse to start it off, so it is said to be myogenic – that is, 'started by the muscle'.
The pacemaker's rate can be adjusted by nerves transmitting impulses to the pacemaker from the brain.

2 As the muscle in the SAN contracts, it produces an electrical impulse which sweeps through all of the muscle in the atria of the heart. This impulse makes the muscle in the atrial walls contract.

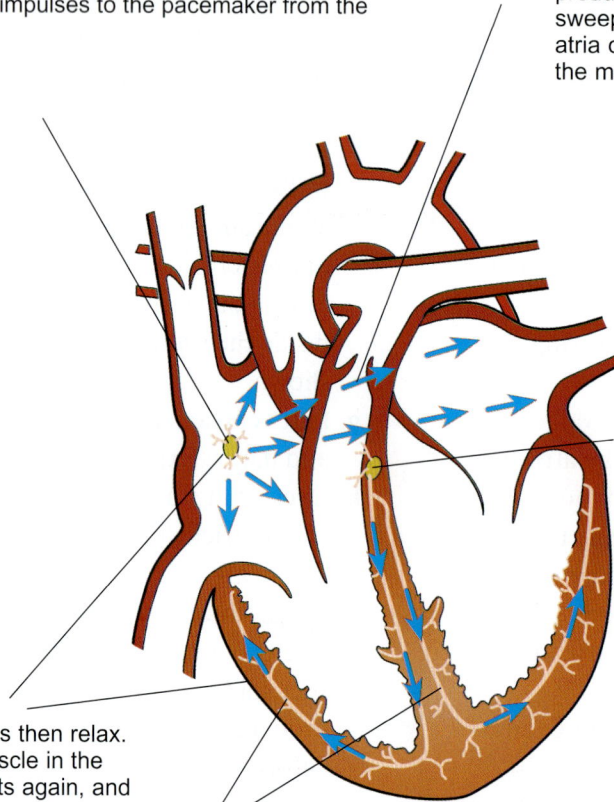

3 The impulse sweeps onwards and reaches another patch of cells called the atrio-ventricular node (AVN). This node is the only way in which the electrical impulse can get down to the ventricles. The AVN delays the impulse for a fraction of a second, before it travels down into the ventricles. This delay means that the ventricles receive the signal to contract after the atria.

5 The ventricles then relax. Then the muscle in the SAN contracts again, and the whole sequence runs through once more.

4 The impulse moves swiftly down through the septum of the heart, along fibres known as Purkyne tissue. Once the impulse arrives at the base of the ventricles it sweeps upwards, through the ventricle walls. The ventricles contract.

Fig 6.8   How electrical impulses move through the heart.

Thus, all the muscle in both atria contracts almost simultaneously.

As we have seen, the muscles of the ventricles do not contract until after the muscles of the atria. (You can imagine what would happen if they all contracted at once.) This delay is caused by a feature of the heart that briefly delays the excitation wave in its passage from the atria to the ventricles.

There is a band of fibres between the atria and the ventricles which does not conduct the excitation wave. As the wave spreads out from the SAN, it cannot pass through these fibres. The only route is through a small patch of conducting fibres, known as the **atrio-ventricular node** or **AVN**. The AVN picks up the excitation wave as it spreads across the atria and, after a delay of about 0.1 s, passes it on to a bunch of conducting fibres, called the **Purkyne tissue** (also called the Bundle of His) which runs down the septum between the ventricles. This transmits the excitation wave very rapidly down to the base of the septum, from where it spreads outwards and upwards through the ventricle walls. As it does so, it causes the cardiac muscle in these walls to contract, from the bottom up, squeezing blood upwards and into the arteries (Figure 6.9).

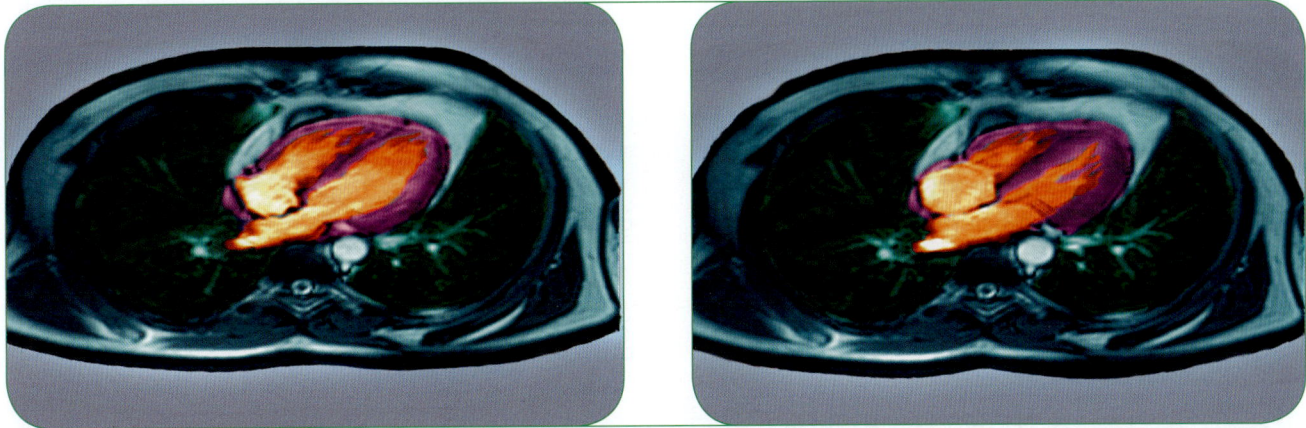

Figure 6.9 Two MRI scans of a man's chest cavity. The orange areas are the ventricles of the heart. In the right-hand image, the ventricles are contracting – the volume inside them is less.

Drugs to help the heart

Two nerves carry impulses from the brain to the SAN. One of these is the **vagus nerve**. It releases a transmitter substance called **acetylcholine** next to the cells in the SAN. Acetylcholine slots into receptors in the plasma membranes of these cells, and makes the cells beat more slowly.

The other nerve, called the **sympathetic nerve**, releases a different chemical called **noradrenaline**. This has the opposite effect to acetylcholine, and makes the cells in the SAN beat more rapidly. The hormone **adrenaline**, released from the adrenal glands just above the kidneys when a person is frightened or excited, does the same.

There are several drugs that can be used to help a person who has problems with their rate of heart beat. Two of these are digoxin and propranolol.

Digoxin inhibits a Na–K pump in the plasma membrane of the heart muscle cells. This pump usually keeps sodium concentration inside the cells at a low level. When the pump is slowed,

Digoxin was discovered in foxgloves.

sodium ions accumulate inside the cells. This also increases the concentration of calcium ions inside them, which increases the force of muscle contraction.

Propranolol has the opposite effect. It belongs to a class of drugs called beta blockers. They work by decreasing the effect of noradrenaline on the SAN, reducing the heart rate. Beta blockers are often given to people with angina, a pain in the chest signalling that the coronary arteries are not supplying enough oxygen to the heart muscle.

Electrocardiograms

It is quite easy to detect and record the waves of electrical excitation as they travel through the heart muscle. Electrodes can be placed on the skin over opposite sides of the heart, and a recording is made of the electrical potentials. The result is essentially a graph of voltage against time. It is called an **electrocardiogram** or **ECG**. Below is an ECG for a healthy heart.

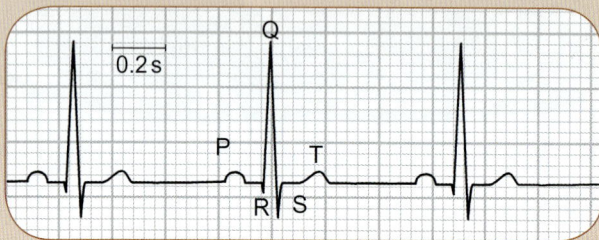

The graphs at the top of the next column show how the peaks and troughs of the ECG relate to the pressure changes we have already looked at. If you look very carefully, you can see that the ups and downs in the ECG happen just before the ups and downs in the pressure graph. For example, the P wave on the ECG comes before the pressure rise in the left atrium. This is because the ECG records the electrical impulses that are spreading over the heart, and these electrical impulses cause the contraction of the muscle in the heart walls. So the P wave in the ECG represents the wave of electrical activity spreading through the walls of the atria, which is quickly followed by the contraction of the atrial muscle and therefore the rise in pressure in the atria.

Below is an example of an abnormal ECG. This is ventricular fibrillation, in which the muscle in the ventricle walls just flutters. This could be because of serious damage to the heart muscle, which has caused it to stop beating – in other words, a heart attack or cardiac arrest.

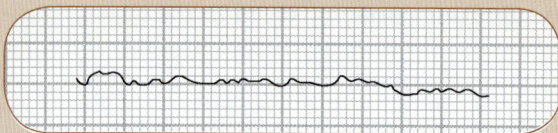

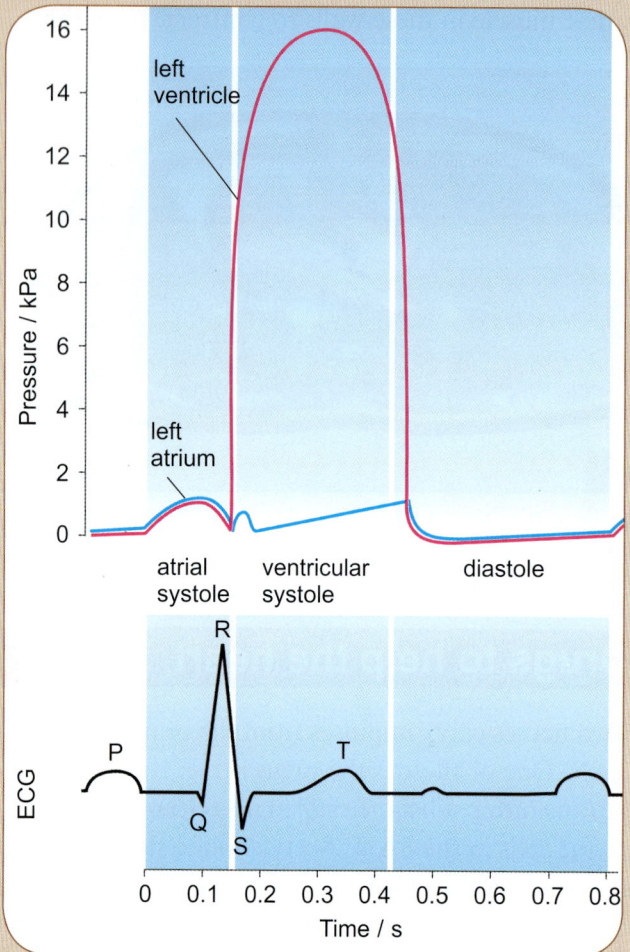

For any chance of survival, the person needs treatment with a defibrillator, which administers electric shocks, to try to get the heart muscle beating normally again.

Another ECG below shows a condition called heart block. There are many different kinds of heart block, a term which refers to problems with the movement of the electrical signals from one part of the heart to another. In this person, the signals are taking much longer than usual to pass from the atria to the ventricles, and you can see that the time interval between the P and R sections is longer than in a normal ECG. This could be caused by damage to the Purkyne fibres.

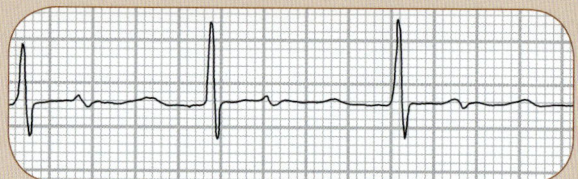

The regulation of cardiac output

The heart is designed to pump out whatever flows into it, over a wide range of values. If an increased volume of blood returns to the heart in the veins, then the heart responds by pumping faster and harder to push it out. This happens because the incoming blood stretches the muscle in the wall of the heart, and the muscle responds by contracting harder than usual, increasing the **stroke volume**. At the same time, the stretching directly stimulates the SAN, which responds by firing action potentials slightly faster than usual, slightly increasing heart rate (Figure 6.10).

During exercise more blood is returned to the heart. This happens because of the drop in oxygen in the blood within blood vessels in active muscles. This drop in oxygen stimulates the cells lining the inside of the blood vessels, causing them to release nitric oxide. The nitric oxide causes muscle to relax in the walls of arterioles supplying blood to the exercising muscles (vasodilation). This increases the rate at which blood is returned to the heart. Increasing the rate of blood returning to the heart increases cardiac output, which results in more oxygen being transported to the muscles.

This mechanism only works up to a certain

Information from the brain

The sympathetic nerves and the hormone adrenaline produce an increase in heart rate and stroke volume.

The increase is caused by (a) nerve impulses from the brain to SAN, AVN and cardiac muscle and (b) impulses from the brain along sympathetic nerves to adrenal glands causing adrenaline secretion into the blood which then circulates to the heart.

Nerve impulses from the brain along the parasympathetic (vagus) nerve to the SAN and AVN decrease heart rate.

Information to the brain

Stretch receptors (baro-receptors) in aorta and carotid arteries are stimulated by high arterial pressure. This causes stimulation of the heart by the vagus nerve.

Low arterial pressure results in sympathetic stimulation.

Chemoreceptors in aortic and carotid bodies monitor the concentration of O_2, CO_2 and H^+ ions in the blood. Low O_2, high CO_2 and high H^+ ions result in sympathetic stimulation of the heart (but their main effect is on breathing).

Sensory input to higher brain centres – emotion, stress, anticipation of events and other factors – can result in sympathetic stimulation, speeding heart rate.

Volume of venous return

The more blood returns to the heart, the more is pumped out. Vasodilation of arteries and arterioles increases the return of blood to the heart. This is partly controlled by local nitric oxide. Vasoconstriction decreases return. This is partly controlled by impulses along sympathetic nerves.

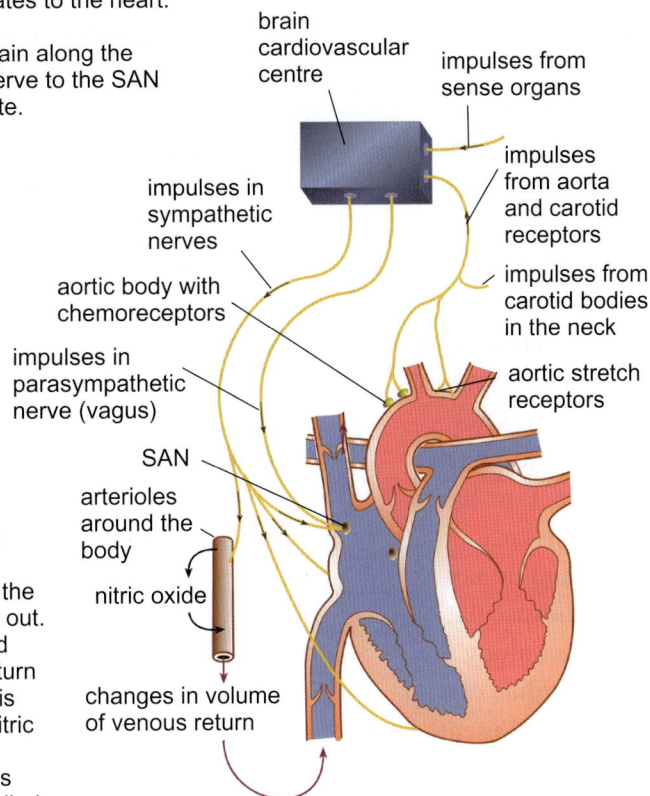

Figure 6.10 Regulation of cardiac output.

maximum cardiac output. However, nervous stimulation can alter the range over which the heart can cope with the blood returning to it. The heart has two types of nerves running to it, the **vagus** (a parasympathetic nerve) and **sympathetic nerves**. These nerves bring impulses from the cardiovascular centre in the medulla of the brain. The vagus nerve brings these impulses from the brain to the SAN and AVN, while the sympathetic nerves bring impulses to many areas of the muscle in the heart walls. If action potentials arrive along a sympathetic nerve, they speed up the heart rate and increase stroke volume. The parasympathetic nerve (vagus) has the opposite effect.

When you are about to exercise, your brain not only sends impulses to your muscles, but also along the sympathetic nerve to your heart, at the same time. This increases the rate of heart beat, even before the increased volume of blood returning to the heart does so, and prepares the heart to cope with the increased blood coming back to it during exercise. The hormone adrenaline, secreted from the adrenal glands in times of nervous anticipation, has similar effects to stimulation by the sympathetic nerves.

These nerves may also be affected by blood pressure. Inside the aorta, and also in the walls of the carotid arteries, are nerve endings which are sensitive to stretching. They are called **baroreceptors** or stretch receptors. If blood pressure rises, this stretches the artery walls, which stimulates these nerve endings. They fire off impulses to the brain, which then sends impulses down the vagus nerve to the heart. This slows the heart rate and reduces stroke volume, which can help to reduce the blood pressure. Low blood pressure has the opposite effect. In this case, the baroreceptors are not stretched and do not send impulses to the brain. The cardiovascular centre in the brain then sends impulses along the sympathetic nerve, which increases cardiac output and thus blood pressure. Impulses are also sent to muscles in the arteriole walls, which contract and narrow the arterioles (vasoconstriction), so increasing blood pressure.

Many factors affect blood pressure, both in the short and long term. Your blood pressure briefly drops, for example, when you stand up after sitting for a while. If you have been relaxing, your heart will be working at a fairly slow rate. When you stand, blood pressure in the vessels in your head and upper body suddenly drops, which can sometimes make you feel faint. This is quickly remedied, as the baroreceptors detect the drop in pressure and set off the processes which increase blood pressure, including an increase in cardiac output.

Yet another factor which can influence the rate of heart beat, through the action of nerves to the heart, is the concentration of carbon dioxide and oxygen in the blood. These are monitored by chemoreceptors, some which are in the brain and others in the walls of the carotid artery and aorta. Higher carbon dioxide concentrations or low oxygen concentrations can increase the rate of heart beat. However, this is usually of little importance compared with other factors.

Blood vessels

When blood first leaves the heart, it is travelling in vessels called **arteries**. Arteries always carry blood away from the heart. The largest arteries divide into smaller ones, and these continue to divide to form much smaller vessels called arterioles. These in turn divide into even smaller vessels called **capillaries**. Capillaries then join up with each other to form venules and these finally merge to form **veins**, which carry blood back to the heart. The structure of arteries, veins and capillaries is shown in Figure 6.11 and Figure 6.12.

Arteries

The function of arteries is to transport blood swiftly and at high pressure to the tissues.

Both arteries and veins have walls made up of three layers:

- an inner endothelium (lining tissue), made up of a layer of flat cells fitting together like jigsaw pieces; called squamous epithelium, this is very smooth, and so reduces friction as blood flows over its surface,
- a middle layer called the tunica media ('middle coat') containing smooth muscle, collagen and elastic fibres,

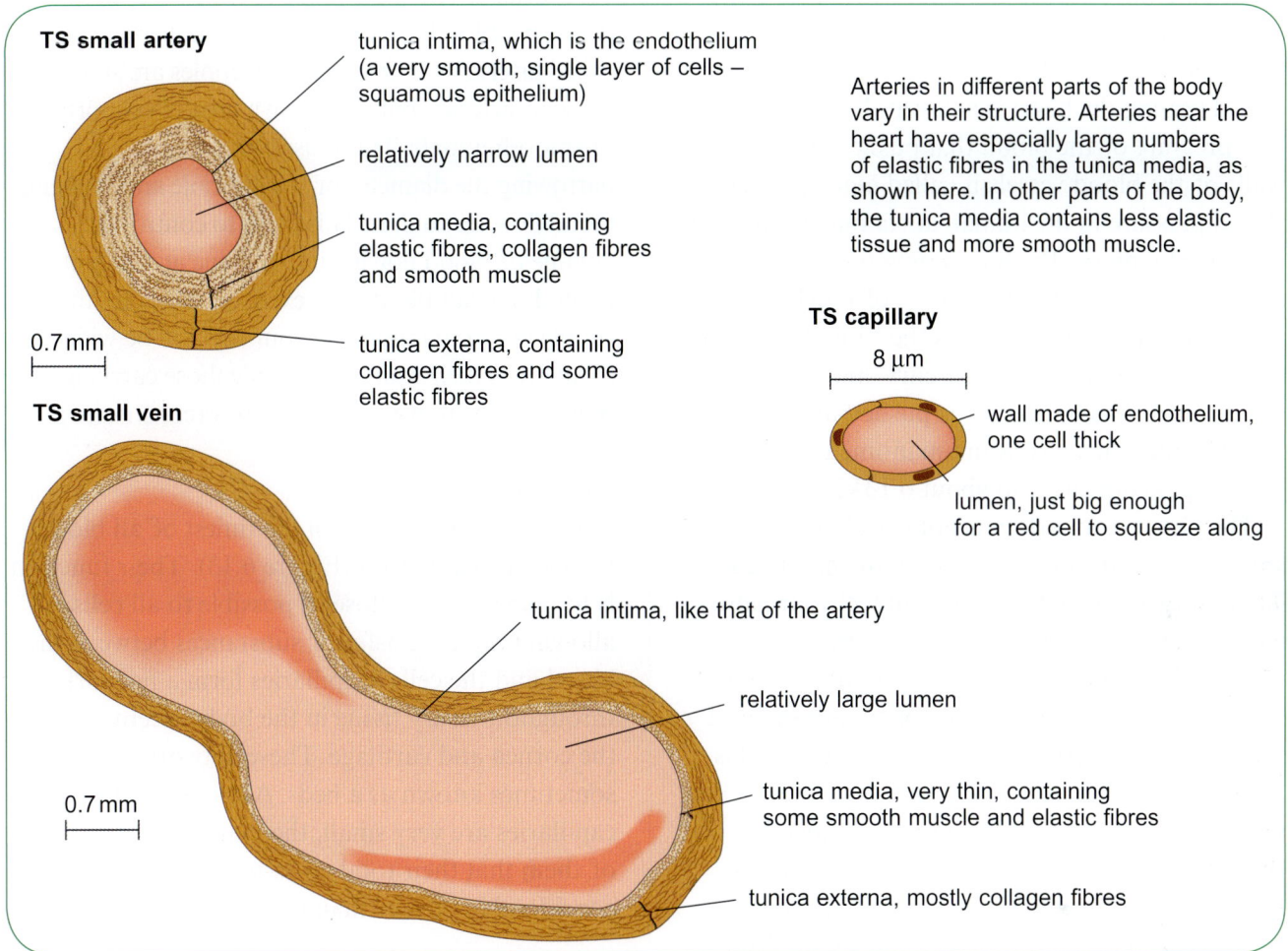

TS small artery

tunica intima, which is the endothelium (a very smooth, single layer of cells – squamous epithelium)

relatively narrow lumen

tunica media, containing elastic fibres, collagen fibres and smooth muscle

0.7 mm

tunica externa, containing collagen fibres and some elastic fibres

TS small vein

Arteries in different parts of the body vary in their structure. Arteries near the heart have especially large numbers of elastic fibres in the tunica media, as shown here. In other parts of the body, the tunica media contains less elastic tissue and more smooth muscle.

TS capillary

8 µm

wall made of endothelium, one cell thick

lumen, just big enough for a red cell to squeeze along

tunica intima, like that of the artery

relatively large lumen

tunica media, very thin, containing some smooth muscle and elastic fibres

0.7 mm

tunica externa, mostly collagen fibres

Figure 6.11 The tissues making up the walls of arteries, capillaries and veins.

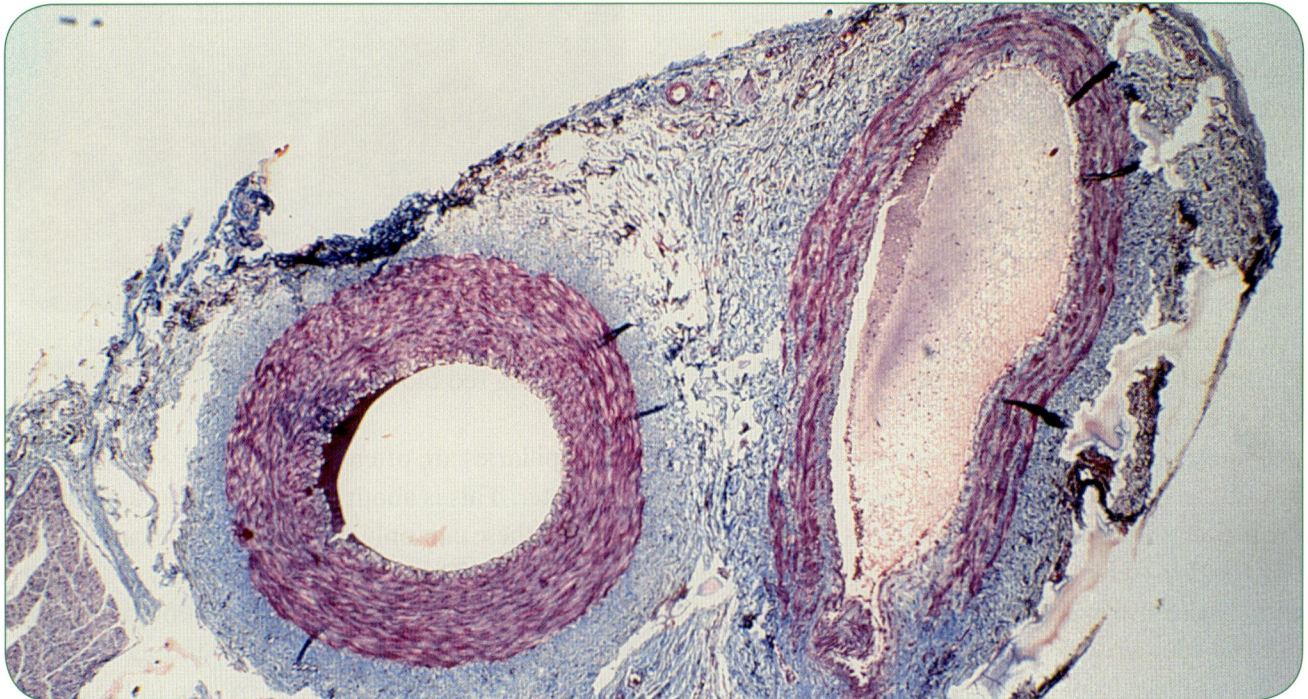

Figure 6.12 Photomicrograph of an artery and vein (×110).

121

- an outer layer called the tunica externa ('outer coat') containing elastic fibres and collagen fibres.

Blood leaving the heart is at a very high pressure. The pressure of the blood that pushes out on the walls of the blood vessels is called **blood pressure**. Blood pressure in the human aorta may be around 120 mm Hg, or 16 kPa. Blood pressure is still usually measured in the old units of mm Hg even though the kPa (kilopascal) is the SI unit – mm Hg stands for 'millimetres of mercury' and refers to the distance which mercury is pushed up the arm of a U-tube when a sphygmomanometer is used. 1 mm Hg is equivalent to about 0.13 kPa.

The blood in an artery is not travelling smoothly, but in surges caused by the heart beat. These surges can be felt when you feel your **pulse** – each pulse corresponds to one heart beat.

To withstand the pressure surges, artery walls must be extremely strong and able to expand and recoil. The distinctive feature of an artery wall is its strength and elasticity. Arteries have the thickest walls of any blood vessel. The human aorta, the largest artery and the one where pressure is highest, has an overall diameter of 2.5 cm close to the heart, and a wall thickness of about 2 mm. Although 2 mm may not seem very great, the composition of the wall provides great strength and resilience. The tunica media, which is by far the thickest part of the wall, contains large numbers of elastic fibres. These allow the wall to stretch as pulses of blood surge through at high pressure as a result of the contraction of the ventricles. As the ventricles relax, the blood pressure drops, and the elastic artery walls recoil inwards.

Therefore, as blood at high pressure enters an artery, the artery becomes wider, which reduces the pressure slightly, so it is a little below what it would be if the wall could not expand. As blood at lower pressure enters an artery, the artery wall recoils inwards, giving the blood a small 'push' and raising the pressure a little. The overall effect is to 'even out' the flow of blood. However, the arteries are not entirely effective in achieving this: if you feel your pulse in your wrist, you can feel the artery, even at this distance from your heart, being stretched outwards with each surge of blood from the heart.

As arteries reach the tissue to which they are delivering blood, they branch into smaller vessels called arterioles. The walls of arterioles are similar to those of arteries, but they have a greater proportion of smooth muscle. This muscle can contract, narrowing the diameter of the arteriole and reducing blood flow through it. This helps to control the volume of blood flowing into a tissue at different times. For example, during exercise, arterioles that supply blood to muscles in your legs will be wide (dilated) as their walls relax, while those carrying blood to the gut wall will be narrow (constricted).

Capillaries

Arterioles branch to form the tiniest of all blood vessels, the capillaries (Figure 6.13). Their function is to take blood as close as possible to all cells, allowing rapid transfer of substances between the blood and the cells. Capillaries form a network throughout every tissue in the body except the cornea and cartilage. These networks are sometimes known as a beds. Although individual capillaries are very small, there are so many of them that their total cross-sectional area is considerably greater than that of the arteries.

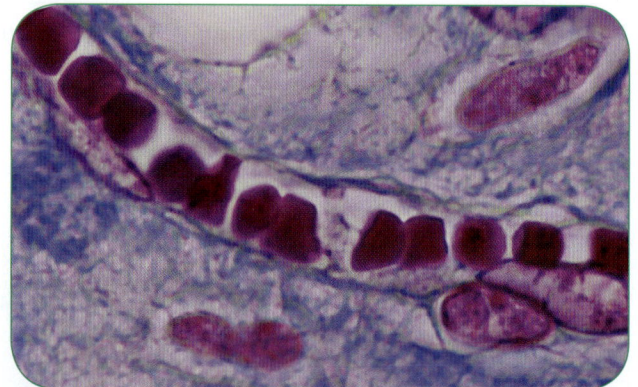

Figure 6.13 Micrograph of a blood capillary containing red blood cells (× 900).

Capillaries are often no more than 8 μm in diameter. This is about the same size as a red blood cell, so these can only pass through the capillaries in single file. This makes sure that every red blood cell, carrying its load of oxygen, is brought as close as possible to the cells in the surrounding tissues. This speeds up the transfer of oxygen to the cells and the removal of carbon dioxide. The gases move by diffusion, down their concentration gradients.

Capillaries have very thin walls, only one cell thick, which also speeds up transfer of materials between the blood and the tissues. Many substances pass across the endothelial cells in vesicles, by endocytosis and exocytosis. The vesicles can even fuse to form tiny holes right through a cell. In most capillaries, there are also tiny gaps between the individual cells that form the endothelium, allowing easy transfer of substances dissolved in the plasma out of the capillary to the surrounding cells.

Veins

As blood leaves a capillary bed, the capillaries join together to form venules and then veins. The function of veins is to return blood to the heart.

The blood which enters veins is at a much lower pressure than in arteries. In humans, a typical value for venous blood pressure is about 5 mm Hg or even less. Veins therefore have no need for thick, elastic walls. The walls are so thin that veins collapse when a section of tissue is cut to make a microscope slide. The walls have the same three layers as arteries, but the tunica media is much thinner with far fewer elastic fibres and muscle fibres.

The low blood pressure in veins creates a problem: how can this blood be returned to the heart? The problem is most obvious if you

consider how blood can return upwards from your legs. Unaided, the blood in your leg veins would sink and accumulate in your feet. Many of the veins run within, or very close to, several leg muscles. Whenever you tense these muscles, they squeeze inwards on the veins, temporarily raising the pressure within them. This in itself would not help to push the blood back towards the heart – blood would just squidge up and down as you walked. To keep the blood flowing in the right direction, veins contain semilunar valves, formed from their endothelium (Figure 6.14). The valves allow blood to move towards the heart, but not away from it. When you contract your leg muscles, the blood in the veins is squeezed through the valves, but cannot drop back past them.

Figure 6.15 shows how blood pressure changes

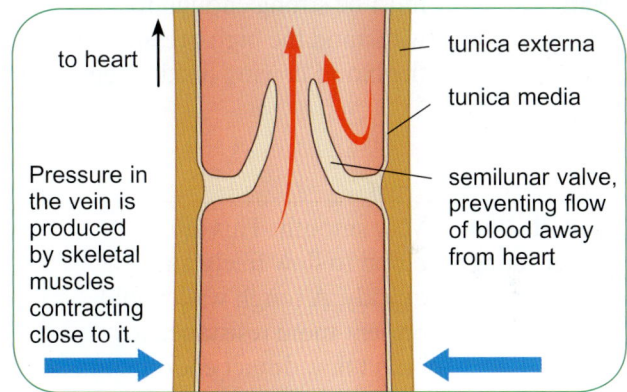

Figure 6.14   Longitudinal section through a small vein and a valve.

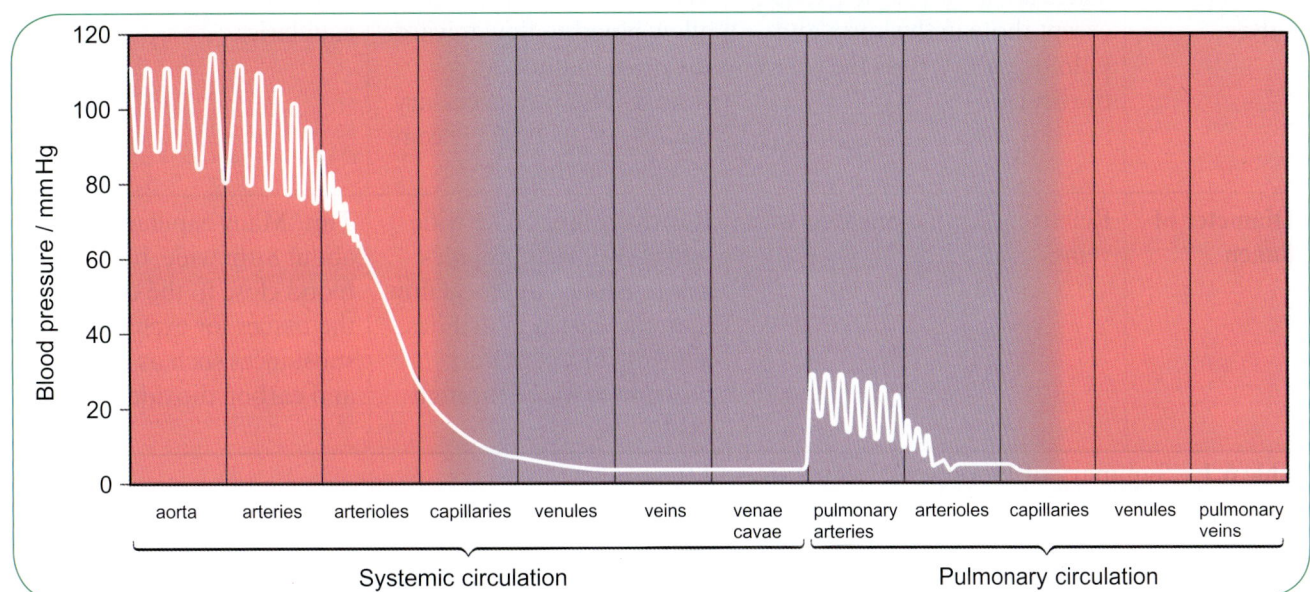

Figure 6.15   Blood pressure in different regions of the human circulatory system.

as it travels on a complete journey from the heart, through the systemic circulatory system, back to the heart and finally through the pulmonary circulatory system. Table 6.1 summarises the differences between arteries, veins and capillaries.

	Artery	Vein	Capillary
Elastic tissue in wall	Large amount, especially in arteries close to the heart. This allows the wall to stretch and recoil as high-pressure blood pulses through.	Small amount. Blood in veins is at low pressure, so there is no need for the walls to be elastic.	None
Smooth muscle in wall	Relatively large amount in small arteries and arterioles. Contraction of this muscle reduces the size of the lumen, which can divert blood from one area to another.	Small amount. All blood in veins is travelling back to the heart, so there is no advantage in being able to divert it to different tissues.	None
Thickness of wall	Relatively thick. Artery walls must be strong enough to withstand the high pressure of the blood flowing inside them.	Relatively thin. The blood in veins is at low pressure, so there is no need for a thick wall.	The wall is only one cell thick. The cells are thin and flattened, so the wall is as thin as possible. This allows rapid transfer of substances by diffusion between the blood and tissue fluid.
Endothelium (inner lining)	Very smooth. This allows blood to flow freely and quickly. A rough wall would present more resistance to blood flow. Intact endothelium decreases the likelihood of a thrombus (blood clot) forming.	As arteries	The wall of a capillary is made of endothelium only, with no other layers of tissue. The thin endothelium and pores speed up exchange of substances with the tissues.
Presence of valves	There are no valves in arteries, except those in the aorta and pulmonary artery as they leave the heart.	Veins have valves, which allow blood to flow towards the heart but not away from it. They are necessary because of the low pressure of blood in the veins.	There are no valves in capillaries.
Diameter of lumen	Relatively small compared with veins.	Relatively large. The wide lumen of a vein provides less resistance to blood flow than the narrower arteries, allowing blood at low pressure to move through easily.	Tiny. Many capillaries are about 8 μm wide, bringing blood close to the cells in the tissues for exchanging substances such as oxygen and carbon dioxide.

Table 6.1 Summary of blood vessel structure and function.

2 Explain what causes each of the following:
   a Blood pressure oscillates (goes up and down) in the arteries.
   b Blood pressure drops in the arterioles and in the capillaries.
   c Blood pressure rises in the pulmonary artery, but not so high as in the aorta.

Measuring blood pressure

A doctor will often measure blood pressure when checking on a person's health. This may be done using a sphygmomanometer (Figure 6.16), which measures the pressure in a large artery close to the elbow joint.

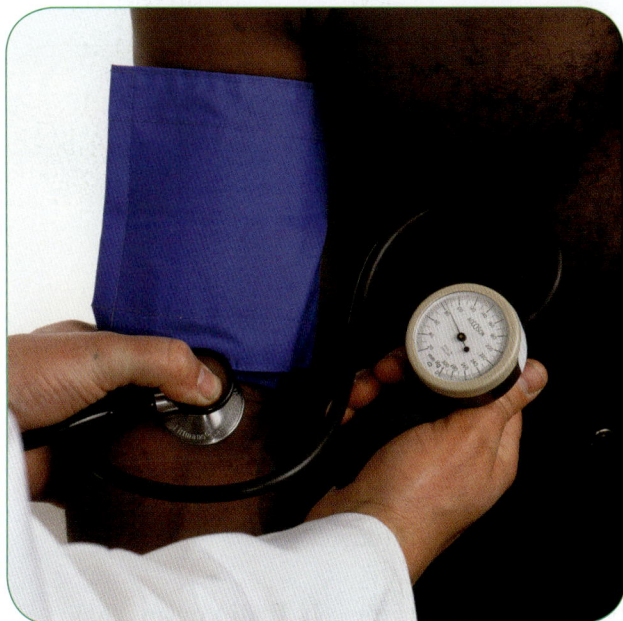

Figure 6.16   A person having their blood pressure taken with a sphygmomanometer.

Both the **systolic pressure** and diastolic pressure are measured. The systolic pressure is the maximum pressure, produced as a result of the contraction of the left ventricle of the heart. The **diastolic pressure** is the lowest pressure, caused by the relaxation of the ventricular muscle in the heart. Although the diastolic pressure is the lower of the two, it is the reading that reveals most about the condition of the circulatory system.

A persistently high diastolic pressure in a person at rest is known as **hypertension** (high blood pressure). This is associated with a higher risk of suffering heart disease, a heart attack or a stroke. High blood pressure can be caused by stiffening of the walls of the arteries, a condition called **atherosclerosis**. This happens naturally to some extent as we age. However, it is also caused by a build-up of cholesterol in the artery walls, forming structures called **plaques**. These narrow the lumen inside the artery (which in itself also increases blood pressure) and make the wall less able to expand and recoil as blood pulses through. You can read more about this, and how diet may affect it, in Chapter 12.

Systolic blood pressure rises temporarily when we exercise or are excited. This is a result of the secretion of adrenaline, or the stimulation of the SAN by the sympathetic nerve, causing the heart to beat more forcefully. This is useful, because it means that the blood moves more rapidly around the circulatory system, delivering oxygen to muscle cells at a greater rate. This allows them to increase their rate of aerobic respiration and produce more ATP for contraction.

Blood

You have about $5\,dm^3$ of blood in your body, with a mass of about 5 kg. Blood is composed of cells floating in a pale yellow liquid called **plasma**. Blood plasma is mostly water, with a variety of substances dissolved in it. These solutes include nutrients, such as glucose, and waste products, such as urea, that are being transported from one place to another in the body. They also include protein molecules, called **plasma proteins**, that remain in the blood all the time.

Suspended in the blood plasma, you have around 2.5×10^{13} **erythrocytes** (red blood cells), 5×10^{11} leucocytes (white blood cells) and 6×10^{12} platelets (Figures 6.17 and 6.18).

The structure of erythrocytes

Erythrocytes are small cells, with no nucleus (Figure 6.19). Their red colour is caused by the red pigment **haemoglobin**, Hb, a globular protein. The main function of erythrocytes is to transport oxygen, and also carbon dioxide, between the lungs and respiring tissues.

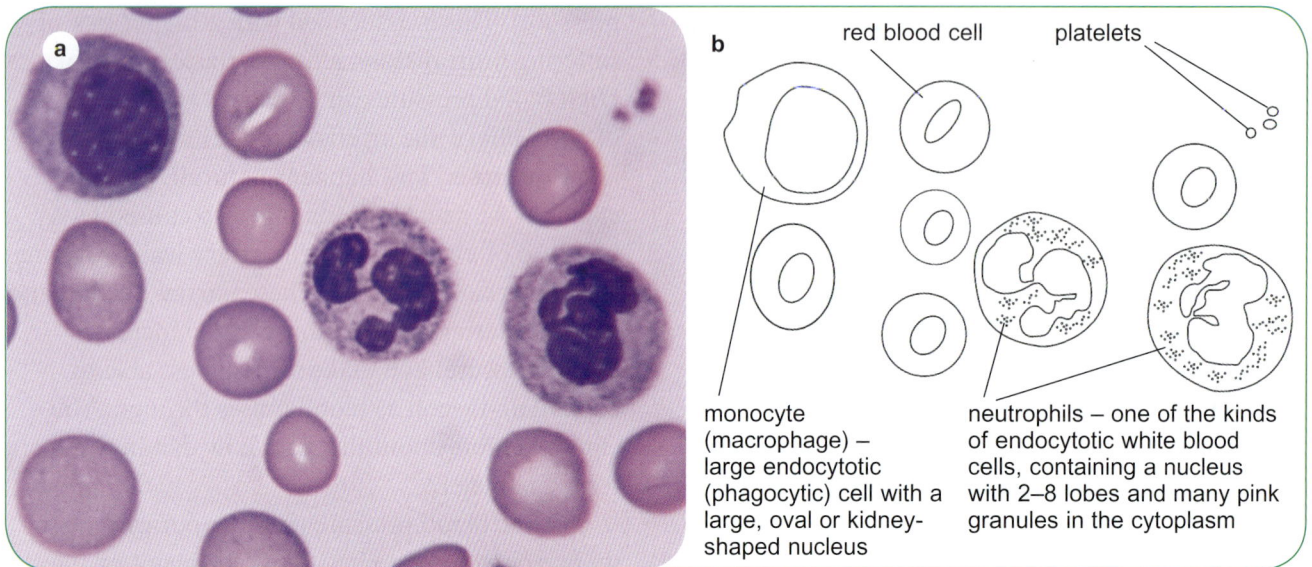

Figure 6.17 **a** Photomicrograph of human blood. It has been stained so that the nuclei of the white cells are dark purple ($\times$ 860), **b** diagram.

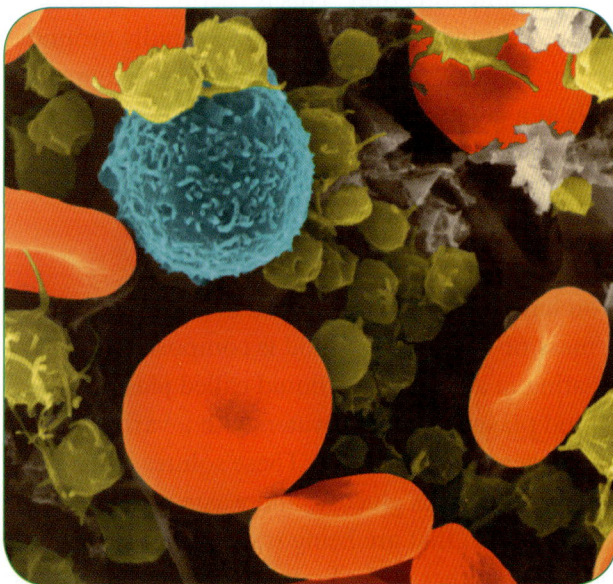

Figure 6.18 SEM of human blood. Red blood cells are coloured red. The blue sphere is a white blood cell. Platelets are coloured yellow ($\times$ 2400).

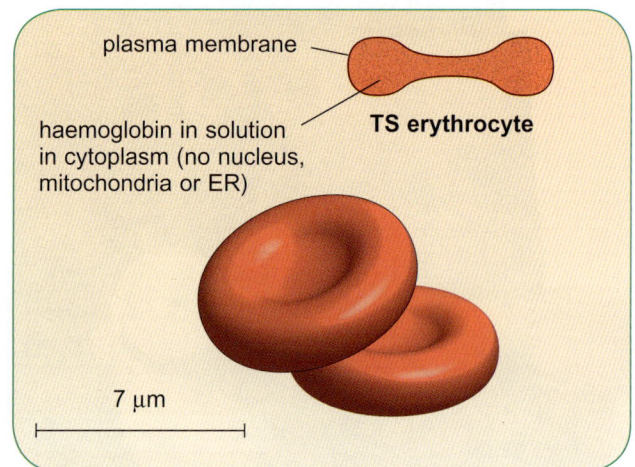

Figure 6.19 Erythrocytes.

Erythrocyte structure is unusual in three ways.

- Erythrocytes are very small. The diameter of a human red blood cell is about 7 μm, compared with the diameter of an 'average' liver cell of 40 μm. This small size means that all haemoglobin molecules within the cell are close to the cell's plasma membrane, and can therefore exchange oxygen easily with the fluid outside the cell. It also means that capillaries can be only 8 μm wide and still allow erythrocytes to squeeze through them, bringing oxygen as close as possible to the cells that require it.
- Erythrocytes are shaped like a biconcave disc. The 'dent' in each side of the cell, like its small size, increases its surface area : volume ratio. This means that oxygen can diffuse rapidly into and out of the cell.
- Erythrocytes have no nucleus, no mitochondria and no endoplasmic reticulum. This leaves more room for haemoglobin.

3 Which of these functions could be carried out in
   a red blood cell? Explain each answer.
   a protein synthesis
   b cell division
   c lipid synthesis

The role of haemoglobin

Oxygen is transported around the body in
combination with haemoglobin. Each haemoglobin
molecule can combine with eight oxygen atoms,
forming **oxyhaemoglobin**. Haemoglobin
combines with oxygen when oxygen is at a high
concentration, and releases it in areas where it is
at a low concentration. This means that it picks
up oxygen at the lungs, and releases it in tissues.

The haemoglobin dissociation curve

To investigate how haemoglobin behaves in
different conditions, samples are extracted
from the blood and then exposed to different
concentrations, known as **partial pressures**, of
oxygen. The amount of oxygen that combines with
each sample of haemoglobin is then measured.

The maximum amount of oxygen with which
a haemoglobin sample can possibly combine is
given a value of 100%. A sample of haemoglobin
that has combined with this maximum amount
is said to be 100% saturated. At lower oxygen
concentrations, less oxygen combines with the
haemoglobin, and so it is less saturated. We can
plot the percentage saturation of haemoglobin
against the different partial pressures of oxygen.
This gives us a curve known as an oxygen
dissociation curve (Figure 6.20).

You can see that, in general, the greater
the partial pressure of oxygen, the greater the
percentage saturation of the haemoglobin. This is
what we would expect. The more oxygen there is,
the more is taken up by the haemoglobin.

Think about the haemoglobin inside an
erythrocyte in a capillary in the lungs. Here,
where the partial pressure of oxygen is high,

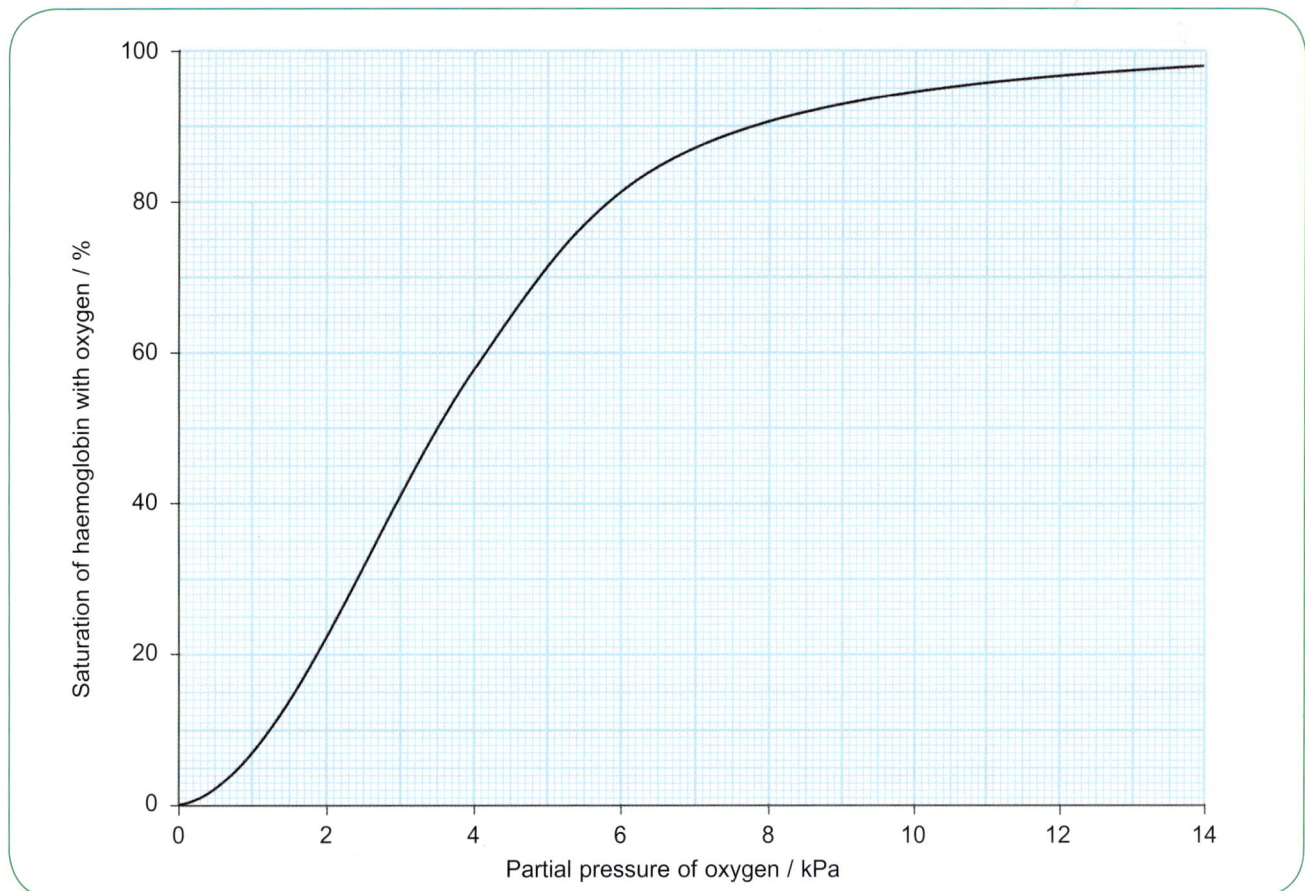

Figure 6.20   The haemoglobin dissociation curve.

the haemoglobin will be 95–97% saturated with oxygen. In an actively respiring muscle, however, where the partial pressure of oxygen is much lower, the haemoglobin will be only about 20–25% saturated with oxygen. This means that the haemoglobin coming from the lungs loses a lot of its oxygen when it arrives at a muscle. The released oxygen diffuses out of the red blood cell and into the muscle, where it can be used in respiration.

The S-shaped curve

You would expect the haemoglobin dissociation curve in Figure 6.20 to look like an enzyme 'rate against substrate concentration' graph, with a straight line from the origin (Figure 6.21a). But the haemoglobin dissociation curve is S-shaped (sigmoidal) (Figure 16.21b). This reflects the way in which a haemoglobin molecule binds with its possible four oxygen molecules.

Imagine a Hb molecule with no oxygen bound to it. It is actually quite hard for the first oxygen molecule to bind. You can see from the dissociation curve in Figure 6.20 that in an oxygen partial pressure of 1 kPa, the Hb molecules are combined with only 7% of their possible full load. You have to increase the partial pressure to 2.2 kPa before reaching a stage where, on average, each Hb molecule is combined with one oxygen molecule.

However, once this first pair of oxygen atoms has bonded with one of the haem groups in the Hb molecule, the shape of the molecule is slightly changed. This is an example of an **allosteric effect**. (Allosteric means 'different shape'.) This makes it

SAQ

4 In a healthy adult human, there are about 150 g of haemoglobin in each dm^3 of blood.
 a 1 g of haemoglobin can combine with 1.3 cm^3 of oxygen at body temperature. How much oxygen can be carried in 1 dm^3 of blood?
 b At body temperature, 0.025 cm^3 of oxygen can dissolve in 1 cm^3 of water. Assuming that blood plasma is mostly water, how much oxygen could be carried in 1 dm^3 of blood if we had no haemoglobin?

5 Use the dissociation curve in Figure 6.20 to answer these questions.
 a i The partial pressure of oxygen in the alveoli of the lungs is about 12 kPa. What is the percentage saturation of haemoglobin in the lungs?
   ii If 1 g of fully saturated haemoglobin is combined with 1.3 cm^3 of oxygen, how much oxygen will 1 g of haemoglobin in the capillaries in the lungs be combined with?
 b i The partial pressure of oxygen in an actively respiring muscle is about 2 kPa. What is the percentage saturation of haemoglobin in the capillaries in this muscle?
   ii How much oxygen will 1 g of haemoglobin in the capillaries of this muscle be combined with?

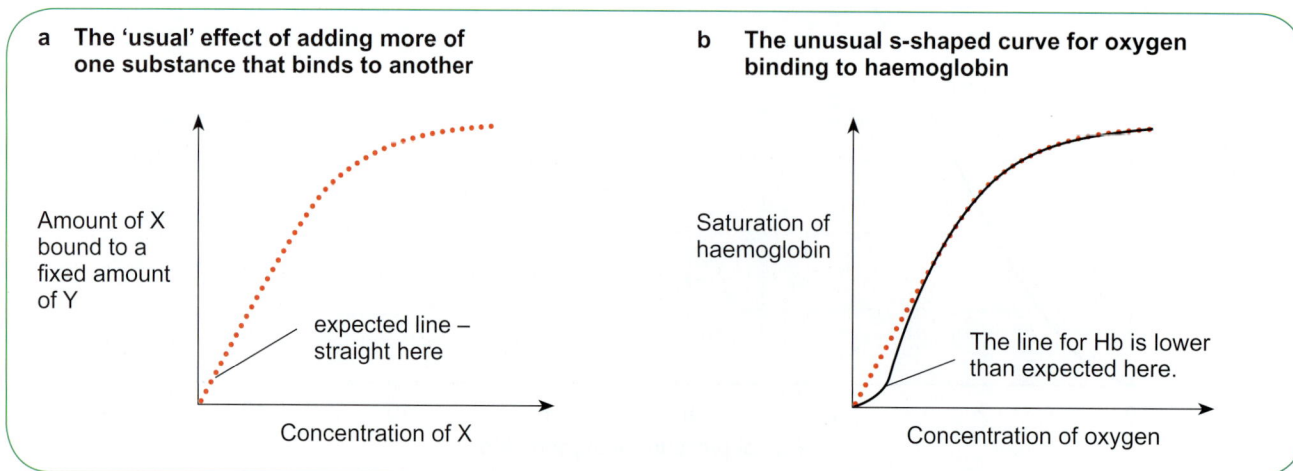

a The 'usual' effect of adding more of one substance that binds to another

Amount of X bound to a fixed amount of Y

expected line – straight here

Concentration of X

b The unusual s-shaped curve for oxygen binding to haemoglobin

Saturation of haemoglobin

The line for Hb is lower than expected here.

Concentration of oxygen

Figure 6.21   The s-shaped haemoglobin dissociation curve.

much easier for the next oxygens to bind with it. The dissociation curve is much steeper now (Figure 6.21b).

This ensures that Hb is very good at delivering large amounts of oxygen to the tissues if required. In the lungs, almost all of the Hb is fully saturated with oxygen – it is very good at combining with oxygen. Once it reaches a respiring muscle, where the oxygen concentration is much lower, the Hb readily releases most of its oxygen. It is just as

important for a respiratory pigment to release its oxygen as it is for it to bind with it. It is the unexpectedly low affinity for oxygen ('affinity' means the ease with which the Hb can pick up oxygen) in the low-oxygen conditions next to respiring tissues that causes saturated blood to release most of its oxygen. This effect allows about 15% more oxygen to be released than you would otherwise expect.

Blood doping

At the 1984 Olympic Games, held in Los Angeles, USA, American cyclists won medals for the first time in 72 years. More surprisingly, no fewer than four of them won medals. It emerged that they had used a technique called 'blood doping' to enhance their performance.

Over the next few years many athletes used blood doping. Several months before competition, $1\,dm^3$ of blood was taken from the athlete and then frozen. As the athlete continued in his or her training, their blood volume would gradually return to normal. Then, a few hours before the competition, the red cells were thawed and transfused back into their body.

Blood doping was done because it raised the quantity of haemoglobin in the athlete's blood. This meant that the blood could carry more oxygen, so the muscles were able to carry out aerobic respiration more quickly. This especially

helped athletes taking part in endurance sports, such as cycling and cross-country skiing.

By 1998, more sophisticated ways of achieving the same effect were being used. These involved a hormone called erythropoetin, or EPO for short. This hormone is produced by the kidneys and increases the rate of production of red blood cells. Some cyclists who took part in the Tour de France in 1998 had injected this hormone.

The use of blood doping is now officially banned. This is because it is seen as being unfair, and also because it can be very dangerous. Blood doping increases the risk of clots developing in blood vessels, and it is thought that several European cyclists died from this between 1987 and 1990. But still people continued to do it. In March 2002, at the Salt Lake City winter Olympics, a cleaner found discarded blood transfusion equipment at the house in which the Austrian skiing team had been staying. Investigations found that three of the skiers had received blood transfusions just before the competition.

Blood doping is very difficult to detect. However, tests are now available that can distinguish between the EPO that is naturally produced in the body and the EPO which can be bought and injected. Another test which is very useful is to measure the haemoglobin concentration in the blood. If this is well above normal, then blood doping is suspected.

Carbon dioxide transport

Carbon dioxide is constantly produced in respiring tissues, and is transported in the blood to the lungs, where it is excreted.

The carbon dioxide from the tissues diffuses into the blood plasma. Then, one of three things can happen to it (Figure 6.22).

● Some of it remains as carbon dioxide molecules, dissolved in the plasma. About 5% of the total carbon dioxide carried in the blood is in this form.

● Some of the carbon dioxide diffuses into the erythrocytes. In the cytoplasm of the erythrocytes, there is an enzyme called **carbonic anhydrase**. This enzyme catalyses the following reaction:

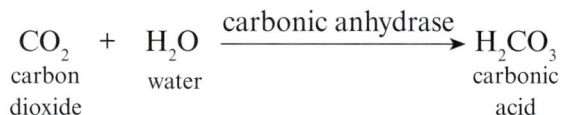

$$CO_2 + H_2O \xrightarrow{\text{carbonic anhydrase}} H_2CO_3$$

carbon dioxide   water   carbonic acid

The carbonic acid then dissociates (splits):

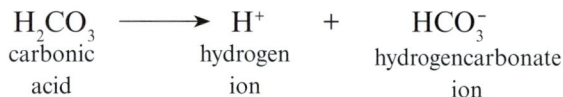

$$H_2CO_3 \longrightarrow H^+ + HCO_3^-$$

carbonic acid   hydrogen ion   hydrogencarbonate ion

The hydrogen ions quickly combine with the haemoglobin molecules inside the erythrocyte. This forms **haemoglobinic acid**, which makes the haemoglobin release the oxygen that it is carrying. The hydrogencarbonate ions diffuse out of the erythrocyte and into the blood plasma. They remain here in solution, and are carried to the lungs. About 85% of carbon dioxide is transported like this.

● Some of the carbon dioxide that diffuses into the erythrocytes escapes the attentions of carbonic anhydrase. Instead, it combines directly with haemoglobin, forming a compound called **carbaminohaemoglobin**. About 10% of the carbon dioxide is transported in this form.

When blood reaches the lungs, all of these reactions go into reverse. Carbon dioxide diffuses out of the blood and into the air in the alveoli. This leaves the haemoglobin molecules free to combine with oxygen, ready to begin another circuit of the body.

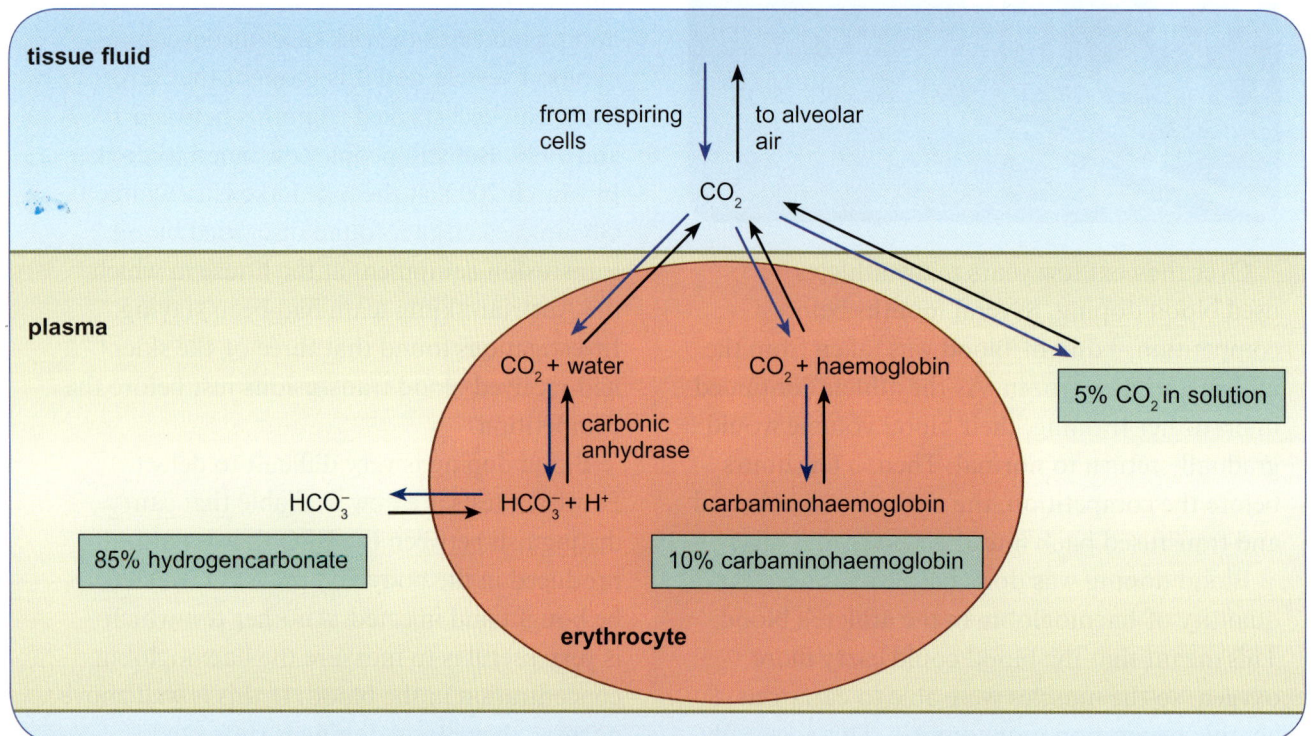

Figure 6.22 Carbon dioxide transport in the blood. The blood carries carbon dioxide partly as undissociated carbon dioxide in solution in the plasma, partly as hydrogencarbonate ions in solution in the plasma and partly combined with haemoglobin in the erythrocytes.

The Bohr shift

We have seen that, when there is a lot of carbon dioxide around, the high concentration of carbon dioxide causes events in the erythrocyte that make the haemoglobin release some of its oxygen. This is called the **Bohr effect**, after Christian Bohr who discovered it in 1904. It is exactly what the body needs. High concentrations of carbon dioxide are found in respiring tissues, which need oxygen. These high carbon dioxide concentrations cause

haemoglobin to release its oxygen even more readily than it would otherwise do.

If a dissociation curve is drawn for haemoglobin at high concentrations of carbon dioxide, the curve lies to the right of and below the 'standard' curve (Figure 6.23). We can say that a high carbon dioxide concentration lowers the affinity of haemoglobin for oxygen.

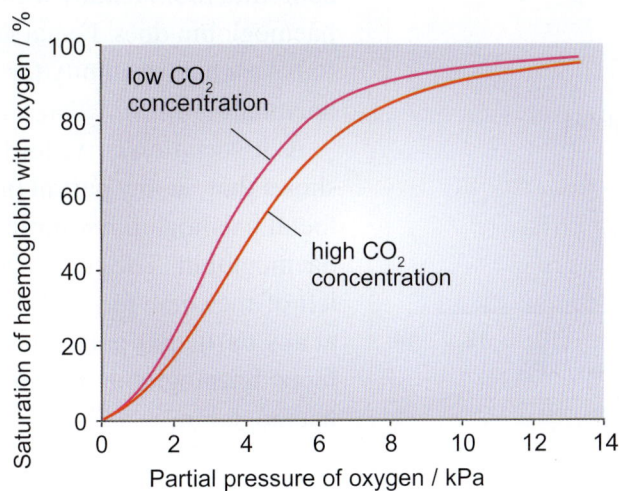

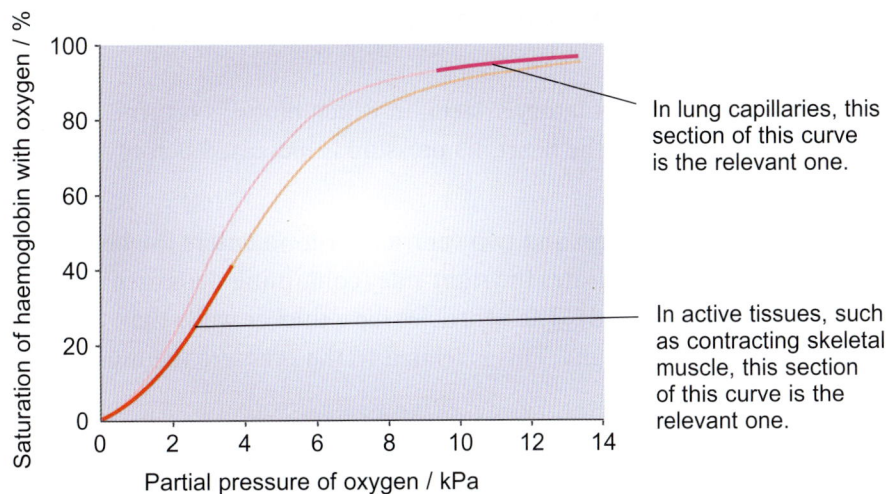

Figure 6.23 Dissociation curves for haemoglobin at two different concentrations of carbon dioxide; the shift of the curve to the right when the haemoglobin is exposed to higher carbon dioxide concentration is called the Bohr effect.

Foetal haemoglobin

A developing foetus obtains its oxygen not from its own lungs, but from its mother's blood. In the placenta, the mother's blood is brought very close to that of the foetus, allowing diffusion of various substances from the mother to the foetus and vice versa.

Oxygen arrives at the placenta in combination with haemoglobin, inside the mother's erythrocytes. The partial pressure of oxygen

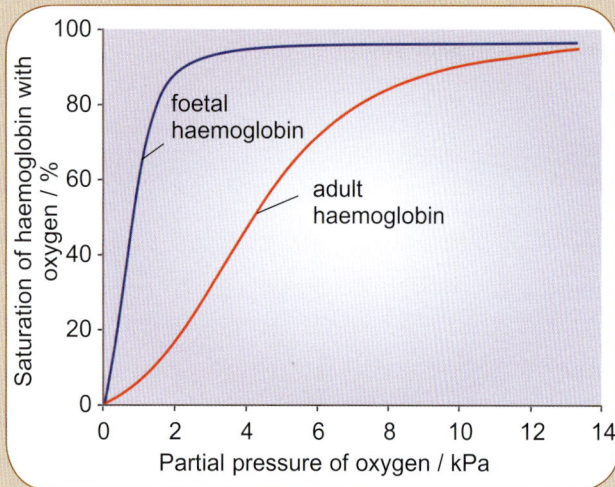

in the blood vessels in the placenta is relatively low, because the foetus is respiring. The mother's haemoglobin therefore releases some of its oxygen, which diffuses from her blood into the foetus's blood.

The partial pressure of oxygen in the foetus's blood is only a little lower than that in its mother's blood, which should mean that the diffusion of oxygen from mother to foetus is very slow. However, the haemoglobin of the foetus is not the same as its mother's. Foetal haemoglobin combines more readily with oxygen than adult haemoglobin does. Foetal haemoglobin is said to have a higher affinity for oxygen than adult haemoglobin.

A dissociation curve for foetal haemoglobin shows that, at any partial pressure of oxygen, foetal haemoglobin is more saturated than adult haemoglobin. The curve lies above and to the left of the curve for adult haemoglobin. So, at any particular partial pressure of oxygen, foetal haemoglobin will take oxygen from adult haemoglobin.

Summary

- Large, multicellular, active organisms need transport systems to deliver oxygen, glucose and other substances to cells, and to remove their waste products, because their surface area : volume ratio is too low for direct diffusion.

- Mammals have a double circulatory system, in which blood is returned to the heart after passing the gas exchange surface. In the heart, its pressure is increased before moving through the systemic system.

- The human heart has two atria and two ventricles. Blood enters the heart by the atria and leaves from the ventricles. A septum separates the right side (containing deoxygenated blood) from the left side (containing oxygenated blood). The ventricles have thicker walls than the atria, and the left ventricle has a thicker wall than the right. This is related to the pressure the muscles in the walls need to produce when they contract.

- Semilunar valves in the veins and in the entrances to the aorta and pulmonary artery, and atrio-ventricular valves, prevent backflow of blood.

continued ...

- The heart is made of cardiac muscle, which is myogenic. The sino-atrial node (SAN) sets the pace for the contraction of muscle in the heart. Excitation waves spread from the SAN across the atria, causing their walls to contract. The AVN slows down the spread to the ventricles. The Purkyne fibres conduct the wave to the base of the ventricles, so these contract after the atria and from the bottom up. One complete cycle of contraction and relaxation is called the cardiac cycle.

- Arteries have thicker, more elastic walls than veins, to allow them to withstand the high pressure of pulsing blood. Veins have thinner walls and valves, to aid the flow of blood at low pressure back to the heart. Capillaries have leaky walls, only one cell thick, which allow rapid transfer of substances between tissues and the blood.

- Erythrocytes carry oxygen in the form of oxyhaemoglobin. Haemoglobin combines with oxygen at high partial pressures of oxygen, and releases it when the partial pressure is low. When carbon dioxide is present, the affinity of haemoglobin for oxygen is lowered, and the dissociation curve lies to the right of and below the normal curve. This is called the Bohr shift.

- Carbon dioxide is carried in the blood as carbon dioxide molecules in solution in the plasma, as HCO_3^- ions in solution in the plasma, and as carbaminohaemoglobin in the erythrocytes. Carbonic anhydrase in the erythrocytes is responsible for the formation of the HCO_3^- ions.

Questions

Multiple choice questions

1   The diagrams below are photomicrographs of transverse sections of an artery and a vein from a sheep.

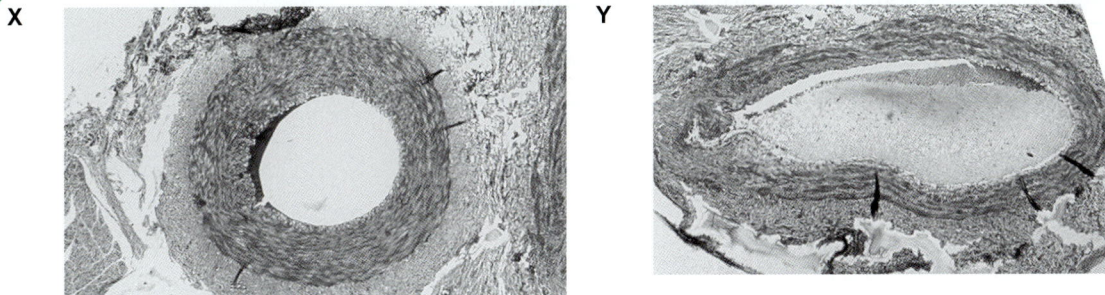

Which of the following correctly identifies the artery and vein?

	X	Y	Reason
A	artery	vein	the artery has thick walls and the vein has thin walls
B	artery	vein	the artery has a thin tunica intima while the vein has a thin tunica media
C	vein	artery	the artery has a thick tunica intima while the vein has a thick tunica media
D	vein	artery	the artery has thin walls and the vein has thick walls

continued ...

2 The diagram below shows the changes in blood pressure as blood flows through the blood vessels.

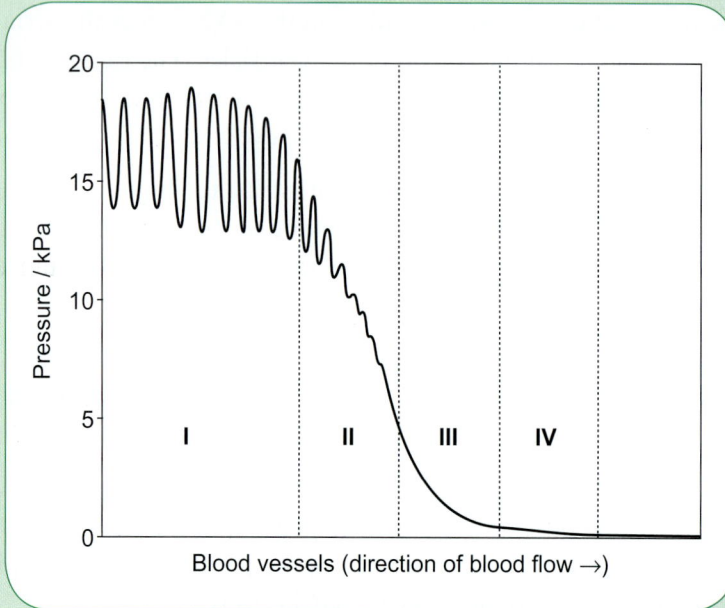

Blood vessels (direction of blood flow →)

Which of the following correctly identifies the vessels labelled **I** to **IV**?

	I	II	III	IV
A	artery	capillary	arteriole	venule
B	arteriole	large artery	venule	capillary
C	artery	arteriole	capillary	venule
D	venule	capillary	arteriole	artery

3 The diagram below shows the internal structure of the mammalian heart with its blood vessels.

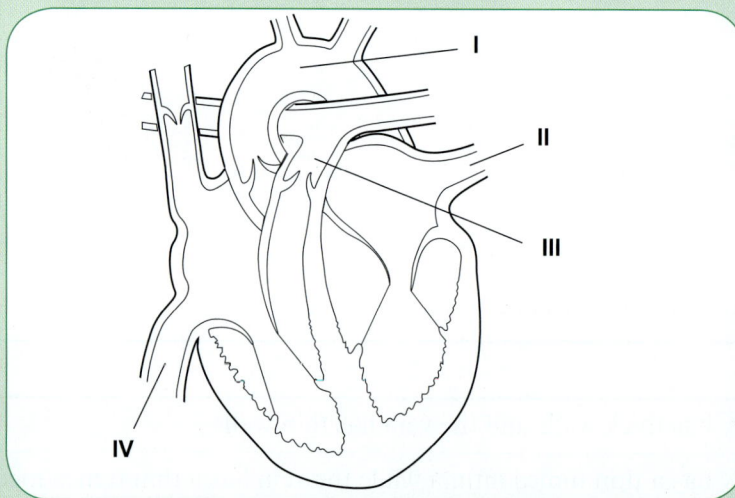

Which of the labelled structures takes oxygenated blood to parts of the body other than the lungs?

A I

B II

C III

D IV

continued …

4 Where is the mammalian heart beat initiated?
  A Purkyne fibres
  B papillary muscle
  C left atrium
  D sino-atrial node

5 Which chamber of the heart shows the greatest pressure changes during one cardiac cycle?
  A left atrium
  B right atrium
  C left ventricle
  D right ventricle

6 The graph below shows the effect of different concentrations of carbon dioxide on oxygen dissociation curves.

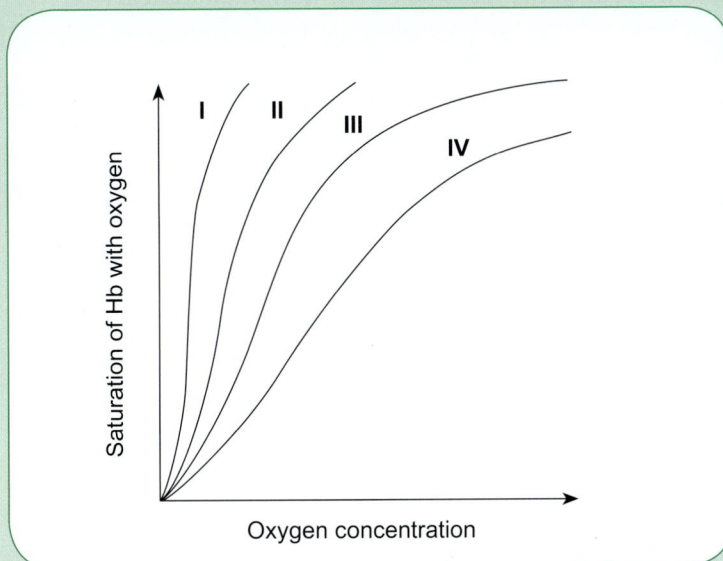

Which of the above curves would you expect to represent the behaviour of haemoglobin in the presence of the highest concentration of carbon dioxide?
  A I
  B II
  C III
  D IV

7 Carbon dioxide is **not** transported by the blood in the form of:
  A hydrogencarbonate ions.
  B carbonic acid.
  C carbaminohaemoglobin.
  D carboxyhaemoglobin.

8 What causes the first heart sound after ventricular systole?
  A closing of the semilunar valves
  B opening of the semilunar valves
  C closing of the atrio-ventricular valves
  D opening of the atrio-ventricular valves

continued…

9 What directly stimulates the sino-atrial node to increase the heart rate?

    A increase in temperature

    B release of adrenaline

    C high blood carbon dioxide concentration

    D high blood oxygen concentration

10 What causes the second heart sound after ventricular systole?

    A closing of the semilunar valves

    B opening of the semilunar valves

    C closing of the atrio-ventricular valves

    D opening of the atrio-ventricular valves

Structured questions

11 The diagram below shows changes that occur in the left side of the mammalian heart during the cardiac cycle.

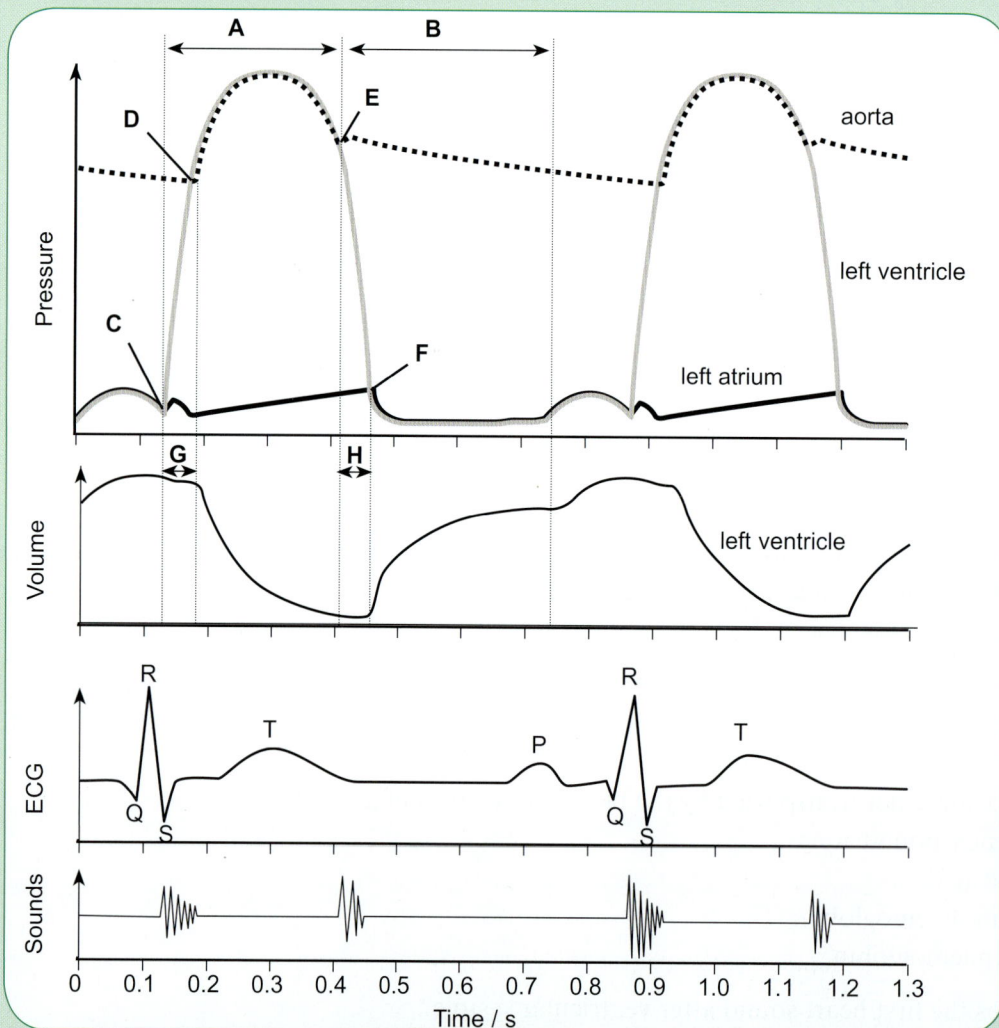

  a State the terms used for the period **A** and period **B**.   [2 marks]

  b Explain what happens at:

     i **C**   **ii** **D**   **iii** **E**   **iv** **F**   [8 marks]

continued …

c Suggest why there is very little change in the volume of the ventricle during the periods **G** and **H**, even though the pressure changes. [2 marks]

d Relate the activities shown in the electrocardiogram to the activity of the heart. [4 marks]

e Explain what causes the heart sounds. [2 marks]

f What causes the pressure of the left ventricle to increase during **G**? [2 marks]

12 The diagram below shows a section of the mammalian heart and its associated blood vessels as seen from the front.

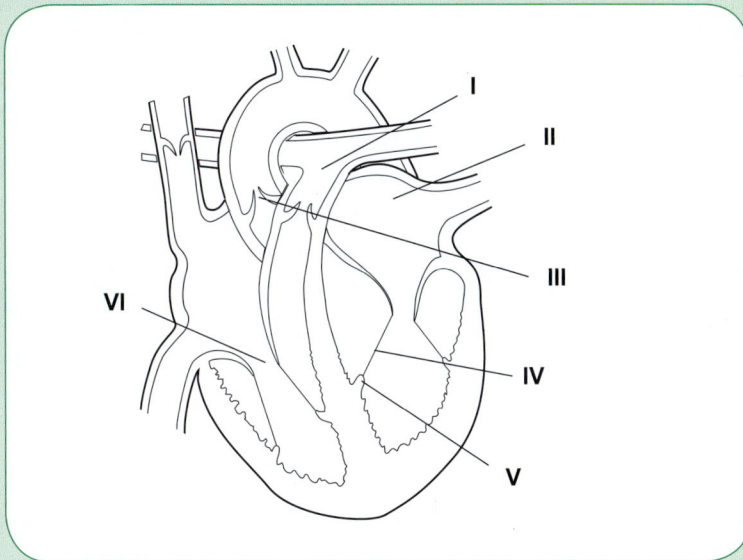

a Identify the structures labelled **I** to **VI**. [3 marks]

b Copy the diagram, and draw arrows to show the direction of blood flow through the left side of the heart. [1 mark]

c Explain the reasons for the relative thickness of the walls of the:
  i atria
  ii left ventricle
  iii right ventricle. [3 marks]

d Even though the thickness of the walls of the left and right ventricles differ, they both pump the same volume of blood with each heart beat. Suggest a reason for this observation. [1 mark]

e Explain how the structures labelled **III** and **IV** help to maintain the flow of blood in one direction through the heart. [2 marks]

f On your diagram, label the location of the
  i sino-atrial node (SAN)
  ii atrio-ventricular node (AVN)
  iii Purkyne fibres / bundle of His. [3 marks]

g Describe the role of the sino-atrial node (SAN) in the maintenance of the heart beat. [2 marks]

continued ...

13 The graph below shows the oxygen dissociation curve for haemoglobin in a mammal.

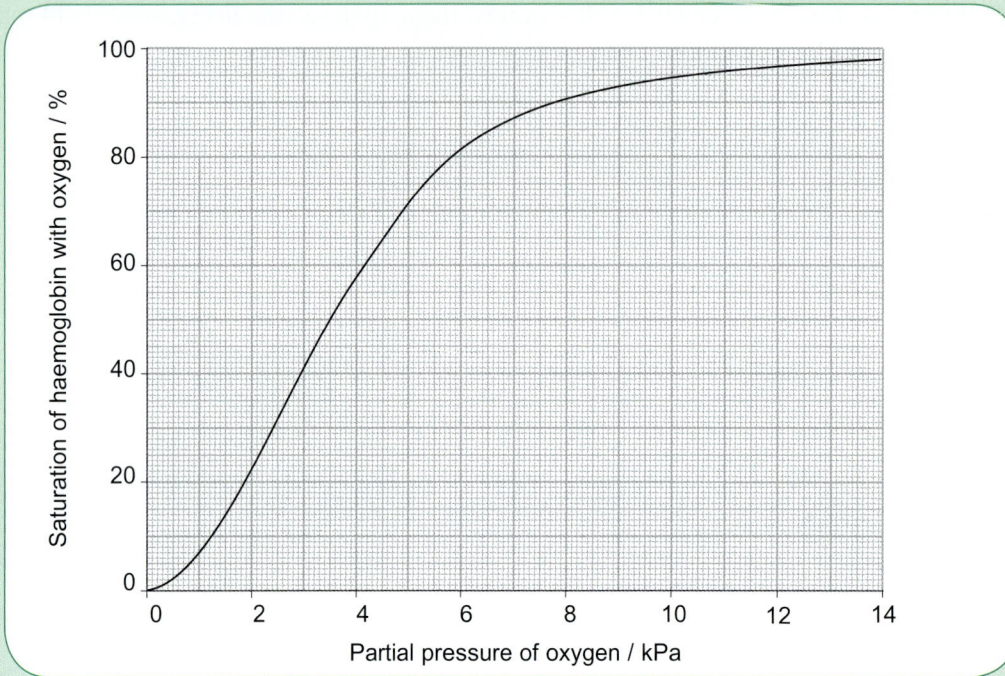

a Why is the oxygen dissociation curve for haemoglobin s-shaped? [2 marks]

b Using the graph, state the partial pressure of oxygen:
   i in the capillaries in the lung if 98% of the haemoglobin is saturated
   ii in capillaries in muscle tissues during vigorous exercise if 20% of the haemoglobin is saturated. [2 marks]

c Oxygen is transported in haemoglobin in red blood cells. Give **two** adaptations of red blood cells and haemoglobin for their function in oxygen transport. [4 marks]

d The oxygen dissociation curve is affected by many factors.
   i Copy the graph above. Draw another curve on your graph to show the curve that you would expect during vigorous exercise. [1 mark]
   ii What is the name of the effect illustrated in **d i**? [1 mark]
   iii Explain the physiological significance of the effect named in **d ii**. [1 mark]

e Haemoglobin acts as a buffer in the blood and this promotes unloading of oxygen. Explain this statement. [4 marks]

continued ...

Essay questions

14 a Veins return blood to the heart. Describe the structure of veins and explain how their structure is adapted to their function. [5 marks]

   b Arteries take blood away from the ventricles. Describe how the structure of an artery is related to its function. [5 marks]

   c Capillaries are adapted for the exchange of materials between blood and tissues. Describe and explain how the structure of capillaries is adapted to their function. [5 marks]

15 a Describe the role of the following structures during the cardiac cycle:
     i sino-atrial node (SAN)
     ii atrio-ventricular node (AVN)
     iii bundle of His / Purkyne fibres
     iv papillary muscle [8 marks]

   b Describe what happens during:
     i atrial diastole
     ii ventricular systole. [4 marks]

   c Explain the internal factors that control heart beat. [3 marks]

16 a i Define the terms 'blood pressure' and 'pulse rate'. [2 marks]
     ii Explain why the pulse rate and heart rate are the same. [3 marks]

   b Discuss **five** factors which affect blood pressure. [5 marks]

   c When one exercises, the heart rate increases. Explain what causes the increase in heart rate. [5 marks]

Chapter 7
Homeostasis and hormonal action

By the end of this chapter you should be able to:

a discuss the concept of homeostasis, including the roles of receptors, effectors, set point, feedback and homeostatic equilibrium;

b outline the general principles of hormonal action in animals, including the roles of ductless glands, target cells and receptors;

c explain how insulin and glucagon regulate blood glucose concentration;

d explain the effect of the plant regulatory molecule, ethylene (ethene), on fruit ripening and respiration;

e discuss the commercial use made of ethylene in supplying market-ready fruit.

Coordinating cell activities

Most animals and plants are complex organisms, made up of many millions of cells. They are said to be **multicellular**. Different parts of the organism perform different functions. It is important that information can pass between these different parts, so that their activities are coordinated.

Sometimes, the purpose of this information transfer is to regulate the levels of some substance within the organism, such as the control of blood glucose concentration in mammals. Or it may be to change the activity of some part of the organism in response to a stimulus, such as salivating when you smell good food cooking, or moving away from someone you do not want to talk to.

In both plants and animals, chemicals called **hormones** (in plants they are sometimes known as **plant growth regulators**) help to transfer information from one part to another. In many animals, including mammals, **nerves** transfer information in the form of electrical impulses. Both of these methods, hormonal and nervous, involve information from one cell being passed on to another, a process called **cell signalling**. We will look in detail at how cell signalling occurs in the hormonal (endocrine) system in this chapter, and how it occurs in the nervous system in Chapter 9.

Homeostasis

One of the most crucial functions of the nervous and hormonal systems in mammals is to control internal conditions, maintaining a stable internal environment. This is called **homeostasis**.

'Internal environment' means the conditions inside the body, in which cells function. For a cell, its immediate environment is the tissue fluid that surrounds it. Many features of this environment affect the activities of the cell. They include:

- **temperature** – low temperatures slow down metabolic reactions; high temperatures can cause proteins to denature, causing damage to enzymes and to cell membranes;

- **amount of water** – lack of water in the tissue fluid causes water to move out of cells by osmosis, which can cause metabolic reactions in the cells to slow down or even stop; too much water in the tissue fluid causes water to move into cells by osmosis, which can cause the cell to swell and burst;

- **concentration of glucose** – glucose is the fuel for respiration in many cells, so a lack of it causes respiration to slow down or halt, as the cells now have no energy source; too much glucose in the tissue fluid can cause water to move out of cells by osmosis, having the same effect as described above.

The principles of homeostasis

It is easiest to understand how homeostasis works by thinking about one particular example. In humans, as in most animals, carbohydrate is transported in the body in the form of the monosaccharide, glucose. The concentration of glucose in the blood is normally kept at about 80 to 100 mg of glucose per 100 cm³ of blood. This can be thought of as the **set point** – the ideal value for blood glucose concentration.

The control of blood glucose concentration involves a mechanism called **negative feedback**. The general principles of negative feedback are shown in Figure 7.1.

A negative feedback system requires a **receptor** (**detector**) and an **effector** and an efficient means of communication between them. The receptor monitors the factor that is being controlled – in this case, the concentration of glucose in the blood. The value of this factor is compared to the set point by a **regulator**. If it is not sufficiently close to the set point, the regulator communicates with the effector. The effector then causes an action that brings the factor back towards normal.

In the control of blood glucose concentration, the communication between regulator and effector involves hormones, but there are other examples of homeostasis (for example, the control of body temperature) that also involve the nervous system. In general, the nervous system brings about rapid, short-term changes, whereas hormones act more slowly but have longer-term effects.

Because there is inevitably a short time delay between a change in the factor, its detection by the receptor, communication with the effector and the action of the effector, the control does not happen instantly. This results in an oscillation around a set value, rather than an absolutely unchanging one. Negative feedback is a dynamic mechanism, in which there are constant small changes, rather than an absolutely steady maintenance of a fixed value.

The mammalian endocrine system

The mammalian **endocrine system** is made up of **endocrine glands**, which secrete chemicals called **hormones**. The hormones travel in blood plasma from the gland where they are made, all over the body. The tissues that they affect are called their **target tissues**.

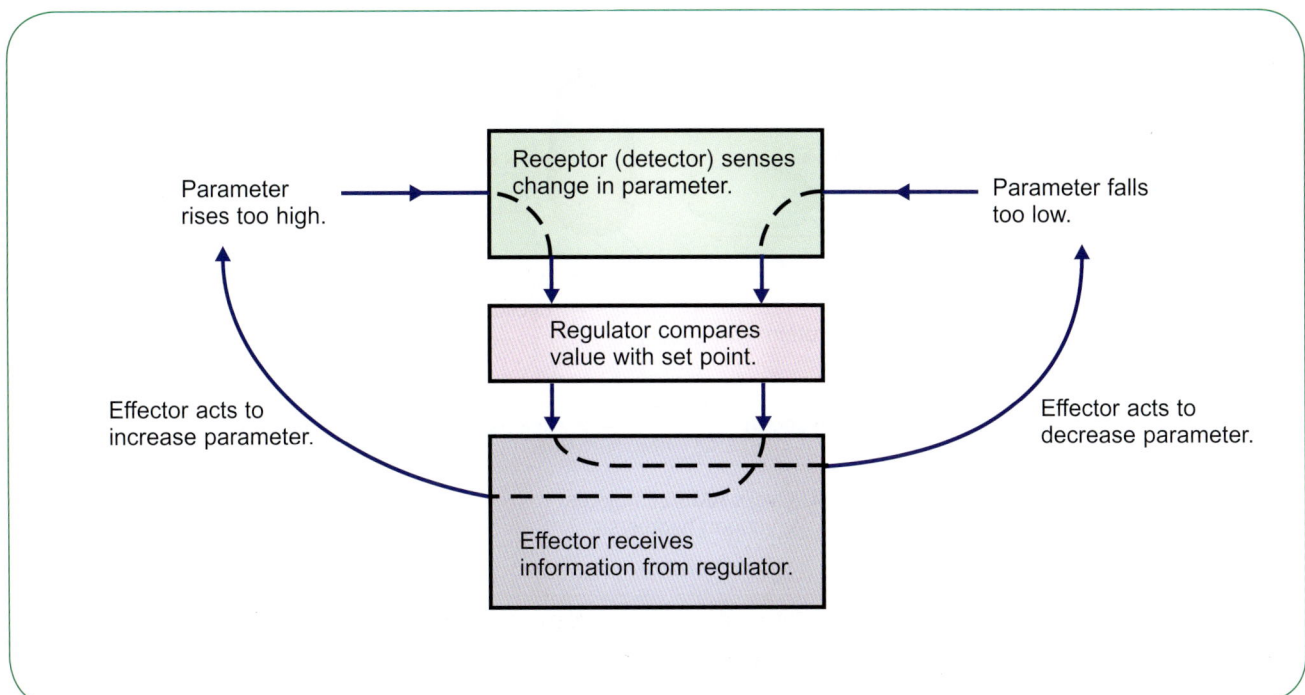

Figure 7.1   Negative feedback.

How adrenaline works using first and second messengers

Hormones affect their target cells by attaching to a specific receptor molecule, which sets into action a series of events within the cell. This is an example of cell signalling. We will look in particular at how adrenaline (sometimes known as epinephrine) affects the activity of liver cells.

Adrenaline is secreted by the adrenal glands – which lie just above the kidneys – in response to excitement, danger or stress. It has a number of target organs and tissues, including the sino-atrial node in the heart, smooth muscle in the wall of the alimentary canal and the muscles in the iris of the eye. Adrenaline brings about changes that prepare the body for vigorous activity, such as might be needed if escaping from danger or fighting against it.

Adrenaline is a catecholamine, synthesised from amino acids and not soluble in lipids. Its target cells – for example, liver cells – therefore have receptors in their plasma membranes, into which adrenaline slots. The binding of adrenaline with its receptor alters the shape of the receptor, causing it to interact with another protein in the membrane called a G-protein. This causes the G-protein to split, and one part of it combines with an inactive enzyme called adenylyl cyclase. This activates the enzyme, which converts ATP to cyclic AMP (cAMP for short).

Now the cAMP binds to another inactive protein, this time an enzyme called protein kinase. Once again, the binding changes the

Outside the liver cell

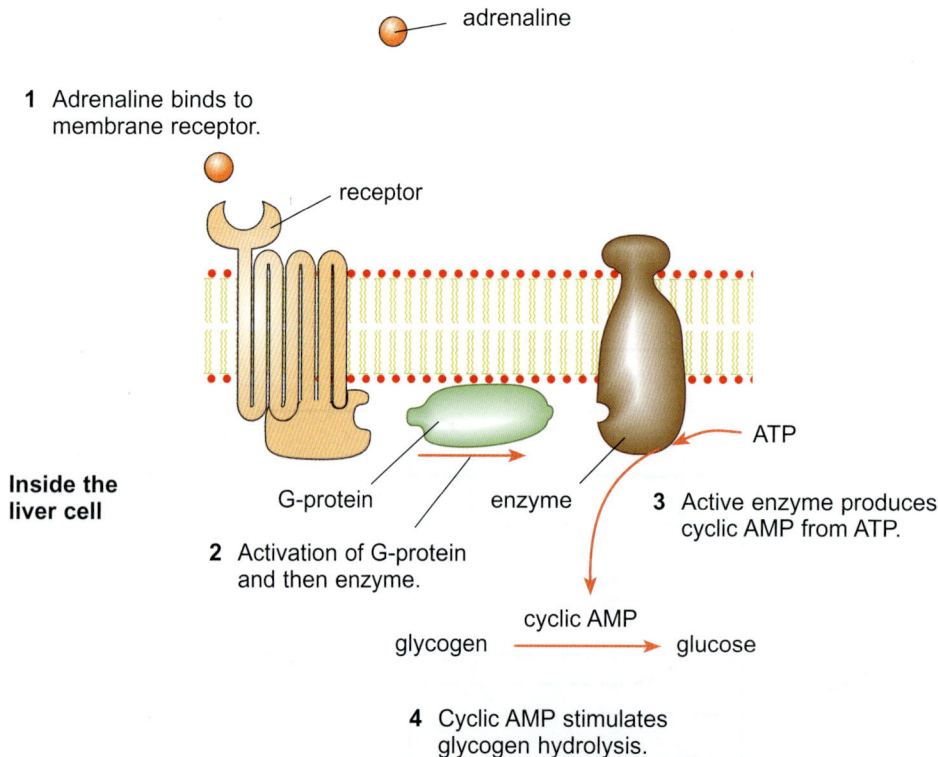

adrenaline

1 Adrenaline binds to membrane receptor.

receptor

Inside the liver cell

G-protein

enzyme

ATP

3 Active enzyme produces cyclic AMP from ATP.

2 Activation of G-protein and then enzyme.

cyclic AMP

glycogen ⟶ glucose

4 Cyclic AMP stimulates glycogen hydrolysis.

continued …

shape of the enzyme, which activates it. The activated protein kinase in turn activates yet another enzyme, this time glycogen phosphorylase kinase, and this then binds to an enzyme called glycogen phosphorylase. Finally, glycogen phosphorylase catalyses the breakdown of glycogen in the liver cell, converting it to glucose.

The secretion of adrenaline has therefore brought about the production of glucose in liver cells, which can be transported in the blood to muscles so that they can respire quickly and generate ATP needed for contraction – to flee or fight the perceived danger. In this response, the adrenaline is known as a **first messenger** and the cAMP is a **second messenger**.

Adrenaline has different effects on other target cells, because the enzymes that are activated by cAMP are not the same in different kinds of cells. For example, it increases the rate of firing of the cells in the sino-atrial node, increasing heart rate. It causes contraction of smooth muscles in arterioles supplying blood to the alimentary canal, reducing the volume of blood flowing through them so that more blood can be diverted to the muscles.

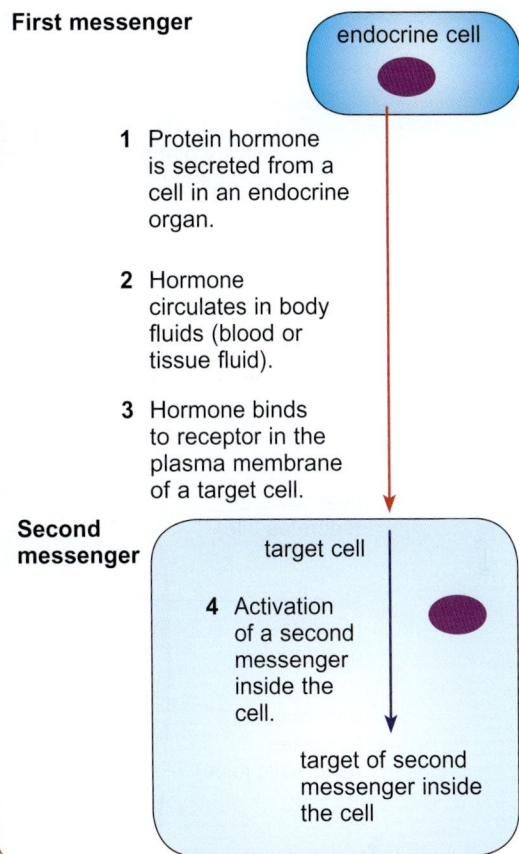

First messenger

endocrine cell

1 Protein hormone is secreted from a cell in an endocrine organ.

2 Hormone circulates in body fluids (blood or tissue fluid).

3 Hormone binds to receptor in the plasma membrane of a target cell.

Second messenger

target cell

4 Activation of a second messenger inside the cell.

target of second messenger inside the cell

A **gland** is a group of cells that produces and releases one or more useful substances, a process known as **secretion**. Endocrine glands contain secretory cells that pass their secretions directly into the blood (Figure 7.2). 'Endocrine' means 'secreting to the inside', a reference to the fact that endocrine glands secrete hormones into blood capillaries inside the gland.

We also have glands of another type, called **exocrine glands**. These secrete substances into a duct, which carries them to a particular part of the body. 'Exocrine' means 'secreting to the outside'. There are many different exocrine glands in the body. One example is the salivary glands – these secrete saliva into salivary ducts that carry it into the mouth.

Mammalian hormones

Mammalian hormones are usually relatively small molecules. Many, such as **insulin**, are polypeptides or proteins. Others, such as testosterone, are steroids. Adrenaline, the 'fight or flight' hormone that is secreted when you are frightened, is a catecholamine, produced from amino acids.

After they have been secreted from an endocrine gland, hormones are transported around the body in the blood plasma. The concentrations of hormones in human blood are very small. For any one hormone, the concentration is rarely more than a few micrograms per cm^3 of blood. Their rate of secretion from endocrine glands is also low, usually of the order of a few micrograms or milligrams a day. These small quantities of hormone can, however, have very large effects on the body.

143

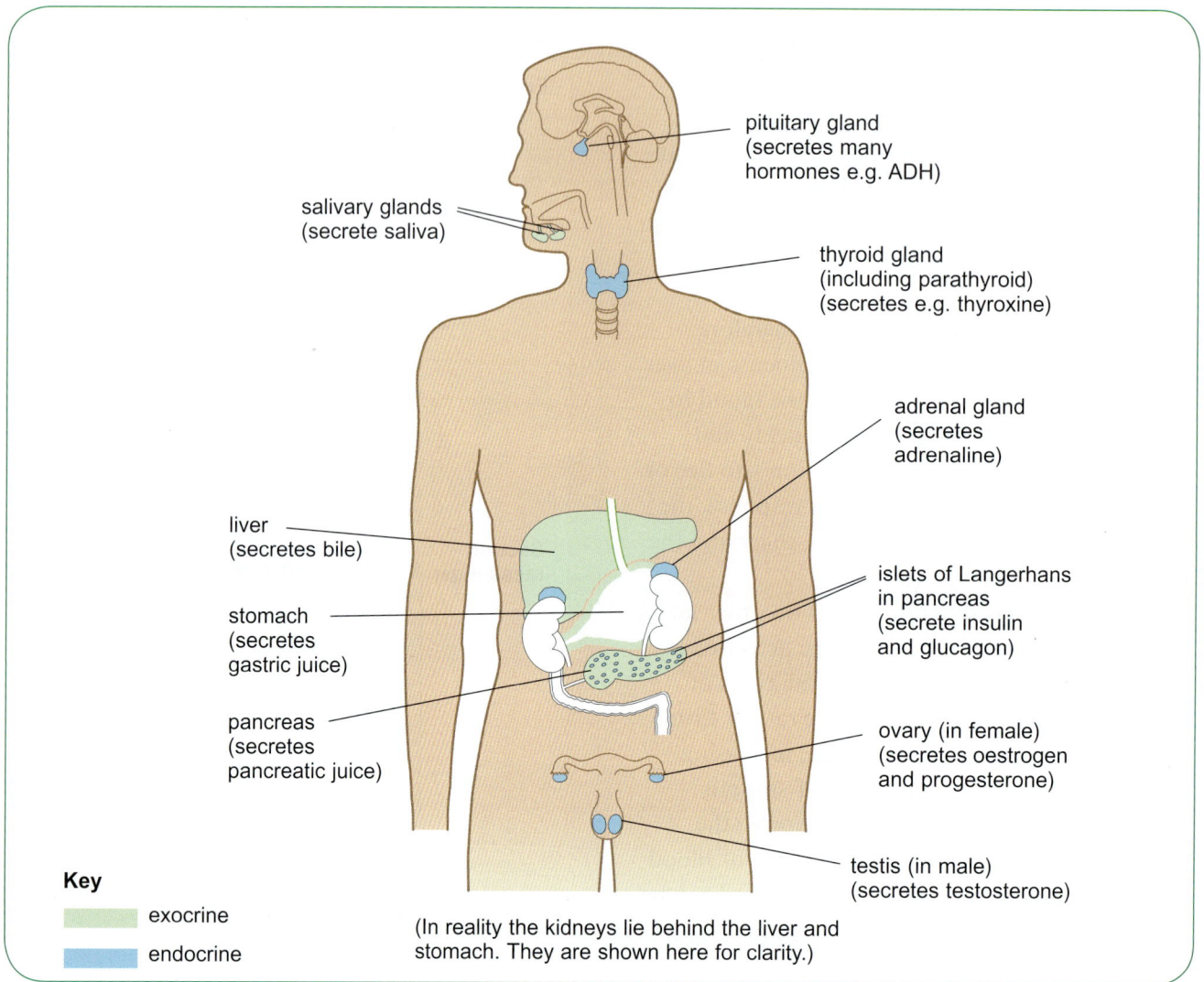

Figure 7.2 The positions of some exocrine and endocrine glands in the human body.

Most endocrine glands can secrete hormones very quickly when an appropriate stimulus arrives. In particular, adrenaline is secreted from the adrenal glands within less than one second of the arrival of a stimulus that elicits fear or excitement.

Many hormones have a very short life in the body. They are broken down by enzymes in the blood or in cells – often in the liver – or are lost in the urine. Insulin, for example, lasts for only around 10 to 15 minutes. Adrenaline lasts for between 1 to 3 minutes.

Although the blood carries hormones to all parts of the body, they only affect their particular target cells. These cells contain receptors for the hormone. The receptors for protein hormones, such as insulin, are in the plasma (cell surface) membrane. The hormones bind with the receptor on the outer surface of the membrane, and bring about a response without actually entering the cell. Steroid hormones, however, are lipid-soluble and they diffuse through the plasma membrane into the cytoplasm. The receptors for steroid hormones are in the cell cytoplasm.

SAQ

1 Explain why steroid hormones can pass easily through the plasma membrane while protein hormones cannot.

The pancreas

Figure 7.3 and Figure 7.4 show the structure of the pancreas.

The pancreas is a very unusual gland, because parts of it function as an exocrine gland, while other parts function as an endocrine gland.

The exocrine function is the secretion of **pancreatic juice**, which flows along the pancreatic duct into the duodenum in the small intestine.

Pancreatic juice contains several enzymes involved in digestion, including:

- lipase, which catalyses the hydrolysis of lipids to fatty acids and glycerol;
- amylase, which catalyses the hydrolysis of starch to maltose;
- trypsin, which catalyses the hydrolysis of proteins to polypeptides.

The endocrine function of the pancreas is the secretion of the hormones **insulin** and **glucagon**, by the cells in the **islets of Langerhans**. **Alpha cells** secrete glucagon, and **beta cells** secrete insulin (Figure 7.5). The islets are well supplied with blood capillaries, and they secrete their hormones directly into the blood.

The control of blood glucose by insulin and glucagon

Carbohydrate is transported through the human bloodstream in the form of glucose, in solution in the blood plasma. For storage, glucose can be

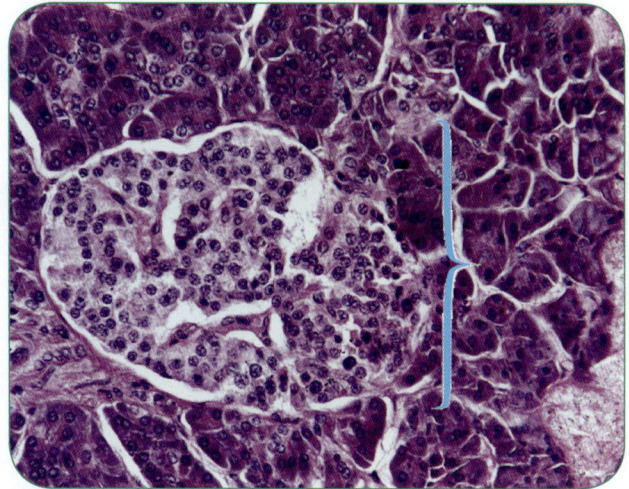

Figure 7.4 The group of cells in the centre of this photomicrograph form an islet of Langerhans (bracketed). The islet is surrounded by cells that secrete pancreatic juice, which does not enter the blood but is collected into branches of the pancreatic duct (× 410).

converted to the polysaccharide **glycogen**, a large, insoluble molecule made up of many glucose units linked together by α1–4 glycosidic bonds with β1–6 branches. Glycogen can be stored inside liver cells and muscle cells.

In a healthy person, each $100\,cm^3$ of blood normally contains between 80 and 120 mg of glucose. If blood glucose concentration drops much below this, then cells may run short of glucose for respiration, and be unable to carry

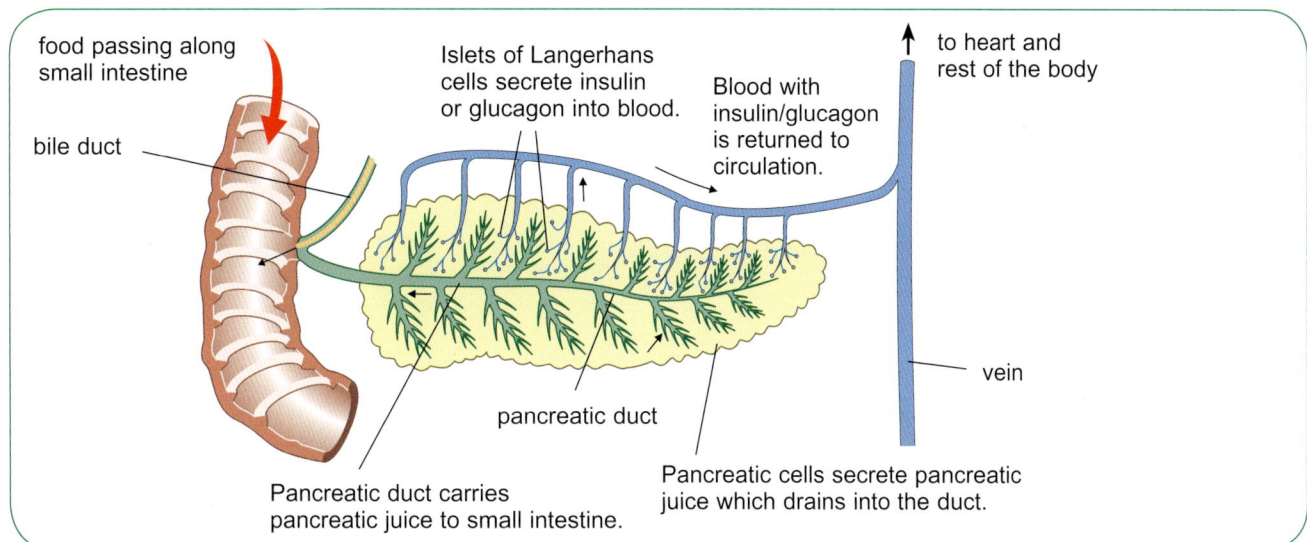

Figure 7.3 The position of the pancreas and its associated organs.

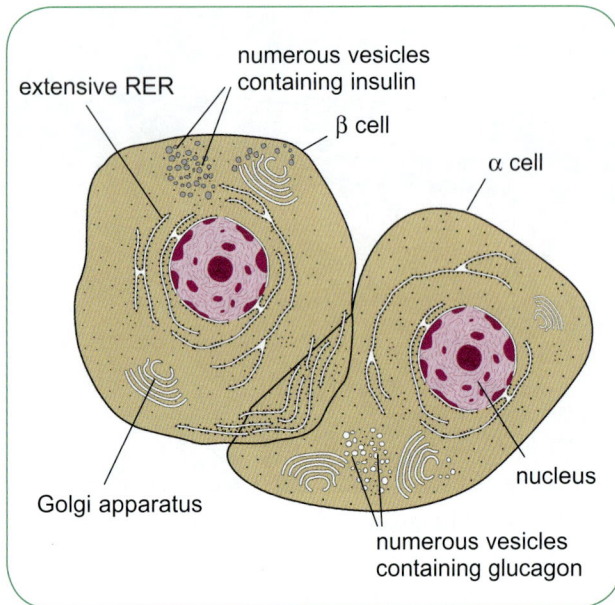

Figure 7.5 These diagrams are based on electron micrographs of alpha cells and beta cells. They look very similar, and it is difficult to tell them apart, but the insulin in beta cells tends to form dark, crystalline deposits that are easier to make out than the glucagon in the alpha cells.

out their normal activities. This is especially important for any cells that can use only glucose for respiration, including brain cells. Very high blood glucose concentrations can also cause severe problems, as the water potential of the blood becomes lower than that inside body cells, which therefore lose water to the blood by osmosis.

After a meal containing carbohydrate, glucose from the digested food is absorbed from the small intestine and passes into the blood. As this blood flows through the pancreas, the alpha and beta cells in the islets of Langerhans detect the raised glucose levels. Alpha cells respond by stopping secretion of glucagon, while beta cells respond by secreting more insulin into the blood plasma. The insulin is carried to all parts of the body.

Insulin affects many cells, especially those in the liver and muscles. The effects on these cells include:

● an increased ability of muscle cells and adipose tissue to absorb glucose from the blood. Glucose can only enter cells through transporter proteins. Muscle cells have glucose transporters called GLUT4, and these are normally kept in the cytoplasm rather than in the plasma membrane (Figure 7.6). When insulin is

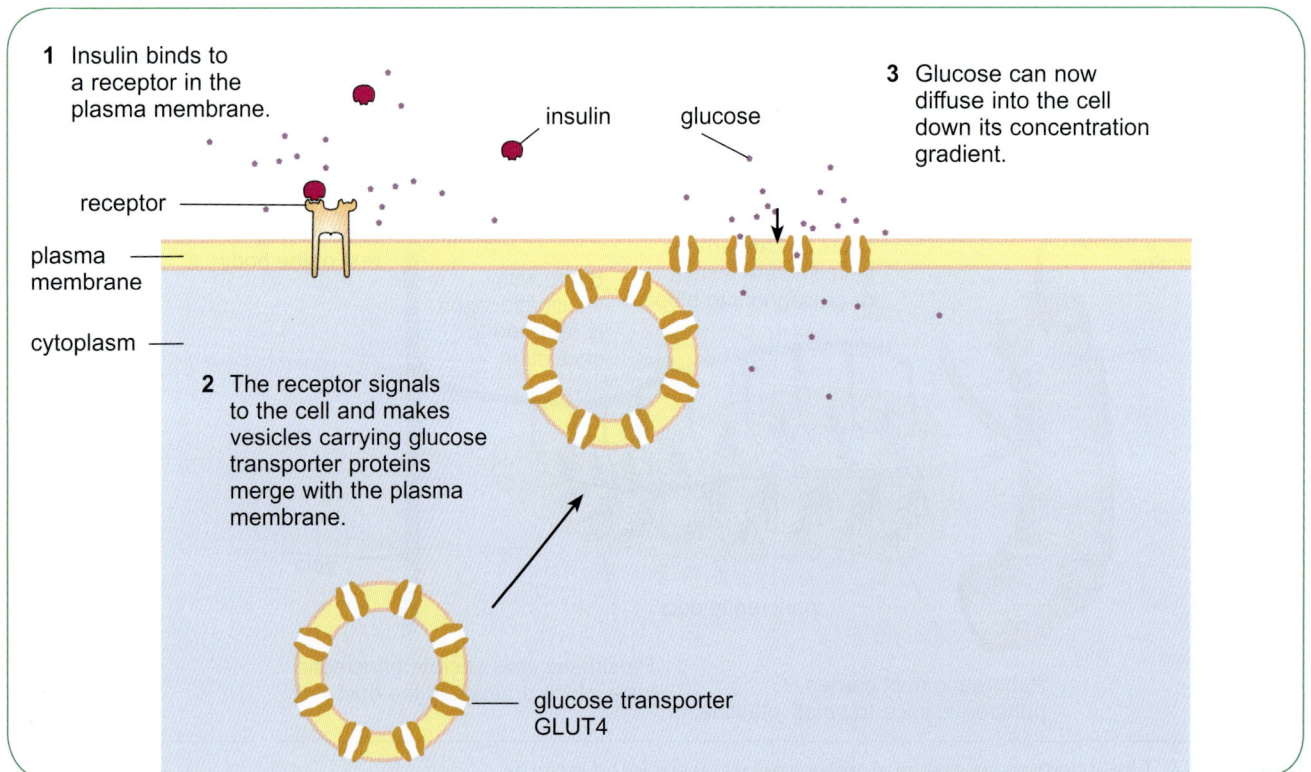

Figure 7.6 How insulin increases membrane permeability to glucose.

detected by a muscle cell, the transporters are moved into the plasma membrane of the cell, where they form channels allowing glucose to enter. (Liver cells and brain cells have a different kind of glucose transporter, which is always present in the plasma membrane and is not affected by insulin, so they are always able to take up glucose.)

- an increase in the rate of production of glycogen from glucose inside liver cells. The arrival of insulin molecules at the receptors on the plasma membranes of liver cells causes the activation of the enzyme **glucokinase**, which phosphorylates glucose. This traps the glucose within the cell, because phosphorylated glucose cannot pass through the transporters in the plasma membrane. The arrival of insulin also brings about the activation of two other enzymes (phosphofructokinase and glycogen synthase), which together cause the glucose molecules to form α1–4 glycosidic

bonds between each other, producing glycogen molecules.

Both of these effects cause the concentration of glucose in the blood to fall. This is sensed by the beta cells in the pancreas, and they reduce their secretion of insulin. You will recognise that this is a negative feedback mechanism (Figure 7.7).

The fall in blood glucose is also detected by the alpha cells in the pancreas, and these respond by secreting more glucagon. Glucagon has several effects, including:

- an increase in the rate of breakdown of glycogen in liver cells. Glucagon binds with receptors in the liver cell plasma membranes, which causes the activation of enzymes within the cell that catalyse the hydrolysis of glycogen to glucose (Figure 7.8). The glucose can then move out of the liver cell through glucose channels, by facilitated diffusion.
- an increase in the production of glucose from other substances in liver cells. This is called

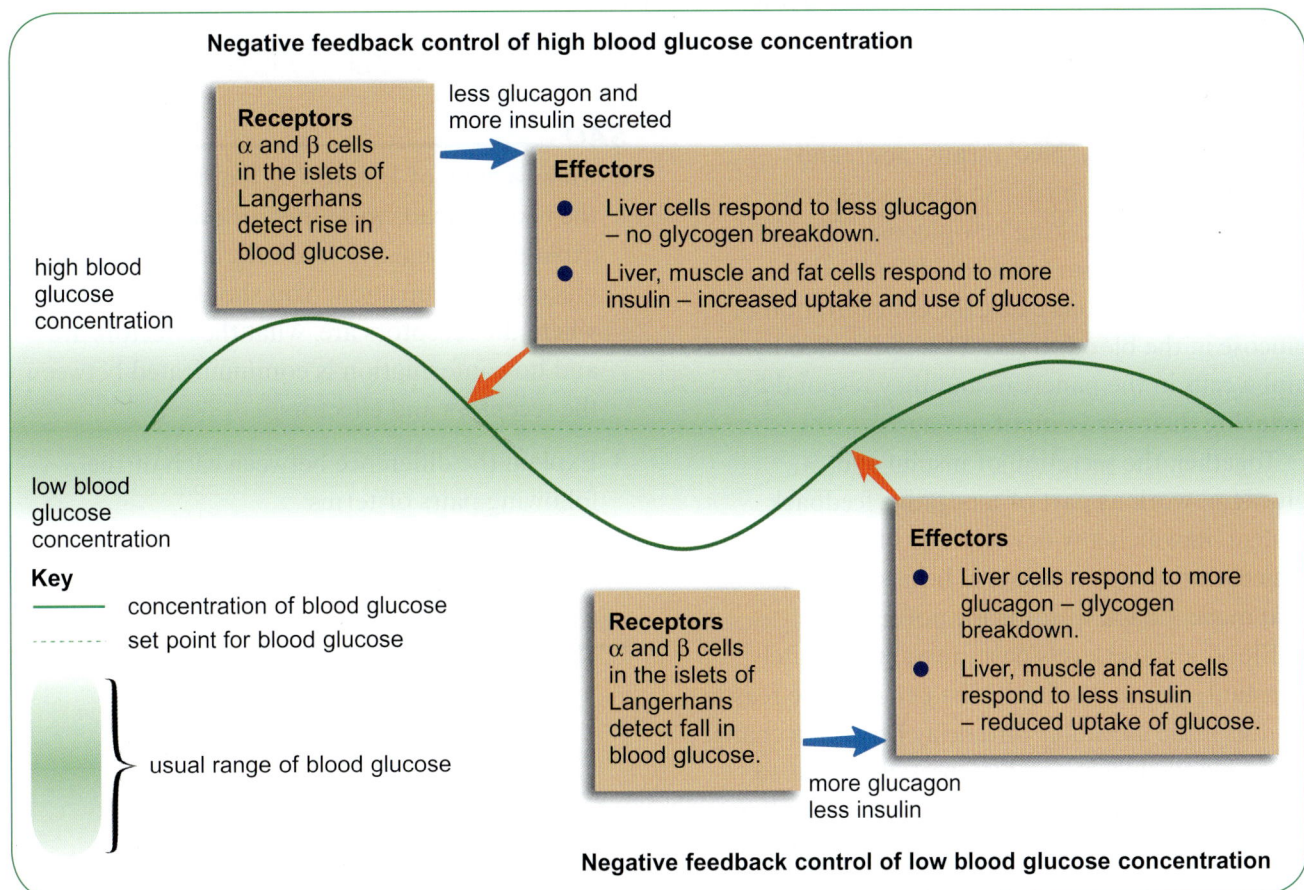

Figure 7.7 The negative feedback control mechanism for blood glucose concentration. In this system, the α and β cells act as both receptors (detectors) and regulators.

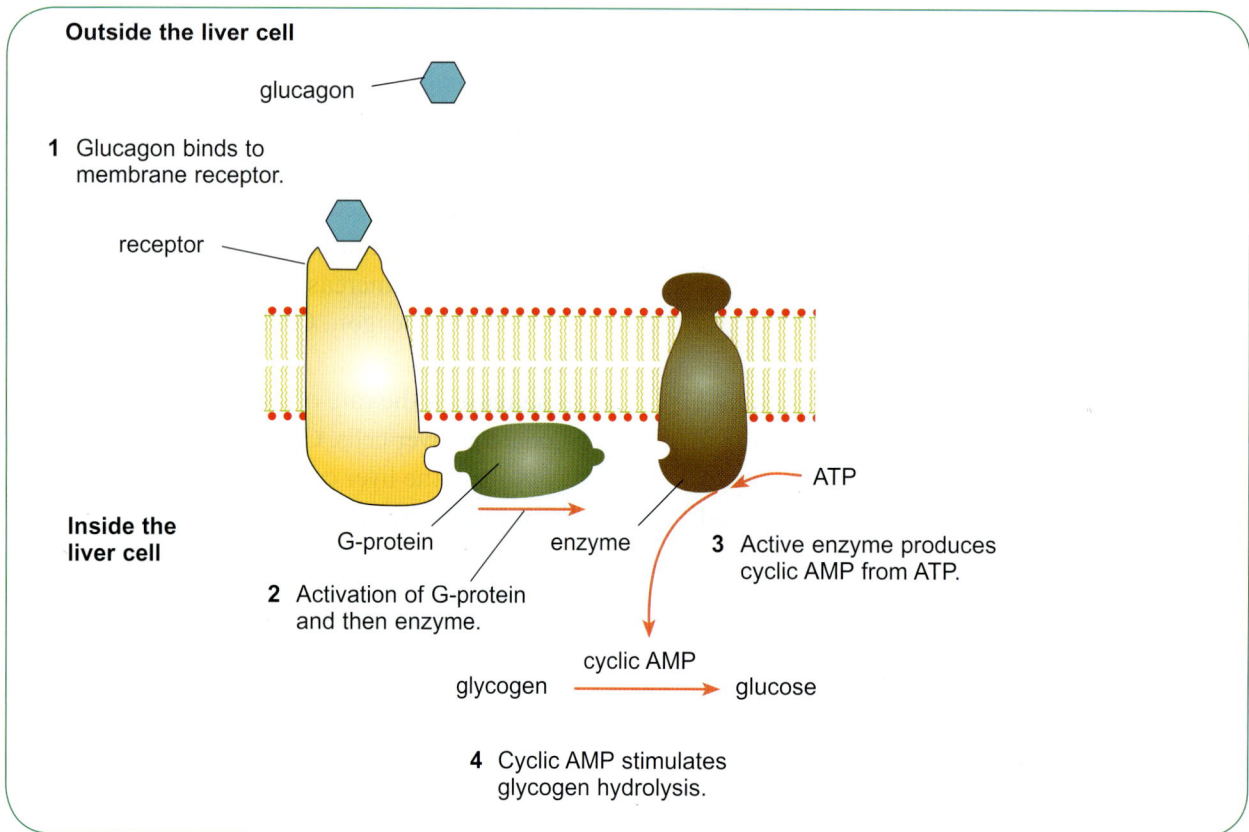

Figure 7.8 How glucagon works.

gluconeogenesis. 'Neo' means 'new', and 'genesis' means 'birth', so gluconeogenesis simply means making new glucose. The glucose can be made from amino acids or lipids. Both of these actions cause the concentration of glucose in the blood to rise. This is detected by the alpha cells in the pancreas, and they respond by reducing their secretion of glucagon.

Together, the secretion of insulin and glucagon work as part of a negative feedback system, in which any deviation of blood glucose concentration from the norm brings about actions that move it back towards the norm.

Blood glucose levels never remain absolutely constant, even in the healthiest person. One reason for this is the inevitable time delay between a change in the blood glucose and the onset of actions to correct it. Time delays in control systems result in oscillations, where things do not stay absolutely constant but sometimes rise slightly above and sometimes drop slightly below the set point.

SAQ

2 Make a copy of Figure 7.1, but do not include the text. Instead, write in your own text to explain how negative feedback controls blood glucose concentration. You should make clear where the receptors are, what the effectors are and how information is communicated between the receptors and effectors.

3 Explain the difference between each of the following pairs of terms.
 a endocrine gland and exocrine gland
 b glycogen and glucagon
 c glycolysis and gluconeogenesis

Control of insulin secretion

We have seen that the beta cells in the islets of Langerhans release insulin in response to raised blood glucose levels. How do they sense this, and how is the amount of insulin that is released controlled?

We still do not fully understand how insulin secretion is controlled. It is a complex process, and research continues to discover new factors that influence it. The description that follows is only a part of a more complex complete picture.

The beta cells contain several types of channels in their plasma membranes, each of which allows a particular type of ion to pass through. These include potassium ion, K⁺, channels and calcium ion, Ca²⁺, channels.

Normally, the K⁺ channels are open, allowing K⁺ ions to pass through the membranes freely. They diffuse from inside the cell to the outside. This helps to maintain a slight positive charge on the outside of the membrane with respect to the inside.

When glucose levels around the beta cell are raised, more glucose than usual passes into the cell through glucose transporter proteins. As the glucose enters the cell, it is phosphorylated by the enzyme glucokinase. The phosphorylated glucose is then metabolised to form ATP.

The K⁺ channels are sensitive to the amount of ATP in the cell, and they respond to this increase by closing. So now the K⁺ ions cannot diffuse out. As a result, the difference in electrical potential between the outside and inside of the membrane becomes less.

Now the Ca²⁺ channels come into the picture. They normally remain closed, but the change in potential difference causes them to open. Calcium ions flood into the cell from the tissue fluid outside it.

The Ca²⁺ ions affect the behaviour of the vesicles containing insulin inside the cell. These vesicles are moved towards the plasma membrane, where they fuse with the membrane and empty their contents outside the cell.

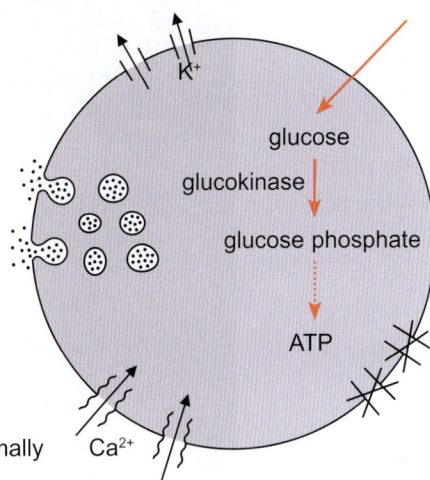

Plant growth regulators

Flowering plants, like mammals, are complex multicellular organisms. Just like mammals, it is important that different parts of the plant are able to communicate with one another to ensure that their activities are coordinated.

Plants produce chemical substances that carry out this function. They have many similarities to hormones in mammals and are often known as plant hormones. However, some biologists prefer to use the term **plant growth regulators**, and that is the term we will use here.

There are many different plant growth regulators, and you may have met some of them in your previous work. They include:

- **auxin**, which is involved in controlling the growth of plants, such as their growth responses to light and gravity;
- **gibberellin**, which is involved in controlling stem elongation and seed germination;
- **abscicic acid**, which is involved in controlling the response of plants to stress, such as causing stomata to close when water is in very short supply;
- **ethylene** (ethene), which is involved in fruit ripening and senescence (ageing processes, such as leaf fall).

Each of these plant growth regulators has many different functions. They interact with one another, and may have different functions in different parts of a plant, or at different stages in the plant's life cycle.

In this chapter, we will concentrate on one plant growth regulator and one of its functions – the role of ethylene in fruit ripening.

Fruit ripening

A fruit develops from the ovary of a flower, after pollination and fertilisation have taken place. A fruit contains seeds, which have each developed from a fertilised ovule. The function of a fruit is to help the seeds to be dispersed away from the parent plant. This enables the plant to colonise new areas, and also reduces competition for light, water and nutrients between the parent plant and its offspring.

Some fruits are adapted for dispersal by animals, and it is this type of fruit that we grow for food. These edible fruits include tomatoes, bananas, mangoes and apples. Each of these fruits has sweet, colourful, aromatic, tasty and nutritious flesh. These features attract animals to the fruit (Figure 7.9). The animal eats the fruit, and may either discard the seeds, or egest them with its faeces. In either case, the animal is likely to spread the seeds to new areas.

The development of a fully mature fruit, with all of these features that are attractive to animals, is called **ripening**. For example, tomatoes and bananas are green and hard when they first develop. As they ripen, numerous changes take place.

- **Colour change**: The green colour of the unripe fruit is due to the presence of chlorophyll in chloroplasts. As the fruit ripens, these chloroplasts change to become chromoplasts. These are organelles with a very similar

Figure 7.9   A fruit bat eating a fruit. The seeds pass out in the bat's faeces and germinate, taking advantage of nutrients in the faeces.

structure to a chloroplast, but containing pigments other than chlorophyll. In chilli peppers, tomatoes and bananas, the chlorophyll breaks down and various colourful carotenoid pigments develop inside the chromoplasts, changing the colour of the fruit flesh to yellow, orange or red (Figure 7.10). Tomatoes contain large amounts of a carotenoid pigment called lycopene, which not only makes the tomatoes red but has strong anti-oxidant properties, making it a good addition to an animal's diet.

- **Softening of texture**: Fruits tend to become softer as they ripen. This is generally the result of the breakdown of their cell walls. The middle lamella (the part of the cell wall midway between two adjoining plant cells, made up largely of pectin) is partially hydrolysed. This makes it easier for the cells to separate from

Figure 7.10 Not only are the ripe fruits of chilli pepper different in flavour from the unripe fruits, but the seeds of fruit just beginning to turn red are seven times less likely to germinate than seeds from fully ripe fruits.

one another. The pectin also becomes more hydrated, which helps to make the fruit juicier.

- **Production of new aromatic compounds**: Each kind of fruit has a typical scent and flavour, which is due to a particular set of chemical substances produced as it ripens. The typical banana flavour, for example, is caused by isopentyl acetate and isobutyl acetate. The amounts of these substances build up as the fruit ripens. Many of these 'flavour' compounds are volatile – that is, they change readily to a gaseous form and spread into the air around the fruit. This means that animals can smell the fruit from some distance away.

- **Increase in sweetness**: As the fruit ripens, starch is changed to sugar. The sugars may include glucose, fructose ('fruit sugar') and sucrose. Unlike starch, sugars dissolve in water inside cells. This decreases the water potential inside the cell, so that more water moves into the cells by osmosis. This makes the fruit juicier. All of these changes add to the attractiveness of the fruit to animals.

The control of fruit ripening

We have seen that the function of fruit ripening is to make the fruit attractive to animals, so that they will eat the fruit and disperse the seeds. It is therefore important that the fruit does not ripen until the seeds are fully developed and ready to be dispersed. It may also be important to ensure that the timing is right in relation to environmental conditions, so that the dispersed seeds will be able to lie dormant for a time, or to germinate straight away, depending on the particular plant species.

The plant growth regulator **ethylene** plays a central role in the control of fruit ripening. If you have studied chemistry, you will be familiar with the group of organic compounds called alkenes, and ethylene is one of these (Figure 7.11).

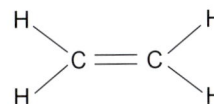

Figure 7.11 Display formula for ethylene (ethene).

Its correct chemical name is ethene, but plant biologists continue to refer to it by its older name of ethylene.

Ethylene has one very unusual property for a hormone or a plant growth regulator – it is a gas. It can therefore spread easily from one fruit to another, by diffusion through the air. Its small, lipid-soluble molecules mean that it is also very easy for it to diffuse freely between cells. Almost every plant tissue that has so far been studied has been shown to produce ethylene at some stage in its development.

In many fruits, known as **climacteric fruits** (Table 7.1), there is a sudden burst of ethylene production as they begin to ripen. This is accompanied by a sudden rise in the rate of respiration (Figure 7.12).

Ethylene is synthesised from the amino acid methionine, in a metabolic pathway involving several enzymes, including ACC synthase and ACC oxidase. This pathway is controlled by a positive feedback mechanism. As ethylene is produced, it increases the activity of the enzymes

Climacteric fruits	Non-climacteric fruits
tomato, banana, avocado, melon, mango, apple, pear, peach, plum, citrus fruits, kiwifruit	cherry, strawberry, pineapple

Table 7.1 Some examples of climacteric and non-climacteric fruits.

that synthesise it, meaning that even more ethylene is synthesised.

The increase in ethylene production in the fruit triggers the numerous changes that are involved in fruit ripening. Ethylene has these effects by causing various genes to be switched on. Figure 7.13 shows how the arrival of an ethylene molecule at the plasma membrane of a target cell results in a change of gene activity.

Many of the genes that are directly affected by ethylene are regulatory genes – that is, they control whether or not other genes are turned off

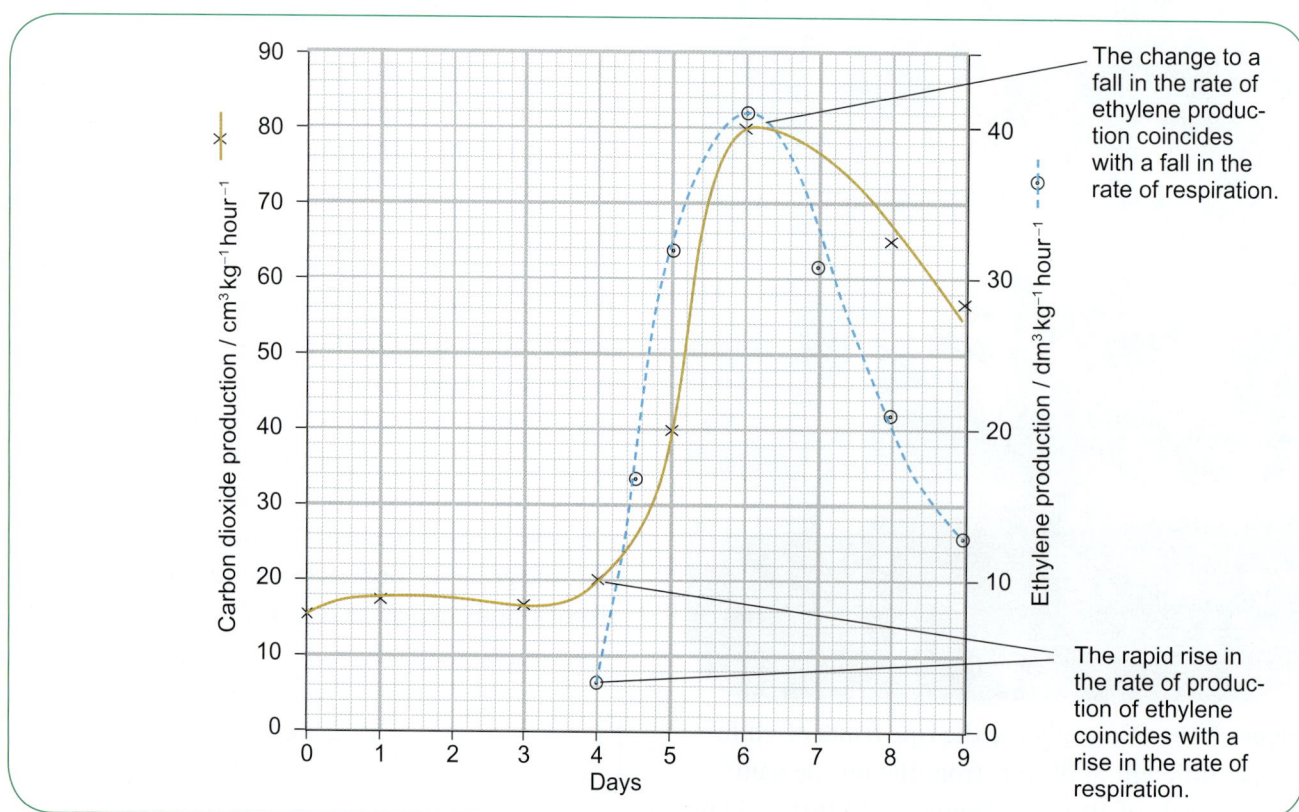

The change to a fall in the rate of ethylene production coincides with a fall in the rate of respiration.

The rapid rise in the rate of production of ethylene coincides with a rise in the rate of respiration.

Figure 7.12 Rate of production of carbon dioxide and ethylene during the ripening of bananas.

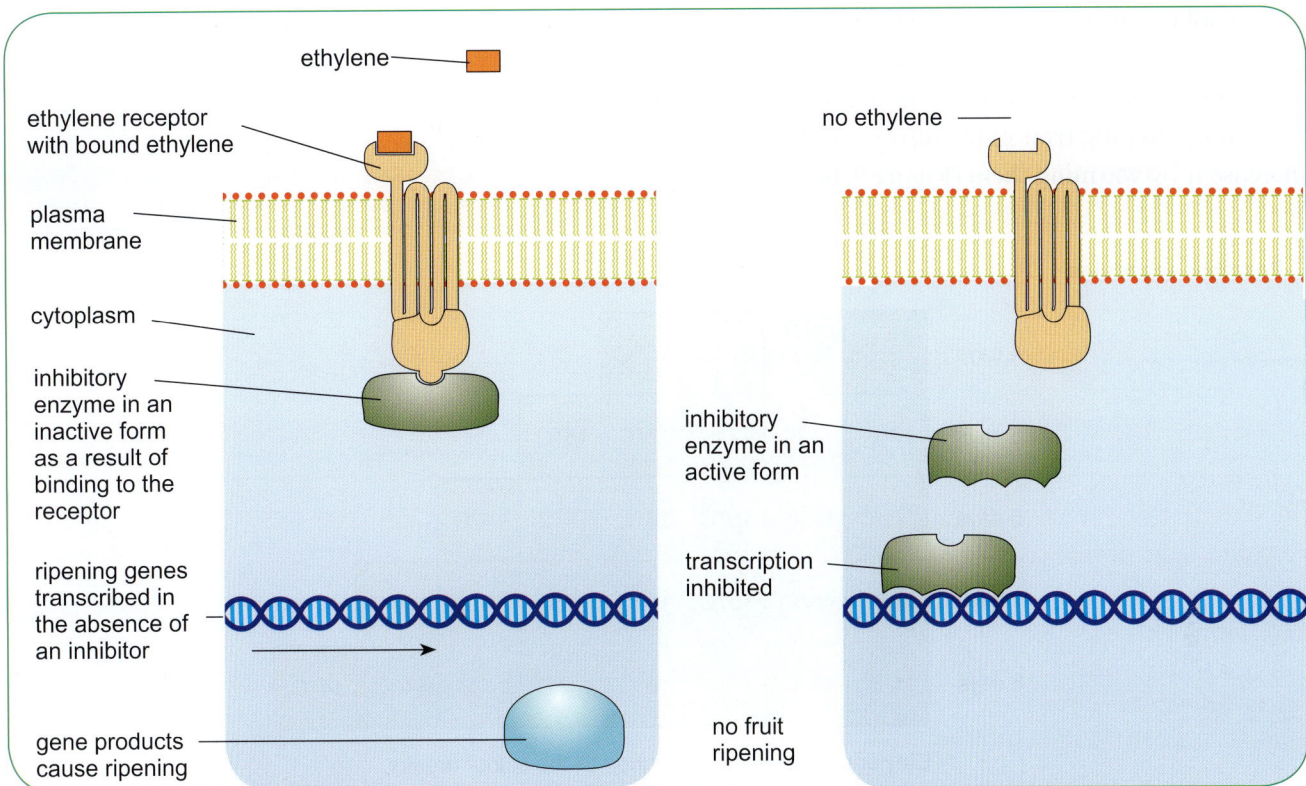

Figure 7.13 How ethylene changes gene activity.

or on. In this way, ethylene triggers a whole range of changes in the fruit. Many different genes are now transcribed to produce mRNA, and this mRNA is translated to produce many different proteins, including numerous enzymes. This is what causes the changes involved in fruit ripening. For example, an increase in the synthesis of amylase causes starch to be converted to sugar. An increase in the synthesis of pectinase brings about cell wall softening.

SAQ

4 a What are the similarities and differences between negative feedback and positive feedback?

b Explain why positive feedback cannot help in homeostasis.

5 Suggest advantages to a plant of the ability of ethylene to diffuse through the air from one developing fruit to another.

Commercial uses of ethylene

The stimulation and control of fruit ripening by ethylene is an entirely natural process. However, it is very easy for chemists to synthesise ethylene, and it is widely used in the fruit marketing industry to ensure that fruits can be supplied to the market in peak condition.

For example, it is often easier and better to pick fruits before they have fully ripened. Unripe fruits are harder and stronger, and therefore are easier to move from place to place without damaging them. Bananas, for example, are usually picked while they are still green. They can easily be distributed all over the world in this state, arriving undamaged at the final distributor's warehouse. They are then placed in a room to which ethylene gas is supplied. This causes them to ripen – all very much at the same time, so that they can be supplied at exactly the right stage of ripeness to the shops where they will be sold.

Like all metabolic reactions, those involved in the ripening process take place more rapidly at higher temperatures. You can slow down the process by keeping fruit in the refrigerator, and increase it by warming them (Figure 7.14).

Possible schedules

4 days	18 °C	18 °C	17 °C	15 °C				
5 days	17 °C	17 °C	17 °C	17 °C	15 °C			
6 days	17 °C	17 °C	15 °C	15 °C	15 °C	14 °C		
7 days	15 °C	15 °C	15 °C	15 °C	15 °C	15 °C	14 °C	
8 days	14 °C	14 °C	14 °C	14 °C	14 °C	14 °C	14 °C	14 °C

Ethylene treatment is continued till the colour breaks.

colour index number	1	2	3	4	5	6	7
colour of peel	green	green – trace of yellow	more green than yellow	more yellow than green	green tip	all yellow	yellow flecked with brown

Figure 7.14 A ripening guide for bananas.

SAQ

6 With reference to the effects of ethylene on the activities of cells, suggest why the burst of ethylene production is accompanied by a sharp rise in the rate of respiration.

7 If you have some unripe tomatoes, mangoes or avocados, you can speed up their ripening by placing them inside a paper bag with a yellow banana. Explain how this works.

8 Plant tissues tend to produce ethylene when they are damaged – for example, by bruising, or by attack from organisms such as insects or fungi. Apples can be stored, unripe, in a cool place to delay ripening. Explain why it is important not to include any damaged apples in the store.

9 a Explain why growers generally pick bananas before they ripen.

  b Suggest why many wholesalers and retailers ripen bananas by exposing them to ethylene, rather than allowing them to ripen naturally.

  c With reference to the schedules in Figure 7.14, describe and explain the effect of temperature on banana ripening.

Summary

- Multicellular organisms, such as animals and plants, have systems to allow cells in different parts of their bodies to communicate so that their activities can be coordinated.

- In mammals, the environment within the body is kept relatively stable. This is called homeostasis.

- Homeostasis involves negative feedback mechanisms, which are dynamic mechanisms that keep a particular parameter close to a set point. Receptors detect small changes in the parameter, and pass information (as nerve impulses or hormones) to effectors. The effectors take action to bring the parameter back towards the set point.

- Hormones are chemicals secreted by endocrine (ductless) glands. They are carried around the body dissolved in blood plasma. They act on target cells, which have receptors in their plasma membranes (or inside the cell) that allow the hormone to bind and bring about changes in the activity of the cell.

- The islets of Langerhans in the pancreas are involved in the control of blood glucose concentration. Alpha cells in the islets secrete glucagon, and beta cells secrete insulin. If blood glucose level rises too high, the beta cells act as receptors and detect this. They secrete more insulin, which acts on muscle cells to cause more glucose to be absorbed from the blood, and also causes liver cells to change glucose to glycogen for storage. If blood glucose level falls too low, the alpha cells secrete glucagon, which causes the liver cells to break down glycogen to glucose.

- Plant growth regulators are similar to animal hormones, but are not made in endocrine glands. Ethylene is a gaseous plant growth regulator that controls fruit ripening. In climacteric fruits, a burst of ethylene production, accompanied by a rise in respiratory activity, begins the ripening process. Ethylene causes numerous genes in its target cells to be switched on. The protein products of these genes bring about changes in the fruit, including changes in colour, texture, flavour and aroma.

- Ethylene is used by commercial growers and distributors of fruit to control the ripening process, allowing unripe fruits to be picked and moved to points of distribution before they are exposed to ethylene to cause them to ripen.

Questions

Multiple choice questions

1 Homeostasis in a mammal is defined as the maintenance of a:
   A constant internal and external environment.
   B constant internal environment, providing a degree of independence from the external environment.
   C variable internal environment, resulting from a variable external environment.
   D constant internal environment with some dependence on the external environment.

2 Which of the following **correctly** identifies the components of a negative feedback system in a mammal?
   A set point, detector, thermostat, regulator
   B thermostat, detector, regulator
   C detector, receptor, set point
   D set point, detector, regulator, effector

3 The cells or tissues which bring about the corrective mechanism restoring a factor to its set point is called the:
   A effector.
   B norm.
   C regulator.
   D detector.

4 Which of the following is a characteristic of an endocrine system?
   A has ducts
   B is ductless
   C secretes enzymes
   D has a poor supply of blood vessels

5 Which of the following statements is true of an endocrine system?
   A causes changes in metabolic activity
   B produces effects in milliseconds
   C effects tend to be short-lived
   D communication is through impulses

6 The following are stages involved in negative feedback systems:
   I   change detected by receptors
   II   corrective mechanism switched off
   III return to set point
   IV   regulator secretes hormones
   What is the correct sequence of stages following a change in a particular factor?
   A I, II, III, IV
   B I, II, IV, III
   C III, I, II, IV
   D I, IV, III, II

continued ...

7   Which does an increase in the secretion of insulin produce?
    A a decrease in glucose metabolism
    B an increase in the conversion of glycogen to glucose
    C an increase in glucose channels in the plasma membranes of muscle cells
    D an increase in blood glucose levels

8   Which of the following correctly identifies the hormones responsible for increases in the processes shown?

	Conversion of glycogen to glucose in liver cells	**Uptake of glucose by muscle cells**	**Respiration of glucose by muscle cells**
A	glucagon	glucagon	insulin
B	insulin	glucagon	insulin
C	glucagon	insulin	insulin
D	insulin	insulin	glucagon

9   Which process increases its rate when ethylene is produced during the ripening of a banana fruit?
    A photosynthesis
    B respiration
    C replication
    D secretion

10 If a shipper of fruits wants to delay fruit ripening, which of the following would be the most appropriate action?
    A increase the oxygen concentration and decrease the ethylene concentration
    B decrease oxygen concentration and raise the nitrogen concentration
    C increase the oxygen concentration and raise the nitrogen concentration
    D decrease the oxygen concentration and raise the ethylene concentration

Structured questions

11 **a i** What do you understand by the term 'homeostasis'?   [1 mark]
   ii Identify **two** factors in mammals which are regulated by homeostatic mechanisms. [2 marks]
   iii State **two** reasons why homeostasis is important.   [2 marks]
   b Negative feedback is the mechanism of delivering homeostasis. What do you
       understand by the term 'negative feedback'?   [2 marks]
   c The diagram below shows a generalised negative feedback system.

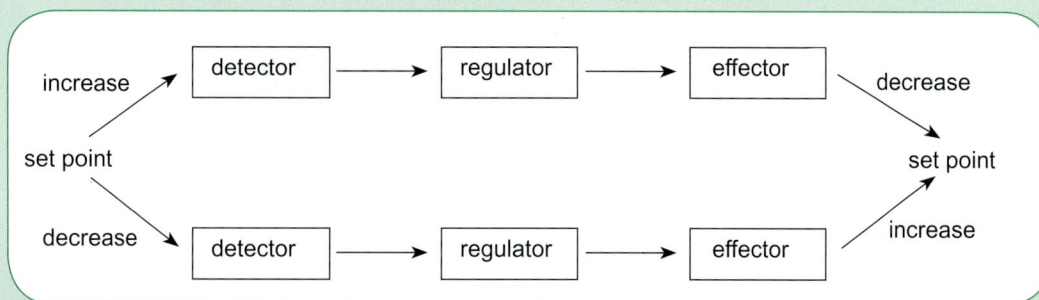

   i What is meant by the term 'set point'? Give an example.   [2 marks]
   ii State the roles of the regulator, effector and detector.   [3 marks]

continued …

iii Name **two** ways by which the regulator conveys information to the effector so that corrective action may be taken. [2 marks]

d Suggest a reason for the complexity of the corrective system shown in **c**. [1 mark]

12 The graph below shows the rate of production of carbon dioxide and ethylene during the ripening of bananas.

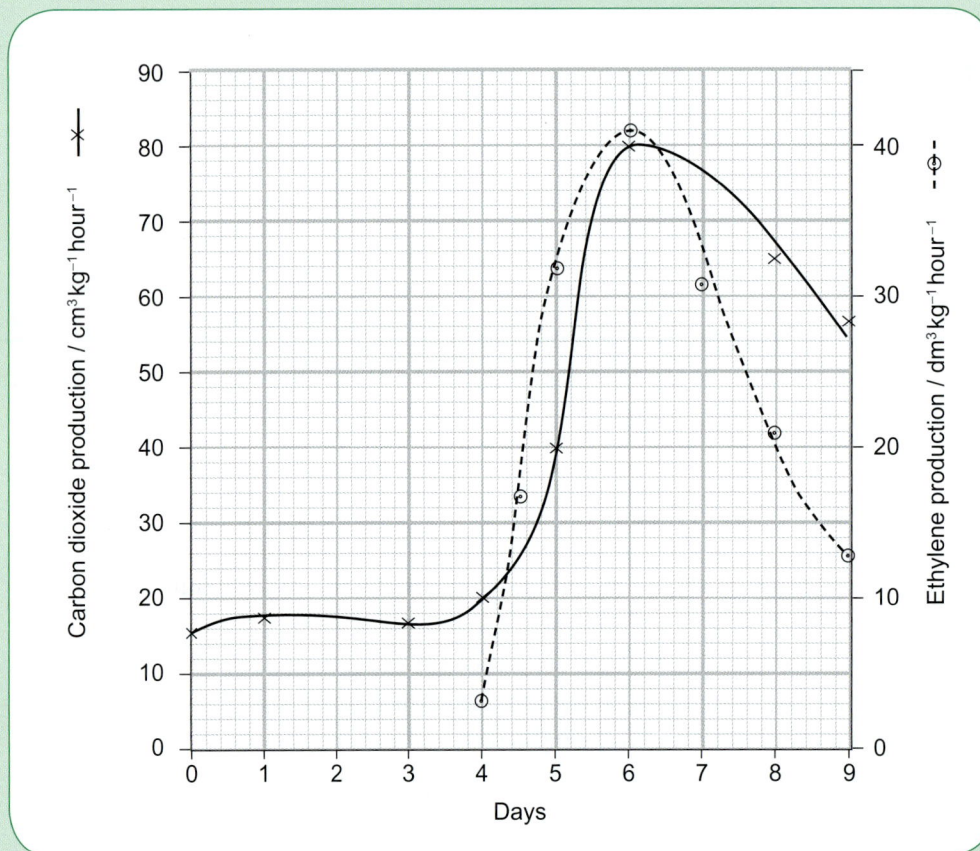

a What process produces the carbon dioxide gas? [1 mark]

b i Describe the curve showing carbon dioxide production during the period shown in the graph. [3 marks]

ii Describe the curve showing ethylene production during the period shown in the graph. [3 marks]

c Which day showed the highest **rate** of production of carbon dioxide and ethylene? [1 mark]

d Briefly describe the changes that occur during the ripening of the banana. [3 marks]

e Banana is a high starch, low fat fruit. Describe how you can determine the stage of ripeness in the fruit. [4 marks]

continued …

13 The graph below shows the relationship between blood sugar levels and the hormones insulin and glucagon in a person before and after a sports drink, containing a high concentration of glucose, was taken.

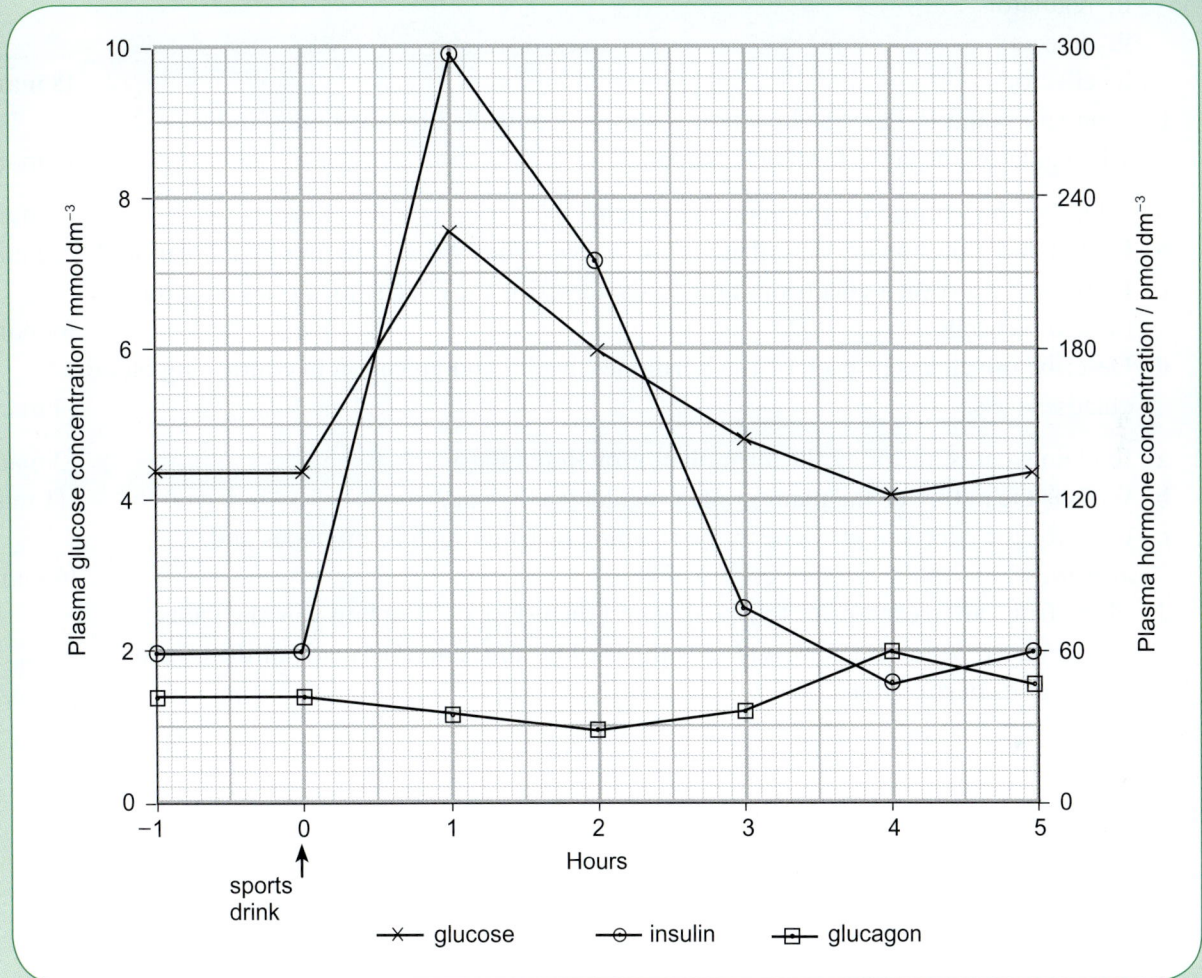

a Name the endocrine tissue which produces insulin and glucagon. [2 marks]

b Using the data in the graph, suggest the concentration of glucose that could be its set point. Give a reason for your answer. [2 marks]

c Suggest a reason why glucose concentration in blood plasma should be kept within limits. [1 mark]

d Describe the changes in plasma glucose concentration after drinking the sports drink. [3 marks]

e With reference to the graph above, explain how the changes in blood glucose cause:

　i an increase in insulin

　ii a subsequent decrease in insulin. [4 marks]

f With reference to the graph above, explain the increase in glucagon at 4 hours. [3 marks]

continued ...

Essay questions

1 a Define the following terms as used in the context of negative feedback.
       i   set point
       ii   regulator
       iii detector
       iv   effector   [8 marks]
    b Using an example, describe how homeostasis is controlled by hormones and a
       self regulatory negative feedback system.   [7 marks]

2 a What are the features of an endocrine system?   [2 marks]
    b Insulin and glucagon are described as hormones. What are the features of a hormone? [3 marks]
    c Hormones exert their effects on target cells. Describe the effects hormones have on
       these target cells.   [6 marks]
    d Describe **two** effects of each of the hormones insulin and glucagon in controlling blood
       glucose levels.   [4 marks]

3 a Explain what is meant by the term plant growth regulator.   [2 marks]
    b What is the nature of the plant growth regulator ethylene?   [1 mark]
    c Describe the effects of ethylene in the ripening of fruits such as mangoes and
       avocados.   [6 marks]
    d Many fruits are picked prior to ripening and then shipped. Explain why the fruits
       are harvested before ripening and how the fruit becomes market ready at the time of
       arrival at its destination.   [6 marks]

Chapter 8
The kidney, excretion and osmoregulation

By the end of this chapter you should be able to:

a explain the need to remove nitrogenous and other excretory products from the body, and review the formation of urea;

b describe the gross structure of the kidney and the detailed structure of the nephron and associated blood vessels, using annotated diagrams;

c make drawings of sections of the kidney from prepared slides;

d explain the function of the kidney in terms of excretion and osmoregulation, including the role of ADH;

e discuss the clinical significance of the presence of glucose and protein in the urine.

Excretion

Many of the metabolic reactions occurring in the body produce unwanted substances. Some of these are toxic (poisonous). The removal from the body of these unwanted products of metabolism is known as **excretion**.

There are several excretory products formed in our bodies, but two are made in much greater quantities than the others. These are **carbon dioxide** and **urea**.

Carbon dioxide is produced continuously by almost every cell in the body, by the reactions of aerobic respiration. The waste carbon dioxide is transported from the respiring cells to the lungs, in the bloodstream. It diffuses from the blood into the alveoli of the lungs, and is excreted in the air that we breathe out.

Urea, however, is produced in only one organ – the **liver**. It is formed from excess amino acids, and is transported from the liver to the kidneys, in solution in blood plasma. The kidneys remove urea from the blood and excrete it, dissolved in water, as urine.

The formation of urea

The human body is unable to store any excess protein that we eat. As many of us eat much more protein than we need, something needs to be done with the excess. This happens in the liver, and it is called **deamination** (Figure 8.1).

In deamination, excess amino acids (from excess protein) are broken down. The amino group is removed, and forms ammonia, NH_3. The rest of the amino acid forms a keto acid, which can be

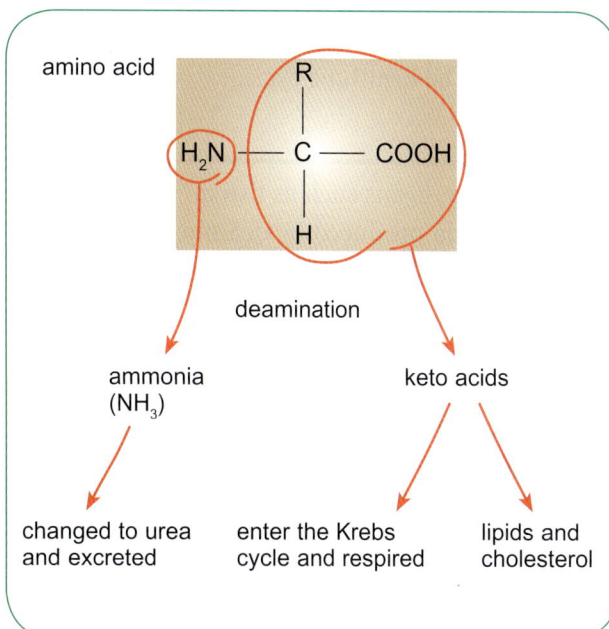

Figure 8.1 Deamination of excess amino acids.

respired to release energy or converted to fat to be stored.

Ammonia is very soluble and very toxic, so it cannot be allowed to remain in the body. Still in the liver, it is combined with carbon dioxide to form urea, $CO(NH_2)_2$. Urea, although still toxic, is much less soluble and much less dangerous than ammonia. The liver releases urea into the blood, where it dissolves in the plasma and is transported all over the body. It is removed from the blood as it passes through the kidneys.

Figure 8.2 shows how ammonia is converted to urea. This series of metabolic reactions is called the **ornithine cycle**. Ornithine is an amino acid, but not one that is used in making proteins. As you can see, the ornithine cycle requires input of energy in the form of ATP.

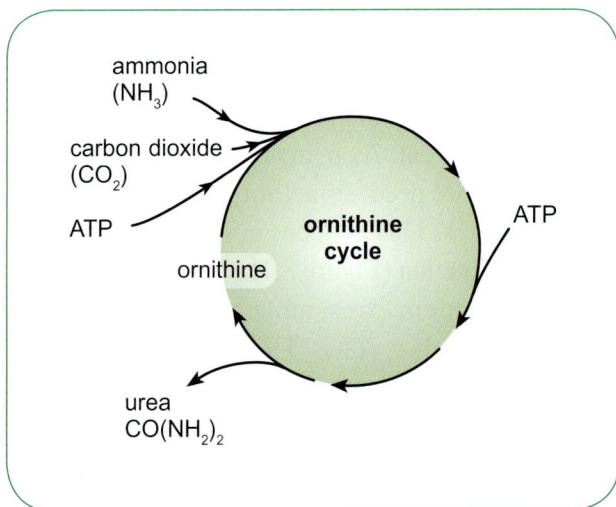

Figure 8.2   The ornithine cycle.

SAQ

1 Aquatic organisms such as fish do not convert the ammonia produced by deamination into urea, but simply excrete it as ammonia into their environment.
   a Explain why it is possible for them to do this, whereas terrestrial animals cannot.
   b Suggest the advantages to aquatic animals of excreting ammonia rather than urea.

The kidneys

The two kidneys lie at the back of the abdominal cavity (that is, close to the backbone). A long tube runs from each of them to the bladder (Figure 8.3). These are the **ureters**, and they carry urine away from the kidneys to the **bladder**, where it is stored before being expelled via the **urethra**.

Each kidney is supplied with blood though a **renal artery**, which branches off from the aorta. A **renal vein** returns blood to the vena cava.

Figure 8.4 shows the gross structure of a human kidney. Kidney tissue is a deep, dark red. Seen with the naked eye, the surface of a kidney section shows it to be made up of an outer **cortex** and an inner paler **medulla**. A whitish area, the **pelvis**, lies in the centre of one edge.

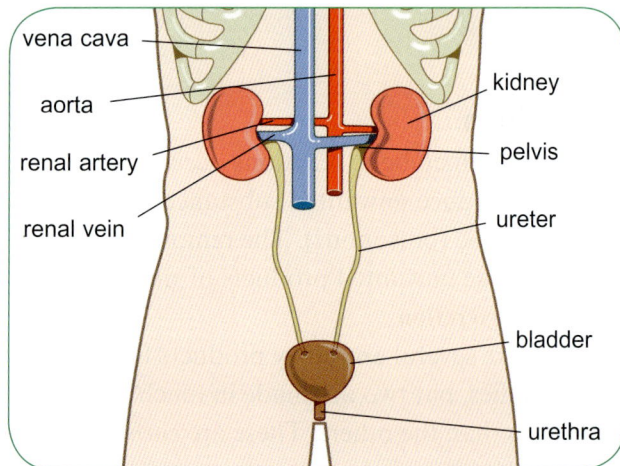

Figure 8.3   Position of the kidneys and associated structures in the human body.

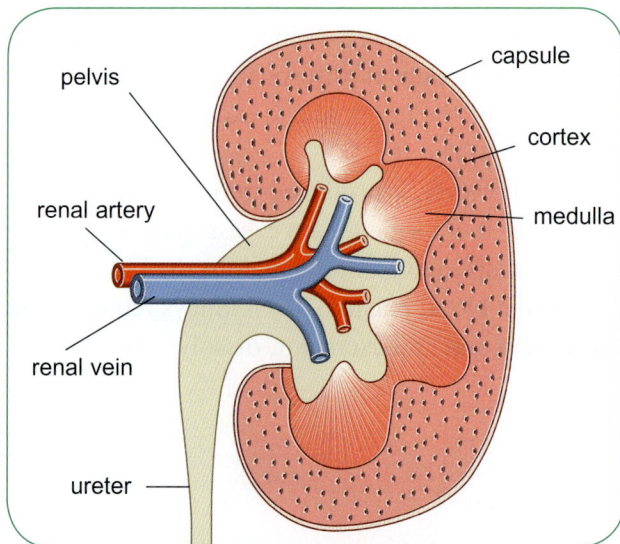

Figure 8.4   A kidney cut in half vertically.

The structure of a nephron

Each kidney is made up of thousands of tiny tubules called **nephrons** (Figure 8.5 and Figure 8.6). These are much too small to be seen with the naked eye, and even with a microscope you will not find it easy to see them clearly. This is because the nephrons take a very winding route from the outer parts of the cortex to the pelvis, so that when a kidney is cut through, the cut passes through tiny bits of many different nephrons (Figure 8.7).

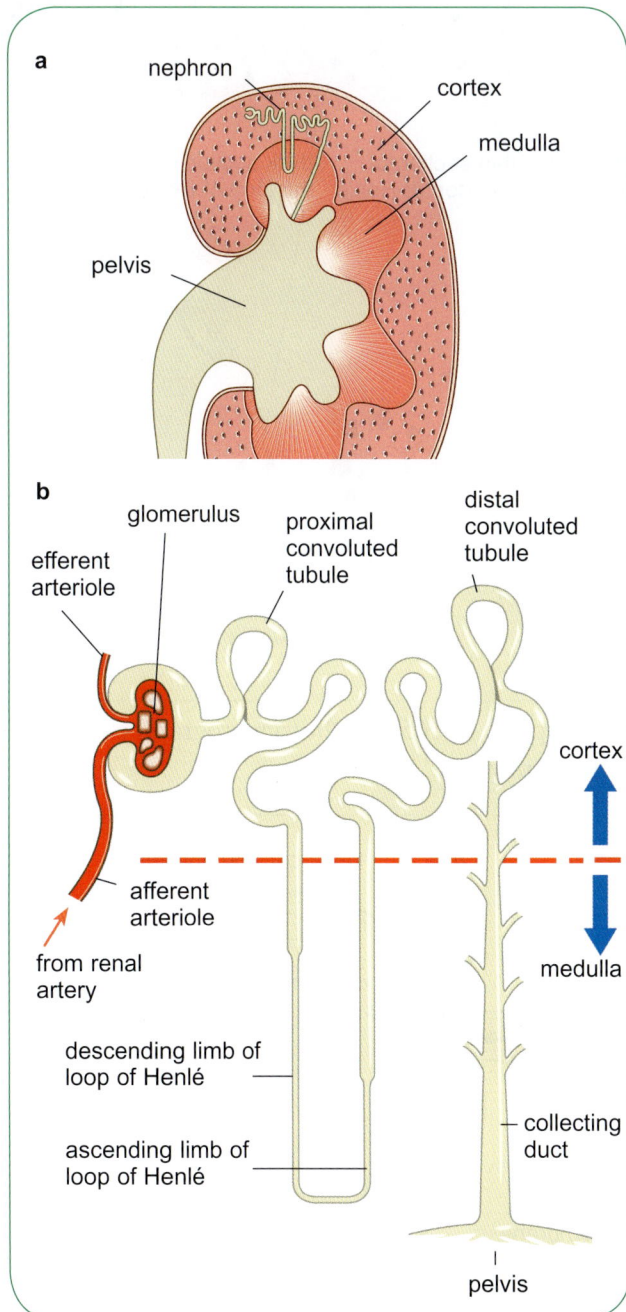

Each nephron begins as a cup-shaped structure called a **renal (Bowman's) capsule**. The renal capsules of all the nephrons are in the cortex of the kidney. From the renal capsule, the tube runs towards the centre of the kidney, first forming a twisted region called the **proximal convoluted tubule** and then a long hairpin loop in the medulla, the **loop of Henlé**. The tubule then turns back up through the cortex and forms another twisted region called the **distal convoluted tubule**. Finally, it joins a **collecting duct**, which leads down through the medulla and into the pelvis of the kidney. Here the collecting ducts join the ureter.

Blood vessels are closely associated with the nephrons. Each renal capsule is supplied with blood by a branch of the renal artery called an **afferent arteriole**. This splits into a tangle of capillaries in the 'cup' of the renal capsule, called a **glomerulus**. The capillaries of the glomerulus rejoin to form an **efferent arteriole**. This leads off to form a network of capillaries running closely alongside the rest of the nephron, before linking

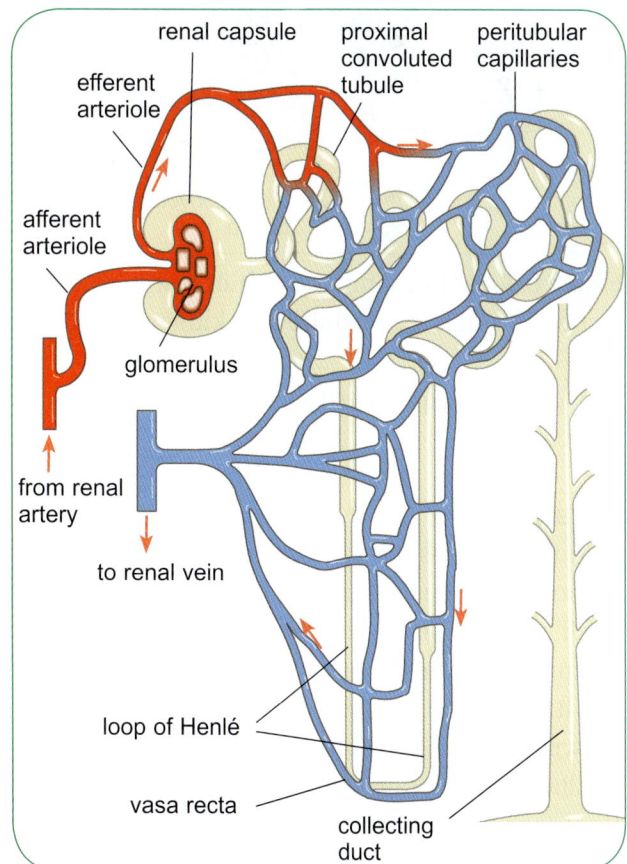

Figure 8.5 **a** Section through a kidney to show the position of one nephron, **b** a nephron.

Figure 8.6 The blood supply associated with a nephron.

163

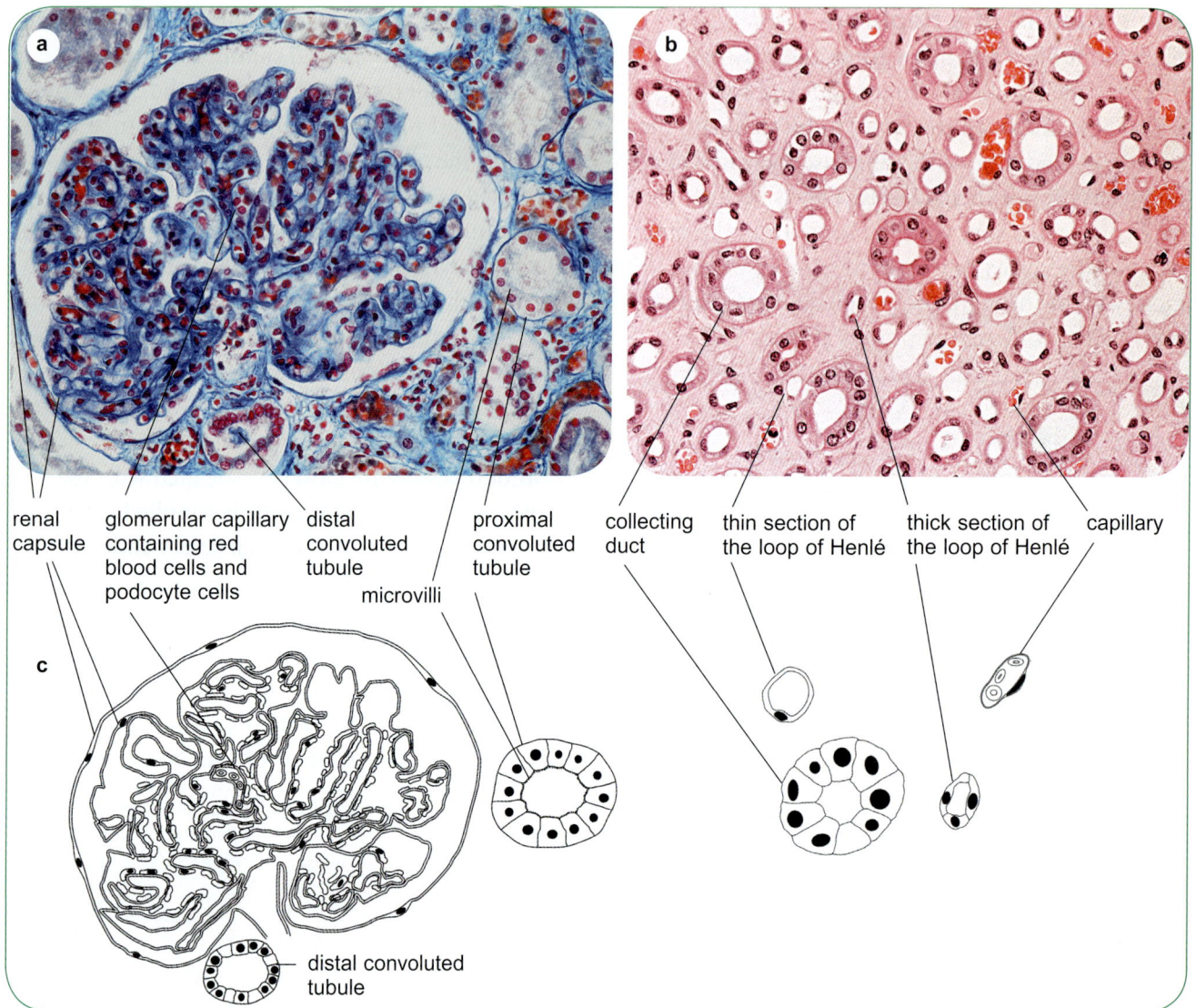

Figure 8.7 **a** Photomicrograph of a section through a renal capsule (×165), **b** photomicrograph of a section through the medulla of a kidney (×300), **c** interpretive drawings.

up with other capillaries to feed into a branch of the renal vein.

Ultrafiltration

Ultrafiltration, as the name suggests, involves filtration on a micro-scale. This process filters out small molecules from the blood and these pass into the lumens of the nephrons.

Ultrafiltration happens in the renal capsules (Bowman's capsules). The blood in the glomerular capillaries is separated from the lumen of the renal capsule by two cell layers and a basement membrane (Figure 8.8).

The first cell layer is the lining, called the **endothelium**, of the blood capillary. This, like

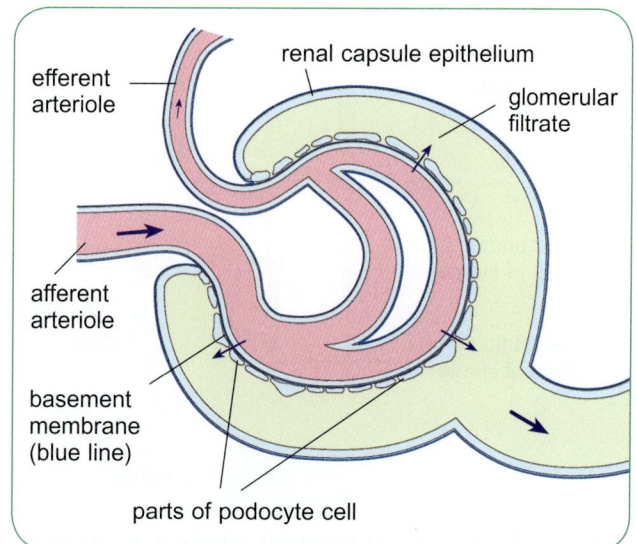

Figure 8.8 A renal capsule (Bowman's capsule).

that of most capillaries, has many small pores in it through which plasma can seep out. Lying closely against the endothelium is a basement membrane, and against that is the layer of cells making up the lining of the renal capsule. These cells are called **podocytes**. 'Pod' means 'foot', and these cells have a very unusual structure. They have many projecting fingers (or feet) that wrap themselves closely around the capillary loops of the glomerulus (Figure 8.9). Tiny slits are left between the interlocking podocyte fingers.

The diameter of the afferent arteriole that brings blood to the glomerulus is greater than the diameter of the efferent arteriole that carries it away. This results in a build-up of hydrostatic pressure inside the glomerular capillaries. As a result, blood plasma is forced out through the pores in the capillaries, through the basement membrane and then through the slits between the podocytes. The fluid that seeps through, into the cavity of the renal capsule, is known as **glomerular filtrate** (Figure 8.10). It is the basement membrane that acts as the filter. In kidney dialysis for a person with kidney failure, the dialysis membrane carries out a similar role to that of the basement membrane.

No cells can get through this filter. And not quite all the components of blood plasma can pass through, either. Large proteins with a relative molecular mass of more than about 65 000 to 69 000 remain dissolved in the blood. Table 8.1 shows the composition of blood plasma and glomerular filtrate.

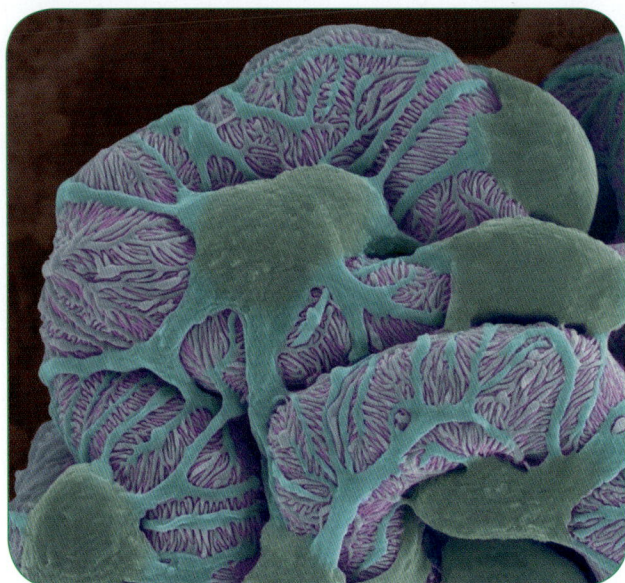

Figure 8.9 A false colour scanning electron micrograph of podocyte cells (× 3900). The podocytes are the blue cells, with their 'fingers' wrapped around the purple blood capillary.

Selective reabsorption

As you can see from Table 8.1, glomerular filtrate is identical to blood plasma minus most proteins. It is therefore inevitable that it will contain many substances that the body should keep, as well as others that need to be got rid of. Selective reabsorption, which happens as the filtrate flows along the nephron, takes these wanted substances back into the blood.

Most of this reabsorption takes place in the proximal convoluted tubule. The walls of this part of the nephron are made up of a layer of cuboidal cells with microvilli on their inner surfaces

Substance	Concentration in blood plasma / $g\,dm^{-3}$	Concentration in glomerular filtrate / $g\,dm^{-3}$
water	900	900
inorganic ions	7.2	7.2
urea	0.3	0.3
uric acid	0.04	0.04
glucose	1.0	1.0
amino acids	0.5	0.5
proteins	80.0	0.05

Table 8.1 Comparison of the composition of blood plasma and glomerular filtrate.

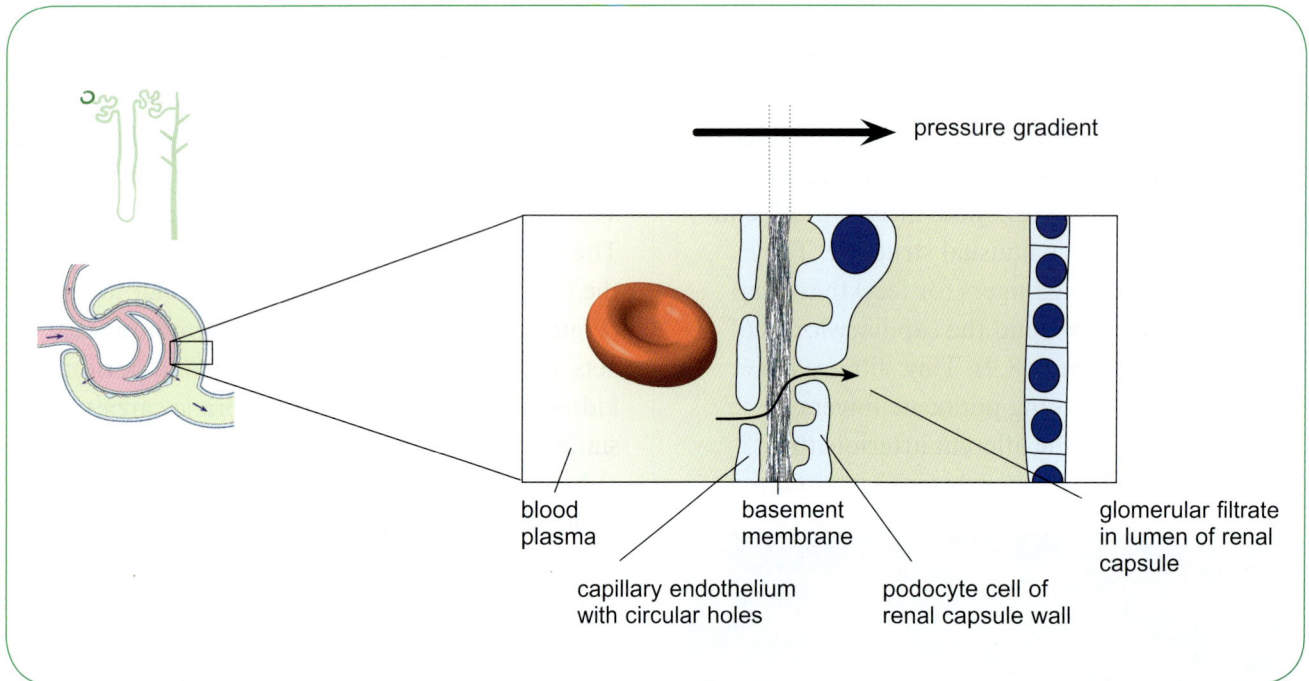

pressure gradient

blood plasma

basement membrane

glomerular filtrate in lumen of renal capsule

capillary endothelium with circular holes

podocyte cell of renal capsule wall

Figure 8.10 Ultrafiltration.

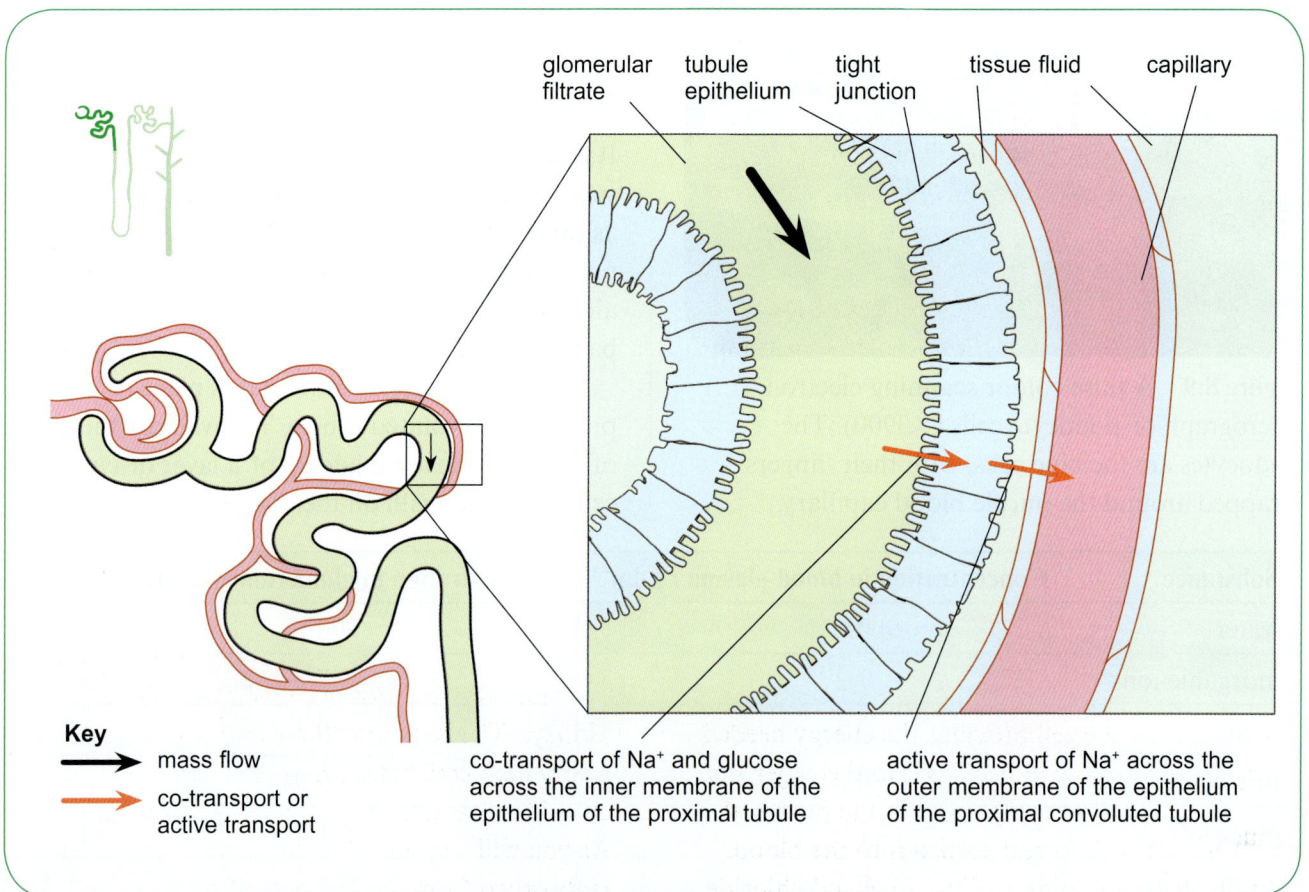

glomerular filtrate

tubule epithelium

tight junction

tissue fluid

capillary

Key

mass flow

co-transport or active transport

co-transport of Na$^+$ and glucose across the inner membrane of the epithelium of the proximal tubule

active transport of Na$^+$ across the outer membrane of the epithelium of the proximal convoluted tubule

Figure 8.11 Selective reabsorption from the proximal convoluted tubule.

(Figure 8.11). The cells have tight junctions which hold adjacent cells tightly together preventing any water or mineral ions passing out of the nephron between the cells. Because of these tight junctions, movement of water, glucose, amino acids and mineral ions has to take place across the cells and through their plasma membranes and can, therefore, be regulated.

Blood capillaries lie very closely against the outer surface of the tubule. The blood in these capillaries has come directly from the glomerulus, so it has much less plasma in it than usual and has lost much of its water and many of the ions, small proteins and other substances that it was carrying as it entered the glomerulus. It still contains all its cells, and its large soluble proteins.

The outer membranes of the cells of the proximal convoluted tubule walls actively transport sodium ions out of the cytoplasm. This lowers the concentration of sodium ions inside the cells. As a result, there is a concentration gradient for sodium ions from the contents of the tubule (relatively high concentration) into the cytoplasm. The sodium ions diffuse down this gradient from the fluid inside the tubule into the cells, passing through transporter proteins in their plasma membranes.

There are several different varieties of these transporters, and each one transports something else at the same time as sodium ions. They can even do this against a concentration gradient. For example, a sodium ion diffusing through one kind of transporter might carry a glucose molecule with it, *up* the concentration gradient for glucose. This is called **co-transport**. The passive movement of the sodium ion down its gradient provides the energy to move the glucose molecule up its gradient. So, indirectly, the active transport of sodium ions out of one side of the cell provides the energy needed to transport glucose molecules into the other side.

In this way, all of the glucose in the proximal convoluted tubule is reabsorbed into the blood. Amino acids, vitamins, sodium ions and chloride ions are also reabsorbed here.

The removal of all these solutes from the glomerular filtrate greatly increases its water potential. But the water potential inside the cells in the nephron walls, and inside the blood capillaries, is decreasing as these solutes move into them. So a water potential gradient builds up. Water molecules move down this gradient, out of the nephron and into the blood. About 65% of the water in the filtrate is reabsorbed here. As the blood flows away, the water and other reabsorbed substances are carried away with it.

Surprisingly, quite a lot of urea is reabsorbed too. Urea is a small molecule, which passes easily through cell membranes. Its concentration in the glomerular filtrate is considerably higher than in the capillaries so it diffuses passively through the wall of the proximal convoluted tubule and into the blood. About half of the urea in the filtrate is reabsorbed in this way.

All of this reabsorption greatly decreases the volume of the liquid remaining in the tubule. In an adult human, around $125\,cm^3$ of filtrate enters the proximal tubules each minute, and all but $45\,cm^3$ is reabsorbed.

SAQ

2 Although almost half of the urea in the glomerular filtrate is reabsorbed from the proximal convoluted tubule, the concentration of urea in the fluid that remains inside the nephron actually increases. Explain why.

3 Explain how each of these features of the cells in the walls of the proximal convoluted tubules adapt them for their functions.
   a microvilli
   b large numbers of mitochondria.

The loop of Henlé

About one third of our nephrons have long loops of Henlé, dipping down into the medulla of the kidneys. The function of these loops is to create a very high concentration of sodium ions and chloride ions in the tissue fluid in the medulla. As you will see, this allows a lot of water to be reabsorbed from the contents of the nephron as they pass through the collecting duct. This means that very concentrated urine can be produced, conserving water in the body and preventing dehydration.

The first part of the loop of Henlé is called the **descending limb** and the second part is the **ascending limb**. These differ in their permeabilities to water. The descending limb is water-permeable, while the ascending limb is impermeable to water (Figure 8.12).

It is a bit easier to understand how it works if you begin at the 'wrong' end – in the ascending limb. The cells in the upper part of this limb actively transport sodium and chloride ions out of

the nephron and into the surrounding tissues. This increases the water potential of the fluid inside the nephron and decreases the water potential outside it. Water cannot pass out of the nephron at this point, because the walls are impermeable to it.

Now think about the descending limb. We have seen that its walls are permeable to water. As the fluid from the proximal convoluted tubule flows through the descending limb, it passes through the tissues into which sodium and chloride ions have been pumped. So there is a water potential gradient, and water moves down this gradient from inside the descending limb into the tissues outside it.

The fluid that now begins to go up the ascending limb is very concentrated – it has lost a lot of its water, so the concentration of the ions that remain is large. This makes it relatively easy to pump these ions out of the tubule as the fluid moves up.

Having the two limbs of the loop running next to each other like this, with the fluid flowing down one side and up the other, enables the maximum concentration of solutes to be built up both inside and outside the tube at the bottom of the loop. It is called a **counter-current system**.

The longer the loop of Henlé, the greater the concentration of solutes that can be built up at the bottom of the loop. We have seen that about one third of our nephrons have long loops. In desert-living mammals, such as gerbils, almost all of the loops are very long. This is useful because, as we shall see, the very low water potential that they build up in the medulla helps water to be conserved and not lost in the urine.

Reabsorption in the distal convoluted tubule and collecting duct

The fluid now continues along the nephron, entering the distal convoluted tubule and finally the collecting duct. The cells in the walls of the distal convoluted tubule actively transport sodium ions out of the fluid, while potassium ions are actively transported into it.

As the fluid flows through the collecting duct, deep in the medulla, it passes through the same regions as the deep parts of the loops of Henlé. The very low water potential in this region once more provides a water potential gradient, so that

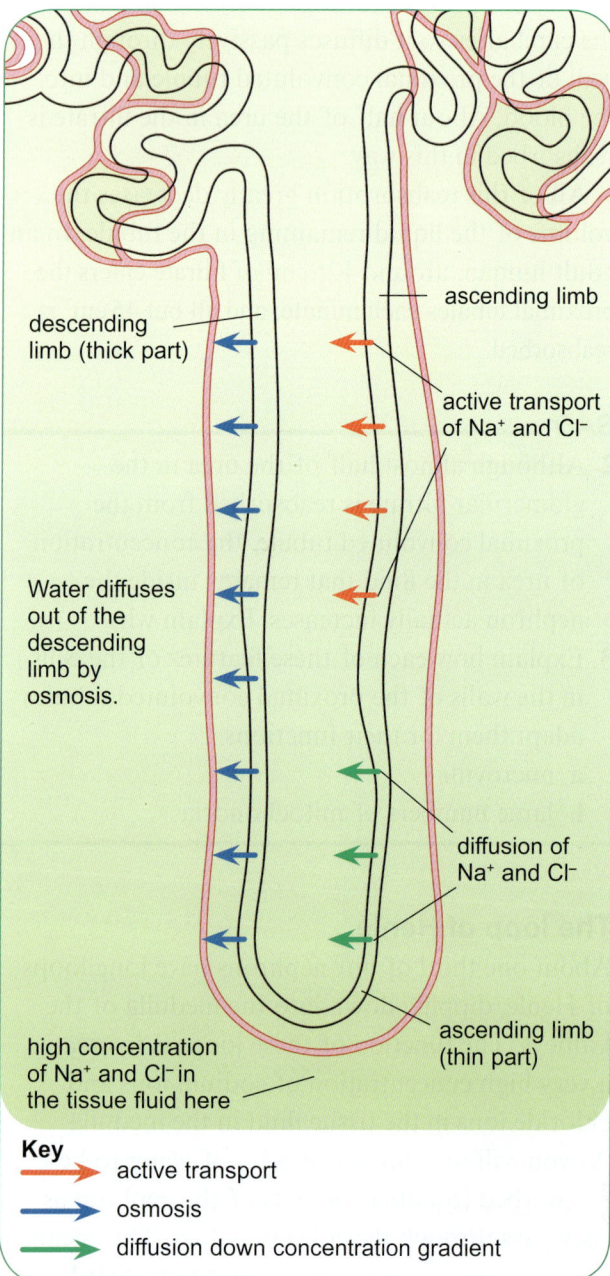

Figure 8.12 The loop of Henlé.

water moves out of the collecting duct and into the tissues around it. It moves into the blood capillaries (the **vasa recta**) and is transported away (Figure 8.13).

The loop of Henlé helps to conserve water. The lower the water potential it can build up, the greater will be the water potential gradient between the fluid inside the collecting ducts and the tissues outside the duct. This enables more water to be drawn out of the collecting duct, resulting in a smaller volume of more concentrated urine.

Osmoregulation

Osmoregulation is the control of the water content of the body. This is a vital part of homeostasis, and it involves the kidneys, the pituitary gland and a part of the brain called the hypothalamus. It works by means of negative feedback.

The **hypothalamus** contains sensory neurones called **osmoreceptors**. They are sensitive to the water potential of the blood that passes through the hypothalamus. Their cell bodies produce a hormone called **anti-diuretic hormone**, **ADH**. ADH is a small peptide, made up of just nine amino acids.

However, the osmoreceptor cells don't secrete this hormone directly into the blood. Instead, the ADH passes along their axons, which terminate in the **posterior pituitary gland** (Figure 8.14).

If the water potential in the blood is too low (that is, the blood does not contain enough water), some of this ADH will be released from the ends of these axons, just like a transmitter substance at a synapse. However, ADH is released into the blood, not into a synaptic cleft. The ADH is therefore secreted from the posterior pituitary gland, even though it was synthesised in the hypothalamus.

We have seen that water is reabsorbed from the fluid in the nephron and back into the blood as the fluid passes through the collecting ducts. Water is drawn out of the collecting ducts by osmosis, moving down its water potential gradient. The water balance of the body can be controlled by adjusting the water permeability of the plasma membranes of the collecting duct cells. Make them more permeable, and more water is reabsorbed and less is lost in the urine. Make them impermeable and no

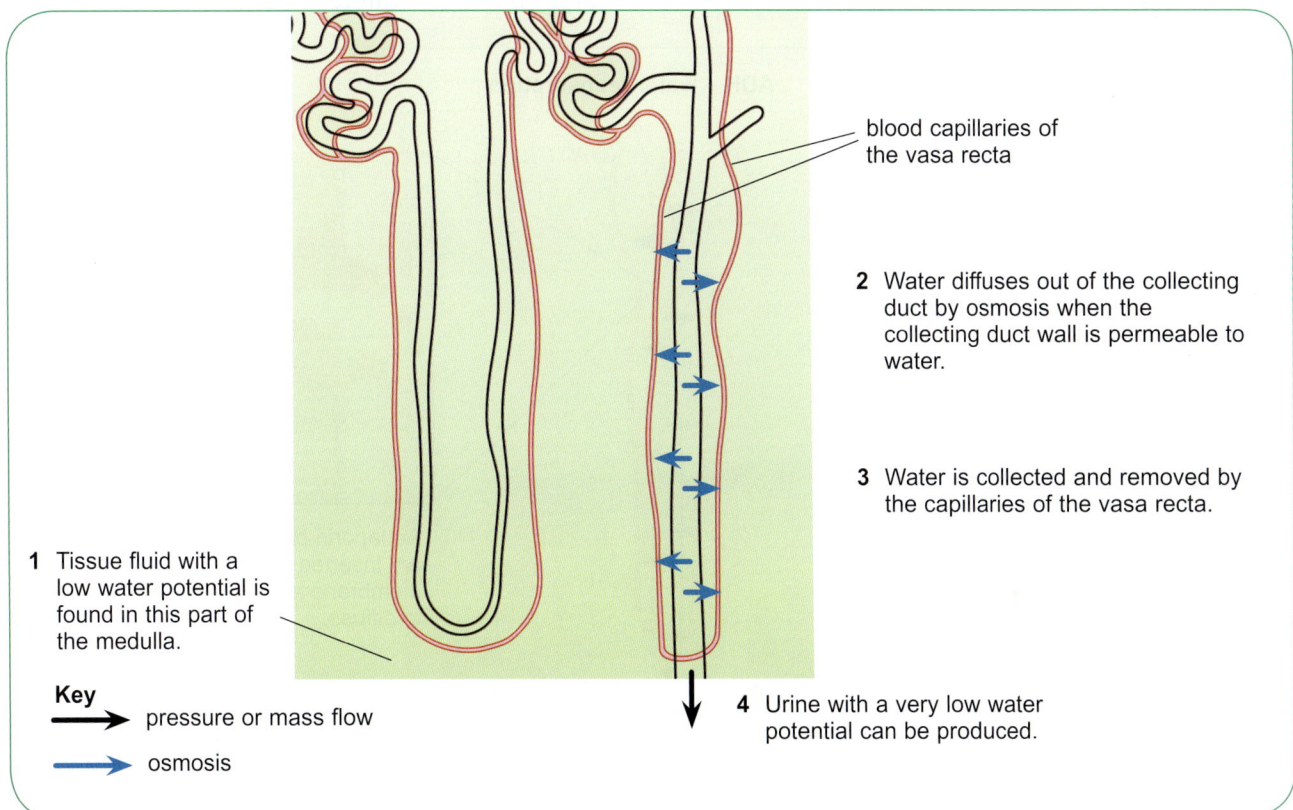

blood capillaries of the vasa recta

2 Water diffuses out of the collecting duct by osmosis when the collecting duct wall is permeable to water.

3 Water is collected and removed by the capillaries of the vasa recta.

1 Tissue fluid with a low water potential is found in this part of the medulla.

Key

→ pressure or mass flow

→ osmosis

4 Urine with a very low water potential can be produced.

Figure 8.13 Reabsorption of water from the collecting duct.

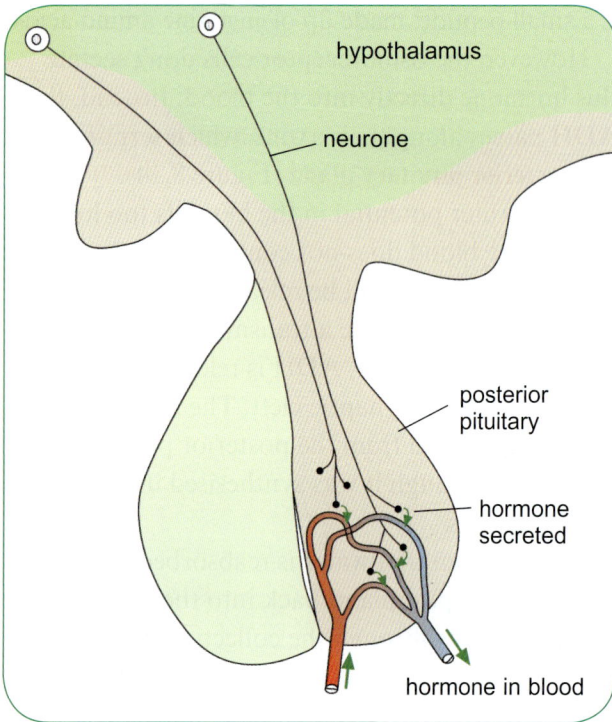

Figure 8.14 ADH is produced in the hypothalamus and moves along axons to be released into the blood from the posterior pituitary gland.

water is reabsorbed, so more is lost in the urine.

These cells are the target cells for ADH. ADH molecules slot into receptors on their plasma membranes. This causes little groups of protein molecules in their cytoplasm, called **aquaporins**, to move to the plasma membrane and insert themselves into it (Figure 8.15). They form channels that allow water molecules to pass through.

So, with ADH in position, water can move freely out of the collecting ducts and back into the blood. A smaller volume of urine is therefore formed, which has a much lower osmotic potential than blood plasma (hypertonic), and the body conserves water.

Everything goes into reverse if the blood contains too much water. The osmoreceptors in the hypothalamus are not stimulated, and so only a little ADH is released into the blood. Much less ADH binds to receptors in the plasma membranes of the collecting duct cells, and the aquaporins move back into the cytoplasm. Now the walls of the collecting ducts are quite impermeable to water, so most of the water in the fluid inside the collecting ducts flows along and into the bladder. Large volumes of dilute urine are produced.

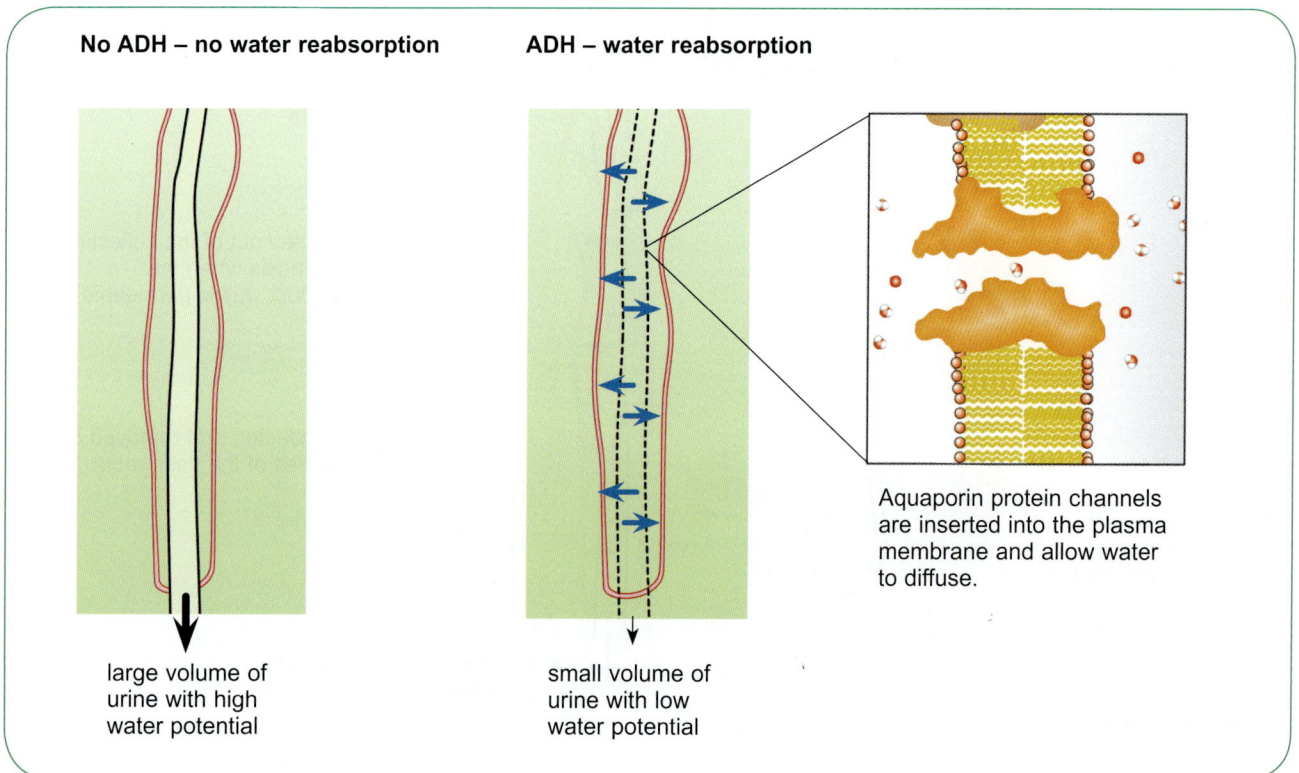

Aquaporin protein channels are inserted into the plasma membrane and allow water to diffuse.

Figure 8.15 ADH and water reabsorption.

SAQ

4 The graph shows the relative concentrations of four substances in the glomerular filtrate as it passes along a nephron.

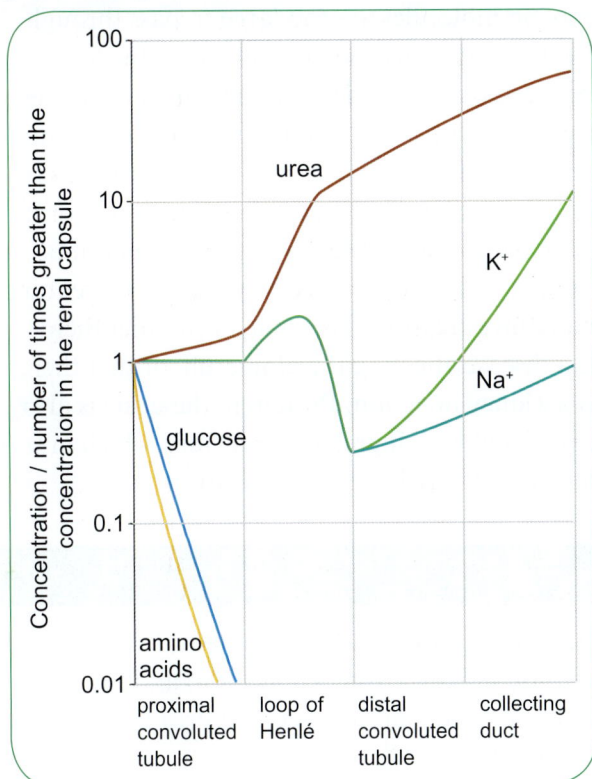

a What is unusual about the y-axis of the graph? Why is it shown this way?

b Take each curve in turn, and explain why it is this shape.

5 The graph shows the rates at which fluid flows through different parts of a nephron.

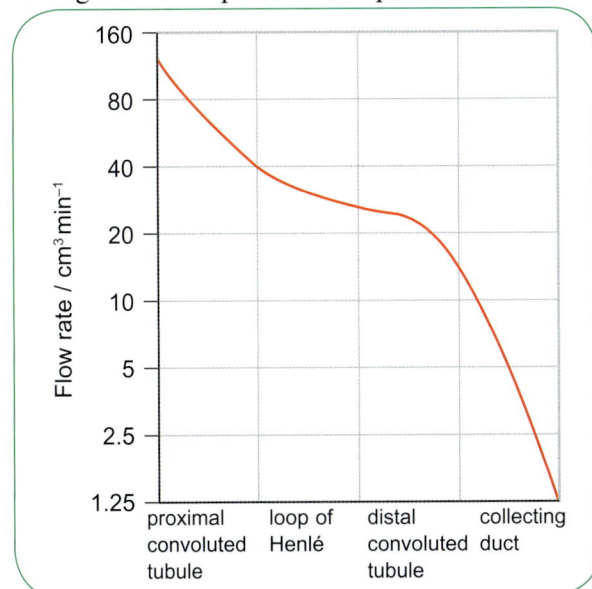

If water flows into an impermeable tube like a hosepipe, it flows out of the far end at the same rate as it flows in. However, this clearly does not happen in a nephron. Suggest an explanation for the shape of the graph.

6 Make a copy of Figure 7.1 on page 141, but do not include the text. Instead, write in your own text to explain how negative feedback controls the water content of the blood. You should make clear where the receptors are, what the effectors are and how information is communicated between the receptors and effectors.

7 The table shows the percentage of nephrons that have long loops of Henlé in five mammals, and also the maximum concentration of the urine that they can produce.

Mammal	Percentage of long loops	Maximum concentration of urine (arbitrary units)
beaver	0	0.96
desert mouse	100	9.2
human	14	2.6
jerboa	33	12.0
pig	3	2.0

a Describe any relationship that you can see between the percentage of long loops of Henlé and the environment in which a mammal lives.

b Describe any relationship that you can see between the percentage of long loops of Henlé and the maximum concentration of urine produced.

c Suggest reasons for the relationships you have described.

Using urine for diagnosis

It is much easier to collect a urine sample from a person than to collect a blood sample. Simple tests on urine can give early indications of health problems, which can then be investigated more thoroughly. Dipsticks can be used to test for a range of different substances, including glucose and protein.

The presence of glucose in urine indicates that a person may have diabetes – a disorder in which the normal blood glucose control mechanisms do not work properly. This is described in Chapter 10. Normally, all the glucose from the glomerular filtrate is reabsorbed into the blood as it passes through the proximal convoluted tubules, so there will be none at all in the urine. However, if blood glucose concentration rises too high, it is not possible for all of the glucose in the filtrate to be reabsorbed, and some will remain in the urine.

The presence of protein in urine may indicate that something is wrong with the kidneys. Most protein molecules are too large to pass through the basement membrane that acts as the filter between the capillaries and the lumen of the renal capsule. It is not uncommon for there to be small amounts of protein in urine for short periods of time – for example, after vigorous exercise, or if someone has a high fever – but large amounts, or the persistent presence of protein, will require more investigation. They may mean that there is a disease affecting the glomeruli, or that there is a kidney infection. Protein in the urine is also associated with high blood pressure, which in turn increases the risk of heart disease.

Summary

- Excretion is the removal of the waste products of metabolism, some of which are toxic, from the body. The main excretory products of mammals are carbon dioxide (from respiration) and urea (from the deamination of excess amino acids). Deamination occurs in the liver, and urea is produced via the ornithine cycle.

- The kidneys are supplied with blood through the renal arteries, and the renal veins deliver blood to the vena cava. Each kidney contains many tubules called nephrons. Blood is delivered to the renal capsule of each nephron in an afferent arteriole, which forms a glomerulus in the cup of the capsule. A narrower vessel, the efferent arteriole, takes blood away.

- Ultrafiltration occurs as fluid is forced, under pressure, from the capillaries of the glomerulus, through the endothelium of the capillary, through the basement membrane of the renal capsule, and between the podocytes. The filter is the basement membrane. Only small molecules can pass through, so all blood cells and large molecules (including almost all proteins) remain in the blood.

- As the filtrate flows through the proximal convoluted tubule, all the glucose, most of the water and a high proportion of ions such as sodium and chloride are reabsorbed into the blood. Some of this occurs by diffusion, and some by active transport. Glucose is moved by co-transport (indirect active transport) along with sodium ions.

- A counter-current mechanism builds up a high concentration (low water potential) in the tissues surrounding the loop of Henlé. The collecting ducts run through these areas, so water tends to move out of the collecting ducts by osmosis, down a water potential gradient.

- The permeability of the collecting duct walls is affected by ADH, a hormone secreted by the posterior pituitary gland when the concentration of the blood is too high. ADH makes the walls more permeable, so more water is reabsorbed and small quantities of concentrated urine are excreted.

- The presence of glucose in urine indicates the possibility of diabetes, and the presence of protein may indicate disease affecting the glomeruli.

Questions

Multiple choice questions

1 Humans excrete nitrogen in the form of urea because it is:
   A more toxic and more alkaline than ammonia.
   B less soluble than ammonia and less toxic.
   C an extremely soluble gas.
   D able to maintain the pH of the blood.

2 Which of the following statements about urea synthesis is **correct**?
   A It is made in the kidney in the ornithine cycle from deaminated amino acids and carbon dioxide.
   B It is produced from excess amino acids alone.
   C It does not require energy to combine ammonia and carbon dioxide.
   D It is made in the liver in the ornithine cycle from deaminated amino acids and carbon dioxide.

3 The diagram below represents a kidney tubule. Where in the tubule is the most glucose reabsorbed?

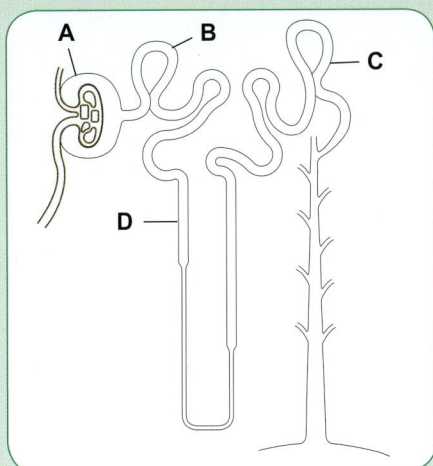

4 The diagram below shows a nephron of a mammalian kidney.

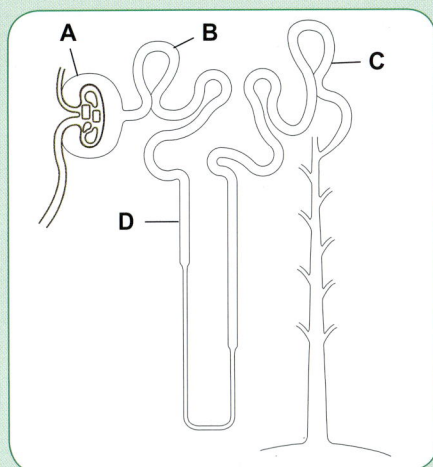

Which of the labelled structures has walls that have variable permeability to water and so affect the final concentration and volume of the urine excreted?

continued ...

5 The diagrams below shows the nephrons of three different mammals: the house mouse which can survive with a water supply every few days, the beaver which has a large supply of water and the kangaroo rat which can live in the desert without drinking water at all.

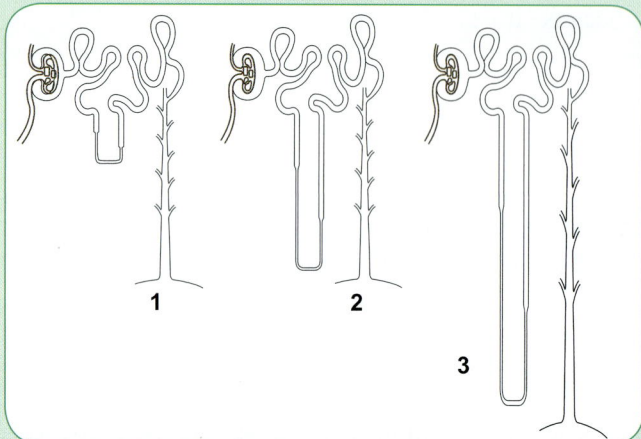

Which of the following correctly identifies the nephron of each animal?

	House mouse	Beaver	Kangaroo rat
A	2	1	3
B	1	2	3
C	3	2	1
D	3	1	2

6 The diagram below shows a glomerulus and Bowman's capsule of a mammalian nephron.

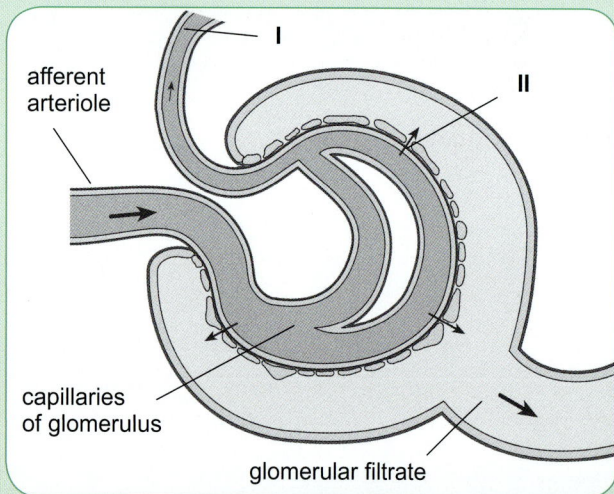

Which of the following correctly identifies the diameter of vessel **I** and the process shown at **II**?

	I	II
A	wider than afferent arteriole	ultrafiltration
B	narrower than afferent arteriole	ultrafiltration
C	narrower than afferent arteriole	selective reabsorption
D	wider than afferent arteriole	selective reabsorption

continued ...

7 A function of the loop of Henlé is to:
   A vary its permeability to maintain the water potential of the body.
   B actively transport glucose from the lumen to the capillaries.
   C concentrate sodium ions in the medulla.
   D absorb water from the collecting duct.

8 Proteins larger than relative molecular mass 68 000 are not filtered from the glomerulus into the space of the Bowman's capsule because:
   A the gaps in the endothelium of the capillary are very small.
   B the slit pores of the podocytes are 25 nm wide.
   C the basement membrane acts a dialysing membrane.
   D the filtration pressure is high.

9 The micrograph shown below is a cross-section of the cortex of the kidney.

   Which of the labelled structures correctly identifies a distal convoluted tubule (DCT)?

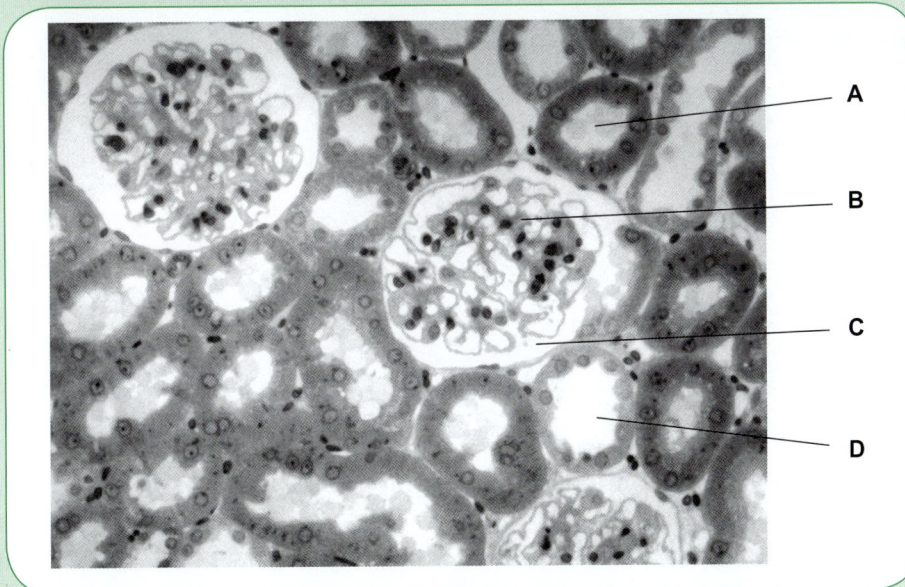

10 Even though glucose is filtered out of the glomerulus it is not found in urine in mammals. This is because:
   A glucose is actively reabsorbed with sodium ions in the proximal convoluted tubule.
   B glucose is actively reabsorbed in the loop of Henlé.
   C the glucose enters the efferent arteriole from the Bowman's capsule.
   D glucose is used in respiration in the nephron.

continued ...

Structured questions

11 a Draw a large labelled diagram to illustrate the detailed structure of a nephron of a mammalian kidney. [6 marks]

b On the diagram, indicate:
   i the direction of movement of small molecules in the glomerulus
   ii the movement of sodium ions in the loop of Henlé
   iii the direction of increasing osmotic potential
   iv counter-current flow
   v the direction of flow of water if ADH is present. [5 marks]

c Give **three** features of the proximal convoluted tubule necessary for its role in selective reabsorption. [3 marks]

d Give **one** feature of the collecting duct which allows it to control the water content of the body. [1 mark]

12 The electron micrograph below is of a section of a part of the kidney nephron unit.

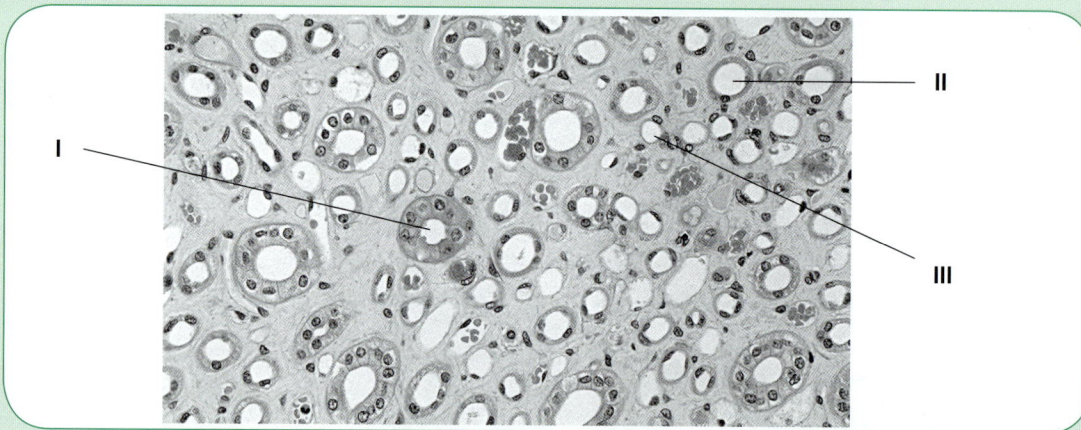

a Suggest which region of the kidney is shown on the micrograph. Give a reason for your answer. [2 marks]

b Identify the structures labelled **I** to **III**. [3 marks]

c Make a drawing of the structure labelled **I** at a magnification of ×2. [3 marks]

d Suggest a reason for the differences observed between structure **II** and **III**. [2 marks]

e The table below shows the amounts of some substances in both blood plasma and urine. [1 mark]

Substance	Percentage in plasma	Percentage in urine	Increase
water	90	95	-
protein	8	0	-
glucose	0.1	0	-
urea	0.03	2	67×
Na⁺	0.32	0.35	1×

i Explain why there is no protein or glucose in urine. [2 marks]

ii What is the role of sodium ions in the functioning of the kidneys? [1 mark]

continued ...

f Copy the graph below, and draw the curves for urea and glucose in various parts of the nephron. [2 marks]

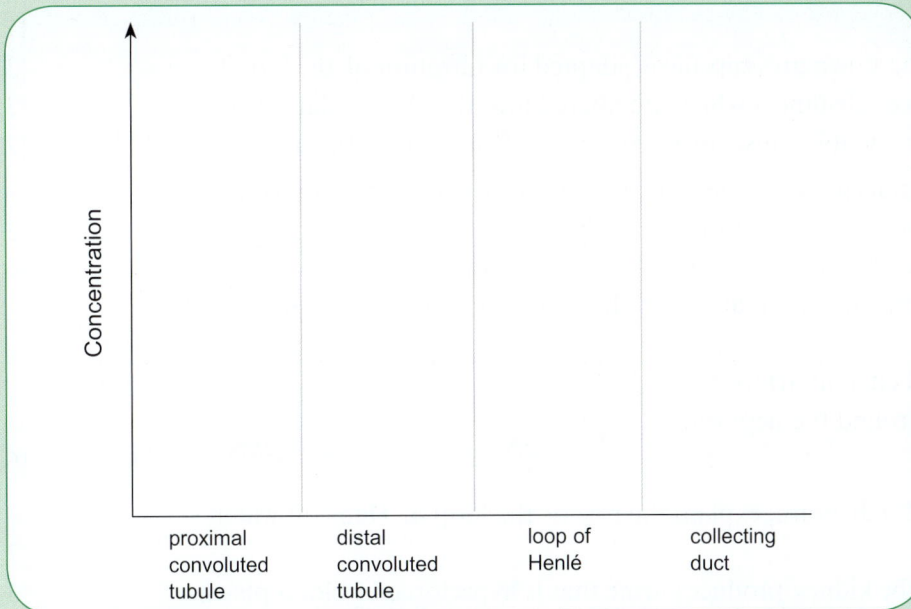

13 The figure below shows a section through the wall of the proximal convoluted tubule of a kidney nephron as seen under the electron microscope.

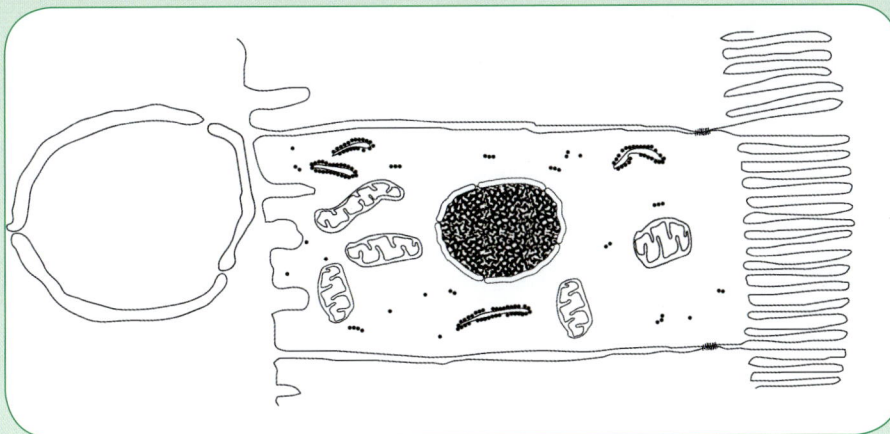

a Copy the diagram above. On your diagram label the following structures: microvilli, tight junction, capillary, mitochondrion, lumen [3 marks]

b i What is the main process which occurs in the proximal convoluted tubule? [1 mark]

ii State how the following assist in the process named in b i: mitochondria, tight junction, capillary, microvilli [5 marks]

c Briefly describe how glucose, small proteins, sodium ions and water are taken up from the lumen of the tubule into the peritubular capillaries. [4 marks]

d What is the clinical significance of the presence of glucose in urine? [2 marks]

continued…

Essay questions

14 **a** Describe how ultrafiltration occurs in the Bowman's capsule to form glomerular filtrate. [7 marks]

    b Explain how the Bowman's capsule is adapted for filtration of the blood. [3 marks]

    c **i** Identify **three** substances which are filtered into the glomerular filtrate. [3 marks]

       ii Outline one possible cause for the presence of proteins in the urine. [2 marks]

15 **a** What do you understand by the term 'excretion'? Explain the importance of removing nitrogenous waste from the body. [3 marks]

    b Briefly describe why and how urea is formed in mammals. [6 marks]

    c Describe the roles and adaptations of the following blood vessels in the kidney nephron.

       i afferent and efferent arterioles

       ii capillaries around the nephron

       iii vasa recta [6 marks]

16 **a** With the aid of a diagram, explain the role of the loop of Henlé in water conservation. [7 marks]

    b Describe how the kidney produces urine that is hypertonic to blood plasma. [6 marks]

    c A student observes that when he drinks coffee while studying, he has to urinate more than if he drinks the same volume of water. Suggest an explanation for this observation. [2 marks]

Chapter 9
Nervous coordination

By the end of this chapter you should be able to:

a   describe the structure of motor and sensory neurones;

b   explain the role of nerve cell membranes in establishing and maintaining the resting potential;

c   describe the conduction of an action potential along the nerve cell membrane, including the role of myelin in increasing the speed of transmission;

d   explain synaptic transmission, including the structure of a cholinergic synapse;

e   outline the roles of synapses.

The human nervous system

The human nervous system is made up of the **brain** and **spinal cord**, which form the **central nervous system**; and **nerves**, which form the **peripheral nervous system**. Nerves themselves, and also much of the central nervous system, are made up of highly specialised cells called **neurones**.

Information is transferred along neurones in the form of **action potentials**, sometimes known as **nerve impulses**. These are fleeting changes in the electrical charge on either side of the plasma membranes.

Neurones

Figure 9.1 shows the structure of a **motor neurone**. This type of neurone transmits action potentials from the central nervous system to an effector such as a muscle or a gland.

The cell body of a motor neurone lies within the spinal cord or the brain. The nucleus of a neurone is in the cell body (Figure 9.2). Often, dark specks can be seen in the cytoplasm. These are groups of ribosomes involved in protein synthesis.

Many thin cytoplasmic processes extend from the cell body. In a motor neurone, all but one of these are quite short. These short processes conduct impulses towards the cell body, and they are called **dendrites**. One process is much longer, and this conducts impulses away from the cell body. This is called the **axon**. A motor neurone with its cell body in your spinal cord might have its axon running all the way to a toe, so axons can be very long.

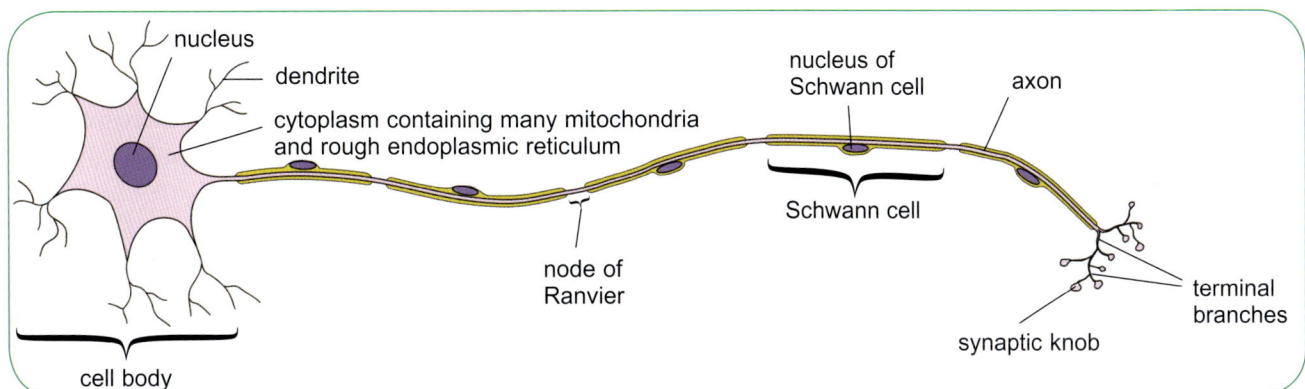

Figure 9.1   A motor neurone.

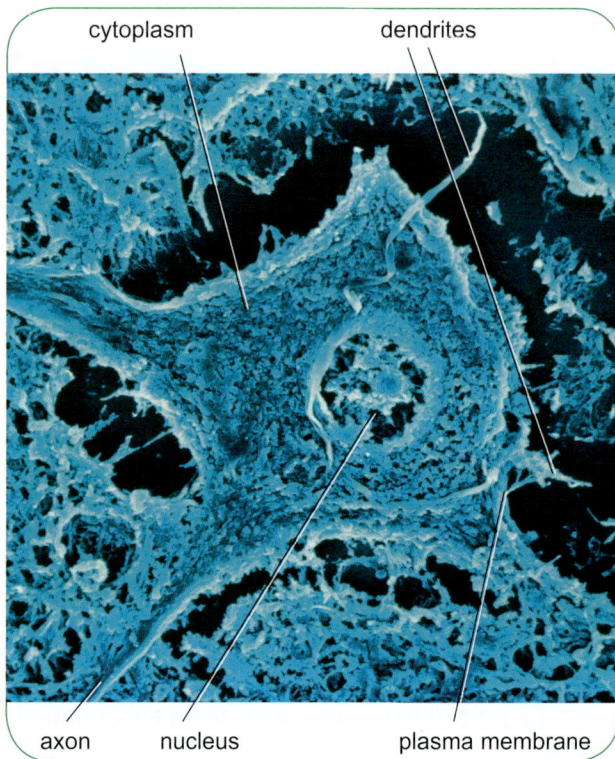

Figure 9.2 An electron micrograph of the cell body of a motor neurone within the spinal cord (×1390).

cytoplasm   dendrites

axon   nucleus   plasma membrane

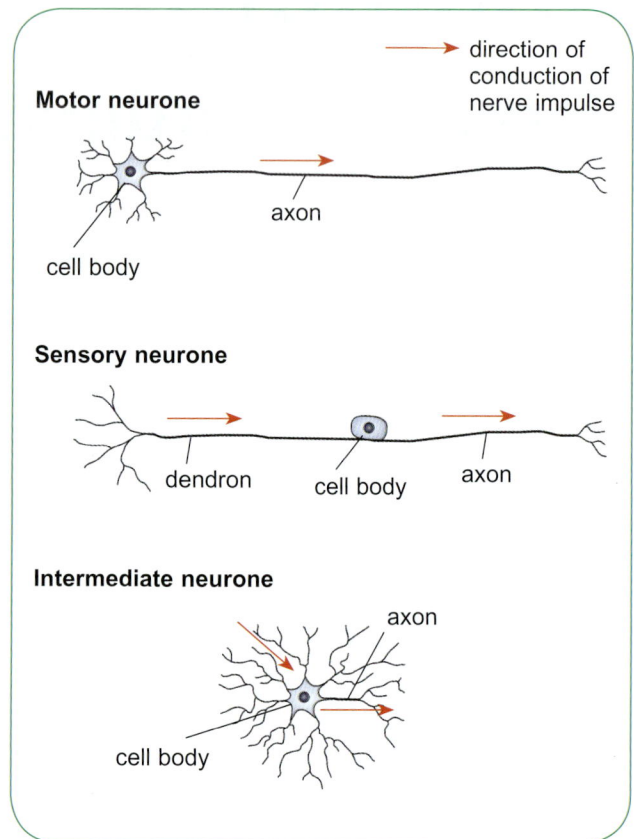

Figure 9.3 Types of neurones.

Motor neurone

direction of conduction of nerve impulse

axon

cell body

Sensory neurone

dendron   cell body   axon

Intermediate neurone

axon

cell body

Within the cytoplasm, all the usual organelles, such as endoplasmic reticulum, Golgi body and mitochondria, are present. Particularly large numbers of mitochondria are found at the tips of the terminal branches of the axon, together with many vesicles containing chemicals called **transmitter substances**. These are involved in passing nerve impulses from the neurone to a muscle.

Sensory neurones (Figure 9.3) carry impulses via a **dendron** from sense organs to the brain or spinal cord. Their cell bodies are inside structures called **dorsal root ganglia**, just outside the spinal cord.

Intermediate neurones, sometimes called **relay neurones** (Figure 9.3), have their cell bodies and their cytoplasmic processes inside the brain or spinal cord. They are adapted to carry impulses from and to numerous other neurones.

SAQ

1 Describe two differences between the structures of a motor neurone and a sensory neurone.

Myelin

In some neurones, cells called **Schwann cells** wrap themselves around the axon all along its length. Figure 9.4 shows one such cell, viewed as the axon is cut transversely. The Schwann cell spirals around, enclosing the axon in many layers of its plasma membrane. This enclosing sheath, called the **myelin sheath**, is made largely of lipid, together with some proteins.

There are small uncovered gaps along the axons, where there are spaces between the Schwann cells. These are known as **nodes of Ranvier**. They occur about every 1–3 mm.

About one third of our motor and sensory neurones are myelinated. The sheath increases the speed of conduction of the nerve impulses, and this is described on pages 186–187.

A reflex arc

Figure 9.5 shows how sensory, intermediate and motor neurones are arranged in the body to form a **reflex arc**. In the example in Figure 9.5, a spinal

Myelinated axon

- node of Ranvier
- axon
- Schwann cell forming myelin sheath

Cross-section of the myelin sheath and axon

- plasma membrane of a Schwann cell
- axon
- nucleus of Schwann cell
- cytoplasm of Schwann cell

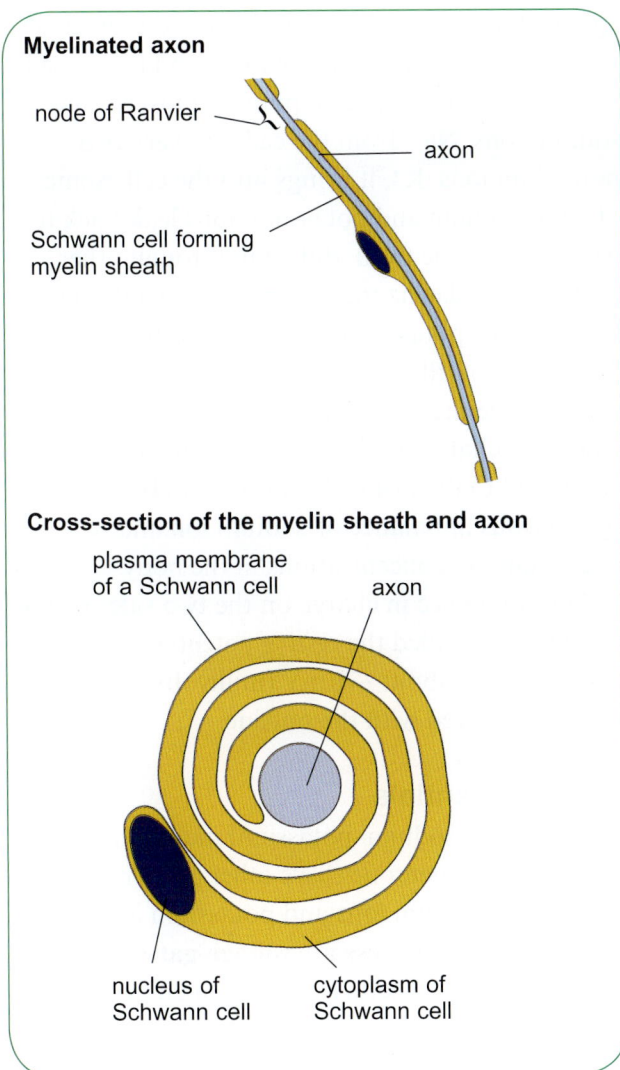

Figure 9.4 A myelinated axon.

reflex arc is shown, in which the nerve impulses are carried into and out of the spinal cord. Other reflex arcs may involve the brain.

A reflex arc is the pathway along which impulses are carried from a receptor to an effector, without involving any conscious thought. You may remember that an effector is a part of the body that responds to a stimulus. Muscles and glands are effectors.

The impulse arrives along the sensory neurone and passes through the dorsal root ganglion into the spinal cord. Here it may be passed directly to the motor neurone, or to an intermediate neurone and then the motor neurone. The impulse sweeps along the axon of the motor neurone, arriving at the effector within less than one second of the receptor having picked up the stimulus.

The response by the effector can be extremely rapid. It is called a **reflex action**. A reflex action is a fast, stereotyped response to a particular stimulus. Reflex actions help us to avoid danger, by allowing us to respond immediately to a potentially harmful situation without having to spend time thinking about it. For example, a sharp pinprick on the bottom of your foot will probably result in contraction of muscles in your leg, pulling the leg away from the stimulus.

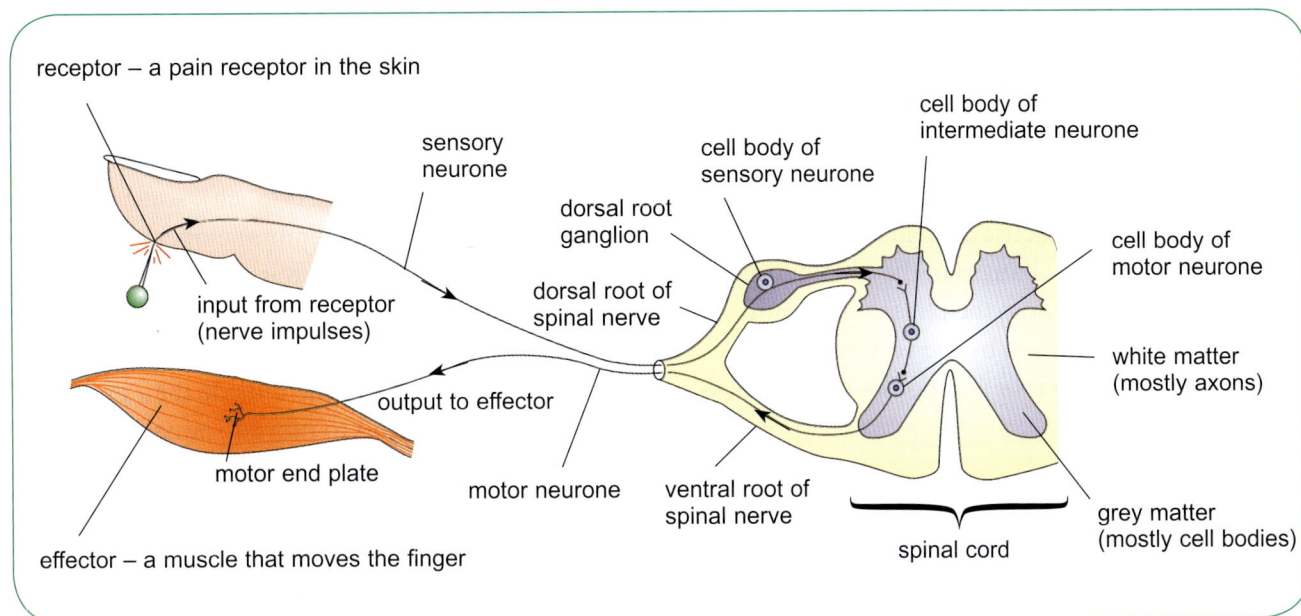

Figure 9.5 A spinal reflex arc.

2 Some reflex actions appear to be innate (inborn). They appear to be 'hard-wired' into our brains from birth. Other reflex actions are learned during our lifetimes.

  a Think of a reflex action that almost everyone shows, and that is therefore likely to be innate. Name:
- the stimulus
- the receptor
- the effector
- the response.

  b Do the same for a reflex action that you have learned.

  c What, if any, are the survival values of the reflex actions you have described?

Structure of a nerve

Axons of neurones are almost always found in bundles. There may be several thousand of them, lying side by side and surrounded by a protective covering called the **perineurium** (Figure 9.6). It is like a cable with lots of electrical wires inside it.

Some nerves contain only sensory neurones, some only motor neurones, and some contain a mixture of both. These are respectively known as sensory nerves, motor nerves and mixed nerves. In each type of nerve, some of the axons are myelinated and some not.

Transmission of nerve impulses

Neurones transmit impulses as electrical signals. These signals travel very rapidly from one end of the neurone to the other. They are not a flow of electrons, like an electric current. Rather, the signals are very brief changes in the distribution of electrical charge across the plasma membranes. These changes are caused by the very rapid movement of sodium ions and potassium ions into and out of the axon.

Resting potential

Even a resting neurone is very active. The sodium–potassium pumps in its plasma membrane (Figure 9.7) constantly move sodium ions out of the cell and potassium ions into it. These movements are

against the concentration gradients, so they involve active transport. Large amounts of ATP are used.

The sodium–potassium pump removes three sodium ions, Na^+, from the cell for every two potassium ions, K^+, it brings into the cell. Some of these sodium and potassium ions leak back to where they came from, diffusing through other parts of the plasma membrane. The membrane is leakier for potassium ions than sodium ions. As a result of all of this, there are more positive ions outside the membrane than inside. There is a positive charge on the outside of the membrane compared to the inside. Neurones can be affected by a serious imbalance of sodium ion and potassium ion concentrations in the body.

This difference in charge on the two sides of the membrane is called the **resting potential**. In most neurones, it is about $-70\,mV$ (millivolts) on the inside compared with the outside.

Action potentials

As well as the sodium–potassium pump, the plasma membranes of neurones have other protein channels that will let sodium ions and potassium ions pass through. Some of these are **voltage-gated channels**. This means that whether they are open or closed depends on the potential difference (voltage) across the membrane. When the membrane is at its resting potential, with a potential difference of $-70\,mV$ inside, these voltage-gated channels are closed.

Other channels are caused to open or close depending on stimuli such as touch. Imagine a touch receptor in your hand. The receptor is actually the end of a sensory neurone. When the receptor receives a stimulus (touch), some sodium channels in the plasma membrane open. The sodium ions that had been pumped out now flood back into the cell. They do this because there is an electrical gradient for them – the membrane has more positive charge on the outside than on the inside, so the ions tend to move to equal out the charges on the two sides. There is also a chemical gradient – there are more sodium ions outside than inside, so they tend to diffuse inwards down their concentration gradient. This 'double gradient' is known as an **electrochemical gradient**.

Within a very short space of time, the resting

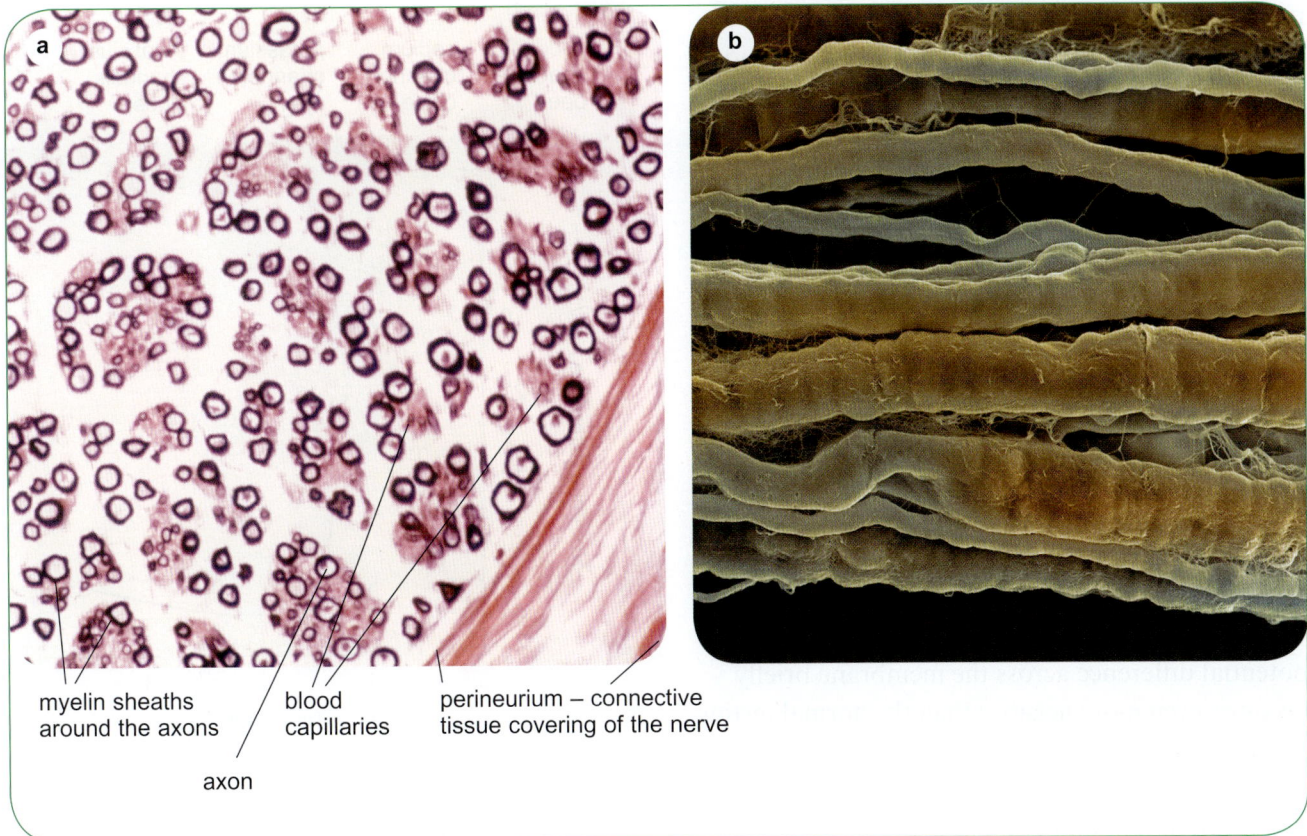

Figure 9.6   a A photomicrograph of a transverse section across a small part of a nerve (×960). **b** This is a scanning electron micrograph of a few of the axons in a nerve (×4000). Each axon belongs to a different neurone. You can see that the axons are not all the same size.

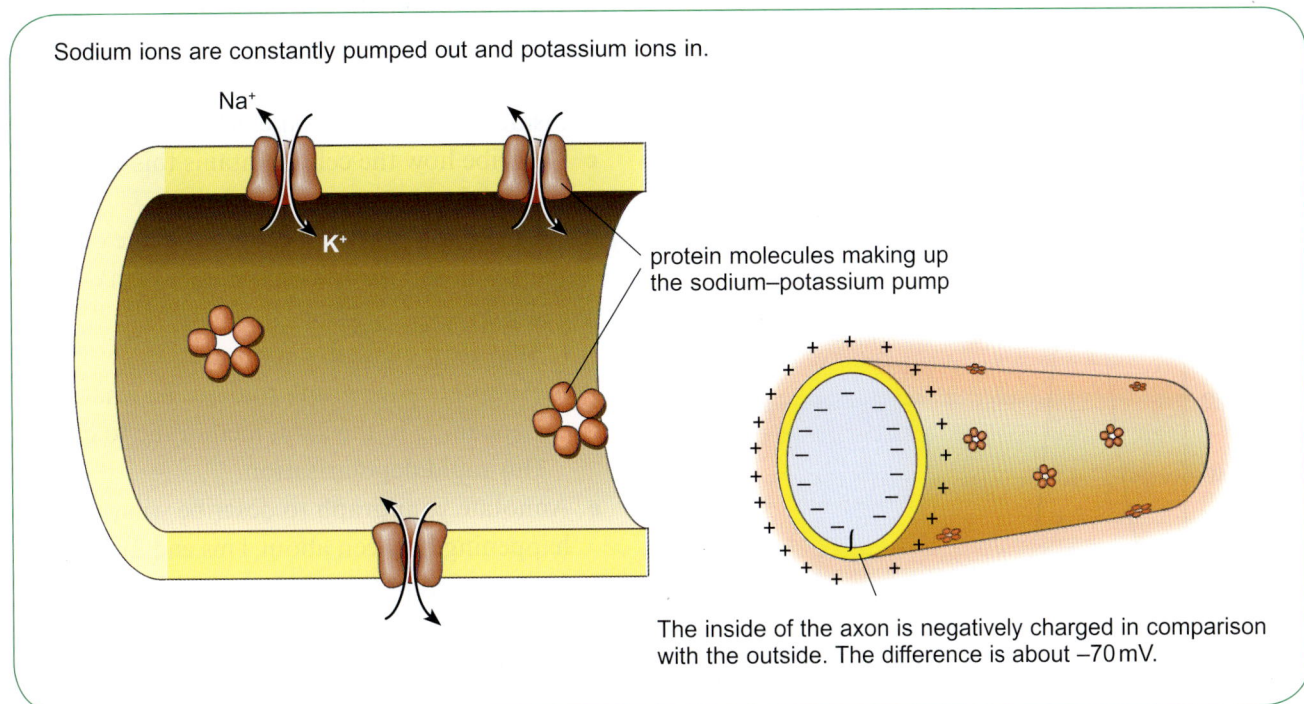

Figure 9.7   The activity of the sodium–potassium pump in maintaining the potential in a 'resting' neurone.

potential has gone. There is no longer a negative charge inside the axon compared with the outside. The axon membrane is now **depolarised**.

So many sodium ions flood in so quickly that they 'overshoot'. For a brief moment, the axon actually becomes positively charged inside, rather than negatively. Then the sodium channels close, so sodium ions stop moving into the axon.

At this point, in response to the voltage changes that have been taking place, the potassium channels open. Potassium ions therefore diffuse out of the axon, down their electrochemical gradient. This movement of the potassium ions removes positive charge from inside the axon to the outside, so the charge across the membrane begins to return to normal. This is called **repolarisation**.

So many potassium ions leave the axon that the potential difference across the membrane briefly becomes even more negative than the normal resting potential. The Na^+/K^+ channels then close, and the sodium–potassium pumps restore the normal distribution of sodium and potassium ions across the membrane, which restores the resting potential.

This sequence of events is called an **action potential**. These changes in electrical charge can be measured and displayed using an oscilloscope. Figure 9.8 shows what an action potential looks like, and Figure 9.9 shows what is happening at the Na^+ and K^+ channels during the action potential.

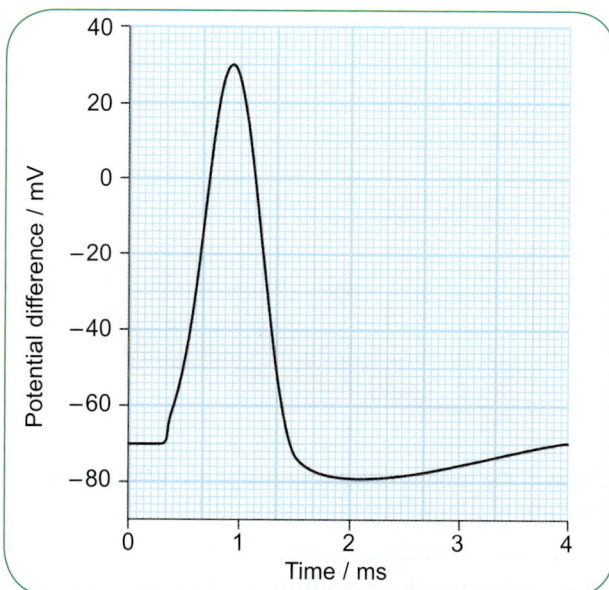

Figure 9.8 Changes in potential difference across a membrane during an action potential.

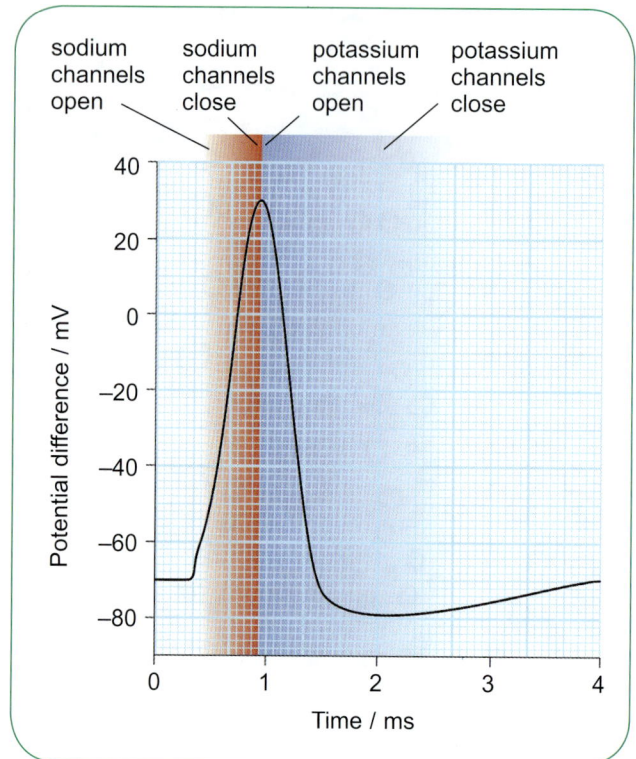

Figure 9.9 The behaviour of ion channels during an action potential.

SAQ

3 Make a copy of Figure 9.8.
  a On your graph, draw a horizontal line right across it to represent the resting potential.
  b The resting potential is said to be $-70\,mV$ inside. What does this mean?
  c Describe how the cell maintains this resting potential.
  d As an action potential begins, the line on the graph shoots upwards from $-70\,mV$ to $+30\,mV$.
    i Why is this called 'depolarisation'?
    ii Annotate your graph to describe what is happening in the axon membrane to cause this rapid depolarisation.
  e Annotate your graph to describe what is happening between about 1 ms and 2 ms.
  f If the action potential starts at time 0, how long does it take between the start of depolarisation and the restoration of the resting potential?

Threshold potentials

Not every touch on your hand will generate an action potential. If the touch is very light, then no action potential will be produced and you will not feel the touch.

Action potentials are only generated if the depolarisation of the axon membrane reaches a value called the **threshold potential** (Figure 9.10). This value varies in different neurones, but is often around −50 mV to −60 mV. If the depolarisation is less than this, nothing more happens. If it is more than this, then a full-size action potential is produced.

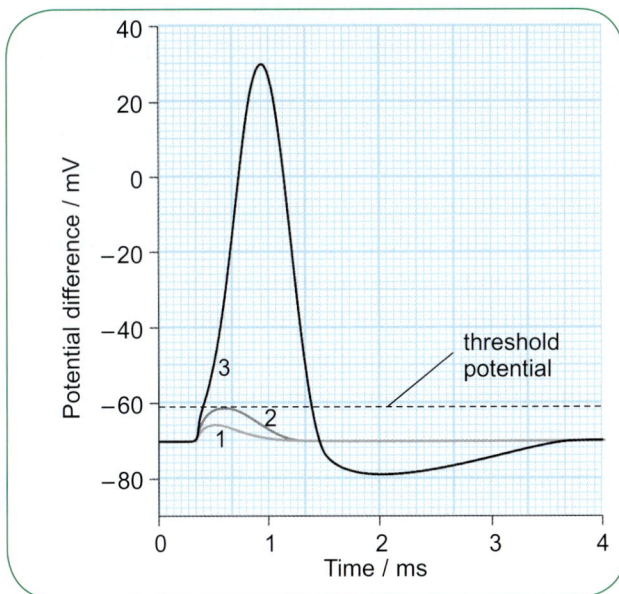

Figure 9.10 A small depolarisation (1 or 2) does not result in an action potential. The depolarisation must meet the threshold potential before an action potential is generated.

Transmission of an action potential

The graphs in Figure 9.8 and Figure 9.9 show the events that take place at one point in the axon membrane. However, the function of a neurone is to transmit information, in the form of action potentials, along itself. How do action potentials move along a neurone?

An action potential at any point in an axon's membrane triggers the production of an action potential in the part of the membrane just next to it. Figure 9.11 shows how it does this. The temporary depolarisation of the membrane where the action potential is causes a 'local circuit' to be set up between the depolarised region and the

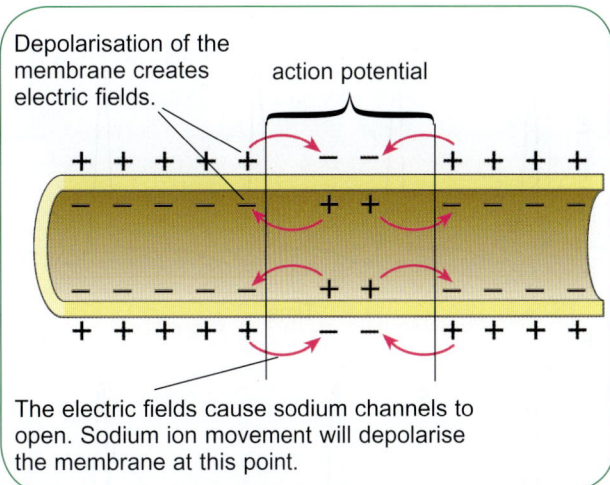

Figure 9.11 How local circuits cause an action potential to move along an axon.

resting regions on either side of it. This depolarises these adjoining regions and so causes voltage-gated sodium and then potassium channels to open. Sodium ions flood in, and a few milliseconds later potassium ions flood out, causing an action potential. In this way, the action potential sweeps all along the membrane of the neurone.

In normal circumstances, nerve cell axons only transmit an action potential in one direction. A 'new' action potential is only generated ahead of the action potential, not behind it. This is because the region behind it is still recovering from the action potential it has just had. The distribution of Na^+ and K^+ in this region is still not back to normal. It is therefore temporarily incapable of generating an action potential. The time it takes to recover is called the **refractory period**.

How action potentials carry information

Action potentials are always the same size. A light touch on your hand will generate exactly the same size of action potentials as a strong touch. Either an action potential is generated, or it is not. This is sometimes known as the 'all-or-nothing' law.

So how does your brain distinguish between a light touch and a strong touch? This is done using a different frequency of action potentials. A heavy touch generates more frequent action potentials than a light touch. The brain interprets a stream of closely spaced action potentials as meaning 'strong stimulus' (Figure 9.12).

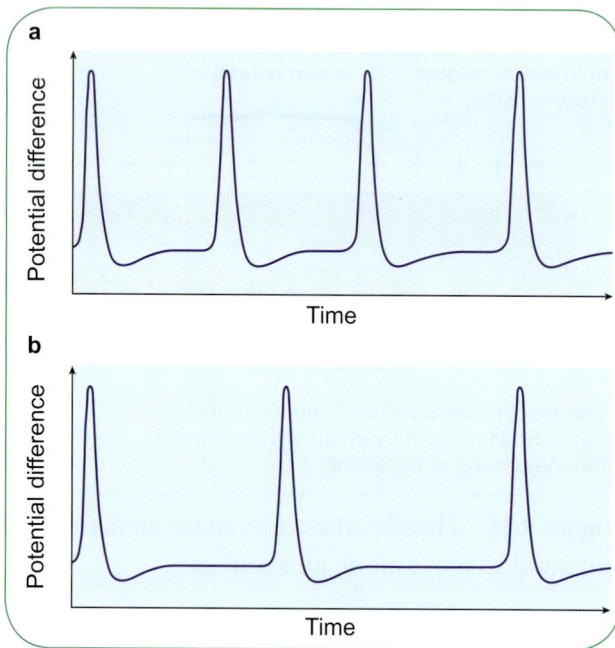

Figure 9.12 **a** A high frequency of impulses is produced when a receptor is given a strong stimulus. **b** A lower frequency of impulses is produced when a receptor is given a weak stimulus. Notice that the size of each action potential remains the same. Only their frequency changes.

Moreover, a strong stimulus is likely to stimulate more neurones than a weak stimulus. While a weak stimulus might result in action potentials being generated in just one or two neurones, a strong stimulus could produce action potentials in many more.

The brain can therefore interpret the frequency of action potentials passing along the axon of a sensory neurone, and the number of neurones carrying action potentials, to get information about the strength of the stimulus detected by the receptor. The nature of the stimulus – whether it is light, heat or touch, for example – is deduced from the position of the sensory neurone bringing the information. If the neurone is from the retina of the eye, then the brain will interpret the information as meaning 'light'. If for some reason a different stimulus, such as pressure, stimulates a receptor cell in the retina, the brain will still interpret the action potentials from this receptor as meaning 'light'. This is why rubbing your eyes when they are shut can cause you to 'see' patterns of light.

Speed of conduction

The speed at which an action potential sweeps along an axon is not the same for every neurone. It depends partly on the diameter of the axon, and partly on whether or not it is myelinated (Figure 9.13).

The wider the axon, the faster the speed of transmission. For example, in a relatively small human axon it may be no more than $15\,\mathrm{m\,s^{-1}}$. Earthworms have 'giant axons' which can transmit action potentials at around $25\,\mathrm{m\,s^{-1}}$. This enables an action potential to sweep along the whole length of the body very quickly, so the earthworm can respond very rapidly to a peck from a bird and escape into its burrow.

Giant axons work well for an earthworm, but humans use a different system for speeding up the transmission of nerve impulses. Myelin insulates axons, and this speeds up the rate of transmission of an action potential along them. Sodium and potassium ions cannot flow through the myelin sheath, so it is not possible for depolarisation or action potentials to occur in parts of the axon that are surrounded by it. These can only happen in the gaps between the sheath, at the nodes of Ranvier.

Figure 9.14 shows how an action potential is transmitted along a myelinated axon. The local circuits that are set up stretch from one node to the next. Thus action potentials 'jump' from one node

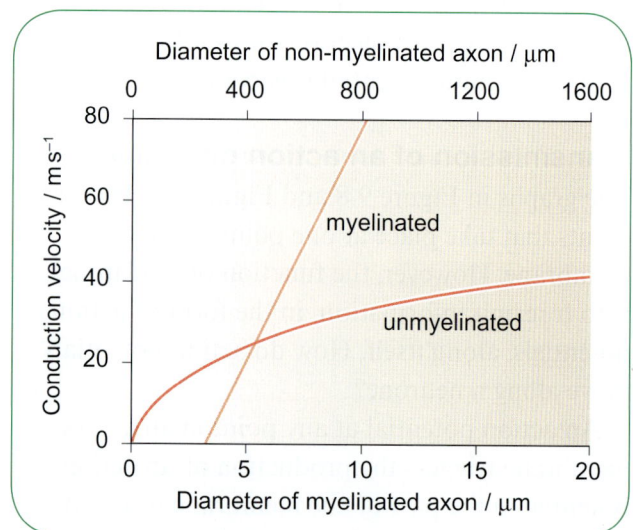

Figure 9.13 Speed of transmission in myelinated and non-myelinated axons of different diameters.

Multiple sclerosis

Multiple sclerosis, MS, is a chronic (long-lasting) disease that generally occurs in people between the ages of 20 and 40. No-one knows what causes it, but for some reason the body's own immune system attacks the myelin sheaths around neurones in the brain and spinal cord. Some researchers think that this inappropriate immune response might be triggered by a virus.

The photograph shows an MRI scan showing a transverse section of the brain of a person with multiple sclerosis. The white areas are places where the myelin sheaths around neurones have been broken down.

The damage to the neurones can cause a wide range of symptoms, including problems with vision, balance and muscle weakness. Usually, there are periods where these symptoms occur, interspersed with periods when the person is almost entirely free of them. In some, the symptoms get progressively worse, but in others the disease remains relatively mild over a long period of time.

At the moment, there is no treatment that completely cures MS, although several different drugs can be used to help to relieve the symptoms. Research is focused on finding ways of quietening the T-lymphocytes that are responsible for the attacks of the immune system on the myelin sheaths.

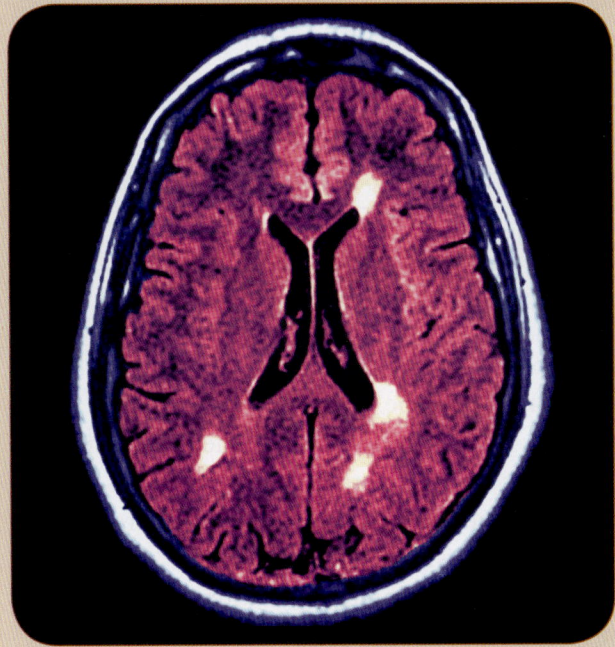

to the next, a distance of between 1 and 3 mm. This is called **saltatory conduction**. It can increase the speed of transmission by up to 50 times.

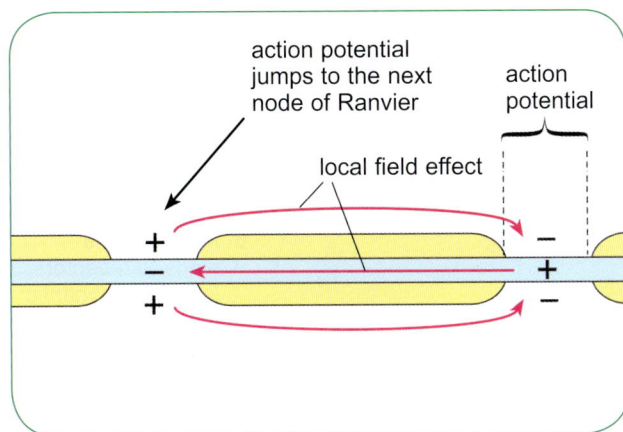

Figure 9.14 Saltatory conduction of an action potential along a myelinated neurone.

Synapses

Where two neurones meet, they do not quite touch each other. There is a very small gap, usually about 20 nm wide, between them. This gap is called a **synaptic cleft**. The parts of the neurones near to the cleft, plus the cleft itself, make up a **synapse** (Figure 9.15).

How impulses cross synapses

Action potentials cannot jump across synapses. Instead, the signal is passed across by a chemical, known as a **transmitter substance**. In outline, an action potential arriving along the plasma membrane of the **presynaptic neurone** causes it to release transmitter substance into the cleft. The transmitter substance molecules diffuse across the cleft, which takes less than a millisecond as the distance is so small. This may set up an

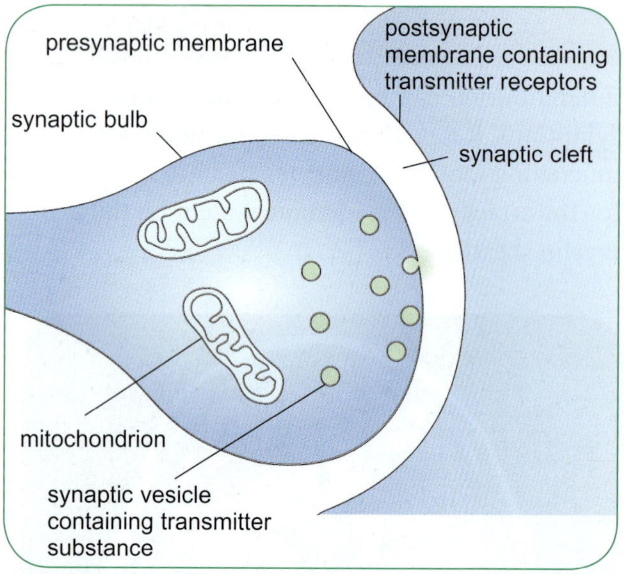

Figure 9.15 A synapse.

action potential in the plasma membrane of the **postsynaptic neurone**.

This is shown in Figure 9.16. The cytoplasm of the presynaptic neurone contains vesicles of transmitter substance. More than 40 different transmitter substances are known. **Noradrenaline** and **acetylcholine** (sometimes abbreviated to ACh) are found throughout the nervous system, while others such as dopamine and glutamate occur only in the brain. We will look at synapses which use acetylcholine as the transmitter substance; they are known as **cholinergic synapses**.

You will remember that, as an action potential sweeps along the plasma membrane of a neurone, local circuits depolarise the next piece of membrane. This opens voltage-gated Na^+ channels and propagates the action potential. In the part of the membrane of the presynaptic neurone that is next to the synaptic cleft, the action potential also causes **calcium ion channels** to open. So the action potential causes not only sodium ions but also calcium ions to flood into the cytoplasm.

This influx of calcium ions causes vesicles of acetylcholine to move to the presynaptic membrane and fuse with it, emptying their contents into the synaptic cleft. (This is an example of exocytosis.) Each action potential causes just a few vesicles to do this, and each vesicle contains up to 10 000 molecules of acetylcholine. The acetylcholine rapidly diffuses across the cleft, usually in less than 0.5 ms.

The plasma membrane of the postsynaptic neurone contains **receptor proteins**. Part of the receptor protein molecule has a complementary shape to part of the acetylcholine molecule, so that the acetylcholine molecules can bind with the receptors. This changes the shape of the protein, opening channels through which sodium ions can pass (Figure 9.17). Sodium ions rush into the cytoplasm of the postsynaptic neurone, depolarising the membrane and starting off an action potential.

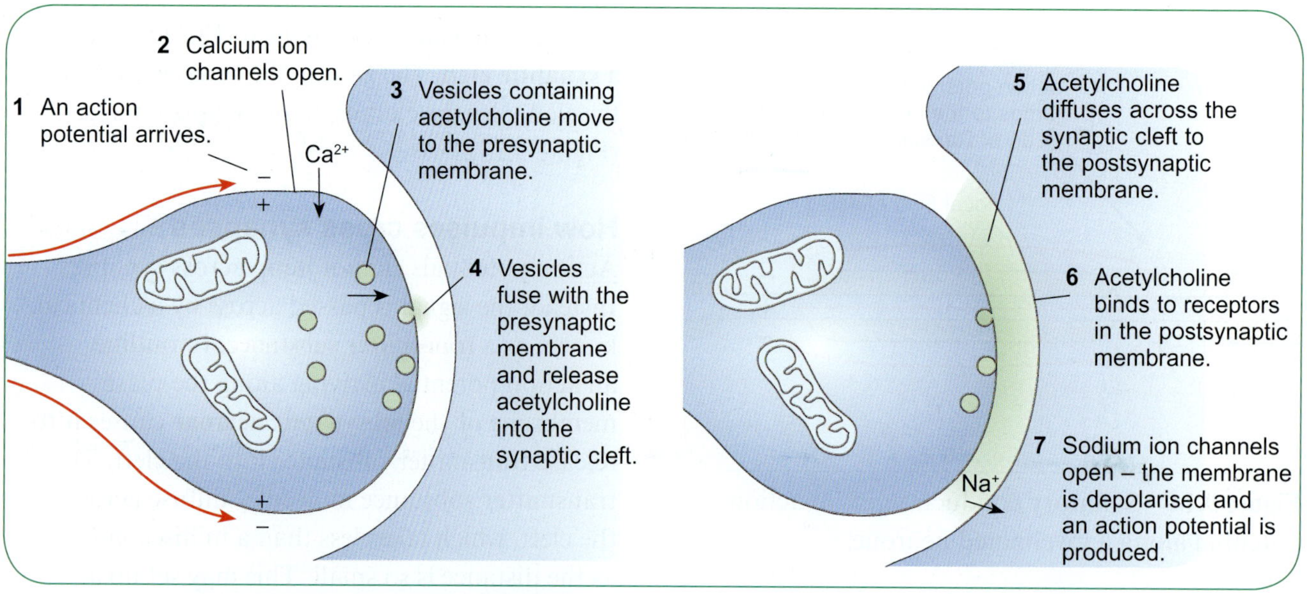

Figure 9.16 How an impulse crosses a synapse.

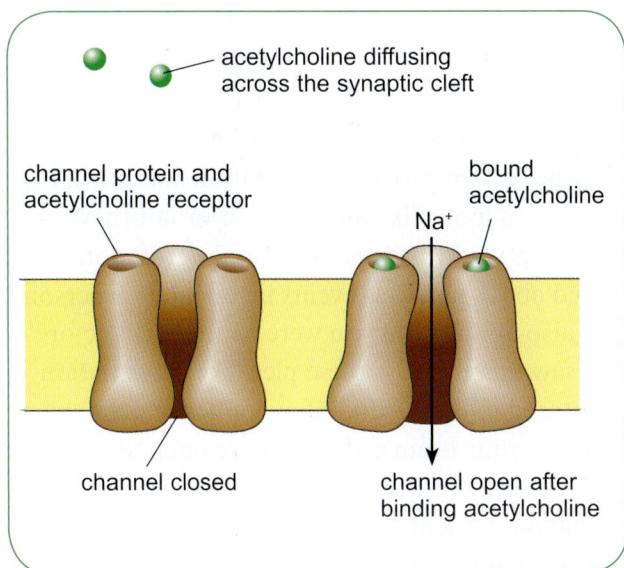

acetylcholine diffusing across the synaptic cleft

channel protein and acetylcholine receptor

bound acetylcholine

Na$^+$

channel closed

channel open after binding acetylcholine

Figure 9.17 How an acetylcholine receptor works.

A **neuromuscular junction** is a synapse between the end of a motor neurone and a muscle. Here, the plasma membrane of the muscle fibre is the postsynaptic membrane, and acetylcholine sets up an action potential in it in just the same way as in a postsynaptic neurone. The action potential sweeps along the plasma membrane of the muscle fibre and causes the fibre to contract.

Recharging the synapse

If the acetylcholine remained bound to the postsynaptic receptors, the sodium ion channels would remain open. Action potentials might fire continuously, or it might be impossible to reinstate the resting potential across the membrane, so that there could be no new action potentials generated.

Action potentials in plants

Plants have action potentials, too. They do not have specific 'nerve cells', but many of their cells transmit waves of electrical activity that are very similar to those transmitted along the neurones of animals. The action potentials generally last much longer and travel more slowly than in animal neurones (see graph below).

Almost all animal and plant cells have sodium–potassium pumps, which maintain an electrochemical gradient across the plasma membrane, and it is this that produces the resting potential. As in animals, plant action potentials are triggered when the membrane is depolarised. Just as in animals, there is a refractory period following each action potential.

Many different types of stimuli have been shown to trigger action potentials in plants. In Venus fly traps, for example, the touch of a fly on one of the hairs on the leaf starts an action potential that travels across the leaf and causes it to fold over and trap the fly. This is quite fast as plant responses go, taking only about 0.5 s between the stimulus and the action.

Chemicals coming into contact with the plant's surface also trigger action potentials. For example, dripping a solution of acid of a similar pH to acid rain onto soya bean leaves causes action potentials to sweep across them. In potato plants, Colorado beetle larvae feeding on the leaves has been shown to induce action potentials, of the shape shown in the graph here. These travel only slowly, from the leaves down the stem and all the way to the tubers beneath the soil. At the moment, we don't know what effect, if any, these action potentials have, but it is thought that they might bring about changes in the metabolic reactions taking place in some parts of the plant.

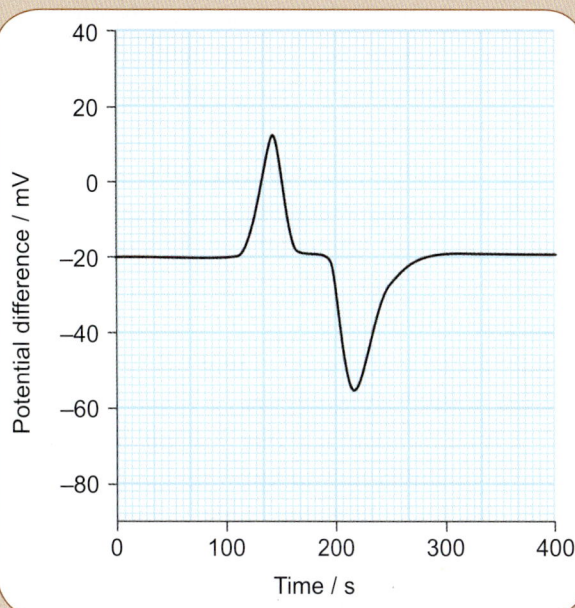

To prevent either of these events from happening, and also to avoid wasting the acetylcholine, it is recycled. The synaptic cleft contains an enzyme, **acetylcholinesterase**, which splits each acetylcholine molecule into acetate and choline.

The choline is taken back into the presynaptic neurone, where it is combined with acetyl CoA to form acetylcholine once more. This resynthesis requires energy from ATP, supplied by mitochondria. The acetylcholine is then transported into the presynaptic vesicles, ready for the next action potential. The entire sequence of events, from initial arrival of the action potential to the re-formation of acetylcholine, takes about 5–10 ms.

The functions of synapses
It isn't at first obvious why we have synapses. Action potentials could move much more swiftly through the nervous system if they did not have to cross synapses. In fact, synapses have numerous functions.

Ensuring one-way transmission
Signals can only pass in one direction at synapses. This ensures that signals can be directed along specific pathways, rather than spreading at random through the nervous system.

Interconnecting nerve pathways
Synapses allow a wider range of behaviour than could be generated in a nervous system in which neurones were directly 'wired up' to each other. At most synapses, many different neurones converge, so that many different possible pathways for the impulses are brought together. It may be necessary for action potentials to arrive along several neurones simultaneously before an action potential can be set up in another. This is known as **summation**. The arrival of impulses at certain synapses actually reduces the likelihood of an action potential starting up in that neurone. These are called 'inhibitory' synapses.

Think for a moment of your possible behaviour when you see someone you know across the street. You can call out to them and walk to meet them, or you can pretend not to see them and hurry away. It is events at your synapses that help to determine which of these two responses, or any number of others, you decide to make.

Your nervous system is receiving information from various sources about the situation. Receptors in your eyes send action potentials to your brain that provide information about what the person looks like and whether or not they have seen you. Inside your brain, information is stored about previous events involving this person, and also about what you were about to do before you saw them. All of these pieces of information are stored in the myriad of synaptic connections between your brain cells. They are integrated with each other, and as a result action potentials will or will not be sent to your leg muscles to take you towards your acquaintance.

Memory and learning
Despite much research, we still do not fully understand how memory operates. But we do know that it involves synapses. For example, if your brain frequently receives information about two things at the same time – say, the sound of a particular voice and the sight of a particular face – then new synapses form in your brain that link the neurones involved in the passing of information along the particular pathways from your ears and eyes. In future, when you hear the voice, information flowing from your ears along this pathway automatically flows into the other pathway too, so that your brain 'pictures' the face that goes with the voice.

Effects of other chemicals at synapses
Many drugs and other chemicals act by affecting the events at synapses.

Nicotine, found in tobacco, has a molecule with a similar shape to acetylcholine, which will fit into the acetylcholine receptors on postsynaptic membranes (Figure 9.17). This produces similar effects to acetylcholine, initiating action potentials in the postsynaptic neurone or muscle fibre. Unlike acetylcholine, however, nicotine is not rapidly broken down by enzymes, and so remains in the receptors for longer than acetylcholine. A large dose of nicotine can be fatal.

The **botulinum toxin** (Botox) is produced by an anaerobic bacterium which occasionally

Electric eels

The electric eel, *Electrophorus electricus*, is a fresh-water fish that lives in rivers in South America. It is a carnivore, and it captures its prey by giving it a high-voltage electric shock.

The eels have highly specialised effector cells, called electrocytes, that produce the electrical discharge. The electrocytes maintain a resting potential across themselves, negative inside, using the sodium–potassium pump.

Each electrocyte has a motor neurone that forms a synapse with it. The electrocytes are disc-shaped, and the motor neurone synapses with one of its surfaces. When an action potential arrives at the presynaptic membrane (on the motor neurone), acetylcholine is released and diffuses across the cleft, just as in an ordinary synapse. The acetylcholine slots into receptors on the postsynaptic membrane (on the electrocyte) and depolarises it.

But this only happens on one side of the electrocyte. The other side of the cell, where there is no synapse with a motor neurone, remains polarised. Momentarily, there is a difference in electrical potential on the two sides of the cell.

This difference is only 0.15 V, but electric eels greatly amplify it by having lots of electrocytes – as many as 200 000 – stacked up together, each facing in the same direction. It is like connecting a lot of electrical cells in series. The potential difference (voltage) produced by each cell adds up, producing a voltage that is enough to stun and often kill quite large prey.

This only works if all of the electrocytes discharge exactly in unison. This happens as the result of an 'electrocytes fire!' signal from the brain. When the eel detects prey, action potentials are sent off from the brain along the motor neurones that lead to the electrocytes. As each electrocyte has its own motor neurone, it is important that an action potential arrives at the end of each motor neurone simultaneously. But the electrocytes are not all the same distance from the brain. So, to achieve perfect synchronisation, motor neurones leading to electrocytes that are closer to the brain take a longer route than they might need to, or are narrower than others, slowing down the nerve impulses in them.

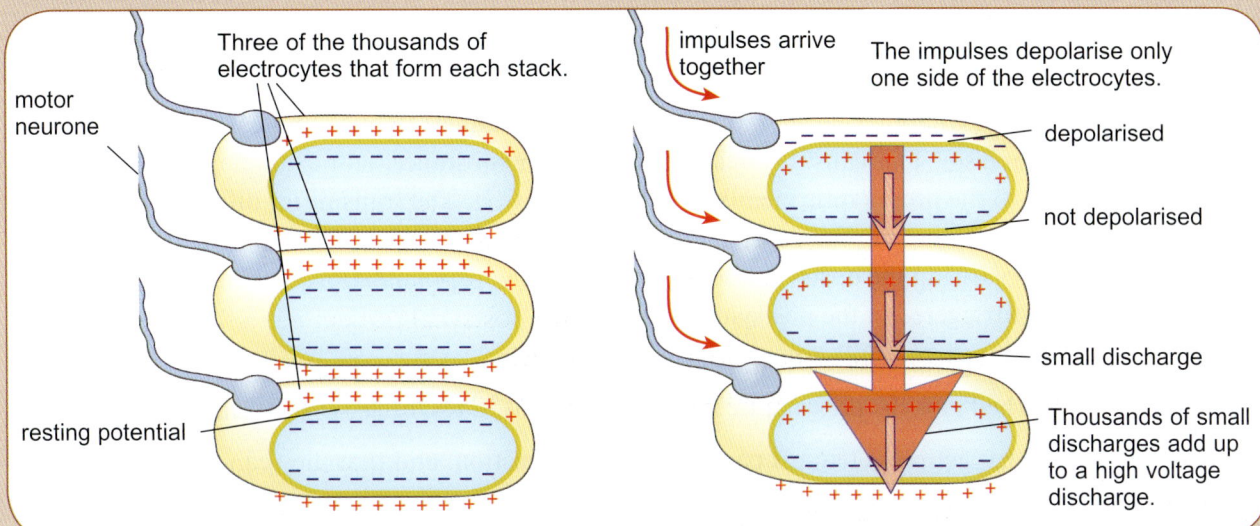

motor neurone

Three of the thousands of electrocytes that form each stack.

resting potential

impulses arrive together

The impulses depolarise only one side of the electrocytes.

depolarised

not depolarised

small discharge

Thousands of small discharges add up to a high voltage discharge.

breeds in contaminated canned food. It acts at the presynaptic membrane, where it prevents the release of acetylcholine. Eating food that contains this bacterium is often fatal. However, the toxin does have important medical uses. In some people, for example, the muscles of the eyelids contract permanently, so that they cannot open their eyes. Injections of tiny amounts of the botulinum toxin into these muscles can cause them to relax, allowing the lids to be raised. Botox injections are widely used to smooth wrinkles in skin, especially around the eyes.

Organophosphorous insecticides inhibit the action of acetylcholinesterase, thus allowing acetylcholine to cause continuous production of action potentials in the postsynaptic membrane. Many flea sprays and collars for cats and dogs contain these insecticides, so great care should be taken when using them, for the health of both the pet and the owner. Contamination from organophosphorous sheep dip (used to combat infestation by ticks) has been linked to illness in farm workers. Several nerve gases also work in this way.

Summary

- Neurones are highly specialised cells that transfer electrical impulses, in the form of action potentials, from one part of the body to another. Sensory neurones transfer impulses from receptors to the central nervous system, and motor neurones transfer them from the central nervous system to effectors.

- The axons of some neurones are sheathed with myelin, which insulates them and speeds up conduction of action potentials along them.

- Neurones maintain a resting potential of about −70 mV inside, by means of the sodium–potassium pump in the plasma membrane.

- If the plasma membrane is depolarised, voltage-gated sodium ion channels open and an action potential may be generated. This sweeps along the axon by depolarising the section of membrane just ahead of it. In myelinated axons, the action potential jumps between nodes of Ranvier.

- During an action potential, the membrane briefly reaches a potential difference of +30 mV as sodium ions rush in through the voltage-gated sodium channels. Then voltage-gated potassium channels open, and the membrane returns to a potential difference that is negative inside, as potassium ions move out. The membrane cannot transmit another action potential until all the ion channels have returned to their normal state, and this period of time is called the refractory period.

- All action potentials are the same size. The stronger the stimulus, the greater the frequency of action potentials, and the more neurones carry action potentials.

- Synapses are found where two neurones meet. The arrival of an action potential along the plasma membrane of the presynaptic neurone causes calcium ion channels to open and calcium ions then rush into the cytoplasm. This causes vesicles of transmitter substance – for example, acetylcholine (ACh) – to move to the presynaptic membrane and fuse with it. The transmitter diffuses across the cleft and slots into receptors in the postsynaptic membrane. This opens sodium channels and sodium ions flood in, depolarising the postsynaptic membrane. If the depolarisation is great enough, an action potential is triggered in the postsynaptic neurone.

- Acetylcholinesterase in the synaptic cleft quickly breaks down acetylcholine into acetate and choline, which are reabsorbed into the presynaptic neurone and used to resynthesise acetylcholine.

- Synapses ensure that action potentials pass in only one direction, and that they can travel along a range of different pathways, but not at random. They are also involved in memory.

Questions

Multiple choice questions

1   The diagram below shows a type of neurone found in mammals.

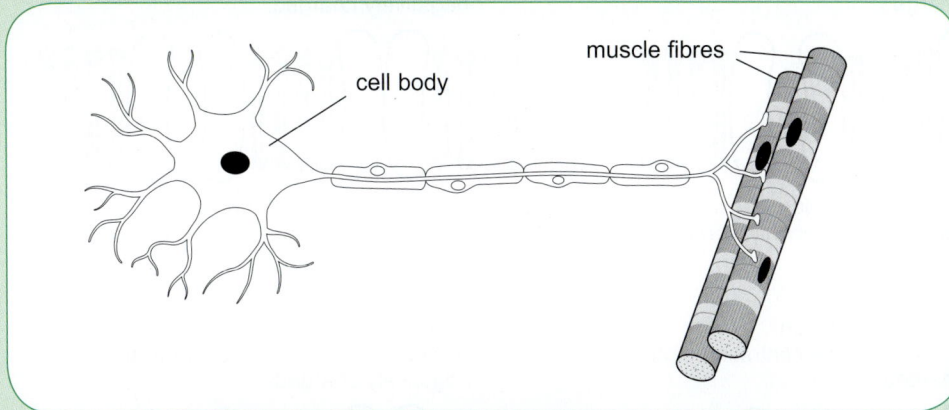

Which of the following correctly identifies the type of neurone and the direction of nerve impulse?

	Type of neurone	Direction of nerve impulse
A	sensory	towards muscle fibres
B	sensory	towards cell body
C	motor	towards muscle fibres
D	motor	towards cell body

2   The diagram represents a transverse section through a myelinated neurone as seen under an electron microscope.

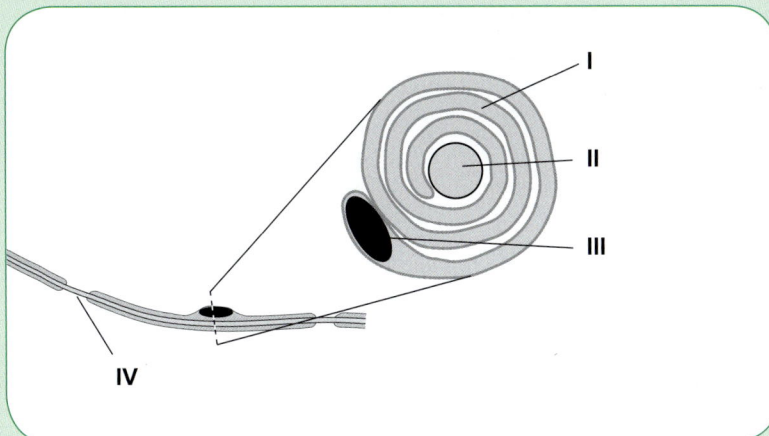

Which of the labelled structures represents the myelin sheath?

A I

B II

C III

D IV

continued...

3 The diagrams below show the distribution of sodium and potassium ions in a section of an axon. Which is at resting potential?

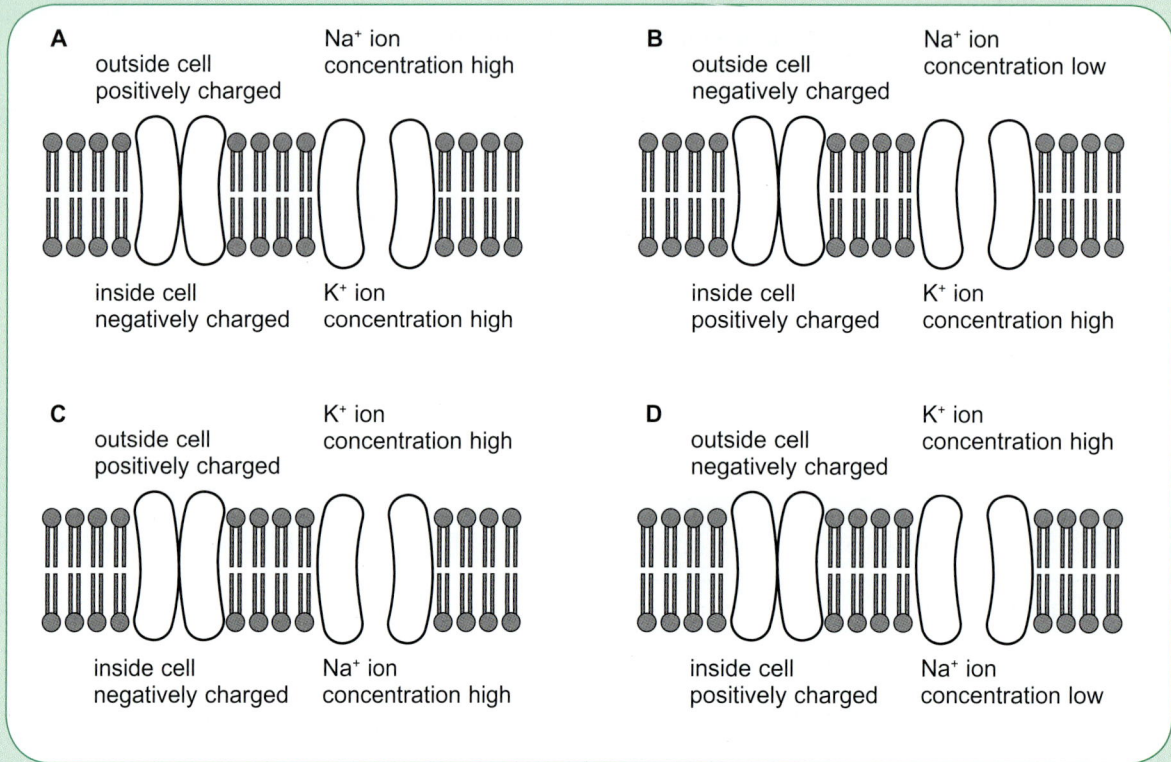

A outside cell positively charged — Na⁺ ion concentration high

inside cell negatively charged — K⁺ ion concentration high

B outside cell negatively charged — Na⁺ ion concentration low

inside cell positively charged — K⁺ ion concentration high

C outside cell positively charged — K⁺ ion concentration high

inside cell negatively charged — Na⁺ ion concentration high

D outside cell negatively charged — K⁺ ion concentration high

inside cell positively charged — Na⁺ ion concentration low

4 The diagram below shows a section through a cholinergic synapse.

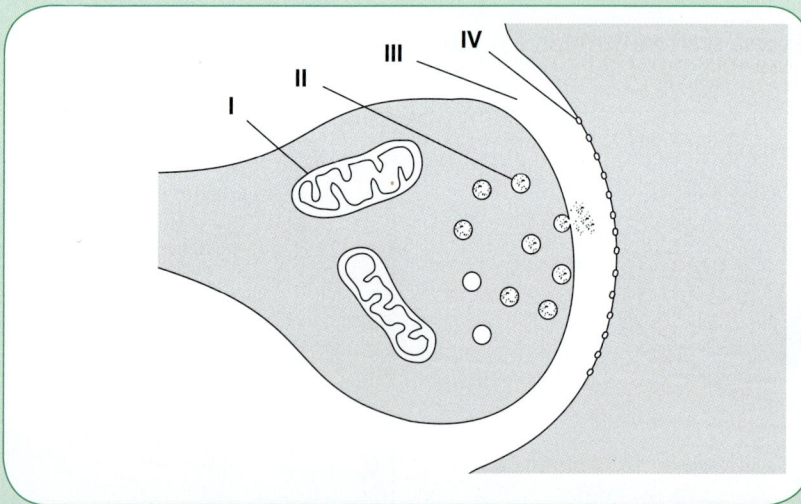

Which of the labelled structures is the receptor for acetylcholine molecules?

A I
B II
C III
D IV

continued ...

5 The diagram below shows the changes in the potential difference across the plasma membrane of a neurone when a stimulus is applied.

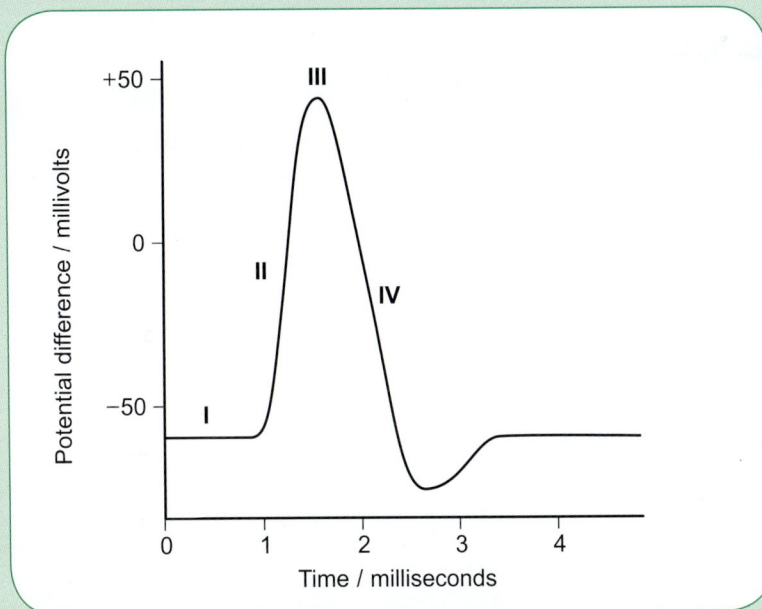

Which of the following correctly identifies the stages labelled **I** to **IV**?

	I	II	III	IV
A	repolarisation	resting potential	depolarisation	action potential
B	depolarisation	repolarisation	resting potential	action potential
C	resting potential	depolarisation	action potential	repolarisation
D	depolarisation	action potential	repolarisation	resting potential

6 Which of the following is a difference between a motor neurone and a sensory neurone?
   A A sensory neurone has its cell body in the white matter.
   B A motor neurone synapses with the effector.
   C A sensory neurone carries impulses away from the spinal cord.
   D A motor neurone is not myelinated.

7 A change which initiates depolarisation along a neurone is known as a:
   A response.
   B stimulus.
   C synapse.
   D receptor.

8 Which of the following structures is responsible for saltatory conduction along a myelinated neurone?
   A node of Ranvier
   B acetylcholine
   C dendrites
   D axon

continued ...

9 What is a function of a dendrite?
   A connect axon to dendron
   B carry impulses to the cell body
   C carry impulses away from the cell body
   D synapse with the effector

10 Which of the following processes is responsible for the secretion of acetylcholine into the synaptic cleft?
   A endocytosis
   B active transport
   C diffusion
   D exocytosis

Structured questions

11 The diagram below shows a neurone.

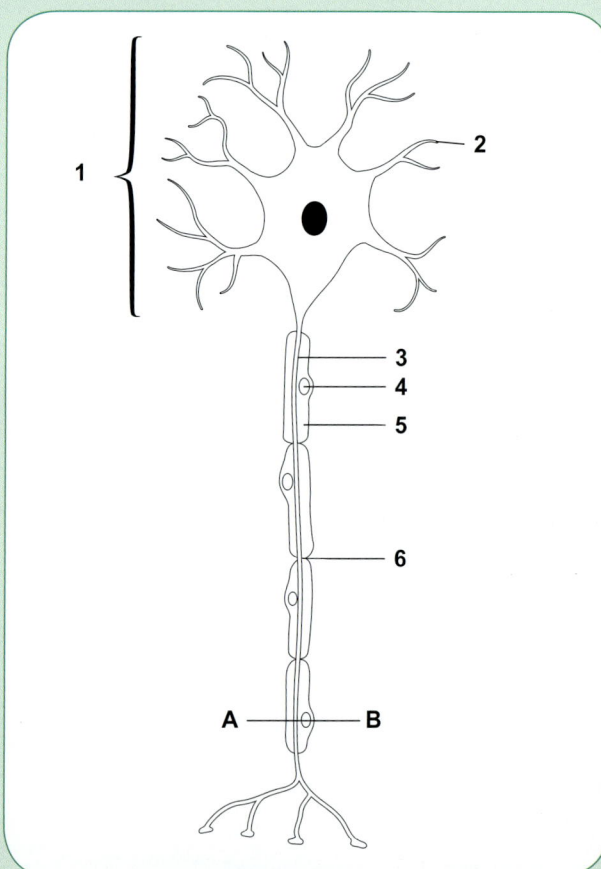

   a i Which type of neurone is shown in the diagram?   [1 mark]
      ii Give a reason for your answer.   [1 mark]
   b Identify the structures labelled **1** to **6**.   [6 marks]
   c Make a copy of the diagram. On your copy, draw the position of the effector.   [1 mark]
   d Use an arrow to indicate the direction in which the nerve impulse travels.   [1 mark]

continued ...

e State the functions of the structures labelled **3**, **5** and **6**.   [3 marks]

f Based on your knowledge of the structure of a neurone, draw a labelled transverse
   section of the neurone across the line labelled **A** to **B**.   [2 marks]

12 The diagram below shows an action potential.

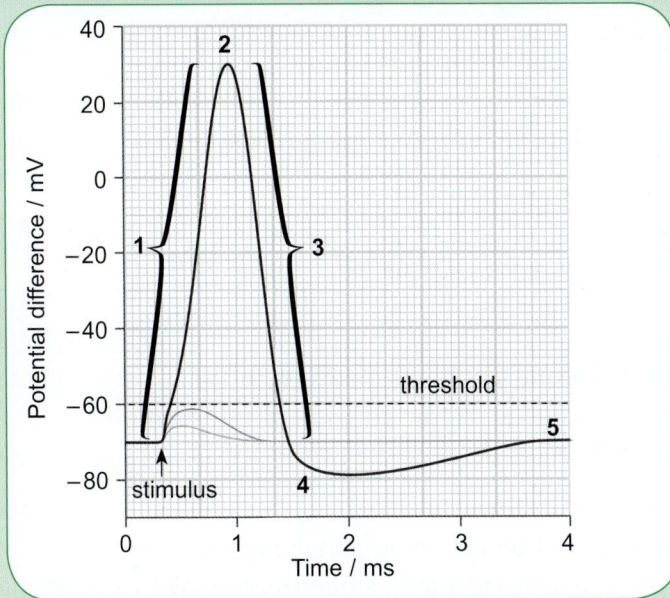

a What is meant by the term 'threshold' as shown on the graph?   [1 mark]

b Why were there failed initiations after the stimulus?   [2 marks]

c State the names of stages **1** to **5** and explain what is happening to the sodium and
   potassium channels in the neurone at:
   i 1   ii 2   iii 3   iv 4   v 5   [10 marks]

d Explain what takes the membrane of an axon from the resting potential to the
   threshold potential as an action potential approaches.   [2 marks]

13 The diagram below shows a section through a cholinergic synapse between two neurones.

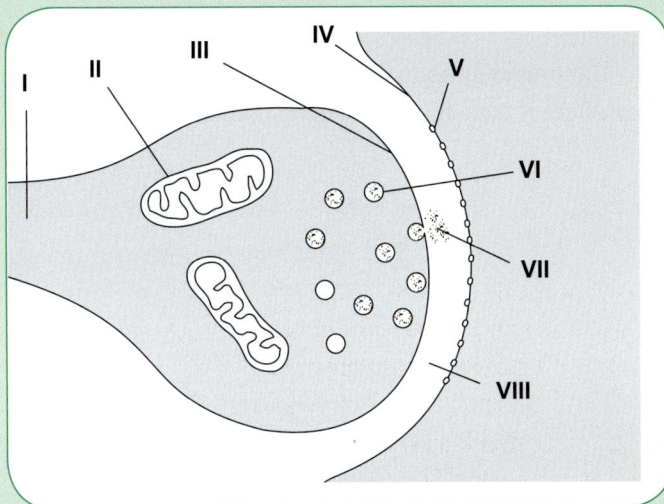

continued …

    a Name the structures labelled **I** to **VIII**.   [4 marks]

    b Describe the direction of the impulse across the synapse.   [1 mark]

    c Give **two** roles of the synapse in the nervous system.   [2 marks]

    d Describe the roles of the following in the transmission of an impulse across a synapse in the nervous system of a mammal:

        i   structure **II**

        ii structure **V**

        iii structure **VI**   [6 marks]

    e What is the role of calcium ions in the passage of impulses across the synapse?   [3 marks]

Essay questions

14 a By means of an annotated diagram only, describe the structure of a myelinated sensory neurone.   [5 marks]

     b Describe the function of the myelin sheath.   [3 marks]

     c Describe how a nerve impulse is transmitted along a non-myelinated neurone.   [4 marks]

     d Both the nervous and endocrine systems coordinate the transmission of information in the body of a mammal. Explain **three** differences between the two systems.   [3 marks]

15 a Describe how a resting potential is maintained in a neurone.   [4 marks]

     b Describe the events that lead to the generation of an action potential and the subsequent return to the resting potential in a neurone after a stimulus is applied.   [6 marks]

     c Action potentials can travel along axons at speeds of $0.1–100\,\text{ms}^{-1}$. Suggest **three** factors which may influence their speed.   [3 marks]

     d Explain why there is a delay in transmission of an impulse across a synapse.   [2 marks]

16 a Describe the sequence of events in the transmission of an impulse across a synapse (you may use an annotated diagram).   [7 marks]

     b The transmission of impulses across a synapse may be modified in various ways. Explain the role of the synapse in the following:

        i   unidirectional transmission of an impulse

        ii summation of impulses

        iii inhibition of impulses   [6 marks]

     c Botulin is a neurotoxin which attaches to the presynaptic membrane and prevents the release of acetylcholine. Suggest what effect it may have on the transmission of an impulse across the synapse.   [2 marks]

Chapter 10
Health and disease

By the end of this chapter you should be able to:

a   discuss the meaning of the term 'health', focusing on the physical, mental and social aspects;

b   explain the categories of disease or illness, to include physical, mental, social, chronic, infectious, degenerate, inherited, self-inflicted, and deficiency, with examples;

c   discuss reasons for the regional distribution of diabetes, including the effects of diet, obesity and prenatal malnutrition;

d   discuss reasons for the regional distribution of cancer, including the roles of environmental hazards, food additives, viruses, genetic factors, implications of symptom awareness and failure to seek treatment in management of the disease;

e   discuss reasons for the regional distribution of acquired immune deficiency syndrome (AIDS);

f   analyse data involving incidence and mortality rates of disease to draw conclusions or make predictions.

What is health?

You know what you mean when you say that you are 'healthy' – but it is not easy to give this term a definition that everyone will agree with. The World Health Organization (WHO) defines **health** as being 'a state of complete physical, mental and social well-being and not merely the absence of disease or infirmity'.

So, being healthy means more than just not being ill. It means that a person's body is working properly, so that they can lead an active and enjoyable life. They feel well in themselves, and are mentally sound. They fit easily into society, in whatever way suits them best.

The WHO definition of health includes the word **disease**, and this is another term that deserves some consideration. Many people use the word to mean an illness such as tuberculosis (TB) or perhaps cancer, but it can be used more widely than that. Disease is anything that impairs the normal functioning of the body. It certainly includes infectious diseases such as TB, and also problems that arise as we get older, such as coronary heart disease, or mental illnesses such as Alzheimer's

disease, schizophrenia or clinical depression. There are also diseases that are inherited, such as cystic fibrosis.

Categories of disease

It is sometimes useful to classify a disease into a particular category, and some examples are given below. However, it is important to realise that many diseases 'fit' into more than one category.

Physical disease

A physical disease is one that involves some kind of damage or malfunction somewhere in the body. Almost all diseases fit into this category. The only diseases that are sometimes not considered to be physical diseases are some mental diseases, where (as yet) no-one has been able to link the disease to any physical abnormalities in the brain.

Mental disease

A mental disease is one that affects the mind. Most of them are known as 'disorders' rather than diseases. As research into these conditions progresses, more and more mental disorders are now at least partly explained by measurable changes in the structure or function of particular parts of the brain. For example, Alzheimer's disease is associated with the deterioration of tissues in the hippocampus and other parts of the cerebral cortex. Its symptoms include loss of memory and the ability to think logically. In other cases, much less is known about the causes. For example, despite much research into schizophrenia, there is still no clear understanding about exactly what causes it, although there is increasing evidence that it is associated with measurable changes in the structure and physiology of certain regions of the brain.

Social disease

Social diseases are ones that are strongly associated with the social setting in which a person spends their life. For example, poor housing or sanitation can greatly increase the risk of developing infectious diseases such as tuberculosis. Living in a polluted environment may have adverse effects on the respiratory system, causing an increase in bronchitis. Not having access to a good diet increases the risk of developing deficiency diseases such as rickets (caused by a lack of vitamin D), or becoming obese – which in turn increases the risk of developing diabetes or cardiovascular disease. Having a job that exposes a person to potentially damaging conditions – such as working in an environment where there are asbestos particles in the air, or where they are exposed to cigarette smoke – can cause respiratory illnesses such as silicosis or lung cancer.

Chronic disease

A chronic disease is one that lasts for a long time. For example, people who smoke cigarettes may develop bronchitis which never really clears up – it is a disease that they live with day after day.

Infectious disease

An infectious disease is one that is caused by another organism that enters the body and reproduces there. These organisms are called **pathogens**. For example, the common cold is caused by a virus; cholera is caused by a

bacterium; malaria is caused by a single-celled protoctist. There is much more information about infectious diseases and how the body responds to invasion by a pathogen in Chapter 11.

Degenerative disease

A degenerative disease is one that results from the gradual loss of function of some part of the body. Many degenerative diseases are associated with ageing, such as Alzheimer's disease. Others can afflict younger people, such as muscular dystrophy, in which muscle function is lost (this is an inherited disease) and multiple sclerosis, in which nerve axons lose their myelin sheaths and fail to work correctly.

Inherited disease

An inherited disease is one that is caused by the combination of alleles that a person inherits from their parents. Examples include sickle cell anaemia, cystic fibrosis and haemophilia (Unit 1 Chapter 7).

Self-inflicted disease

Self-inflicted diseases are those that can be considered to have been caused by a person's own choices about their lifestyle. For example, a person who smokes cigarettes greatly increases their chance of developing numerous diseases such as chronic bronchitis, emphysema, heart disease, lung cancer and many other cancers. Misusing alcohol can lead to cirrhosis of the liver and brain damage.

Deficiency disease

A deficiency disease is one that results from the lack of a particular nutrient in the diet. For example, lack of vitamin C can lead to scurvy, because not enough collagen can be made in the body. Lack of iron can cause anaemia, because not enough haemoglobin can be synthesised.

In the rest of this chapter we will look at three particular diseases to see how they affect people, and reasons why they are more likely to affect people living in some regions of the world than others. These three diseases are:

- HIV/AIDS – an infectious disease whose incidence is greatly affected by lifestyle;
- diabetes – a chronic disease that is related to

lifestyle and also has a genetic component;
- cancer – which includes a wide range of very different degenerative diseases, each with their own particular group of risk factors and causes.

Incidence, prevalence and mortality

The distribution of different diseases in different parts of the world is of great interest to many health professionals. Often, it can provide clues about the factors that increase the risk of acquiring a disease, which in turn can help to suggest ways in which this risk can be reduced. Governments can use these data to see how the risk of a particular disease in their country compares with that in others around the world, and this can help them to decide how to allocate funds for disease prevention and control.

The study of the pattern of distribution of disease, and of the factors that influence how common it is within a particular population, is called **epidemiology**. Three types of data are often of particular interest.

- **Incidence** of a disease: this is the number of new cases of a disease that arise in a population over a given time period, generally one year.
- **Prevalence** of a disease: this is the number of people with a disease in the population at a certain time.
- **Mortality**: this is the number of people who die from a particular disease in one year.

For all of these measures, it is usually much more informative to calculate the numbers in relation to the size of the total population. They are often expressed as the number of people per 100 000. If a disease is especially common, it is sometimes expressed as the number of people per 100 – that is, as a percentage.

Acquired immune deficiency syndrome

This disease is caused by the human immunodeficiency virus, usually known as HIV. The disease is generally known as HIV/AIDS.

Figure 10.1 shows the structure of this virus. It is a retrovirus, containing RNA rather than DNA.

Viruses are not cellular, and most are very much smaller than bacteria. HIV is basically a

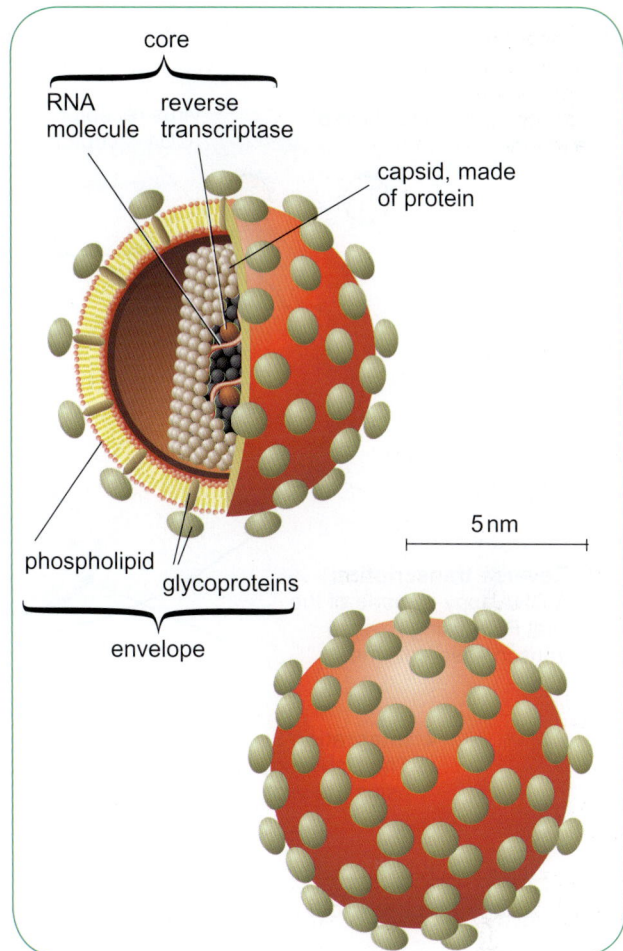

Figure 10.1   The structure of HIV.

ball of protein and lipid around a core containing **RNA** (its genetic material) and the enzyme **reverse transcriptase**, which is required once the virus has entered a cell. The enzyme makes a 'DNA version' of the virus's RNA. The infected cell then follows the code on the DNA to make new viruses. The virus essentially hijacks the human cell's protein-making machinery.

Like all viruses, HIV can only reproduce when it is inside a host cell. HIV infects a type of blood cell called a T-lymphocyte (Figure 10.2), specifically ones with CD4 receptors in their plasma membranes. You can read more about this in Chapter 11.

HIV is passed from person to person when body

SAQ

1   Compare the structure of HIV with the structure of a bacterium.

1 Transmission
Virus particles are carried from the body fluid of one person to the body fluid of another.

virus receptor (CD4 receptor)

lysis   budding

9 Release
HIV particles are released from the cell by budding. The cell then lyses (bursts).

8 Assembly and maturation
Viral particles are assembled and become infective.

2 Infection
Virus protein binds to receptors and the virus enters a T-lymphocyte. Viral RNA is released.

7 Translation
Viral proteins are synthesised.

6 Transcription
Viral proteins direct mRNA synthesis.

3 Reverse transcription
A DNA copy is made of the viral RNA using reverse transcriptase enzyme.

Years later ...

4 Integration
The DNA copy is inserted into a chromosome using the viral integrase enzyme.

5 The lymphocyte divides normally, still with viral DNA in a chromosome, but the cell remains normal (latent virus).

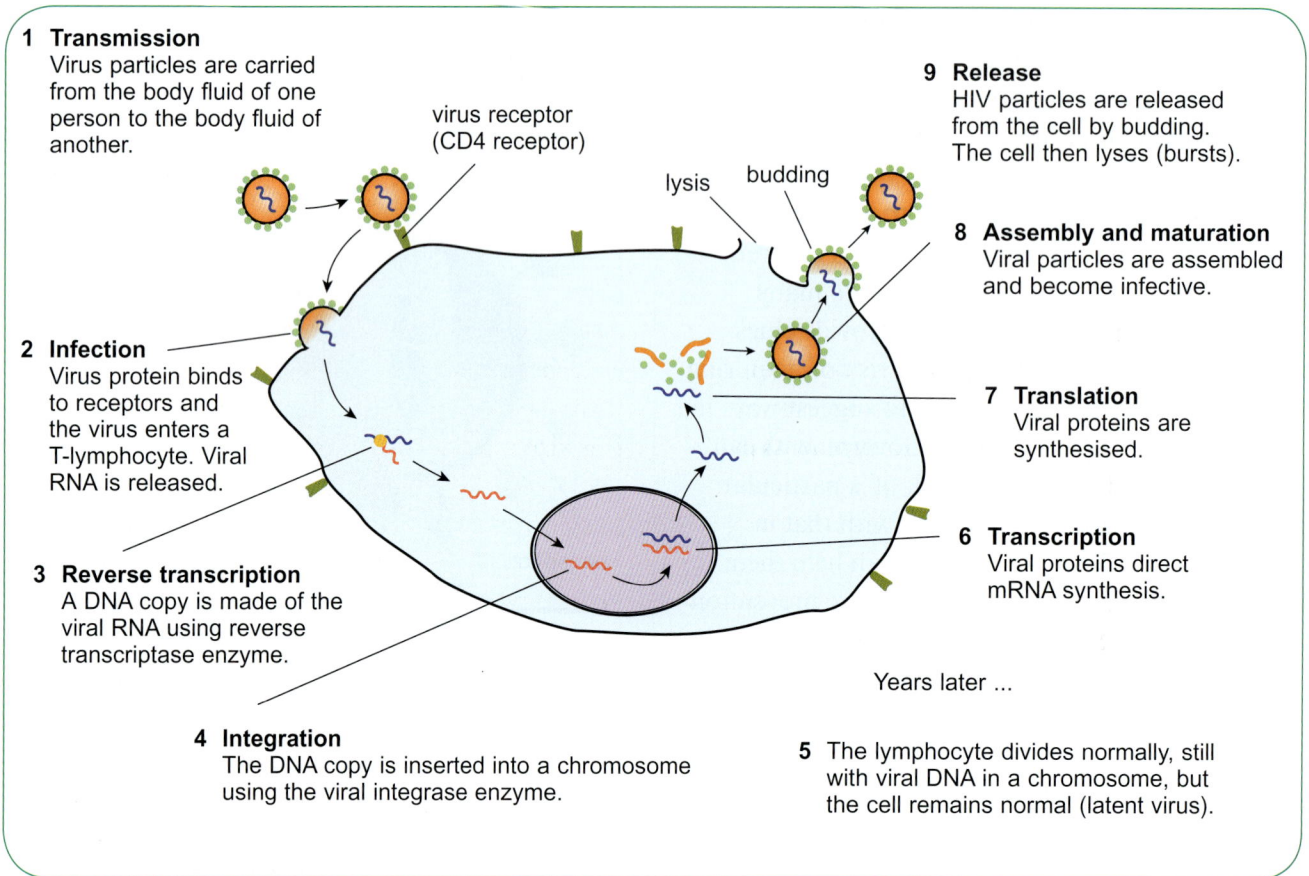

Figure 10.2   The life cycle of HIV.

fluids come into direct contact. The virus cannot survive outside the human body, except in blood. The main ways in which HIV is passed on are:

- during sexual intercourse – especially (but not only) if this involves damage to the linings of the vagina or anus, because the virus is most easily spread via blood;
- sharing hypodermic needles – a needle used by someone with HIV may contain a small amount of fluid with the virus in it, which can enter the body of another person if they re-use the needle;
- transfusions of blood from a person infected with HIV to another person;
- from a mother to her unborn child – it is sometimes possible for the virus to cross the placenta, but it is more likely that the virus can be passed from the mother's blood to her baby's during the birth process.

Most people who are infected with HIV eventually go on to develop AIDS. At first the virus lies low inside the T-lymphocytes that it has infected. The cell makes copies of the virus's DNA and

incorporates them into its own chromosomes. While this is happening – normally for about two to four weeks – the person has no symptoms. This is called the incubation period. Following this, they are likely to develop flu-like symptoms, which are almost always just put down to a cold or flu. However, if the person takes a blood test, antibodies (page 231) against HIV will be detected. The person is said to be HIV-positive.

Later, the virus may become active, producing many copies of itself inside the infected CD4$^+$ cells and then destroying the cells as they bud out or the cell bursts. More and more cells are infected and destroyed. The person is now said to have AIDS. The United States agency, the Center for Disease Control and Prevention (CDC) defines AIDS as being HIV-positive and having a CD4$^+$ cell count of less than 200 per µL of blood, or where the percentage of CD4$^+$ cells is less than 14. The length of time between the initial infection and the development of AIDS can be as short as two weeks, and as long as 20 years or more. This means that a person may have HIV in their body for 20 years, and not know that they are HIV-positive.

T-lymphocytes are a very important group of cells because they help to protect us against infectious diseases, especially viral diseases. In a person infected by HIV, as T-lymphocytes are destroyed, opportunistic diseases begin to occur (Table 10.1). The fall in T-lymphocyte numbers and the occurrence of opportunistic infections are evidence of AIDS. Opportunistic infections include pneumonia and otherwise rare forms of cancer such as Kaposi's sarcoma (a type of skin cancer). The body becomes weaker, more and more infectious diseases take hold, and the person eventually dies. Globally, the infectious disease tuberculosis, TB, is the main cause of death for people with AIDS (Figure 10.3). Symptoms of AIDS are summarised in Table 10.2.

Stage 1	Infection with HIV. No symptoms. Not classified as AIDS.
Stage 2	Minor opportunistic infections occur, especially respiratory tract infections.
Stage 3	More severe opportunistic infections occur, including long-term diarrhoea and bacterial infections such as TB.
Stage 4	Severe opportunistic infections of the brain and respiratory organs; Kaposi's sarcoma; these are symptomatic of AIDS.

Table 10.1 Stages in the development of AIDS.

persistent tiredness and weight loss
night sweats
persistent diarrhoea
blurred vision
white spots on the tongue or mouth
dry cough and shortness of breath
persistent fever or swollen glands

Table 10.2 Summary of AIDS symptoms.

There is currently no cure for HIV/AIDS but there are now some very successful drug therapies for HIV infection available, which can enable an HIV-positive person to live a long and healthy life. However, these drugs are expensive and not freely available to people in many developing countries.

The global distribution of HIV/AIDS

AIDS has become an **epidemic** – that is, a very widespread outbreak of an infectious disease, with many people being infected at the same time. It is also a **pandemic** – a disease that has spread worldwide. Today, it is easy for many people to travel from one part of the world to another. No country can consider itself to be safely isolated from the spread of this disease.

In 2009 it is estimated that 7000 people were newly infected with HIV every single day. Of these, 97% were in countries where the average level of income is low or medium. About 1000 of these infections were in children under 15 years of age. Of the other 6000, about 51% were in women, and 41% were in young people between the ages of 15 and 24.

It is difficult to use these simple numbers to give us a real idea of the importance of HIV/AIDS in a particular region. To do that, it is more helpful to look at the *percentages* of people in a population who are infected. Table 10.3 includes information about the percentage of people who had HIV/AIDS, as well as the numbers of those who were infected with it, living with it or died from it, in 2009.

HIV/AIDS in the Caribbean

Table 10.3 shows that the Caribbean has some of the highest rates of infection with HIV in the world, second only to Sub-Saharan Africa. The rates of infection, and also the death rates, vary considerably between different countries in this region. Table 10.4 (page 206) shows some statistics for HIV and AIDS in the Caribbean in 2009.

What are the possible reasons for these high rates of infection with HIV in the Caribbean?

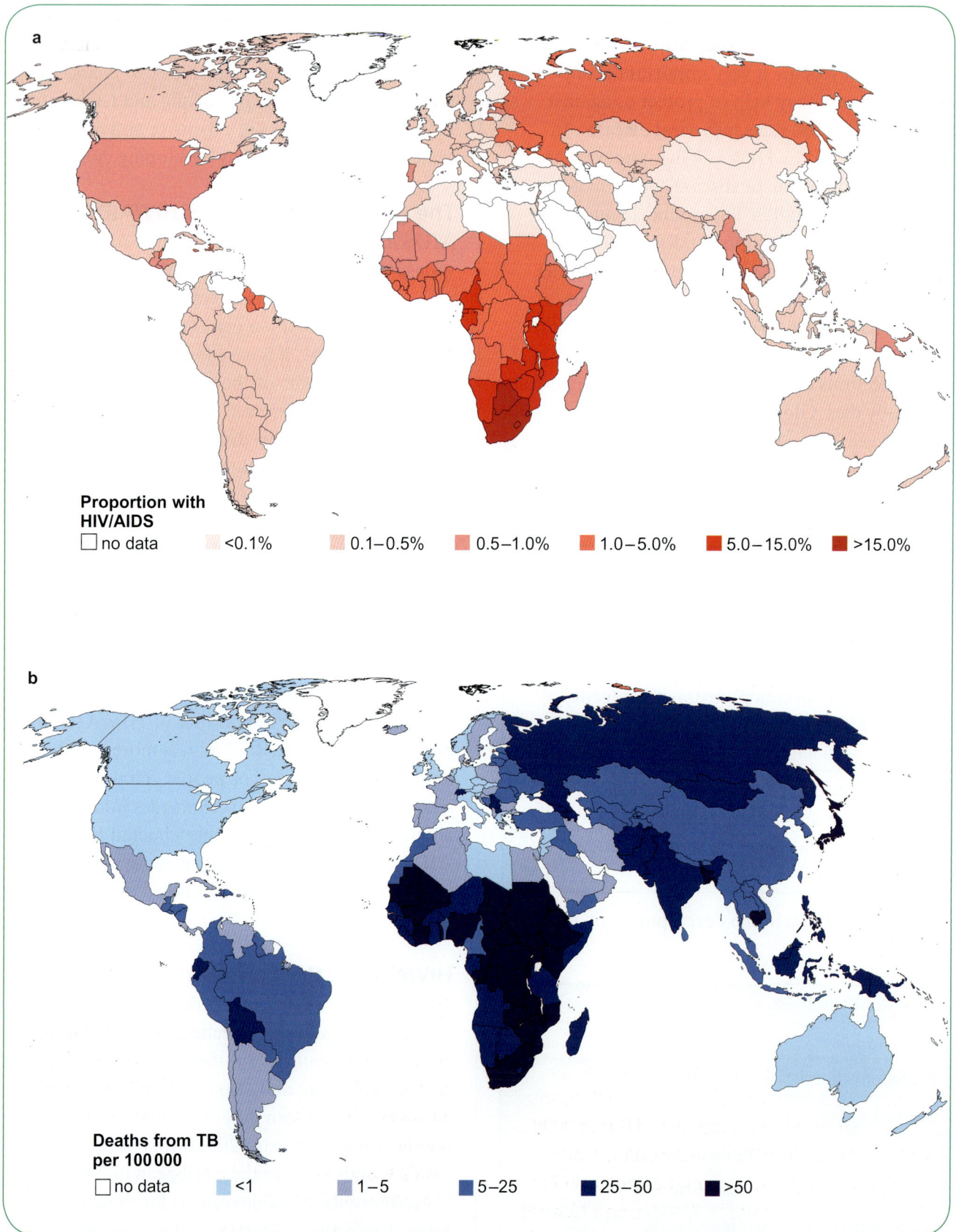

Figure 10.3 **a** Global distribution of HIV/AIDS (proportion of the population living with AIDS, data from World Health Organization, 2010), **b** Global distribution of TB (estimated deaths, data from World Health Organization, 2004–2008).

Region	Number of people newly infected with HIV (incidence)	Number of people living with HIV (prevalence)	Percentage of the population with HIV (prevalence)	Number of people who died from AIDS (mortality)
Sub-Saharan Africa	1.8 million	22.5 million	5.0%	1.3 million
Middle East and North Africa	75 000	460 000	0.2%	24 000
South and South-East Asia	270 000	4.1 million	0.3%	260 000
East Asia	82 000	770 000	0.1%	36 000
Central and South America	92 000	1.4 million	0.5%	58 000
Caribbean	17 000	240 000	1.0%	12 000
Eastern Europe and Central Asia	130 000	1.4 million	0.8%	76 000
Western and Central Europe	31 000	820 000	0.2%	8500
North America	70 000	1.5 million	0.5%	26 000
Oceania	4500	57 000	0.3%	1400
Total	2.6 million	33.3 million	0.8%	1.8 million

Table 10.3   Global HIV/AIDS statistics for 2009.

2 a Compare the distribution of HIV/AIDS and TB, shown in Figure 10.3.

  b Explain why a high prevalence of HIV/AIDS in a country may be related to a high level of TB.

3 a Which global region is most greatly affected by HIV/AIDS? Use figures from Table 10.3 to support your answer.

  b Where does the Caribbean rank, in terms of percentage prevalence of HIV, in relation to other global regions?

  c For Sub-Saharan Africa, the ratio of the number of people dying from AIDS to the number of people living with HIV in 2009 was 1.3 million : 22.5 million. This works out at 0.06 : 1. Do a similar calculation for the Caribbean and for Western and Central Europe.

  d Suggest reasons for the differences between the ratios you calculated in c.

Unprotected sexual intercourse

In the Caribbean as a whole, the main way in which HIV is transmitted from one person to another is through unprotected sexual intercourse (that is, not using a condom).

Multiple partners

High levels of poverty and unemployment often appear to be associated with high levels of HIV infection. In these situations, it is more likely that a young girl may become a sex worker, perhaps as a way of earning money for herself or because she is forced to do so by others. Unprotected sex between sex workers and clients is a major method of spread of HIV in the Caribbean. In Guyana, a study undertaken in 2006 found that 31% of sex workers were HIV-positive.

Country	Total number of people with HIV/AIDS	Percentage of 15–49 year olds with HIV/AIDS	Number of deaths due to AIDS
Haiti	120 000	1.9%	7100
Dominican Republic	57 000	0.9%	2300
Jamaica	32 000	1.7%	1200
Trinidad and Tobago	15 000	1.5%	less than 1000
Cuba	7100	0.1%	less than 100
Bahamas	6600	3.1%	less than 500
Barbados	2100	1.4%	less than 100

Table 10.4 HIV/AIDS in the Caribbean in 2009.

Unwillingness to admit to being HIV-positive

In many parts of the Caribbean, there is still a considerable stigma associated with being HIV-positive, so people may be unwilling to be tested, or unwilling to admit that they have the virus. This increases the risk that the virus can be passed on to someone else.

Nevertheless, the overall picture is hopeful. Rates of infection are no longer increasing in most countries. Good education in many countries has been shown to have greatly improved people's understanding of the methods of transmission, and surveys show that most people are able to identify important risk factors. However, this has not always been translated into changes in behaviour, and many people still put themselves at risk by having unprotected sexual intercourse.

SAQ

4 Discuss how each of the following have contributed to the global pandemic of HIV/AIDS. You may wish to do some research on the internet for supporting evidence.
  a the length of the incubation period, in which a person has no symptoms
  b the ease of global travel
  c the common practice in some countries of having many different sexual partners
  d the high cost of effective drugs to treat HIV/AIDS
  e poor education about the ways in which HIV is spread

Diabetes mellitus

Diabetes mellitus, usually just called diabetes, is an illness in which the blood glucose control mechanism (Chapter 7) has partly or completely broken down. It is very important to diagnose and control this disease as early as possible, because wildly swinging blood glucose levels are highly dangerous to many body organs. Good treatment can keep things well under control and allow people with diabetes to live almost entirely normal lives.

There are two types of diabetes. **Type 1 diabetes**, sometimes known as insulin-dependent diabetes, begins at a very early age. The pancreas is incapable of secreting enough insulin, so that blood glucose levels may soar after a carbohydrate-containing meal. **Type 2 diabetes**, also known as non-insulin-dependent diabetes, typically begins later in life. The pancreas does secrete insulin, but the liver and other target organs do not respond to it adequately.

Risk factors for diabetes

The risk factors for Type 1 diabetes are not known. It is thought that the development of this illness may be affected by a person's genes, but there also seem to be some environmental risk factors. In particular, it has been suggested that the person's own immune system may attack their beta cells, although why this should happen is not yet understood.

Type 2 diabetes is most likely to develop in people with an excessively high body weight, especially those with a BMI (body mass index) above 27. (To calculate your BMI, divide your weight, in kilograms, by your height, in metres, squared.) People with 'apple-shaped' figures (most fat carried around the middle) are at greater risk than those with 'pear-shaped' figures (most fat carried around the hips and thighs). A sedentary lifestyle also increases the risk.

There is even more evidence for a genetic link for Type 2 diabetes than there is for Type 1. The first contributory gene was tracked down in the year 2000. It lies on chromosome 2. Since then, others have been discovered and it is expected that more will be found as research progresses.

Several research studies also point to a link between prenatal malnutrition and the risk of developing Type 2 diabetes. Children whose mothers were malnourished while they were pregnant may be more likely to develop diabetes when they are older. Once again, research into this effect is ongoing, and by the time you read this there may be more information about the strength of this effect, and how it works. Table 10.5 summarises the risk factors for Type 2 diabetes.

SAQ

This question will help you to revise your earlier work on the control of blood glucose concentration, as well as giving you insights into some of the health issues related to diabetes.

5 A glucose tolerance test can be used to diagnose diabetes. A person fasts overnight, and then is given a drink containing a known mass of glucose. Their blood glucose levels are measured over the next few hours. The graphs show the results of glucose tolerance tests carried out on a normal person and a person with Type 2 diabetes.

a These questions are about the graphs for the normal person.

   i Explain why the blood glucose concentration rises during the first 20 minutes.

   ii Explain why the insulin level also rises during this time.

   iii Suggest **two** reasons why the blood glucose level begins to fall after 45 minutes.

   iv Suggest why the insulin level does not begin to fall as soon as the blood glucose level begins to decrease.

b Now look at both graphs.

   i Describe how the pattern of blood glucose concentration for the person with diabetes differs from that for the normal person.

   ii Describe how the pattern of blood insulin concentration for the person with diabetes differs from that for the normal person.

   iii Suggest explanations for these differences.

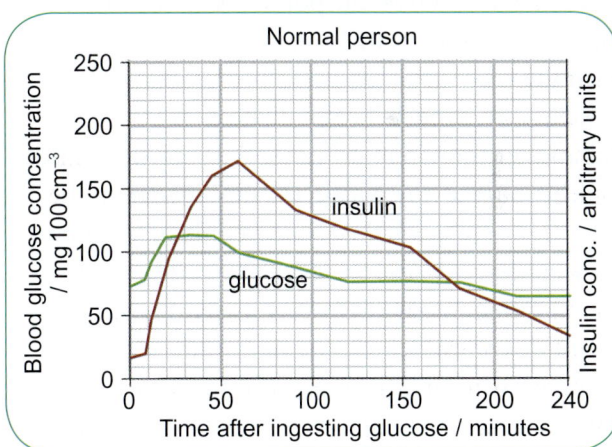

Normal person

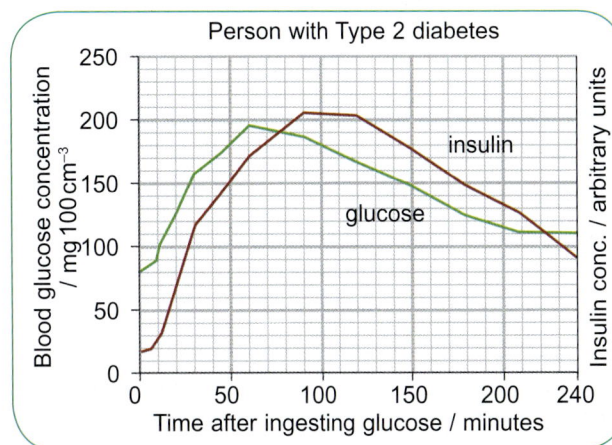

Person with Type 2 diabetes

being overweight, especially if BMI is above 27
being aged 45 or over
being physically inactive
having a close relative with diabetes
being of Asian or African descent
having high blood pressure or coronary artery disease
having low levels of HDL cholesterol in the blood

Table 10.5   Summary of factors that increase the risk of developing Type 2 diabetes.

Diabetes in the Caribbean

Figure 10.4 shows the prevalence of diabetes in different countries around the world, and in the Caribbean, in 2009. Figure 10.5 shows the new cases, per 100 000 of the population, of Type 1 diabetes in children in 2010.

In the Caribbean, about 95% of cases of diabetes are Type 2. Type 2 diabetes is much commoner than in many other parts of the world. At least part of the reason for this appears to be genetic, as statistics show that people of Asian or African descent have a higher risk of developing diabetes than others. However, there is also no doubt that lifestyle plays an important part, and that a person can do a great deal to reduce their risk of developing diabetes by eating a good diet, keeping their BMI below 27 and taking plenty of exercise.

SAQ

This question is about the data in Figures 10.4 and 10.5.

6 a Compare the prevalence of diabetes in the Caribbean and in the rest of the world.

  b Compare the incidence of Type 1 diabetes in children in the Caribbean and in the rest of the world.

Cancer

Cancer is a disease in which the normal control of cell division breaks down. The timing of mitosis is controlled by a number of different genes within a cell. If these genes are altered, then the cell may begin to divide uncontrollably.

These continuously dividing cells may eventually form a lump, called a **tumour**. This may not be harmful if the tumour stays in one place and does not grow too much. A tumour like this is said to be **benign**. But if the tumour invades tissues around it or spreads around the body, this is dangerous and is a **cancer**. The most dangerous behaviour is when cells break away and start producing more tumours elsewhere in the body, which is known as **metastasis**. This type of tumour is said to be **malignant**.

There is no doubt that cancer is a serious disease, and is often fatal. But it is also important to remember that many cancers can be cured, and the percentage of people who are successfully treated for cancer is going steadily upwards. The earlier the cancer is detected, the better the chance of a cure. This is because, in its early stages, a tumour may be benign, only later becoming malignant.

As with most diseases, prevention is much better than cure. We are learning a great deal about the factors that can cause cancer to develop, and many of these are things that relate to lifestyle.

What causes cancer?

The older a person is, the more likely they are to develop cancer. Cancers often only appear after a number of separate events have each damaged a cell. The older you are, the more likely that this has happened in a cell, which then may become a cancer.

A person's risk of getting cancer is affected both by their genes and by their lifestyle. Our cells contain many different genes which regulate cell division. They are responsible for making sure that cells do divide when needed, but also that they do not divide when they shouldn't.

Some of these regulatory genes, called **proto-oncogenes**, can mutate to form slightly different ones called **oncogenes**. Oncogenes can cause

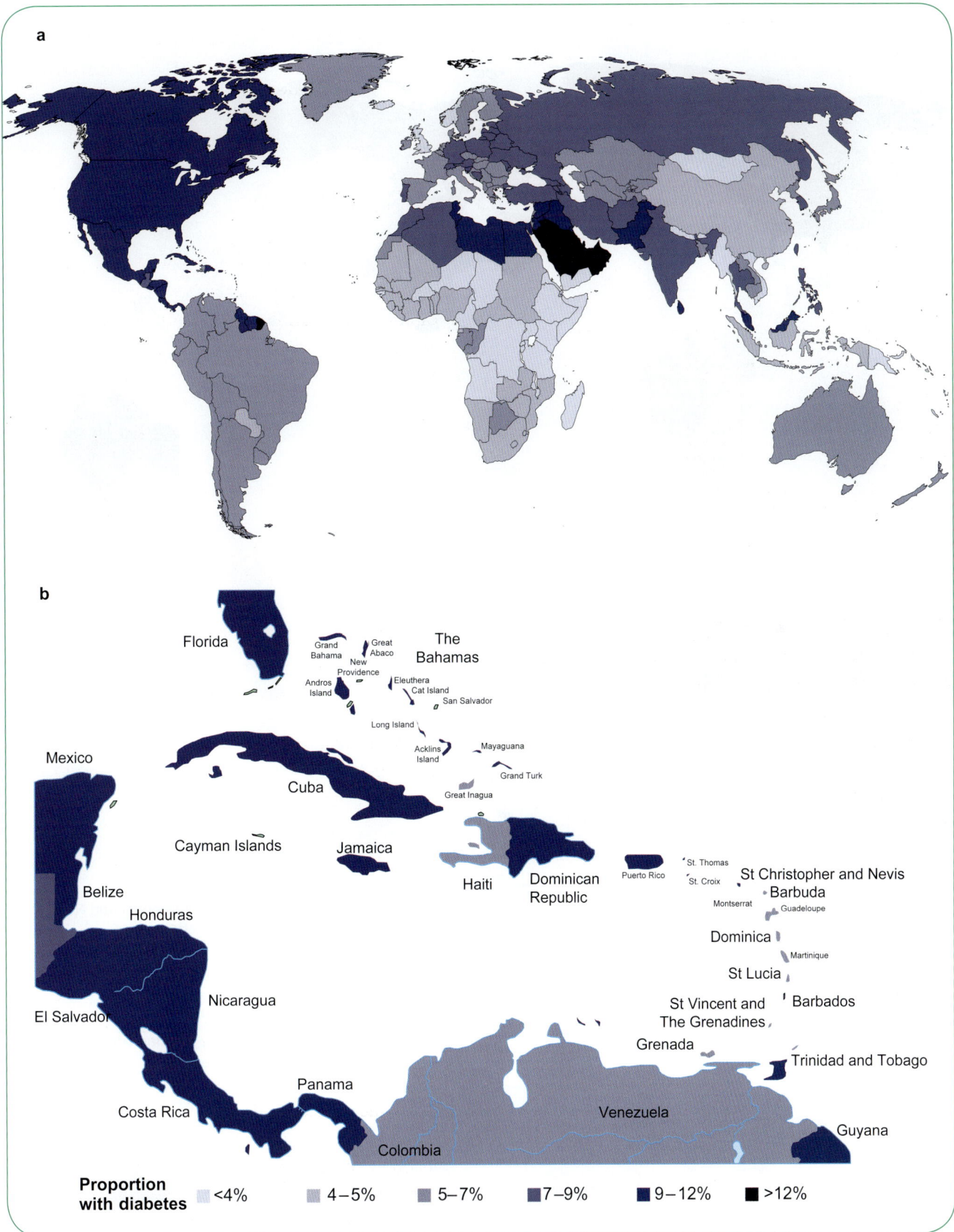

Figure 10.4 Proportion of people aged 20–79 with diabetes in 2009, **a** world, **b** Caribbean (data – International Diabetes Federation).

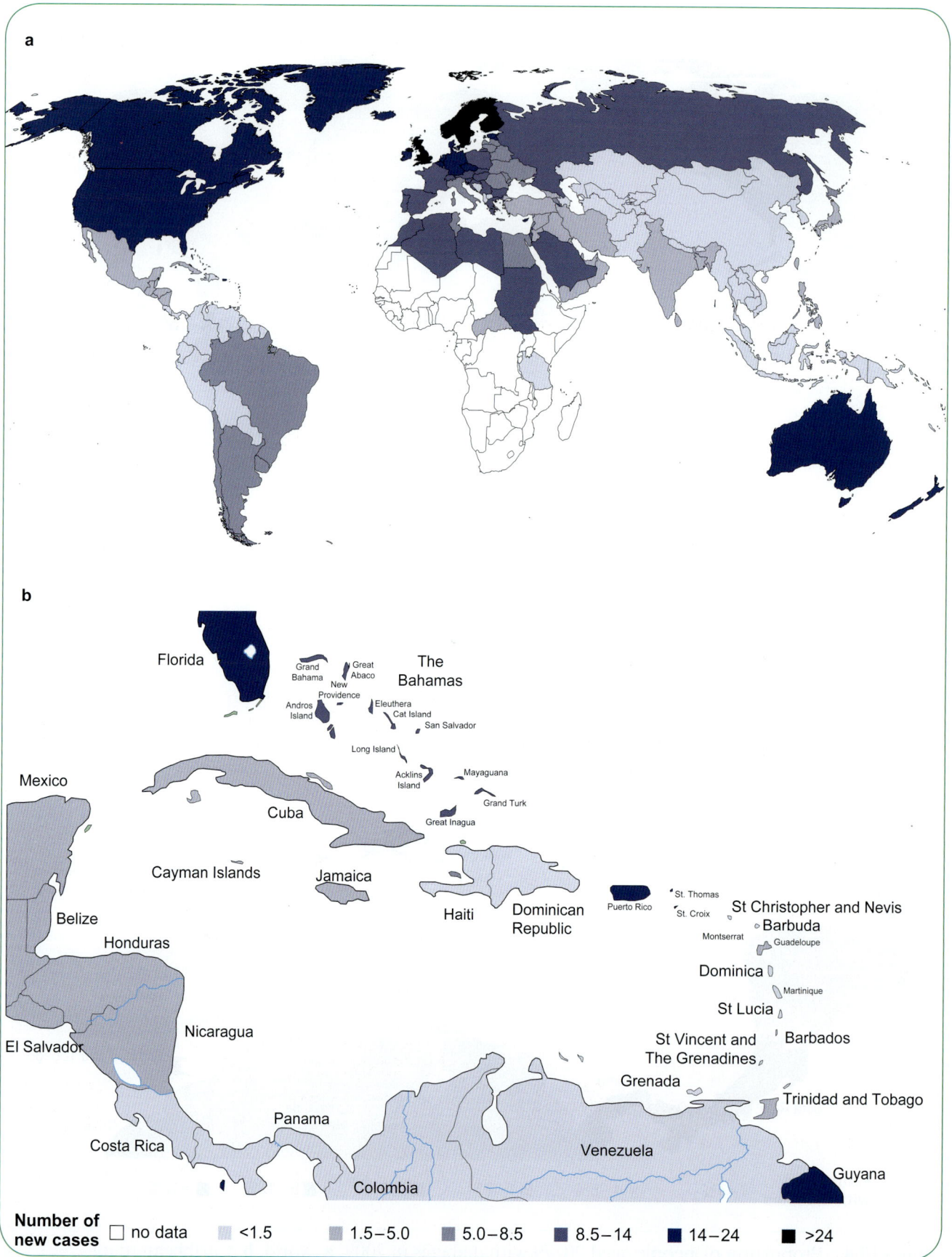

Figure 10.5   Number of new cases of Type 1 diabetes in children less than 14 years old in 2010 per 100 000 of the population, **a** world, **b** Caribbean (data – International Diabetes Federation).

cancer, because they allow the cell to divide uncontrollably, over and over again.

Cells also contain **repressor genes**. These genes normally inhibit cell division. They can mutate so that they lose their function, which once again allows uncontrollable division to take place (Figure 10.6).

Cells contain a number of different proto-oncogenes and repressor genes, and usually more than one mutation is needed to start off a cancer. Our cells contain many more different proto-oncogenes than repressor genes, and often several of these must mutate before cancer develops. But there are different versions of these genes, and some of them are more likely to mutate than others. Some people may therefore have versions which make them more susceptible to certain types of cancer than others.

This helps to explain why cancers become more common as people get older. The longer you live, the more chance there is that several regulatory genes in a cell may become altered.

So, if we want to know what causes cancer, we must look for what makes proto-oncogenes and repressor genes mutate. This can happen absolutely randomly, because mistakes do occasionally get made when DNA replication occurs. But the risk of mutations happening can also be increased by many different environmental factors, known as **carcinogens**. They include:

- ionising radiation, such as X-rays and cosmic rays;
- ultraviolet light;
- some chemicals, such as mustard gas, aflatoxin and chromium;
- infection by certain kinds of viruses.

All of these damage DNA, changing base sequences and therefore changing the primary structure of the proteins for which they code. These proteins are often enzymes, and they affect metabolic reactions in the cell.

Ionising radiation

Ionising radiation includes X-rays, alpha radiation and beta radiation. We are all exposed to some of it all the time, and this is known as background radiation. Exposure increases when we are given X-rays or if we are exposed to radon gas (which can leak out of some kinds of rocks and build up inside houses) or to nuclear fall-out from a nuclear bomb. Some forms of ionising radiation can penetrate deep into the body, and so can cause cancer in any of the organs. Ionising radiation contains great quantities of energy, and is powerful enough to break bonds in DNA molecules. This can change the base sequences in DNA. For reasons that are not fully understood, cells seem to be most vulnerable to ionising radiation during the latter part of interphase and during mitosis.

Ultraviolet light

Ultraviolet light is electromagnetic radiation with wavelengths just a little shorter than our eyes can detect. Ultraviolet light has less energy than

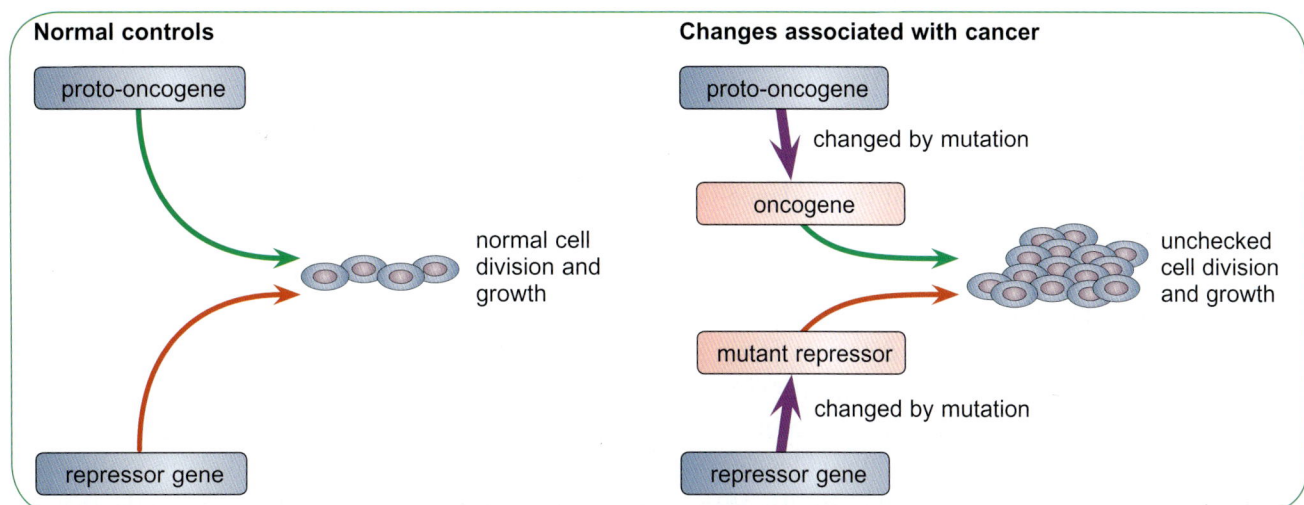

Figure 10.6 How mutations can cause cancer.

ionising radiation, so it cannot penetrate beneath our skin and the cancers it causes are skin cancers. Dark skins provide a great deal of protection against ultraviolet light, because the pigment melanin absorbs it, protecting the cells beneath. Cells are most sensitive to ultraviolet light when they are in early interphase.

Chemicals

An ever-increasing number of chemicals are being found to act as carcinogens. Mustard gas, used in the First World War, has been known for a long time to increase the rate of cancers of the nose, bronchus and larynx. Like most other chemical carcinogens, it has its effect by directly reacting with DNA molecules and altering their structure.

Tobacco smoke contains several different kinds of carcinogens, including nitrosamines and oxides of nitrogen, and smoking greatly increases the risk of developing many different kinds of cancer. You can read more about this, especially in relation to lung cancer, in Chapter 13. Nitric oxide is a type of free radical – that is, a chemical which can oxidise other chemicals, including DNA, in our cells. It has been thought that the action of free radicals can be counterbalanced by eating a diet containing plenty of anti-oxidants, such as vitamins A, C and E. However, recent research has cast doubt on this idea. All the same, it is still not a bad idea to try to eat a diet that contains plenty of anti-oxidants, as there is still plenty of evidence that they do protect against heart disease.

Drinking large amounts of alcohol over a prolonged period considerably increases the risk of developing several types of cancer. You can read more about this in Chapter 13.

Some **food additives** have come under suspicion of increasing the risk of cancer, but the evidence for this is limited. Food additives are substances that are added to foods before sale, to improve qualities such as appearance, taste, or the ability to be kept for a long time without deterioration. Food additives are tested carefully for health risks before they are licensed for use, and their safety is regularly reviewed. If there is scientific evidence that a food additive may be harmful to health, then

it is withdrawn from use. For example, in the past, amaranth was used as a dye in food and cosmetics. In 1971, a Russian study found a link between the use of this dye and cancer, and the dye is no longer permitted to be used.

The artificial sweeteners cyclamate and saccharin have caused cancer in laboratory rats when they were fed extremely high doses of them, but there is no evidence that they cause cancer in humans. All the same, it would be sensible to use these in moderation.

Recent studies have found that some food dyes may even help to protect against cancer, at least in laboratory animals. Most researchers consider that natural chemicals present in our food probably present more risk than additives.

Viruses

It is known that some viruses can cause cancer. The best known is the human papilloma virus, HPV. Some types of this virus only cause us the slightest of problems – for example, a wart on the hand. Warts are not dangerous because they are not invasive; they are benign tumours. But some kinds of HPV carry a code for a protein that interacts with a region of our DNA coding for a protein called p53. Alteration of the p53 gene is involved in the cause of very many human cancers. HPV is especially associated with cervical cancer. The virus is passed on during sexual intercourse.

Weakened immune system

Research suggests that many cells in all of us become potentially cancerous. Normally, however, our own immune system (Chapter 11) spots them as being different and destroys them well before they develop into noticeable tumours.

If someone's immune system is badly impaired, then this protective device breaks down. For example, many patients with HIV/AIDS, in which T-lymphocytes are destroyed, develop the otherwise rare skin cancer, Kaposi's sarcoma.

Genetics

Some alleles of genes are more likely to mutate and cause cancer than others. For example, the gene *BRCA1* has an important role in cells, where it codes for a protein that repairs damaged DNA strands. There are many different alleles of this gene, which occur as a result of mutation of the normal gene, and many of these alleles don't produce a working version of the repair protein. People with these faulty alleles are therefore more likely to get cancer. For example, women with a faulty version of the *BRCA1* gene have a 60% risk of developing breast cancer before they reach the age of 90, and also an increased risk of developing ovarian cancer.

Cancer in the Caribbean

Table 10.6 shows the incidence and mortality rates for four types of cancer in nine countries in the Caribbean and in the USA.

There are many reasons for the difference in incidence of the various cancers in these countries. Some of these are well known – for example, the close linking of the incidence of lung cancer with the number of people who smoke. The greater incidence of cervical cancer in the Caribbean than in the USA may be linked to more people having unprotected sexual intercourse, as this cancer is

caused by the human papilloma virus, transmitted through sexual intercourse. It is important that people are educated about the risk factors for cancer, so that they can choose a lifestyle that decreases their chances of developing these diseases.

The mortality rates are very much affected by how quickly people are diagnosed with cancer, and how easy it is for them to get good treatment once they have been diagnosed. The earlier that cancer is detected, the more likely it is that it can be successfully treated. Countries where people are on the look-out for early symptoms of cancer, and prepared to visit their doctor for a check-up if they are worried, tend to have much lower mortality rates. Compare the mortality and incidence rates for breast cancer in the USA, and in the Caribbean countries, shown in Table 10.6. Screening programmes, such as giving women the opportunity to have a mammogram (breast X-ray), can pick up cancer in its early stages, enabling it to be treated successfully. It is therefore important to ensure that people are aware of the early signs and symptoms of cancer, and encouraged to go for a health check if they think they may have them.

Country	Breast cancer		Cervical cancer		Lung cancer				Colorectal cancer			
	Incidence	Mortality	Incidence	Mortality	Incidence		Mortality		Incidence		Mortality	
	Women	Women	Women	Women	Women	Men	Women	Men	Women	Men	Women	Men
USA	76.0	14.7	5.7	1.7	36.2	49.5	24.1	38.2	25.0	34.1	7.7	9.9
Bahamas	61.0	24.1	17.6	9.4	4.1	16.4	4.1	15.6	11.9	18.4	8.9	10.8
Barbados	74.0	29.3	20.8	9.9	4.0	9.2	4.0	9.2	22.1	23.1	13.9	15.6
Cuba	38.5	15.5	23.1	8.9	20.2	43.9	18.5	40.6	17.5	16.0	11.9	10.7
Dominican Republic	32.7	12.1	29.7	13.7	9.7	14.0	8.7	12.9	9.5	8.8	6.2	5.6
Haiti	23.9	10.6	16.0	10.1	7.0	7.9	6.5	7.3	8.9	7.3	6.0	5.0
Jamaica	56.8	22.9	45.7	20.2	8.3	24.8	7.8	22.3	13.4	12.3	9.0	7.9
Puerto Rico	54.2	12.3	7.5	2.8	6.5	15.8	5.8	12.9	16.8	24.9	8.3	11.2
Trinidad and Tobago	36.0	16.8	15.8	11.5	3.3	21.4	3.3	18.1	10.8	19.9	6.9	13.3

Table 10.6 Breast, cervical, lung and colorectal cancer in the Caribbean and the USA, per 100 000, in 2008. (Data from the GLOBOCAN program of the International Agency for Research in Cancer (IARC).)

SAQ

7 This question is about the data in Table 10.6.

a Which of the cancers in the table is more common in the Caribbean than in the USA?

b Suggest reasons why the incidence of breast cancer is much greater in the USA than in any of the Caribbean countries in the table.

c Compare the incidence of lung cancer in men and women in the Caribbean countries.

d Suggest reasons for the differences you have described in your answer to **c**.

e Which cancer has the highest mortality rate compared with incidence? Suggest a reason for this.

Summary

- Health is defined by the World Health Organization as a state of complete physical, mental and social well-being and not merely the absence of disease or infirmity.

- Diseases can be classified into various different categories. Any one disease may belong in two or more categories.

- The incidence of a disease is the number of new cases per year. Prevalence is the number of people with the disease at any one time. Mortality is the number of people who die from a disease per year. These figures are normally expressed per 100 000 people in the population, or as a percentage.

- AIDS is caused by the human immunodeficiency virus, HIV. The worldwide pandemic has resulted partly from the current ease of global travel, and is also due to the fact that the virus may be present in a person's body for many years without causing symptoms, so that they may unknowingly pass the virus to a sexual partner. Differences in lifestyles, availability of drugs and education about the disease contribute to differences in incidence and mortality in different countries.

- Type 2 diabetes is common in the Caribbean. It is a disorder of the homeostatic mechanism that controls blood glucose concentration. Lifestyle contributes to the risk of developing Type 2 diabetes, in particular being overweight (BMI above 27), not taking exercise and eating a poor diet, including malnutrition of a mother during pregnancy. There is also a genetic element.

- Cancer is, in fact, a multitude of different diseases, each with their own causes and risk factors. In general, however, it results from damage to the genes that normally control cell division by mitosis. This may be a result of exposure to carcinogens, such as the chemicals in cigarette smoke; infection with viruses, such as HPV; or inheriting particular alleles, such as the *BRCA1* allele. Awareness of symptoms can decrease mortality, because a person seeking early diagnosis has a much better chance of receiving successful treatment.

Questions

Multiple choice questions

1 Which of the following definitions **best** describes 'good health'?
  A a state of complete physical and mental well-being
  B a state of complete physical and social well-being
  C a state of complete physical, mental and social well-being
  D a state of complete physical, mental and social well-being and not merely the absence of disease

2 Diseases that are transmitted by a pathogenic organism which invades the body are described as:
  A inherited.   B infectious.   C deficiency.   D mental.

3 The human immunodeficiency virus (HIV) is spread by the exchange of body fluids between an infected person and an uninfected person. In which of the following groups of disease categories can HIV/AIDS be placed?
  A infectious, social, degenerate
  B non-infectious, social, mental
  C deficiency, physical, degenerate
  D inherited, infectious, mental

4 Which of the following diseases is matched to its **most** appropriate definition?

	Category	Definition
A	deficiency	caused by a genetic fault passed on from the parents
B	inherited	caused by poor diet
C	physical	permanent or temporary damage to any part of the body
D	self-inflicted	caused by changes to the mind

5 Which of the following diseases is matched to its most appropriate category?

	Disease	Category
A	scurvy	mental
B	cystic fibrosis	self-inflicted
C	lung cancer	inherited
D	dengue	infectious

6 Which of the following region has the most people living with HIV/AIDS?
  A Latin America and the Caribbean
  B Sub-Saharan Africa
  C North America
  D Asia

continued …

7   Which is **not** a risk factor for Type 2 diabetes?
   A low blood pressure
   B obesity
   C prenatal malnutrition
   D physical inactivity

8   Which of the following reasons **best** explains the distribution of HIV/AIDS in the Caribbean?
   A lack of education, poverty, difficulty in travelling to islands
   B short incubation period, sex tourism, poverty
   C drug use, high cost of HIV/AIDS drugs, poverty
   D lack of education, low cost of drugs, poverty

9   Which of the following is a high risk factor for HIV transmission?
   A working as a nurse
   B living with someone with HIV/AIDS
   C receiving blood from a HIV-negative person
   D sexual intercourse without a condom

10 Which of the following is **not** considered an environmental risk factor in relation to developing cancer?
   A ultraviolet radiation
   B exposure to second-hand smoke (passive smoking)
   C presence of cancer genes
   D X-rays

Structured questions

11 a Define the term 'health'.   [2 marks]
   b Diabetes is a disease. What is meant by the term 'disease'?   [2 marks]
   c Diseases are classified according to certain characteristics.
      Copy and complete the table which gives information about five categories of disease.

Category of disease	Definition	Example
	wilful damage to the body by a person's own actions or behaviour	lung cancer
social		
	inadequate quantity of a nutrient	rickets
mental	causes changes to the mind	
degenerate		osteoarthritis

                                                                                             [6 marks]
   d Some diseases are not easy to place in a particular category. State **two** categories of diseases in which each of the following could be placed.
      i   HIV/AIDS   ii diabetes   iii lung cancer   [3 marks]
   e Some diseases are described as chronic. State with an example what is meant by 'chronic'.   [2 marks]

continued ...

12 A number of health agencies, e.g. WHO and CAREC, collect health statistics. These statistics are reported in a number of ways. Three such statistics are incidence, prevalence and mortality of the particular disease.

a Explain the meanings of each of the following terms:

i incidence **ii** prevalence **iii** mortality [3 marks]

b The following data show the regional statistics for HIV and AIDS at the end of 2008.

Region	Adults and children living with HIV/AIDS	Adults and children newly infected	Adult prevalence*	Deaths of adults and children
Sub-Saharan Africa	22.4 million	1.9 million	5.2%	1.4 million
South and South-East Asia	3.8 million	280 000	0.3%	270 000
Latin America	2.0 million	170,000	0.6%	77 000
Caribbean	240 000	20 000	1.0%	12 000
Eastern Europe and Central Asia	1.5 million	110 000	0.7%	87 000
North America	1.4 million	55 000	0.4%	25 000
Western and Central Europe	850 000	30 000	0.3%	13 000

* Proportion of adults aged 15–49 who were living with HIV/AIDS

i Using evidence from the data given in the table, draw **one** general conclusion. [3 marks]

ii The adult prevalence of HIV/AIDS in Sub-Saharan Africa and the Caribbean is much higher than in North America. Suggest **three** reasons for the difference in the percentages. [3 marks]

c The table below shows the estimated HIV and AIDS prevalence and deaths due to AIDS in 2007.

Country	Prevalence of HIV/AIDS		Deaths due to AIDS
	all ages / number	15–49 year-olds / %	all ages / number
Bahamas	6 200	3.0	<200
Barbados	2 200	1.2	<100
Cuba	6 200	0.1	<100
Dominican Republic	62 000	1.1	3 900
Haiti	120 000	2.2	7 500
Jamaica	27 000	1.6	1 400
Trinidad and Tobago	14 000	1.5	<1 000

continued…

    i Identify the **two** health statistics shown in the table. [2 marks]

    ii Make **one** conclusion based on the data given in the table above. [1 mark]

    iii Suggest **two** reasons for the difference in rates of infection in the Caribbean. [2 marks]

  d Why are health statistics important to health authorities? [1 mark]

13 **a** The graph below shows the results of a study into the causes of deaths by the Caribbean Epidemiology Centre (CAREC) in 21 member countries.

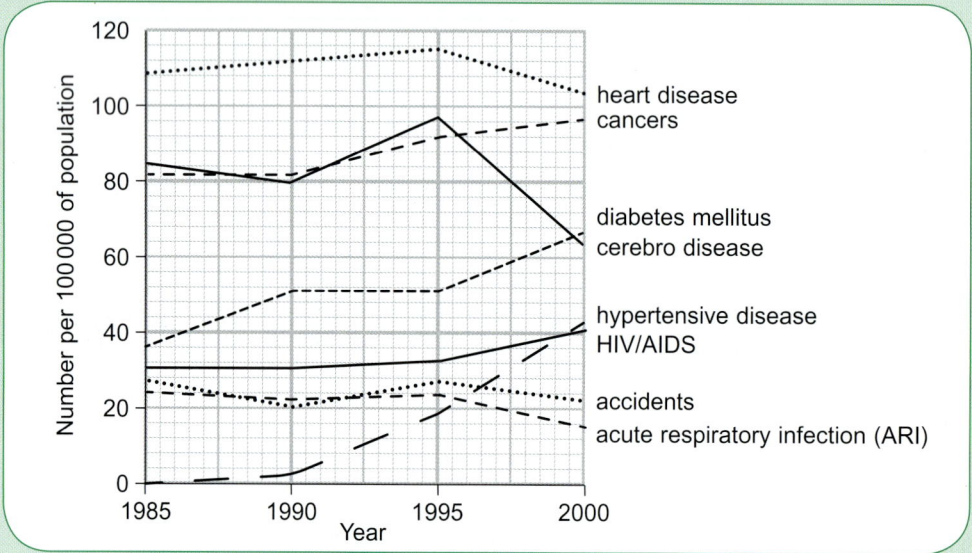

    i Identify **four** diseases whose mortality rates increased between 1995 and 2000. [2 marks]

    ii Calculate the percentage difference in mortality rates for diabetes between 1995 and 2000. [1 mark]

  b CAREC collects statistics on HIV/AIDS and estimates the total number of people who are infected with HIV in its member countries in the Caribbean. The graph below shows the numbers of HIV cases, AIDS cases and AIDS deaths.

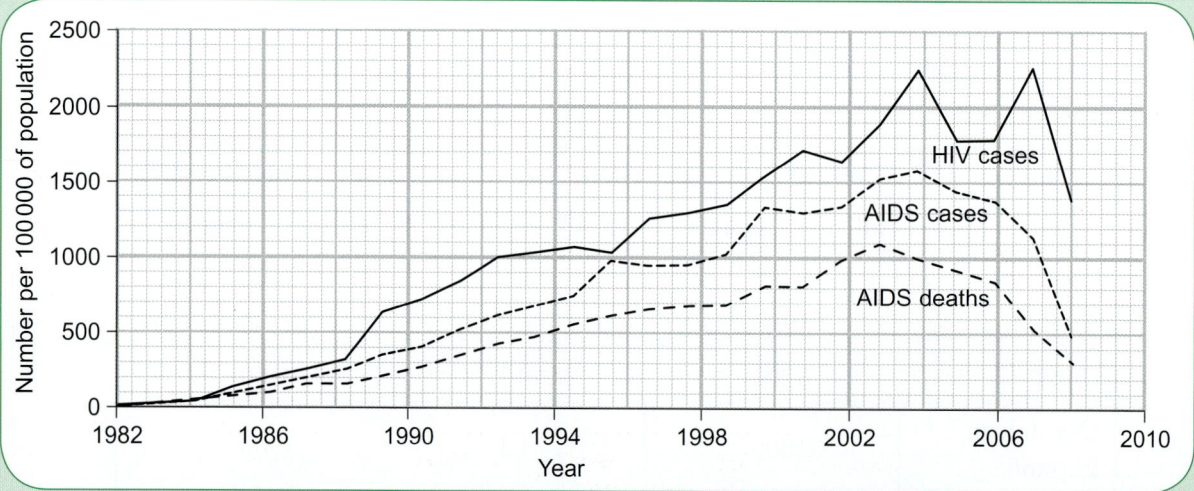

    i Using the data in the graph above, describe the changes that occurred in the numbers of people who were infected with HIV between 1982 and 2007. [3 marks]

    ii Suggest why the number of people actually infected with HIV may be much larger than the data suggest. [1 mark]

continued ...

iii Explain why the number of AIDS cases is always likely to be lower than the number of HIV cases. [2 marks]

iv Explain the decrease in the number of people who have been diagnosed with AIDS and who have died from HIV/AIDS since 2002. [2 marks]

c The bar graphs below show the estimated number of adults with diabetes by age group and year in developed and developing countries for the years 2000 and 2030.

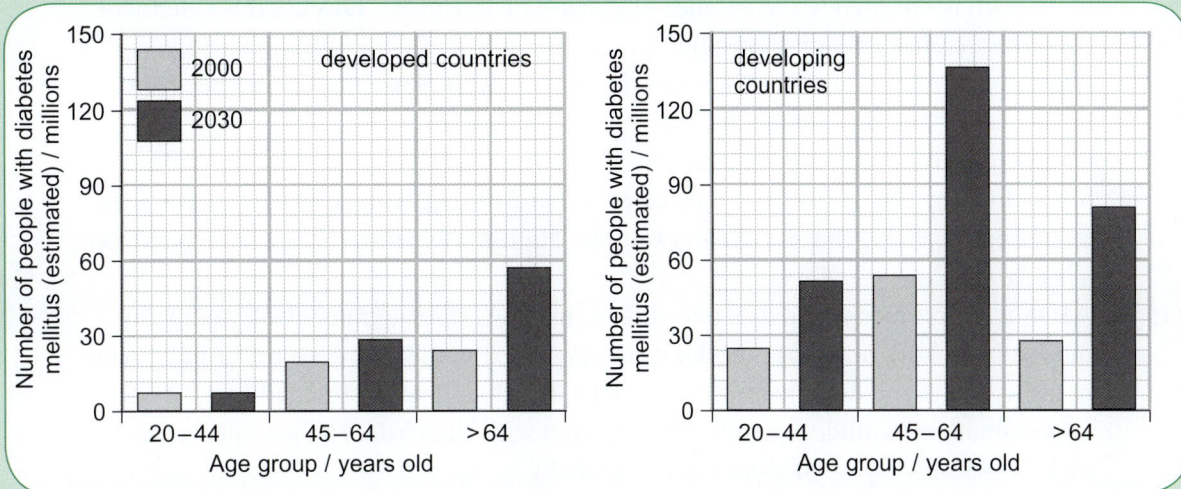

i Describe the similarities and differences between the data for developed and developing countries. [4 marks]

ii Account for the differences observed. [2 marks]

d The graph below shows the incidence of lung cancer and smoking trends in the UK between 1948 and 2008.

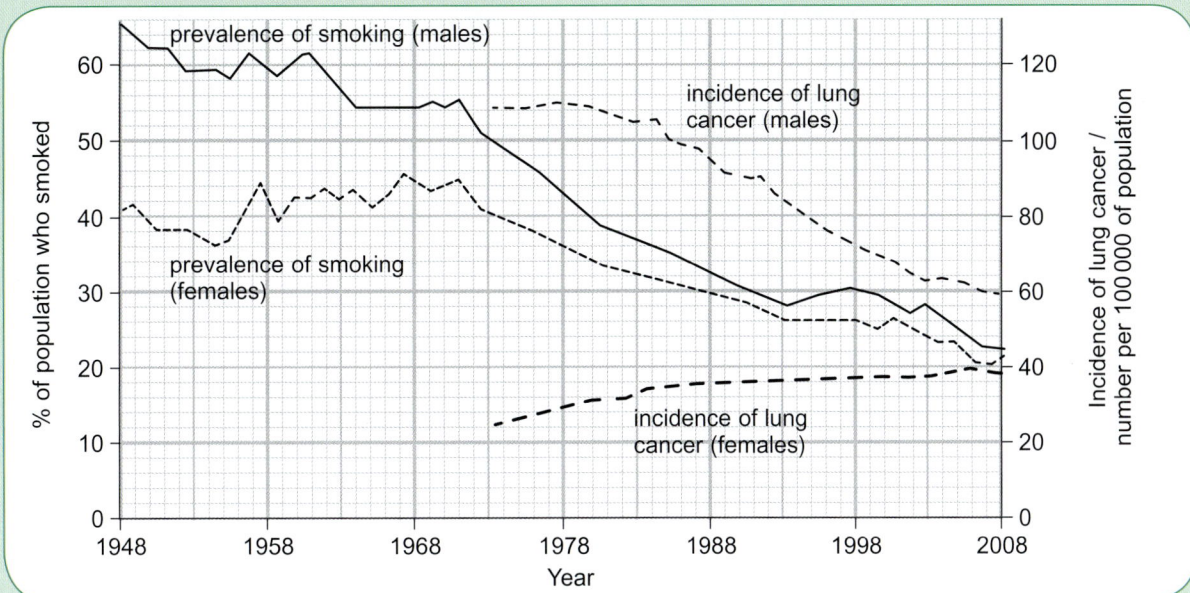

i Describe the changes in prevalence of smoking in both males and females between 1948 and 2008. [4 marks]

ii Explain the relationship between the incidence of lung cancer and the prevalence of smoking. [4 marks]

continued …

Essay questions

14 a James, 55, is a chain smoker, often eats fast foods, rarely eats fruits and vegetables, drives to work, rarely exercises and drinks 4 bottles of beer every day alone at home. James considers himself to be in 'good health' since he has no chronic diseases and does not feel unwell.

  i What do you understand by the term 'chronic diseases'? [2 marks]

  ii 'Health is not merely the absence of disease or infirmity'. Discuss this statement with reference to James's profile. [4 marks]

 b Diseases are placed in different categories. Using examples, differentiate between:

  i deficiency and degenerate diseases

  ii physical and inherited diseases. [6 marks]

 c Some diseases can be placed in one category while others can be placed in more than one category. Using diabetes as an example, discuss why some diseases can be placed in more than one category. [3 marks]

15 a AIDS was first recognised as a new disease in 1981, when a number of young gay men in New York and Los Angeles were diagnosed with symptoms not usually seen in individuals with healthy immune systems. In 2008, it was estimated that approximately 35 million people were infected with the virus. The prevalence rates of HIV/AIDS vary in different regions globally.

  i Explain why the disease spread so rapidly in such a relatively short time span. [2 marks]

  ii Discuss the reasons for the varying prevalence rate of HIV/AIDS throughout the world. [6 marks]

 b Women account for approximately 50% of the HIV/AIDS cases and they live mostly in developing countries. Suggest reasons for these observations. [3 marks]

 c The Caribbean has one of the highest prevalence of HIV/AIDS in the world. Discuss the effects of HIV/AIDS on Caribbean countries. [4 marks]

16 a Cancer is a leading cause of death worldwide: it accounted for 7.4 million deaths (around 13% of all deaths) in 2004.

  i What do you understand by the term 'cancer'?

  ii Describe the global distribution of cancer.

  iii Give **two** examples of major types of cancer in males and females.

  iv Cancers are the result of the interaction between the genetic factors and environmental factors affecting a person. Discuss how named environmental factors result in cancerous cells. [10 marks]

 b Describe and account for the global distribution of diabetes. [5 marks]

Chapter 11
Immunology

By the end of this chapter you should be able to:

a   describe the mode of action of phagocytes;

b   describe the roles of mast cells and histamine production, complement, and phagocytes as antigen-presenting cells;

c   define the term 'immune response';

d   compare the origin and maturation of B- and T-lymphocytes, including the types of T-cells and their functions, and B-cells and their functions;

e   distinguish between the humoral and the cell-mediated immune responses;

f   explain the role of T- and B-memory cells in long-term immunity;

g   relate the molecular structure of a typical antibody molecule to its function, including specificity;

h   distinguish between active and passive immunity, natural and artificial immunity;

i   explain the role of vaccination in providing immunity;

j   state what is meant by a monoclonal antibody;

k   describe the use of monoclonal antibodies in diagnosis and treatment, including pregnancy testing, and the anticancer drug MabThera®.

Parasites and pathogens

Infectious diseases are ones that we can catch from someone else, such as a cold, TB, malaria and HIV/AIDS. These diseases are caused by **pathogens**. A pathogen can be defined as a microorganism that causes disease.

Pathogens are a kind of parasite. A parasite is an organism that lives in a very close relationship with another organism, called its host, and does it harm. The parasite gains from the relationship. So all pathogens are parasites, but not all parasites are pathogens. For example, you might have lice living in your hair, but they are not causing a disease so they are not pathogens.

A well-adapted parasite or pathogen does not kill its host. The parasite or pathogen is most likely to survive, and produce offspring that can move to a new host, if its host survives long enough for this to happen. Most of the infectious diseases that have been around for a long time, such as colds, measles and TB, either do not kill us – or do not kill us quickly.

Pathogens belong to one of four different groups of microorganisms – viruses, bacteria, fungi and protozoa. (Some may argue that viruses are not organisms at all.) Table 11.1 lists some examples of diseases caused by each of these groups.

The immune response

We have numerous defences against invasion of our bodies by pathogens. The first line of defence is to stop them getting in at all. If they do gain access, then the immune system comes into action. The way in which white blood cells respond when pathogens enter the body is called the **immune response**.

Several types of white blood cells (leucocytes) are able to recognise 'foreign' cells or molecules that enter the body. In other words, they can distinguish self from non-self. The immune response is the way in which the immune system responds to the presence of non-self cells or molecules in the body.

Pathogen	Type of microorganism	Disease caused
human immunodeficiency virus (HIV)	virus	acquired immune deficiency syndrome (AIDS)
adenovirus	virus	colds
Mycobacterium	bacterium	tuberculosis (TB)
Tinea pedis	fungus	athlete's foot
Plasmodium	protozoan	malaria

Table 11.1 Causes of some infectious diseases.

Primary lines of defence

The best line of defence against pathogens is to prevent them from getting established in the body.

Skin is impermeable to most pathogens, although there are a few viruses, such as the ones that cause warts, that can penetrate unbroken skin. We have our own 'flora' of harmless bacteria that live on healthy skin, but most pathogenic bacteria cannot survive there, partly because lactic acid and fatty acids secreted from sweat glands and sebaceous glands provide a pH that is too low for them. However, the common bacterium *Staphylococcus aureus* can thrive even on undamaged skin, and it often infects hair follicles and sebaceous glands.

The normal bacterial flora living on our body surfaces can help to prevent infection by other microorganisms. For example, the bacteria that normally live in the vagina keep the pH low by secreting lactic acid. If a person takes antibiotics, these bacteria may be killed. Then the pH of the vagina rises, and this may allow other microorganisms, such as the fungus that causes thrush, *Candida*, to multiply to a much greater population density than usual.

If skin is damaged – for example, by cuts or extensive burns – then the way is open for bacteria to get into the underlying tissues. Blood clotting helps to seal wounds rapidly, until a more permanent repair is produced by mitosis of the cells surrounding the wound. A blood clot forms when soluble, globular fibrinogen is converted to the insoluble, fibrous protein fibrin. This forms a mesh of strands across the wound in which platelets stick and red blood cells get trapped, thus preventing further loss of blood or entry of pathogens.

Moist body surfaces, such as the surface of the eyes and mouth, are bathed in fluids which have some bactericidal action. An enzyme called lysozyme is present in saliva and tears, and this enzyme can damage and destroy many bacteria. Semen contains a bactericide called spermine; milk contains a bactericidal enzyme called lactoperoxidase. The hydrochloric acid secreted into the stomach is very effective in destroying bacteria and other pathogens ingested in food.

Mucus helps to protect the digestive and respiratory tracts from infection. It acts as a barrier so that bacteria cannot make contact with the epithelial cells lining the walls of the tubes. Mucus is produced by goblet cells, which are part of the epithelium. A layer of cells containing goblet cells is sometimes known as a mucous membrane (but don't confuse this 'membrane' with a plasma membrane of a cell). In the trachea and bronchi, the mucus is swept upwards to the back of the throat by cilia and then swallowed. Coughing and sneezing help to expel mucus containing microorganisms from the trachea and bronchi. If the mucus is swallowed, the acid and enzymes in the stomach destroy any bacteria trapped in it.

Phagocytes

If pathogens do get through the body's outer defences, they may be destroyed by patrolling phagocytic white blood cells. The types of white blood cells known as **neutrophils** and **macrophages** are phagocytes. They engulf and digest foreign particles of almost any type or size (Figure 11.1). They crawl around within almost every part of the body – for example, over the surfaces of the alveoli in the lungs.

Neutrophils are found in the blood, where they make up about 60% of the white blood cells. They do not live very long, often dying after they have taken in and destroyed bacteria, and so new neutrophils are constantly being made in the bone marrow. They move around actively, and frequently leave the blood and patrol parts of the body where 'invaders' may be found.

Macrophages also leave the blood. (Indeed, when they are actually in the blood they are given a different name – monocytes.) They are present in especially large numbers in the liver, where they are known as Kupffer cells. They also line the passages through which lymph flows inside lymph nodes and are found on the inside of the alveolar

walls. Unlike neutrophils, they are quite long-lived, tending to survive after taking in foreign particles. They break the particles up into their component molecules and place some of these molecules in their plasma membranes. Cells that do this are called **antigen-presenting cells**. By doing this, they display the molecules to other cells of the immune system, helping these cells to identify the invaders and be able to destroy them. This role is described more fully on pages 224–228.

For phagocytosis to take place, the microorganisms must first adhere to the plasma membrane of the phagocyte. This process is helped by a group of proteins called **complement** (page 228) which are always present in the blood plasma, and also by chemicals called **cytokines**, which are produced by other white blood cells in response to the presence of particular antigens. Cytokines make phagocytes more efficient at killing any microorganisms that they have engulfed.

The way in which phagocytes deal with invading cells or other foreign material is a **non-specific response**. Each phagocyte can attack and destroy any type of non-self material.

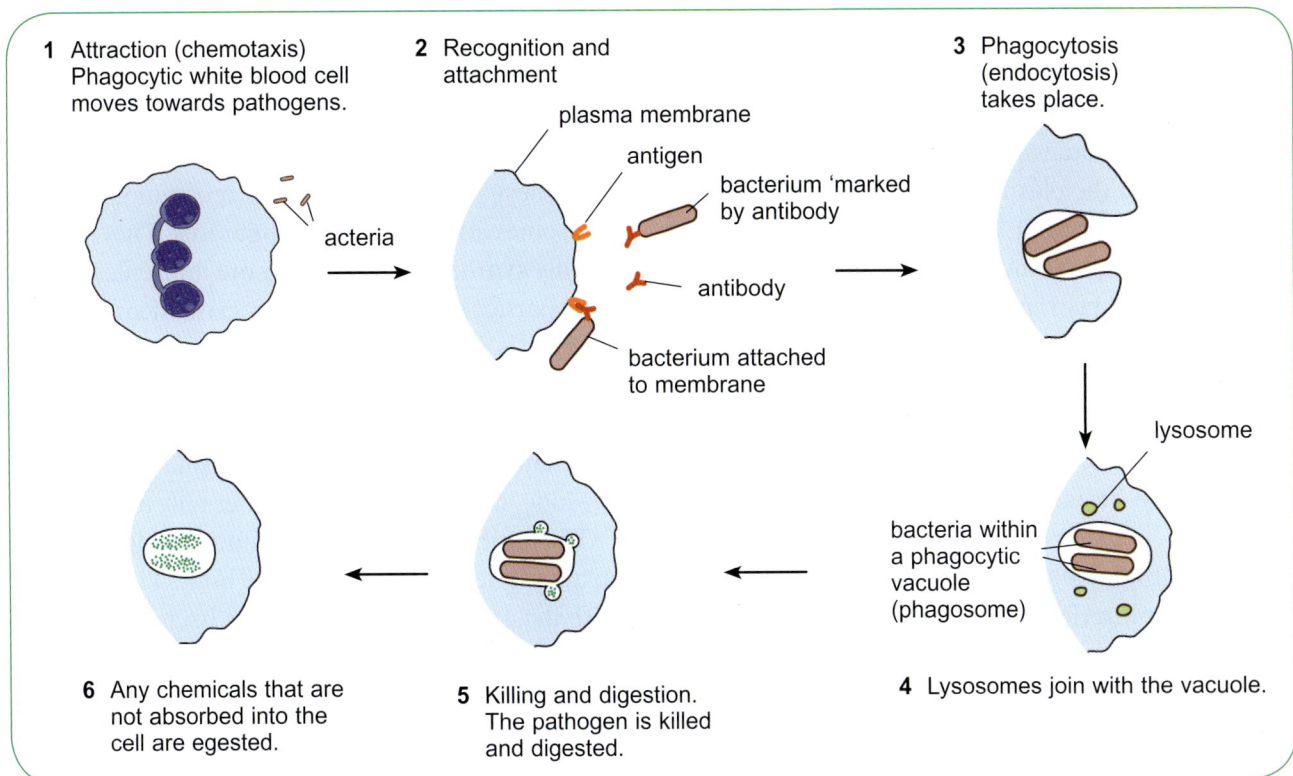

1 Attraction (chemotaxis) Phagocytic white blood cell moves towards pathogens.

2 Recognition and attachment
plasma membrane
antigen
bacterium 'marked by antibody
antibody
bacterium attached to membrane
acteria

3 Phagocytosis (endocytosis) takes place.

lysosome
bacteria within a phagocytic vacuole (phagosome)

4 Lysosomes join with the vacuole.

5 Killing and digestion. The pathogen is killed and digested.

6 Any chemicals that are not absorbed into the cell are egested.

Figure 11.1 Phagocytosis.

Lymphocytes

Lymphocytes are relatively small white blood cells. They are of two types, **B-lymphocytes** and **T-lymphocytes**. These two types look identical, and differ only in their functions. B-lymphocytes are so-called because they develop in the bone marrow, while T-lymphocytes need to spend time in the thymus gland during a person's childhood to become properly developed. This gland is found in the neck. It disappears by the time a person becomes a teenager.

Lymphocytes are stimulated into action when they come into contact with molecules called **antigens**. Invading bacteria and viruses are recognised as foreign because they carry or produce antigens that are different from any of our own molecules. Antigens may be 'free' or they may be part of a bigger structure, such as the cell wall of a bacterium.

We have a huge number of different kinds of lymphocytes in our blood. Each one is capable of recognising and responding to one particular antigen. The response of lymphocytes to non-self molecules is therefore known as a **specific response**.

As they mature, lymphocytes produce small quantities of particular glycoproteins called **antibodies** (page 231). We have perhaps a million different kinds of lymphocytes, each kind producing an antibody which is slightly different from other antibodies. At this stage, the antibodies are placed into the plasma membranes of the lymphocytes (Figure 11.2). Here, the antibodies act as receptors, able to bind with a particular antigen if this should appear in the body.

If bacteria enter the body, there is a good chance that some of the lymphocytes will have receptors that bind with antigens on the surface of the bacteria. If so, then a response is triggered. B-lymphocytes and T-lymphocytes respond differently.

How B-lymphocytes respond to antigens

Most B-lymphocytes will spend all their lives without anything happening to them at all, because they never meet their particular antigen. But if a B-lymphocyte does encounter an antigen which binds to the receptors in its plasma membrane, it is triggered into action. It could simply meet

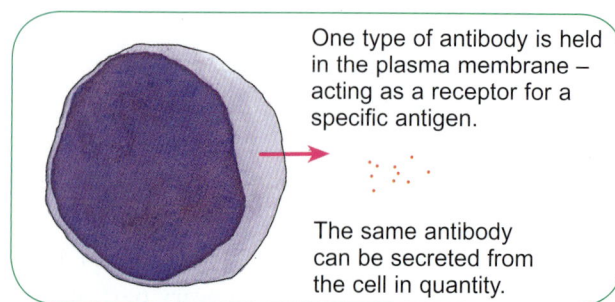

One type of antibody is held in the plasma membrane – acting as a receptor for a specific antigen.

The same antibody can be secreted from the cell in quantity.

Figure 11.2   A lymphocyte can produce one specific type of antibody.

this antigen in the blood, or it could meet it as it is being displayed in the plasma membrane of an antigen-presenting cell (APC) such as a macrophage (Figure 11.3).

You can imagine the macrophages sitting in the lymph channels inside a lymph node, holding out the antigens they have discovered so that the lymphocytes will 'see' them as they pass by.

The B-lymphocyte responds by dividing repeatedly by mitosis. A large number of genetically identical cells is formed – a clone of the stimulated lymphocyte.

The process of the B-lymphocyte binding with its specific antigen is sometimes called **clonal selection**, and its division to form a clone of genetically identical cells is called **clonal proliferation** or clonal expansion.

Some of these cells differentiate into **plasma cells**. These cells develop extra protein-making machinery – more endoplasmic reticulum, more ribosomes and more Golgi apparatus. They rapidly synthesise more and more molecules of their particular antibody and release them by exocytosis. It has been estimated that a plasma cell can produce and release more than 2000 antibody molecules per second. Perhaps as a direct result of this tremendous rate of activity, plasma cells do not live long, mostly disappearing after only a few weeks.

The antibodies are secreted into the blood and so are carried to all parts of the body. They bind with the antigens on the invading bacteria, which results in the destruction of the bacteria – as we shall see on pages 231–233.

Other cells in the clone produced by the original B-lymphocyte's division do not secrete antibodies. Instead, they remain as **memory cells.** These cells

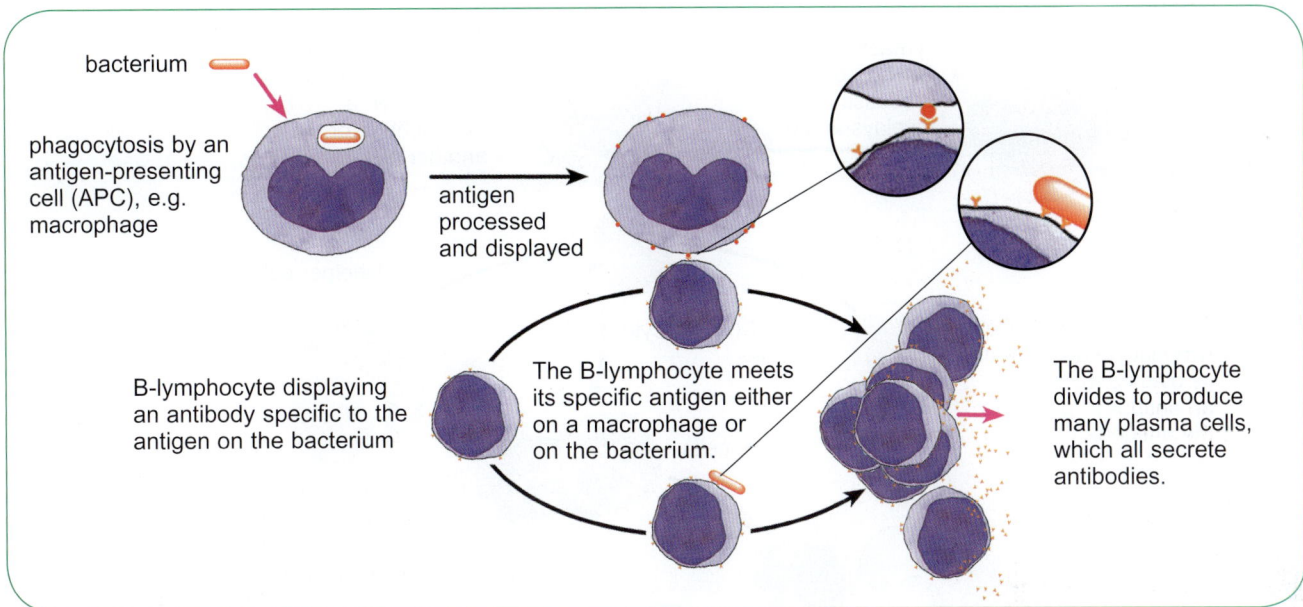

Figure 11.3 B-lymphocyte response to antigen.

live for a long time, and remain circulating in the blood long after the invading bacteria have all been destroyed. They are capable of responding very quickly if the same type of bacterium enters the body again.

How T-lymphocytes respond to antigens

T-lymphocytes, like B-lymphocytes, are activated if and when their particular antigen binds with the specific glycoproteins that are held in their plasma membranes. T-lymphocytes, however, normally only respond to their antigen if they find it in the plasma membrane of another cell. This could be a macrophage that is displaying some of the molecules from a pathogen that it has taken up. Or it could be molecules on a body cell that has been invaded by a virus, and has placed virus particles in its plasma membrane as a 'help' signal (Figure 11.4).

There are several types of T-lymphocytes, including **T-helper cells** and **T-killer cells**. A particular T-helper cell with the complementary receptor binds to the antigen that it has found. It then divides to form a clone of itself. The cloned T-helper cells then begin to secrete chemicals called **cytokines**. These chemicals stimulate other cells to fight against the invaders. For example, they may stimulate macrophages to carry out phagocytosis, or they may stimulate B-lymphocytes specific to

this antigen to divide rapidly and become plasma cells. They also help to stimulate appropriate T-killer cells.

T-killer cells actually destroy the cell to which they have become bound. A body cell displaying virus particles will be destroyed by T-killer cells. This is the only way of destroying the viruses – it can't be done without destroying the cell in which they are multiplying. The T-killer cells destroy the infected cell by secreting chemicals such as hydrogen peroxide. The T-killer cells are our main defence against viral diseases.

We have seen that T-lymphocytes, like B-lymphocytes, divide to form clones when they meet their own particular antigen (Figure 11.5). While most of these cells act as helper cells or killer cells, some of them remain in the blood as memory cells. These, and memory cells formed from B-lymphocytes, help the body to respond more quickly if this same antigen ever invades again.

Complement

Complement is a collection of small proteins (more than 25 different ones) that are always present in the blood plasma. It was first discovered in 1895, and was given this name because it helps, or complements, the activity of antibodies and phagocytes. Complement is very important in fighting bacterial infections.

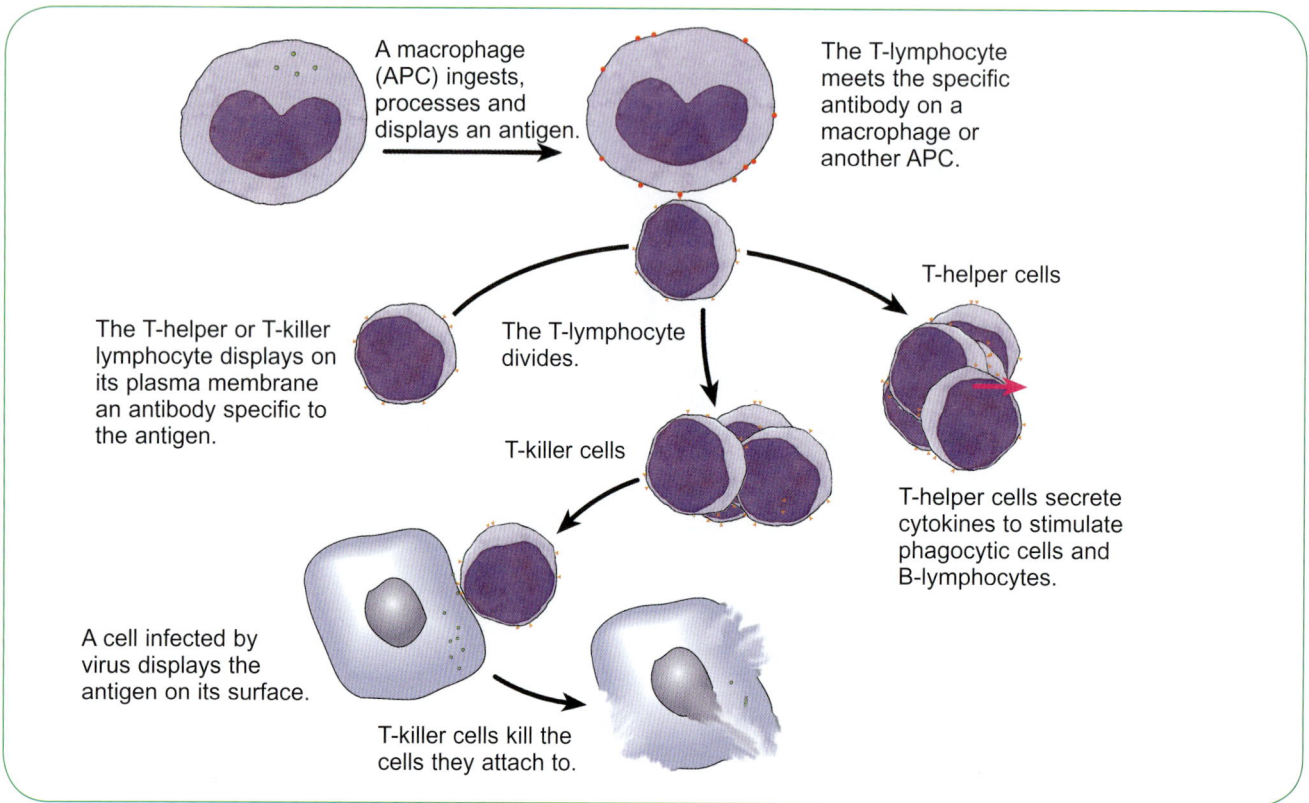

Figure 11.4 T-lymphocyte response to antigen.

Maturation of T-lymphocytes

T-lymphocytes all originate from cells in the bone marrow that divide by mitosis. As a child grows and develops, these immature T-lymphocytes move to the thymus gland in the neck, where they divide to form a large population of T-lymphocytes.

As the T-lymphocytes mature, they begin to produce glycoproteins called CD4 and CD8. These glycoproteins are placed in their plasma membranes, where they act as receptors. Each cell then stops producing one of these types of glycoprotein, and becomes either a CD4$^+$ cell (producing CD4 only) or a CD8$^+$ cell (producing CD8 only).

In general, T-lymphocytes that express the CD4 receptor become T-helper cells, while those that express the CD8 receptor become T-killer cells.

Each T-lymphocyte also produces other receptors, coded for by variant genes in their nuclei that are able to produce a wide range of different glycoproteins. This results in a very large number of different kinds of T-lymphocytes, each producing a different range of receptors.

During their development in the thymus gland, only T-lymphocytes that have a set of receptors enabling them to bind to the protein antigens on the body's own cells (called the MHC complex) are allowed to survive. Moreover, any that interact with the MHC complex too strongly are also destroyed. This ensures that all of the T-lymphocytes that remain in the body are able to recognise the body's own cells, and will not initiate auto-immune reactions in which they attack and harm them. Overall, only about 2% of all the T-lymphocytes that develop in the thymus gland pass these tests and survive.

SAQ

1 With reference to the way in which they respond to antigens, suggest why T-lymphocytes are more effective than B-lymphocytes in dealing with infection by a virus.

B-cells

Specific binding
B-lymphocyte with antibody in its plasma membrane binds to complementary antigen.

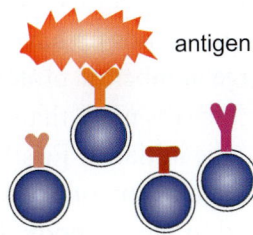

antigen

Clonal selection and proliferation
Stimulated B-lymphocyte divides many times.

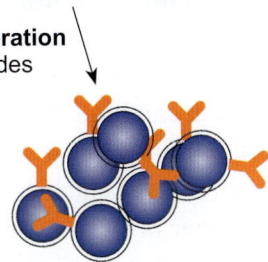

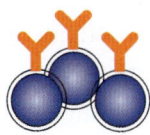

Memory cells
These survive for a long time.

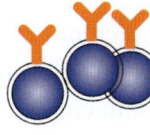

Plasma cells
These secrete large amounts of antibody.

If antigen appears later, the memory cells are stimulated, divide and produce many plasma cells very quickly.

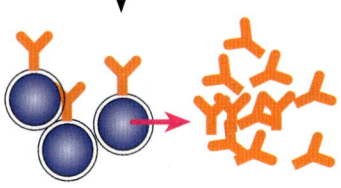

T-cells

Antigen presentation
An APC (macrophage) ingests, processes and presents antigen.

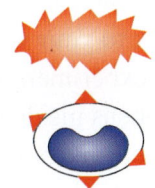

Specific binding
T-helper lymphocyte or T-killer lymphocyte binds to complementary antigen on an APC.

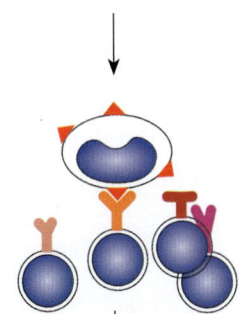

Clonal selection and proliferation
One clone is stimulated and this T-lymphocyte divides many times.

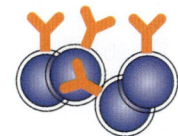

either

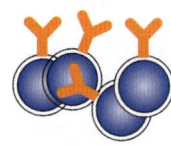

T-killer lymphocytes
These bind to cells presenting the complementary antigen.

T-helper lymphocytes
These secrete cytokines which stimulate phagocytic cells and other lymphocytes.

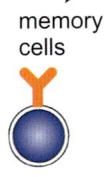

memory cells

memory cells

T-killer cells bind to cells presenting the complementary antigen and kill them.

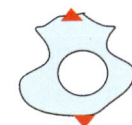

cell killed

Figure 11.5 Summary of B-lymphocyte and T-lymphocyte actions.

2 To answer this question, you will need to think back to your work on cells.

An experiment was carried out to follow what happens inside plasma cells as they make and secrete antibodies. Some cells were cultured in a solution containing amino acids which had been 'labelled' with a radioactive marker. The radioactivity in the Golgi body, endoplasmic reticulum and ribosomes was then measured over the next 40 minutes. The results are shown in the graph.

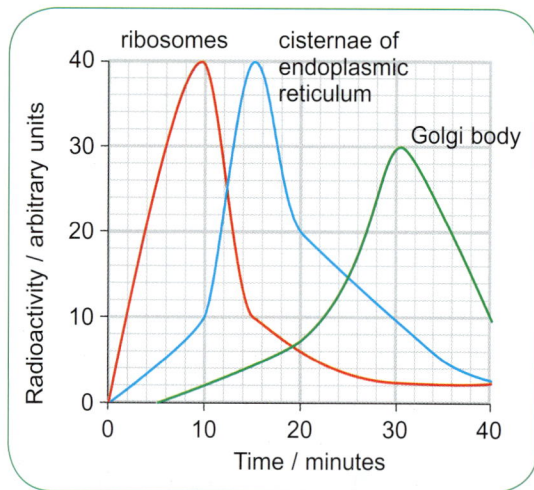

a In which order did the amino acids move through the three organelles? Use the results shown in the graph to justify your answer.

b Using your own knowledge, describe what happened to the amino acids in each organelle.

c Suggest why the peak values for the radioactivity in the ribosomes and the endoplasmic reticulum are the same, whereas the peak value for the Golgi body is lower. (There may be more than one possibility.)

d Suggest how the amino acids would have been taken up into the cell at the beginning of the experiment.

e Describe how the antibody molecules would be secreted from the cell.

Many of the proteins that make up complement are precursors of enzymes. When a piece of their molecule is removed, they become active. Once one of them has been activated in this way, it acts as a catalyst for the activation of another complement protein. This becomes a **cascade process**, in which one small action (whatever activates the first protein) ends up having a very large effect on a large number of protein molecules (Figure 11.6).

There is more than one way in which the cascade can be initiated. Firstly, when an antibody binds to an antigen, one of the complement proteins can bind to the antibody. This changes the shape of the complement protein, activating it and setting off the cascade. Alternatively, a different complement protein can bind directly with a pathogen (or any other 'non-self' surface). Once again, this changes its shape and starts off the cascade. The result of either of these events is the production of various proteins that can help to destroy invading microorganisms. There are three ways in which they do this.

- **Opsonisation** – Some of the proteins produced when the complement cascade is activated bind to the surface of bacteria, coating them with a layer of protein called **opsonin**. Phagocytic cells have receptors which bind to opsonin, and this stimulates them to engulf and destroy the coated bacterium.

- **Attracting macrophages** and other cells to the site of infection – Some of the newly produced complement proteins drift away from the place where they were formed, into the tissue fluid and blood. Their presence attracts phagocytes and other white blood cells, which move towards the site. (Cell movement in the direction of a chemical stimulus is an example of chemotaxis.) This is important in the inflammatory response.

- **Destroying foreign cells** – A third kind of complement protein directly destroys the cells that stimulated its production, by making holes in their plasma membranes.

The inflammatory response

If a pathogen gets into a particular area of your body and begins to multiply, it is no use having your phagocytes and lymphocytes spread all over the body – you need them to be concentrated in the danger area. The process that brings this about is called the **inflammatory response**, and it results in inflammation (Figure 11.7).

Complement is a group of short-lived soluble proteins always present in blood plasma. Complement is activated by contact with antibody bound to antigen, or with a foreign surface. Activation of complement triggers a cascade which results in the production of active proteins.

The active proteins help destroy foreign cells.

activation

a complement protein

inactive enzyme → active enzyme

inactive enzyme → active enzyme

inactive complement protein → active complement protein

Opsonins coat a foreign cell which encourages phagocytosis.

Phagocytes are attracted to the area by active complement protein.

Foreign cells are destroyed by active complement protein.

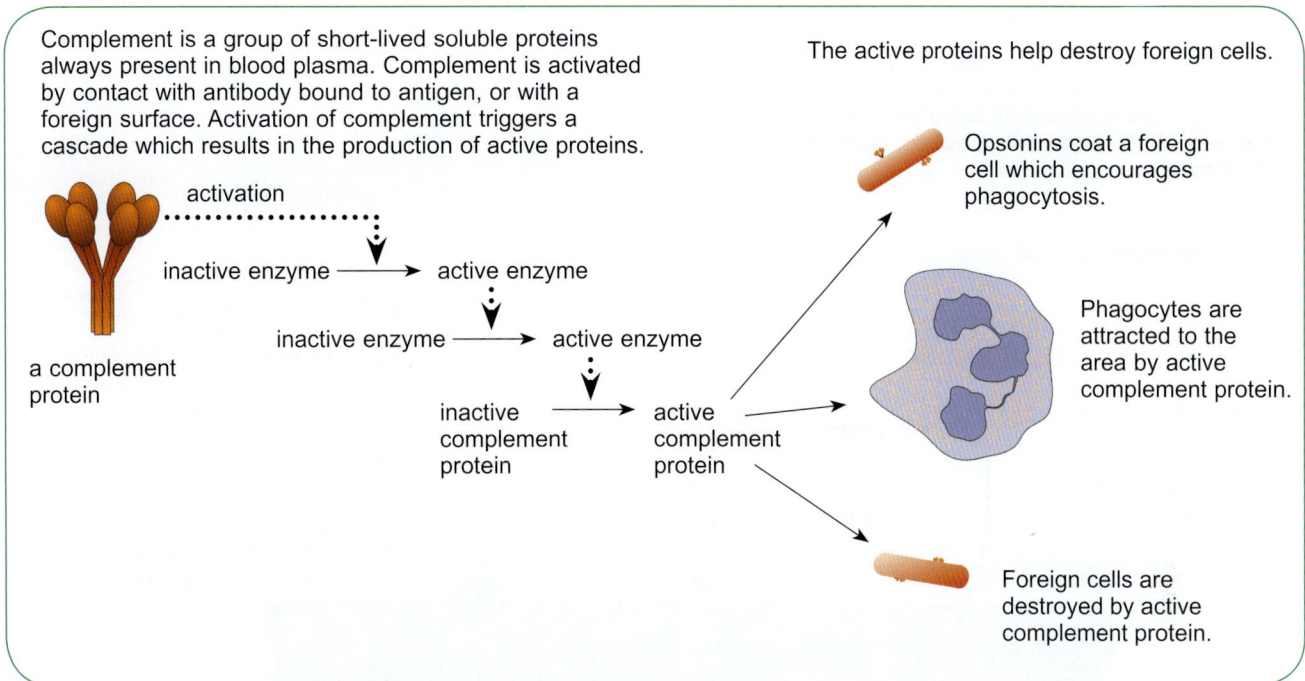

Figure 11.6 Complement.

Imagine, for example, that a thorn has penetrated deep under your skin. Bacteria on the thorn begin to multiply. The presence of antigens on the bacteria, and your own damaged tissues, activate the complement system. Chemicals are released that increase the blood supply to the area and make the capillaries more permeable. This brings more phagocytes and lymphocytes to the infected tissues. Phagocytes are attracted to the area by the chemicals, and they crawl out of the blood into the infected tissues.

The extra blood supply makes the area look red, and the leakage of fluid from the blood makes it swollen. If all goes well, your body will win the battle against the pathogens, and the swelling and redness will subside as the infection is brought under control. Sometimes, a thick white mixture of dead bacteria, lymphocytes and phagocytes builds up, known as pus.

Mast cells

Mast cells are cells that are found in all tissues, generally lying close to the walls of blood vessels and nerves. Their cytoplasm is packed full of granules (Figure 11.8), which contain numerous chemicals, especially **histamine** and **heparin**.

We know a lot about mast cells because they are very much involved in allergies and auto-immune diseases. Both of these result from the immune system behaving inappropriately, causing illness. However, it is also thought that mast cells do have a useful role to play, probably in helping the immune system to fight intestinal worms and other parasites.

Mast cells must be activated before they begin to do anything. There are three main ways in which this happens.

- They may respond directly to injury. This could be physical, or it could be caused by toxic chemicals such as alcohol.
- The membranes of mast cells have receptors that bind tightly to a type of antibody called IgE, so each mast cell is completely coated with IgE molecules. If the protein that fits into the IgE molecule binds with them, the IgE molecules become linked together, and this activates the mast cell. Unfortunately, this often happens not in response to a potentially dangerous pathogen, but to a harmless antigen such as a protein in the surface of a pollen grain, or on a cell in a peanut. These substances that should be harmless, but that act as antigens and bring about a strong and inappropriate immune response, are known as **allergens**.

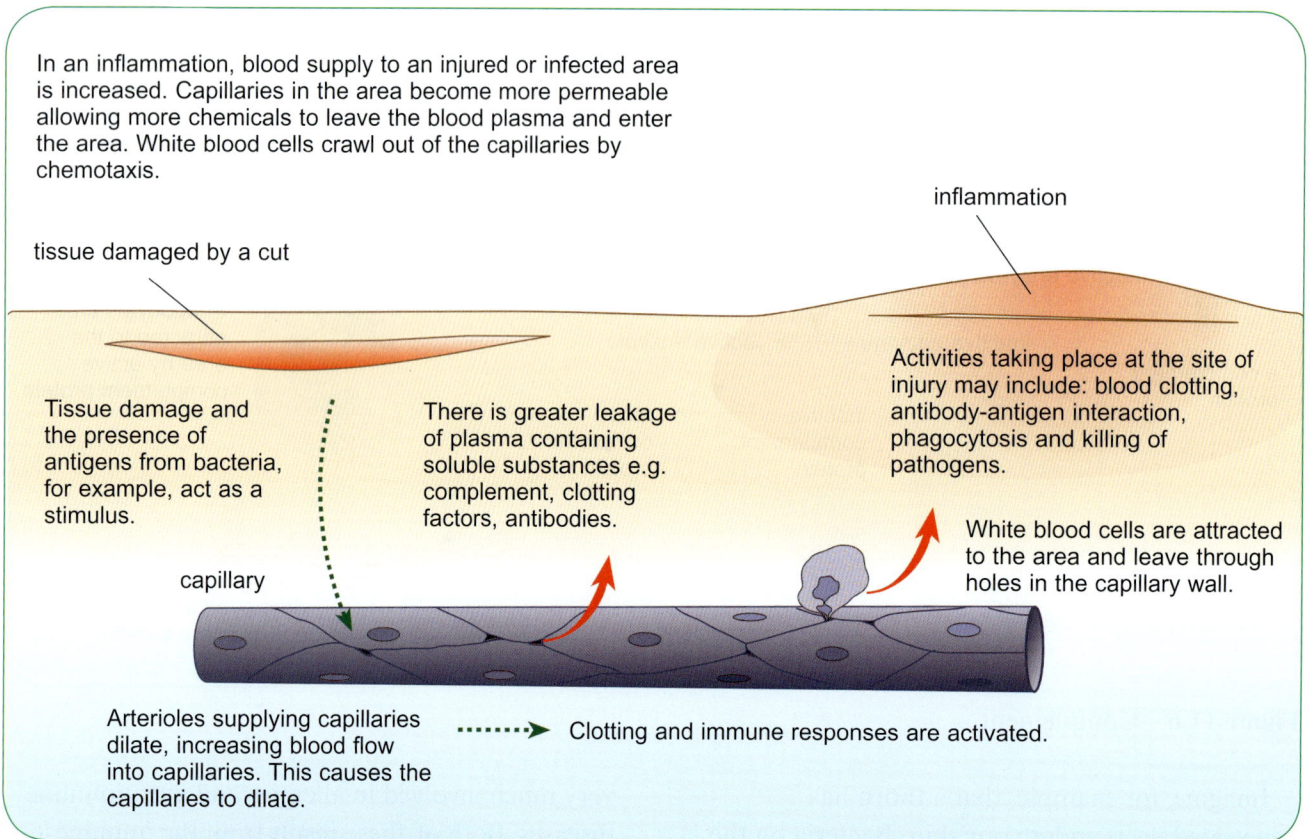

In an inflammation, blood supply to an injured or infected area is increased. Capillaries in the area become more permeable allowing more chemicals to leave the blood plasma and enter the area. White blood cells crawl out of the capillaries by chemotaxis.

tissue damaged by a cut

inflammation

Tissue damage and the presence of antigens from bacteria, for example, act as a stimulus.

There is greater leakage of plasma containing soluble substances e.g. complement, clotting factors, antibodies.

Activities taking place at the site of injury may include: blood clotting, antibody-antigen interaction, phagocytosis and killing of pathogens.

capillary

White blood cells are attracted to the area and leave through holes in the capillary wall.

Arterioles supplying capillaries dilate, increasing blood flow into capillaries. This causes the capillaries to dilate.

Clotting and immune responses are activated.

Figure 11.7 Inflammation.

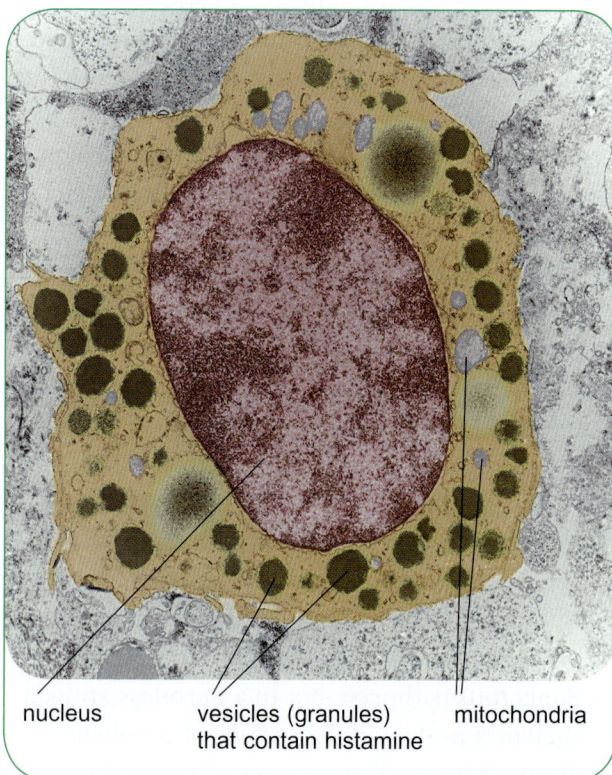

nucleus   vesicles (granules)   mitochondria
that contain histamine

Figure 11.8 A coloured electronmicrograph of a mast cell ($\times 12\,000$).

- Activated complement proteins can also activate mast cells.

An activated mast cell releases the contents of its granules. These include histamine and several cytokines. These cause an acute inflammatory reaction, in which blood vessels dilate, smooth muscle in airways contracts, rashes appear on the skin and tissues swell as fluid accumulates in them. In a severe allergic reaction, mast cells all over the body release their contents at the same time, causing a massive inflammatory response that can be life-threatening.

Several diseases are the result of a misdirected attack of the immune system on a person's own tissues, and these are known as **auto-immune diseases**. Mast cells are known to play a major part in many of these, including rheumatoid arthritis (in which the joints become inflamed) and multiple sclerosis (in which the myelin sheaths of neurones are destroyed). Despite much research, there is still no clear picture of what causes these diseases to develop. There does seem to be some genetic component, because auto-immune diseases may have a tendency to run in families. However, there is also an environmental component, because the development of an auto-immune disease often seems to follow infection by a virus.

Humoral and cell-mediated responses

Early studies of the immune system suggested that the body had two different ways of attacking pathogens. One involved cells – the phagocytes and T-lymphocytes – and was called the **cell-mediated response**. The other involved chemicals, especially antibodies produced by B-lymphocytes, and was called the **humoral response**. It is now known that, in reality, there are constant and complex interactions between cells and chemicals, as you will have appreciated from what you have read earlier in this chapter.

HIV/AIDS and the immune system

The human immunodeficiency virus infects a particular group of T-helper cells called CD4+ cells, and also some types of macrophages. In the disease AIDS, the presence of the virus causes a reduction in the numbers of CD4+ cells. This can be because the virus itself destroys the cell as it reproduces inside it and bursts out from it; or because other T-lymphocytes recognise that the CD4+ cell is infected, and attack and destroy it.

The reduction in numbers of the CD4+ cells greatly weakens the ability of the immune system to respond to infection, and it is this that causes the symptoms of AIDS.

Antibodies

Antibodies are glycoproteins. Their molecules contain chains of amino acids, and also sugar units. Figure 11.9 shows the structure of an antibody molecule.

Antibodies are also known as **immunoglobulins**. There are several different kinds of them, given names such as **IgG** and **IgA**.

Each antibody contains a **variable region** that can bind specifically with a particular antigen. We have millions of different antibodies with different variable regions. The particular part of the antigen that is recognised by the immune system, and to which the antibody attaches, is called an **epitope**.

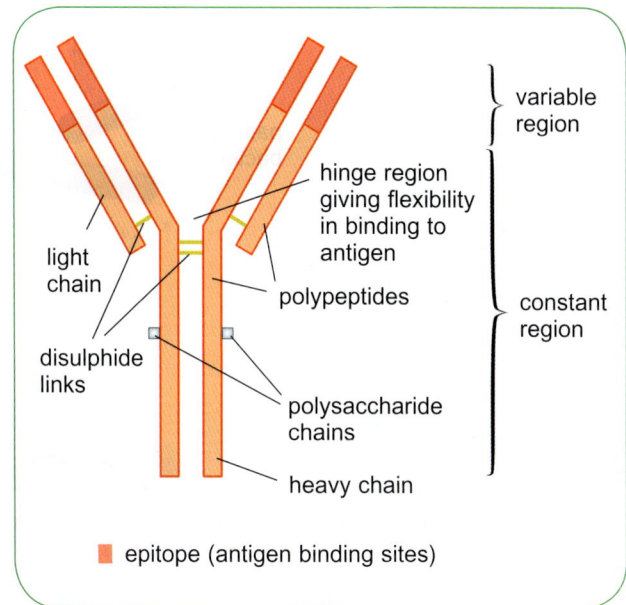

Figure 11.9 The structure of an antibody molecule.

When an antibody molecule meets its specific antigen, it binds with it. The effect that this has depends on what the antigen is, and on what type of immunoglobulin has bound to it.

Some antibodies directly neutralise the antigen – for example, by binding with a toxin produced by a bacterium. Others may encourage phagocytes to destroy the pathogen, sometimes by making the pathogens clump together. Yet others may stop pathogens getting a foothold on body surfaces, by preventing them from attaching to cells or tissues (Figure 11.10 and Figure 11.11).

How immunity develops

When a pathogen first enters the body, there will be only a few lymphocytes with receptors that fit into its antigens. It takes time for these lymphocytes to encounter and bind with these pathogens. It takes more time for them to divide to form clones, and for the B-lymphocytes to secrete enough antibodies to destroy the pathogens, or for enough T-lymphocytes to be produced to be able to destroy all the cells that are infected by them.

During this delay, the pathogens have the opportunity to divide repeatedly, forming large populations in the body tissues. The damage that they cause, and toxins that they may release, can make the person ill. It may be several days, or even

to make clones of themselves, so no memory cells have been formed. Passive immunity lasts only as long as the antibodies or antitoxins last. The body actually 'sees' them as being foreign, and they will be removed and destroyed quite quickly by cells in the liver and spleen.

Vaccination

Vaccination is an excellent way of preventing a person from acquiring an infectious disease. The larger the proportion of people who are vaccinated in a population, the lower the chance that anyone – even those who have not been vaccinated – will get that disease. This is called **herd immunity**. For most diseases, at least 80–85% of the population need to be vaccinated to achieve herd immunity.

Vaccination involves giving a person a dose of a preparation that will cause the immune system to react as though an antigen from a pathogenic organism has entered the body. Most vaccinations are given by injection, but the polio vaccine is given by mouth. Many vaccines contain an attenuated (weakened) form of the bacterium or virus that causes the disease, while others contain a modified toxin produced by them.

When the vaccine enters the body, lymphocytes that recognise the antigen respond to it as if they had encountered live bacteria or viruses. They form clones of plasma cells, which secrete antibodies, and also memory cells. In most cases, a

second 'booster' dose of the vaccine is given later on. This raises the antibody level much higher than the first dose, and helps to ensure that protection against the antigen lasts for some time (Figure 11.14).

Monoclonal antibodies

We have seen that there is a huge number of different antibodies that can be made by human B-lymphocytes, and that each lymphocyte can make only one kind. In the 1970s, researchers wanted to be able to obtain large amounts of one particular antibody at a time, so that they could study it without interference from all the other antibodies that are usually present in a mammal's blood. Their aim was to produce a large clone of a particular type of B plasma cell, all secreting identical antibodies, known as **monoclonal antibodies**.

There is one problem in achieving this – B-lymphocytes that divide to form clones of plasma cells do not secrete antibodies, and plasma cells that secrete antibodies do not divide. In 1975, a technique was developed to get around this problem (Figure 11.15). B-lymphocytes were fused with cancer cells, which – unlike other body cells – go on dividing indefinitely. The product of this fusion is called a **hybridoma** cell. The hybridoma divides repeatedly to form a clone of cells that secrete monoclonal antibodies.

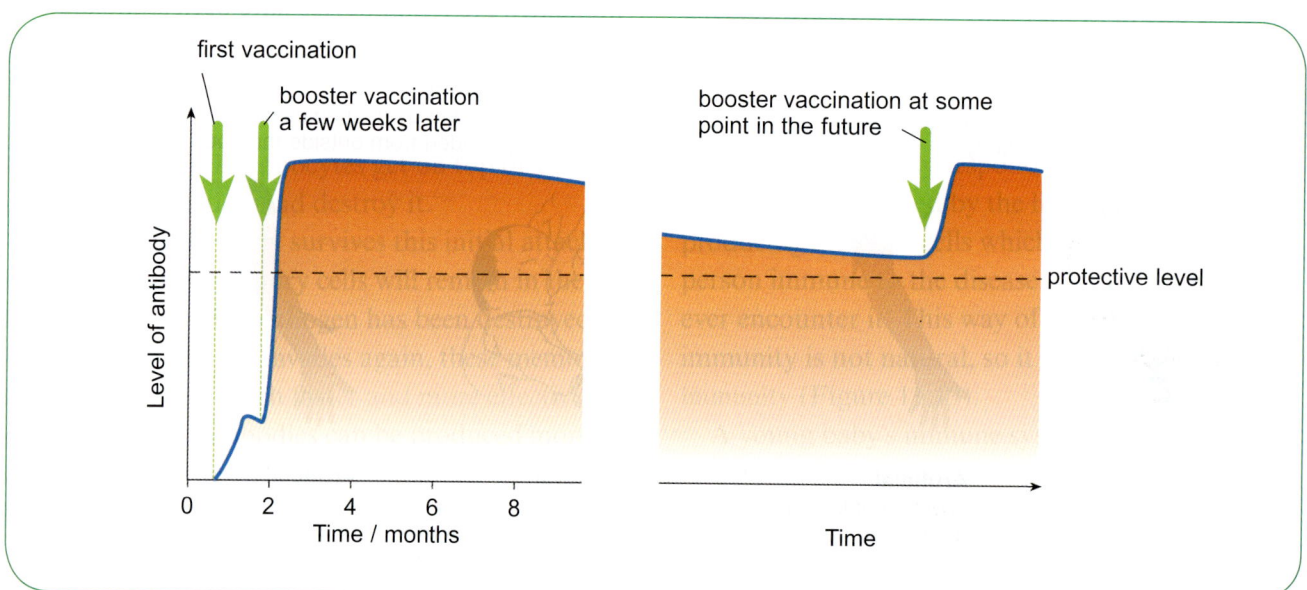

Figure 11.14   Antibody levels after vaccination.

When this technique was first invented, no-one really knew what uses might be made of it. Since then, many applications have been found for monoclonal antibodies, both in research and in various areas such as medical diagnosis and treatment. Their uses derive from the fact that any particular monoclonal antibody binds very specifically to a particular molecule.

Using monoclonal antibodies for diagnosis

Monoclonal antibodies can be used to help to diagnose a particular condition, or to find out where particular types of cells are present in the body.

Monoclonal antibodies can be used to locate places where blood clots have formed in the body of a person suspected of suffering from deep-vein thrombosis (a blood clot in a vein, often in the leg). First, a mouse is injected with human fibrin, a protein found in blood clots. The fibrin acts as an antigen in the mouse. Mouse B-lymphocytes with the antibody for human fibrin proliferate, especially in the spleen. After a month or so, the spleen contains large quantities of these lymphocytes.

The mouse spleen cells are then mixed with cancer cells to form hybridomas, which are checked to see which antibody they secrete. Hybridomas secreting the anti-fibrin antibody are selected and cultured in a fermenter, so that large amounts of the antibody are made. The antibody can be 'labelled' by attaching it to a radioactive chemical that produces gamma radiation.

The labelled antibodies are then introduced into the patient's blood. As they are carried around the body in the blood stream, they bind to fibrin molecules. A gamma camera can be used to detect the position of the antibodies, an therefore of any blood clots, in the patient's body.

A very different diagnostic application is in testing for pregnancy. Any couple who are trying for a baby will want to know as soon as possible if the woman has become pregnant. There are now many different pregnancy testing kits on the market which can be used at home. Most of them use monoclonal antibodies to test for the presence of a hormone called human chorionic gonadotrophin (HCG) in her urine. This hormone is only secreted during pregnancy.

Monoclonal antibodies are made, using mouse lymphocytes, that will bind specifically with HCG. In one type of pregnancy-testing kit, these HCG-specific antibodies are bound to atoms of gold. The antibody–gold complexes are then used to coat the end of a dipstick (Figure 11.16). Another type of monoclonal antibody is also made, which will specifically bind with HCG–antibody–gold complexes. These antibodies are impregnated into a region further up the dipstick, called the Patient Test Result region.

To use the dipstick, it is dipped into a urine sample. Any HCG in the urine will bind to the antibodies at the end of the stick, which will be carried upwards as the urine seeps up the stick.

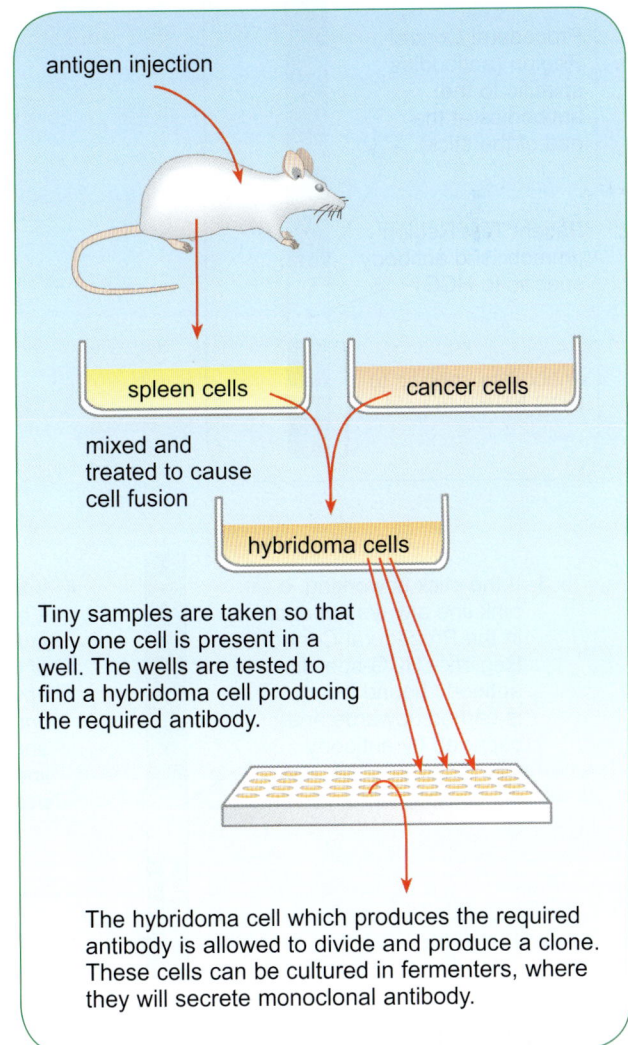

Figure 11.15 Monoclonal antibody production.

As the HCG–antibody–gold complexes reach the test result region of the stick, they bind with the antibodies there and are held firmly in position. As more and more gold atoms arrive there, a pink colour (or another colour, dependent on the brand) builds up.

The stick also contains an area called the Procedural Control Region, which contains yet another type of immobilised monoclonal antibody. These are from goats, and they are anti-mouse antibodies. They bind with the antibody–gold complexes even if these have not encountered any HCG in the urine sample. This strip therefore goes pink even if the test result is negative.

Other uses are for producing reagents used to determine a person's blood group, the identification and location of some types of cancer and following the progression of an HIV infection.

Using monoclonal antibodies for treatment

The anticancer drug **MabThera**® is a monoclonal antibody. MabThera® is a trade name for the drug **rituximab**.

Rituximab is a monoclonal antibody that binds to a protein called CD20. This protein is found

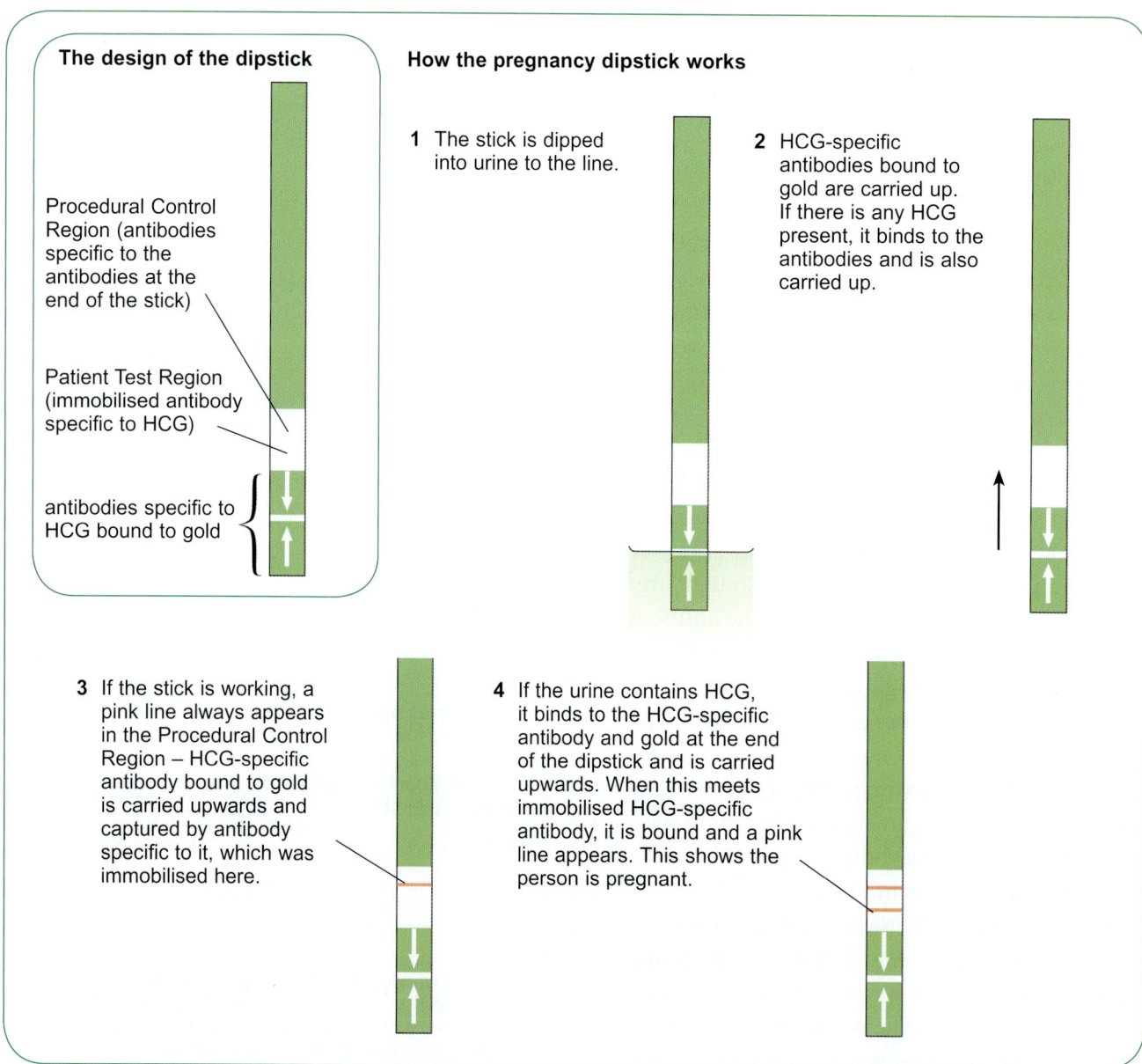

The design of the dipstick

Procedural Control Region (antibodies specific to the antibodies at the end of the stick)

Patient Test Region (immobilised antibody specific to HCG)

antibodies specific to HCG bound to gold

How the pregnancy dipstick works

1 The stick is dipped into urine to the line.

2 HCG-specific antibodies bound to gold are carried up. If there is any HCG present, it binds to the antibodies and is also carried up.

3 If the stick is working, a pink line always appears in the Procedural Control Region – HCG-specific antibody bound to gold is carried upwards and captured by antibody specific to it, which was immobilised here.

4 If the urine contains HCG, it binds to the HCG-specific antibody and gold at the end of the dipstick and is carried upwards. When this meets immobilised HCG-specific antibody, it is bound and a pink line appears. This shows the person is pregnant.

Figure 11.16 How one type of pregnancy-testing kit works.

SAQ

3 Suggest the purpose of the Procedural Control Region on the pregnancy test dip stick.

only on the surface of B-lymphocytes. When rituximab binds to these lymphocytes, it destroys them, although the exact mechanism by which it does this is not yet understood.

Rituximab is used to treat a cancer called non-Hodgkin lymphoma, in which it is the B-lymphocytes that are the cancerous cells, dividing out of control and producing very large numbers in the body. They form tumours in the lymph nodes. The drug kills both the abnormal (cancerous) B-lymphocytes and also any normal ones, because all of them have CD20 on their surfaces. However, the body continues to produce new B-lymphocytes which are usually normal, rather than cancerous, ones.

Rituximab is also used to treat some auto-immune diseases in which overactive B-lymphocytes are implicated, such as rheumatoid arthritis.

Summary

- The body's immune system responds to the presence of non-self cells or molecules by attacking the foreign material. This is done by various white blood cells (leucocytes), including phagocytes and lymphocytes. This response is called the immune response. A molecule that initiates an immune response is called an antigen.

- Phagocytes are mobile cells that are found in almost all parts of the body. They engulf and digest foreign cells or other materials. They include neutrophils and macrophages. Phagocytes often act as antigen-presenting cells, placing antigens from the foreign cells they have engulfed in their plasma membranes, where other cells of the immune system may come into contact with them.

- Lymphocytes are cells that exist in many different varieties. Unlike phagocytes, each individual lymphocyte is able to respond only to one particular antigen.

- When a B-lymphocyte meets its specific antigen, it responds by dividing to form a clone of genetically identical plasma cells. These all secrete antibodies that bind to the antigen.

- When a T-lymphocyte meets its specific antigen on the surface of an antigen-presenting cell, it responds by dividing to form a clone of T-helper cells or T-killer cells. T-helper cells bind to the antigen and secrete cytokines, which stimulate other cells to attack the antigen. T-killer cells also bind to the antigen, and then destroy the cell on which the antigen is present.

- Both B-lymphocytes and T-lymphocytes also form clones of memory cells, which remain in the body and are able to mount a rapid attack if the same antigen invades the body again.

- The blood plasma contains numerous small protein molecules which together form complement. When antigens are present in the body, the complement system is activated. The shape of one of the proteins is altered, causing it to become active as an enzyme and remove part of the molecule of another of the complement proteins. This activates the second protein, and so on down the chain, eventually producing large quantities of proteins that help to destroy invading pathogens.

continued...

- Mast cells contain granules of substances such as heparin and histamine. When activated, they release their granules and this causes inflammation to occur. The inflammatory response involves the dilation of blood vessels, bringing more lymphocytes and phagocytes to the area. Although mast cells may have a useful role to play, they are involved in inappropriate immune responses to harmless substances, called allergens. They are also involved in some auto-immune diseases.

- HIV invades a particular type of T-lymphocyte called $CD4^+$ cells. This eventually destroys these cells, weakening the immune system and allowing other pathogens to proliferate in the body.

- Antibodies are glycoproteins. They are also known as immunoglobulins. Most of them are Y-shaped molecules, with binding sites for specific antigens at the tips of the Y.

- Active immunity develops when a person's body has responded to the presence of an antigen, and has produced a clone of memory cells that can react promptly if the same antigen invades again. This can be achieved through natural exposure to the antigen (natural active immunity) or through vaccination (artificial active immunity).

- Passive immunity develops when antibodies from elsewhere are introduced into the body. Babies acquire antibodies from their mother through the placenta and in breast milk (natural passive immunity). Antibodies may also be injected into the body (artificial passive immunity). Passive immunity does not last as long as active immunity, because there are no memory cells involved.

- Monoclonal antibodies are identical antibodies produced from a clone of hybridoma cells. These are produced by fusing a lymphocyte with a cancer cell. Monoclonal antibodies can be used in diagnosis (e.g. in pregnancy tests) or in the treatment of diseases (e.g. MabThera® for the treatment of non-Hodgkin lymphoma and rheumatoid arthritis).

Questions

Multiple choice questions

1   The following are the steps involved in the process of phagocytosis of a bacterium by a macrophage.
    I   recognition and attachment of bacterium to the phagocyte
    II   attraction of the bacterium and movement of the phagocyte by chemotaxis
    III intracellular killing and digestion of bacterium
    IV   egestion of epitopes and antigen presentation
    V   fusion of lysosome with a vesicle produced by endocytosis (phagosome)
    VI   engulfment of the bacterium by phagocyte

    Which of the following shows the **correct** sequence of the process of phagocytosis?
    A I → II → III → IV → V → VI
    B II → III → I → IV → V → VI
    C IV → II → I → III → VI → V
    D II → I → VI → V → III → IV

continued …

2 An immune response is **best** defined as:

   A a defensive reaction by the immune system.

   B a bodily defence reaction which recognises an invading substance and produces a range of cellular and chemical agents directed at the substance.

   C a reaction which recognises an invading substance.

   D the body's reaction to infection.

3 The diagram shows the origin and maturation of B and T-lymphocytes.

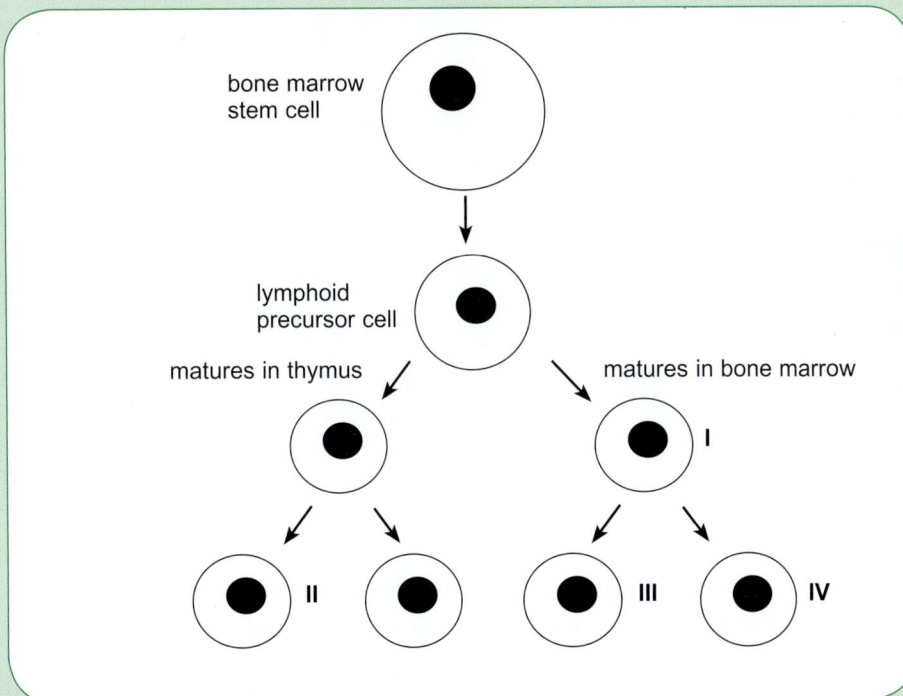

Which of the following correctly identifies cells **I, II, III** and **IV**?

	I	II	III	IV
A	T-cells	B-cells	plasma cells	memory cells
B	plasma cells	memory cells	B-cells	T-cells
C	B-cells	T-cells	plasma cells	memory cells
D	memory cells	plasma cells	B-cells	T-cells

4 Which of the following parts of statements are correct about cell-mediated and humoral immunity?

	Cell-mediated	Humoral
A	involves T-killer cells	involves B-cells
B	involves B-cells	involves T-killer cells
C	produces antibodies	produces antibodies
D	does not involve cell-to-cell interaction	involves cell-to-cell interaction

continued ...

5   Why is passive immunity effective for only a short time?
    A Memory cells are produced.
    B Antibodies are broken down rapidly.
    C Antigens enter the body.
    D Plasma cells are stimulated.

6   Students in a class were exposed to the chicken pox virus by an infected student. What type of immunity would the students obtain if they also became infected?
    A artificial active immunity
    B artificial passive immunity
    C natural active immunity
    D natural passive immunity

7   Which of the following is **not** true about antibodies? They:
    A neutralise toxins.
    B bind to specific antigens.
    C activate the complement system.
    D are effective only when attached to the T-cells.

8   Immune responses may be specific or non-specific. Which response is a specific immune response?
    A capillaries becoming 'leaky'
    B phagocytosis
    C release of histamines
    D production of memory cells

9   Any of the highly specific antibodies produced in large quantity by the clones of a single hybrid cell formed in the laboratory by the fusion of a B cell with a tumour cell are known as:
    A IgG antibodies.
    B monoclonal antibodies.
    C IgM antibodies.
    D IgA antibodies.

10 Monoclonal antibodies are used in all of the following **except**:
    A blood typing for transfusions.
    B the identification of the location of some types of cancer.
    C the stimulation of the immune system.
    D following the progression of HIV infection.

continued …

Structured questions

11 a i What do you understand by the term 'non-specific immunity'? [1 mark]

ii Give **two** examples of non-specific immunity. [2 marks]

b The diagram below shows the events occurring during a non-specific response.

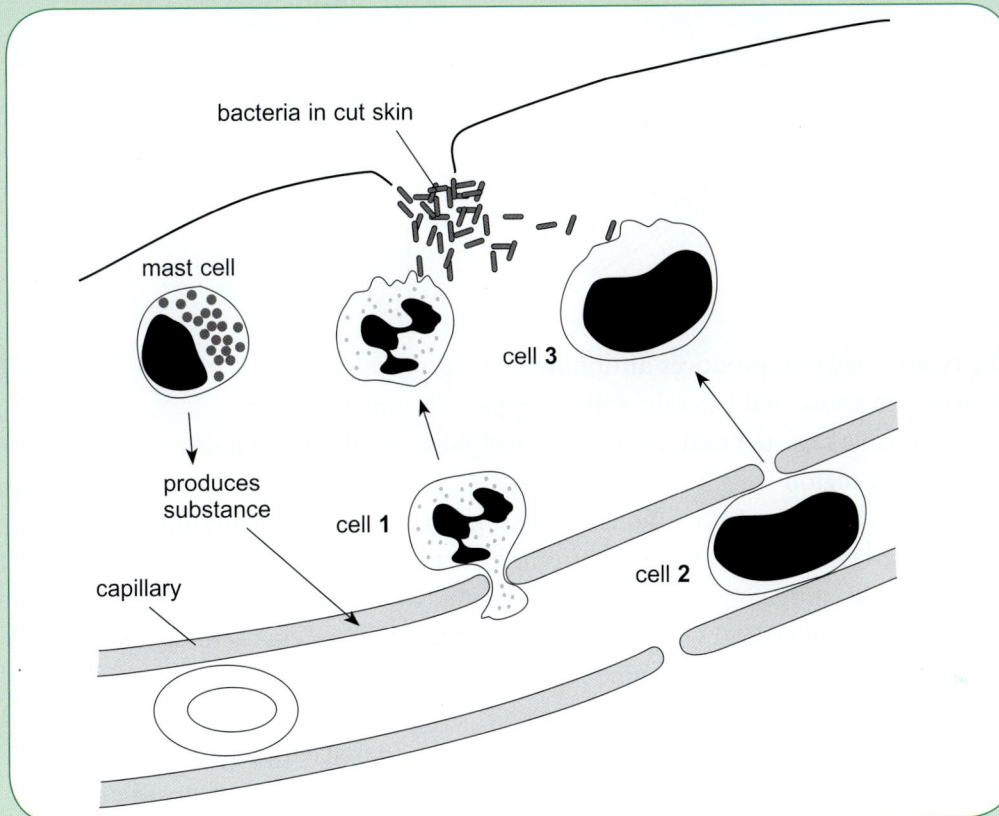

i Name the substance produced by the mast cell. [1 mark]

ii What are the functions of the substance identified in **b i**? [2 marks]

iii Identify cells **1**, **2** and **3**. [2 marks]

iv Explain the role of the complement system in non-specific immunity. [3 marks]

v If the infection lasts for a while the specific immune system is stimulated. What do you understand by the term 'specific immunity'? [1 mark]

vi Explain the role of cell **3** in stimulating the specific immune system. [3 marks]

continued ...

12 The diagram below shows the structure of an antibody.

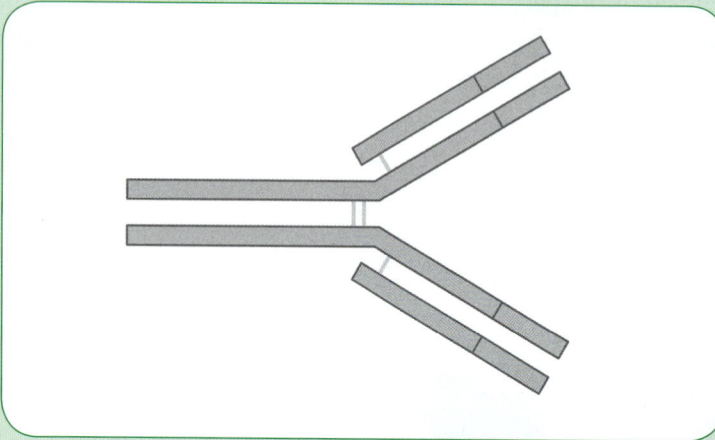

  a Name the type of cell that produces antibodies. [1 mark]

  b Copy the diagram above and label the following parts of an antibody: binding site, variable region, constant region, disulphide bonds, light chain, heavy chain, hinge region [3 marks]

  c State **one** function for each of the following parts: hinge region and disulphide bonds. [2 marks]

  d Explain why a variable region is necessary in the structure of the molecule. [1 mark]

  e Vaccines contain the antigens of pathogens. There are two types of polio vaccine. The Salk vaccine contains dead viral particles while the Sabin vaccine is made of a live attenuated polio virus. The Sabin vaccine replaced the Salk vaccine.

    i What do you understand by the term 'antigen'? [1 mark]

    ii State **one** advantage of using living attenuated viruses to make a vaccine. [2 marks]

  f The graph below shows the concentration of antibody in the blood of a baby after the first oral vaccine and booster shot for polio.

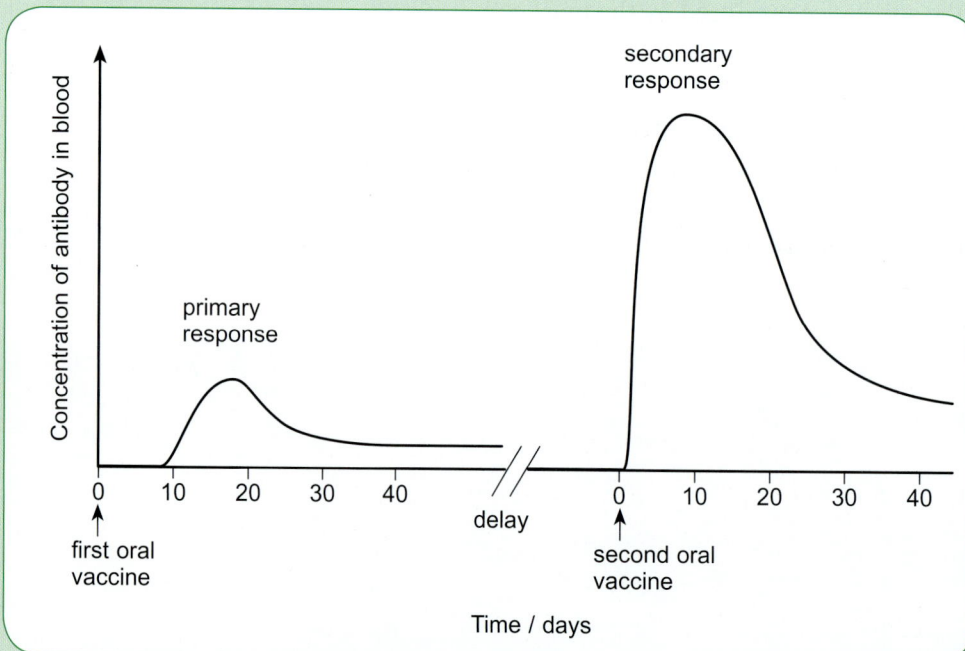

continued …

    i Why is there a delay between the time of the first oral vaccine and the first appearance of antibodies in the blood? [2 marks]

    ii State **two** ways in which the immune system's primary response differs from the secondary response. [2 marks]

    iii Explain the differences shown between the primary and secondary responses. [2 marks]

13 a Distinguish between:
    i natural and artificial immunity
    ii active and passive immunity. [4 marks]

  b Copy and complete the table below to indicate the type of immunity attained in each case.

Example	Type of immunity
baby feeding on breast milk	
child exposed to a friend with chicken pox	
receiving the MMR vaccine as a child	
receiving the H1N1 vaccine as an adult	
getting an emergency tetanus injection after stepping on a rusty nail	

[5 marks]

  c Describe how an effective vaccine can provide long-term immunity. [4 marks]

  d Explain how passive immunity provides protection to a person who has been bitten by a snake. [2 marks]

Essay questions

14 a Describe the mode of action of phagocytes. [3 marks]
  b Define the term 'immune response'. [2 marks]
  c i Describe the origin and maturation of T-lymphocytes. [2 marks]
    ii Describe the changes that occur to T-lymphocytes during an immune response. [3 marks]
  d i Describe how B-lymphocytes are involved in the immune response. [3 marks]
    ii Describe the importance of B memory cells in immunity. [2 marks]

15 a i Define the term 'antibody'. [1 mark]
    ii Make an annotated schematic drawing of an antibody molecule. [4 marks]
    iii Describe how an antibody acts on bacteria. [2 marks]
  b i What are monoclonal antibodies? [2 marks]
    ii Monoclonal antibodies are used for diagnosis and treatment. Identify **two** examples of each use. [2 marks]
    iii Describe the use of monoclonal antibodies in pregnancy kits. [4 marks]

16 a Distinguish between humoral and cell-mediated immunity. [3 marks]
  b Draw a flow diagram to illustrate the stages of the immune response to an invading pathogen. [7 marks]
  c Explain what is meant by clonal selection and clonal expansion. [5 marks]

Chapter 12
Social and preventative medicine

By the end of this chapter you should be able to:

a discuss the causative relationships among diet, obesity and diabetes;

b describe the effects of fats on the cardiovascular system, including reference to plaque formation, atherosclerosis, coronary heart disease, hypertension and stroke;

c investigate the immediate effects of exercise on the body;

d discuss the consequences of exercise on the body and the benefits of maintaining a physically fit body, with reference to the prevention of chronic diseases, VO_2 max and cardiac efficiency;

e describe the mechanisms of infection for AIDS and dengue fever and their causative agents, including the process of infection and the replication of the disease-causing organisms;

f explain how AIDS and dengue fever are transmitted;

g assess the impacts of AIDS and dengue fever regionally, including reference to social and economic issues;

h discuss the roles of social, economic and biological factors in the prevention and control of AIDS and dengue fever.

Diet and health

What a person eats, and how much they eat, can have a very large effect on their health. Eating a balanced diet is a good way to increase the chance of having a long and healthy life. A balanced diet can be defined as a diet containing all of the different nutrients required by the body, and that supplies the appropriate amount of energy. Table 12.1 lists the main nutrients that should be present in the diet, and describes how these nutrients are used in the body.

SAQ

1 a Which of the nutrients listed in Table 12.1 are organic chemicals?

b Which of the nutrients listed in Table 12.1 can be used by the body in respiration, to release energy and make ATP?

Obesity

We have already seen how eating too much and exercising too little can cause a person to become seriously overweight, and that this greatly increases the risk of developing Type 2 diabetes (page 187).

A person who is very overweight is said to be **obese**. Obesity is sometimes defined as having a body mass index (BMI) greater than 27. The formula for calculating BMI is:

$$\frac{\text{weight in kilograms}}{(\text{height in metres})^2}$$

Obesity results from consistently eating nutrients that contain more energy than the body uses. The 'spare' energy is stored in the form of fat, which builds up as **adipose tissue** underneath the skin and around the body organs. Obesity seriously increases the risk of developing not only Type 2 diabetes, but also heart disease and arthritis (Figure 12.1 and Figure 12.2).

Nutrient	Function	Good food sources	Notes
carbohydrates	providing energy, which is released by respiration inside body cells	bread, rice, potatoes, pulses (beans, lentils and peas), breakfast cereals	carbohydrates include sugars and starches; starches are better than sugars because they take longer to digest and the energy in them is released more steadily
proteins	formation of new cells and tissues, and of many important substances, including haemoglobin, collagen and enzymes; can be respired to provide energy	meat, eggs, fish, dairy products, pulses	proteins contain 20 different amino acids, of which 8 are essential in the diet as the body cannot make them from other amino acids
lipids	making cell membranes, and steroid hormones; providing energy when broken down in respiration–fats provide twice as much energy per gram as carbohydrates or proteins	dairy products, red meat, oily fish, plant oils	lipids contain several different fatty acids, of which two are essential in the diet; foods containing lipids are also important sources of fat-soluble vitamins
vitamin A (fat soluble)	making the pigment rhodopsin, found in the rod cells in the eye and essential for vision	meat, egg yolks, carrots	daily doses at around 100 times the recommended daily intake are toxic
vitamin C (water soluble)	making collagen	citrus fruits, blackcurrants, potatoes	
vitamin D (fat soluble)	formation of bones and teeth	dairy foods, oily fish, egg yolks	this vitamin is also made in the skin when exposed to sunlight
iron	formation of haemoglobin	meat, beans, chocolate, shellfish, eggs	shortage of iron in the diet is a common cause of anaemia
calcium	bone formation and blood clotting	dairy products, fish	lack of calcium in the diet can increase the risk of osteoporosis

Table 12.1 Nutrients and their roles in the body.

The incidence of obesity has been steadily increasing. Most people have easy access to as much food as they want, and much of this food is very 'energy-dense'–it contains a lot of kilojoules per gram. This is often true of fast food, such as burgers and fries. On the other side of the coin, many people do not use up a great deal of energy each day; we have become much more sedentary, spending more time sitting and relaxing rather than walking or playing sport. The combination of eating more and exercising less is building up what

Figure 12.1 A normal mouse and an obese mouse.

Figure 12.2 Obesity is most damaging when fat accumulates around the abdomen. It greatly increases the risk of developing Type 2 diabetes.

many nutritionists are calling the 'obesity time bomb'. The increasing number of people who are obese now will result in an increasing number of people with obesity-related diseases in the future.

Diet, obesity and diabetes

In Chapter 10, we saw that there are many different risk factors for Type 2 diabetes. The prevalence of diabetes in the Caribbean is increasing, and–as people's genes are not changing–it appears that this is due to changes in lifestyle.

Obesity is a major risk factor for diabetes (page 187). Some research suggests that, at least in the West, around 90% of cases of Type 2 diabetes are caused by being overweight. Worryingly, more and more children are becoming obese, and this is believed to be greatly increasing the numbers of people who are likely to develop diabetes as they get older. Figure 12.3 shows the change in the percentages of young people who are obese in the USA, and a similar situation exists in the Caribbean.

What causes obesity?

There's no doubt that some people have a much greater tendency to put on weight than others. While quite a bit of this can be put down to environment and lifestyle–including the diet eaten, amount of exercise taken and straightforward willpower–scientists have long believed that there is also a strong genetic influence on our likelihood of becoming obese. For example, studies of identical twins show that they have a very high resemblance in their tendency to become obese, even if they are brought up in completely different environments.

It seems likely that genetic influences on obesity are polygenic–that is, there are many different genes that each have a small effect. There are just a few examples of a single gene that can have a large effect, but they are very rare. For example, a two-year-old boy who weighed almost 30 kg was found to have a mutation in a gene that normally codes for a protein called leptin, which has been linked to the control of appetite.

The discovery of leptin was first made in mice, in 1994. Various strains of mice are kept and bred in laboratories, and one of these strains is extremely obese (Figure 12.1). The obese mice were found to have a single gene mutation that prevented them from making leptin. Leptin is made in fat storage cells, in adipose tissue. The more fat there is, the more leptin is made. Leptin travels in the blood to all parts of the body, where it has several different target organs. Among these is the brain–leptin provides an 'I am full' signal to the brain, suppressing appetite. As fat stores dwindle, less leptin is produced and the mouse feels hungrier. The obese mice have no leptin, so their brains never get a 'full' signal, and they always feel hungry.

There were high hopes that this discovery might help to explain obesity in humans.

continued ...

We also produce leptin, and it was thought that perhaps giving people leptin might suppress their appetites and help them to lose weight. But results of trials have not been encouraging. Leptin may play a role in our desire to eat, but it isn't a magic bullet that can reduce obesity. Indeed, many obese people already have high levels of leptin in their blood, and it seems that the problem is more in the way the brain responds to it than the actual production of leptin by the fat cells.

Various other studies have found potential candidate genes that might affect the tendency to put on weight. One of the best studies was reported in 2007. A group of researchers in Europe had been looking for a genetic link to the tendency to develop Type 2 diabetes. They had screened 2000 people with Type 2 diabetes, and found a strong correlation with the presence of a particular allele called FTO. The link was so strong that the team decided to expand their study, and to look not only at diabetes but also

obesity. They used a huge sample of 38 759 people, from Britain, Italy and Finland. They found that people who were heterozygous for this allele were, on average, 1.2 kg heavier than people who did not have it. People who were homozygous for the allele were, on average, 3 kg heavier. Around 50% of people were heterozygous and 16% homozygous.

It looks as though this research has identified one of the many genes that are probably involved in determining the likelihood of becoming obese. There must be many more yet to be discovered. But we cannot put all the blame on genes. There is no suggestion that our genes have changed in the last 50 years, but there is no doubt that the proportion of obese people has increased greatly. This can only be down to lifestyle. Some of us may find it more difficult than others to keep our weight down, but we can still take care over diet and exercise and try to maintain weight at a healthy level.

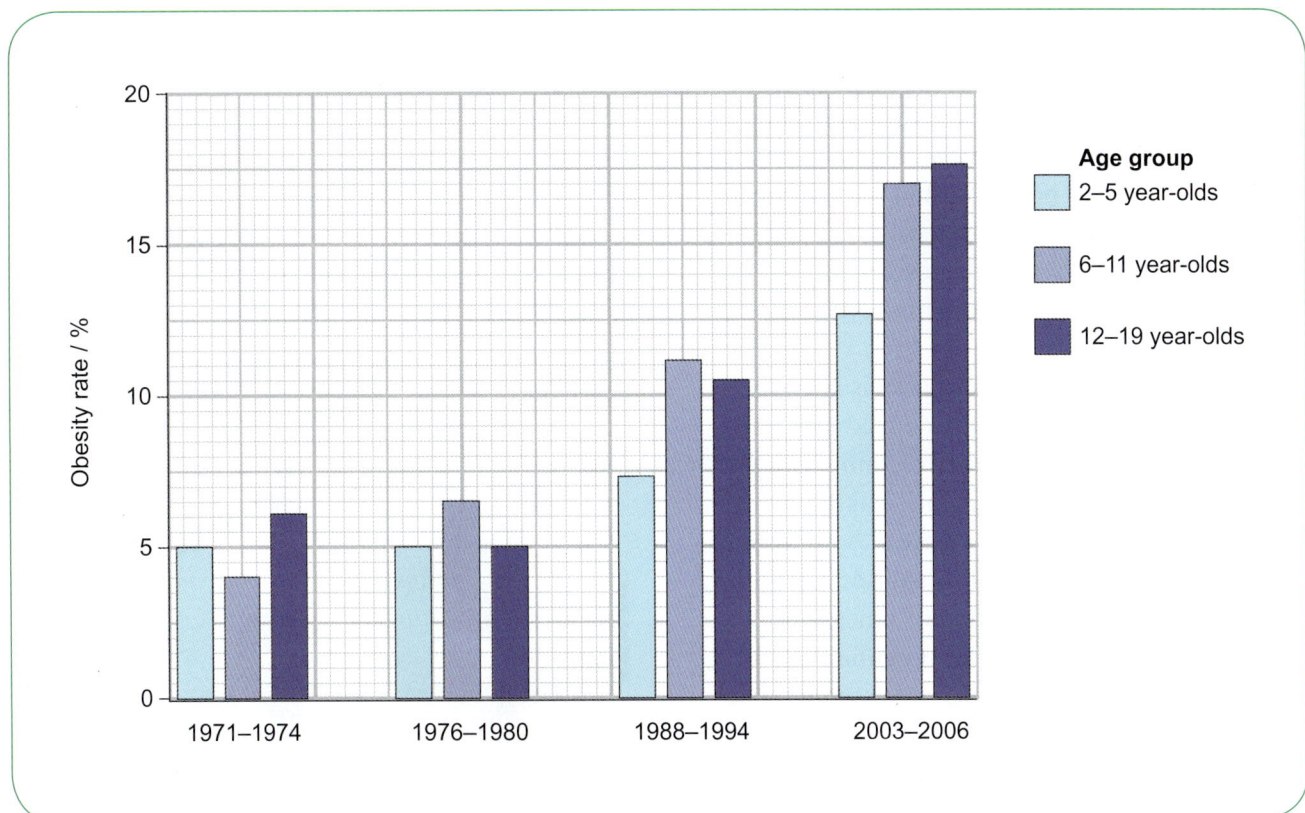

Figure 12.3   Change in percentages of young people who are obese (data from the USA).

Symptoms of diabetes

Studies in the Caribbean indicate that at least 50% of people with diabetes do not know that they have it. Every second person who is diagnosed with diabetes already has developed some complications, as a result of having the disease for some time but not being treated for it. There is no doubt that diagnosing the disease early allows the person to manage their diabetes successfully, and helps them to maintain a much higher level of health.

Many people have Type 2 diabetes for years without knowing it. First symptoms can go unrecognised. The person may feel tired or thirsty all the time, but as the development of these symptoms is slow they may just creep up stealthily and be unnoticed.

An understanding of what is going wrong can explain these symptoms. Imagine that a diabetic person eats a meal containing a lot of sugar. As this is absorbed, blood glucose levels go well above normal, but the liver and muscle cells are not alerted and do not take corrective action.

The very high blood glucose levels mean that the kidneys (Chapter 8) are not able to stop glucose being excreted in the urine. Instead of being stored in the liver as glycogen, much of the glucose is lost from the body. Later, when the glucose in the blood has been used in respiration, and if the person does not eat again, blood glucose levels may drop well below normal. The liver cells have not stored any as glycogen, so they cannot release glucose to bring up the level in the blood. The person feels very tired and may even become unconscious.

Having a high blood glucose level is known as **hyperglycaemia**. It is usually defined as a level above about 250 mg per 100 cm^3 (15 mmol dm^{-3}). In the short term, hyperglycaemia makes the person feel unwell. They may have a dry mouth and blurred vision. They may also feel very thirsty, because the high concentration of glucose in the body fluids reduces their water potential; this is detected by the hypothalamus, which sends nerve impulses to parts of the brain that control feelings of thirst. The person may be confused. Sometimes hyperglycaemia is associated with **ketoacidosis**, caused by the presence of substances called

ketone bodies in the blood. The ketone bodies are produced from fatty acids in the liver, and can be used as respiratory substrates. However, in diabetes they may be produced faster than they are used and high concentrations of them can be dangerous. Up to 10% of diabetic people admitted to hospital with ketoacidosis die.

Having a low blood glucose level is known as **hypoglycaemia**. The person feels exceptionally tired and may become confused and show irrational behaviour. Hypoglycaemia is not restricted to people with diabetes. Many normal people can become mildly hypoglycaemic if they have not eaten for a while, and be quite unaware that their mood and behaviour have changed as a result. However, a person with diabetes is more likely to suffer severe attacks of hypoglycaemia. If caught early, hypoglycaemia is easily treated by eating something sugary.

Treating diabetes

As yet, there is no cure for diabetes. The management of diabetes mellitus revolves around keeping blood glucose concentrations reasonably constant. The patient may need to check their blood glucose regularly, which is generally done with a simple sensor providing a digital readout (Figure 12.4).

Urine can also be checked for glucose, using a dipstick, for example (Figure 12.5). If the illness is under control, then there should be no more than very small amounts of glucose present in urine.

In Type 2 diabetes, a well-controlled diet may

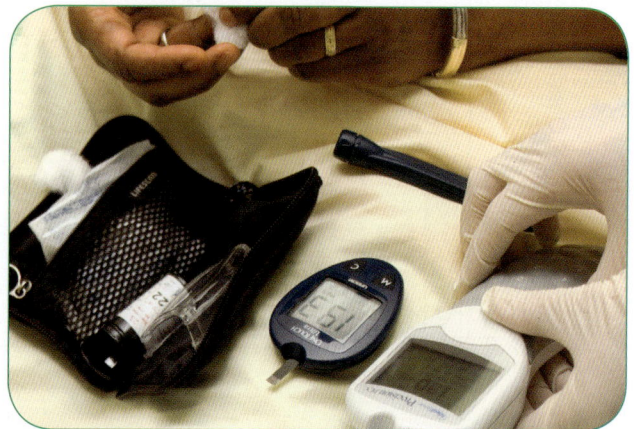

Figure 12.4   Measuring blood glucose concentration.

Figure 12.5 Measuring glucose concentration in urine.

be able to keep symptoms at bay. If the patient is obese, then weight loss through diet and exercise will be the first target. It is often possible to manage Type 2 diabetes, at least in the early stages, through diet alone. The person needs to eat small meals at reasonably regular intervals, never flooding their blood with excess glucose and never allowing blood glucose levels to drop too low. Polysaccharides are a better carbohydrate source than sugars, because it takes time for them to be digested and then absorbed, spreading out the time over which sugars are absorbed into the blood and avoiding a sharp 'spike' in blood glucose concentration.

SAQ

2 Suggest why testing the concentration of glucose in blood is more useful than testing the concentration of glucose in urine.

SAQ

3 The graph shows the changes in blood glucose concentration in a person who ate 50 g of carbohydrate as wholemeal bread, and others who ate 50 g of carbohydrate as lentils and as soya beans.

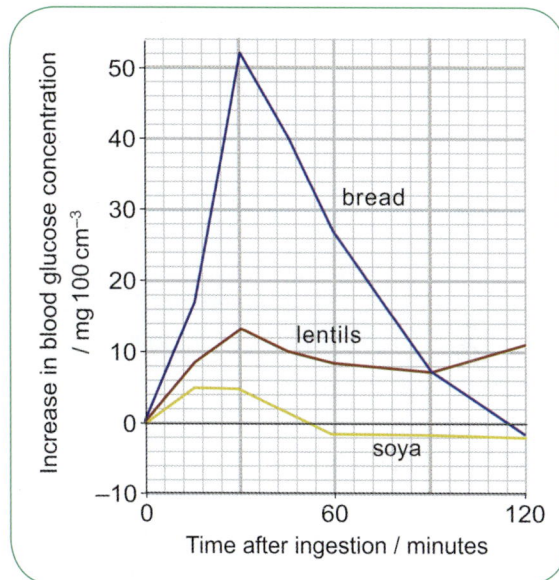

a Explain the shape of the curve when bread was eaten.
b Describe the differences between this curve and the ones showing the results after lentils and soya beans were eaten.
c Suggest reasons for these differences.

Diet and heart disease

If you live to be 80 years old, your heart will beat at least 2.5 billion times. Your lungs will inflate and deflate at least 600 million times. Inevitably the body systems become less efficient as we get older, but there is a great deal that we can do to help to keep both the cardiovascular system and the gaseous exchange system working strongly, even as we age.

Coronary heart disease, often abbreviated to **CHD**, is a common disorder of the blood vessels that supply the heart muscle with oxygenated blood. It is the leading cause of death in the Caribbean (Figure 12.6).

The ability of the cardiac muscle to contract depends on it receiving a continuous supply of

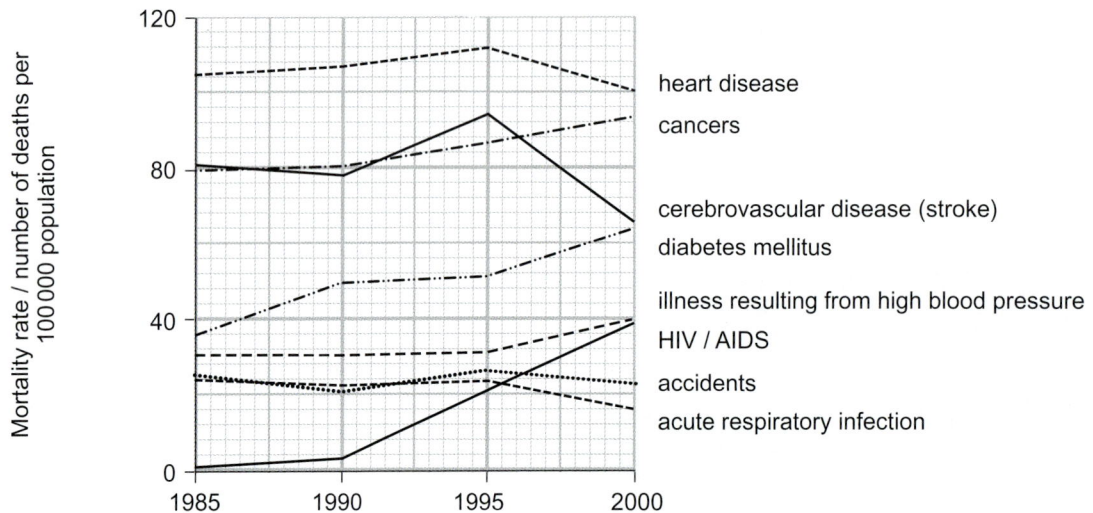

Figure 12.6 The eight leading causes of death in the Caribbean between 1985 and 2000.

oxygen. The muscle uses the oxygen for aerobic respiration, which provides the energy that it uses for contraction. If the oxygen supply fails, then the muscle cannot contract. Heart muscle lacking oxygen quickly dies.

CHD is caused by **atherosclerosis** in the coronary arteries (page 110). Atherosclerosis is sometimes known as 'hardening of the arteries'.

Atherosclerosis can lead to the coronary arteries becoming blocked. Usually, the blockage is due to the build-up of material inside the artery walls, which makes the space through which blood can flow–the lumen–much narrower. Atherosclerosis

can also occur in other arteries, including those supplying the brain.

Atherosclerosis develops slowly, and people do not normally show any symptoms until they are at least 40 years old. It occurs naturally as part of the ageing process. However, in some people it progresses more rapidly and this can be due to a variety of factors that tend to damage the lining of arteries. These include high blood pressure, the presence of harmful chemicals such as those in tobacco smoke, or low-density lipoproteins (LDLs, described on pages 252–253). The damage, and the attempts by the body to repair itself, build up tissue and chemicals in the artery wall. These deposits are known as an **atheromatous plaque** (Figure 12.7).

Once the plaque has reduced the lumen of a coronary artery by 50% or more, the flow of blood through the artery cannot keep up with the oxygen requirements of the heart muscle during exercise. The person experiences pain when exercising, known as **angina**. The pain is often in the left shoulder, chest and arm, but for some people also in the neck or the left side of the face.

Blood clots can form on and around the plaque. Such a blood clot is called a **coronary thrombosis**. This happens because platelets in the blood come

SAQ

4 These questions are about the data in Figure 12.6.
  a What was the major cause of death in the Caribbean countries in each of the years shown in the graph?
  b Describe the changes in mortality due to diabetes between 1985 and 2000, and suggest reasons for these changes.
  c Describe the changes in mortality due to HIV/AIDS between 1985 and 2000, and suggest reasons for these changes.

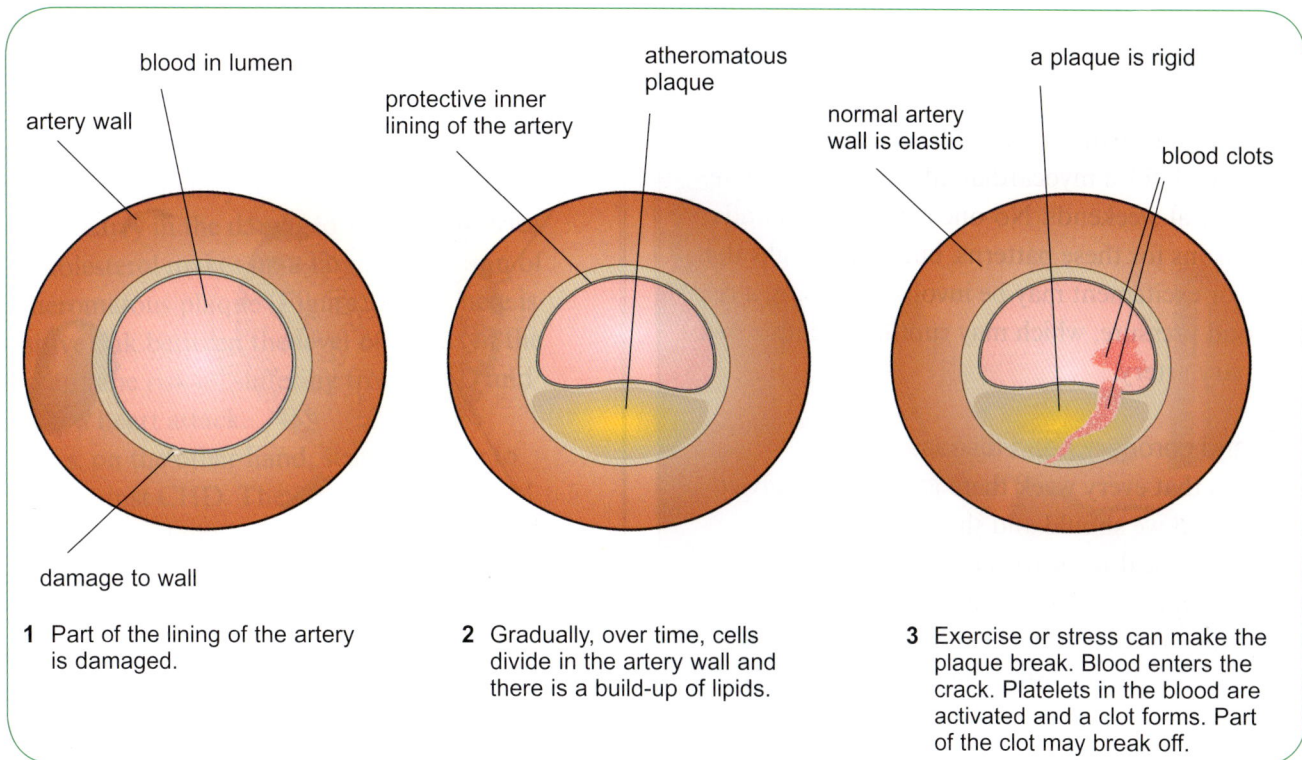

blood in lumen

artery wall

protective inner
lining of the artery

atheromatous
plaque

normal artery
wall is elastic

a plaque is rigid

blood clots

damage to wall

1   Part of the lining of the artery
    is damaged.

2   Gradually, over time, cells
    divide in the artery wall and
    there is a build-up of lipids.

3   Exercise or stress can make the
    plaque break. Blood enters the
    crack. Platelets in the blood are
    activated and a clot forms. Part
    of the clot may break off.

Figure 12.7   The development of an atheromatous plaque.

into contact with collagen in the artery wall. The platelets then secrete chemicals that stimulate the blood to form a clot.

The blood clot narrows the artery even more. It may break off and get stuck in a smaller vessel. The part of the heart that is supplied by this blood vessel stops beating, and some of the muscle cells may die. This is known as a **myocardial infarction** and is an extremely dangerous condition.

Myocardial infarction

'Myo' means 'muscle', and the myocardium is the muscular wall of the heart. 'Infarction' is a term describing the loss of sufficient blood flow to a tissue to allow it carry out its normal activity. Around 90% of instances of myocardial infarction are caused by a coronary thrombosis.

If the infarction involves a large amount of muscle, the person may die almost immediately. Severe myocardial infarction may cause the heart to stop beating. This is called cardiac arrest (heart attack) (Figure 12.8). No pulse can be felt, and the victim rapidly loses consciousness.

Others may not lose consciousness, but experience such severe pain that they call for help

straight away. If less muscle is affected, the pain may be less severe, and the patient may wait several hours before calling a doctor. Sometimes, they may not even realise that they have had a minor infarction, and do nothing. The pain is usually felt near the centre of the thorax, behind the sternum, and is described as 'crushing' or 'bursting'.

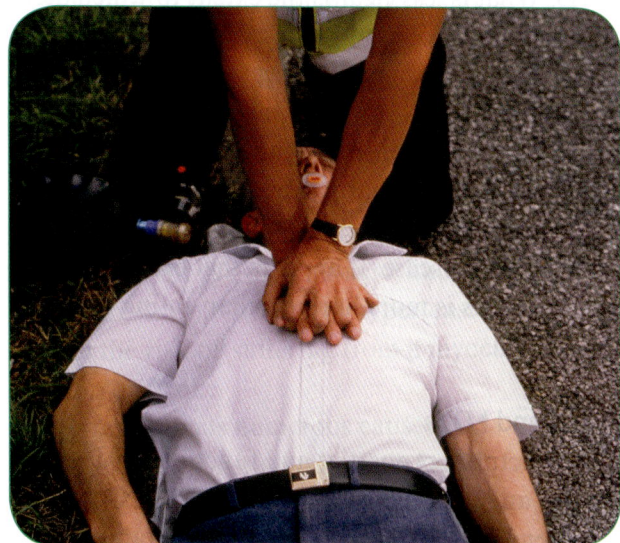

Figure 12.8   A paramedic applying chest compressions to get the heart to beat again after cardiac arrest.

SAQ

5 A study followed 639 people with a family history of CHD over a period of 14 years. Some had an LDL:HDL of more than 8, while some had an LDL:HDL of less than or equal to 8. The graph shows the probability of survival of a person in each of these groups over the 14 years of the study.

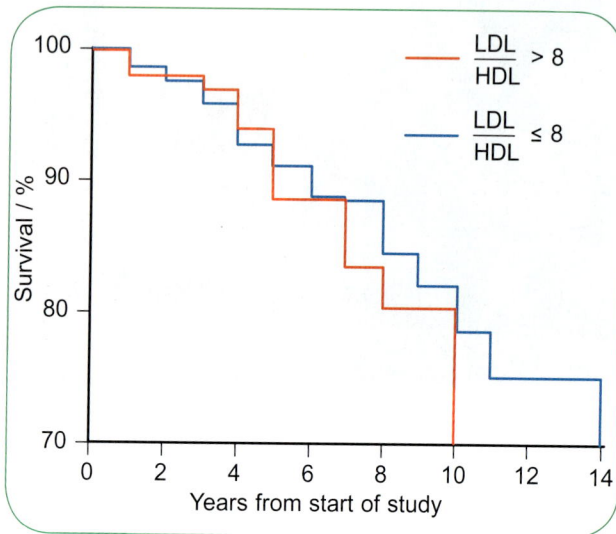

a Explain why the survival probability is 100% at 0 years.

b Suggest why the graph is drawn so that it goes down in steps rather than in a smooth line.

c Describe the conclusions that can be drawn from these data.

6 Statins are drugs that inhibit an enzyme in liver cells which catalyses one of the reactions involved in the synthesis of cholesterol. In July 2002, the results of a five-year study, involving more than 20 000 people, were published. Half of the people had been given 40 mg of statin each day over this period. The other half were given a placebo–a pill that looked like a statin pill but did not contain any drug. Neither the people in the trial, nor the researchers who collected and analysed the results, knew which people were taking the statin and which were taking the placebo. The table shows the results.

Events during study period	Given statin	Given placebo
total number of people who died	1328	1507
number who died from CHD	587	707
number who died from other circulatory diseases	194	230
number who suffered a first, non-fatal heart attack	898	1212

a Suggest why those people who did not take statins were given a placebo.

b Suggest why the trial was organised so that the researchers interacting with the people, and collecting the results, did not know who was given statins and who was taking the placebo.

c Discuss what the results suggest about the effectiveness of statins in reducing the risk of developing coronary heart disease.

d Suggest how statins bring about the effects you have described in **c**.

Stroke

A **stroke** is an acute instance of damage to the brain, caused by problems with the blood vessels supplying it. About 80% of strokes are caused by a blood clot that forms in a vessel as the result of atherosclerosis. The remaining 20% are caused by bleeding into brain tissue (Figure 12.11).

The risk factors for stroke are, as might be expected, the same as those for coronary heart disease. A person with hypertension has a considerably increased risk of stroke. The risk doubles with each 1 kPa (7 mm Hg) rise in diastolic blood pressure.

Brain cells have a metabolic rate, and must have good supplies of oxygen and glucose for respiration. They begin to die if deprived of these for more than a few minutes.

The effects of the stroke will depend on the parts of the brain in which neurones die. For example, a stroke in the right side of the cerebrum is likely to affect movement on the left side of the body. As this side of the brain is concerned with spatial

Proving the link

For many years, doctors have urged people with high blood pressure to eat less salt, to decrease their risk of developing coronary heart disease or having a stroke.

But there was no hard evidence to support this recommendation. Despite doctors' and scientists' suspicions, no-one had actually shown that reducing the salt in your diet is good for your health. Because the evidence was so shaky (and some people suggested that the little evidence there was even showed that a low-salt diet was bad for you) many people did not follow their doctor's advice.

It was not until April 2007 that a careful piece of research actually showed that this link genuinely exists–yes, eating less salt really is good for your health.

The research followed 2400 people with high blood pressure–all volunteers–over a period of 15 years. Half were shown how to look for low-salt foods when they were shopping, and eat a low-salt diet, while half ate a 'normal' diet, with as much salt as they wanted.

The results showed that those eating a low-salt diet had a 20% lower risk of death from all causes. In all, 200 people had developed cardiovascular disease. Of these, 112 came from the group that had not been recommended to eat a low-salt diet. Only 88 were in the low-salt group.

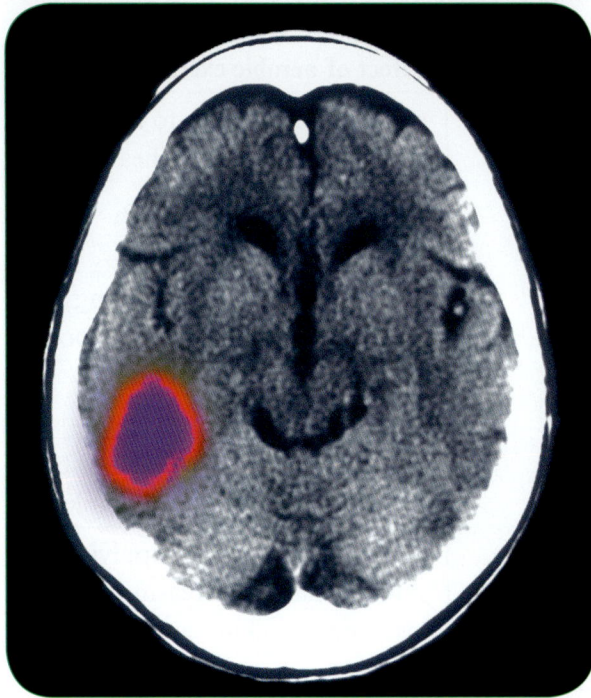

Figure 12.11 CT scan of a section through the head of a woman who has suffered a stroke on the left side of the brain.

awareness, the person may have problems with judging distance and so find difficulty with walking or picking up objects. A stroke in the left side of the cerebrum will affect language. Memory is often harmed no matter which side of the brain the stroke affects.

Exercise and health

Numerous studies show that taking regular exercise has very great beneficial effects on health. It reduces the incidence of chronic diseases such as coronary heart disease and Type 2 diabetes. It affects processes in the brain, and in most people it makes them feel happier, more energetic and more positive about their lives.

Aerobic exercise

Muscles need oxygen and an energy source such as glucose to provide them with the ATP they need for contraction. The oxygen is used to allow aerobic respiration to take place. If oxygen is not supplied to the muscles fast enough, they can get by on anaerobic respiration for a while. But this produces lactate (lactic acid), and as this builds up the muscles stop working.

An endurance athlete is therefore limited in his or her performance by the rate at which oxygen can be supplied to the muscles. The harder the muscles are working, the faster the rate at which they use energy, and therefore the faster the rate that oxygen must be supplied to them. Marathon runners will try to run at the maximum speed that they can keep up for several hours. Their training increases the ability of the heart and lungs to get oxygen to the muscles as fast as possible over a long period of time.

Even if you have no intention of becoming a marathon runner, your fitness and general health will almost certainly benefit from regular **aerobic exercise**–that is, exercise in which the muscles get most of their energy from aerobic respiration. It can take almost any form you like to mention, so long as it is done at a rate that you can keep up for a reasonable amount of time. Walking, swimming, dancing and cycling, as well as long-distance running, are all forms of aerobic exercise (Figure 12.12).

Short-term effects of aerobic exercise

The ways in which aerobic exercise affects the circulatory and gaseous exchange systems are summarised in Table 12.3.

Effects on the circulatory system

When you are about to start exercising, your brain sends nerve impulses along a **sympathetic nerve** to the **sino-atrial node** (SAN)–the heart's pacemaker–stimulating it to contract at a faster rate. So your heart starts beating faster even before you have begun the exercise. You might also begin to secrete more of the hormone **adrenaline** into the blood, which has the same effect on the heart as the sympathetic nerve.

Once exercise begins, and the muscles are respiring at a faster rate, cardiac output is further increased. This is brought about by **nitric oxide**, a gas which acts as a hormone. When muscles are using up oxygen quickly, the concentration of oxygen in the blood vessels in the muscles falls, and the cells in the blood vessel walls respond to the lowered oxygen concentration by secreting nitric oxide. The nitric oxide makes the muscles in the walls of arterioles relax, which widens the lumen of the arterioles (vasodilation) and allows more blood to flow through and more quickly. This in turn increases the rate at which blood flows back to the heart in the veins.

The heart is designed so that it pumps out blood at the same rate that blood flows into it. (You can imagine what might happen if it did not do this.) So extra blood flowing in, stretching the muscles in the heart wall, causes the heart to contract more

Figure 12.12   Students on campus at Fouillole University Pointe a Pitre Grande Terre Guadeloupe, French West Indies. Walking and running are the two most common methods of taking effective aerobic exercise.

	Effect of aerobic exercise
Circulation	more nerve impulses to the heart pacemaker, increasing heart rate
	more adrenaline secretion, increasing heart rate
	nitric oxide secretion, dilating arterioles, which increases blood flow back to the heart and increases cardiac output
	diversion of blood to muscles by changes in dilation of arterioles
	dilation of arterioles supplying skin capillaries, increasing heat loss from the skin
Gaseous exchange	breathing rate increases
	tidal volume increases
	increases in the acidity of the blood are detected by chemoreceptors; information is then sent to the brain, which increases rate and extent of diaphragm and intercostal muscle contractions

Table 12.3   Short-term effects of exercise.

forcefully. This increases the **stroke volume**–the volume of blood forced out of the heart each time the ventricles contract. The stretching also stimulates the SAN, increasing the rate at which it fires off nerve impulses.

The blood vessels in various parts of the body also respond to the increased demand for oxygen and glucose by the muscles. We have seen that arterioles in the muscles widen (dilate). At the same time, arterioles supplying blood to other parts of the body whose needs are less urgent, such as the digestive system, contract and reduce blood flow. This allows more blood to flow to the muscles. At rest, the percentage of the blood flowing through the muscles is around 20%, but during strenuous exercise it can be over 80%.

All this muscular activity generates a lot of heat in the body. It is important that it can escape, and this is speeded up by dilation of the arterioles supplying blood to the skin surface. This increases the rate at which heat is lost by radiation.

Effects on the gaseous exchange system
Just as heart rate increases during exercise, so does ventilation rate. Breathing becomes faster and deeper, increasing the rate at which oxygen diffuses into the blood in the lungs, and carbon dioxide diffuses out.

The increased rate of respiration in the muscles causes an increased quantity of carbon dioxide to diffuse from them into the blood. **Chemoreceptors** in the medulla of the brain and in the walls of the carotid arteries (which carry blood from the aorta to the head) detect this by monitoring the pH of the blood. A high concentration of carbon dioxide lowers the pH, making the blood more acidic.

If a low pH is detected, nerve impulses will be sent from the respiratory centre in the medulla to the intercostal muscles and the diaphragm muscles, making them contract harder and more quickly. This increases the rate at which new air is brought into the lungs and stale air removed, which in turn maintains a large concentration gradient between the alveoli and the capillaries. At rest, ventilation rate may be about 10 dm^3 min^{-1}. During intense exercise, values of well over 100 dm^3 min^{-1} are achieved.

SAQ

7 For each of the changes described in Table 12.3, explain how they help the body to cope with aerobic exercise.

Investigating the immediate effects of exercise on the body
A convenient type of exercise to carry out is a step test. This has the advantage that it can be done in exactly the same way by different people, or by the same person at different times.

A platform of some kind – a gym bench or a firmly positioned chair – is required. The height of the platform is usually between 10 cm and 25 cm high.

The person being investigated first rests for several minutes, and their resting pulse rate is measured at least twice. They then step up and down onto the platform a given number of times, or until they are exhausted. Their pulse rate is then measured again every minute after the exercise has stopped, until it has returned to normal.

If a metronome is available, then the rate of stepping can be controlled. The metronome is set to a particular number of beats per minute (for example, 24 steps per minute) and the person matches their stepping to this rhythm.

Long-term effects of aerobic exercise
Taking regular aerobic exercise over a long period of time can cause major changes to take place in the muscles, circulatory system and gaseous exchange systems. The magnitude of these changes is, in general, proportional to the amount and intensity of training that is done. However, different people can respond very differently to identical training, and there seems to be a strong genetic component to this.

Changes in the muscles

Many changes take place in the muscles that are used in training. These changes are specific–they do not affect other muscles. They include:

- an increase in the cross-sectional area of slow-twitch muscle fibres (see page 259) This increases the mass of muscle that can be used during aerobic exercise, as well as increasing the overall size of the muscles.
- an increase in the number of capillaries in the muscle, and also in the ratio of capillaries to muscle fibres. This increases the volume of blood in the muscle, improving oxygen supply.
- an increase in the concentration of **myoglobin** in the muscle. Myoglobin is a respiratory pigment that stores oxygen, so this increases the amount of oxygen stored within the muscle.
- an increase in the number and size of mitochondria in the muscle fibres and therefore an increase in respiratory enzymes. Mitochondria are the sites where the Krebs cycle and oxidative phosphorylation occur, so this increases the rate at which these processes can occur within the muscle.
- an increase in the glycogen stores, which can be rapidly broken down to glucose for use as a respiratory substrate.

Changes in VO_2 max and the circulatory system

When a person increases the rate at which they are exercising, their rate of oxygen consumption increases too. However, there comes a point where they can no longer get any more oxygen to their muscles, or where their muscles just cannot use oxygen any faster, at which point the muscles have to switch over to anaerobic respiration. The maximum rate at which oxygen is used, before the muscles have to make the switch, is called **VO_2 max**.

VO_2 max increases with training. A trained athlete can have a higher work rate before their muscles switch to the less energy-efficient anaerobic respiration. The changes in the muscles described above contribute to this. Changes in the cardiovascular system also contribute to this

improvement, by increasing the rate at which oxygen can be supplied to the muscles. The changes include:

- an increased number of red blood cells. This increases the ability of the blood to carry oxygen.
- an increase in the size of the heart muscle, especially in the walls of the left ventricle. This increases the force with which the muscle can contract and force blood out of the heart.
- an increase in **stroke volume**–that is, the volume of blood that is forced out of the heart with each beat.
- an increase in **cardiac efficiency**–that is, the work output that the heart produces for each unit of oxygen that it uses.

As a result of these changes, the heart rate of the trained person decreases when they are resting, because the greater stroke volume means that the same quantity of blood can be moved around the body using a slower heart rate. However, the maximum possible stroke volume is considerably increased, so the person can exercise harder and still manage to get enough blood into their muscles to supply the oxygen that they need. The heart rate recovery period–that is, the time taken for the heart rate to return to normal after exercise–decreases with training. This is often used as a good measure of how a person's fitness is improving during a training programme.

Changes in the gaseous exchange system

Training increases the rate at which oxygen can be brought into the body and carbon dioxide removed. Everyone's breathing rate and depth increase when they exercise, but the degree to which this happens is improved by regular aerobic training. For example, while a 'normal' person might be able to increase their ventilation rate by up to ten times, a really fit endurance athlete may be able to increase theirs by as much as 20 times. Top Olympic-standard rowers may have ventilation rates of 200 dm^3 min^{-1}. Maximum oxygen intake is also achieved more quickly in a trained person.

Slow-twitch and fast-twitch muscle fibres

There are two different types of muscle fibres in the skeletal muscles in the human body. They are known as slow-twitch and fast-twitch fibres.

During aerobic exercise, it is mostly the slow-twitch fibres that are working. These fibres are adapted for continuous aerobic respiration. They contain a lot of myoglobin, which makes them look dark red, so they are sometimes known as 'red fibres'.

During intensive, short-term exercise, such as sprinting, the fast-twitch fibres are used. They are adapted for producing ATP by anaerobic respiration. They therefore do not require stores of oxygen, and do not contain much myoglobin. They are sometimes known as 'white fibres'.

See if you can explain how each of the structural differences between slow-twitch and fast-twitch fibres, shown in the diagram, adapt them for their different ways of generating ATP.

Slow-twitch fibres

produce ATP through aerobic respiration

contain large numbers of mitochondria

contain large quantities of myoglobin

have a relatively small diameter

are supplied by large numbers of capillaries

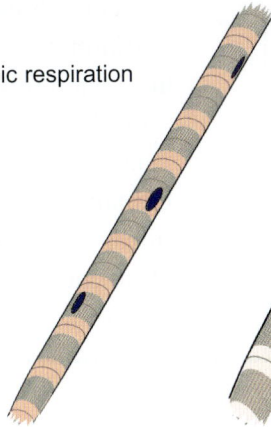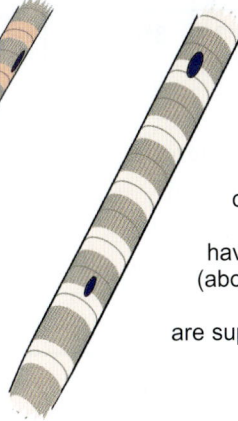

Fast-twitch fibres

produce ATP through anaerobic respiration

contain few mitochondria

contain little myoglobin

have a relatively large diameter (about twice that of a slow-twitch fibre)

are supplied by relatively few capillaries

SAQ

8 A group of untrained people undertook a training programme involving aerobic exercise over a period of 13 weeks. The graph shows the mean VO_2 max of these people during the training period.

a Explain the meaning of the term 'VO_2 max'.

b Describe the changes in VO_2 max during this training programme.

c Suggest reasons for the changes that you describe.

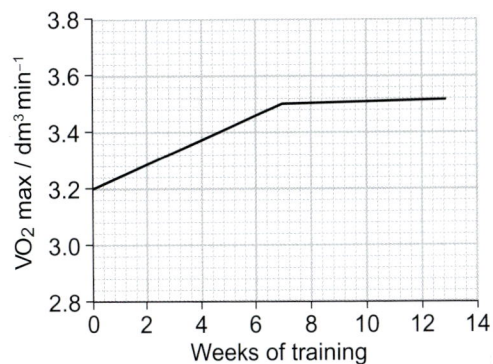

SAQ

9 During aerobic exercise, most respiration taking place in the muscles is aerobic. However, even at low rates of exercise some anaerobic respiration also happens.

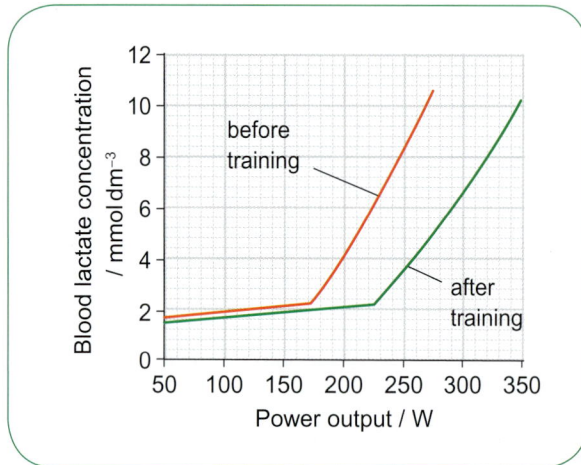

A person undertook a programme of aerobic training. The graph shows the relationship between the intensity of exercise, measured as power output in watts, and the concentration of lactate in the blood for this person before and after the training programme.

a i Describe the relationship between blood lactate concentration and intensity of exercise, up to a power output of 175 W.

ii Suggest reasons for this relationship.

b The lactate threshold is the point at which more lactate is being produced than can be cleared from the blood.

i Name the organ that is responsible for breaking down lactate.

ii Use the graph to determine the power outputs at which the person reached their lactate threshold before training, and after training.

iii Explain three changes in the body that could contribute to this increase in the lactate threshold after training.

c Explain how an increase in lactate threshold could improve the performance of an endurance athlete such as a rower or marathon runner.

Infectious diseases

There are many infectious diseases that can cause serious illness. In the Caribbean, two infectious diseases that are having a considerable impact on society are HIV/AIDS, and dengue fever.

The effects of HIV/AIDS on society

We have already looked at HIV/AIDS in some detail. In Chapter 10, we described how the human immunodeficiency virus is transmitted from one person to another, and looked at its life cycle. In Chapter 11 we saw how the virus affects the immune system and causes AIDS.

Understanding how HIV is transmitted from one person to another (page 202), and how the virus affects $CD4^+$ T-lymphocytes, helps us to find ways of preventing the spread and development of the disease. The prime method of reducing infections is to educate people to modify their sexual behaviour, particularly by reducing the number of sexual partners and by using condoms if having sexual intercourse with someone whose HIV status is not known. Testing blood for HIV before allowing it be used for transfusions, and treating HIV-positive pregnant women with anti-retroviral drugs (ARVs) can also greatly reduce the spread of this virus.

ARVs can be very effective at slowing the development of AIDS in a person infected with HIV. The best current treatment uses a cocktail of three different drugs. These are reverse transcriptase inhibitors – proteins that inhibit the enzyme used to transcribe DNA from the virus's RNA (Figure 10.2 on page 202). While these drugs greatly slow down the development of AIDS in many people who are treated with them, they do not kill the virus and so do not get rid of the infection. They are, however, very effective in reducing the risk that a mother will pass on the virus to her child. But these drugs are expensive, and they are not available to many people in developing countries who could benefit from them.

Unlike most diseases, it is people in the prime of their lives who are most likely to be affected by

HIV/AIDS, and most likely to die as a result of this infection. This means that many children are left with no parents to care for them. Older people, who depended on their grown-up children for care and support, may lose this essential support to help them to continue to live independent lives.

This puts an extra burden on the State and on charities, who have to step in to care for people who have lost essential members of their families.

The workforce of the Caribbean is also affected, as many people who would be important members of the working community can no longer continue to do their jobs normally.

HIV/AIDS is a significant drain on the resources available for healthcare. Money is spent on education, testing and diagnosis (for example, all pregnant women are routinely tested for HIV) and treatment. Where drugs are available, they will need to be taken for the rest of a patient's life.

Dengue fever

Dengue fever is a disease caused by a virus. The virus is transmitted by the mosquito *Aedes aegypti*. These mosquitoes are therefore **vectors** for dengue fever.

The dengue fever virus, often abbreviated to DENV, belongs to a family of viruses called flaviviruses. The structure of a mature virus particle is shown in Figure 12.13, and the way in which the virus reproduces inside human cells is shown in Figure 12.14. There are several different forms (serotypes) of the virus and, unfortunately,

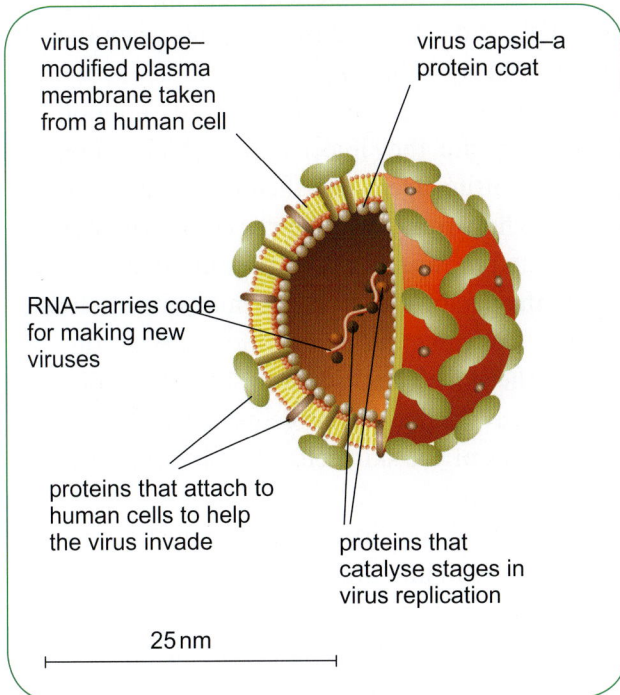

Figure 12.13 The dengue virus

virus envelope–modified plasma membrane taken from a human cell

virus capsid–a protein coat

RNA–carries code for making new viruses

proteins that attach to human cells to help the virus invade

proteins that catalyse stages in virus replication

25 nm

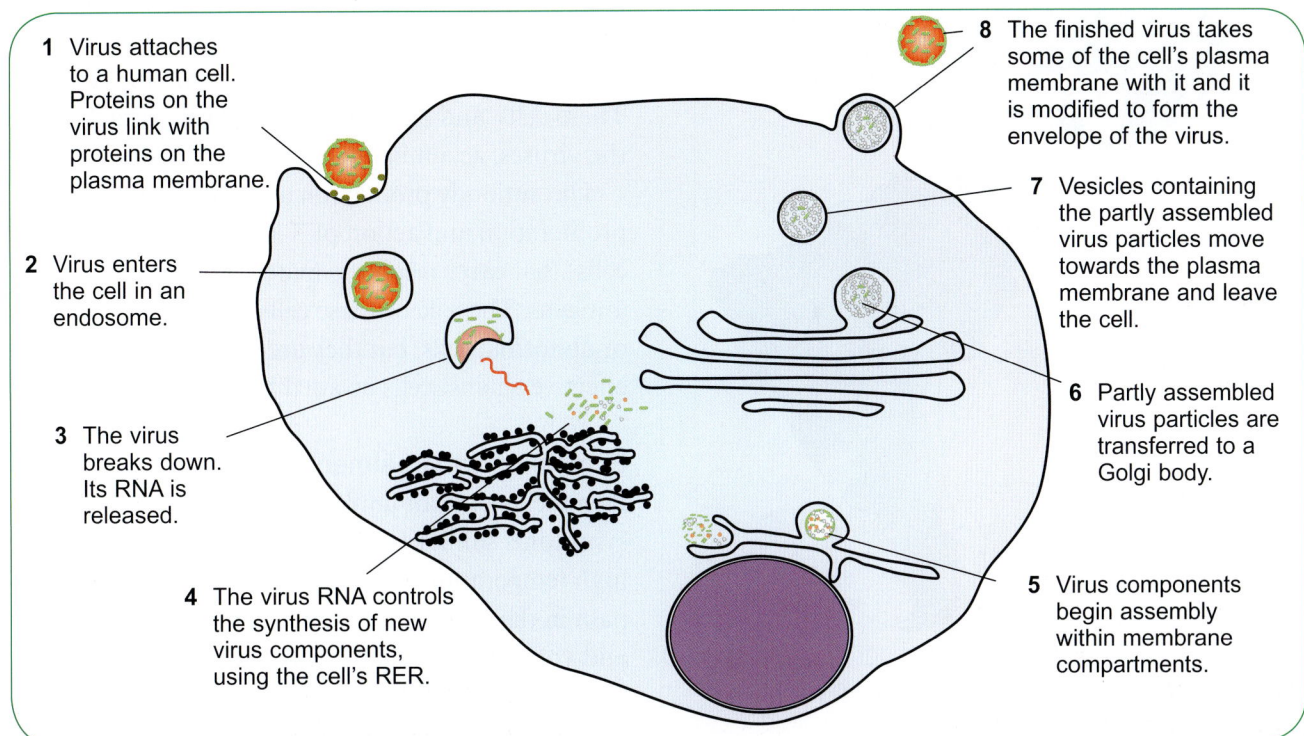

1 Virus attaches to a human cell. Proteins on the virus link with proteins on the plasma membrane.

2 Virus enters the cell in an endosome.

3 The virus breaks down. Its RNA is released.

4 The virus RNA controls the synthesis of new virus components, using the cell's RER.

5 Virus components begin assembly within membrane compartments.

6 Partly assembled virus particles are transferred to a Golgi body.

7 Vesicles containing the partly assembled virus particles move towards the plasma membrane and leave the cell.

8 The finished virus takes some of the cell's plasma membrane with it and it is modified to form the envelope of the virus.

Figure 12.14 Replication of the dengue virus.

immunity against one form does not provide immunity against the others.

Dengue fever was originally confined to tropical countries, but recently it has been spreading to countries further north and south of the equator. Figure 12.15 shows the distribution of dengue fever in the Americas in 2006. Dengue fever is a serious disease in the Caribbean, and in some years, such as 2010, the numbers of infections rise to epidemic proportions. The number of cases of dengue fever are increasing worldwide, and it is considered to be a serious public health problem. In 2010, there were 30 times more cases worldwide than in 1960. No-one is quite sure why this is, but it may be a combination of the greater number of people travelling around the globe, and global warming increasing the breeding range of the *Aedes aegypti* mosquitoes.

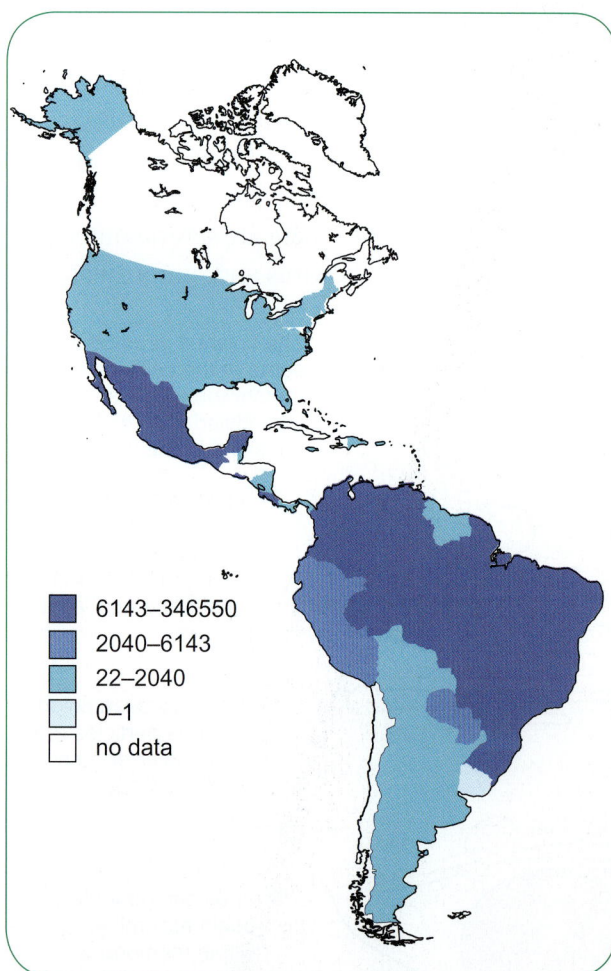

Figure 12.15 Distribution of dengue fever in the Americas (number of cases in 2006).

Infection with the dengue virus

The *A. aegypti* mosquitoes that transmit the dengue virus breed in any small pools of water that they find–for example, in old tyres, water storage containers and old oil drums. This means that they are present in both cities and in rural areas. The mosquitoes are most active during the day, especially at dawn and dusk, which is when they are most likely to bite a person.

Female *A. aegypti* mosquitoes feed on blood. When they bite, they inject saliva, which contains an anti-clotting agent and therefore enables the blood to flow freely into their mouthparts. When an infected mosquito bites a person, the virus enters the person's body in the mosquito's saliva.

The virus can enter many different types of cells in the skin. The proteins in the outer coat of the virus can bind to proteins in the plasma membranes of the skin cells, allowing the virus to enter the cells.

The entry of the virus stimulates the body's immune system into action. Cytokines are produced, which stimulate the generation of antibodies by B-lymphocytes. Some of the antibodies bind to the viral proteins, which causes phagocytes to engulf the viruses. Unfortunately, in many cases the phagocytes do not kill the virus effectively, but instead harbour viruses that actually continue to duplicate themselves inside the cells. These cells, and other white blood cells attacked by the viruses, accumulate in the lymph nodes.

The antibody production also causes the proliferation and action of T-killer cells (T-cytotoxic cells) that carry receptors matching the viral antigens. The role of these cells is to kill infected or abnormal cells, but they are not particularly effective against cells invaded by this virus.

Symptoms and treatment

Dengue fever is an unpleasant illness, with symptoms similar to influenza. The person has a high temperature, a rash, a severe headache and pain in the muscles and joints. They may feel sick and vomit, and probably will not want to eat. The illness generally lasts up to 10 days, but many people will not feel fully better for up to one month.

Although dengue fever is very unpleasant, it is not a particularly dangerous illness. However, in some cases a serious condition develops, called dengue haemorrhagic fever. This results from damage to the cells lining the blood vessels (the endothelium), and disruption of the normal blood-clotting process. Fluid leaks from the blood vessels and accumulates in the tissues. This may happen in many different organs, and can result in very serious illness that is fatal in about 5% of cases.

As for many viral diseases, there are no drugs that can be taken to kill the dengue fever virus. (Antibiotics only work against bacteria.) Treatment consists of making the person as comfortable as possible, and ensuring that they take plenty of fluids, especially if they are losing liquid through vomiting. This can often be done at home, but in serious cases the person may need to be connected to an intravenous drip in hospital. Paracetamol can be taken to reduce the pain, but aspirin and ibuprofen should be avoided, because they can worsen the bleeding that may occur. The great majority of people make a full recovery.

Prevention

As yet, no vaccine has been developed to immunise people against dengue fever. Researchers are currently working on this, trying to produce a vaccine that will protect people against all the different forms of the virus. There are already some possible vaccines undergoing trials, and there is hope that there could be a useful vaccine available by as early as 2015.

For the moment, however, the only way to prevent yourself getting dengue fever is to avoid being bitten by the *A. aegypti* mosquitoes. If you know that you are in an area where dengue fever is present, you can use insecticides such as DEET on your skin to deter the mosquitoes, and wear clothing that covers your arms and legs. Everyone can help by clearing up rubbish that may collect water and provide breeding grounds for the mosquitoes. Another approach, useful with larger bodies of water, is to introduce fish or other organisms that will feed on the mosquito larvae.

Summary

- Obesity is defined as having a body mass index greater than 27. Being obese increases the risk of developing Type 2 diabetes. People become obese through eating a diet that contains more energy than their body uses.

- Atherosclerosis is a condition that develops when the walls of the blood vessels lose their elasticity. If this happens in the coronary arteries, a person has coronary heart disease (CHD). Atherosclerosis develops as plaques form in artery walls, due to the build-up of cholesterol.

- A diet rich in saturated fats increases the risk of developing CHD. Having a low ratio of HDL:LDL cholesterol also increases this risk.

- Hypertension (high blood pressure) is often associated with atherosclerosis. Other risk factors include a diet containing a lot of salt, and smoking cigarettes. Hypertension increases the likelihood of developing CHD, and also of suffering a stroke.

- Aerobic exercise helps to maintain fitness. Regular exercise increases the maximum rate at which oxygen can be used by the body, known as VO_2 max, and cardiac efficiency. Exercise can help to maintain body weight at a healthy level, and reduce the risk of the development of chronic diseases such as Type 2 diabetes.

- AIDS and dengue fever are serious infectious diseases that are caused by viruses. The dengue fever virus is transmitted by the mosquito vector *Aedes aegypti*. The mosquitoes breed in any body of water, so an important method of control is to remove rubbish in which water may collect, or to add predators of mosquito larvae to ponds.

Questions

Multiple choice questions

1 Which of following **best** describes a 'balanced diet'?

A one which provides an adequate intake of nutrients needed for maintenance of body and good health

B one which contains carbohydrates, lipids and proteins

C one which provides an adequate intake of energy and nutrients needed for maintenance of body and good health

D one which provides an adequate intake of energy needed for maintenance of body and good health

2 One way of defining obesity is by the Body Mass Index (BMI). The formula for BMI is:

A $\dfrac{\text{body mass in kg}}{\text{height in metres}}$

B $\dfrac{\text{body mass in g}}{\text{height in metres}}$

C $\dfrac{(\text{height in metres})^2}{\text{body mass in kg}}$

D $\dfrac{\text{body mass in kg}}{(\text{height in metres})^2}$

3 Image **I** shows a healthy coronary artery while image **II** shows the artery when it became unhealthy.

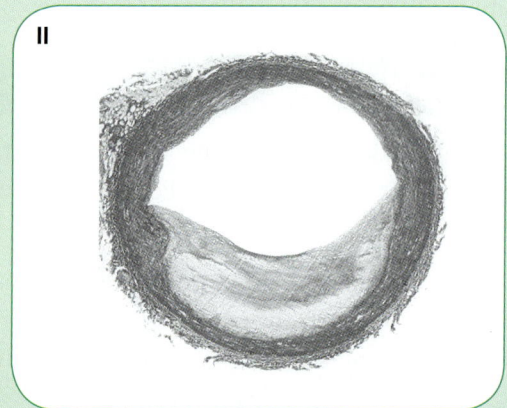

What is the name of the disease and a cause that is characterised by image **II**?

A coronary heart disease–diet high in saturated fats

B plaque formation–diet high in cholesterol

C atherosclerosis–diet high in fish oils

D coronary heart disease–diet high in unsaturated fats

4 Which of the following is **not** an immediate effect of exercise on the body?

A increased heart rate

B vasoconstriction in skeletal muscles

C rise in blood pressure

D vasodilation in skeletal muscles

continued ...

5   A girl has been running every day to improve her level of physical fitness. Which of the following is a long-term benefit to the girl in improving her physical fitness?

    A less glycogen and fat stored in skeletal muscle

    B reduction in blood cholesterol concentration

    C increase in number of alveoli in lung

    D reduction in tidal volume at rest

6. What is the causative pathogen of dengue fever?

    A protoctist

    B bacterium

    C virus

    D fungus

7   What is the vector of dengue fever?

    A the female *Aedes aegypti* mosquito

    B the male *Aedes aegypti* mosquito

    C the female *Anopheles* mosquito

    D the male *Anopheles* mosquito

8   Which of the following is **not** a method by which HIV is transmitted?

    A from mother to child across the placenta

    B receiving blood through transfusions

    C sharing needles without sterilisation

    D sharing eating utensils

9   Which of the following is an impact of HIV/AIDS in the Caribbean region?

    A It has little effect on the work force.

    B It is not a major cause of death in the region.

    C It does not drain resources for education.

    D It has improved educational awareness of sexually transmitted disease.

10 Which cells of the immune system are susceptible to HIV?

    A T-helper cells with CD8 receptors

    B T-cytotoxic cells with $CD4^+$ receptors

    C T-helper cells with $CD4^+$ receptors

    D T-cytotoxic cells with CD8 receptors

continued ...

Structured questions

11 a What are the components of a balanced diet? [3 marks]

    b Obesity is now a global problem.

      i Define the term 'obesity'. [1 mark]

      ii Explain how poor diet can lead to obesity. [3 marks]

      iii A man is 1.65 m tall and weighs 82 kg. Calculate his Body Mass Index (BMI). Show calculations. [2 marks]

      iv Comment on the BMI value obtained in **iii**. [1 mark]

    c Obesity is linked to many diseases including diabetes.

      i Distinguish between Type 1 and Type 2 diabetes. [2 marks]

      ii Explain how obesity is linked to Type 2 diabetes. [3 marks]

12 a Students performed an experiment to determine their cardiovascular efficiency by observing their pulse rates during various activities. They first took their resting pulse rate, then performed various activities. The duration of the stepping exercise was 3 minutes.

      i What do you understand by the term 'resting pulse rate'? [1 mark]

      ii Explain why resting pulse rate is taken as a measure of one's physical fitness. [2 marks]

      iii Why was the resting pulse rate taken before the exercise began? [2 marks]

      iv Suggest how the students could use a step test during this experiment. Students were provided with a stepping stool of 4 cm, a stopwatch and a digital pulse meter. [3 marks]

The results below are from one of the students from the class.

Activity	At rest	Standing	Exercise	Recovery after 1 min
Pulse rate per minute	76	101	130	89

      v Using the formula below, calculate the student's cardiovascular efficiency.

$$\text{cardiovascular efficiency} = \frac{\text{duration of exercise in seconds} \times 100}{\text{recovery pulse} \times 5.6}$$

[2 marks]

      vi Using the information below, assess the student's cardiovascular efficiency. [1 mark]
Cardiovascular efficiency is assessed as:

      0–27 = very poor   28–38 = poor   39–48 = fair

      49–59 = good   60–70 = very good   71–100 = excellent

    b State **three** short term effects of exercise on the body. [3 marks]

    c State **three** long term effects of exercise on the body [3 marks]

13 HIV is described as a retrovirus and is transmitted in a variety of ways.

    a Explain why HIV is described as a retrovirus. [1 mark]

    b Describe **three** ways in which HIV is transmitted. [3 marks]

    c The figure below shows the infection cycle of HIV in a T-helper lymphocyte.

continued …

The table below describes the various steps of the infection but they are not in order.

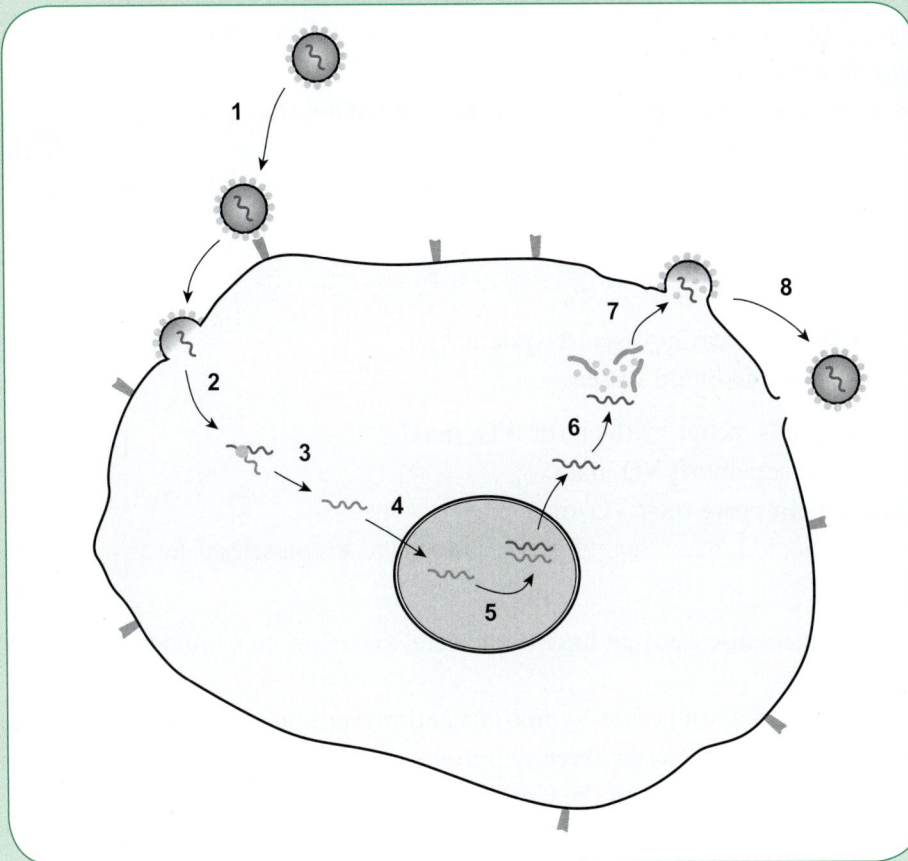

Identify stages **1– 8**.

Description	Stage
reverse transcription: making of DNA copy from viral RNA	
transcription: special enzymes create mRNA	
binding: attachment of HIV proteins to CD4⁺ surface receptor of T-helper cell	
viral assembly and maturation: new viral particles are assembled and become more infectious	
translation: new viral proteins are produced	
budding: T-helper cell lyses and releases infectious new viral cells	
RNA from virus is released into T-helper cell	
integration: HIV DNA is added into the cell's DNA using viral enzyme, integrase	

[4 marks]

continued …

d The drug therapy that is employed to treat people infected with HIV is known as HAART (highly active anti-retroviral therapy). This therapy contains a combination of drugs which target different stages of the viral infection cycle. Suggest **two** ways that these drugs may slow the onset of HIV.   [2 marks]

e AIDS is the final and most serious stage of HIV infection. What are the signs indicating that this stage has been reached?   [2 marks]

f Explain why the number of people who are infected with HIV is usually greater than the number of people with AIDS.   [3 marks]

Essay questions

14 a Discuss the effects of fats on the cardiovascular system.   [10 marks]

b Explain how plaque is formed in blood vessels.   [5 marks]

15 a Using a graph, explain what is meant by the term 'VO$_2$ max'.   [4 marks]

b What factors may influence a person's VO$_2$ max?   [4 marks]

c Suggest how a person may improve their VO$_2$ max.   [4 marks]

d A footballer has reached his VO$_2$ max. Suggest what happens to his muscles if he continues playing.   [3 marks]

16 Both HIV/AIDS and dengue are diseases that have both social and economic impact on the Caribbean region.

a Discuss the transmission, incubation period, symptoms and prevention of dengue.   [8 marks]

b HIV infections can lead to AIDS. Describe **three** symptoms of AIDS.   [3 marks]

c Discuss the impact of AIDS and dengue in the Caribbean.   [4 marks]

Chapter 13
Substance abuse

By the end of this chapter you should be able to:

a   discuss the meaning of the term 'substance abuse', with reference to legal and illegal drugs;

b   distinguish between psychological and physical dependence;

c   describe the short-term and long-term consequences of alcohol consumption on the nervous system and the liver, with reference to fatty liver, hepatitis, cirrhosis, cancer, impaired nervous transmission, demyelination, and dehydration of the brain cells;

d   discuss the social consequences of excessive alcohol use;

e   describe the effects of the components of cigarette smoke on the respiratory and cardiovascular systems, including reference to passive smoking.

Legal and illegal drugs

A **drug** can be defined as a substance that alters the body's physiology. Drugs may be used to treat specific health problems, and this is known as **therapeutic** drug use. There are also drugs that people use to change their mood, such as caffeine, alcohol, nicotine, cannabis and heroin.

Although all of these drugs can have beneficial effects in some circumstances, most of them also have the potential to cause enormous problems for their users and others if they are abused. Drug (or substance) abuse means using the drug in a way that causes harm, either to oneself or to others. Misuse of drugs seriously damages the physical and mental health of many people in the Caribbean each year, as well as harming their families and other members of the society in which they live and work.

Many of the most harmful drugs are illegal. However, the fact that a drug is legal does not mean that it is harmless. Most doctors agree that alcohol, although it is a legal drug, does more harm each year than any of the illegal drugs. It has been suggested that, if alcohol was discovered for the first time today, it would immediately be banned as being extremely dangerous to health.

In this chapter, we will look in detail at two legal drugs which, between them, contribute to very large numbers of deaths and serious illness each year. These are alcohol and nicotine.

Drug dependency

Many drugs affect what happens at synapses, either in the brain or elsewhere in the body. Postsynaptic neurones contain receptors in their plasma membranes into which the transmitter substance used at that synapse precisely fits. Drugs that act at synapses may do so by mimicking the action of the transmitter substance; that is, they have the same shape and affect the postsynaptic neurone in the same way that the transmitter would. They may prevent the breakdown of the transmitter – for example, by inhibiting the enzyme that normally does this. Or they may inhibit the action of the transmitter itself.

If the drug is taken over a period of time, then the body may adjust to its use. For example, if the drug blocks particular receptors at synapses, then new receptors may be produced to make up for the ones that are no longer in use. This means that more drug has to be taken to have the same effect. This is known as **tolerance** to the drug. An increasing tolerance is an indication of increasing dependence on the drug.

The ways in which people use mood-changing drugs such as nicotine, heroin and alcohol are sometimes classified according to how much control a person has over their drug-taking behaviour.

- **Recreational use** involves a person taking a drug occasionally, in such a way that they do not suffer any health problems as a result, nor does their use of the drug affect their behaviour in ways that cause problems for anyone else. For example, having a glass of wine or beer with a meal would be classed as recreational use of alcohol.

- **Abuse** occurs when the drug starts to damage the health of the person taking it, or of people around them or in their families. An example of drug abuse would be a person drinking enough alcohol to make them aggressive and cause them to act violently.

- **Dependency** occurs when, as a result of changes in the brain and other parts of the body, the person can no longer manage without the drug. Their life begins to revolve around getting the drug and using it.

Dependency can be classified as physical or psychological. This distinction is useful in working out the best way to help a person to escape from the hold that the drug has over them. However, there is no sharp dividing line between these two types of dependency, and in the end they both probably result from changes that occur in the body as a result of taking the drug.

- **Physical dependency** occurs because there have been changes in the structure and physiology of neurones in the brain. If the person stops taking the drug, they suffer from **withdrawal symptoms** (**abstinence syndrome**). Withdrawal from heroin produces some of the very worst withdrawal symptoms. The person will feel anxious, restless and irritable. They will not be able to sleep. Their eyes water and nose runs, and they salivate excessively, and may vomit, have abdominal pain and diarrhoea. The pupils of

their eyes dilate and they may feel pain all over the body. These extremely unpleasant symptoms start about 8 to 16 hours after withdrawal begins, and then can last for a week. The person will feel cravings for the drug for many weeks afterwards, as well as a general feeling of being unwell and being unable to relax or sleep.

- **Psychological dependency** is also due to what is happening in the brain as a result of taking the drug, but the person does not experience unpleasant withdrawal symptoms when they stop taking it. They do, however, constantly crave the drug. It seems as essential to them as food or water does to you when you feel very hungry or very thirsty. They may have begun taking it to help them to get through a particular problem in their lives, and if that situation re-emerges they may start taking it again. Their drug-taking may also have led them to experience an environment that they enjoyed – for example, injecting drugs along with others; they may miss all the paraphernalia associated with this environment and feel a tremendous need to go back to it. Indeed, psychological dependency may be harder to get over than physical dependency.

Alcohol

Alcohol – more correctly **ethanol** – has been used by humans for thousands of years. It was drunk in beer, wine and other drinks produced by the fermentation of substances such as grapes by yeasts. It was also widely used as a solvent in the preparation of herbal remedies.

As you will see below, drinking too much alcohol can cause serious damage to the liver, brain and other parts of the body. Health professionals recommend that each person should stay within daily alcohol limits (DALs) of no more than 2 or 3 units for a woman, and no more than 3 or 4 units for a man. A 'unit' is explained on page 274.

How alcohol affects the body

Alcohol molecules dissolve very easily in the fatty acid tails of phospholipids that make up cell surface membranes. This distorts the proteins that form channels in the membranes. In particular, it affects the shape of receptors in the membranes of neurones in the brain that respond to a neurotransmitter called **GABA**, which inhibits the formation of action potentials. Alcohol increases and prolongs the effects of GABA.

Alcohol also affects another, stimulatory, neurotransmitter called **glutamate**. This is the commonest neurotransmitter in the brain, and is responsible for much of the interaction between neurones. Alcohol blocks the receptors on cell membranes that glutamate would normally bind to.

So, alcohol increases the effect of the inhibitory neurotransmitter GABA and reduces the effect of the stimulatory neurotransmitter glutamate. Both of these actions reduce or depress the activity of the brain, so alcohol is a **depressant**. The effects are especially great in the cortex of the cerebrum and in the cerebellum. As the activity of the cortex is depressed, the person becomes less able to think clearly and logically and to make decisions. Inhibitions are reduced, and this helps some people to relax and interact socially. Depression of the activity of the cerebellum inhibits coordination of movements.

If drunk in large amounts, alcohol can kill. Inhibition of various areas of the brain causes drowsiness and eventually unconsciousness. It can cause coma. When the nervous stimulation of the muscles used in breathing is inhibited by alcohol, breathing movements stop and the person may die.

Alcohol is broken down inside the cells of the liver, the hepatocytes. The enzyme that catalyses the breakdown of ethanol is **ethanol dehydrogenase**, also known as **alcohol dehydrogenase**. Ethanol is first converted to ethanal by this enzyme, and then to ethanoate by **aldehyde dehydrogenase**. Ethanoate can enter the Krebs cycle in mitochondria and be metabolised to produce ATP (Figure 13.1).

If large quantities of alcohol are consumed on a regular basis, then the tissues within the liver can be damaged. You can see, in Figure 13.1, that the breakdown of ethanol produces reduced NAD. In its oxidised state, NAD is involved in oxidising fatty acids in the liver cells. If the NAD has been reduced, then it cannot do this. The fatty acids accumulate and are converted to fats, which are

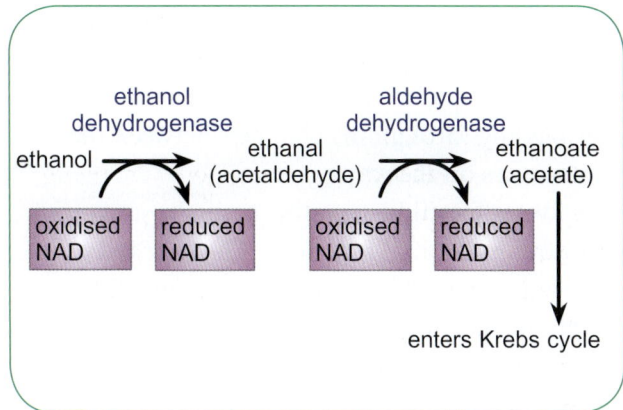

Figure 13.1   Detoxification of alcohol in the liver.

deposited in the liver. There is a strong correlation between the amount of alcohol consumed and the amount of fat deposited in a person's liver. The fat is stored in the hepatocytes, and can severely reduce their efficiency at carrying out their other functions. This condition is known as **fatty liver** (Figure 13.2). (Alcohol consumption is not the only cause of fatty liver – other risk factors include diabetes and obesity.)

Excessive intake of alcohol may also cause the liver to become inflamed, a condition known as **hepatitis**.

A combination of the excess storage of fat in the hepatocytes, plus the direct damage done to hepatocytes by ethanol, can lead to a condition known as **cirrhosis**. The damaged hepatocytes are replaced by fibrous tissue. The structure of

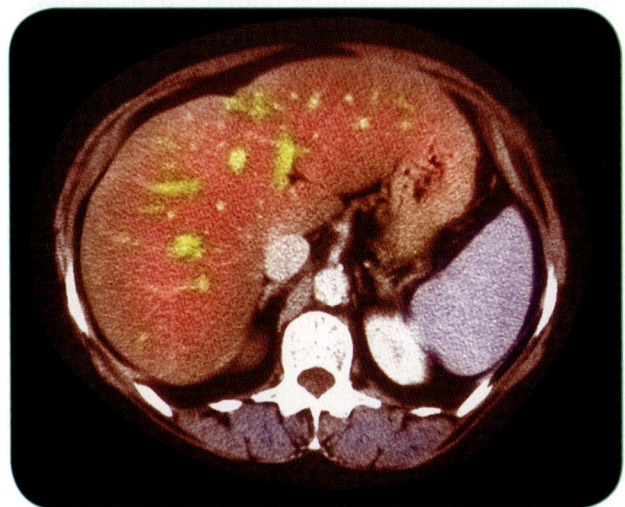

Figure 13.2   This is an MRI scan of a person suffering from fatty liver. The fat deposits can be seen as yellow patches in the liver.

the blood supply is lost, so that some blood that arrives in the hepatic portal vein simply goes straight past and into the hepatic vein, without ever passing through the channels between the hepatocytes on the way.

A liver affected by hepatitis or cirrhosis cannot carry out its normal functions. The liver has a very wide range of roles, involving many different metabolic reactions, so damage to it has far-reaching effects on the body. For example, the hepatocytes can no longer convert ammonia into urea, so ammonia concentration in the blood increases and can cause major damage to the central nervous system. In severe cases, coma and even death may result.

Long-term alcohol consumption also causes high blood pressure which in turn increases the risk of heart attacks and strokes. Alcohol can damage the lining of the stomach. It increases the loss of water in urine, so can cause dehydration. Brain cells are especially susceptible to this. The neurones in some parts of the brain also tend to lose their myelin sheaths, a process known as demyelination. This severely affects brain function.

Alcohol is a major cause of cancer. People who regularly drink large quantities of alcohol have a greatly increased risk of developing cancer in the mouth, oesophagus, liver, breast or bowel.

Some people are able to drink large amounts of alcohol without becoming dependent on it, but others run the risk of developing dependency. It is not understood why some people become alcoholics (dependent on alcohol) while others do not. Alcoholics experience unpleasant withdrawal symptoms if they have to go for any length of time without drinking it. If they wish to give up drinking alcohol, they can be helped through these withdrawal symptoms with the use of drugs such as diazepam. However, a person who has once been dependent on alcohol can easily fall back into the same dependency again, unless they completely give up drinking alcohol or control their drinking very rigorously.

Social consequences of alcohol abuse
Drinking and driving

Drinking alcohol increases reaction time, and adversely affects judgment. Both of these effects mean that a driver who has drunk alcohol is much less likely to react appropriately and rapidly to danger. A high proportion of accidents involve drivers who have been drinking. They often also involve pedestrians who have been drinking.

Many Caribbean countries have laws that limit the amount of alcohol that a driver can legally have in their blood. In the majority, this is 0.08% – that is, 80 mg of alcohol in every 100 cm³ of blood. In Jamaica, the limit is higher than this, at 0.35%. In Barbados and Cuba, the limit is zero.

How can you judge your blood alcohol concentration? Just going by how you feel doesn't work, as people generally greatly underestimate the effect that alcohol has on them. It helps to think about 'units' of alcohol. One unit can be considered to be half a pint of low strength beer, or just under one half of a 'regular' glass of wine with an ABV (alcohol by volume) of 13% (Figure 13.3). These each contain 8 g of alcohol.

Figure 13.3   Units of alcohol in some drinks.

To calculate the number of units in a drink, multiply the volume of the drink in ml by its ABV, and divide by 1000:

$$\text{number of units} = \frac{\text{volume of drink} \times \text{ABV}}{1000}$$

On average, each unit increases blood alcohol concentration by 15 mg per 100 cm³ (though this may be higher in a small person, and tends always to be higher in women). The liver breaks down about one unit each hour.

Many people, however, think that the best rule is not to drink at all if you are going to drive (Figure 13.4). There really is no 'safe limit' for drinking and driving. Young people on an evening out often appoint a 'designated driver', who doesn't drink

Figure 13.4 The amount of alcohol in the breath is directly related to the concentration of alcohol in the blood.

alcohol at all, and gets all of his or her (non-alcoholic) drinks paid for by the rest of the group.

Violence

Some people become aggressive and violent when they have been drinking alcohol. They may be almost unaware of this effect on them, thinking that they are just behaving normally and like everyone else. However, this kind of behaviour can have very severe effects on others who get caught up in it. Alcohol-fuelled violence happens not only out in the streets, but also within the home. Family members may suffer at the hands of a drunken parent or partner. Each year, many families break up as a result of aggressive behaviour caused by drinking alcohol.

Crime

We have seen that drinking alcohol damages judgment and weakens inhibitions. In some people, this can lead to them committing crimes such as theft, which they would not commit if they were not drunk.

SAQ

1 The graphs show the number of people who were admitted to hospital in one part of the USA in the year 2000 for drug-related illnesses. In all cases, the drug was being abused and was a direct cause of the need for admission.
   a Describe the pattern of alcohol abuse that resulted in hospital admission, amongst men of different ages.
   b Compare the pattern you have described in **a** with that shown by cannabis.
   c Compare the pattern you have described in **a** with the pattern of admissions for alcohol amongst women of different ages.
   d Explain why these data do not give useful information about the percentage of people who were using these different categories of drugs.

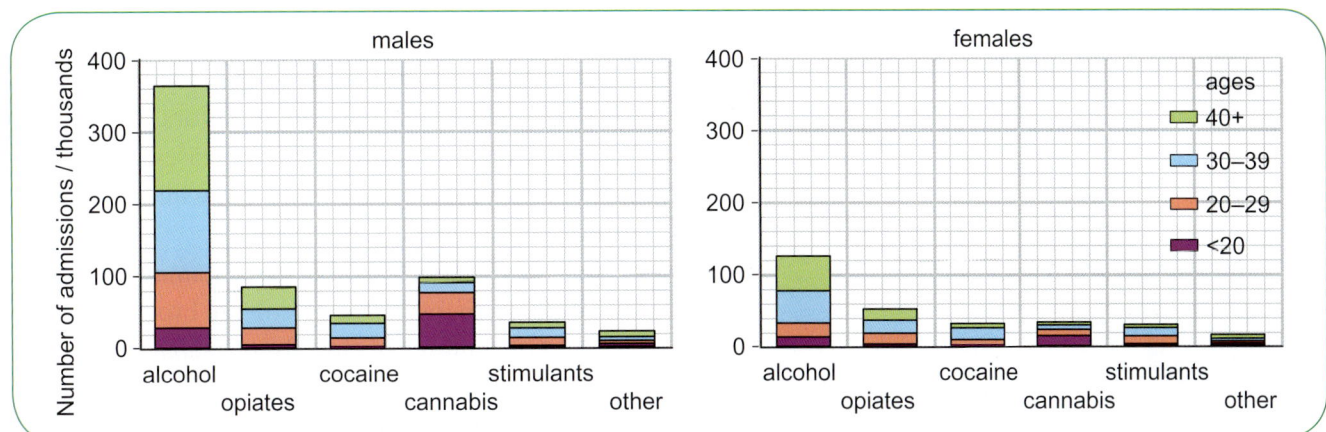

Smoking

Tobacco smoke contains many different chemicals. These include:

- **tar** – a mixture of substances, some of which can cause cancer;
- **nicotine** – the addictive substance in cigarette smoke; it affects the brain and other parts of the nervous system, and also the cardiovascular system;
- **carbon monoxide** – a gas, produced by incomplete oxidation of some of the substances in tobacco, which reduces the oxygen-carrying capacity of the blood;
- **particulates** – tiny particles, mostly of carbon, that cause irritation in the lungs and airways.

Each of these substances is potentially harmful to health. Compounds found in cigarette smoke are the direct cause of serious lung diseases, and increase the risk of developing CHD or suffering a stroke. Even breathing in someone else's cigarette smoke – passive smoking (Figure 13.5) – significantly increases the risk of developing these health problems.

Figure 13.5   Passive smoking.

Lung diseases

Lung diseases are a major cause of illness and death. They include:

- **chronic obstructive pulmonary disease** (**COPD**) – this includes many related diseases, such as **emphysema**, that prevent the normal flow of air through the gaseous exchange system;
- **lung cancer**, where cells in the lungs divide uncontrollably and form a tumour;
- illnesses caused by infectious organisms (pathogens), such as **bronchitis**.

Chronic obstructive pulmonary disease

COPD is an illness in which the airflow into and out of the lungs gradually and progressively becomes more and more obstructed. COPD happens to everyone to a certain extent as they get older, but it is hugely accelerated and worsened by smoking. It is thought that around 600 million people worldwide suffer from COPD, and that 300 million die from it each year. Somewhere between 80% and 90% of these cases are caused by smoking cigarettes.

Cigarette smoke contains a wide range of different chemicals, many of which stimulate neutrophils – a type of white blood cell (Figure 13.6) – to come to the scene. Neutrophils are an important part of the body's defence against infectious disease, but here they behave inappropriately and actually cause illness.

The neutrophils secrete an enzyme called neutrophil elastase. This enzyme is a protease and, as its name suggests, it breaks down elastin, which forms the elastic fibres in the tissues of the airways. Usually, there are inhibitors present that prevent this enzyme from doing very much harm. But, in a smoker, the balance between the concentrations of the protease enzymes and inhibitors tips too far in favour of the enzymes. The proteases gradually break down the elastin tissues in the lungs, causing irreversible damage.

One of the effects of this tissue damage is that the walls of many of the alveoli are broken down. Instead of millions of tiny alveoli, separated from blood capillaries by exceptionally thin walls, the lungs become filled with larger spaces, much more widely separated from the blood capillaries. What's

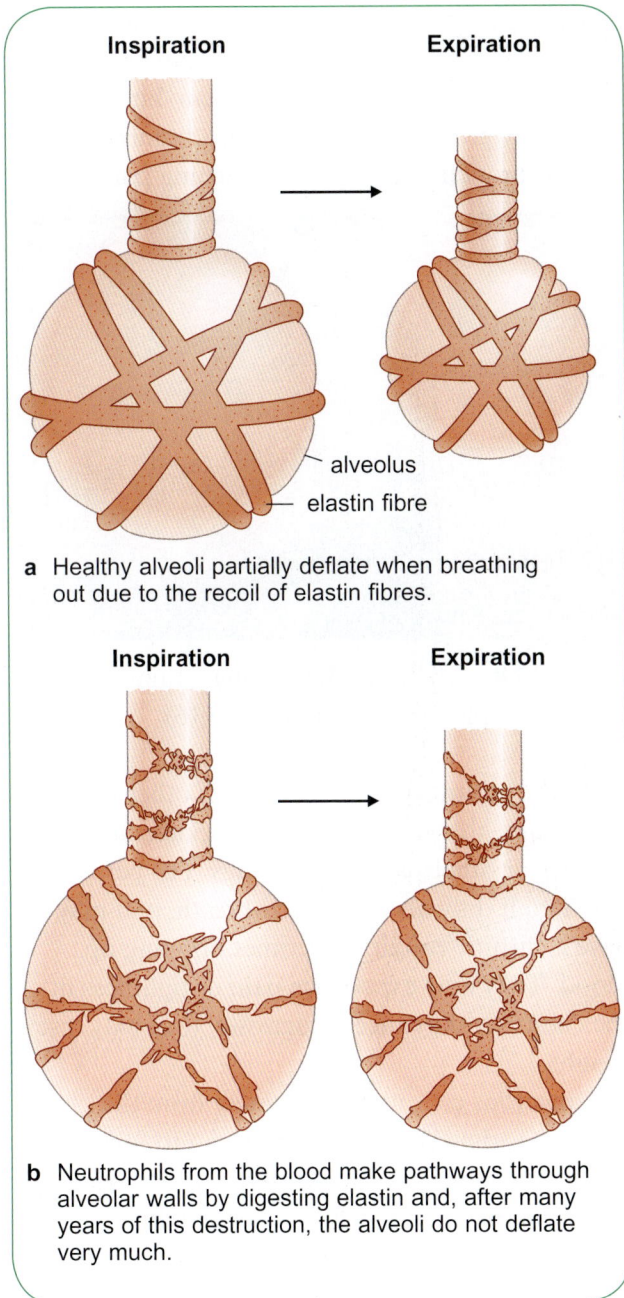

a Healthy alveoli partially deflate when breathing out due to the recoil of elastin fibres.

b Neutrophils from the blood make pathways through alveolar walls by digesting elastin and, after many years of this destruction, the alveoli do not deflate very much.

Figure 13.6 The development of emphysema.

more, many of these capillaries also disappear. The total surface area for gaseous exchange is therefore greatly reduced. This condition is called emphysema (Figure 13.7). Not surprisingly, someone with emphysema has great difficulty in getting enough oxygen into their blood.

The progressive damage to the lungs causes them to lose their elasticity, while damage to the airways causes their walls to thicken. This happens because the attempts by the tissue to repair itself cause it to become fibrous. Both of these changes

make it more difficult for air to move into and out of the lungs.

The damage to the airways also involves the ciliated cells and the goblet (mucus-producing) cells, which normally help to keep the lungs clear of dust, bacteria and other foreign particles in the air that is breathed in. In smokers, the goblet cells often proliferate, producing much larger numbers than in a non-smoker. The production of large

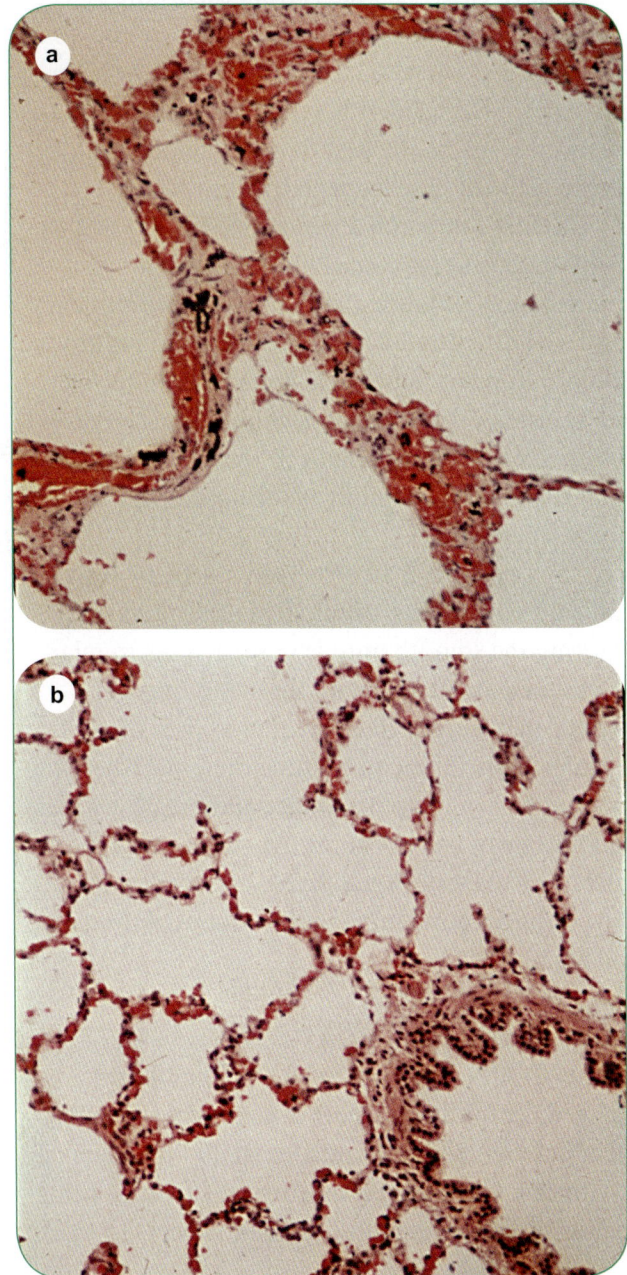

Figure 13.7 **a** Photomicrograph of lung tissue from a person with chronic emphysema, showing large spaces where there should be many tiny alveoli, **b** photomicrograph of normal lung tissue.

numbers of 'extra' cells is called **hyperplasia**. As a result, more mucus is produced, but the cilia do not beat and so there is nothing to carry the mucus up and out of the bronchi and trachea. Instead, mucus accumulates in the airways, where it provides a breeding ground for bacteria. People with this condition therefore tend to suffer from bacterial infections of the bronchi, called bronchitis. They may have a chronic cough, as they attempt to clear the mucus from their lungs.

There is not really a great deal that can be done to help a person who has COPD. Once the tissues have been damaged, it is very difficult for them to recover. Usually, the best that can be done is to prevent the disease from getting any worse.

The first thing that anyone with COPD will be told to do is to stop smoking. This will almost immediately produce a reduction in the frequency and severity of infections, and may also reduce the cough. Ciliated cells and goblet cells can recover to a certain extent. But it is unlikely that large improvements will be made in the breathlessness that is caused by emphysema. Emphysema appears to be irreversible.

Many patients may be helped a little by drugs called beta agonists, which dilate the airways by causing the smooth muscle in their walls to relax.

As the patient ages, and the symptoms get worse, they may need to breathe oxygen on a regular basis. This can be done at home, where the patient has an oxygen cylinder and breathing mask that they can use whenever they need to. In the advanced stages of the disease, even walking a few steps becomes impossible without getting out of breath.

Lung cancer

While COPD causes about 15% of smoking-related deaths, lung cancer causes almost double that number. Smokers are almost 20 times as likely to die from lung cancer as are non-smokers. Lung cancer is one of the most difficult cancers to treat successfully.

Cigarette smoke contains several chemicals that are carcinogenic. Carcinogens are substances that damage the control of cell division. Cells may begin to divide much more than they should,

forming a lump of disorganised cells called a tumour (Figure 13.8). The tumour can be almost anywhere in the gas exchange system, but most frequently grows where the trachea branches into the two bronchi, or at other branching points.

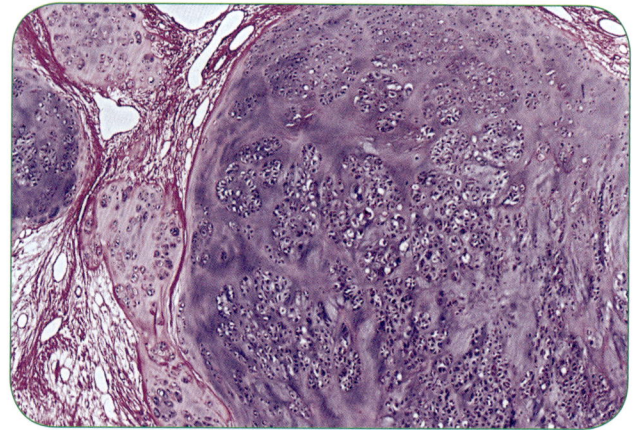

Figure 13.8 Micrograph showing a tumour (darker purple) in a human lung (×16).

As the tumour grows, it displaces other tissues. Eventually, this can lead to the blockage of the airways or other parts of the lungs. The person may find it difficult to get their breath, and may have a chronic cough, sometimes bringing up blood. They may experience pain or tightness in the chest. As the cancer progresses, they may lose weight.

Cancerous cells may break away from the primary (original) tumour and begin to form secondary tumours in other parts of the body. If this happens, survival rates are very low.

Some of the carcinogenic substances enter the bloodstream in the lungs, and are carried all over the body. It is therefore not surprising that smoking significantly increases the risk of developing cancers in almost every part of the body.

Smoking and the cardiovascular system

Smoking increases the risk of developing CHD. Nearly everyone who develops CHD in their 30s or early 40s is a smoker. Smoking can cause high blood pressure. A smoker with high blood pressure has a 20 times greater risk of stroke than a non-smoker who does not have high blood pressure.

Nicotine

One of the culprits is the nicotine in cigarettes. Nicotine is a neurotoxin – a chemical that damages the nervous system. It is used as an insecticide. Nicotine is extremely addictive, and this is the reason why smokers find it so difficult to give up.

Nicotine molecules are relatively small, and they easily move out of the blood and into every part of the body, including the brain. Nicotine increases the levels of a transmitter substance called dopamine in the parts of the brain that are known as 'reward circuits'. Activation of these circuits gives feelings of pleasure, and this is why people enjoy smoking.

Nicotine also causes the release of adrenaline into the blood. Adrenaline increases the rate of heart beat, blood pressure and breathing rate.

Nicotine is a vasoconstrictor – it causes the smooth muscle in the walls of arteries and arterioles to contract, narrowing the lumen and therefore making it harder for blood to be pumped through. This, too, tends to increase blood pressure and the risk of blood clots forming (page 250).

Carbon monoxide

Carbon monoxide diffuses from the alveoli into the blood in the lung capillaries. Here it combines with haemoglobin, forming a bright red compound called **carboxyhaemoglobin**. It holds on tightly; haemoglobin has a very high affinity for carbon monoxide. With a proportion of the haemoglobin tied up in this way, there is less available for the transport of oxygen. Smoking therefore reduces the delivery of oxygen to the tissues, including the heart muscle. Smokers have less energy available to their muscles when they exercise.

The body may respond to the oxygen shortage by producing larger numbers of red blood cells. A hormone called **erythropoetin**, produced by the kidneys, is secreted in larger amounts when the amount of oxygen in the blood is low. This hormone stimulates the production of red blood cells by the stem cells in the bone marrow. and smokers usually have a higher red blood cell count (the number of red cells per unit volume of blood). This might seem to be a good thing, but it can sometimes cause problems such as dizziness, weakness, headache and joint pain.

Hypertension, CHD and stroke

We have seen that nicotine increases blood pressure, which can increase the risk of developing atherosclerosis and CHD (Chapter 12). It is not only the coronary arteries that are affected – atherosclerosis can develop in any arteries in the body. Smokers run a higher risk than non-smokers of atherosclerosis developing in blood vessels that supply the brain. This greatly increases the risk of suffering a stroke (page 254).

Smokers tend to have more viscous blood than non-smokers. This can increase the risk of blood clots forming inappropriately, which once again increases the risk of stroke.

SAQ

2 The chart below is used to work out how likely a person is to have a heart attack or stroke.

a Use the chart to find the predicted risk for:
  - a 56-year-old woman who smokes, has a blood pressure of 160/95 and whose total cholesterol : HDL-cholesterol ratio is 5
  - a 45-year-old man who does not smoke, whose blood pressure reading is 160/95 and whose total cholesterol : HDL-cholesterol ratio is 8.

b What could each of these people do to reduce their risk of having a heart attack or stroke?

c Suggest how a risk calculator like this could be produced.

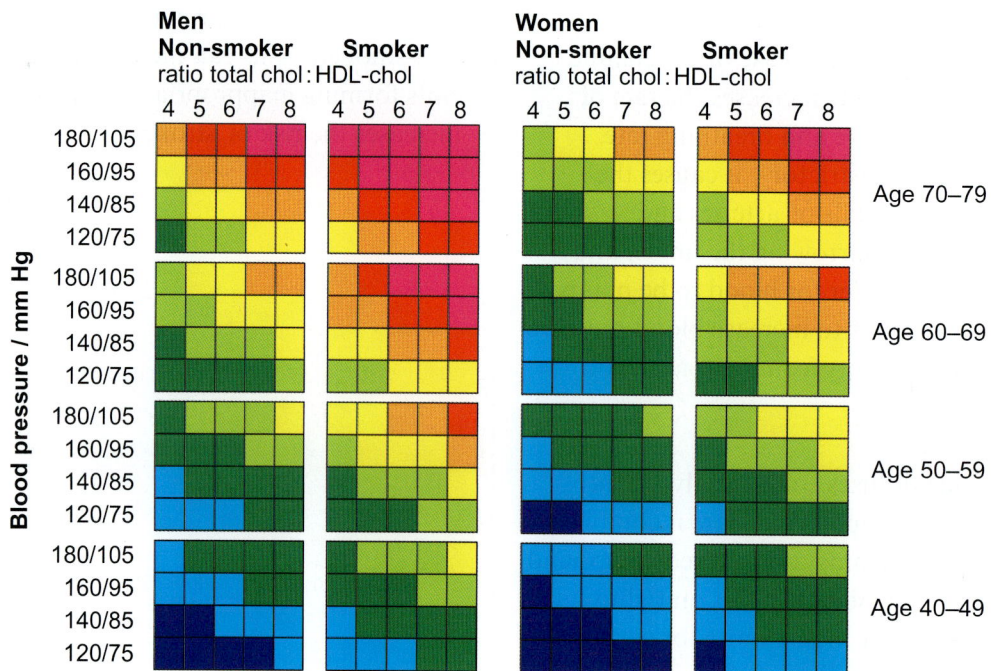

Risk – 5 yr cardiovascular fatal + non-fatal events		Events prevented per 100 treated for 5 yrs
very high	>30%	>10
	25–30%	9
	20–25%	7.5
high/moderate	15–20%	6
	10–15%	4
mild	5–10%	2.5
	2.5–5%	1.25
	<2.5%	<0.8

Notes:
1 'ratio total chol : HDL-chol' is the ratio of the total amount of cholesterol in the blood to the amount of cholesterol transported in high density lipoprotein in the blood.

2 A 'cardiovascular event' in this table is referring to newly diagnosed angina, myocardial infarction, death from CHD or stroke.

Summary

- Substance abuse is the misuse of a drug or other substance, so that it causes harm to the user or to other people.

- Although alcohol and nicotine (in cigarettes) are legal drugs, their use can cause serious health problems.

- Physical dependency on a drug occurs when the structure and physiology of the body is changed by the drug use, so that withdrawal symptoms are experienced when the drug is no longer taken. Psychological dependency occurs when the person feels they cannot manage without the drug, even if no withdrawal symptoms are experienced. There is no sharp dividing line between physical and psychological dependency.

- In the short-term, alcohol affects the neurotransmitters GABA and glutamate in the brain, which together causes the activity of the brain to slow down. It is therefore a depressant. Inhibitions are reduced, coordination is lost and nervous transmission is slowed, lengthening reaction time. If so much alcohol is drunk that the breathing muscles are inhibited, the person may die.

- Alcohol is broken down in the liver by the hepatocytes. Long-term excessive consumption of alcohol often leads to fatty liver, hepatitis and cirrhosis and also greatly increases the risk of developing many types of cancer.

- Alcohol consumption is a causative factor in many vehicle and other accidents, in incidents involving violence and aggression, and in petty crime.

- Smoking cigarettes, and the inhalation of smoke from other people's cigarettes, causes a very wide range of serious health problems. These include COPD and lung cancer, CHD and stroke.

Questions

Multiple choice questions

1 Drug abuse is:
   A the use of a drug for personal gratification, causing damage to health.
   B the compulsion to use a drug on a periodic or continuous basis to avoid discomfort from its absence.
   C the need for increasing quantities of the drug to produce the same effect.
   D the occasional use of the drug to lessen pain.

2 Which of the following **best** describes 'physical dependence'?
   A the emotional changes if the drug is withheld
   B the need for an increasing dose of the drug to produce the same effect
   C when a drug or one of its metabolites has become necessary for the continued functioning of the body
   D a mild form of dependence that does not produce withdrawal symptoms

continued ...

3 Which of the following is **not** a consequence of long-term use of alcohol?

  A the development of swollen cells with wispy cytoplasm in the liver cells

  B the accumulation of fat in the liver cells

  C the constriction of blood vessels in the liver

  D the development of fibrous tissue in the liver

4 How many grams of absolute (pure) alcohol does one 'unit' of alcohol contain?

  A 7

  B 8

  C 15

  D 25

5 Fat accumulates in the liver when alcohol is consumed regularly because:

  A fat absorbs alcohol and helps detoxify it.

  B alcohol is used to synthesise fat molecules in the liver.

  C liver cells use alcohol instead of fat as an energy source.

  D alcohol prevents liver cells from secreting fat molecules.

6 Which component of tobacco smoke causes an increased risk of lung cancer?

  A nicotine

  B carbon dioxide

  C carbon monoxide

  D tar

7 How does nicotine in cigarette smoke increase the risk of cardiac disease?

  A by reducing the diameter of arterioles

  B by attaching to haemoglobin

  C by stimulating the sino-atrial node directly

  D by forming plaque in blood vessels

8 Which of the components of tobacco smoke lowers the capacity of haemoglobin to transport oxygen?

  A carbon monoxide

  B nicotine

  C tar

  D carcinogens

continued …

9 The images below are enlarged views of alveoli from a non-smoker and a smoker.

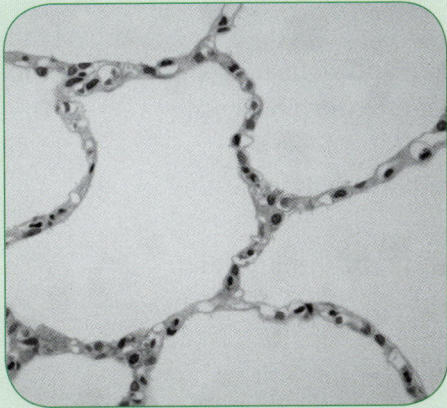

alveoli of a non-smoker

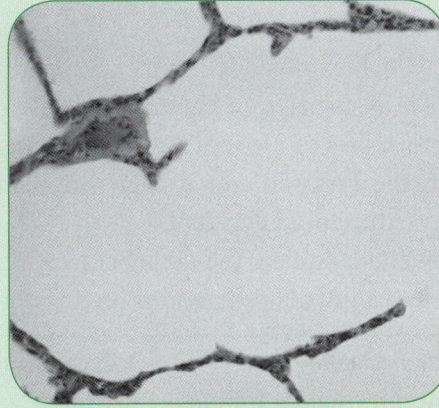

alveoli of a smoker

Why may a smoker have to consciously contract his muscles to breathe out?

A increased mucus production by goblet cells

B paralysis of the cilia

C excess tar in the alveoli

D loss of elasticity in the alveolar walls

Structured questions

10 a What do you understand by the following terms?

  i   drug

  ii   drug abuse

  iii drug dependence

  iv   drug tolerance

  v   abstinence syndrome (withdrawal symptoms)   [10 marks]

   b Distinguish between:

  i   physical and psychological dependence

  ii   legal and illegal drugs.   [5 marks]

11 The following drinking guidelines have been developed for people over 18 years of age, based on medical advice.

4 day
21 week

Men
It is recommended that men drink no more than 3 to 4 units of alcohol a day and no more than 21 units over the course of the week.

3 day
14 week

Women
It is recommended that women drink no more than 2 to 3 units of alcohol a day and no more than 14 units over the course of the week.

continued ...

a What do you understand by the term 'unit of alcohol'? [1 mark]

b Why are the recommended units given in both units per day as well as units per week? [2 marks]

c Why are the recommended units per day of alcohol for men and women different? [4 marks]

d Alcohol is absorbed quickly from the gastrointestinal tract into the blood. What properties of alcohol facilitate the fast absorption rates? [2 marks]

e Recently the Trinidad and Tobago Government introduced breathalyzer testing in order to reduce road accidents.

    i Copy and complete the table below which shows the effects of drinking and blood alcohol concentrations on driving behaviour.

Blood alcohol concentration / g 100 cm^{-3}	Effects of alcohol on driving
0.02–0.05	
0.05–0.08	

[4 marks]

    ii The legal limit for drinking in Trinidad and Tobago is 0.08 g per 100 cm³ blood. Explain why a breathalyzer test can be used to determine whether a driver is above this limit. [2 marks]

12 a Name **three** main constituents of cigarette smoke that are harmful to the body. [3 marks]

Diagram **a** below shows the alveoli of a smoker and non-smoker during expiration, and image **b** shows the coronary artery of a smoker.

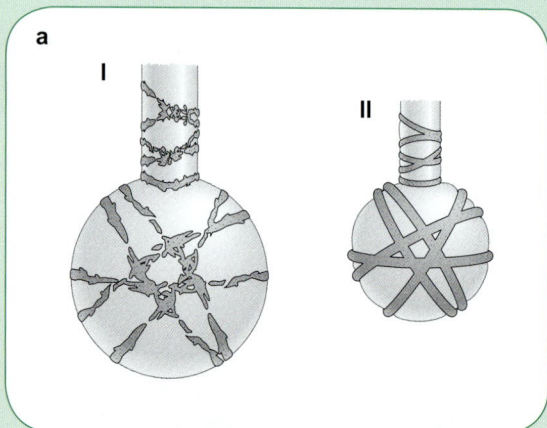

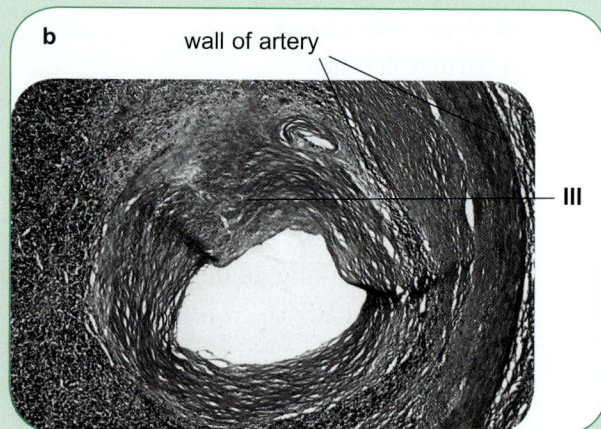

b Identify the alveoli of the smoker and the non-smoker. Give a reason for your answer. [3 marks]

c i Name the disease that is characterised by the alveoli of the smoker. [1 mark]

   ii Explain why the smoker would have difficulty in breathing. [2 marks]

d i Identify structure **III** in image **b**. [1 mark]

   ii Name the disease that is characterised by image **b**. [1 mark]

  iii State **four** symptoms that might be experienced by a person whose artery has been narrowed as shown in image **b**. [2 marks]

  iv Explain how cigarette smoking may account for the appearance of the artery. [2 marks]

continued …

Essay questions

13 Explain the following terms using alcohol and the components of cigarette smoke as examples.
- **a** physical dependence
- **b** psychological dependence
- **b** tolerance
- **b** abstinence syndrome (withdrawal symptoms) [15 marks]

14 Cigarette smoke contains many substances that are harmful to the body and which cause disease. Explain how the components of cigarette smoke increase the risk of developing the following diseases.
- **a** coronary heart disease
- **b** lung cancer
- **c** chronic bronchitis
- **d** emphysema
- **e** hypertension
- **f** strokes [15 marks]

15 a Briefly describe the short-term and long-term consequences of alcohol consumption on:
- **i** the liver
- **ii** the nervous system. [9 marks]
- **b** Discuss the factors which affect blood alcohol level. [3 marks]
- **c** Discuss the social consequences of excessive alcohol consumption. [3 marks]

when environmental conditions are ideal for photosynthesis. Tropical rainforest has a greater density of plants.

d Alfalfa plants are young and growing, so much of the carbon they fix in photosynthesis is incorporated into new cells rather than being respired. In the rainforest, the trees are mostly mature and amounts of growth will be small. Alfalfa is a nitrogen-fixer and this, together with the probable application of fertiliser to the crop, could allow greater rates of growth than in the rainforest.

4 a The lack of water in a desert limits the density of plants that can grow there, and also their rate of photosynthesis.

b There is a much greater total leaf surface area in a forest than in grassland, so more light is intercepted and more of it is transferred to chemical potential energy during photosynthesis.

Chapter 4

1 a abiotic **b** biotic **c** abiotic **d** biotic

2 a Perhaps individual grasses with different genotypes taste different, so the geese may have chosen to eat some and leave others. You may be able to think of other possibilities.

b An experiment would need to be set up in which the independent variable is the genotype of the seagrass, and the dependent variable is the amount eaten by geese. All other variables would be controlled. You would need large numbers of seagrass plants of each genotype. Plant a bed of seagrass in which there are square patches of each genotype. Plant other beds identical in every way, except that the pattern in which the different genotypes is arranged is different. Introduce geese to each bed and leave for a set amount of time. Record the numbers of shoots of each genotype eaten.

3 • to clear land for growing crops, either subsistence farming or large-scale

production such as banana plantations
*   to provide wood for fuel
*   to provide timber for building and other purposes
*   to clear land for building roads, houses or factories

4 a Behaviour patterns, including mating behaviour, may be adversely affected by the conditions in captivity. There are a large number of possible reasons for this. For example, animals may need a particular cycle of light and dark; if they are in a part of the world at a different latitude, they may not experience this. They may need to be able to roam across large territories in order to stimulate mating behaviour. They may need a different diet from the one provided in captivity. They may need to be able to choose a mate from a large number of individual animals, whereas in captivity they are likely to be introduced to only one potential mate.

b Inbreeding increases the chance of deleterious recessive alleles coming together in an individual. It reduces the range of different alleles in the population, which will make it more difficult for these animals to adapt to changing conditions in the future, or when reintroduced back into the wild.

5 a Selection pressures in the natural habitat might include grazing, wide variations in rainfall or competition with other species. In the seed bank, none of these selection pressures will apply. Here, the greatest selection pressure will be the conditions in which the seeds are stored for long periods of time – seeds best able to survive storage will be the most successful.

b It is possible that plants grown from the saved seeds will not have the best set of characteristics for surviving the different selection pressures they will encounter in their natural habitat. This could reduce the chances of success when returning them to the wild.

Chapter 5

1 Plants have a large surface area : volume ratio because of their branching shape. This allows gases to move quickly between the atmosphere and the cells by diffusion. Plants also have a relatively low metabolic rate, so they do not need such fast supplies of gases.

2 It has a large surface area, which increases the quantity of water and mineral ions that can cross this surface at a given moment in time. Like all plant cells, it has a fully permeable cell wall that allows water and mineral ions to pass freely through, and a partially permeable membrane that allows water (but not most solutes) to pass through. Again like all plant cells, its cytoplasm and cell sap have a lower water potential than the external solution, so water enters passively down a water potential gradient.

3 Scale bar length = 12 mm

    = 12 000 μm

magnification = $\dfrac{\text{size of image}}{\text{real size of object}}$

$= \dfrac{12\,000\,\mu m}{100\,\mu m} = \times 120$

diameter of vessel above the scale bar in image

    = 20 mm

    = 20 000 μm

real size of object = $\dfrac{\text{size of image}}{\text{magnification}}$

$= \dfrac{20\,000\,\mu m}{120}$

= 167 μm

4 a The total lack of cell contents provides an uninterrupted pathway for the flow of water.

   b Lack of end walls also provides an uninterrupted pathway for the flow of water.

   c The wider the diameter, the more water can be moved up through a xylem vessel per unit time. However, if the vessels are too wide, there is an increased tendency for the water column to break. The diameter of the xylem vessels is a compromise between these two requirements.

   d The lignified walls provide support, preventing the vessels from collapsing inwards. The lignin waterproofs the walls, keeping most of the water inside the vessel.

   e Pits in the walls of the vessels allow water to move into and out of them.

5 Sucrose, amino acids and plant growth substances are synthesised by the plant.

6 a Sink. b Sink. c Source. d Sink.

7 See table at the bottom of this page.

Chapter 6

1 a i   0.7–0.8 seconds

      ii $\dfrac{60}{0.75} = 80$ beats per minute

   For b, c, d, e and f, see graph on next page. The periods that are not atrial systole are atrial diastole.

   g Blood is flowing from the ventricle into the aorta, pushed out by the contraction of the muscle in the ventricle walls.

   h Between 0.46 s and 0.87 s.

   i See graph on next page.

Feature	Xylem vessels	Phloem sieve tubes
cell contents	none	cytoplasm and organelles, but no nucleus
cell walls	contain lignin and cellulose	contain cellulose but not lignin
diameter	between 0.01 mm and 0.2 mm	can be smaller than xylem vessels
substances transported	water and mineral ions	substances made by the plant, especially sucrose and amino acids; also some mineral ions (but not nitrate)
method of transport	driven by the transpiration stream – a passive process	driven by active loading of sucrose – an active process

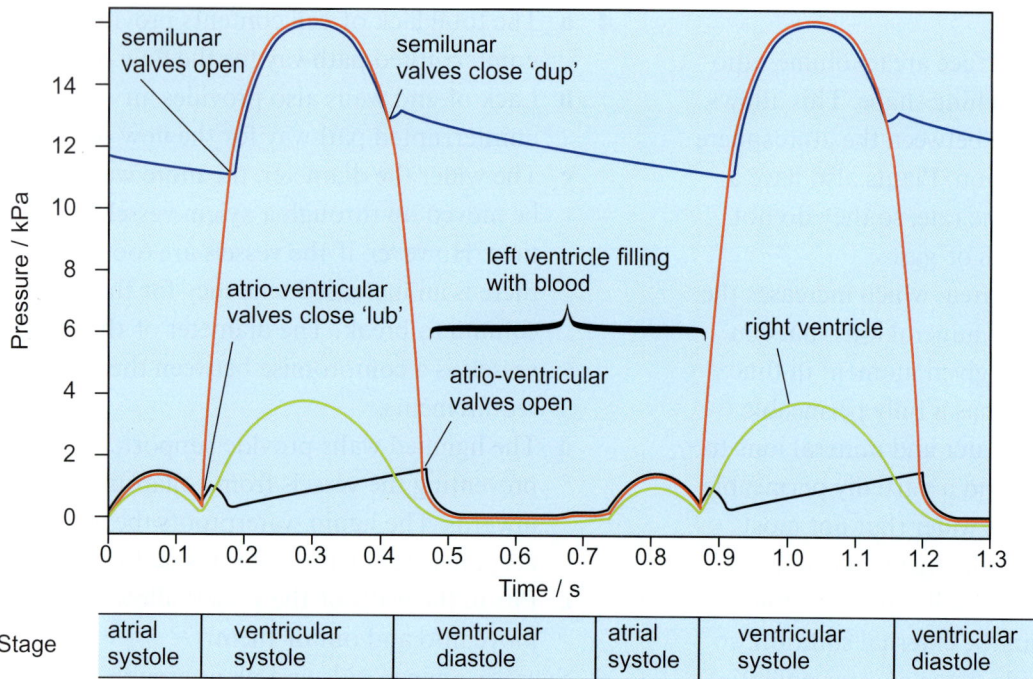

Stage	atrial systole	ventricular systole	ventricular diastole	atrial systole	ventricular systole	ventricular diastole

2 a The arteries carry blood that has just come from the heart. When the ventricles contract, the blood surges into the arteries at high pressure, and the pressure falls when the ventricles relax.

b Blood pressure drops because the total cross-sectional area of the arterioles and capillaries is greater than that of the arteries. The same quantity of blood is therefore spread out into a larger volume, so its pressure is lower. Pressure also falls as plasma leaks out of the capillaries.

c The high blood pressure in the pulmonary artery is produced by the contraction of the right ventricle, and that in the aorta is produced by the contraction of the left ventricle. The muscle in the wall of the right ventricle is not as thick as in the left ventricle, so it does not produce as much force when it contracts.

3 a Protein synthesis – no; there is no DNA.

b Cell division – no; there are no chromosomes, so mitosis cannot occur.

c Lipid synthesis – no; this occurs on the smooth endoplasmic reticulum, and there is no SER in the cell.

4 a About 195 cm3

b 25 cm3

5 a i 96.5%

ii 1.25 cm^3

b i 22.0%

ii 0.29 cm^3

Chapter 7

1

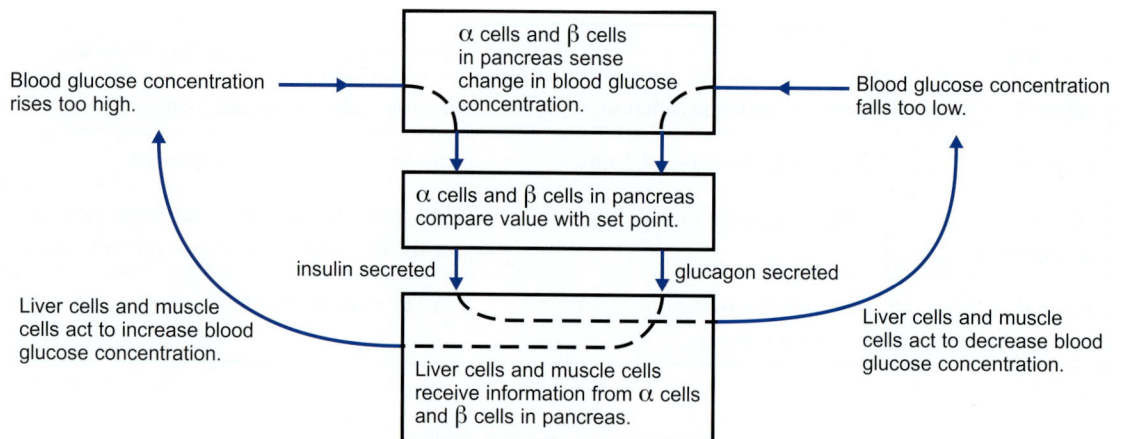

2 Steroids are soluble in lipids, so they can diffuse through the phospholipid bilayer. Protein hormones are not lipid-soluble.

3 **a** An endocrine gland secretes its product directly into the blood, whereas an exocrine gland secretes its product into a duct. An endocrine gland secretes hormones, whereas an exocrine gland secretes other substances, such as digestive juices containing enzymes.

   b Glycogen is a polysaccharide storage substance, made from glucose molecules linked through α1–4 glycosidic bonds, with α 1–6 branching. Glucagon is a peptide hormone secreted by the β cells in the pancreas.

   c Glycolysis is the first stage of respiration, which takes place in the cytoplasm, in which glucose is converted to pyruvate in a series of small steps, with the generation of ATP. Gluconeogenesis is the production of glucose from amino acids or lipids.

4 **a** In both positive and negative feedback, a receptor detects changes in a parameter and communicates with an effector which acts to cause further change in the same parameter. In positive feedback, this further change is in the same direction as the initial change, whereas in negative feedback it is in the opposite direction.

   b Positive feedback has the effect of amplifying the initial change, and so could not help to bring back the parameter to its set point. Negative feedback moves the parameter back towards its set point, and so can help to keep internal conditions constant.

5 This can help different fruits on the same plant – or even on different plants – to ripen at the same time. This could encourage many animals to come to that plant to feed on the fruits, thereby increasing the chances of the seeds being dispersed.

6 Ethylene causes many genes to be switched on, which in turn causes many proteins to be synthesised. Protein synthesis uses ATP. To generate this extra ATP, respiration increases.

7 The yellow banana secretes ethylene into the air, which affects the cells of the unripe fruit and speeds the ripening process.

8 The bruised tissue secretes ethylene, which could affect all the other apples in the store, making them ripen too rapidly and shortening the time for which they can be stored.

9 **a** Unripe bananas are easier to transport without damage. They can remain in this state for a long time, allowing transport overseas.

   b This gives control over when the bananas ripen, so the sellers are able to produce bananas of a particular ripeness exactly when required.

   c The higher the temperature, the faster the bananas ripen. For example, if the bananas are held at 18 °C for two days, they are turning yellow by the third day, whereas if they are held at 14 °C they do not begin to turn yellow until the sixth day. This is because metabolic reactions take place faster at higher temperatures.

Chapter 8

1 **a** The ammonia will quickly dissolve in the large volumes of water around them, and be so diluted that it will not harm the fish.

   b Turning ammonia into urea requires energy in the form of ATP, so by excreting ammonia rather than urea energy is saved.

2 A large percentage of the water in the fluid is reabsorbed in the proximal convoluted tubule, so the volume of water in which the urea is dissolved decreases. This decrease in the volume of water is greater than the decrease in the quantity of urea, so this increases the concentration of urea in the fluid.

3 **a** Microvilli increase the surface area of the cells that are in contact with the glomerular filtrate inside the proximal convoluted tubules. This increases the number of transporter proteins available for the transfer of substances such as glucose and sodium ions out of the filtrate and into the cell.

b Mitochondria produce ATP by the Krebs cycle and oxidative phosphorylation. Much of this ATP is used for active transport. For example, it is used to actively transport sodium ions out of the cells, thereby creating a concentration gradient for sodium ions. As the ions move down their concentration gradient into the cell, they pull glucose molecules with them, moving the glucose molecules up their concentration gradient.

4 a The *y*-axis is shown as 'number of times greater'. This is done because the actual concentrations of each substance are very different from each other, so each would need a separate scale. It is also a logarithmic scale, so that it can accommodate a very wide range of values. It has no 0, because a value of ×1 means 'no greater'. Values above 1 represent an increase in concentration, and values below 1 represent a decrease.

b Amino acids and glucose are virtually all reabsorbed into the blood from the proximal convoluted tubule.

A small amount of urea is reabsorbed in the proximal convoluted tubule, but its concentration increases because there is now less water present. As more water is reabsorbed throughout the loop of Henlé, the concentration of urea continues to increase.

Although both sodium ions and potassium ions are reabsorbed in the proximal convoluted tubule, their concentration does not change because water is also reabsorbed here. The concentrations of both increase as they go down the descending limb of the loop of Henlé, because water is lost from here by osmosis into the tissue fluid around it. As the fluid passes up the ascending limb, sodium ions are actively pumped out, so their concentration inside the tubule decreases. More water is lost from the filtrate in the distal convoluted tubule and collecting duct, so the concentrations of both ions increase. (Potassium ions are actively transported into the distal convoluted tubule, which explains why their concentration rises more than that of sodium ions.)

5 Flow rate is highest at the beginning of the proximal convoluted tubule, where fluid is entering via filtration into the renal capsule. As the fluid flows along the proximal convoluted tubule, a large percentage of it is reabsorbed, thus decreasing its volume. There is thus less fluid to flow, so less passes a given point in unit time; in other words, its flow rate decreases.

This reabsorption happens all along the nephron, which is why the flow rate continues to drop. The rate of flow decreases rapidly in the collecting duct, as a high proportion of the water may be reabsorbed here.

6 See the diagram below.

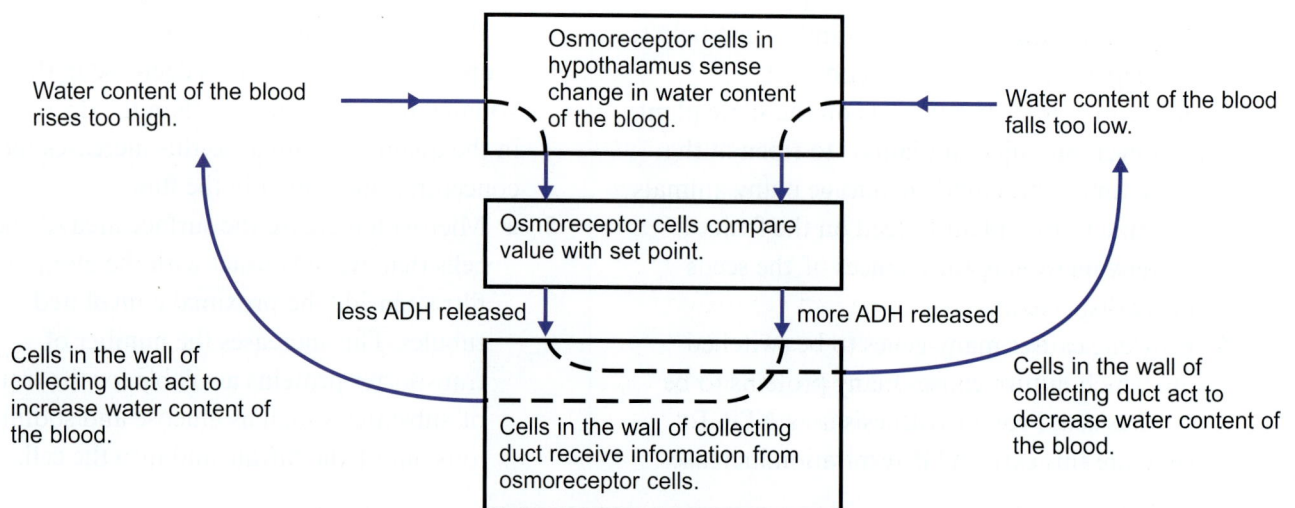

7 a There appears to be a positive correlation between the percentage of long loops of Henlé and the dryness of a mammal's environment. For example, desert mice have 100% long loops, while beavers (which spend a lot of time in fresh water) have none.

b There appears to be a positive correlation between the percentage of long loops of Henlé and the maximum concentration of urine that can be produced. However, jerboas don't quite fit this pattern: they have only 33% long loops but still produce urine of a higher concentration than desert mice, which have 100% long loops.

c Long loops of Henlé can produce very high concentrations (low water potentials) in the kidney medulla. The lower the water potential here, the more water can be drawn out of the collecting duct rather than being lost in urine. Animals that live in conditions where water is in short supply therefore benefit by having long loops of Henlé because more of their water can be kept in the body and less lost in urine.

Chapter 9

1 • Motor neurones have a single long axon, while sensory neurones have a long axon and a long dendron.
 • Motor neurones have many short dendrites – short cytoplasmic processes from the cell body – but sensory neurones do not have these.

2 There are many different possible answers to each section of this question.

3 a The line should be drawn at about −70 mV.

b The inside of the axon has a charge of −70 mV compared with the outside.

c By active transport using ATP to power the sodium–potassium pumps in the membrane of the axon. Both sodium and potassium ions are positively charged. Three sodium ions are pumped out for every two potassium ions pumped in, so this builds up a positive charge outside compared with inside the axon.

d i It is called depolarisation because the axon was polarised so that it had a negative charge inside and a positive charge outside. Now this is altered and there is a negative charge outside and a positive charge inside.

ii Sodium channels in the membrane open and allow sodium ions to flow in down their electrochemical gradient. As they enter the axon, their positive charge causes the negative charge inside the axon to be brought to zero and then continue to become more positive until it reaches about 30 mV.

e Between 1 ms and 2 ms the axon is repolarised. The sodium channels close again, and potassium channels open. Potassium ions flood out of the axon and therefore make the outside more positive than the inside. The potential overshoots the resting potential, temporarily becoming even more negative inside than it was before. Then the sodium–potassium pump kicks in again and the resting potential is restored (see Figure 9.9 on page 184).

f About 4 ms.

Chapter 10

1

Bacterium	HIV
cellular	not cellular
has a plasma membrane	has an envelope
has cytoplasm	no cytoplasm
much larger than a virus	much smaller than a bacterium
contains DNA	contains RNA
does not contain reverse transcriptase	contains reverse transcriptase
no capsid	has a capsid made of protein

c In all countries, more men than women develop lung cancer each year. Figures should be quoted to support this statement – for example, in Jamaica, the incidence for men is four times greater than for women.

d By far the most important cause of lung cancer is smoking tobacco. It is likely that more men than women are smokers.

e Lung cancer. In each country, the mortality rate is only a little lower than the incidence, suggesting that this disease is almost always fatal. Lung cancer is one of the most difficult cancers to cure.

Chapter 11

1 Viruses enter body cells, where they hijack the cell's machinery to reproduce themselves. If a cell is infected by a virus, it cuts up some of the virus molecules and puts them in its plasma membrane. T-lymphocytes respond to antigens in the plasma membrane, so they recognise when a cell is infected by a virus. T-helper lymphocytes then secrete cytokines, which alert other cells to respond. T-killer lymphocytes bind to the cell that is infected by the virus and kill it.

B-lymphocytes, however, respond by secreting antibodies. These will not reach viruses that are safely inside a cell. Antibodies cannot cross plasma membranes to get into a cell.

2 a The results show that the radioactivity (and therefore the amino acids) was found first in the ribosomes, then in the endoplasmic reticulum, and then in the Golgi body. As the radioactivity in ribosomes declines, it rises in the ER. As it declines in the ER, it rises in the Golgi body.

b At the ribosomes, the labelled amino acids would have been used to make protein molecules. The ribosomes are attached to the membranes of the endoplasmic reticulum, and the proteins move into the cisternae of the endoplasmic reticulum as they are made. Pieces of the ER then break off to form small vesicles, containing the proteins. These vesicles travel to the Golgi body, where they

fuse with its membranes. In the Golgi body, carbohydrates are added to the proteins to convert them to glycoproteins.

c This suggests that most of the proteins made on the ribosomes moved into the ER. However, not all of these proteins were transported to the Golgi body. Some of them might have gone straight into the cytoplasm of the cell. Another possibility is that the radioactivity of the amino acids decreased over time.

d The amino acids might have been taken up by phagocytosis (endocystosis). In this case, the cell would have formed a vacuole containing amino acids and a droplet of the liquid surrounding them.
They could have been taken up by active transport, through a protein channel in the plasma membrane.

e Small vesicles would pinch off from the Golgi body, and travel to the plasma membrane. They would then fuse with this membrane, emptying the contents of the vesicles outside the cell. This is an example of exocytosis.

3 If this region changes colour, it shows that the dipstick is working – that is, that urine has moved up the stick and that the antibodies on the stick are present and active.

Chapter 12

1 a Carbohydrates, proteins, lipids and the three vitamins.

b Carbohydrates, proteins and lipids.

2 There will only be glucose in urine when it has risen above a particular level in the blood, so testing urine for glucose won't tell you anything about blood glucose levels below this value. Glucose in urine has moved into the urine from the blood over a period of time, whereas if you test blood directly for glucose you know what the blood value is at a particular moment in time.

3 a Bread contains starch, which is made up of thousands of alpha glucose units linked together. When the bread is eaten, amylase in the saliva begins to hydrolyse the starch to maltose. When the food reaches the small intestine, amylase from pancreatic juice continues the conversion of starch to maltose, and then the maltose itself is hydrolysed to glucose by maltase. Only then can the glucose be absorbed. This explains the fact that a peak in blood glucose concentration does not occur until 30 minutes after the bread has been ingested.

The fall from 30 minutes up to 120 minutes will have been brought about by increased secretion of insulin by the beta cells in the islets of Langerhans in the pancreas. This takes a short while to happen, which is why the blood glucose does not begin to fall until 30 minutes after ingestion.

b All three foods produced a maximum level of blood glucose after 30 minutes. This maximum increase was much lower in the lentils and soya, at 13 and 5 mg 100 cm^{-3} respectively, compared with a value of 52 mg 100 cm^{-3} when bread was eaten. The blood glucose level then fell very rapidly for bread, but much less so for lentils and soya, and these continued to provide a relatively steady blood glucose level throughout the rest of the 120 minutes. At the end of this time, the blood glucose increases for bread and soya were identical at −2 mg 100 cm^{-3}, while that for lentils was still relatively high at 11 mg 100 cm^{-3}.

c It appears that the carbohydrate in the lentils and soya is less easy to digest, so it takes longer for glucose to be produced and for it to be absorbed into the blood. This would explain the fact that the blood glucose level did not rise as quickly, and, for lentils, stayed at a relatively high value throughout the rest of the experiment; we can guess that it might have continued at this level for some time afterwards.

Another possibility is that some of the carbohydrate in the lentils and soya could be cellulose, which we are not able to digest at all.

Another possibility is that some of the carbohydrate in the lentils and soya was made up of monosaccharides other than glucose – fructose, for example.

4 a Heart disease.

b In 1985, diabetes accounted for about 36 deaths in every 100 000 people. By 2000, this had risen to about 64 deaths per 100 000. This is an increase of 78%. As people's genes will not have changed in this time period, the difference must be due to changes in lifestyle. It is likely to be the effect of a more energy-rich diet and less exercise being taken, both of which increase the risk of becoming obese and developing Type 2 diabetes.

c In 1985, the mortality rate for HIV/AIDS was only just above 0, whereas by 2000 it was 40 deaths per 100 000 people. In 1985, HIV had only recently begun to spread through the human population, and relatively few people were infected. Over time, the virus has spread more widely. Moreover, death from AIDS generally occurs many years after the person has first become infected with the virus, so even if many people were infected with the virus in 1985, they would not be expected to die until much later.

5 a This means that everyone was alive at the start of the study.

b Data were probably collected once a year, so the researchers did not know what happened in between. If one or more people died in a year, the graph goes down by a step.

c There seems to be a clear difference between the results for people with an LDL : HDL ratio greater than 8 (red line) and those with an LDL : HDL ratio of less than or equal to 8 (blue line). Those with the higher ratio had a greater probability of survival.

6 a This was to act as a control. The only difference between the two groups was that one took statins and the other took identical pills that did not contain statins.

b This ensured that the people collecting the data would not be biased in any way, which makes the data more reliable. Even if the researchers thought they were being meticulously careful, it is possible that if they knew that one person had taken statins while another had taken a placebo, it could have affected the way they recorded or interpreted the results.

c The data do not tell us anything about the risk of developing coronary heart disease. However, they do tell us that taking stains reduces the risk of dying from coronary heart disease. For example, the total number of people who died from CHD was 17% lower. Similar calculations can be done for the other categories.

d Statins reduce the quantity of cholesterol synthesised by the liver. People taking statins are therefore likely to have lowered blood cholesterol levels, reducing the risk of developing atheromatous plaques.

7 Increase in heart rate increases the rate at which oxygen is delivered to the respiring muscles so they can respire faster and make more ATP. The secretion of adrenaline helps to increase the heart rate. The secretion of nitric oxide, which dilates the arterioles, helps to increase blood flow back to the heart. This stimulates the heart to beat faster and harder, which also increases the delivery of oxygen to muscles.

Dilation of arterioles delivering blood to the muscles again increases oxygen supply to them. Dilation of arterioles delivering blood to the skin increases the rate of heat loss, which prevents the heat produced during muscle activity from increasing the core body temperature.

The increase of tidal volume and breathing rate helps to maintain a large concentration gradient, for both oxygen and carbon dioxide, between the air in the alveoli and the blood in the lung capillaries. This increases the rate at which oxygen is taken up by the blood and at which carbon dioxide is lost from it. This in turn increases the rate at which oxygen is supplied to the respiring muscles and carbon dioxide is removed from them.

Detection of high acidity (low pH) by chemoreceptors increases the rate and extent of contractions of the diaphragm and intercostal muscles. This increases tidal volume and breathing rate, as described above. It is important to remove carbon dioxide rapidly, as otherwise it would lower the pH of the blood plasma and reduce the activity of enzymes.

8 a VO_2 max is the maximum rate at which the body can use oxygen before it has to switch to anaerobic respiration.

b During the first seven weeks of the training, VO_2 max rose steadily from $3.2\,dm^3\,min^{-1}$ to $3.5\,dm^3\,min^{-1}$. This is an overall increase of $0.3\,dm^3\,min^{-1}$. The rate of increase is $0.04\,dm^3\,min^{-1}$ per week. There was little change from seven weeks onwards.

c The increase in VO_2 max is brought about by the following changes.

The muscle fibres that tend to be used during exercise are slow-twitch fibres, which respire aerobically. The increased cross-sectional area of these fibres increases the quantity of muscle that is used during aerobic exercise.

The increased number of capillaries in the muscles increases the blood flow to them, which brings more oxygen and takes away carbon dioxide more effectively.

The increased concentration of myoglobin increases the quantity of oxygen stored in the muscles, which they are able to use for aerobic respiration when their oxygen concentration is very low.

Mitochondria are the sites of the link reaction, the Krebs cycle and the electron transfer chain. The increase in number and size of mitochondria, and hence the quantity of respiratory enzymes that they contain, therefore results in an increase in the amount of aerobic respiration that can take place at the same time.

An increase in VO_2 max means that muscles can respire aerobically for longer. This is achieved by having more red blood cells, which can bring more oxygen to the muscles. The rate at which oxygen is supplied to the muscles is also increased by the development of more heart muscle and the increase in stroke volume. Resting heart rate is lower. Increases in maximum breathing rate and volume of air breathed in also help oxygen to be supplied more rapidly to the muscles.

9 a i As power output increases, so does the concentration of lactate in the blood. The relationship is directly proportional. However, the increase in lactate concentration is slight, only rising from about 1.8 mmol dm^{-3} to 2.1 mmol dm^{-3} as power output increases from 50 W to 175 W. This is an approximate increase of 0.002 mmol dm^{-3} for a 1 W increase in power.

ii The muscles are able to respire mostly aerobically up to a power output of 175 W. However, some anaerobic respiration does occur and this is the source of the lactate in the blood. As power increases, anaerobic respiration also increases, but only slightly.

b i The liver.

ii Before training: 175 W
After training: 225 W

iii Any long-term changes that bring more oxygen to the muscles more swiftly, or allow muscle fibres to carry out more aerobic respiration, can help to explain these figures. They are listed and explained in the answer to **8 c**.

c An increase in lactate threshold means that an athlete can go on using aerobic respiration in their muscles even when they are working hard. This allows trained endurance athletes to work faster or harder for a longer period of time than an untrained person.

Chapter 13

1 a More than 360 000 men were admitted to hospital in 2000 as a direct result of alcohol abuse. The majority of these (more than 140 000) were over the age of 40. The next most frequent age group was the 30–39 year-olds, followed by 20–29 year-olds and then

men below 20 years of age. So the number of admissions increased with age.

b Less than 100 000 admissions were due to cannabis use, so there were 3.6 times as many admissions due to alcohol than due to cannabis. Here, the number of admissions decreased with age, in contrast to the increase with age seen for alcohol abuse. By the age of 40, only a very few admissions occurred.

c The pattern of increase in admissions due to alcohol abuse with age in women is similar to that seen in men, but here there are 2.9 times fewer overall – 125 000 instead of 360 000. The difference is shown throughout all four age ranges, but is greatest in the 20–29 and the 40+ age ranges.

d For every person admitted to hospital following abuse of a drug, there will be many more who are using the drug but do not need hospital admission. This number will differ for different drugs. For example, it is likely the the percentage of cocaine users who are admitted to hospital is greater than the percentage of alchol users.

2 a The woman: high/moderate risk, 10–15%. The man: mild risk, 5–10%.

b The woman should give up smoking, as this is by far the greatest factor contributing to her risk of having a heart attack or stroke. She should also try to reduce her total cholesterol : HDL-cholesterol ratio, perhaps by reducing the quantity of saturated fats in her diet, or by taking statins.

The man needs to reduce his total cholesterol : HDL-cholesterol ratio. The fact that it is so high raises the possibility that he may be genetically liable to high cholesterol levels, in which case he will need to take statins or a prescribed medicine and not just try to get the level down by changing his diet.

c The risk calculators are built up by studying a large number of people over many years, recording various factors about their lifestyles (smoker or not, blood pressure readings, blood cholesterol levels) and all the cardiovascular events they have. These findings are then used to search for relationships between a particular lifestyle factor and the likelihood of suffering a cardiovascular event.

Glossary

abiotic factor a non-living component of the environment that affects the distribution and abundance of a species

abscicic acid a plant hormone produced in conditions of stress, which brings about responses such as stomatal closure

absorption spectrum a graph showing the wavelengths of light absorbed by a pigment

abuse (of drug) use of a drug in such a way as to cause harm to oneself or others

accessory pigment a pigment other than the main light-absorbing pigment (chlorophyll) – for example, carotenoids; it helps to absorb more wavelengths of light than would be absorbed by chlorophyll alone, and may also have a protective effect

acetyl CoA coenzyme A with an acetate group attached

acetylcholine a transmitter substance released at some synapses in the nervous system

acetylcholinesterase an enzyme that breaks down (hydrolyses) acetylcholine to acetate and choline

action potential a fleeting reversal of the resting potential, generally to about +30 mV inside, which sweeps along an axon

active immunity the ability to produce antibodies to destroy a pathogen

active transport the movement of molecules or ions through transport proteins across a cell membrane, against their concentration gradient or electrochemical gradient, involving the use of energy from ATP

adenosine triphosphate (ATP) an energy-containing substance that acts as the energy currency of a cell, supplying an instantly available energy source that the cell can use

ADH (anti-diuretic hormone) a hormone that is secreted by the posterior pituitary gland, which increases the permeability of the collecting duct walls and so allows the production of small volumes of concentrated urine

adhesion a force that attracts water molecules to a surface, by hydrogen bonding

adipose tissue a tissue made up of cells containing large lipid droplets

adrenaline a catecholamine hormone, secreted by the adrenal glands in times of stress, fear or excitement, which prepares the body for fight or flight

aerobic exercise any exercise that increases the rate of aerobic respiration in muscles

aerobic respiration the sequence of reactions – including glycolysis, the link reaction, the Krebs cycle and the electron transport chain – that result in the complete oxidation of glucose in a cell

afferent arteriole the blood vessel that delivers blood to a glomerulus

aldehyde dehydrogenase an enzyme found in liver cells that converts ethanal to ethanoate

allergen a substance that brings about an inappropriate immune response

alpha cells cells in the islets of Langerhans in the pancreas that secrete glucagon

ammonification the production of ammonia from nitrogen-containing compounds such as proteins, amino acids or urea

anaerobic respiration the partial oxidation of glucose to supply a small amount of energy; it involves glycolysis followed by either the lactate pathway or the ethanol pathway

angina a pain felt in the chest and left arm, caused by poor blood flow in the coronary arteries

anti-diuretic hormone (ADH) a hormone that is secreted by the posterior pituitary gland, which increases the permeability of the collecting duct walls and so allows the production of small volumes of concentrated urine

antibody a small protein secreted by B-lymphocytes in response to a particular antigen

antigen a molecule or cell that is recognised as foreign by the immune system

antigen-presenting cell a cell that takes in a pathogen, or molecules from it, and holds them in its plasma membrane where they may be encountered by a lymphocyte

decarboxylation a chemical reaction in which carbon dioxide is removed

decomposer an organism that breaks down organic remains, returning matter from them to the soil and air

dehydrogenase an enzyme that can remove hydrogens from a substance

dendrites short cytoplasmic processes that transmit action potentials from other neurones towards the cell body of a motor neurone

dendron a long cytoplasmic process that transmits action potentials towards the cell body of a neurone

denitrification the production of nitrogen gas from nitrite or nitrate ions

deoxyribonucleic acid (DNA) the genetic material contained in chromosomes; a polynucleotide in which the five-carbon sugar is deoxyribose

dependency a condition in which a person feels they cannot manage without a drug

depolarisation the loss or reversal of the resting potential

depressant a drug that reduces or slows the activity of the nervous system

descending limb the part of the loop of Henlé which carries fluid downwards from the cortex to the medulla

detritivore an organism that feeds on detritus

detritus remains of plants and animals, such as dead leaves, used as a nutrient source by decomposers and detritivores

diabetes mellitus a condition in which blood glucose levels are not fully controlled; in Type 1 diabetes, insulin is not secreted, while in Type 2 diabetes insulin is secreted but has little effect on the target tissues

diastolic pressure the pressure exerted by blood on the wall of an artery when the ventricles are relaxing

distal convoluted tubule the second coiled part of a nephron

DNA (deoxyribonucleic acid) the genetic material contained in chromosomes; a polynucleotide in which the five-carbon sugar is deoxyribose

dorsal root ganglion (pl. ganglia) a swelling on the dorsal root of the spinal nerve in which cell bodies of sensory neurones are found

drug a chemical that affects the physiology of the body

ECG (electrocardiogram) a recording of the heart's electrical activity

ecological niche the role of an organism in an ecosystem; the effects that it has on other components of the ecosystem, and the effects that they have on it

ecosystem the interactions between all the organisms, and their environment, in a particular area

effector an organ that carries out an action in response to a stimulus, such as a muscle that contracts or a gland that secretes a substance

efferent arteriole the blood vessel that carries blood away from a glomerulus

efficiency the total energy put into a system divided by the useful energy obtained; it is often multiplied by 100 and stated as a percentage

electrocardiogram (ECG) a recording of the heart's electrical activity

electrochemical gradient a situation in which the concentration and charge on one side of a membrane differs from that on the other

electron carrier one of the components of the electron transport chain, that picks up electrons from one substance and passes them on to another

electron transport chain a series of molecules that successively gain and release electrons provided by a reduced coenzyme such as NADP; as the electron is passed along it loses energy, and the energy is used to synthesise ATP

emphysema a disorder caused by the breakdown of the alveolar walls, making it difficult to obtain sufficient oxygen in the blood

endemic species a species that is found naturally in only one country or area

endocrine gland an organ that secretes hormones directly into the blood

endocrine system the body organs that secrete hormones

endodermis the outer layer of the stele in a plant root

endothelium a tissue lining the inner surface of an organ – for example, the inside of a blood vessel

envelope a pair of membranes surrounding some organelles; that is, chloroplast, mitochondrion and nucleus

epidemiology the study of patterns of disease in populations, in order to work out the causes of the disease

epitope the part of an antigen to which an antibody binds

erythrocyte a red blood cell

erythropoetin a hormone that increases the rate of production of red blood cells

ethanol dehydrogenase an enzyme in liver cells that breaks down ethanol

ethylene (ethene) a gaseous plant growth substance that brings about fruit ripening

ex situ **conservation** maintaining or increasing the numbers of an endangered species in a place other than its natural habitat, e.g. a zoo or botanical garden

excretion the removal of toxic waste products of metabolism

exocrine gland a gland that secretes something into a duct

facilitated diffusion the diffusion of a substance through protein channels in a cell membrane; the proteins provide hydrophilic areas that allow the molecules or ions to pass through a membrane that would otherwise be less permeable to them

FAD flavine adenine dinucleotide; a coenzyme that is required to allow dehydrogenases to remove hydrogens; the FAD accepts them and becomes reduced

fatty liver a condition in which fat deposits are formed in the liver, often as a result of the excessive consumption of alcohol

food additive a non-nutritious substance added to processed foods during manufacture

food chain a diagram showing a sequence of organisms in which chemical energy passes from one organism to the next

food web many interconnecting food chains

GABA a transmitter substance found in the brain

GALP an alternative name for triose phosphate (TP)

gibberellin a plant hormone that affects stem elongation and seed germination; it acts by causing certain genes to be transcribed

gland an organ that secretes a useful substance

glomerular filtrate the fluid that is filtered from the blood and passes into a renal capsule

glomerulus a network of blood capillaries in the cup of a renal capsule

glucagon a hormone secreted in response to low blood glucose levels, which brings about an increase in the rate of production of glucose from glycogen and other substances in the liver

glucokinase an enzyme that adds a phosphate group to a glucose molecule

gluconeogenesis the production of glucose from non-carbohydrate substances, such as amino acids or lipids

glutamate a transmitter substance found in the brain

glycerate 3-phosphate (GP) a three-carbon substance formed following the reaction between RuBP and carbon dioxide, in the Calvin cycle

glycogen a storage polysaccharide found in liver cells and muscle cells, made of many α-glucose units linked by glycosidic bonds

glycolysis the first set of reactions in respiration; it takes place in the cytoplasm and results in the conversion of glucose to pyruvate, with the net gain of two ATPs per glucose molecule

GP (glycerate 3-phosphate) a three-carbon substance formed following the reaction between RuBP and carbon dioxide, in the Calvin cycle

GPP (gross primary productivity) the total quantity of energy transferred by plants from sunlight into plant tissues

granum (pl. grana) stack of thylakoids

gross primary productivity (GPP) the total quantity of energy transferred by plants from sunlight into plant tissues

habitat a place where an organism lives

haemoglobin the red pigment found in red blood cells; it transports oxygen and carbon dioxide between lungs and body cells

haemoglobinic acid the compound formed when hydrogen ions combine with haemoglobin

HDL high-density lipoprotein

heparin a cytokine secreted by mast cells

hepatitis inflammation of the liver

herd immunity immunity possessed by a large proportion of individuals in a population, lowering the chances of even those individuals that are not immune from getting an infectious disease

heterotroph an organism that requires organic nutrients to supply it with a source of carbon

histamine a cytokine secreted by mast cells, often involved in allergic reactions

homeostasis the maintenance of a stable internal environment

hormone a chemical secreted by an endocrine gland, which brings about a response in an organ elsewhere in the body

humidity the quantity of water vapour held in the air

humoral response the part of the immune response brought about by antibodies and cytokines

hybridoma a cell formed by the fusion of a cancer cell and a plasma cell, used in the production of monoclonal antibodies

hyperglycaemia having a blood glucose level that is too high

hyperplasia an abnormal increase in the number of cells

hypertension high blood pressure

hypoglycaemia having a blood glucose level that is too low

hypothalamus a small part of the brain in the very centre of the head, which contains receptors involved in temperature regulation and osmoregulation; it is closely associated with the pituitary gland and controls the secretion of hormones from that gland

immune response the way in which lymphocytes respond to infection by pathogens

immunoglobulin an antibody; a small protein molecule that is able to bind with a specific antigen

***in situ* conservation** maintaining or increasing the numbers of a species in its natural habitat

insulin a hormone secreted in response to high blood glucose levels, which brings about an increase in the uptake of glucose from the blood and its conversion to glycogen

intermediate neurone a neurone in the central nervous system that transmits nerve impulses between a sensory neurone and a motor neurone

islets of Langerhans groups of cells in the pancreas that secrete insulin and glucagon

isomerisation the rearrangement of atoms in a molecule to make a different molecule, with no loss or addition of atoms

ketoacidosis a dangerous condition caused by an excessive amount of ketone bodies in the blood

ketone bodies substances produced from fatty acids in the liver

Krebs cycle the cycle of reactions that takes place in the matrix of a mitochondrion, in which pyruvate is oxidised to oxaloacetate; ATP, reduced NAD and reduced FAD are produced, and carbon dioxide is given off

lactic fermentation anaerobic respiration resulting in the formation of lactate

lamellae sheets; in a chloroplast, the lamellae are membranes within it

LDL low-density lipoprotein

light-dependent stage the stage of photosynthesis in which light energy is absorbed by chlorophyll and used to split water and make ATP and reduced NADP

light-independent stage the stage of photosynthesis in which carbon dioxide reacts with RuBP, and carbohydrates are produced; it requires ATP and reduced NADP from the light-dependent stage

lignin a strong, waterproof substance found in the walls of xylem elements

limiting factor a factor that is preventing a reaction or other process from going any faster; if the supply of the factor is increased, then the reaction rate will increase; with respect to populations, any factor that prevents the growth of the population above a certain value

link reaction a reaction taking place in the matrix of a mitochondrion, in which pyruvate reacts with CoA to form acetyl CoA and carbon dioxide

lipoprotein a tiny ball of lipid and protein; the form in which cholesterol and other lipids are transported in the blood

liver a large organ situated just beneath the diaphragm; its cells carry out a very wide range of metabolic reactions, including deamination and the interconversion of glucose and glycogen

loop of Henlé the section of a nephron that dips down into the medulla and then back up into the cortex of the kidney

lung cancer a disorder caused by uncontrollable cell division in the lungs, producing tumours

lysis breaking apart

MabThera® a monoclonal antibody used in the treatment of leukaemia

macrophage a type of leucocyte; it is a large cell and it destroys bacteria and other foreign material by phagocytosis; also known as a monocyte when in the blood

malignant (tumour) a tumour whose cells break away and produce new tumours in other parts of the body

mass flow the movement of a bulk liquid, like water flowing in a river

mast cell a cell found in all body tissues, which produces histamine and heparin when activated

matrix the 'background material' inside a mitochondrion, where the link reaction and the Krebs cycle take place

medulla the inner part of a kidney, in which loops of Henlé and collecting ducts are found

metabolic pathway a series of chemical reactions taking place in an organism, in which each step is usually catalysed by an enzyme

metabolic reactions (metabolism) the chemical reactions that take place in living organisms

metastasis the spreading of cancer from its initial site to other parts of the body

monoclonal antibodies antibodies (immunoglobulins) all of one type

motor neurone a neurone that transmits action potentials from the central nervous system to an effector

multicellular made of many cells

muscle cells cells making up muscle tissue; they contain the proteins actin and myosin that are able to use energy from ATP to slide along each other and shorten the cell

mutualism a close relationship between two organisms in which both benefit

myelin sheath an insulating layer around an axon or dendron

myocardial infarction death of muscle cells in the heart wall

myogenic a property of cardiac muscle; its contraction is initiated within the muscle itself, not by impulses from a nerve

myoglobin a pigment in muscle which combines with oxygen and acts as an oxygen store

NAD nicotinamide adenine dinucleotide; a coenzyme that is required in respiration to allow dehydrogenases to remove hydrogens; the NAD accepts them and becomes reduced

NADP nicotinamide adenine dinucleotide phosphate; a coenzyme that is required in photosynthesis to allow dehydrogenases to remove hydrogens; the NADP accepts them and becomes reduced

natural immunity immunity acquired naturally – for example, following an infection or through breast-feeding

negative feedback a mechanism by which a change in a parameter is detected and which brings about a response that moves the parameter back towards the norm

nephron a kidney tubule

nerve a group of axons and dendrons, surrounded by a protective covering

nerve impulse an action potential

net primary productivity (NPP) the energy left as chemical energy after plants have supplied their own needs by respiration

neuromuscular junction a synapse between a motor neurone and a muscle fibre

neurone a nerve cell, specialised for the rapid transmission of electrical impulses called action potentials

neutrophil a leucocyte (white blood cell) which destroys pathogens by phagocytosis

niche the role of an organism in an ecosystem; the effects that it has on other components of the ecosystem, and the effects that they have on it

nicotine a substance found in cigarette smoke, whose molecules have a similar shape to part of the acetylcholine molecule, and that can slot into acetylcholine receptors on postsynaptic membranes

nitrification the production of nitrate and nitrite ions by the oxidation of ammonium ions

nitrifying bacteria bacteria that oxidise ammonium ions to nitrite or nitrate; they include *Nitrobacter* and *Nitrosomonas*

nitrogen fixation the conversion of nitrogen from unreactive nitrogen gas to a more reactive form such as ammonium or nitrate ions

nitrogenase an enzyme that catalyses the conversion of nitrogen gas to ammonium ions

node of Ranvier a gap in the myelin sheath

noradrenaline a transmitter substance

NPP (net primary productivity) the energy left as chemical energy after plants have supplied their own needs by respiration

obese seriously overweight; having a body mass index of more than 27–30

omnivore an animal that eats both animals and plants

oncogene a gene that causes a cell to divide uncontrollably

opsonin a molecule that attaches to bacteria, or other antigens, targetting them for phagocytosis

ornithine cycle a metabolic pathway that takes place in liver cells, in which urea is produced from excess amino acids

osmoreceptor a cell that detects changes in the concentration of a fluid

osmoregulation the regulation of the water content of body fluids

oxaloacetate a four-carbon compound that is involved in the Krebs cycle

oxidation addition of oxygen, loss of hydrogen or loss of electrons

oxidative phosphorylation the production of ATP via the electron transport chain in a mitochondrion

oxygen debt the extra oxygen required by the body after exercise has taken place partly fuelled by anaerobic respiration; the extra oxygen is needed to convert the lactic acid that has been formed to pyruvate

pancreatic juice a digestive secretion produced by the pancreas; it contains several digestive enzymes that act in the duodenum

pandemic a worldwide outbreak of a disease

partial pressure a measure of the concentration of a gas

particulates tiny carbon particles, found for example in cigarette smoke and exhaust fumes from diesel engines, that accumulate in lungs and cause irritation

passive immunity possessing antibodies that were produced in another organism's body

pathogen an organism that causes disease

pelvis (of kidney) the innermost part of a kidney, where the nephrons merge into the ureter

perineurium protective connective tissue surrounding neurones

peripheral nervous system all of the nervous system apart from the brain and spinal cord, made up of nerves (containing axons and dendrons of neurones)

phosphorylation the addition of a phosphate group to a molecule

photolysis the splitting of water molecules using energy from light

photophosphorylation the production of ATP using energy from light; it takes place on the thylakoid membranes in a chloroplast

photorespiration an undesirable reaction between RuBP and oxygen, which takes place at high temperatures and high light intensities in some plants

photosynthesis the manufacture of carbohydrates from inorganic substances (carbon dioxide and water) using energy from light; the light is transformed to chemical energy

photosynthetic pigment a molecule that absorbs some colours of light but not others, and transfers the light energy to chemical energy

photosystem a cluster of pigment and protein molecules that harvest light energy and channel it to chlorophyll molecules

physical dependency (on drug) a condition in which a person can no longer manage without a drug, because of changes in the structure and physiology of neurones in the brain

phytoplankton microscopic photosynthetic protoctists that float in the upper layers of the sea or fresh water

pit part of a xylem element wall in which there is no lignin

plant growth regulator a chemical produced in one part of a plant that affects the growth or development of another part of the plant – examples include cytokinin, gibberellin, ethylene and auxin; plant growth regulators are also known as plant growth substances and plant hormones

plaque (arterial) a build-up of cholesterol and other substances in the wall of an artery

plasma the liquid part of blood

plasma cell a cell derived from a B-lymphocyte, which secretes antibodies

plasma proteins proteins that are dissolved in blood plasma; they include albumin and fibrinogen

plasmodesma (pl. plasmodesmata) a direct connection between the cytoplasm of one plant cell and an adjacent cell, made up of plasma membrane and endoplasmic reticulum running between the two cells

podocyte a cell that makes up the inner wall of a renal capsule

population a group of organisms of the same species, living in the same place at the same time and able to breed with each other

postsynaptic neurone the nerve cell on the side of a synapse towards which the transmitter substance diffuses

potometer apparatus for measuring the rate of water uptake of a shoot

predator an animal that kills and eats other animals

presynaptic neurone the nerve cell on the side of a synapse where the action potential first arrives

primary consumer the first consumer in a food chain; a herbivore

primary producer an organism that transfers energy from light or an inorganic compound to organic compounds; plants are producers, using light energy to produce carbohydrates and other organic substances

primary productivity the energy transferred from sunlight to chemical potential energy by plants, usually measured in $kJ\,m^{-2}\,year^{-1}$

primary response the response of the immune system when an antigen is encountered for the first time

producer an organism that transfers energy from light or an inorganic compound to organic compounds; plants are producers, using light energy to produce carbohydrates and other organic substances

productivity the rate at which new biomass is produced

proto-oncogene a gene which can mutate to form an oncogene

PSI photosystem I, involved in both cyclic and non-cyclic photophosphorylation

PSII photosystem II, involved in non-cyclic photophosphorylation but not cyclic photophosphorylation

pulmonary artery an artery that carries blood from the heart to the lungs

Purkyne tissue cells that conduct an electrical impulse very rapidly down through the septum of the heart

pyruvate a three-carbon molecule that is the end-product of glycolysis

reaction centre the part of a photosystem to which light energy is funnelled; it contains two chlorophyll *a* molecules that emit electrons

receptor a cell that detects a stimulus

receptor protein a protein in a plasma membrane to which a particular molecule or ion can bind

recreational use (of drug) the occasional use of a drug for non-medical reasons, and with no harm to health

reduced NAD NAD that has picked up hydrogens

reduction the loss of oxygen, the gain of hydrogen or the gain of electrons

reflex action a fast, stereotyped response to a stimulus, not involving conscious thought

reflex arc the path travelled by an action potential from a receptor to an effector to bring about a reflex action

refractory period the time immediately following an action potential when an axon cannot transmit another action potential, because of the time needed to restore the resting potential

regulator the component of a negative feedback loop that compares the value of a parameter against the set point

relay neurone a neurone in the central nervous system that transmits nerve impulses between a sensory neurone and a motor neurone

renal artery the blood vessel that carries oxygenated blood to a kidney

renal capsule also known as a Bowman's capsule; the cup-shaped part at the beginning of a nephron, into which ultrafiltration takes place

renal vein the blood vessel that carries deoxygenated blood from a kidney towards the heart

repolarisation the recovery of the resting potential following depolarisation

repressor protein a protein that can bind to DNA and prevent transcription of a gene

respiration the release of chemical energy from glucose or other substrates by oxidation; most of the energy is used to make ATP; respiration takes place in all living cells

respiratory substrate a substance that can be oxidised in respiration to release energy for the synthesis of ATP

resting potential the potential difference, usually about −70 mV inside, across the plasma membrane of a neurone while it is not transmitting an action potential

reverse transcriptase an enzyme that uses RNA to make a single-stranded molecule of complementary DNA

ribonucleic acid (RNA) a polynucleotide made of nucleotides containing ribose

ribosome one of many thousands of tiny organelles, sometimes free in the cytoplasm and sometimes attached to rough endoplasmic reticulum, where protein synthesis takes place

rituximab the generic name for the drug MabThera®, a monoclonal antibody used to treat leukaemia

RNA (ribonucleic acid) a polynucleotide made of nucleotides containing ribose

root hair extension of a cell in the epidermis of plant roots, which absorbs water and mineral ions from soil

root pressure the hydrostatic pressure generated in xylem vessels in roots, as a result of active transport of ions into the xylem

rubisco ribulose bisphosphate carboxylase; an enzyme that catalyses the reaction of RuBP with carbon dioxide

RuBP ribulose bisphosphate; a substance found in leaves that combines with carbon dioxide during the Calvin cycle

saltatory conduction conduction of an action potential along a myelinated neurone by 'jumping' from one node of Ranvier to the next

SAN (sino-atrial node) the pace-maker of the heart

Schwann cell a cell that wraps itself around an axon producing a multiple layer of membranes, called myelin

secondary consumer a carnivore that feeds on herbivores

secondary response the response of the immune system when an antigen is encountered again

secretion the production and release of a useful substance – for example, salivary glands secrete saliva

sensory neurone a neurone that transmits nerve impulses between a receptor and the central nervous system

set point the 'ideal' value of a parameter controlled by negative feedback

sieve element a cell found in phloem tissue through which sap containing sucrose is transported; the cells have very little cytoplasm, thin cellulose side walls, end walls perforated to form sieve plates, no nucleus

sieve plate the end wall of a sieve element, which has many holes through which water and solutes can pass

sink in plants, an area where sucrose is used

sino-atrial node (SAN) the pace-maker of the heart

source in plants, an area where sucrose is produced

species a group of organisms with similar morphology and physiology, which are able to breed together to produce fertile offspring

species density the number of species per unit area

species diversity (richness) the number of different species in an area

spinal cord the part of the central nervous system that runs from the base of the brain and through the vertebral column

starch grain a structure containing large numbers of starch molecules, inside a chloroplast; it is an energy store

stele the central area of a root, containing xylem and phloem tissues

stoma (pl. stomata) a small hole in the epidermis of a leaf, bounded by two guard cells

stroke damage to the brain caused by a burst or blocked blood vessel

stroke volume the volume of blood pumped out by the heart in one beat

stroma the 'background material' in a chloroplast, in which the light-independent stage of photosynthesis takes place

suberin a waxy, waterproof substance found in tree bark, abscission layers and in some of the cells surrounding xylem vessels in roots

substrate-level phosphorylation the production of ATP directly from a reaction in the Krebs cycle, not involving the electron transport chain

sucrose a carbohydrate made up of two sugar units, α-glucose and β-fructose, linked between carbons 1 and 2

sympathetic nerve a nerve that is part of the sympathetic system; stimulation of the SAN by the sympathetic nerve increases heart rate

symplast pathway a route taken by water as it moves across a plant tissue by passing through the cells

synapse an area where a nerve impulse can be passed from one neurone to another, or from a neurone to an effector

synaptic cleft the tiny gap between two neurones, or between a neurone and an effector, at a synapse

systolic pressure the pressure exerted by blood on the walls of an artery when the ventricles are contracting

T-helper cell a T-lymphocyte that secretes cytokines, stimulating other white cells to destroy a pathogen

T-killer cell a T-lymphocyte that attaches to a cell containing an antigen and destroys the cell

T-lymphocyte a white blood cell that binds to a cell containing a specific antigen and either destroys the cell or stimulates other cells to do so

tar a mixture of chemicals in cigarette smoke, several of which are carcinogenic

target tissue a group of cells that contain receptors for a particular hormone and are therefore affected by it

tertiary consumer a carnivore that feeds on a secondary consumer

therapeutic as a treatment for illness

threshold potential the minimum depolarisation of an axon membrane required to produce an action potential

thylakoid one membrane disc within a stack of discs (granum) inside a chloroplast, where chlorophyll is found and the light-dependent reactions of photosynthesis take place

tolerance (to drug) adaptation of the body to a drug, so that more of the drug needs to be taken in order to achieve the same effect

TP (triose phosphate) a three-carbon phosphorylated sugar, the first carbohydrate to be produced in photosynthesis

translocation the transport of assimilates in phloem sieve tubes

transmitter substance a chemical that is released by a presynaptic neurone and diffuses across the synaptic cleft to slot into receptors on the postsynaptic neurone

transpiration the loss of water vapour from a leaf

transpiration stream the continuous movement of water from soil to air through a plant, brought about by the loss of water vapour from the leaves

triose phosphate (TP) a three-carbon phosphorylated sugar, the first carbohydrate to be produced in photosynthesis

trophic level the stage of a food chain at which an organism feeds

tumour a lump of cells; if these are able to spread around the body and cause tumours elsewhere, the tumour is said to be malignant; if not, then it is said to be benign

ultrafiltration filtration on a molecular scale, as happens in the renal capsules of the kidney nephrons

urea the main nitrogenous excretory product of mammals, made in the ornithine cycle following the deamination of amino acids

ureter one of the tubes that carries urine from the kidneys to the bladder

urethra the tube that carries urine from the bladder to the outside of the body

vaccination the introduction of a harmless antigen to the body, in order to generate an immune response that will protect against a pathogen

vagus nerve a nerve running from the brain to many internal organs; it is part of the parasympathetic nervous system and slows heart rate when it carries impulses to the SAN

vasa recta the blood capillaries associated with the loop of Henlé in a kidney nephron

vector an organism that transmits a pathogen – for example, *Anopheles* mosquitoes are vectors for the malaria pathogen

voltage-gated channel an ion channel in a plasma membrane that responds to a change in voltage (potential difference) across the membrane by opening or closing

withdrawal symptoms unpleasant effects experienced when a person stops taking a drug

xylem element a long, narrow, empty, dead cell with no end walls and with lignified side walls, through which water travels

Z-scheme a diagram illustrating the changes in energy levels of electrons during the light-dependent reactions of photosynthesis

Index

abiotic factors 63–5
abscisic acid 150
absorption spectrum 6
abstinence syndrome 270
accessory pigments 6
acetyl CoA 25
acetylcholine (ACh) 117, 188–90, 191–2
acetylcholinesterase 190, 192
acidification of seawater 66, 67
action potentials 182–9
active immunity 232–3
active transport 21, 85, 88, 91, 99
adenosine diphosphate (ADP) 7, 21–3, 27–8
adenosine monophosphate (AMP) 22
adenosine triphosphate (ATP) 7, 8, 9, 11, 21–3, 25–8
ADH *see* anti-diuretic hormone
adhesion, water transport 90
adipose tissue 244
adrenaline 117, 142–3, 144, 256
aerobic exercise 255–9
aerobic respiration 24–8, 33–4
afferent arteriole 163, 164
agriculture, effect on climate 101
AIDS *see* HIV/AIDS
alcohol 270–3
alcohol dehydrogenase 271
alcoholic drinks, fermentation 32
aldehyde dehydrogenase 271
allergens 230
allosteric effect 128
alpha cells 145, 146, 147, 148
Alzheimer's disease 200
amino acids 32, 53–4, 161–2
ammonia
  conversion to urea 161–2
  and the nitrogen cycle 54–5
  production, Haber process 53
ammonification 54
AMP *see* adenosine monophosphate
anaerobic respiration 30–2
angina 117, 250
anti-diuretic hormone (ADH) 169, 170
antibodies 224–37
antigen-presenting cells 223–5
antigens 224–7, 230–5
apex predators 45

apoplast pathway 87–8
aquaporins 170
arteries 120–2, 124
  coronary 111
  pulmonary 111, 112, 113, 114
artificial immunity 233
ascending limb 168
assimilates 95
atheromatous plaque 250, 251
atherosclerosis 125, 250, 253, 254
ATP *see* adenosine triphosphate
ATPase (ATP synthase) 21–2, 28
atrial systole 112, 113, 114, 118
atrio-ventricular node (AVN) 116, 120
atrio-ventricular valves 112, 113, 114
atrium/atria 112–13
auto-immune diseases 230–1
autotrophs 1
auxins 150
axons 179, 183

B-lymphocytes 224–5, 234–5, 237
bacteria 52–3, 55, 222, 224–5, 232
bananas, ripening of 153–4
baroreceptors 120
benign tumours 208
beta cells 145, 146, 147, 149
bicuspid valve, heart 112
biodiversity hotspots 72, 77
biofuels 12
biological diversity 67–71
biomass 47
biotic factors 62–5
bladder 162
blood 125–32
blood alcohol concentration 272
blood clots 222, 235
blood doping by athletes 129
blood pressure 120, 122, 123–5, 253
blood vessels 120–4
BMI (body mass index) 207, 208, 244
Bohr effect 131
botulinum toxin (Botox) 190, 192
Bowman's capsule 163, 164
brain 179
  and appetite suppression 246–7
  controlling cardiac output 119–20
  effect of alcohol on 270–1, 272
  effect of stroke on 254–5

and mental disorders 199–200
synapses 187–92
bronchitis 274, 276

calcium ion channels 149, 188
callose 98
Calvin cycle 8–9, 11
cAMP *see* cyclic AMP
cancer 208, 211–213, 237, 272
capillaries, blood 122–3, 124
capillarity, water transport 90
captive breeding 75–6
carbaminohaemoglobin 130
carbon dioxide 84, 161
  abiotic factor 63
  and the Bohr effect 131
  and photosynthesis rate 10
  in seawater 66
  transport in the blood 130
carbon monoxide 274, 277
carbonic anhydrase 130
carboxyhaemoglobin 277
carcinogens 211, 212, 276
cardiac arrest 251–3, 272, 278
cardiac cycle 112–18
cardiac efficiency 258
cardiac muscle 111, 115–17
cardiac output 119–20
cardiovascular system
  effects of fats on 252–3
  and smoking 276, 277–8
carotenoids 6
Casparian strip 88
catabolic reaction 22
cell-mediated response 231
cell signalling 140, 142, 146
central nervous system 179
CHD *see* coronary heart disease
chemical carcinogens 212
chemiosmosis 28
chemoreceptors 257
chemotaxis 228, 230
chlorophyll 5–7
chloroplast 4–5
cholesterol 252–3
cholinergic synapses 188
chronic diseases 200
chronic obstructive pulmonary disease (COPD) 274–6
chylomicrons 252–3
cigarettes 274, 276, 277

311

gaseous exchange, plants 4
gene mutation and cancer 208, 211, 212–13
genetic diversity 68, 69
gibberellin 150
glands 143, 144
global warming 67
glomerular filtrate 165, 166
glomerulus, nephron 163
glucagon 145–8
glucokinase 147, 149
gluconeogenesis 148
glucose in respiration 22–3
glucose concentration 140, 141
  control of 145–9
  and diabetes 172, 206, 207
  measuring 248–9
glutamate 271
glycerate 3-phosphate (GP) 9, 11
glycogen 145, 147, 148
glycolysis 22–3, 26, 28
glycoproteins 224, 231
grana 5
gross primary productivity (GPP) 50, 51
guard cells 3, 92

Haber process 53
habitat 42, 43
habitat protection 72–4
haemoglobin 125–31
haemoglobinic acid 130
HCG & pregnancy tests 235–6
HDLs (high-density lipoproteins) 252, 253
health 199
  and diet 244–55
  and exercise 255–9
heart 110–20
heart attack 251–2
heart beat (cardiac cycle) 112–15
  control of 115–17
heart rate
  and aerobic exercise 256, 258
  regulation of 119–20
heparin 229, 230
hepatitis 271, 272
herd immunity 234
heterotrophs 1
histamine 229, 230
HIV/AIDS 201
  in the Caribbean 204–6
  development of AIDS 202
  effects on society 260

global distribution of 204, 205
  and the immune system 231
  incidence & prevalence 203–6
  life cycle of HIV 201–2
  structure of HIV 201
  symptoms of AIDS 202, 204
  transmission of HIV 201–2
homeostasis 140–1, 169–71
hormones
  mammalian 143–9
  plant 150–4
human nervous system 179–92
human papilloma virus (HPV) 212, 213
humidity 63, 93
humoral response 231
hybridoma cells 235
hydrogencarbonate 66
hyperglycaemia 248
hyperplasia 276
hypertension 125, 253–5, 272, 277
hypoglycaemia 248
hypothalamus 169, 170

IgE 229–30
illegal drugs 269
immune response 221–34
immunoglobulins 231
incidence of a disease 201
infectious diseases 200, 222, 260
inflammatory response 228–30
inorganic ions 63, 66
  required by plant cells 84
  uptake of by roots 85, 88
insecticides 192
in situ conservation 71, 74
insulin 143, 144–9, 206, 207
intermediate neurones 180
ionising radiation 211
islets of Langerhans 145, 146
isomerisation 22

ketoacidosis 248
kidneys 162
  loop of Henlé 167–8
  nephron structure 163–4
  selective reabsorption 165–7, 168–9
  ultrafiltration 164–5, 166
Krebs cycle 25–6, 28, 30–1, 271

lactate 30, 31, 255, 260
lactic fermentation 30–1
lamellae 4, 5

LDLs (low-density lipoproteins) 252, 253
leaves 2–4, 90–1, 92, 94
leptin 246–7
leucocytes see white blood cells
light-dependent stage see photosynthesis
light-independent stage see photosynthesis
light intensity
  abiotic factor 63, 64, 66
  effect on transpiration 93
  and photosynthesis 9–10
lignin, xylem vessels 89
limiting factors 10–12
link reaction 24–5
lipids 32, 245, 252–3
lipoproteins 252
liver 161–2, 271–2
liver cells 142–3, 147–8
loop of Henlé 167–8, 169
lung cancer 200, 212, 213, 274, 276
lung diseases 274–6
lymphocytes 224–6, 227
lysis 22

MabThera® 236
macrophages 223, 224–5, 228
malignant tumours 208
mass flow 90, 98–9, 100
mast cells 229–31
matrix, mitochondrion 24, 25
matter, cycling of 51–5
medulla, kidneys 162
memory cells 225, 226, 227
  role in immunity 232, 234
mental diseases 199–200
metabolic pathway 4
metabolic reactions 21
metastasis 208
microorganisms 221, 222
mitochondria 24–30
mitral valve 112
monoclonal antibodies 234–7
mortality 201
motor neurones 179–80
mucus 222
multicellular organisms 140
multiple sclerosis (MS) 187
muscles
  and aerobic exercise 255–7
  cardiac 111, 115–17
  changes in during training 258
  effect of adrenaline on 143

Acknowledgements

The author and publisher are grateful for the permissions granted to reproduce copyright materials. While every effort has been made, it has not always been possible to identify the sources of all the materials used, or to trace all the copyright holders. If any omissions are brought to our notice, we will be happy to include the appropriate acknowledgements on reprinting.

Cover image: Georgette Douwma/Science Photo Library; pp. 3*t*, 3*b*, 4, 14, 71, 72*r*, 75*b*, 117*b* Geoff Jones; pp. 5*t*, 52, 85 Dr Jeremy Burgess/Science Photo Library; p. 5*b* Dr Kenneth R. Miller/ Science Photo Library; pp. 24, 111, 121, 133*l*, 133*r* CNRI/Science Photo Library; p. 29 Dartmouth Education Images; p. 30 Photolibrary; p. 39 ISM/ Science Photo Library; pp. 42, 44, 64*r* Brandon Cole Marine Photography/Alamy; p. 43*l* Michael Stubblefield/Alamy; p. 43*r* Ron Steiner/Alamy; p. 53 Nigel Cattlin/Alamy; p. 55 Maximilian Weinzier/Alamy; p. 62 David Fleetman/Alamy; p. 64*l* Ed BrownUW/Alamy; p. 65 Mark Conlin/ Alamy; p. 70 Richard Ellis/Science Photo Library; p. 72*l* Tommy Trenchard/Alamy; p. 73 Stock Connection Blue/Alamy; p. 74 Michael DeFreitas, Caribbean/Alamy; p. 75*t* National Geographic Image Collection/Alamy; p. 76 David Allan/ Alamy; p. 77 BSIP, Laurent/Science Photo Library; p. 89*l* Eye of Science/Science Photo Library; p. 89*r*, 126*t*, 276 Carolina Biological Supply Company/ Phototake Science; pp. 96, 105, 108*rt*, 183*l*, 264*l*, 264*r*, 275*t*, 275*b* Biophoto Associates/Science Photo Library; p. 97 J.C. Revy, ISM/Science Photo Library; pp. 104, 108*lt* John Adds (The Coachman's House, Rectory Lane, Latchington, Chelmsford, CM3 6HB); p. 108*b* Biodisc, Visuals Unlimited/Science Photo Library; p. 110 Science Photo Library; pp. 117*lt*, 117*rt* Zephyr/Science Photo Library; pp. 122, 145, 281*l*, 281*r* Peter Arnold Images/Photolibrary; p. 125 Saturn Stills/ Science Photo Library; p. 126*b*, p. 165 Phototake/ Alamy; p. 129 Corbis/Photolibrary; p. 150 Martin Harvey/Alamy; p. 151 Daniel Borzynski/Alamy; pp. 164*l*, 180 Manfred Kage/Science Photo Library; pp. 164*r*, 176 Alamy; pp. 175, 183*r* Steve Gschmeissner/Science Photo Library; p. 187 Sovereign, ISM/Alamy; p. 191 Amazon Images/ Alamy; p. 230 Science Photo Library; p. 245 Oak Ridge National Laboratory/US Department of Energy/Science Photo Library; pp. 246, 249 Custom Medical Stock/Science Photo Library; p. 248 Belmonte/Science Photo Library; p. 251 Adam Hart-Davis/Alamy; p. 253 Hattie Young/ Science Photo Library; p. 255 Scott Camazine/ Alamy; p. 256 Robert Fried/Alamy; p. 271 Simon Fraser/Freeman Hospital, Newcastle Upon Tyne/ Science Photo Library; p. 272 Sciencephotos/ Alamy; p. 273 Jim Varney/Science Photo Library; p. 274 AJ Photo/Science Photo Library; p. 282 Frederick C. Skvara, MD/Visuals Unlimited Inc./ Science Photo Library.

l = left, *r* = right, *t* = top, *b* = bottom, *m* = middle

Typesetting and illustration by Greenhill Wood Studios www.greenhillwoodstudios.com